WAYS OF READING

An Anthology for Writers

David Bartholomae
UNIVERSITY OF PITTSBURGH

Anthony Petrosky
UNIVERSITY OF PITTSBURGH

A Bedford Book
ST. MARTIN'S PRESS · NEW YORK

An Instructor's Manual is available. To obtain one, please mail in the enclosed postcard or write College Sales Department, 15th floor, St. Martin's Press, 175 Fifth Avenue, New York, NY 10010

Library of Congress Catalog Card Number: 85–61293

Manufactured in the United States of America
9 8 7 6
f e d c b a
For information, write St. Martin's Press, Inc.,
175 Fifth Avenue, New York, NY 10010
Editorial Offices: Bedford Books of St. Martin's Press,
29 Commonwealth Avenue, Boston, MA 02116
ISBN: 0–312–85828–0

Typography: Anna Post
Cover design: Volney Croswell

ACKNOWLEDGMENTS

Saul Bellow, "A Silver Dish." From *Him with His Foot in His Mouth and Other Stories* by Saul Bellow. Copyright © 1974, 1978, 1982, 1984 by Saul Bellow Limited. "A Silver Dish" originally appeared in *The New Yorker Magazine*. Reprinted by permission of Harper & Row, Publishers, Inc.

John Berger, "Ways of Seeing." From *Ways of Seeing* by John Berger. Copyright © 1972 by Penguin Books Ltd. Reprinted by permission of Viking Penguin Inc. Botticelli, *Venus and Mars;* Leonardo da Vinci, *Virgin of the Rocks* and *The Virgin and Child with St. Anne and St. John the Baptist.* Reproduced by courtesy of the Trustees, The National Gallery, London. Leonardo da Vinci, *Virgin of the Rocks.* Reprinted by permission of the Louvre Museum. Pierre Bourdieu and Alain Darbel, from *L'Amour de l'Art.* Reprinted by permission of Éditions de Minuit. Pieter Breughel the Elder, *The Procession to Calvary.* Reprinted by permission of Kunst Historisches Museum, Vienna. Frans Hals, *Regents of the Old Men's Alms House* and *Regentesses of the Old Men's Alms House.* Reprinted by permission of Frans Halsmuseum. Vincent van Gogh, *Wheatfield with Crows.* Vincent van Gogh Foundation/National Museum Vincent van Gogh, Amsterdam. Reprinted by permission of Stedelijk Museum. Jan Vermeer, *Woman Pouring Milk.* Reprinted by permission of Rijksmuseum-Stichting.

Raymond Carver, "What We Talk about When We Talk about Love." Copyright © 1981 by Raymond Carver. Reprinted from *What We Talk about When We Talk about Love,* by Raymond Carver, by permission of Alfred A. Knopf, Inc.

Robert Coles, "Entitlement." From *Priveleged Ones:* Volume V of *Children of Crisis* by Robert Coles. Copyright © 1977 by Robert Coles. By permission of Little, Brown and Company in association with the Atlantic Monthly Press.

Thomas J. Cottle and Stephen L. Klineberg, "Ted and Ellie Graziano." Reprinted with permission of The Free Press, a Division of Macmillan, Inc. from *The Present of Things Future: Explorations of Time in Human Experience* by Thomas J. Cottle and Stephen L. Klineberg. Copyright © 1974 by The Free Press.

Annie Dillard, "The Fixed." From *Pilgrim at Tinker Creek* by Annie Dillard. Copyright © 1974 by Annie Dillard. Reprinted by permission of Harper & Row, Publishers, Inc.

Dorothy Dinnerstein, "Higamous-Hogamous." From *The Mermaid and the Minotaur: Sexual Arrangements and Human Malaise* by Dorothy Dinnerstein. Copyright © 1976 by Dorothy Dinnerstein. Reprinted by permission of Harper & Row, Publishers, Inc.

Stanley Fish, "How to Recognize a Poem When You See One." Reprinted by permission of the author and publishers from *Is There a Text in This Class? The Authority of Interpretive Communities* by Stanley Fish, Cambridge, Mass.: Harvard University Press, Copyright © 1980 by The President and Fellows of Harvard College.

Paulo Freire, "The 'Banking' Concept of Education." From Chapter 2 of *Pedagogy of the Oppressed* by Paulo Freire. Copyright © 1970 by the author. Reprinted by permission of The Continuum Publishing Company.

Sigmund Freud, "Taboo and the Ambivalence of Emotions." From *Totem and Taboo* in *The Basic Writings of Sigmund Freud* translated and edited by A. A. Brill. Copyright 1938, copyright renewed 1965 by Gioia B. Bernheim and Edmund Brill. Reprinted by permission.

Clifford Geertz, "Deep Play: Notes on the Balinese Cockfight." Reprinted by permission of *Daedalus,* Journal of the American Academy of Arts and Sciences, Volume 101, Numbers 1–2, Winter 1972, Boston, MA.

Thomas S. Kuhn, "The Historical Structure of Scientific Discovery." From *Science,* Volume 136, 1 June 1962, pages 760–764. Copyright © 1962 by the AAAS.

Joyce Carol Oates, "Theft." Copyright Joyce Carol Oates. From *Marya: A Life.* (Originally published in *The Northwest Review.*)

Walker Percy, "The Loss of the Creature." From *The Message in the Bottle* by Walker Percy. Copyright © 1975 by Walker Percy. Reprinted by permission of Farrar, Straus and Giroux, Inc.

Adrienne Rich, "When We Dead Awaken: Writing as Re-Vision" is reprinted from *On Lies, Secrets, and Silence, Selected Prose 1966–1978,* by Adrienne Rich, by permission of W. W. Norton & Company, Inc. Copyright © 1979 by W. W. Norton & Company, Inc.

(Continued on page 628)

Preface

Ways of Reading is designed for a course where students are given the opportunity to work on what they read, and to work on it by writing. When we began developing such courses, we realized the problems our students had when asked to write or talk about what they read were not "reading problems," at least not as these are strictly defined. Our students knew how to move from one page to the next. They could read sentences. They had, obviously, been able to carry out many of the versions of reading required for their education—skimming textbooks, cramming for tests, strip-mining books for term papers.

Our students, however, felt powerless in the face of serious writing, in the face of long and complicated texts—the kinds of texts we thought they should find interesting and challenging. We thought (as many teachers have thought) that if we just, finally, gave them something good to read—something rich and meaty—they would change forever their ways of thinking about English. It didn't work, of course. The issue is not only *what* students read, but what they can learn to *do* with what they read. We learned that the problems our students had lay not in the reading material (it was too hard) or in the students (they were poorly prepared) but in the classroom—in the ways we and they imagined what it meant to work on an essay.

There is no better place to work on reading than in a writing course, and this book is intended to provide occasions for readers to write. You will find a number of distinctive features in *Ways of Reading*. For one thing, it contains selections you don't usually see in a college reader: long, powerful, mysterious pieces like John Berger's "Ways of Seeing," Stanley Fish's "How to Recognize a Poem When You See One," Adrienne Rich's "When We Dead Awaken: Writing as Re-Vision," Clifford Geertz's "Deep Play:

Notes on the Balinese Cockfight," Thomas Kuhn's "The Historical Structure of Scientific Discovery," Sigmund Freud's "Taboo and the Ambivalence of Emotions," and Saul Bellow's "A Silver Dish." These are the sorts of readings we talk about when we talk with our colleagues. We have learned that we can talk about them with our students as well.

When we chose the essays and stories, we were looking for "readable" texts—that is, texts that left some work for a reader to do. We wanted selections that invite students to be active, critical readers, that present powerful readings of common experience, that open up the familiar world and make it puzzling, rich, and problematic. We wanted to choose selections that invite students to be active readers and to take responsibility for their acts of interpretation. So we avoided the short set-pieces you find in so many anthologies. In a sense, those short selections misrepresent the act of reading. They can be read in a single sitting; they make arguments that can be easily paraphrased; they solve all the problems they raise; they wrap up Life and put it into a box; and so they turn reading into an act of appreciation, where the most that seems to be required is a nod of the head. And they suggest that a writer's job is to do just that, to write a piece that is similarly tight and neat and self-contained. We wanted to avoid pieces that were so plainly written or tightly bound that there was little for students to do but "get the point."

We learned that if our students had reading problems when faced with long and complex texts, the problems lay in the way they imagined a reader—the role a reader played, what a reader did, why a reader read (if not simply to satisfy the requirements of a course). When, for example, our students were puzzled by what they read, they took this as a sign of failure. ("It doesn't make any sense," they would say, as though the sense were supposed to be waiting on the page, ready for them the first time they read through.) And our students were haunted by the thought that they couldn't remember everything they had read (as though one could store all of Geertz's "Deep Play" in memory); or if they did remember bits and pieces, they felt that the fragmented text they possessed was evidence that they could not do what they were supposed to do. Our students were confronting the experience of reading, in other words, but they were taking the problems of reading—problems all readers face—and concluding that there was nothing for them to do but give up.

As expert readers, we have all learned what to do with a complex text. We know that we can go back to a text; we don't have to remember it—in fact, we've learned to mark up a text to ease that re-entry. We know that a reader is a person who puts together fragments. Those coherent readings we construct begin with confusion and puzzlement, and we construct those readings by writing and rewriting—by working on a text.

These are the lessons our students need to learn, and it is why a course in reading is also a course in writing. Our students need to learn that there is something they can do once they have first read through a complicated text; successful reading is not just a matter of "getting" an essay the first time. In a very real sense, you can't begin to feel the power a reader has until you realize the problems, until you realize that no one "gets" Geertz or Rich or Kuhn or Bellow all at once. You work on what you read, and then what you have at the end is something that is yours, something you made. And this is what the teaching apparatus in *Ways of Reading* is designed to do. In a sense, it says to students, "OK, let's get to work on these essays; let's see what you can make of them."

This, then, is the second distinctive feature you will find in *Ways of Reading:* reading and writing assignments designed to give students access to the essays and stories. After each selection, for example, you will find "Questions for a Second Reading." We wanted to acknowledge that rereading is a natural way of carrying out the work of a reader, just as rewriting is a natural way of completing the work of a writer. It is not something done out of despair or as a punishment for not getting things right the first time. The questions we have written highlight what we see as central textual or interpretive problems. Geertz, for example, divides his essay into seven sections, each written in a different style. By going back through the essay with this in mind and by asking what Geertz is doing in each case (what his method is and what it enables him to accomplish), a student is in a position to see the essay as the enactment of a method and not just as a long argument with its point hidden away at the end. These questions might serve as preparations for class discussion or to direct students' work in journals. Whatever the case, they both honor and direct the work of rereading.

Each selection is also followed by two sets of writing assignments, "Assignments for Writing" and "Making Connections." The first set directs students back into the work they have just read. While the assignments vary, there are some basic principles behind them. They ask students to work on the essay by working on difficult or problematic moments in the text; they ask students to work on the author's examples, extending and testing his or her methods of analysis; or they ask students to apply the method of the essay (its way of seeing and understanding the world) to settings or experiences of their own. Students are asked, for example, to give a "Geertzian" reading to scenes from their own immediate culture (the behavior of teenagers at a shopping mall, characteristic styles in decorating a dorm room) and they are asked to imagine that they are working alongside Geertz and making his project their own. Or they are asked to consider the key examples in Rich's "When We Dead Awaken" (poems from various points in her career) to see how as writers they might use the key terms of her argument ("structures of oppression," "re-naming") in a discussion of their own. The latter assignments—"Making Connections"—invite students to read one essay in the context of another, to see, for example, if Kuhn's account of the "historical structure" of a discovery might be used to chart the stages in the development of Rich's poems or in Geertz's work on the Balinese cockfight. In a sense, then, the essays are offered as models, but not as "prose models" in the strictest sense. What they model, rather, is a way of seeing or reading the world, of both imagining problems and imagining methods to make those problems available to a writer.

At the end of the book, we have included several longer assignment sequences. In some cases, these incorporate single assignments from earlier in the book; in most cases they involve students in projects that extend over several weeks, that include several of the stories or essays in the anthology, and that require a series of separate drafts and revisions. In academic life, readers seldom read single essays in isolation, as though one were "finished" with Geertz after a week or two. They read, rather, with a purpose—with a project in mind or a problem to solve. The assignment sequences are designed to give students a feel for the rhythm and texture of an extended academic project. They offer, that is, one more way of reading and writing. Because these assignment sequences lead students through intellectual projects proceeding from one week to the next, they enable them to develop authority as specialists, to feel the difference between being an expert and a "common" reader on a single subject. And, with the luxury of time available for self-reflection, students can look back on what they have done, not only to revise what they know and the methods that enable what they know, but also to take stock and comment on the value and direction of their work.

Because of their length, it is difficult to summarize the assignment sequences. Perhaps the best way to see what we have done is to turn to the back of the book and look at them. We have made them short enough to leave room for an individual instructor's desire to add assignments, to spend additional time on single essays, or to mix one sequence with another. They are meant to frame a project for students, but to leave open possibilities for new directions.

You will also notice that there are few "glosses" appended to the essays. We have not added many editors' notes to define difficult words or to identify names or allusions to other authors or artists. We've omitted them because their presence suggests something we feel is false about reading. They suggest that good readers know all the words or pick up all the allusions or recognize every name that is mentioned. This is not true. Good readers do what they can and try their best to fill in the blanks; they ignore seemingly unimportant references and look up the important ones. There is no reason for students to feel they lack the knowledge necessary to complete a reading of these texts. We have translated foreign phrases and glossed some technical terms, but we have kept the selections as clean and open as possible.

Several of our reviewers asked us why we had included short stories in the collection. Perhaps the best answer is because we love to teach them. We think of them as having a similar status to the nonfiction case studies in the book: Thomas Cottle and Stephen Klineberg's on Ted and Ellie Graziano, Studs Terkel's on Roberta Victor and Eric Nesterenko, John Wideman's on his brother Robby, Gloria Steinem's on her mother, or Robert Coles's on the children of privileged families. They offer thick, readable slices of life—material rich enough for a reader's time and effort. We realize that we are ignoring traditional distinctions between fiction and nonfiction, but we are not sure that these are key distinctions in a course that presents reading as an action to be completed by writing. Students can work on Bellow's story about Woody Selbst just as they can work on Cottle and Klineberg's representation of the Grazianos.

We have also been asked on several occasions whether the readings aren't finally just too hard for students. The answer is no. Students will have to work on the selections, but that is the point of the course and the reason, as we said above, why a reading course is also a course in writing. College students want to believe that they can strike out on their own, make their mark, do something they have never done before. They want to *be* experts, not just hear from them. This is the great pleasure, as well as the great challenge, of undergraduate instruction. It is not hard to convince students they ought to be able to speak alongside of (or even speak back to) Clifford Geertz, Adrienne Rich, or Sigmund Freud. And, if a teacher is patient and forgiving—willing, that is, to let a student work out a reading of Freud, willing to keep from saying, "No, that's not it" and filling the silence with the "right" reading of Freud—then students can, with care and assistance, learn to speak for themselves. It takes a certain kind of classroom, to be sure. A teacher who teaches this book will have to be comfortable turning the essays over to the students, even with the knowledge that they will not do immediately on their own what a professional could do—at least not completely, or not with the same grace and authority.

In our own teaching, we have learned that we do not have to be an expert on every figure or every area of inquiry represented in this book. And, frankly, that has come as a great relief. We can have intelligent, responsible conversations about Geertz's "Deep Play" without being experts on Geertz or on anthropology or ethnography. We needed to prepare ourselves to engage and direct students as readers, but we did not have to prepare ourselves to lecture on Freud or Geertz or Rich or Kuhn and what they have to say. The classes we have been teaching, and they have been some of the most exciting we have ever taught, have been classes where students—together and with their instructors—work on what these essays might mean.

So here we are, imagining students working shoulder to shoulder with Geertz and Rich and Freud, even talking back to them as the occasion arises. There is a wonderful Emersonian bravado in all this. But such is the case with strong and active readers. If we allow students to work on powerful texts, they will want to share the power. This is the heady fun of academic life, the real pleasure of thinking, reading, and writing. There is no reason to keep it secret from our students.

Acknowledgments. We owe much to the friendship and wisdom of the people with whom we have worked: Paul Kameen, Mariolina Salvatori, Nick Coles, Bill Coles, Phil Smith, Bill Smith, Bob Marshall, Steve Carr, Marilyn DeMario, Bill Hendricks, Susan Wall, John Repp.

We also owe much to colleagues at other schools who have followed our work with interest and offered their support and criticism, particularly Nancy Sommers, Kurt Spellmeyer, Donald McQuade, and Kris Gutierrez and her staff. Don McQuade gave a close and careful reading to the many drafts of the book. He is a remarkably wise and attentive reader; his own carefully crafted writing is perhaps the best evidence of this. We were fortunate to have a number of outstanding reviewers on the project: Miriam Dow, Anne Gere, Shirley Morahan, Mike Rose, Kurt Spellmeyer, and Josephine Koster Tarvers.

Chuck Christensen of Bedford Books showed us how to write a book for others, not just for ourselves. We owe our greatest debt to Joan Feinberg, a fine and thoughtful friend as well as a fine and thoughtful editor. She was quick to understand what we wanted to do in our book and helped to keep everyone on track when there was a danger of becoming lost or distracted, and she did it all with her characteristic grace and good humor. Chris Rutigliano was the unsung hero in putting the book into print; she gave an incredible amount of time and care to allow us to make the necessary changes to have the book we wanted. We would also like to thank the rest of the talented group at Bedford Books: Nancy Lyman, Elizabeth Schaaf, and Steve Scipione.

And, finally, we are grateful to Joyce Dunlop Bartholomae and to Jesse, Daniel, and Catherine Bartholomae; to Ellen Bishop and Matthew and Benjamin Petrosky, for their love and support and for seeing to it that life went on even when we weren't there.

Contents

Introduction: Ways of Reading

Making a Mark

READING involves a fair measure of push and shove. You make your mark on a book and it makes its mark on you. Reading is not simply a matter of hanging back and waiting for a piece, or its author, to tell you what the writing has to say. In fact, one of the difficult things about reading is that the pages before you will begin to speak only when the authors are silent and you begin to speak in their place, sometimes for them, doing their work, continuing their projects, and sometimes for yourself, following your own agenda.

This is an unusual way to talk about reading, we know. We have not mentioned finding information or locating an author's purpose or identifying main ideas, useful though these skills are, because the purpose of our book is to offer you occasions to imagine other ways of reading. We think of reading as a social interaction—sometimes peaceful and polite, sometimes not so peaceful and polite.

We'd like you to imagine that when you read the essays and stories we've collected here, somebody is saying something to you, and we'd like you to imagine that you are in a position to speak back, to say something of your own in turn. In other words, we are not presenting our book as a miniature library (a place to find information) and we do not think of you, the reader, as a term-paper writer (a person looking for information to write down on three-by-five cards).

When you read, you hear an author's voice as you move along; you believe a person with something to say is talking to you. You pay attention, even when you don't completely understand what is being said, trusting that it will all make sense in the end, relating what the author says to what you already know or expect to hear or learn. Even if you don't quite grasp everything you are reading at every moment (and you won't), and even if you don't remember everything you've read (no reader does—at least not in long, complex pieces), you begin to see the outlines of the author's project, the patterns and rhythms of that particular way of seeing and interpreting the world.

When you stop to talk or write about what you've read, the author is silent; you take over—it is your turn to write, to begin to respond to what the author said. At that point this author and his or her text become something you construct out of what you remember or what you notice as you go back through the text a second time, working from passages or examples but filtering them through your own predisposition to see or read in particular ways.

In "The Achievement of Desire," one of the essays in this book, Richard Rodriguez tells the story of his education, of how he was drawn to imitate his teachers because of his desire to think and speak like them. His is not a simple story of hard work and success, however. In a sense, Rodriguez's education gave him what he wanted—status, knowledge, a way of understanding himself and his position in the world. At the same time, his education made it difficult to talk to his parents, to share their point of view; and to a degree, he felt himself becoming consumed by the powerful ways of seeing and understanding represented by his reading and his education. The essay can be seen as Rodriguez's attempt to weigh what he had gained against what he had lost.

If ten of us read this essay, each would begin with the same words on the page, but when we discuss the chapter (or write about it), each will retell and interpret Rodriguez's story differently; we emphasize different sections—some, for instance, would want to discuss the strange way Rodriguez learned to read, others would be taken by his difficult and changing relations to his teachers, and still others would want to think about Rodriguez's remarks about his mother and father.

Each of us will come to his or her own sense of what is significant, of what the point is, and the odds are good that what each of us makes of the essay will vary from one to another. Each of us will understand Rodriguez's story in his or her own way, even though we read the same piece. At the same time, if we are working with Rodriguez's essay (and not putting it aside or ignoring its peculiar way of thinking about education), we will be working within a framework he has established, one that makes education stand, metaphorically, for a complicated interplay between permanence and change, imitation and freedom, loss and achievement.

In "The Achievement of Desire," Rodriguez tells of reading a book by Richard Hoggart, *The Uses of Literacy.* He was captivated by a section of this book in which Hoggart defines a particular kind of student, the "scholarship boy." Here is what Rodriguez says:

> Then one day, leafing through Richard Hoggart's *The Uses of Literacy,* I found, in his description of the scholarship boy, myself. For the first time I realized that there were other students like me, and so I was able to frame the meaning of my academic success, its consequent price—the loss.

For Rodriguez, this phrase, "scholarship boy," became the focus of Hoggart's book. Other people, to be sure, would read that book and take different phrases or sections as the key to what Hoggart has to say. Some might argue that Rodriguez misread the book; that it is really about something else, about British culture, for example, or about the class system in England. The power and value of Rodriguez's reading, however, is represented by what he was able to *do* with what he read, and what he was able to do was not record information or summarize main ideas but, as he says, "frame the meaning of my academic success." Hoggart provided a frame, a way for Rodriguez to think and talk about his own history as a student. As he goes on in his essay, Rodriguez not only uses this frame to talk about his experience, but he resists it, argues with it. He casts his experience in Hoggart's terms but then makes those terms work for him by seeing both what they can and cannot do. This combination of reading, thinking, and writing is what we mean by *strong reading,* a way of reading we like to encourage in our students.

When we have taught "The Achievement of Desire" to our students, it was almost impossible for them not to see themselves in Rodriguez's description of the scholarship boy (and this was true of students who were not minority students and not literally on scholarships). They, too, have found a way of framing (even inventing) their own lives as students—students whose histories involve both success and loss. When we have asked our students to write about this essay, however, some students have argued, and quite convincingly, that Rodriguez had either to abandon his family and culture or remain ignorant. Other students have argued equally convincingly that Rodriguez's anguish was destructive and self-serving, that he was trapped into seeing his situation in terms that he might have replaced with others. He did not necessarily have to turn his back on his family. Some have contended that Rodriguez's problems with his family had nothing to do with what he says about education, that he himself shows how imitation need not blindly lead a person away from his culture, and these student essays, too, have been convincing.

Reading, in other words, can be the occasion for you to put things together, to notice this idea or theme rather than that one, to follow a writer's announced or secret ends while simultaneously following your own. When this happens, when you forge a reading of a story or an essay, you make your mark on it, casting it in your terms. But the story makes its mark on you as well, teaching you not only about a subject (Rodriguez's struggles with his teachers and his parents, for example) but about a way of seeing and understanding a subject. The text provides the opportunity for you to see through someone else's powerful language, to imagine your own familiar settings through the images, metaphors, and ideas of others. Rodriguez's essay, in other words, can make its mark on readers, but they, too, if they are strong, active readers, can make theirs on it.

Readers learn to put things together by writing. It is not something you can do, at least not to any degree, while you are reading. It requires that you work on what you have read, and that work best takes shape when you sit down to write. We will have more to say about this kind of thinking in a later section of the introduction, but for now let us say that writing gives you a way of going to work on the text you have read. To write about a story or essay, you go back to what you have read to find phrases or passages that define what for you are the key moments, that help you interpret sections that seem difficult or troublesome or mysterious. If you are writing an essay of your own, the work that you are doing gives a purpose and a structure to that rereading.

Writing also, however, gives you a way of going back to work on the text of your own reading. It allows you to be self-critical. You can revise not just to make your essay neat or tight or tidy but to see what kind of reader you have been, to examine the pattern and consequences in the choices you have made. Revision, in other words, gives you the chance to work on your essay, but it also gives you an opportunity to work on your reading—to qualify or extend or question your interpretation of, say, "The Achievement of Desire."

We can describe this process of "re-vision," or re-seeing, fairly simply. You should not expect to read "The Achievement of Desire" once and completely understand the essay or know what you want to say. You will work out what you have to say while you write. And once you have constructed a reading—once you have completed a draft of your essay, in other words—you can step back, see what you have done, and go back to work on it. Through this activity—writing and rewriting—we have seen our students become strong, active, and critical readers.

Not everything a reader reads is worth that kind of effort. The essays and stories we have chosen for this book all provide, we feel, powerful ways of seeing (or framing) our common experience. The selections cannot be quickly summarized. They are striking, surprising, sometimes troubling in how they challenge common ways of seeing the world. Some of them (we're thinking of pieces by Thomas Kuhn, Stanley Fish, Clifford Geertz, and Sigmund Freud) have captured and altered the way our culture sees and understands daily experience. The essays have changed the ways people think and write. In fact, every selection in the book is one that has given us, our students, and colleagues that dramatic experience, almost like a discovery, when we suddenly saw things as we had never seen them before and, as a consequence, we had to work hard to understand what had happened and how our thinking had changed.

If we recall, for example, the first time we read Walker Percy's essay, "The Loss of the Creature" or John Berger's "Ways of Seeing," we know that they have radically shaped our thinking. We carry these essays with us in our minds, mulling over them, working through them, hearing Percy and Berger in sentences we write or sentences we read; we introduce the essays in classes we teach whenever we can; we are surprised, reading them for the third or fourth time, to find things we didn't see before. It's not that we failed to "get" these essays the first time around. In fact, we're not sure we have captured them yet, at least not in any final sense, and we disagree in basic ways about what Percy and Berger are saying or about how those essays might best be used. Essays like these are not the sort that you can "get" like a loaf of bread at the store. We're each convinced that the essays are ours in that we know best what's going on in them, and yet we have also become theirs, creatures of these essays, because of the ways they have come to dominate our seeing, talking, reading, and writing. This captivity is something we welcome, yet it is also something we resist.

Our experience with these texts is a remarkable one and certainly hard to provide for others, but the challenges and surprises are reasons we read—we hope to be taken and changed in just these ways. Or, to be more accurate, it is why we read outside the daily requirements to keep up with the news or conduct our business. And it is why we bring reading into our writing courses.

Ways of Reading

Before explaining how we organized this book, we would like to say more about the purpose and place of the kind of strong, aggressive, labor-intensive reading we've been referring to.

Readers face many kinds of experiences, and certain texts are written with specific situations in mind and invite specific ways of reading. Some texts, for instance, serve very practical purposes—they give directions or information. Others, like the short descriptive essays often used in English textbooks and anthologies, celebrate common ways of seeing and thinking and ask primarily to be admired. These texts seem self-contained; they announce their own meanings with little effort and ask little from the reader, making it clear how they want to be read and what they have to say. They ask only for a nod of the head or for the reader to take notes and give a sigh of admiration ("yes, that was very well said"). They are clear and direct. It is as though the authors could anticipate all the questions their own essays might raise and solve all the problems a reader might imagine. There is not much work for a reader to do, in other words, except, perhaps, to take notes and, in the case of textbooks, to work step-by-step, trying to remember as much as possible.

This is how assigned readings are often presented in university classrooms. Introductory textbooks (in biology or business, for instance) are good examples of books that ask little of readers outside of note-taking and memorization. In these texts the writers are experts and your job, as novice, is to digest what they have to say. And, appropriately, the task set before you is to summarize—so you can speak again what the author said, so you can better remember what you read. Essay tests are an example of the writing tasks that often follow this kind of reading. You might, for instance, study the human nervous system through textbook readings and lectures and then be asked to write a summary of what you know from both sources. Or a teacher might ask you during a class discussion to paraphrase a paragraph from a textbook describing chemical cell communication to see if you understand what you've read.

Another typical classroom form of reading is reading for main ideas. With this kind of reading you are expected to figure out what most people (or most people within a certain specialized group of readers) would take as the main idea of a selection. There are good reasons to read for main ideas. For one, it is a way to learn how to imagine and anticipate the values and habits of a particular group—test-makers or, if you're studying business, Keynesian economists, perhaps. If you are studying business, to continue this example, you must learn to notice what Keynesian economists notice—for instance, when they analyze the problems of growing government debt—to share key terms, to know the theoretical positions they take, and to adopt for yourself their common examples and interpretations, their jargon, and their established findings.

There is certainly nothing wrong with reading for information or reading to learn what experts have to say about their fields of inquiry. These are not, however, the only ways to read, although they are the ones most often taught. Perhaps because we think of ourselves as writing teachers, we are concerned with presenting other ways of reading in the college and university curriculum.

A danger arises in assuming that reading is only a search for information or main ideas. There are ways of thinking through problems and working with written texts which are essential to academic life but which are not represented by summary and paraphrase or by note-taking and essay exams.

Student readers, for example, can take responsibility for determining the meaning of the text. They can work as though they were doing something other than finding ideas already there on the page and they can be guided by their own impressions or questions as they read. We are not, now, talking about finding hidden meanings. If such things as hidden meanings can be said to exist, they are hidden by readers' habits and prejudices (by readers' assumptions that what they read should tell them what they already know), or by readers' timidity and passivity (by their unwillingness to take the responsibility to speak their minds and say what they notice).

Reading to locate meaning in the text places a premium on memory, yet a strong reader is not necessarily a person with a good memory. This point may seem minor, but we have seen too many students haunted because they could not remember everything they read or retain a complete essay in their minds. A reader could set herself the task of remembering as much as she could from Percy's "The Loss of the Creature," an essay filled with stories about tourists at the Grand Canyon and students in a biology class, but a reader could also do other things with that essay; a reader might figure out, for example, how both students and tourists might be said to have a common problem seeing what they want to see. Students who read Percy's essay as a memory test end up worrying about bits and pieces (bits and pieces they could go back and find if they had to) and turn their attention away from the more pressing problem of how to make sense of a difficult and often ambiguous essay.

A reader who needs to have access to something in the essay can use simple memory aids. A reader can go back and scan, for one thing, to find passages or examples that might be worth reconsidering. Or a reader can construct a personal index, making marks in the margin or underlining passages that seem interesting or mysterious or difficult. A mark is a way of saying, "This is something I might want to work on later." If you mark the selections in this book as you read them, you will give yourself a working record of what, at the first moment of reading, you felt might be worth a second reading.

If Percy's essay presents problems for a reader, they are problems of a different order from summary and recall altogether. The essay is not the sort that tells you what it says. You would have difficulty finding one sentence that sums up or announces, in a loud and clear voice, what he is talking about. At the point you think Percy is about to summarize, he turns to one more example that complicates the picture, as though what he is discussing defies his attempts to sum things up. Percy is talking about tourists and students, about such things as individual "sovereignty" and our media culture's "symbolic packages," but if he has a point to make, it cannot be stated in a sentence or two.

In fact, Percy's essay is challenging reading in part because it does not have a single, easily identifiable main idea. A reader could infer that it has several points to make, none of which can be said easily and some of which, perhaps, are contradictory. To search for information, or to ignore the rough edges in search of a single, paraphraseable idea, is to divert attention from the task at hand, which is not to remember what Percy says but to speak about the essay and what it means to you, the reader. In this sense, the Percy essay is not the sum of its individual parts, it is, more accurately, what its readers make of it.

A reader could go to an expert on Percy to solve the problem of what to make of the essay—perhaps to a teacher, perhaps to a book in the library. And if the reader pays attention, he could remember what the expert said or she could put down notes on paper. But in doing either, the reader only rehearses what he or she has been told, abandoning the responsibility to make the essay meaningful. There are ways of reading, in other words, in which Percy's essay, "The Loss of the Creature," is not what it means to the experts but what it means to you as a reader willing to take the chance to construct a reading. You can be the authority on Percy; you don't have to turn to others. The meaning of the essay, then, is something you develop as you go along, something for which you must take final responsibility. The meaning is forged from reading the essay, to be sure, but it is determined by what you do with the essay, by the connections you can make and your explanation of why those connections are important, and by your account of what Percy might mean when he talks about "symbolic packages" or a "loss of sovereignty" (phrases Percy uses as key terms in the essay). This version of Percy's essay will finally be yours; it will not be exactly what Percy said. (Only his words in the order he wrote them would say exactly what he said.) You will choose the line to take through his essay and support it as you can with arguments, explanations, examples, and commentary.

If an essay or story is not the sum of its parts but something you as a reader create by putting together those parts that seem to matter personally, then the way to begin, once you have read a selection in this collection, is by reviewing what you recall, by going back to those places that stick in your memory—or, perhaps, to those sections you marked with checks or notes in the margins. You begin by seeing what you can make of these memories and notes. You should realize that with essays as long and complex as those we've included in this book, you will never feel, after a single reading, as though you have command of everything you read. This is not a problem. After four or five readings (should you give any single essay that much attention), you may still feel that there are parts you missed or don't understand. This sense of incompleteness is part of the experience of reading, at least the experience of reading serious work. And it is part of the experience of a strong reader. No reader could retain one of these essays in her mind, no matter how proficient her memory or how experienced she might be. No reader, at least no reader we would trust, would admit that he understood everything that Sigmund Freud or Clifford Geertz or Walker Percy had to say. What strong readers know is that they have to begin, and they have to begin regardless of their doubts or hesitations. What you have after your first reading of an essay is a starting place, and you begin with your marked passages or examples or notes, with questions to answer, or with problems to solve. Strong readings, in other words, put a premium on individual acts of attention and composition.

Strong Readers, Strong Texts

We chose essays and stories for this book that invite strong readings. The selections require more attention than an easy summary or a quick reduction to main ideas. They are written for readers who delight in contradictory and puzzling matters. The challenges they present, however, do not make them inaccessible to college students. The essays are not specialized studies; they have interested, pleased, or piqued both general and specialist audiences. To say they are challenging is to say, then, that they leave some work for a reader to do. They require readers willing to accept the challenge and the responsibility of reading. These readers need not be experts on the subject matter. Perhaps the most difficult problem for students is to believe that this is true.

You do not need experts to explain these stories and essays, although you probably could find an expert guide to any selection we've included. Let's take, for example, the selection from Dorothy Dinnerstein's unsettling book about men and women, *The Mermaid and the Minotaur*. The chapter we included, "Higamous-Hogamous," discusses why men and women are unable to understand each other and links the problem with the fact that as young children, both boys and girls are raised primarily by women. You could go to the library to find out how Dinnerstein is regarded by experts, by psychologists, for example; you could learn how her ideas fit into standard theories about the effects of child-rearing on men and women.

You could see how experts define and understand some of Dinnerstein's key terms: "mother-raising," "erotic impulsivity," or "personal sentiment."

But Dinnerstein can also be read outside any official system of interpretation. She is talking, after all, about our daily experience. When she says "we" are affected by unfair sexual standards initiated in early childhood, she means all of us. The question, then, is not what "erotic impulsivity" might mean to a group of psychologists, but what you, the reader, can make of the phrase and Dinnerstein's use of it, given your own immediate experience. In this sense, *The Mermaid and the Minotaur* is not what it means to others (those who have already decided what it means) but what it means to you, and this meaning is something you compose when you write about the essay; it is your account of what she says and how it makes sense.

A teacher, poet, and critic we admire, I. A. Richards, once said, "Read as though it made sense and perhaps it will." To take command of complex material like the essays and stories in this book, you need not subordinate yourself to experts; you can assume the authority to provide such a reading on your own. This means you must allow yourself a certain tentativeness and recognize your limits. You should not assume that it is your job to solve the problems between men and women. You can speak with authority while still acknowledging that complex issues *are* complex.

There is a paradox here. On the one hand, the essays are rich, magnificent, too big for anyone to completely grasp all at once, and before them, as before inspiring spectacles, it seems appropriate to stand humbly, admiringly. And yet, on the other hand, a reader must speak with authority.

In "The American Scholar" (an essay included in this book), Ralph Waldo Emerson said, "Meek young men grow up in libraries, believing in their duty to accept the views, which Cicero, which Locke, which Bacon, have given, forgetful that Cicero, Locke, and Bacon were only young men in libraries when they wrote these books." What Emerson offers here is not a fact but an attitude. There is creative reading, he says, as well as creative writing. It is up to you to treat authors as your equals, as people who will allow you to speak too. At the same time, you must respect the difficulty and complexity of their texts and of the issues and questions they examine. Little is to be gained, in other words, by turning Dinnerstein's essay into a message that would fit on a poster in a dorm room: "Be Yourself" or "Stand on Your Own Two Feet."

Reading and Writing: The Questions and Assignments

Strong readers, we've said, remake what they have read to serve their own ends, putting things together, figuring out how ideas and examples relate, explaining as best they can material that is difficult or problematic, translating phrases like Richard Rodriguez's "scholarship boy" into their own terms. At these moments, it is hard to distinguish the act of reading from the act of writing. In fact, the connection between reading and writing can be seen as almost a literal one, since the best way you can show your reading of a rich and dense essay like "The Achievement of Desire" is by writing down your thoughts, placing one idea against another, commenting on what you've done, taking examples into account, looking back at where you began, perhaps changing your mind, and moving on.

Readers, however, seldom read a single essay in isolation, as though their only job were to arrive at some sense of what an essay has to say. Although we couldn't begin to provide examples of all the various uses of reading in academic life, it is often the case that readings provide information and direction for investigative projects, whether they are philosophical or scientific in nature. The reading and writing assignments that follow each selection in this book are designed to point you in certain directions, to give you ideas and projects to work with, and to challenge you to see one writer's ideas through another's.

Strong readers often read critically, weighing, for example, an author's claims and interpretations against evidence—evidence provided by the author in the text, evidence drawn from other sources, or the evidence that is assumed to be part of a reader's own knowledge and experience. Critical reading can produce results as far-reaching as a biochemist publicly challenging the findings and interpretations in an article on cancer research in the *New England Journal of Medicine* or as quiet as a student offering a personal interpretation of a story in class discussion.

You will find that the questions we have included in our reading and writing assignments often direct you to test what you think an author is saying by measuring it against your own experience. Paulo Freire, for example, in "The 'Banking' Concept of Education," talks about the experience of the student, and one way for you to develop or test your reading of his essay is to place what he says in the context of your own experience, searching for examples that are similar to his and examples that differ. If the writers in this book are urging you to give strong readings of your common experience, you have access to what they say because they are not only talking to you but about you. Freire has a method that he employs when he talks about the classroom—one that compares "banking" education with "problem-posing" education. You can try out his method and his terms on examples of your own, continuing his argument as though you were working with him on a common project. Or you can test his argument as though you want to see not only where and how it will work but where and how it will not.

You will also find questions that ask you to extend the argument of the essay by looking in detail at some of the essay's own examples. John Berger, for example, gives a detailed analysis of two paintings by Franz Hals in "Ways of Seeing." Other paintings in the essay he refers to only briefly. One way of working on his essay is to look at the other examples, trying to do with them what he has done for you earlier.

It is seldom the case, however, that readers read a single essay in isolation, as though having once worked out a reading of Walker Percy's "The Loss of the Creature," it was time to go on to something else, something unrelated. It is unusual for anyone, at least in an academic setting, to read in so random a fashion. Readers read most often because they have a project in hand—a question they are working on or a problem they are trying to solve. For example, if as a result of reading Percy's essay you are studying why people fail to see that which is around them, or how some can see while others remain blind, then other essays in the book can be read through the frame of Percy's essay. If you have a project in mind, that project will help determine how you use these other essays. Sections of a story that might otherwise seem unimportant suddenly become important—when, for instance, Berger uses terms that may be similar to Percy's or when Annie Dillard, in "The Fixed," provides examples of someone struggling to see what she would otherwise miss in nature. Percy might enable you to discover something you would have overlooked in Berger. Berger may cause you to change your mind or alter your point of view on Percy.

In a sense, then, you do have the chance to become an expert reader, a reader with a project in hand, one who has already done some reading, who has watched others at work, and who has begun to develop a method of analysis and a set of key terms. You might read Saul Bellow's story "The Silver Dish," for example, in the context of Sigmund Freud's discussion of the taboo of the dead, or use Thomas Kuhn's system for charting the internal structure of a discovery to examine the process of Clifford Geertz's discoveries concerning cockfights in Bali, or use Robert Coles's concept of entitlement to understand Richard Rodriquez and his concern about what he did and did not deserve to get from his education. Imagining yourself operating alongside of some of the major figures in contemporary thought can be great fun and heady work—particularly when you have the occasion to speak back to them.

In every case, then, the material we provide to direct your work on the essay will have you constructing a reading, but then doing something with what you have read—using the essay as a frame through which you can understand (through which you can "read") your own experience, the examples of others, or the ideas and methods of other writers.

You may find that you have to alter your sense of who a writer is and what a writer does as you work on your own writing. Writers are often told that they need to begin with a clear sense of what they want to do and what they want to say. The writing assignments we've written, we believe, give you a sense of what you want (or need) to do. We define a problem for you to work on, and the problem will frame the task for you. You will have to decide where you will go in the texts you have read to find material to work with, the primary materials that will give you a place to begin as you work on your essay. It would be best, however, if you did not feel that you need to have a clear sense of what you want to say before you begin. In one sense, you will begin to develop a sense of what you want to say while you are writing—as you begin, for example, to examine the way Annie Dillard studies insects in light of what Emerson says about studying nature. In another sense, however, the subjects you will be writing about are too big for you to assume that you need to have all the answers or that it is up to you to have the final word or to solve the problems once and for all. When you work on your essays, you should cast yourself in the role of one who is exploring a question, examining what might be said, and speculating on possible rather than certain conclusions. If you consider your responses to be provisional, examples of what might be said by a bright and serious student at this point in time, you will be in a position to learn more, as will those who read what you write. Think of yourself, then, as a writer intent on opening a subject up rather than closing one down.

Let us turn briefly now to the various categories of reading and writing assignments you will find in the book.

Questions for a Second Reading

Immediately following each selection are questions designed to guide your second reading. You may, as we've said, prefer to follow your own instincts as you search for the materials to build your understanding of the essay or story. These questions are meant to assist that process or develop those instincts. Most of the essays and stories in the book are longer and more difficult than those you may be accustomed to reading. They are difficult enough that any reader would have to reread them and work to understand them; the second reading questions are meant to suggest ways of beginning that work.

The second reading questions characteristically ask you to consider the relations between ideas and examples in what you have read or to test specific statements in the essays against your own experience (so that you can get a sense of the author's habit of mind, his or her way of thinking about subjects that are available to you, too). Some turn your attention to what we take to be key terms or concepts, asking you to define these terms by observing how the writer uses them throughout the essay.

These are the questions that seemed "natural" to us; they reflect our habitual way of reading and, we believe, the general habits of mind of the academic community. These questions have no simple answers; you will not find a correct answer hidden somewhere in the selection. In short, they are not the sorts of questions asked on SAT or ACT exams. They are real questions, questions that ask about the basic methods of an essay or about the issues the essay raises. They pose problems for interpretation or indicate sections where, to our minds, there is some interesting work for a reader to do. They are meant to reveal possible ways of reading the text, not to indicate that there is only one correct way, and that we have it.

You may find it useful to take notes as you read through each selection a second time, perhaps in a journal you can keep as a sourcebook for more formal written work.

Assignments for Writing

This book actually offers three different kinds of writing assignments: assignments that ask you to write about a single essay or story; assignments that ask you to read one selection through the frame of another; and longer sequences of assignments that define a project within which three or four of the selections serve as primary sources. All of these assignments serve a dual purpose. Like the second reading questions, they suggest a way for you to reconsider the stories or essays; they give you access from a different perspective. The assignments also encourage you to be strong readers and actively interpret what you have read. In one way or another, they all invite you to use a story or an essay as a way of framing experience, as a source of terms and methods to enable you to interpret something else—some other text, events and objects around you, or your own memories and experience. The assignment sequences can be found at the end of the book. The others (titled Assignments for Writing and Making Connections) come immediately after each selection.

Assignments for Writing ask you to write about a single selection. Although some of these assignments call for you to paraphrase or reconstruct difficult passages, most ask you to interpret what you have read with a specific purpose in mind. The work you are to do is generally of two sorts. For most of the essays, one question asks you to interpret a moment from your own experience through the frame of the essay. This, you will remember, is the use that Rodriguez made of Richard Hoggart's *The Uses of Literacy*.

An essay by Thomas Kuhn, "The Historical Structure of Scientific Discovery," provides a method for analyzing the internal structure of scientific discoveries. Although we cannot assume that you have made a scientific discovery, we can assume that at some point you have discovered something—about yourself, your friends, your school, or the world around you. Thus, one assignment asks you to describe a discovery that gave you a new view of something familiar and to then give that discovery a Kuhnian analysis, to examine it as though you were continuing Kuhn's work in a project of your own. The point of this exercise is to develop your command of Kuhn's method and key terms by applying them to a separate case, by seeing how this essay on great moments in science might connect with moments in your own life. We believe that by doing such an assignment you will learn about Kuhn and the work he does, but we also believe that through Kuhn you can come to a new understanding of your own experience.

Other assignments, however, ask you to turn an essay back on itself or to extend the conclusions of the essay by reconsidering the examples the writer has used to make his or her case. Adrienne Rich's essay, "When We Dead Awaken: Writing as Re-Vision," is built around a series of poems she wrote at various stages in her career. She says that the development represented by these poems reflects her growing understanding of the problems women in a patriarchal society have in finding a language for their own experience. She presents the poems as examples but offers little detailed discussion of them. One of the assignments, then, asks you to describe the key differences in these poems. It next asks you to comment on the development of her work and to compare your account of that development with hers.

In her essay, Rich also says that writing is "re-naming." This is an interesting and, one senses, a potentially powerful term. For it to be useful, however, a reader must put it to work, to see what results when you accept the challenge of the essay and think about writing as re-naming. Another assignment, then, asks you to apply this term to one of her poems and to discuss the poem as an act of re-naming. The purpose of this assignment is not primarily to develop your skill as a reader of poems but to develop your sense of the method and key terms of Rich's argument.

Making Connections

The connections questions will have you work with two readings at a time. These are not so much questions that ask you to compare or contrast the essays or stories as they are directions on how you might use one text as the context for interpreting another. Freud, for example, talks in "Taboo and the Ambivalence of Emotions" about our complicated attitudes toward death and how these attitudes affect our behavior. And Saul Bellow's story, "A Silver Dish," begins with the central character saying, "What do you do about death—in this case, the death of an old father?" Accordingly, there is an assignment that asks you to give a Freudian reading of the

Bellow story, where the Freud you are working with is the Freud you have seen at work in "Taboo and the Ambivalence of Emotions." (You are not, in other words, expected to know everything there is to know about Freud.) Other assignments follow this pattern. You are asked to see Annie Dillard's journey to Tinker Creek through Emerson's eyes and to consider how closely she is following his program for studying nature. Emerson can give you a way of looking at Dillard that you would not have been able to invent on your own. In another assignment you are asked to examine the case study of Ted and Ellie Graziano in the context of Dorothy Dinnerstein's argument about why men and women are unable to understand each other.

The purpose of all of these assignments is to demonstrate how the work of one author can be used as a frame for reading and interpreting the work of another. This can be exciting work, and it demonstrates a basic principle of liberal arts education: students should be given the opportunity to adopt different points of view, including those of scholars and writers who have helped to shape modern thought. These kinds of assignments give you the chance, even as a novice, to try your hand at the work of professionals.

The Assignment Sequences

The assignment sequences are more broad-ranging versions of the making connections assignments; in the sequences several reading and writing assignments are linked and directed toward a single goal. They allow you to work on projects that require more time and incorporate more readings than would be possible in a single assignment. And they encourage you to develop your own point of view in concert with those of the professionals who wrote the essays and stories you are reading.

The assignments in a sequence build on each other, each relying on the ones before. In one sequence, for example, you begin with Walker Percy's essay "The Loss of the Creature," an essay that considers the problems tourists and students have in seeing and understanding that which lies before them. You are given the chance to work on the essay, to determine what, so far as you are concerned, it is saying about both the nature of this problem and how it might be overcome. The second assignment asks you to comment on experiences you have had as a student or a tourist using Percy's terms, writing about yourself as though you were carrying out a project Percy had begun.

The opening assignments are followed by others that have you working on essays by other writers who consider why people do or don't see things. You have a chance to look at a student (Richard Rodriguez) and a tourist (Clifford Geertz) in order to test Percy's views and those of the other writers. And, finally, you are asked to carve out a position of your own, to see what, after studying all these essays, you might add to an ongoing conversation about tourists and students and the problems people have seeing and understanding the world around them.

The sequences allow you to participate in an extended academic project, one in which you take a position, revise it, look at a new example, hear what someone else has to say, revise it again, and see what conclusions you can draw about your subject. These projects always take time—they go through stages and revisions as a writer develops a command over his or her material, pushing against habitual ways of thinking, learning to examine an issue from different angles, rejecting quick conclusions, seeing the power of understanding that comes from repeated effort, and feeling the pleasure writers take when they find their own place in the context of others whose work they admire. This is the closest approximation we can give you of the rhythm and texture of academic life, and we offer our book as an introduction to its characteristic ways of reading, thinking, and writing.

The Readings

SAUL BELLOW

SAUL BELLOW is one of our most celebrated contemporary American writers. He won the Nobel Prize for literature in 1976, the Pulitzer Prize for fiction (for Humboldt's Gift*), and several National Book Awards (for* The Adventures of Augie March, Herzog, *and* Mr. Sammler's Planet*). Bellow was born in Lachine, Quebec, in 1915, but grew up in Chicago, which is the setting for much of his fiction.*

Bellow earned a B.S. in sociology and anthropology from Northwestern University in 1937. He abandoned his studies after a short stay in graduate school—because, he said, "every time I worked on my thesis, it turned out to be a story." While he made a career telling stories, his writing has always exemplified the social scientist's concern for closely observed, carefully recorded scenes of daily life. Bellow's fiction is not showy or self-consciously experimental. He seems to invite a reader into familiar territory; these familiar landscapes, however, become rich, mysterious, and unsettling. Bellow once commented that "perhaps the deepest readers are those who are least sure of themselves." Bellow's great talent is telling stories of ordinary people and places that allow readers those deep, if disquieting, moments of uncertainty.

After working in the WPA Writer's Project during the Great Depression and serving with the Merchant Marine in World War II, Bellow taught at the University of Minnesota, New York University, and Princeton University, among others, and has been a member of the University of Chicago's English department since 1963. The following story, "A Silver Dish," appeared in Bellow's most recent collection, Him with His Foot in His Mouth and Other Stories.

A Silver Dish

What do you do about death—in this case, the death of an old father? If you're a modern person, sixty years of age, and a man who's been around, like Woody Selbst, what do you do? Take this matter of mourning, and take it against a contemporary background. How, against a contemporary background, do you mourn an octogenarian father, nearly blind, his heart enlarged, his lungs filling with fluid, who creeps, stumbles, gives off the odors, the moldiness or gassiness, of old men. I *mean!* As Woody put it, be realistic. Think what times these are. The papers daily give it to you—the Lufthansa pilot in Aden is described by the hostages on his knees, begging the Palestinian terrorists not to execute him, but they shoot him through the head. Later they themselves are killed. And still others shoot others, or shoot themselves. That's what you read in the press, see on the tube, mention at dinner. We know now what goes daily through the whole of the human community, like a global death-peristalsis.

Woody, a businessman in South Chicago, was not an ignorant person. He knew more such phrases than you would expect a tile contractor (offices, lobbies, lavatories) to know. The kind of knowledge he had was not the kind for which you get academic degrees. Although Woody had studied for two years in a seminary, preparing to be a minister. Two years of college during the Depression was more than most high-school graduates could afford. After that, in his own vital, picturesque, original way (Morris, his old man, was also, in his days of nature, vital and picturesque), Woody had read up on many subjects, subscribed to *Science* and other magazines that gave real information, and had taken night courses at De Paul and Northwestern in ecology, criminology, existentialism. Also he had traveled extensively in Japan, Mexico, and Africa, and there was an African experience that was especially relevant to mourning. It was this: on a launch near the Murchison Falls in Uganda, he had seen a buffalo calf seized by a crocodile from the bank of the White Nile. There were giraffes along the tropical river, and hippopotamuses, and baboons, and flamingos and other brilliant birds crossing the bright air in the heat of the morning, when the calf, stepping into the river to drink, was grabbed by the hoof and dragged down. The parent buffaloes couldn't figure it out. Under the water the calf still threshed, fought, churned the mud. Woody, the robust traveler, took this in as he sailed by, and to him it looked as if the parent cattle were asking each other dumbly what had happened. He chose to assume that there was pain in this, he read brute grief into it. On the White Nile, Woody had the impression that he had gone back to the pre-Adamite past, and he brought reflections on this impression home to South Chicago. He brought also a bundle of hashish from Kampala. In this he took a chance with the customs inspectors, banking perhaps on his broad build, frank face, high color. He didn't look like a wrongdoer, a bad guy; he looked like a good guy. But he liked taking chances. Risk was a wonderful stimulus. He threw down his trenchcoat on the customs counter. If the inspectors searched the pockets, he was prepared to say that the coat wasn't his. But he got away with it, and the Thanksgiving turkey was stuffed with hashish. This was much enjoyed. That was practically the last feast at which Pop, who also relished risk or defiance, was present. The hashish Woody had tried to raise in his backyard from the Africa seeds didn't take. But behind his warehouse, where the Lincoln Continental was parked, he kept a patch of marijuana. There was no harm at all in Woody, but he didn't like being entirely within the law. It was simply a question of self-respect.

After that Thanksgiving, Pop gradually sank as if he had a slow leak. This went on for some years. In and out of the hospital, he dwindled, his mind wandered, he couldn't even concentrate enough to complain, except in exceptional moments on the Sundays Woody regularly devoted to him. Morris, an amateur who once was taken seriously by Willie Hoppe, the great pro himself, couldn't execute the simplest billiard shots anymore. He could only conceive shots; he began to theorize about impossible three-cushion combinations. Halina, the Polish woman with whom Morris had lived for over forty years as man and wife, was too old herself now to run to the hospital. So Woody had to do it. There was Woody's mother, too—a Christian convert—needing care; she was over eighty and frequently hospitalized. Everybody had diabetes and pleurisy and arthritis and cataracts and cardiac pacemakers. And everybody had lived by the body, but the body was giving out.

There were Woody's two sisters as well, unmarried, in their fifties, very Christian, very straight, still living with Mama in an entirely Christian bungalow. Woody, who took full responsibility for them all, occasionally had to put one of the girls (they had become sick girls) in a mental institution. Nothing severe. The sisters were wonderful women, both of them gorgeous once, but neither of the poor things was playing with a full deck.

And all the factions had to be kept separate—Mama, the Christian convert; the fundamentalist sisters; Pop, who read the Yiddish paper as long as he could still see print; Halina, a good Catholic. Woody, the seminary forty years behind him, described himself as an agnostic. Pop had no more religion than you could find in the Yiddish paper, but he made Woody promise to bury him among Jews, and that was where he lay now, in the Hawaiian shirt Woody had bought for him at the tilers' convention in Honolulu. Woody would allow no undertaker's assistant to dress him, but came to the parlor and buttoned the stiff into the shirt himself, and the old man went down looking like Ben-Gurion in a simple wooden coffin, sure to rot fast. That was how Woody wanted it all. At the graveside, he had taken off and folded his jacket, rolled up his sleeves on thick freckled biceps, waved back the little tractor standing by, and shoveled the dirt himself. His big face, broad at the bottom, narrowed upward like a Dutch house. And, his small good lower teeth taking hold of the upper lip in his exertion, he performed the final duty of a son. He was very fit, so it must have been emotion, not the shoveling, that made him redden so. After the funeral, he went home with Halina and her son, a decent Polack like his mother, and talented, too—Mitosh played the organ at hockey and basketball games in the Stadium, which took a smart man because it was a rabble-rousing kind of occupation—and they had some drinks and comforted the old girl. Halina was true blue, always one hundred percent for Morris.

Then for the rest of the week Woody was busy, had jobs to run, office responsibilities, family responsibilities. He lived alone; as did his wife; as did his mistress: everybody in a separate establishment. Since his wife, after fifteen years of separation, had not learned to take care of herself, Woody did her shopping on Fridays, filled her freezer. He had to take her this week to buy shoes. Also, Friday night he always spent with Helen—Helen was his wife de facto. Saturday he did his big weekly shopping. Saturday night he devoted to Mom and his sisters. So he was too busy to attend to his own feelings except, intermittently, to note to himself, "First Thursday in the grave." "First Friday, and fine weather." "First Saturday; he's got to be getting used to it." Under his breath he occasionally said, "Oh, Pop."

But it was Sunday that hit him, when the bells rang all over South Chicago—the Ukrainian, Roman Catholic, Greek, Russian, African Methodist churches, sounding off one after another. Woody had his offices in his warehouse, and there had built an apartment for himself, very spacious and convenient, in the top story. Because he left every Sunday morning at seven to spend the day with Pop, he had forgotten by how many churches Selbst Tile Company was surrounded. He was still in bed when he heard the bells, and all at once he knew how heartbroken he was. This sudden big heartache in a man of sixty, a practical, physical, healthy-minded, and experienced man, was deeply unpleasant. When he had an unpleasant condition, he believed in taking something for it. So he thought: What shall I take? There were plenty of remedies available. His cellar was stocked with cases of Scotch whisky, Polish vodka, Armagnac, Moselle, Burgundy. There were also freezers with steaks and with game and with Alaskan king crab. He bought with a broad hand—by the crate and by the dozen. But in the end, when he got out of bed, he took nothing but a cup of coffee. While the kettle was heating, he put on his Japanese judo-style suit and sat down to reflect.

Woody was moved when things were *honest*. Bearing beams were honest, undisguised concrete pillars inside high-rise apartments were honest. It was bad to cover up anything. He hated faking. Stone was honest. Metal was honest. These Sunday bells were very straight. They broke loose, they wagged and rocked, and the vibrations and the banging did something for him—cleansed his insides, purified his blood. A bell was a one-way throat, had only one thing to tell you and simply told it. He listened.

He had had some connections with bells and churches. He was after all something of a Christian. Born a Jew, he was a Jew facially, with a hint of Iroquois or Cherokee, but his mother had been converted more than fifty years ago by her brother-in-law, the Reverend Doctor Kovner. Kovner, a rabbinical student who had left the Hebrew Union College in Cincinnati to become a minister and establish a mission, had given Woody a partly Christian upbringing. Now, Pop was on the outs with these fundamentalists. He said that the Jews came to the mission to get coffee, bacon, canned pineapple, day-old bread, and dairy products. And if they had to listen to sermons, that was okay—this was the Depression and you couldn't be too particular—but he knew they sold the bacon.

The Gospels said it plainly: "Salvation is from the Jews."

Backing the Reverend Doctor were wealthy fundamentalists, mainly Swedes, eager to speed up the Second Coming by converting all Jews. The foremost of Kovner's backers was Mrs. Skoglund, who had inherited a large dairy business from her late husband. Woody was under her special protection.

Woody was fourteen years of age when Pop took off with Halina, who worked in his shop, leaving his difficult Christian wife and his converted son and his small daughters. He came to Woody in the backyard one spring day and said, "From now on you're the man of the house." Woody was practicing with a golf club, knocking off the heads of dandelions. Pop came into the yard in his good suit, which was too hot for the weather, and when he took off his fedora the skin of his head was marked with a deep ring and the sweat was sprinkled over his scalp—more drops than hairs. He said, "I'm going to move out." Pop was anxious, but he was set to go—determined. "It's no use. I can't live a life like this." Envisioning the life Pop simply *had* to live, his free life, Woody was able to picture him in the billiard parlor, under the El tracks in a crap game, or playing poker at Brown and Koppel's upstairs. "You're going to be the man of the house," said Pop. "It's okay. I put you all on welfare. I just got back from Wabansia Avenue, from the relief station." Hence the suit and the hat. "They're sending out a caseworker." Then he said, "You got to lend me money to buy gasoline—the caddie money you saved."

Understanding that Pop couldn't get away without his help, Woody turned over to him all he had earned at the Sunset Ridge Country Club in Winnetka. Pop felt that the valuable life lesson he was transmitting was worth far more than these dollars, and whenever he was conning his boy a sort of high-priest expression came down over his bent nose, his ruddy face. The children, who got their finest ideas at the movies, called him Richard Dix. Later, when the comic strip came out, they said he was Dick Tracy.

As Woody now saw it, under the tumbling bells, he had bankrolled his own desertion. Ha ha! He found this delightful; and especially Pop's attitude of "That'll teach you to trust your father." For this was a demonstration on behalf of real life and free instincts, against religion and hypocrisy. But mainly it was aimed against being a fool, the disgrace of foolishness. Pop had it in for the Reverend Doctor Kovner, not because he was an apostate (Pop couldn't have cared less), not because the mission was a racket (he admitted that the Reverend Doctor was personally honest), but because Doctor Kovner behaved foolishly, spoke like a fool, and acted like a fiddler. He tossed his hair like a Paganini (this was Woody's addition; Pop had never even heard of Paganini). Proof that he was not a spiritual leader was that he converted Jewish women by stealing their hearts. "He works up all those broads," said Pop. "He doesn't even know it himself, I swear he doesn't know how he gets them."

From the other side, Kovner often warned Woody, "Your father is a dangerous person. Of course, you love him; you should love him and forgive him, Voodrow, but you are old enough to understand he is leading a life of wice."

It was all petty stuff: Pop's sinning was on a boy level and therefore made a big impression on a boy. And on Mother. Are wives children, or what? Mother often said, "I hope you put that brute in your prayers. Look what he has done to us. But only pray for him, don't see him." But he saw him all the time. Woodrow was leading a double life, sacred and profane. He accepted Jesus Christ as his personal redeemer. Aunt Rebecca took advantage of this. She made him work. He had to work under Aunt Rebecca. He filled in for the janitor at the mission and settlement house. In winter, he had to feed the coal furnace, and on some nights he slept near the furnace room, on the pool table. He also picked the lock of the storeroom. He took canned pineapple and cut bacon from the flitch with his pocketknife. He crammed himself with uncooked bacon. He had a big frame to fill out.

Only now, sipping Melitta coffee, he asked himself: Had he been so hungry? No, he loved being reckless. He was fighting Aunt Rebecca Kovner when he took out his knife and got on a box to reach the bacon. She didn't know, she couldn't prove that Woody, such a frank, strong, positive boy, who looked you in the eye, so direct, was a thief also. But he was also a thief. Whenever she looked at him, he knew that she was seeing his father. In the curve of his nose, the movements of his eyes, the thickness of his body, in his healthy face, she saw that wicked savage Morris.

Morris, you see, had been a street boy in Liverpool—Woody's mother and her sister were British by birth. Morris's Polish family, on their way to America, abandoned him in Liverpool because he had an eye infection and they would all have been sent back from Ellis Island. They stopped awhile in England, but his eyes kept running and they ditched him. They slipped away, and he had to make out alone in Liverpool at the age of twelve. Mother came of better people. Pop, who slept in the cellar of her house, fell in love with her. At sixteen, scabbing during a seamen's strike, he shoveled his way across the Atlantic and jumped ship in Brooklyn. He became an American, and America never knew it. He voted without papers, he drove without a license, he paid no taxes, he cut every corner. Horses, cards, billiards, and women were his lifelong interests, in ascending order. Did he love anyone (he was so busy)? Yes, he loved Halina. He loved his son. To this day, Mother believed that he had loved her most and always wanted to come back. This gave her a chance to act the queen, with her plump wrists and faded Queen Victoria face. "The girls are instructed never to admit him," she said. The Empress of India speaking.

Bell-battered Woodrow's soul was whirling this Sunday morning, indoors and out, to the past, back to his upper corner of the warehouse, laid out with such originality—the bells coming and going, metal on naked metal, until the bell circle expanded over the whole of steel-making, oil-refining, power-producing mid-autumn South Chicago, and all its Croatians, Ukrainians, Greeks, Poles, and respectable blacks heading for their churches to hear Mass or to sing hymns.

Woody himself had been a good hymn singer. He still knew the hymns. He had testified, too. He was often sent by Aunt Rebecca to get up and tell a churchful of Scandihoovians that he, a Jewish lad, accepted Jesus Christ. For this she paid him fifty cents. She made the disbursement. She was the bookkeeper, fiscal chief, general manager of the mission. The Reverend Doctor didn't know a thing about the operation. What the Doctor supplied was the fervor. He was genuine, a wonderful preacher. And what about Woody himself? He also had fervor. He was drawn to the Reverend

Doctor. The Reverend Doctor taught him to lift up his eyes, gave him his higher life. Apart from this higher life, the rest was Chicago—the ways of Chicago, which came so natural that nobody thought to question them. So, for instance, in 1933 (what ancient, ancient times!), at the Century of Progress World's Fair, when Woody was a coolie and pulled a rickshaw, wearing a peaked straw hat and trotting with powerful, thick legs, while the brawny red farmers—his boozing passengers—were laughing their heads off and pestered him for whores, he, although a freshman at the seminary, saw nothing wrong, when girls asked him to steer a little business their way, in making dates and accepting tips from both sides. He necked in Grant Park with a powerful girl who had to go home quickly to nurse her baby. Smelling of milk, she rode beside him on the streetcar to the West Side, squeezing his rickshaw puller's thigh and wetting her blouse. This was the Roosevelt Road car. Then, in the apartment where she lived with her mother, he couldn't remember that there were any husbands around. What he did remember was the strong milk odor. Without inconsistency, next morning he did New Testament Greek: The light shineth in darkness—*to fos en te skotia fainei*—and the darkness comprehended it not.

And all the while he trotted between the shafts on the fairgrounds he had one idea, nothing to do with these horny giants having a big time in the city: that the goal, the project, the purpose was (and he couldn't explain why he thought so; all evidence was against it)—God's idea was that this world should be a love world, that it should eventually recover and be entirely a world of love. He wouldn't have said this to a soul, for he could see himself how stupid it was—personal and stupid. Nevertheless, there it was at the center of his feelings. And at the same time, Aunt Rebecca was right when she said to him, strictly private, close to his ear even, "You're a little crook, like your father."

There was some evidence for this, or what stood for evidence to an impatient person like Rebecca. Woody matured quickly—he had to—but how could you expect a boy of seventeen, he wondered, to interpret the viewpoint, the feelings, of a middle-aged woman, and one whose breast had been removed? Morris told him that this happened only to neglected women, and was a sign. Morris said that if titties were not fondled and kissed, they got cancer in protest. It was a cry of the flesh. And this had seemed true to Woody. When his imagination tried the theory on the Reverend Doctor, it worked out—he couldn't see the Reverend Doctor behaving in that way to Aunt Rebecca's breasts! Morris's theory kept Woody looking from bosoms to husbands and from husbands to bosoms. He still did that. It's an exceptionally smart man who isn't marked forever by the sexual theories he hears from his father, and Woody wasn't all that smart. He knew this himself. Personally he had gone far out of his way to do right by women in this regard. What nature demanded. He and Pop were common, thick men, but there's nobody too gross to have ideas of delicacy.

The Reverend Doctor preached, Rebecca preached, rich Mrs. Skoglund preached from Evanston, Mother preached. Pop also was on a soapbox. Everyone was doing it. Up and down Division Street, under every lamp, almost, speakers were giving out: anarchists, Socialists, Stalinists, single-taxers, Zionists, Tolstoyans, vegetarians, and fundamentalist Christian preachers—you name it. A beef, a hope, a way of life or salvation, a protest. How was it that the accumulated gripes of all the ages took off so when transplanted to America?

And that fine Swedish immigrant Aase (Osie, they pronounced it), who had been the Skoglunds' cook and married the eldest son, to become his rich, religious widow—she supported the Reverend Doctor. In her time she must have been built like a chorus girl. And women seem to have lost the secret of putting up their hair in the high basketry fence of braid she wore. Aase took Woody under her special protection and paid his tuition at the seminary. And Pop said . . . But on this Sunday, at peace as soon as the bells stopped banging, this velvet autumn day when the grass was finest and thickest, silky green: before the first frost, and the blood in your lungs is redder than summer air can make it and smarts with oxygen, as if the iron in your system was hungry for it, and the chill was sticking it to you in every breath . . . Pop, six feet under, would never feel this blissful sting again. The last of the bells still had the bright air streaming with vibrations.

On weekends, the institutional vacancy of decades came back to the warehouse and crept under the door of Woody's apartment. It felt as empty on Sundays as churches were during the week. Before each business day, before the trucks and the crews got started, Woody jogged five miles in his Adidas suit. Not on this day still reserved for Pop, however. Although it was tempting to go out and run off the grief. Being alone hit Woody hard this morning. He thought: Me and the world; the world and me. Meaning that there always was some activity to interpose, an errand or a visit, a picture to paint (he was a creative amateur), a massage, a meal—a shield between himself and that troublesome solitude which used the world as its reservoir. But Pop! Last Tuesday, Woody had gotten into the hospital bed with Pop because he kept pulling out the intravenous needles. Nurses stuck them back, and then Woody astonished them all by climbing into bed to hold the struggling old guy in his arms. "Easy, Morris, Morris, go easy." But Pop still groped feebly for the pipes.

When the tolling stopped, Woody didn't notice that a great lake of quiet had come over his kingdom, the Selbst Tile warehouse. What he heard and saw was an old red Chicago streetcar, one of those trams the color of a stockyard steer. Cars of this type went out before Pearl Harbor—clumsy, big-bellied, with tough rattan seats and brass grips for the standing passengers. Those cars used to make four stops to the mile, and ran with a wallowing motion. They stank of carbolic or ozone and throbbed when the air compressors were being charged. The conductor had his knotted signal cord to pull, and the motorman beat the foot gong with his mad heel.

Woody recognized himself on the Western Avenue line and riding through a blizzard with is father, both in sheepskins and with hands and faces raw, the snow blowing in from the rear platform when the doors opened and getting into the longitudinal cleats on the floor. There wasn't warmth enough inside to melt it. And Western Avenue was the longest car line in the world, the boosters said, as if it was a thing to brag about. Twenty-three miles long, made by a draftsman with a T square, lined with factories, storage buildings, machine shops, used-car lots, trolley barns, gas stations, funeral parlors, six-flats, utility buildings, and junkyards, on and on from the prairies on the south to Evanston on the north. Woodrow and his father were going north to Evanston, to Howard Street, and then some, to see Mrs. Skoglund. At the end of the line they would still have about five blocks to hike. The purpose of the trip? To raise money for Pop. Pop had talked him into this. When they found out, Mother and Aunt Rebecca would be furious, and Woody was afraid, but he couldn't help it.

Morris had come and said, "Son, I'm in trouble. It's bad."

"What's bad, Pop?"

"Halina took money from her husband for me and has to put it back before old Bujak misses it. He could kill her."

"What did she do it for?"

"Son, you know how the bookies collect? They send a goon. They'll break my head open."

"Pop! You know I can't take you to Mrs. Skoglund."

"Why not? You're my kid, aren't you? The old broad wants to adopt you, doesn't she? Shouldn't I get something out of it for my trouble? What am I—outside? And what about Halina? She puts her life on the line, but my own kid says no."

"Oh, Bujak wouldn't hurt her."

"Woody, he'd beat her to death."

Bujak? Uniform in color with his dark-gray work clothes, short in the legs, his whole strength in his tool-and-die-maker's forearms and black fingers; and beat-looking—there was Bujak for you. But, according to Pop, there was big, big violence in Bujak, a regular boiling Bessemer inside his narrow chest. Woody could never see the violence in him. Bujak wanted no trouble. If anything, maybe he was afraid that Morris and Halina would gang up on him and kill him, screaming. But Pop was no desperado murderer. And Halina was a calm, serious woman. Bujak kept his savings in the cellar (banks were going out of business). The worst they did was to take some of his money, intending to put it back. As Woody saw him, Bujak was trying to be sensible. He accepted his sorrow. He set minimum requirements for Halina: cook the meals, clean the house, show respect. But at stealing Bujak might have drawn the line, for money was different, money was vital substance. If they stole his savings he might have had to take action, out of respect for the substance, for himself—self-respect. But you couldn't be sure that Pop hadn't invented the bookie, the goon, the theft—the whole thing. He was capable of it, and you'd be a fool not to suspect him. Morris knew that Mother and Aunt Rebecca had told Mrs. Skoglund how wicked he was. They had painted him for her in poster colors—purple for vice, black for his soul, red for Hell flames: a gambler, smoker, drinker, deserter, screwer of women, and atheist. So Pop was determined to reach her. It was risky for everybody. The Reverend Doctor's operating costs were met by Skoglund Dairies. The widow paid Woody's seminary tuition; she bought dresses for the little sisters.

Woody, now sixty, fleshy and big, like a figure for the victory of American materialism, sunk in his lounge chair, the leather of its armrests softer to his fingertips than a woman's skin, was puzzled and, in his depths, disturbed by certain blots within him, blots of light in his brain, a blot combining pain and amusement in his breast (how did *that* get there?). Intense thought puckered the skin between his eyes with a strain bordering on headache. Why had he let Pop have his way? Why did he agree to meet him that day, in the dim rear of the poolroom?

"But what will you tell Mrs. Skoglund?"

"That old broad? Don't worry, there's plenty to tell her, and it's all true. Ain't I trying to save my little laundry-and-cleaning shop? Isn't the bailiff coming for the fixtures next week?" And Pop rehearsed his pitch on the Western Avenue car. He counted on Woody's health and his freshness. Such a straightforward-looking body was perfect for a con.

Did they still have such winter storms in Chicago as they used to have? Now they somehow seemed less fierce. Blizzards used to come straight down from Ontario, from the Arctic, and drop five feet of snow in an afternoon. Then the rusty green platform cars, with revolving brushes at both ends, came out of the barns to sweep the tracks. Ten or twelve streetcars followed in slow processions, or waited, block after block.

There was a long delay at the gates of Riverview Park, all the amusements covered for the winter, boarded up—the dragon's-back high-rides, the Bobs, the Chute, the Tilt-a-Whirl, all the fun machinery put together by mechanics and electricians, men like Bujak the tool-and-die-maker, good with engines. The blizzard was having it all its own way behind the gates, and you couldn't see far inside; only a few bulbs burned behind the palings. When Woody wiped the vapor from the glass, the wire mesh of the window guards was stuffed solid at eye level with snow. Looking higher, you saw mostly the streaked wind horizontally driving from the north. In the seat ahead, two black coal heavers, both in leather Lindbergh flying helmets, sat with shovels between their legs, returning from a job. They smelled of sweat, burlap sacking, and coal. Mostly dull with black dust, they also sparkled here and there.

There weren't many riders. People weren't leaving the house. This was a day to sit legs stuck out beside the stove, mummified by both the outdoor and the indoor forces. Only a fellow with an angle, like Pop, would go and buck such weather. A storm like this was out of the compass, and you kept the human scale by having a scheme to raise fifty bucks. Fifty soldiers! Real money in 1933.

"That woman is crazy for you," said Pop.

"She's just a good woman, sweet to all of us."

"Who knows what she's got in mind. You're a husky kid. Not such a kid, either."

"She's a religious woman. She really has religion."

"Well, your mother isn't your only parent. She and Rebecca and Kovner aren't going to fill you up with their ideas. I know your mother wants to wipe me out of your life. Unless I take a hand, you won't even understand what life is. Because they don't know—those silly Christers."

"Yes, Pop."

"The girls I can't help. They're too young. I'm sorry about them, but I can't do anything. With you it's different."

He wanted me like himself, an American.

They were stalled in the storm, while the cattle-colored car waited to have the trolley reset in the crazy wind, which boomed, tingled, blasted. At Howard Street they would have to walk straight into it, due north.

"You'll do the talking at first," said Pop.

Woody had the makings of a salesman, a pitchman. He was aware of this when he got to his feet in church to testify before fifty or sixty people. Even though Aunt Rebecca made it worth his while, he moved his own heart when he spoke up about his faith. But occasionally, without notice, his heart went away as he spoke religion and he couldn't find it anywhere. In its absence, sincere behavior got him through. He had to rely for delivery on his face, his voice—on behavior. Then his eyes came closer and closer together. And in this approach of eye to eye he felt the strain of hypocrisy. The twisting of his face threatened to betray him. It took everything he had to keep looking honest. So, since he couldn't bear the cynicism of it, he fell back on mischievousness. Mischief was where Pop came in. Pop passed straight through all those divided fields, gap after gap, and arrived at his side, bent-nosed and broad-faced. In regard to Pop, you thought of neither sincerity nor insincerity. Pop was like the man in the song: he wanted what he wanted when he wanted it. Pop was physical; Pop was digestive, circulatory, sexual. If Pop got serious, he talked to you about washing under the arms or in the crotch or of drying between your toes or of cooking supper, of baked beans and fried onions, of draw poker or of a certain horse in the fifth race at Arlington. Pop was elemental. That was why he gave such relief from religion and paradoxes, and things like that. Now, Mother *thought* she was spiritual, but Woody knew that she was kidding herself. Oh, yes, in the British accent she never gave up she was always talking to God or about Him—please God, God willing, praise God. But she was a big substantial bread-and-butter down-to-earth woman, with down-to-earth duties like feeding the girls, protecting, refining, keeping pure the girls. And those two protected doves grew up so overweight, heavy in the hips and thighs, that their poor heads looked long and slim. And mad. Sweet but cuckoo—Paula cheerfully cuckoo, Joanna depressed and having episodes.

"I'll do my best by you, but you have to promise, Pop, not to get me in Dutch with Mrs. Skoglund."

"You worried because I speak bad English? Embarrassed? I have a mockie accent?"

"It's not that. Kovner has a heavy accent, and she doesn't mind."

"Who the hell are those freaks to look down on me? You're practically a man and your dad has a right to expect help from you. He's in a fix. And you bring him to her house because she's bighearted, and you haven't got anybody else to go to."

"I got you, Pop."

The two coal trimmers stood up at Devon Avenue. One of them wore a woman's coat. Men wore women's clothing in those years, and women men's, when there was no choice. The fur collar was spiky with the wet, and sprinkled with soot. Heavy, they dragged their shovels and got off at the front. The slow car ground on, very slow. It was after four when they reached the end of the line, and somewhere between gray and black, with snow spouting and whirling under the street lamps. In Howard Street, autos were stalled at all angles and abandoned. The sidewalks were blocked. Woody led the way into Evanston, and Pop followed him up the middle of the street in the furrows made earlier by trucks. For four blocks they bucked the wind and then Woody broke through the drifts to the snowbound mansion, where they both had to push the wrought-iron gate because of the drift behind it. Twenty rooms or more in this dignified house and nobody in them but Mrs. Skoglund and her servant Hjordis, also religious.

As Woody and Pop waited, brushing the slush from their sheepskin collars and Pop wiping his big eyebrows with the ends of his scarf, sweating and freezing, the chains began to rattle and Hjordis uncovered the air holes of the glass storm door by turning a wooden bar. Woody called her "monk-faced." You no longer see women like that, who put no female touch on the face. She came plain, as God made her. She said, "Who is it and what do you want?"

"It's Woodrow Selbst. Hjordis? It's Woody."

"You're not expected."

"No, but we're here."

"What do you want?"

"We came to see Mrs. Skoglund."

"What for do you want to see her?"

"Just tell her we're here."

"I have to tell her what you came for, without calling up first."

"Why don't you say it's Woody with his father, and we wouldn't come in a snowstorm like this if it wasn't important."

The understandable caution of women who live alone. Respectable old-time women, too. There was no such respectability now in those Evanston houses, with their big verandas and deep yards and with a servant like Hjordis, who carried at her belt keys to the pantry and to every closet and every dresser drawer and every padlocked bin in the cellar. And in High Episcopal Christian Science Women's Temperance Evanston, no tradespeople rang at the front door. Only invited guests. And here, after a ten-mile grind through the blizzard, came two tramps from the West Side. To this mansion where a Swedish immigrant lady, herself once a cook and now a philanthropic widow, dreamed, snowbound, while frozen lilac twigs clapped at her storm windows, of a new Jerusalem and a Second Coming and a Resurrection and a Last Judgment. To hasten the Second Coming, and all the rest, you had to reach the hearts of these scheming bums arriving in a snowstorm.

Sure, they let us in.

Then in the heat that swam suddenly up to their mufflered chins Pop and Woody felt the blizzard for what it was; their cheeks were frozen slabs. They stood beat, itching, trickling in the front hall that *was* a hall, with a carved newel post staircase and a big stained-glass window at the top. Picturing Jesus with the Samaritan woman. There was a kind of Gentile closeness to the air. Perhaps when he was with Pop, Woody made more Jewish observations than he would otherwise. Although Pop's most Jewish characteristic was that Yiddish was the only language he could read a paper in. Pop was with Polish Halina, and Mother was with Jesus Christ, and Woody ate uncooked bacon from the flitch. Still, now and then he had a Jewish impression.

Mrs. Skoglund was the cleanest of women—her fingernails, her white neck, her ears—and Pop's sexual hints to Woody all went wrong because she was so intensely clean, and made Woody think of a waterfall, large as she was, and grandly built. Her bust was big. Woody's imagination had investigated this. He thought she kept things tied down tight, very tight. But she lifted both arms once to raise a window and there it was, her bust, beside him, the whole unbindable thing. Her hair was like the raffia you had to soak before you could weave with it in a basket class—pale, pale. Pop, as he took his sheepskin off, was in sweaters, no jacket. His darting looks made him seem crooked. Hardest of all for these Selbsts with their bent noses and big, apparently straightforward faces was to look honest. All the signs of dishonesty played over them. Woody had often puzzled about it. Did it go back to the muscles, was it fundamentally a jaw problem—the projecting angles of the jaws? Or was it the angling that went on in the heart? The girls called Pop Dick Tracy, but Dick Tracy was a good guy. Whom could Pop convince? Here Woody caught a possibility as it flitted by. Precisely because of the way Pop looked, a sensitive person might feel remorse for condemning unfairly or judging unkindly. Just because of a face? Some must have bent over backward. Then he had them. Not Hjordis. She would have put Pop into the street then and there, storm or no storm. Hjordis was religious, but she was wised up, too. She hadn't come over in steerage and worked forty years in Chicago for nothing.

Mrs. Skoglund, Aase (Osie), led the visitors into the front room. This, the biggest room in the house, needed supplementary heating. Because of fifteen-foot ceilings and high windows, Hjordis had kept the parlor stove burning. It was one of those elegant parlor stoves that wore a nickel crown, or miter, and this miter, when you moved it aside, automatically raised the hinge of an iron stove lid. That stove lid underneath the crown was all soot and rust, the same as any other stove lid. Into this hole you tipped the scuttle and the anthracite chestnut rattled down. It made a cake or dome of fire visible through the small isinglass frames. It was a pretty room, three-quarters paneled in wood. The stove was plugged into the flue of the marble fireplace, and there were parquet floors and Axminster carpets and cranberry-colored tufted Victorian upholstery, and a kind of Chinese étagère, inside a cabinet, lined with mirrors and containing silver pitchers, trophies won by Skoglund cows, fancy sugar tongs and cut-glass pitchers and goblets. There were Bibles and pictures of Jesus and the Holy Land and that faint Gentile odor, as if things had been rinsed in a weak vinegar solution.

"Mrs. Skoglund, I brought my dad to you. I don't think you ever met him," said Woody.

"Yes, Missus, that's me, Selbst."

Pop stood short but masterful in the sweaters, and his belly sticking out, not soft but hard. He was a man of the hard-bellied type. Nobody intimidated Pop. He never presented himself as a beggar. There wasn't a cringe in him anywhere. He let her see at once by the way he said "Missus" that he was independent and that he knew his way around. He communicated that he was able to handle himself with women. Handsome Mrs. Skoglund, carrying a basket woven of her own hair, was in her fifties—eight, maybe ten years his senior.

"I asked my son to bring me because I know you do the kid a lot of good. It's natural you should know both of his parents."

"Mrs. Skoglund, my dad is in a tight corner and I don't know anybody else to ask for help."

This was all the preliminary Pop wanted. He took over and told the widow his story about the laundry-and-cleaning business and payments overdue, and explained about the fixtures and the attachment notice, and the bailiff's office and what they were going to do to him; and he said, "I'm a small man trying to make a living."

"You don't support your children," said Mrs. Skoglund.

"That's right," said Hjordis.

"I haven't got it. If I had it, wouldn't I give it? There's bread lines and soup lines all over town. Is it just me? What I have I divvy with. I give the kids. A bad father? You think my son would bring me if I was a bad father into your house? He loves his dad, he trusts his dad, he knows his dad is a good dad. Every time I start a little business going I get wiped out. This one is a good little business, if I could hold on to that little business. Three people work for me, I meet a payroll, and three people will be on the street, too, if I close down. Missus, I can sign a note and pay you in two months. I'm a common man, but I'm a hard worker and a fellow you can trust."

Woody was startled when Pop used the word "trust." It was as if from all four corners a Sousa band blew a blast to warn the entire world: "Crook! This is a crook!" But Mrs. Skoglund, on account of her religious preoccupations, was remote. She heard nothing. Although everybody in this part of the world, unless he was crazy, led a practical life, and you'd have nothing to say to anyone, your neighbors would have nothing to say to you, if communications were not of a practical sort, Mrs. Skoglund, with all her money, was unworldly—two-thirds out of this world.

"Give me a chance to show what's in me," said Pop, "and you'll see what I do for my kids."

So Mrs. Skoglund hesitated, and then she said she'd have to go upstairs, she'd have to go to her room and pray on it and ask for guidance—would they sit down and wait. There were two rocking chairs by the stove. Hjordis gave Pop a grim look (a dangerous person) and Woody a blaming one (he brought a dangerous stranger and disrupter to injure two kind Christian ladies). Then she went out with Mrs. Skoglund.

As soon as they left, Pop jumped up from the rocker and said in anger, "What's this with the praying? She has to ask God to lend me fifty bucks?"

Woody said, "It's not you, Pop, it's the way these religious people do."

"No," said Pop. "She'll come back and say that God wouldn't let her."

Woody didn't like that; he thought Pop was being gross and he said, "No, she's sincere. Pop, try to understand: she's emotional, nervous, and sincere, and tries to do right by everybody."

And Pop said, "That servant will talk her out of it. She's a toughie. It's all over her face that we're a couple of chiselers."

"What's the use of us arguing," said Woody. He drew the rocker closer to the stove. His shoes were wet through and would never dry. The blue flames fluttered like a school of fishes in the coal fire. But Pop went over to the Chinese-style cabinet or étagère and tried the handle, and then opened the blade of his penknife and in a second had forced the lock of the curved glass door. He took out a silver dish.

"Pop, what is this?" said Woody.

Pop, cool and level, knew exactly what this was. He relocked the étagère, crossed the carpet, listened. He stuffed the dish under his belt and pushed it down into his trousers. He put the side of his short thick finger to his mouth.

So Woody kept his voice down, but he was all shook up. He went to Pop and took him by the edge of his hand. As he looked into Pop's face, he felt his eyes growing smaller and smaller, as if something were contracting all the skin on his head. They call it hyperventilation when everything feels tight and light and close and dizzy. Hardly breathing, he said, "Put it back, Pop."

Pop said, "It's solid silver; it's worth dough."

"Pop, you said you wouldn't get me in Dutch."

"It's only insurance in case she comes back from praying and tells me no. If she says yes, I'll put it back."

"How?"

"It'll get back. If I don't put it back, you will."

"You picked the lock. I couldn't. I don't know how."

"There's nothing to it."

"We're going to put it back now. Give it here."

"Woody, it's under my fly, inside my underpants. Don't make such a noise about nothing."

"Pop, I can't believe this."

"For cry-ninety-nine, shut your mouth. If I didn't trust you I wouldn't have let you watch me do it. You don't understand a thing. What's with you?"

"Before they come down, Pop, will you dig that dish out of your long johns."

Pop turned stiff on him. He became absolutely military. He said, "Look, I order you!"

Before he knew it, Woody had jumped his father and begun to wrestle with him. It was dangerous to clutch your own father, to put a heel behind him, to force him to the wall. Pop was taken by surprise and said loudly, "You want Halina killed? Kill her! Go on, you be responsible." He began to resist, angry, and they turned about several times, when Woody, with a trick he had learned in a Western movie and used once on the playground, tripped him and they fell to the ground. Woody, who already outweighed the old man by twenty pounds, was on top. They landed on the floor beside the stove, which stood on a tray of decorated tin to protect the carpet. In this position, pressing Pop's hard belly, Woody recognized that to have wrestled him to the floor counted for nothing. It was impossible to thrust his hand under Pop's belt to recover the dish. And now Pop had turned furious, as a father has every right to be when his son is violent with him, and he freed his hand and hit Woody in the face. He hit him three or four times in midface. Then Woody dug his head into Pop's shoulder and held tight only to keep from being struck and began to say in his ear, "Jesus, Pop, for Christ sake remember where you are. Those women will be back!" But Pop brought up his short knee and fought and butted him with his chin and rattled Woody's teeth. Woody thought the old man was about to bite him. And because he was a seminarian, he thought: Like an unclean spirit. And held tight. Gradually Pop stopped threshing and struggling. His eyes stuck out and his mouth was open, sullen. Like a stout fish. Woody released him and gave him a hand up. He was then overcome with many bad feelings of a sort he knew the old man never suffered. Never, never. Pop never had these groveling emotions. There was his whole superiority. Pop had no such feelings. He was like a horseman from Central Asia, a bandit from China. It was Mother, from Liverpool, who had the refinement, the English manners. It was the preaching Reverend Doctor in his black suit. You have refinements, and all they do is oppress you? The hell with that.

The long door opened and Mrs. Skoglund stepped in, saying, "Did I imagine, or did something shake the house?"

"I was lifting the scuttle to put coal on the fire and it fell out of my hand. I'm sorry I was so clumsy," said Woody.

Pop was too huffy to speak. With his eyes big and sore and the thin hair down over his forehead, you could see by the tightness of his belly how angrily he was fetching his breath, though his mouth was shut.

"I prayed," said Mrs. Skoglund.

"I hope it came out well," said Woody.

"Well, I don't do anything without guidance, but the answer was yes, and I feel right about it now. So if you'll wait, I'll go to my office and write a check. I asked Hjordis to bring you a cup of coffee. Coming in such a storm."

And Pop, consistently a terrible little man, as soon as she shut the door, said, "A check? Hell with a check. Get me the greenbacks."

"They don't keep money in the house. You can cash it in her bank tomorrow. But if they miss that dish, Pop, they'll stop the check, and then where are you?"

As Pop was reaching below the belt, Hjordis brought in the tray. She was very sharp with him. She said, "Is this a place to adjust clothing, Mister? A men's washroom?"

"Well, which way is the toilet, then?" said Pop.

She had served the coffee in the seamiest mugs in the pantry, and she bumped down the tray and led Pop down the corridor, standing guard at the bathroom door so that he shouldn't wander about the house.

Mrs. Skoglund called Woody to her office and after she had given him the folded check said that they should pray together for Morris. So once more he was on his knees, under rows and rows of musty marbled-cardboard files, by the glass lamp by the edge of the desk, the shade with flounced edges, like the candy dish. Mrs. Skoglund, in her Scandinavian accent—an emotional contralto—raising her voice to Jesus-uh Christ-uh, as the wind lashed the trees, kicked the side of the house, and drove the snow seething on the windowpanes, to send light-uh, give guidance-uh, put a new heart-uh in Pop's bosom. Woody asked God only to make Pop put the dish back. He kept Mrs. Skoglund on her knees as long as possible. Then he thanked her, shining with candor (as much as he knew how), for her Christian generosity and he said, "I know that Hjordis has a cousin who works at the Evanston YMCA. Could she please phone him and try to get us a room tonight so that we don't have to fight the blizzard all the way back? We're almost as close to the Y as to the car line. Maybe the cars have even stopped running."

Suspicious Hjordis, coming when Mrs. Skoglund called to her, was burning now. First they barged in, made themselves at home, asked for money, had to have coffee, probably left gonorrhea on the toilet seat. Hjordis, Woody remembered, was a woman who wiped the doorknobs with rubbing alcohol after guests had left. Nevertheless, she telephoned the Y and got them a room with two cots for six bits.

Pop had plenty of time, therefore, to reopen the étagère, lined with reflecting glass or German silver (something exquisitely delicate and tricky), and as soon as the two Selbsts had said thank you and goodbye and were in midstreet again up to the knees in snow, Woody said, "Well, I covered for you. Is that thing back?"

"Of course it is," said Pop.

They fought their way to the small Y building, shut up in wire grille and resembling a police station—about the same dimensions. It was locked, but they made a racket on the grille, and a small black man let them in and shuffled them upstairs to a cement corridor with low doors. It was like the small-mammal house in Lincoln Park. He said there was nothing to eat, so they took off their wet pants, wrapped themselves tightly in the khaki army blankets, and passed out on their cots.

First thing in the morning, they went to the Evanston National Bank and got the fifty dollars. Not without difficulties. The teller went to call Mrs. Skoglund and was absent a long time from the wicket. "Where the hell has he gone?" said Pop.

But when the fellow came back, he said, "How do you want it?"

Pop said, "Singles." He told Woody, "Bujak stashes it in one-dollar bills."

But by now Woody no longer believed Halina had stolen the old man's money.

Then they went into the street, where the snow-removal crews were at work. The sun shone broad, broad, out of the morning blue, and all Chicago would be releasing itself from the temporary beauty of those vast drifts.

"You shouldn't have jumped me last night, Sonny."

"I know, Pop, but you promised you wouldn't get me in Dutch."

"Well, it's okay. We can forget it, seeing you stood by me."

Only, Pop had taken the silver dish. Of course he had, and in a few days Mrs. Skoglund and Hjordis knew it, and later in the week they were all waiting for Woody in Kovner's office at the settlement house. The group included the Reverend Doctor Crabbie, head of the seminary, and Woody, who had been flying along, level and smooth, was shot down in flames. He told them he was innocent. Even as he was falling, he warned that they were wronging him. He denied that he or Pop had touched Mrs. Skoglund's property. The missing object—he didn't even know what it was—had probably been misplaced, and they would be very sorry on the day it turned up. After the others were done with him, Dr. Crabbie said that until he was able to tell the truth he would be suspended from the seminary, where his work had been unsatisfactory anyway. Aunt Rebecca took him aside and said to him, "You are a little crook, like your father. The door is closed to you here."

To this Pop's comment was "So what, kid?"

"Pop, you shouldn't have done it."

"No? Well, I don't give a care, if you want to know. You can have the dish if you want to go back and square yourself with all those hypocrites."

"I didn't like doing Mrs. Skoglund in the eye, she was so kind to us."

"Kind?"

"Kind."

"Kind has a price tag."

Well, there was no winning such arguments with Pop. But they debated it in various moods and from various elevations and perspectives for forty years and more, as their intimacy changed, developed, matured.

"Why did you do it, Pop? For the money? What did you do with the fifty bucks?" Woody, decades later, asked him that.

"I settled with the bookie, and the rest I put in the business."

"You tried a few more horses."

"I maybe did. But it was a double, Woody. I didn't hurt myself, and at the same time did you a favor."

"It was for me?"

"It was too strange of a life. That life wasn't *you,* Woody. All those women . . . Kovner was no man, he was an in-between. Suppose they made you a minister? Some Christian minister! First of all, you wouldn't have been able to stand it, and second, they would throw you out sooner or later."

"Maybe so."

"And you wouldn't have converted the Jews, which was the main thing they wanted."

"And what a time to bother the Jews," Woody said. "At least *I* didn't bug them."

Pop had carried him back to his side of the line, blood of his blood, the same thick body walls, the same coarse grain. Not cut out for a spiritual life. Simply not up to it.

Pop was no worse than Woody, and Woody was no better than Pop. Pop wanted no relation to theory, and yet he was always pointing Woody toward a position—a jolly, hearty, natural, likable, unprincipled position. If Woody had a weakness, it was to be unselfish. This worked to Pop's advantage, but he criticized Woody for it, nevertheless. "You take too much on yourself," Pop was always saying. And it's true that Woody gave Pop his heart because Pop was so selfish. It's usually the selfish people who are loved the most. They do what you deny yourself, and you love them for it. You give them your heart.

Remembering the pawn ticket for the silver dish, Woody startled himself with a laugh so sudden that it made him cough. Pop said to him after his expulsion from the seminary and banishment from the settlement house, "You want in again? Here's the ticket. I hocked that thing. It wasn't so valuable as I thought."

"What did they give?"

"Twelve-fifty was all I could get. But if you want it you'll have to raise the dough yourself, because I haven't got anymore."

"You must have been sweating in the bank when the teller went to call Mrs. Skoglund about the check."

"I was a little nervous," said Pop. "But I didn't think they could miss the thing so soon."

That theft was part of Pop's war with Mother. With Mother, and Aunt Rebecca, and the Reverend Doctor. Pop took his stand on realism. Mother represented the forces of religion and hypochondria. In four decades, the fighting never stopped. In the course of time, Mother and the girls turned into welfare personalities and lost their individual outlines. Ah, the poor things, they became dependents and cranks. In the meantime, Woody, the sinful man, was their dutiful and loving son and brother. He maintained the bungalow—this took in roofing, pointing, wiring, insulation, air-conditioning—and he paid for heat and light and food, and dressed them all out of Sears, Roebuck and Wieboldt's, and bought them a TV, which they watched as devoutly as they prayed. Paula took courses to learn skills like macramé-making and needlepoint, and sometimes got a little job as recreational worker in a nursing home. But she wasn't steady enough to keep it. Wicked Pop spent most of his life removing stains from people's clothing. He and Halina in the last years ran a Cleanomat in West Rogers Park—a so-so business resembling a laundromat—which gave him leisure for billiards, the horses, rummy and pinochle. Every morning he went behind the partition to check out the filters of the cleaning equipment. He found amusing things that had been thrown into the vats with the clothing—sometimes, when he got lucky, a locket chain or a brooch. And when he had fortified the cleaning fluid, pouring all that blue and pink stuff in from plastic jugs, he read the *Forward* over a second cup of coffee, and went out, leaving Halina in charge. When they needed help with the rent, Woody gave it.

After the new Disney World was opened in Florida, Woody treated all his dependents to a holiday. He sent them down in separate batches, of course. Halina enjoyed this more than anybody else. She couldn't stop talking about the address given by an Abraham Lincoln automaton. "Wonderful, how he stood up and moved his hands, and his mouth. So real! And how beautiful he talked." Of them all, Halina was the soundest, the most human, the most honest. Now that Pop was gone, Woody and Halina's son, Mitosh, the organist at the Stadium, took care of her needs over and above Social Security, splitting expenses. In Pop's opinion, insurance was a racket. He left Halina nothing but some out-of-date equipment.

Woody treated himself, too. Once a year, and sometimes oftener, he left his business to run itself, arranged with the trust department at the bank to take care of his gang, and went off. He did that in style, imaginatively, expensively. In Japan, he wasted little time on Tokyo. He spent three weeks in Kyoto and stayed at the Tawaraya Inn, dating from the seventeenth century or so. There he slept on the floor, the Japanese way, and bathed in scalding water. He saw the dirtiest strip show on earth, as well as the holy places and the temple gardens. He visited also Istanbul, Jerusalem, Delphi, and went to Burma and Uganda and Kenya on safari, on democratic terms with drivers, Bedouins, bazaar merchants. Open, lavish, familiar, fleshier and fleshier but (he jogged, he lifted weights) still muscular—in his naked person beginning to resemble a Renaissance courtier in full costume—becoming ruddier every year, an outdoor type with freckles on his back and spots across the flaming forehead and the honest nose. In Addis Ababa he took an Ethiopian beauty to his room from the street and washed her, getting into the shower with her to soap her with his broad, kindly hands. In Kenya he taught certain American obscenities to a black woman so that she could shout them out during the act. On the Nile, below Murchison Falls, those fever trees rose huge from the mud, and hippos on the sandbars belched at the passing launch, hostile. One of them danced on his spit of sand, springing from the ground and coming down heavy, on all fours. There, Woody saw the buffalo calf disappear, snatched by the crocodile.

Mother, soon to follow Pop, was being lightheaded these days. In company, she spoke of Woody as her boy—"What do you think of my Sonny?"—as though he was ten years old. She was silly with him, her behavior was frivolous, almost flirtatious. She just didn't seem to know the facts. And behind her all the others, like kids at the playground, were waiting their turn to go down the slide: one on each step, and moving toward the top.

Over Woody's residence and place of business there had gathered a pool of silence of the same perimeter as the church bells while they were ringing, and he mourned under it, this melancholy morning of sun and autumn. Doing a life survey, taking a deliberate look at the gross side of his case—of the other side as well, what there was of it. But if this heartache continued, he'd go out and run it off. A three-mile jog—five, if necessary. And you'd think that this jogging was an entirely physical activity, wouldn't you? But there was something else in it. Because, when he was a seminarian, between the shafts of his World's Fair rickshaw, he used to receive, pulling along (capable and stable), his religious experiences while he trotted. Maybe it was all a single experience repeated. He felt truth coming to him from the sun. He received a communication that was also light and warmth. It made him very remote from his horny Wisconsin passengers, those farmers whose whoops and whore cries he could hardly hear when he was in one of his states. And again out of the flaming of the sun would come to him a secret certainty that the goal set for this earth was that it should be filled with good, saturated with it. After everything preposterous, after dog had eaten dog, after the crocodile death had pulled everyone into his mud. It wouldn't conclude as Mrs. Skoglund, bribing him to round up the Jews and hasten the Second Coming, imagined it, but in another way. This was his clumsy intuition. It went no further. Subsequently, he proceeded through life as life seemed to want him to do it.

There remained one thing more this morning, which was explicitly physical, occurring first as a sensation in his arms and against his breast and, from the pressure, passing into him and going into his breast.

It was like this: When he came into the hospital room and saw Pop with the sides of his bed raised, like a crib, and Pop, so very feeble, and writhing, and toothless, like a baby, and the dirt already cast into his face, into the wrinkles—Pop wanted to pluck out the intravenous needles and he was piping his weak death noise. The gauze patches taped over the needles were soiled with dark blood. Then Woody took off his shoes, lowered the side of the bed, and climbed in and held him in his arms to soothe and still him. As if he were Pop's father, he said to him, "Now, Pop. Pop." Then it was like the wrestle in Mrs. Skoglund's parlor, when Pop turned angry like an unclean spirit and Woody tried to appease him, and warn him, saying, "Those women will be back!" Beside the coal stove, when Pop hit Woody in the teeth with his head and then became sullen, like a stout fish. But this struggle in the hospital was weak—so weak! In his great pity, Woody held Pop, who was fluttering and shivering. From those people, Pop had told him, you'll never find out what life is, because they don't know what it is. Yes, Pop—well, what is it, Pop? Hard to comprehend that Pop, who was dug in for eighty-three years and had done all he could to stay, should now want nothing but to free himself. How could Woody allow the old man to pull the intravenous needles out? Willful Pop, he wanted what he wanted when he wanted it. But what he wanted at the very last Woody failed to follow, it was such a switch.

After a time, Pop's resistance ended. He subsided and subsided. He rested against his son, his small body curled there. Nurses came and looked. They disapproved, but Woody, who couldn't spare a hand to wave them out, motioned with his head toward the door. Pop, whom Woody thought he had stilled, only had found a better way to get around him. Loss of heat was the way he did it. His heat was leaving him. As can happen with small animals while you hold them in your hand, Woody presently felt him cooling. Then, as Woody did his best to restrain him, and thought he was succeeding, Pop divided himself. And when he was separated from his warmth, he slipped into death. And there was his elderly, large muscular son, still holding and pressing him when there was nothing anymore to press. You could never pin down that self-willed man. When he was ready to make his move, he made it—always on his own terms. And always, always, something up his sleeve. That was how he was.

. . . .

QUESTIONS FOR A SECOND READING

1. The story begins with a question: "What do you do about death—in this case, the death of an old father? If you're a modern person, sixty years of age, and a man who's been around, like Woody Selbst, what do you do?" What *does* Woody do about the death of his father? What does the story offer as his characteristic ways of thinking and acting in this situation? And what can you conclude from this about Woody Selbst?
2. What attitude do you suppose Bellow intends you to take toward Woody? (How, for example, are you supposed to read the reference to Woody as a "modern person," "a man who's been around"? Are these references ironic?) As you read back through the story, mark those passages that best represent the narrator's attitude (or attitudes) toward Woody. What attitude do you think the narrator expects the reader to take in each case? What attitudes *do* you take, and how do they change or develop as you read from the first page to the last?

ASSIGNMENTS FOR WRITING

1. Aunt Rebecca said that Woody was a "little crook," just like his father. Woody said that Pop "wanted me like himself, an American." Is Woody like his father? What part of his father does Woody carry with him? What lessons? Write an essay in which you discuss what Woody inherits from his father and explain what he does (or does not do) with his inheritance.
2. At one point (on page 41) the narrator says:

> Pop was no worse than Woody, and Woody was no better than Pop. Pop wanted no relation to theory, and yet he was always pointing Woody toward a position—a jolly, hearty, natural, likable, unprincipled position. If Woody had a weakness, it was to be unselfish. This worked to Pop's advantage, but he criticized Woody for it, nevertheless. "You take too much on yourself," Pop was always saying. And it's true that Woody gave Pop his heart because Pop was so selfish. It's usually the selfish people who are loved the most. They do what you deny yourself, and you love them for it. You give them your heart.

This paragraph sounds like one of the statements an author makes to sum up a character—in this case, to give the final word on Woody Selbst and his relationship to his father. Write an essay in which you discuss whether you think this summation is an adequate description of the relationship. What parts of Woody's behavior does it seem to explain? What won't it account for? (Who is speaking in that passage? to what end?)

MAKING CONNECTIONS

1. John Berger, in "Ways of Seeing" (p. 51), says "The past is never there waiting to be discovered, to be recognized for exactly what it is. History always constitutes the relation between a present and its past." If the past is not just *there*, waiting to be recognized for exactly what it is, then the past has to be created, or re-created, by a person with a particular point of view, a particular way of reading the memories, stories, documents, or artifacts that provide a connection to a time that would otherwise be gone.

   John Wideman, in "Our Time" (p. 519), says that he is writing to "recover" his brother Robby from the past. Woody Selbst, it might be said, is doing the same thing. As the story "A Silver Dish" takes us inside his thinking and his memories, we watch him trying to put together his past and, in doing so, understand his father.

   Take John Wideman and Woody Selbst as examples of people working on the past. (To do this, you will have to assume that "A Silver Dish" represents Woody's train of thought.) Pay particular attention to the characteristic ways that each selects, arranges, and interprets (or comments on) the material they gather to represent the past. Write an essay, then, in which you use these two texts, "Our Time" and "A Silver Dish," to test and explain Berger's statement that "history always constitutes the relation between a present and its past."

2. Write an essay in which you use Woody Selbst as an example to test what you see to be the most powerful and pertinent arguments in "Higamous-Hogamous" (p. 169). You will need to take time to represent the sections of Dinnerstein's argument that you feel have bearing on Woody's case, and you want to be sure, as you turn to the story, to consider the parts of Woody's character that defy this form of explanation. Dinnerstein will give you a powerful way of framing Woody's character. You should keep an eye out for what you miss.

JOHN BERGER

JOHN BERGER (b. 1926), like few other art critics, elicits strong and contradictory reactions to his writing. He has been called (and sometimes in the same review) "preposterous" as well as "stimulating," "pompous" yet "exciting." He has been accused of falling prey to "ideological excesses" and of being a victim of his own "lack of objectivity," but he has been praised for his "scrupulous" and "cogent" observations on art and culture. He is one of Europe's most influential Marxist critics, yet his work has been heralded and damned by leftists and conservatives alike. Although Berger's work speaks powerfully, its tone is quiet, thoughtful, measured. According to the poet and critic Peter Schjeldahl, "The most mysterious element in Mr. Berger's criticism has always been the personality of the critic himself, a man of strenuous conviction so loath to bully that even his most provocative arguments sit feather-light on the mind."

The following selection is the first chapter from Ways of Seeing, *a book which began as a series on BBC television. In fact, the show was a forerunner of those encyclopedic television series later popular on public television stations in the United States:* Civilization, The Ascent of Man, Cosmos. *Berger's show was less glittery and ambitious, but in its way it was more serious in its claims to be educa-*

tional. As you watched the screen, you saw a series of images (like those in the following text). These were sometimes presented with commentary, but sometimes in silence, so that you constantly saw one image in the context of another—for example, classic presentations of women in oil paintings interspersed with images of women from contemporary art, advertising, movies, and "men's magazines." The goal of the exercise, according to Berger, was to "start a process of questioning," to focus his viewer's attention not on a single painting in isolation but on "ways of seeing" in general, on the ways we have learned to look at and understand the images that surround us, and on the culture that teaches us to see things as we do. The method of Ways of Seeing, *a book of art history, was used by Berger in another book,* A Seventh Man, *to document the situation of the migrant worker in Europe.*

Berger has written poems, novels, essays, and film scripts, including G, A Fortunate Man, The Success and Failure of Picasso, *and* About Looking. *He lived and worked in England for years, but he currently lives in a small peasant village in France, where he is writing a series of three novels on peasant life. The first of these was titled* Pig Earth.

Ways of Seeing

Seeing comes before words. The child looks and recognizes before it can speak.

But there is also another sense in which seeing comes before words. It is seeing which establishes our place in the surrounding world; we explain that world with words, but words can never undo the fact that we are surrounded by it. The relation between what we see and what we know is never settled. Each evening we *see* the sun set. We *know* that the earth is turning away from it. Yet the knowledge, the explanation, never quite fits the sight. The Surrealist painter Magritte commented on this always-present gap between words and seeing in a painting called *The Key of Dreams.*

The way we see things is affected by what we know or what we believe. In the Middle Ages when men believed in the physical existence of Hell the sight of fire must have meant something different from what it means today. Nevertheless their idea of Hell owed a lot to the sight of fire consuming and the ashes remaining—as well as to their experience of the pain of burns.

When in love, the sight of the beloved has a completeness which no

The Key of Dreams by Magritte 1898–1967

words and no embrace can match: a completeness which only the act of making love can temporarily accommodate.

Yet this seeing which comes before words, and can never be quite covered by them, is not a question of mechanically reacting to stimuli. (It can only be thought of in this way if one isolates the small part of the process which concerns the eye's retina.) We only see what we look at. To look is an act of choice. As a result of this act, what we see is brought within our reach—though not necessarily within arm's reach. To touch something is to situate oneself in relation to it. (Close your eyes, move round the room and notice how the faculty of touch is like a static, limited form of sight.) We never look at just one thing; we are always looking at the relation between things and ourselves. Our vision is continually active, continually moving, continually holding things in a circle around itself, constituting what is present to us as we are.

Soon after we can see, we are aware that we can also be seen. The eye of the other combines with our own eye to make it fully credible that we are part of the visible world.

If we accept that we can see that hill over there, we propose that from that hill we can be seen. The reciprocal nature of vision is more fundamental than that of spoken dialogue. And often dialogue is an attempt to ver-

balize this—an attempt to explain how, either metaphorically or literally, "you see things," and an attempt to discover how "he sees things."

In the sense in which we use the word in this book, all images are man-made [see above]. An image is a sight which has been recreated or reproduced. It is an appearance, or a set of appearances, which has been detached from the place and time in which it first made its appearance and preserved—for a few moments or a few centuries. Every image embodies a way of seeing. Even a photograph. For photographs are not, as is often assumed, a mechanical record. Every time we look at a photograph, we are aware, however slightly, of the photographer selecting that sight from an infinity of other possible sights. This is true even in the most casual family snapshot. The photographer's way of seeing is reflected in his choice of subject. The painter's way of seeing is reconstituted by the marks he makes on the canvas or paper. Yet, although every image embodies a way of seeing, our perception or appreciation of an image depends also upon our own way of seeing. (It may be, for example, that Sheila is one figure among twenty; but for our own reasons she is the one we have eyes for.)

Images were first made to conjure up the appearances of something that was absent. Gradually it became evident that an image could outlast what it represented; it then showed how something or somebody had once looked—and thus by implication how the subject had once been seen by other people. Later still the specific vision of the image-maker was also recognized as part of the record. An image became a record of how X had seen Y. This was the result of an increasing consciousness of individuality, accompanying an increasing awareness of history. It would be rash to try to date this last development precisely. But certainly in Europe such consciousness has existed since the beginning of the Renaissance.

No other kind of relic or text from the past can offer such a direct testimony about the world which surrounded other people at other times. In this respect images are more precise and richer than literature. To say this is not to deny the expressive or imaginative quality of art, treating it as mere documentary evidence; the more imaginative the work, the more profoundly it allows us to share the artist's experience of the visible.

Yet when an image is presented as a work of art, the way people look at it is affected by a whole series of learnt assumptions about art. Assumptions concerning:

Beauty
Truth
Genius
Civilization
Form
Status
Taste, etc.

Many of these assumptions no longer accord with the world as it is. (The world-as-it-is is more than pure objective fact, it includes consciousness.) Out of true with the present, these assumptions obscure the past. They mystify rather than clarify. The past is never there waiting to be discovered, to be recognized for exactly what it is. History always constitutes the relation between a present and its past. Consequently fear of the present leads to mystification of the past. The past is not for living in; it is a well of conclusions from which we draw in order to act. Cultural mystification of the past entails a double loss. Works of art are made unnecessarily remote. And the past offers us fewer conclusions to complete in action.

When we "see" a landscape, we situate ourselves in it. If we "saw" the art of the past, we would situate ourselves in history. When we are prevented from seeing it, we are being deprived of the history which belongs to us. Who benefits from this deprivation? In the end, the art of the past is being mystified because a privileged minority is striving to invent a history which can retrospectively justify the role of the ruling classes, and such a justification can no longer make sense in modern terms. And so, inevitably, it mystifies.

Regents of the Old Men's Alms House by Hals 1580–1666

Regentesses of the Old Men's Alms House by Hals 1580–1666

Let us consider a typical example of such mystification. A two-volume study was recently published on Frans Hals.[1] It is the authoritative work to date on this painter. As a book of specialized art history it is no better and no worse than the average.

The last two great paintings by Frans Hals [above] portray the Gover-

[1] Seymour Slive, *Frans Hals* (Phaidon, London)

nors and the Governesses of an Alms House for old paupers in the Dutch seventeenth-century city of Haarlem. They were officially commissioned portraits. Hals, an old man of over eighty, was destitute. Most of his life he had been in debt. During the winter of 1664, the year he began painting these pictures, he obtained three loads of peat on public charity, otherwise he would have frozen to death. Those who now sat for him were administrators of such public charity.

The author records these facts and then explicitly says that it would be incorrect to read into the paintings any criticism of the sitters. There is no evidence, he says, that Hals painted them in a spirit of bitterness. The author considers them, however, remarkable works of art and explains why. Here he writes of the Regentesses:

> Each woman speaks to us of the human condition with equal importance. Each woman stands out with equal clarity against the *enormous* dark surface, yet they are linked by a firm rhythmical arrangement and the subdued diagonal pattern formed by their heads and hands. Subtle modulations of the *deep,* glowing blacks contribute to the *harmonious fusion* of the whole and form an *unforgettable contrast* with the *powerful* whites and vivid flesh tones where the detached strokes reach *a peak of breadth and strength.* (our italics)

The compositional unity of a painting contributes fundamentally to the power of its image. It is reasonable to consider a painting's composition. But here the composition is written about as though it were in itself the emotional charge of the painting. Terms like *harmonious fusion, unforgettable contrast,* reaching *a peak of breadth and strength* transfer the emotion provoked by the image from the plane of lived experience, to that of disinterested "art appreciation." All conflict disappears. One is left with the unchanging "human condition," and the painting considered as a marvellously made object.

Very little is known about Hals or the Regents who commissioned him. It is not possible to produce circumstantial evidence to establish what their relations were. But there is the evidence of the paintings themselves: the evidence of a group of men and a group of women as seen by another man, the painter. Study this evidence and judge for yourself [p. 54].

The art historian fears such direct judgement:

> As in so many other pictures by Hals, the penetrating characterizations almost seduce us into believing that we know the personality traits and even the habits of the men and women portrayed.

What is this "seduction" he writes of? It is nothing less than the paintings working upon us. They work upon us because we accept the way

Hals saw his sitters. We do not accept this innocently. We accept it in so far as it corresponds to our own observation of people, gestures, faces, institutions. This is possible because we still live in a society of comparable social relations and moral values. And it is precisely this which gives the paintings their psychological and social urgency. It is this—not the painter's skill as a "seducer"—which convinces us that we *can* know the people portrayed.

The author continues:

> In the case of some critics the seduction has been a total success. It has, for example, been asserted that the Regent in the tipped slouch hat, which hardly covers any of his long, lank hair, and whose curiously set eyes do not focus, was shown in a drunken state. [p. 55]

This, he suggests, is a libel. He argues that it was a fashion at that time to wear hats on the side of the head. He cites medical opinion to prove that the Regent's expression could well be the result of a facial paralysis. He insists that the painting would have been unacceptable to the Regents if one of them had been portrayed drunk. One might go on discussing each of these points for pages. (Men in seventeenth-century Holland wore their hats on the side of their heads in order to be thought of as adventurous and pleasure-loving. Heavy drinking was an approved practice. Etcetera.) But such a discussion would take us even farther away from the only confrontation which matters and which the author is determined to evade.

In this confrontation the Regents and Regentesses stare at Hals, a destitute old painter who has lost his reputation and lives off public charity;

he examines them through the eyes of a pauper who must nevertheless try to be objective; i.e., must try to surmount the way he sees as a pauper. This is the drama of these paintings. A drama of an "unforgettable contrast."

Mystification has little to do with the vocabulary used. Mystification is the process of explaining away what might otherwise be evident. Hals was the first portraitist to paint the new characters and expressions created by capitalism. He did in pictorial terms what Balzac did two centuries later in literature. Yet the author of the authoritative work on these paintings sums up the artist's achievement by referring to

> Hals's unwavering commitment to his personal vision, which enriches our consciousness of our fellow men and heightens our awe for the ever-increasing power of the mighty impulses that enabled him to give us a close view of life's vital forces.

That is mystification.

In order to avoid mystifying the past (which can equally well suffer pseudo-Marxist mystification) let us now examine the particular relation which now exists, so far as pictorial images are concerned, between the present and the past. If we can see the present clearly enough, we shall ask the right questions of the past.

Today we see the art of the past as nobody saw it before. We actually perceive it in a different way.

This difference can be illustrated in terms of what was thought of as perspective. The convention of perspective, which is unique to European art and which was first established in the early Renaissance, centres everything on the eye of the beholder. It is like a beam from a lighthouse—only instead of light travelling outwards, appearances travel in. The conventions called those appearances *reality*. Perspective makes the single eye the centre of the visible world. Everything converges on to the eye as to the vanishing point of infinity. The visible world is arranged for the spectator as the universe was once thought to be arranged for God.

According to the convention of perspective there is no visual reciprocity. There is no need for God to situate himself in relation to others: he is himself the situation. The inherent contradiction in perspective was that it structured all images of reality to address a single spectator who, unlike God, could only be in one place at a time.

After the invention of the camera this contradiction gradually became apparent.

Still from *Man with a Movie Camera* by Vertov

> I'm an eye. A mechanical eye. I, the machine, show you a world the way only I can see it. I free myself for today and forever from human immobility. I'm in constant movement. I approach and pull away from objects. I creep under them. I move alongside a running horse's mouth. I fall and rise with the falling and rising bodies. This is I, the machine, manoeuvring in the chaotic movements, recording one movement after another in the most complex combinations.
>
> Freed from the boundaries of time and space, I coordinate any and all points of the universe, wherever I want them to be. My way leads towards the creation of a fresh perception of the world. Thus I explain in a new way the world unknown to you.[2]

The camera isolated momentary appearances and in so doing destroyed the idea that images were timeless. Or, to put it another way, the camera showed that the notion of time passing was inseparable from the experience of the visual (except in paintings). What you saw depended upon where you were when. What you saw was relative to your position in time and space. It was no longer possible to imagine everything converging on the human eye as on the vanishing point of infinity.

This is not to say that before the invention of the camera men believed that everyone could see everything. But perspective organized the visual field as though that were indeed the ideal. Every drawing or painting that used perspective proposed to the spectator that he was the unique centre of the world. The camera—and more particularly the movie camera—demonstrated that there was no centre.

The invention of the camera changed the way men saw. The visible came to mean something different to them. This was immediately reflected in painting.

For the Impressionists the visible no longer presented itself to man in order to be seen. On the contrary, the visible, in continual flux, became fugitive. For the Cubists the visible was no longer what confronted the single eye, but the totality of possible views taken from points all round the object (or person) being depicted [p. 58, top].

The invention of the camera also changed the way in which men saw paintings painted long before the camera was invented. Originally paintings were an integral part of the building for which they were designed. Sometimes in an early Renaissance church or chapel one has the feeling that the images on the wall are records of the building's interior life, that

---

[2]This quotation is from an article written in 1923 by Dziga Vertov, the revolutionary Soviet film director.

Still Life with Wicker Chair by Picasso 1881–1973

Church of St. Francis at Assisi

together they make up the building's memory—so much are they part of the particularity of the building [p. 58, bottom].

The uniqueness of every painting was once part of the uniqueness of the place where it resided. Sometimes the painting was transportable. But it could never be seen in two places at the same time. When the camera reproduces a painting, it destroys the uniqueness of its image. As a result its meaning changes. Or, more exactly, its meaning multiplies and fragments into many meanings.

This is vividly illustrated by what happens when a painting is shown on a television screen. The painting enters each viewer's house. There it is surrounded by his wallpaper, his furniture, his mementoes. It enters the atmosphere of his family. It becomes their talking point. It lends its meaning to their meaning. At the same time it enters a million other houses and, in each of them, is seen in a different context. Because of the camera, the painting now travels to the spectator rather than the spectator to the painting. In its travels, its meaning is diversified.

One might argue that all reproductions more or less distort, and that therefore the original painting is still in a sense unique. Here [p. 60] is a reproduction of the *Virgin of the Rocks* by Leonardo da Vinci.

Having seen this reproduction, one can go to the National Gallery to look at the original and there discover what the reproduction lacks. Alternatively one can forget about the quality of the reproduction and simply be reminded, when one sees the original, that it is a famous painting of which somewhere one has already seen a reproduction. But in either case the uniqueness of the original now lies in it being *the original of a reproduction*. It is no longer what its image shows that strikes one as unique; its first meaning is no longer to be found in what it says, but in what it is.

This new status of the original work is the perfectly rational consequence of the new means of reproduction. But it is at this point that a process of mystification again enters. The meaning of the original work no

Virgin of the Rocks by Leonardo da Vinci 1452–1519. Reproduced by courtesy of the Trustees, The National Gallery, London

longer lies in what it uniquely says but in what it uniquely is. How is its unique existence evaluated and defined in our present culture? It is defined as an object whose value depends upon its rarity. This market is affirmed and gauged by the price it fetches on the market. But because it is nevertheless "a work of art"—and art is thought to be greater than commerce—its market price is said to be a reflection of its spiritual value. Yet the spiritual value of an object, as distinct from a message or an example, can only be explained in terms of magic or religion. And since in modern society neither of these is a living force, the art object, the "work of art," is enveloped in an atmosphere of entirely bogus religiosity. Works of art are discussed and presented as though they were holy relics: relics which are first and foremost evidence of their own survival. The past in which they originated is studied in order to prove their survival genuine. They are declared art when their line of descent can be certified.

Before the *Virgin of the Rocks* the visitor to the National Gallery would be encouraged by nearly everything he might have heard and read about the painting to feel something like this: "I am in front of it. I can see it. This painting by Leonardo is unlike any other in the world. The National Gallery has the real one. If I look at this painting hard enough, I should

National Gallery

Virgin of the Rocks by Leonardo da Vinci 1452–1519.
Louvre Museum

somehow be able to feel its authenticity. The *Virgin of the Rocks* by Leonardo da Vinci: it is authentic and therefore it is beautiful."

To dismiss such feelings as naïve would be quite wrong. They accord perfectly with the sophisticated culture of art experts for whom the National Gallery catalogue is written. The entry on the *Virgin of the Rocks* is one of the longest entries. It consists of fourteen closely printed pages. They do not deal with the meaning of the image. They deal with who commissioned the painting, legal squabbles, who owned it, its likely date, the families of its owners. Behind this information lie years of research. The aim of the research is to prove beyond any shadow of doubt that the painting is a genuine Leonardo. The secondary aim is to prove that an almost identical painting in the Louvre is a replica of the National Gallery version.

French art historians try to prove the opposite [see above].

The Virgin and Child with St. Anne and St. John the Baptist by Leonardo da Vinci 1452–1519. Reproduced by courtesy of the Trustees, The National Gallery, London.

The National Gallery sells more reproductions of Leonardo's cartoon of *The Virgin and Child with St. Anne and St. John the Baptist* [above] than any other picture in their collection. A few years ago it was known only to scholars. It became famous because an American wanted to buy it for two and a half million pounds.

Now it hangs in a room by itself. The room is like a chapel. The drawing is behind bullet-proof perspex. It has acquired a new kind of impressiveness. Not because of what it shows—not because of the meaning of its image. It has become impressive, mysterious, because of its market value.

The bogus religiosity which now surrounds original works of art, and which is ultimately dependent upon their market value, has become the substitute for what paintings lost when the camera made them reproducible. Its function is nostalgic. It is the final empty claim for the continuing values of an oligarchic, undemocratic culture. If the image is no longer unique and exclusive, the art object, the thing, must be made mysteriously so.

The majority of the population do not visit art museums. The following table shows how closely an interest in art is related to privileged education.

National proportion of art museum visitors according to level of education:
Percentage of each educational category who visit art museums

	Greece	Poland	France	Holland		Greece	Poland	France	Holland
With no educational qualification	0.02	0.12	0.15	—	Only secondary education	10.5	10.4	10	20
Only primary education	0.30	1.50	0.45	0.50	Further and higher education	11.5	11.7	12.5	17.3

Source: Pierre Bourdieu and Alain Darbel, *L'Amour de l'Art,* Editions de Minuit, Paris 1969, Appendix 5, table 4

The majority take it as axiomatic that the museums are full of holy relics which refer to a mystery which excludes them: the mystery of unaccountable wealth. Or, to put this another way, they believe that original masterpieces belong to the preserve (both materially and spiritually) of the rich. Another table [below] indicates what the idea of an art gallery suggests to each social class.

In the age of pictorial reproduction the meaning of paintings is no longer attached to them; their meaning becomes transmittable: that is to say it becomes information of a sort, and, like all information, it is either put to

Of the places listed below which does a museum remind you of most?

	Manual workers	*Skilled and white collar workers*	*Professional and upper managerial*
	%	%	%
Church	66	45	30.5
Library	9	34	28
Lecture hall	—	4	4.5
Department store or entrance hall in public building	—	7	2
Church and library	9	2	4.5
Church and lecture hall	4	2	—
Library and lecture hall	—	—	2
None of these	4	2	19.5
No reply	8	4	9
	100 (n = 53)	100 (n = 98)	100 (n = 99)

Source: as above, Appendix 4, table 8

use or ignored; information carries no special authority within itself. When a painting is put to use, its meaning is either modified or totally changed. One should be quite clear about what this involves. It is not a question of reproduction failing to reproduce certain aspects of an image faithfully; it is a question of reproduction making it possible, even inevitable, that an image will be used for many different purposes and that the reproduced image, unlike an original work, can lend itself to them all. Let us examine some of the ways in which the reproduced image lends itself to such usage.

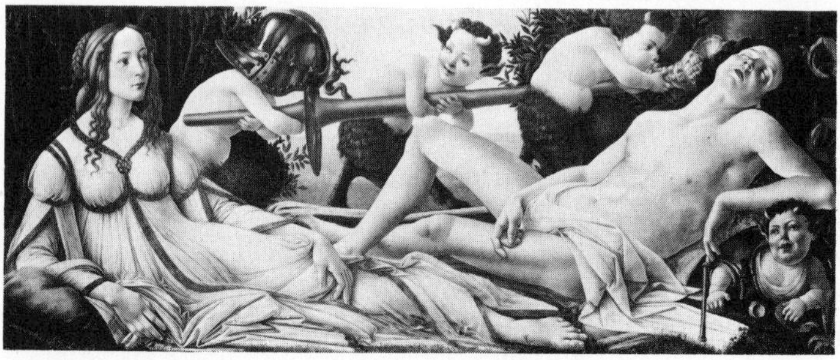

Venus and Mars by Botticelli 1445–1510. Reproduced by courtesy of the Trustees, The National Gallery, London

Reproduction isolates a detail of a painting from the whole. The detail is transformed. An allegorical figure becomes a portrait of a girl [p. 64].

When a painting is reproduced by a film camera it inevitably becomes material for the film-maker's argument.

A film which reproduces images of a painting leads the spectator, through the painting, to the film-maker's own conclusions. The painting lends authority to the film-maker. This is because a film unfolds in time and a painting does not. In a film the way one image follows another, their succession, constructs an argument which becomes irreversible. In a painting all its elements are there to be seen simultaneously. The spectator may need time to examine each element of the painting but whenever he reaches a conclusion, the simultaneity of the whole painting is there to reverse or qualify his conclusion. The painting maintains its own authority [below]. Paintings are often reproduced with words around them [p. 66, top].

Procession to Calvary by Breughel 1525–1569

This is a landscape of a cornfield with birds flying out of it. Look at it for a moment [below]. Then turn the page [p. 67, top].

It is hard to define exactly how the words have changed the image but undoubtedly they have. The image now illustrates the sentence.

In this essay each image reproduced has become part of an argument which has little or nothing to do with the painting's original independent meaning. The words have quoted the paintings to confirm their own verbal authority. . . .

Wheatfield with Crows by Van Gogh 1853–1890

This is the last picture that Van Gogh painted before he killed himself.

Reproduced paintings, like all information, have to hold their own against all the other information being continually transmitted [below].

Consequently a reproduction, as well as making its own references to the image of its original, becomes itself the reference point for other images. The meaning of an image is changed according to what one sees immediately beside it or what comes immediately after it. Such authority as it retains, is distributed over the whole context in which it appears [see p. 68].

Because works of art are reproducible, they can, theoretically, be used by anybody. Yet mostly—in art books, magazines, films, or within gilt frames in living-rooms—reproductions are still used to bolster the illusion that nothing has changed, that art, with its unique undiminished authority, justifies most other forms of authority, that art makes inequality seem noble and hierarchies seem thrilling. For example, the whole concept of the Na-

and the Labour Party

STEPHEN JOHNS

MASS UNEMPLOYMENT is the reality facing the Clyde. This will mean poverty and degradation for thousands of workers and their families.

Going at £1,680,000
'It will fit perfectly over my fireplace...'

British tea planters shot by Khan's troops

Bridge contract

ᴿCH 8 1972 13

ᵏdrop

Subject and significance in Titian's Death of Actaeon

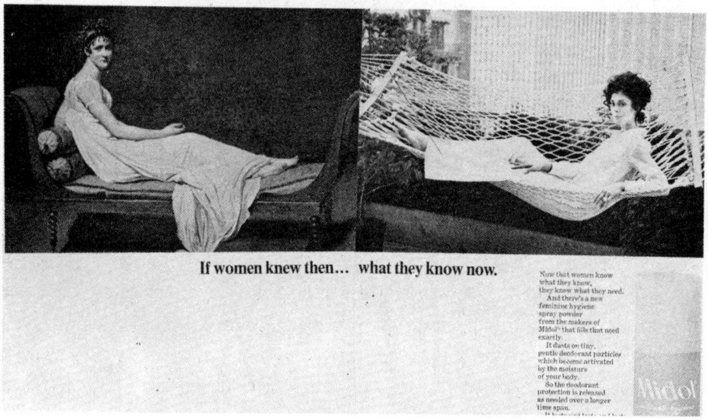

tional Cultural Heritage exploits the authority of art to glorify the present social system and its priorities.

The means of reproduction are used politically and commercially to disguise or deny what their existence makes possible. But sometimes individuals use them differently [p. 69].

Adults and children sometimes have boards in their bedrooms or living-rooms on which they pin pieces of paper: letters, snapshots, reproductions of paintings, newspaper cuttings, original drawings, postcards. On each board all the images belong to the same language and all are more or less equal within it, because they have been chosen in a highly personal way to match and express the experience of the room's inhabitant. Logically, these boards should replace museums.

What are we saying by that? Let us first be sure about what we are not saying.

We are not saying that there is nothing left to experience before original

works of art except a sense of awe because they have survived. The way original works of art are usually approached—through museum catalogues, guides, hired cassettes, etc.—is not the only way they might be approached. When the art of the past ceases to be viewed nostalgically, the works will cease to be holy relics—although they will never re-become what they were before the age of reproduction. We are not saying original works of art are now useless.

Original paintings are silent and still in a sense that information never is. Even a reproduction hung on a wall is not comparable in this respect for in the original the silence and stillness permeate the actual material, the paint, in which one follows the traces of the painter's immediate gestures. This has the effect of closing the distance in time between the painting of the picture and one's own act of looking at it. In this special sense all paintings are contemporary. Hence the immediacy of their testimony. Their historical moment is literally there before our eyes. Cézanne made a similar observation from the painter's point of view. "A minute in the world's life passes! To paint it in its reality, and forget everything for that! To become that minute, to be the sensitive plate . . . give the image of what we see, forgetting everything that has appeared before our time . . ." What we make of that painted moment when it is before our eyes depends upon what we expect of art, and that in turn depends today upon how we have already experienced the meaning of paintings through reproductions.

Nor are we saying that all art can be understood spontaneously. We are not claiming that to cut out a magazine reproduction of an archaic Greek

Woman Pouring Milk by Vermeer 1632–1675

head, because it is reminiscent of some personal experience, and to pin it to a board beside other disparate images, is to come to terms with the full meaning of that head.

The idea of innocence faces two ways. By refusing to enter a conspiracy, one remains innocent of that conspiracy. But to remain innocent may also be to remain ignorant. The issue is not between innocence and knowledge (or between the natural and the cultural) but between a total approach to art which attempts to relate it to every aspect of experience and the esoteric approach of a few specialized experts who are the clerks of the nostalgia of a ruling class in decline. (In decline, not before the proletariat, but before the new power of the corporation and the state.) The real question is: to whom does the meaning of the art of the past properly belong? To those who can apply it to their own lives, or to a cultural hierarchy of relic specialists?

The visual arts have always existed within a certain preserve; originally this preserve was magical or sacred. But it was also physical: it was the place, the cave, the building, in which, or for which, the work was made.

The experience of art, which at first was the experience of ritual, was set apart from the rest of life—precisely in order to be able to exercise power over it. Later the preserve of art became a social one. It entered the culture of the ruling class, whilst physically it was set apart and isolated in their palaces and houses. During all this history the authority of art was inseparable from the particular authority of the preserve.

What the modern means of reproduction have done is to destroy the authority of art and to remove it—or, rather, to remove its images which they reproduce—from any preserve. For the first time ever, images of art have become ephemeral, ubiquitous, insubstantial, available, valueless, free. They surround us in the same way as a language surrounds us. They have entered the mainstream of life over which they no longer, in themselves, have power.

Yet very few people are aware of what has happened because the means of reproduction are used nearly all the time to promote the illusion that nothing has changed except that the masses, thanks to reproductions, can now begin to appreciate art as the cultured minority once did. Understandably, the masses remain uninterested and sceptical.

If the new language of images were used differently, it would, through its use, confer a new kind of power. Within it we could begin to define our experiences more precisely in areas where words are inadequate. (Seeing comes before words.) Not only personal experience, but also the essential historical experience of our relation to the past: that is to say the experience of seeking to give meaning to our lives, of trying to understand the history of which we can become the active agents.

The art of the past no longer exists as it once did. Its authority is lost. In its place there is a language of images. What matters now is who uses that language for what purpose. This touches upon questions of copyright for reproduction, the ownership of art presses and publishers, the total policy of public art galleries and museums. As usually presented, these are narrow professional matters. One of the aims of this essay has been to show that what is really at stake is much larger. A people or a class which is cut off from its own past is far less free to choose and to act as a people or class than one that has been able to situate itself in history. This is why—and this is the only reason why—the entire art of the past has now become a political issue.

Many of the ideas in the preceding essay have been taken from another, written over forty years ago by the German critic and philosopher Walter Benjamin.

His essay was entitled The Work of Art in the Age of Mechanical Reproduction. *This essay is available in English in a collection called* Illuminations *(Cape, London, 1970).*

• • • • • • • • • • • •

QUESTIONS FOR A SECOND READING

1. Berger says, "The past is never there waiting to be discovered, to be recognized for exactly what it is. History always constitutes the relation between a present and its past." And he says, "If we 'saw' the art of the past, we would situate ourselves in history. When we are prevented from seeing it, we are being deprived of the history which belongs to us." As you reread this essay, pay particular attention to Berger's uses of the word "history." What does it stand for? What does it have to do with looking at pictures? How might you define the term if your definition were based on its use in this essay?

   You might take Berger's discussion of the Hals painting as a case in point. What is the relation Berger establishes between the past and the present. If he has not "discovered" the past or recognized it for exactly what it is, what has Berger done in writing about these paintings? What might it mean to say that he has "situated" us in history or has returned a history that belongs to us?

2. Berger argues forcefully that the account of the Hals painting offered by the unnamed art historian is a case of "mystification." How would you characterize Berger's account of that same painting? Would you say that he sees what is "really" there? If so, why wasn't it self-evident? Why does it take an expert to see "clearly"? As you read back over the essay, look for passages you could use to characterize the way Berger looks at images or paintings. If, as he says, "The way we see things is affected by what we know or what we believe," what does he know and what does he believe?

ASSIGNMENTS FOR WRITING

1. Berger says that the real question is this: "To whom does the meaning of the art of the past properly belong?" Let's say, in Berger's spirit, that it belongs to you. Look again at the painting by Vermeer, *Woman Pouring Milk,* that is included in the essay. Berger includes the painting but without much discussion, as though he were, in fact, leaving it for you. Write an essay that shows others how they might best look at and see that painting. You should offer this lesson in the spirit of John Berger. Imagine that you are doing this work for him, perhaps as his apprentice.
2. Berger says, "In order to avoid mystifying the past . . . let us now examine the particular relation which now exists, so far as pictorial images are concerned, between the present and the past. If we can see the present clearly enough, we shall ask the right questions of the past."

   In "Ways of Seeing," the discussion that follows this passage presents Berger's account of the relation that exists between the present and the past, "so far as pictorial images are concerned." It takes some work from a reader, however, to be able to say what we might see if we saw the present clearly enough or what we should ask if we were to ask the right questions of the past. Use one of the paintings from this section of the essay *(Virgin of the Rocks, Venus and Mars, Procession to Calvary, Wheatfield with Crows,* or *Woman Pouring Milk*) to explain what you think Berger is saying about the relation that exists between the past and the present so far as pictorial images are concerned. What must you see in the present? What might you ask of the past? (Berger gives only a few sentences to each of these individual works; your essay should continue and extend what he has to say.)

MAKING CONNECTIONS

1. Walker Percy, in "The Loss of the Creature" (p. 394), like Berger in "Ways of Seeing," talks about the problems people have seeing things. "How can the sightseer recover the Grand Canyon?" Percy asks. "He can recover it in any number of ways, all sharing the common strategem of avoiding the approved confrontation of the tour and the Park Service." There is a way in which Berger also tells a story about tourists—tourists going to a museum to see paintings, to buy postcards, gallery guides, reprints, and T-shirts featuring the image of the Mona Lisa. "The way original works of art are usually approached—through museum catalogues, guides, hired cassettes, etc.—is not the only way they might be approached. When the art of the past ceases to be viewed nostalgically, the works will cease to be holy relics—although they will never re-become what they were before the age of reproduction."

   Write an essay in which you describe four possible "approaches" to a painting in a museum, approaches that could provide for a better understanding or a more complete "recovery" of that painting than would be possible to a casual viewer, to someone who just wandered in, for example, with no strategy in mind. You should think of your essay as providing real advice to a real person. (You might, if you can, work with a particular painting in a particular museum.) What should that person do? How should that person prepare? What would the consequences be?

Two of your approaches should reflect Percy's best advice to a viewer who wanted to develop a successful strategy; two should represent the best you feel Berger would have to offer. When you've finished explaining these four approaches, go on in your essay to examine the differences between those you associate with Percy and those you associate with Berger. What are the key differences? And what do they say about the different ways these two thinkers approach the problem of why we do or do not see that which lies before us?

2. Clifford Geertz, in "Deep Play" (p. 299) argues that the cockfights are a "Balinese reading of Balinese experience; a story they tell themselves about themselves." They are not, then, just cockfights. Or, as Geertz says, the cockfights can be seen as texts "saying something of something." Berger's essay, "Ways of Seeing," offers a view of our culture and, in particular, of the way our culture reproduces and uses images from the past. They are placed in museums, on bulletin boards, on T-shirts, and in advertisements. They are described by experts in certain predictable tones or phrases. It is interesting to look at our use of those images as a story we tell ourselves about ourselves, as a practice that says something about something else.

   Geertz's analysis of the cockfight demonstrates this way of seeing and interpreting a feature of a culture. Write an essay in which you use Geertz's methods to interpret the examples that Berger provides of the ways our culture reproduces and uses images from the past. If these practices say something about something else, what do they say, and about what do they say it? What story might we be telling ourselves about ourselves?

   Note: For this assignment, you should avoid drawing the conclusion Berger draws—that the story told here is a story about the ruling class and its conspiracy against the proletariat. You should see, that is, what other interpretation you can provide. You may, if you choose, return to Berger's conclusions in your paper, but only after you have worked on some of your own.

RAYMOND CARVER

RAYMOND CARVER writes about people who, at first glance, might well be our neighbors. They have everyday problems with work, love, and friendships, yet Carver's people seem caught or trapped, unable or unwilling to do much to change their lives; even their conversations seem destined to go nowhere, to leave them spinning their wheels. Some readers find his stories, like his characters, to be "cold." Carver's style is spare and quiet; he relies on implication, nuance, and omission. But Carver's fictional world is not filled with automatons, nor does it lack a counterpoint of spirit and life. As Irving Howe observed, " there creeps into Mr. Carver's stories a note of disdain toward the people he creates. . . . [He] grows impatient with, even grieved by, the resignation of his characters. It's as if he wished they would rebel against the constrictions of their lives, rebel even against the stylized constraints he puts upon them." One of the reasons Carver's latest collection of short stories, Cathedral, *has met with so much acclaim may be that his characters are beginning to have some success in their rebellions against those constrictions.*

Raymond Carver was born in Clatskanie, Oregon, in 1938 and was educated at Humboldt State College, graduating with a B.A. in 1963. After attending the

University of Iowa for further study, Carver worked for several years as an editor for Science Research Associates before holding a series of positions as a teacher of creative writing. He has been professor of English at Syracuse University since 1980. In addition to Cathedral, *his collections of fiction include* Will You Please Be Quiet Please, Furious Seasons, *and* What We Talk about When We Talk about Love. *His latest volume of poetry is entitled* When Water Comes Together with Other Water.

What We Talk about When We Talk about Love

My friend Mel McGinnis was talking. Mel McGinnis is a cardiologist, and sometimes that gives him the right.

The four of us were sitting around his kitchen table drinking gin. Sunlight filled the kitchen from the big window behind the sink. There were Mel and me and his second wife, Teresa—Terri, we called her—and my wife, Laura. We lived in Albuquerque then. But we were all from somewhere else.

There was an ice bucket on the table. The gin and the tonic water kept going around, and we somehow got on the subject of love. Mel thought real love was nothing less than spiritual love. He said he'd spent five years in a seminary before quitting to go to medical school. He said he still looked back on those years in the seminary as the most important years in his life.

Terri said the man she lived with before she lived with Mel loved her so much he tried to kill her. Then Terri said, "He beat me up one night. He dragged me around the living room by my ankles. He kept saying, 'I love you, I love you, you bitch.' He went on dragging me around the living room. My head kept knocking on things." Terri looked around the table. "What do you do with love like that?"

She was a bone-thin woman with a pretty face, dark eyes, and brown hair that hung down her back. She liked necklaces made of turquoise, and long pendant earrings.

"My God, don't be silly. That's not love, and you know it," Mel said. "I don't know what you'd call it, but I sure know you wouldn't call it love."

"Say what you want to, but I know it was," Terri said. "It may sound crazy to you, but it's true just the same. People are different, Mel. Sure, sometimes he may have acted crazy. Okay. But he loved me. In his own way maybe, but he loved me. There was love there, Mel. Don't say there wasn't."

Mel let out his breath. He held his glass and turned to Laura and me. "The man threatened to kill me," Mel said. He finished his drink and reached for the gin bottle. "Terri's a romantic. Terri's of the kick-me-so-I'll-know-you-love-me school. Terri, hon, don't look that way." Mel reached across the table and touched Terri's cheek with his fingers. He grinned at her.

"Now he wants to make up," Terri said.

"Make up what?" Mel said. "What is there to make up? I know what I know. That's all."

"How'd we get started on this subject, anyway?" Terri said. She raised her glass and drank from it. "Mel always has love on his mind," she said. "Don't you, honey?" She smiled, and I thought that was the last of it.

"I just wouldn't call Ed's behavior love. That's all I'm saying, honey," Mel said. "What about you guys?" Mel said to Laura and me. "Does that sound like love to you?"

"I'm the wrong person to ask," I said. "I didn't even know the man. I've only heard his name mentioned in passing. I wouldn't know. You'd have to know the particulars. But I think what you're saying is that love is an absolute."

Mel said, "The kind of love I'm talking about is. The kind of love I'm talking about, you don't try to kill people."

Laura said, "I don't know anything about Ed, or anything about the situation. But who can judge anyone else's situation?"

I touched the back of Laura's hand. She gave me a quick smile. I picked up Laura's hand. It was warm, the nails polished, perfectly manicured. I encircled the broad wrist with my fingers, and I held her.

"When I left, he drank rat poison," Terri said. She clasped her arms with her hands. "They took him to the hospital in Santa Fe. That's where we lived then, about ten miles out. They saved his life. But his gums went crazy from it. I mean they pulled away from his teeth. After that, his teeth stood out like fangs. My God," Terri said. She waited a minute, then let go of her arms and picked up her glass.

"What people won't do!" Laura said.

"He's out of the action now," Mel said. "He's dead."

Mel handed me the saucer of limes. I took a section, squeezed it over my drink, and stirred the ice cubes with my finger.

"It gets worse," Terri said. "He shot himself in the mouth. But he bungled that too. Poor Ed," she said. Terri shook her head.

"Poor Ed nothing," Mel said. "He was dangerous."

Mel was forty-five years old. He was tall and rangy with curly soft hair.

His face and arms were brown from the tennis he played. When he was sober, his gestures, all his movements, were precise, very careful.

"He did love me though, Mel. Grant me that," Terri said. "That's all I'm asking. He didn't love me the way you love me. I'm not saying that. But he loved me. You can grant me that, can't you?"

"What do you mean, he bungled it?" I said.

Laura leaned forward with her glass. She put her elbows on the table and held her glass in both hands. She glanced from Mel to Terri and waited with a look of bewilderment on her open face, as if amazed that such things happened to people you were friendly with.

"How'd he bungle it when he killed himself?" I said.

"I'll tell you what happened," Mel said. "He took this twenty-two pistol he'd bought to threaten Terri and me with. Oh, I'm serious, the man was always threatening. You should have seen the way we lived in those days. Like fugitives. I even bought a gun myself. Can you believe it? A guy like me? But I did. I bought one for self-defense and carried it in the glove compartment. Sometimes I'd have to leave the apartment in the middle of the night. To go to the hospital, you know? Terri and I weren't married then, and my first wife had the house and kids, the dog, everything, and Terri and I were living in his apartment here. Sometimes, as I say, I'd get a call in the middle of the night and have to go in to the hospital at two or three in the morning. It'd be dark out there in the parking lot, and I'd break into a sweat before I could even get to my car. I never knew if he was going to come up out of the shrubbery or from behind a car and start shooting. I mean, the man was crazy. He was capable of wiring a bomb, anything. He used to call my service at all hours and say he needed to talk to the doctor, and when I'd return the call, he'd say, 'Son of a bitch, your days are numbered.' Little things like that. It was scary, I'm telling you."

"I still feel sorry for him," Terri said.

"It sounds like a nightmare," Laura said. "But what exactly happened after he shot himself?"

Laura is a legal secretary. We'd met in a professional capacity. Before we knew it, it was a courtship. She's thirty-five, three years younger than I am. In addition to being in love, we like each other and enjoy one another's company. She's easy to be with.

"What happened?" Laura said.

Mel said, "He shot himself in the mouth in his room. Someone heard the shot and told the manager. They came in with a passkey, saw what had happened, and called an ambulance. I happened to be there when they brought him in, alive but past recall. The man lived for three days.

His head swelled up to twice the size of a normal head. I'd never seen anything like it, and I hope I never do again. Terri wanted to go in and sit with him when she found out about it. We had a fight over it. I didn't think she should see him like that. I didn't think she should see him, and I still don't."

"Who won the fight?" Laura said.

"I was in the room with him when he died," Terri said. "He never came up out of it. But I sat with him. He didn't have anyone else."

"He was dangerous," Mel said. "If you call that love, you can have it."

"It was love," Terri said. "Sure, it's abnormal in most people's eyes. But he was willing to die for it. He did die for it."

"I sure as hell wouldn't call it love," Mel said. "I mean, no one knows what he did it for. I've seen a lot of suicides, and I couldn't say anyone ever knew what they did it for."

Mel put his hands behind his neck and tilted his chair back. "I'm not interested in that kind of love," he said. "If that's love, you can have it."

Terri said, "We were afraid. Mel even made a will out and wrote to his brother in California who used to be a Green Beret. Mel told him who to look for if something happened to him."

Terri drank from her glass. She said, "But Mel's right—we lived like fugitives. We were afraid. Mel was, weren't you, honey? I even called the police at one point, but they were no help. They said they couldn't do anything until Ed actually did something. Isn't that a laugh?" Terri said.

She poured the last of the gin into her glass and waggled the bottle. Mel got up from the table and went to the cupboard. He took down another bottle.

"Well, Nick and I know what love is," Laura said. "For us, I mean," Laura said. She bumped my knee with her knee. "You're supposed to say something now," Laura said, and turned her smile on me.

For an answer, I took Laura's hand and raised it to my lips. I made a big production out of kissing her hand. Everyone was amused.

"We're lucky," I said.

"You guys," Terri said. "Stop that now. You're making me sick. You're still on the honeymoon, for God's sake. You're still gaga, for crying out loud. Just wait. How long have you been together now? How long has it been? A year? Longer than a year?"

"Going on a year and a half," Laura said, flushed and smiling.

"Oh, now," Terri said. "Wait awhile."

She held her drink and gazed at Laura.

"I'm only kidding," Terri said.

Mel opened the gin and went around the table with the bottle.

"Here, you guys," he said. "Let's have a toast. I want to propose a toast. A toast to love. To true love," Mel said.

We touched glasses.

"To love," we said.

Outside in the backyard, one of the dogs began to bark. The leaves of the aspen that leaned past the window ticked against the glass. The afternoon sun was like a presence in this room, the spacious light of ease and generosity. We could have been anywhere, somewhat enchanted. We raised our glasses again and grinned at each other like children who had agreed on something forbidden.

"I'll tell you what real love it," Mel said. "I mean, I'll give you a good example. And then you can draw your own conclusions." He poured more gin into his glass. He added an ice cube and a sliver of lime. We waited and sipped our drinks. Laura and I touched knees again. I put a hand on her warm thigh and left it there.

"What do any of us really know about love?" Mel said. "It seems to me we're just beginners at love. We say we love each other and we do, I don't doubt it. I love Terri and Terri loves me, and you guys love each other too. You know the kind of love I'm talking about now. Physical love, that impulse that drives you to someone special, as well as love of the other person's being, his or her essence, as it were. Carnal love and, well, call it sentimental love, the day-to-day caring about the other person. But sometimes I have a hard time accounting for the fact that I must have loved my first wife too. But I did, I know I did. So I suppose I am like Terri in that regard. Terri and Ed." He thought about it and then he went on. "There was a time when I thought I loved my first wife more than life itself. But now I hate her guts. I do. How do you explain that? What happened to that love? What happened to it, is what I'd like to know. I wish someone could tell me. Then there's Ed. Okay, we're back to Ed. He loves Terri so much he tries to kill her and he winds up killing himself." Mel stopped talking and swallowed from his glass. "You guys have been together eighteen months and you love each other. It shows all over you. You glow with it. But you both loved other people before you met each other. You've both been married before, just like us. And you probably loved other people before that too, even. Terri and I have been together five years, been married for four. And the terrible thing, the terrible thing is, but the good thing too, the saving grace, you might say, is that if something happened to one of us—excuse me for saying this—but if something happened to one of us tomorrow, I think the other one, the other person, would grieve for a while, you know, but then the surviving party would go out and love again, have someone else soon enough. All this, all of this love we're talking about, it would just be a memory. Maybe not even a memory. Am I wrong? Am I way off base? Because I want you to set me straight if you think I'm wrong. I want to know. I mean, I don't know anything, and I'm the first one to admit it."

"Mel, for God's sake," Terri said. She reached out and took hold of his wrist. "Are you getting drunk? Honey? Are you drunk?"

"Honey, I'm just talking," Mel said. "All right? I don't have to be drunk to say what I think. I mean, we're all just talking, right?" Mel said. He fixed his eyes on her.

"Sweetie, I'm not criticizing," Terri said.

She picked up her glass.

"I'm not on call today," Mel said. "Let me remind you of that. I am not on call," he said.

"Mel, we love you," Laura said.

Mel looked at Laura. He looked at her as if he could not place her, as if she was not the woman she was.

"Love you too, Laura," Mel said. "And you, Nick, love you too. You know something?" Mel said. "You guys are our pals," Mel said.

He picked up his glass.

Mel said, "I was going to tell you about something. I mean, I was going to prove a point. You see, this happened a few months ago, but it's still going on right now, and it ought to make us feel ashamed when we talk like we know what we're talking about when we talk about love."

"Come on now," Terri said. "Don't talk like you're drunk if you're not drunk."

"Just shut up for once in your life," Mel said very quietly. "Will you do me a favor and do that for a minute? So as I was saying, there's this old couple who had this car wreck out on the interstate. A kid hit them and they were all torn to shit and nobody was giving them much chance to pull through."

Terri looked at us and then back at Mel. She seemed anxious, or maybe that's too strong a word.

Mel was handing the bottle around the table.

"I was on call that night," Mel said. "It was May or maybe it was June. Terri and I had just sat down to dinner when the hospital called. There'd been this thing out on the interstate. Drunk kid, teenager, plowed his dad's pickup into this camper with this old couple in it. They were up in their mid-seventies, that couple. The kid—eighteen, nineteen, something—he was DOA. Taken the steering wheel through his sternum. The old couple, they were alive, you understand. I mean, just barely. But they had everything. Multiple fractures, internal injuries, hemorrhaging, contusions, lacerations, the works, and they each of them had themselves concussions. They were in a bad way, believe me. And, of course, their age was two strikes against them. I'd say she was worse off than he was. Ruptured spleen along with everything else. Both kneecaps broken. But they'd been wearing their seatbelts and, God knows, that's what saved them for the time being."

"Folks, this is an advertisement for the National Safety Council," Terri said. "This is your spokesman, Dr. Melvin R. McGinnis, talking." Terri laughed. "Mel," she said, "sometimes you're just too much. But I love you, hon," she said.

"Honey, I love you," Mel said.

He leaned across the table. Terri met him halfway. They kissed.

"Terri's right," Mel said as he settled himself again. "Get those seatbelts on. But seriously, they were in some shape, those oldsters. By the time I got down there, the kid was dead, as I said. He was off in a corner, laid out on a gurney. I took one look at the old couple and told the ER nurse to get me a neurologist and an orthopedic man and a couple of surgeons down there right away."

He drank from his glass. "I'll try to keep this short," he said. "So we took the two of them up to the OR and worked like fuck on them most of the night. They had these incredible reserves, those two. You see that once in a while. So we did everything that could be done, and toward morning we're giving them a fifty-fifty chance, maybe less than that for her. So here they are, still alive the next morning. So, okay, we move them into the ICU, which is where they both kept plugging away at it for two weeks, hitting it better and better on all the scopes. So we transfer them out to their own room."

Mel stopped talking. "Here," he said, "let's drink this cheapo gin the hell up. Then we're going to dinner, right? Terri and I know a new place. That's where we'll go, to this new place we know about. But we're not going until we finish up this cut-rate, lousy gin."

Terri said, "We haven't actually eaten there yet. But it looks good. From the outside, you know."

"I like food," Mel said. "If I had it to do all over again, I'd be a chef, you know? Right, Terri?" Mel said.

He laughed. He fingered the ice in his glass.

"Terri knows," he said. "Terri can tell you. But let me say this. If I could come back again in a different life, a different time and all, you know what? I'd like to come back as a knight. You were pretty safe wearing all that armor. It was all right being a knight until gunpowder and muskets and pistols came along."

"Mel would like to ride a horse and carry a lance," Terri said.

"Carry a woman's scarf with you everywhere," Laura said.

"Or just a woman," Mel said.

"Shame on you," Laura said.

Terri said, "Suppose you came back as a serf. The serfs didn't have it so good in those days," Terri said.

"The serfs never had it good," Mel said. "But I guess even the knights were vessels to someone. Isn't that the way it worked? But then everyone is always a vessel to someone. Isn't that right? Terri? But what I liked about knights, besides their ladies, was that they had that suit of armor, you know, and they couldn't get hurt very easy. No cars in those days, you know? No drunk teenagers to tear into your ass."

"Vassals," Terri said.

"What?" Mel said.

"Vassals," Terri said. "They were called vassals, not vessels."

"Vassals, vessels," Mel said, "what the fuck's the difference? You knew what I meant anyway. All right," Mel said. "So I'm not educated. I learned my stuff. I'm a heart surgeon, sure, but I'm just a mechanic. I go in and I fuck around and I fix things. Shit," Mel said.

"Modesty doesn't become you," Terri said.

"He's just a humble sawbones," I said. "But sometimes they suffocated in all that armor, Mel. They'd even have heart attacks if it got too hot and they were too tired and worn out. I read somewhere that they were too tired and worn out. I read somewhere that they'd fall off their horses and not be able to get up because they were too tired to stand with all that armor on them. They got trampled by their own horses sometimes."

"That's terrible," Mel said. "That's a terrible thing, Nicky. I guess they'd just lay there and wait until somebody came along and made a shish kebab out of them."

"Some other vessel," Terri said.

"That's right," Mel said. "Some vassal would come along and spear the bastard in the name of love. Or whatever the fuck it was they fought over in those days."

"Same things we fight over these days," Terri said.

Laura said, "Nothing's changed."

The color was still high in Laura's cheeks. Her eyes were bright. She brought her glass to her lips.

Mel poured himself another drink. He looked at the label closely as if studying a long row of numbers. Then he slowly put the bottle down on the table and slowly reached for the tonic water.

"What about the old couple?" Laura said. "You didn't finish that story you started."

Laura was having a hard time lighting her cigarette. Her matches kept going out.

The sunshine inside the room was different now, changing, getting thinner. But the leaves outside the window were still shimmering, and I stared at the pattern they made on the panes and on the Formica counter. They weren't the same patterns, of course.

"What about the old couple?" I said.

"Older but wiser," Terri said.

Mel stared at her.

Terri said, "Go on with your story, hon. I was only kidding. Then what happened?"

"Terri, sometimes," Mel said.

"Please, Mel," Terri said. "Don't always be so serious, sweetie. Can't you take a joke?"

"Where's the joke?" Mel said.

He held his glass and gazed steadily at his wife.

"What happened?" Laura said.

Mel fastened his eyes on Laura. He said, "Laura, if I didn't have Terri and if I didn't love her so much, and if Nick wasn't my best friend, I'd fall in love with you. I'd carry you off, honey," he said.

"Tell your story," Terri said. "Then we'll go to that new place, okay?"

"Okay," Mel said. "Where was I?" he said. He stared at the table and then he began again.

"I dropped in to see each of them every day, sometimes twice a day if I was up doing other calls anyway. Casts and bandages, head to foot, the both of them. You know, you've seen it in the movies. That's just the way they looked, just like in the movies. Little eye-holes and nose-holes and mouth-holes. And she had to have her legs slung up on top of it. Well, the husband was very depressed for the longest while. Even after he found out that his wife was going to pull through, he was still very depressed. Not about the accident, though. I mean, the accident was one thing, but it wasn't everything. I'd get up to his mouth-hole, you know, and he'd say no, it wasn't the accident exactly but it was because he couldn't see her through his eye-holes. He said that was what was making him feel so bad. Can you imagine? I'm telling you, the man's heart was breaking because he couldn't turn his goddamn head and *see* his goddamn wife."

Mel looked around the table and shook his head at what he was going to say.

"I mean, it was killing the old fart just because he couldn't *look* at the fucking woman."

We all looked at Mel.

"Do you see what I'm saying?" he said.

Maybe we were a little drunk by then. I know it was hard keeping things in focus. The light was draining out of the room, going back through the window where it had come from. Yet nobody made a move to get up from the table to turn on the overhead light.

"Listen," Mel said. "Let's finish this fucking gin. There's about enough left here for one shooter all around. Then let's go eat. Let's go to the new place."

"He's depressed," Terri said. "Mel, why don't you take a pill?"

Mel shook his head. "I've taken everything there is."

"We all need a pill now and then," I said.

"Some people are born needing them," Terri said.

She was using her finger to rub at something on the table. Then she stopped rubbing.

"I think I want to call my kids," Mel said. "Is that all right with everybody? I'll call my kids," he said.

Terri said, "What if Marjorie answers the phone? You guys, you've heard us on the subject of Marjorie? Honey, you know you don't want to talk to Marjorie. It'll make you feel even worse."

"I don't want to talk to Marjorie," Mel said. "But I want to talk to my kids."

"There isn't a day goes by that Mel doesn't say he wishes she'd get married again. Or else die," Terri said. "For one thing," Terri said, "she's bankrupting us. Mel says it's just to spite him that she won't get married again. She has a boyfriend who lives with her and the kids, so Mel is supporting the boyfriend too."

"She's allergic to bees," Mel said. "If I'm not praying she'll get married again, I'm praying she'll get herself stung to death by a swarm of fucking bees."

"Shame on you," Laura said.

"Bzzzzzzz," Mel said, turning his fingers into bees and buzzing them at Terri's throat. Then he let his hands drop all the way to his sides.

"She's vicious," Mel said. "Sometimes I think I'll go up there dressed like a beekeeper. You know, that hat that's like a helmet with the plate that comes down over your face, the big gloves, and the padded coat? I'll knock on the door and let loose a hive of bees in the house. But first I'd make sure the kids were out, of course."

He crossed one leg over the other. It seemed to take him a lot of time to do it. Then he put both feet on the floor and leaned forward, elbows on the table, his chin cupped in his hands.

"Maybe I won't call the kids, after all. Maybe it isn't such a hot idea. Maybe we'll just go eat. How does that sound?"

"Sounds fine to me," I said. "Eat or not eat. Or keep drinking. I could head right on out into the sunset."

"What does that mean, honey?" Laura said.

"It just means what I said," I said. "It means I could just keep going. That's all it means."

"I could eat something myself," Laura said. "I don't think I've ever been so hungry in my life. Is there something to nibble on?"

"I'll put out some cheese and crackers," Terri said.

But Terri just sat there. She did not get up to get anything.

Mel turned his glass over. He spilled it out on the table.

"Gin's gone," Mel said.

Terri said, "Now what?"

I could hear my heart beating. I could hear everyone's heart. I could hear the human noise we sat there making, not one of us moving, not even when the room went dark.

• • • • • • • • • • • •

QUESTIONS FOR A SECOND READING

1. The story begins with the statement that Mel is a cardiologist, and sometimes that gives him the right to talk. His part of the conversation dominates the story. What gives him the right to talk about love, and why would the others spend so much time listening to him? What, finally, does he know? What characterizes his manner of speaking?
2. What do we know about Nick, the character who tells the story? As you go back to the story, pay attention to what he has to say about love. What role does he play in the conversation? How does he "read" and respond to what Mel has to say? As a reader, is it important for you to see them as similar or different characters?
3. As you reread, think about the women in this story. What do they have to say? And how does their role in the conversation differ from the men's?

ASSIGNMENTS FOR WRITING

1. Near the end of this conversation, Mel tells a story about an old couple who had been in a terrible car accident. He says the old man was depressed, not so much because he and his wife almost died, but because he couldn't see her through his bandages. This story is important to Mel. Why? And what about you, the reader? How do you read this story of the old couple? Do you take it, for example, as the "conclusion" to Carver's story? Is it an example of "true love"? Do you share Mel's point of view (whatever you take it to be)? Do you think you are supposed to? How do you find a point of view of your own in Carver's story?

Write an essay that discusses the story of the old couple and how it functions for both the characters in the story and for you as a reader.

2. It's possible to read this story a number of times and still keep asking, "What are these people talking about?" Terri, Mel, Laura, and Nick all have something to say, but they never seem to reach any conclusions or agreement, and they have trouble finding words that will work for them. At the same time, it's possible to feel that much has been said here. Write an essay answering the question buried in the title. What, in other words, *do* they talk about when they talk about love?

MAKING CONNECTIONS

1. Saul Bellow's story, "A Silver Dish" (p. 22), is about Woody Selbst's love for his father. In fact, Woody's story (or an episode from it) could serve as a story Mel might tell at the table to Nick, Laura, and Terri. What would he say, and how would he talk about it? What about you—what would you say?

   Write an essay with three sections to it. In the first, tell a story from "A Silver Dish" as Mel might, casting it, if you like, into dialogue that might fit into Carver's story. In the second section, say what you can, as best you can, about Woody and his father as an example of love. When you are done, look at both sections and in a third section, discuss the similarities and differences between the ways the two of you talk about love.
2. In the interview with Ted and Ellie Graziano (p. 124), we hear strong talk about beliefs and values and expectations. Ted and Ellie disagree about much, yet they stay together and they say they love each other. For this assignment, look at the Grazianos and all that they say in the context of the conversation recorded in "What We Talk about When We Talk about Love." What are the interesting differences between Mel, Terri, Nick, and Laura, on the one hand, and Ted and Ellie, on the other, in what they talk about when they talk about love? How might you explain the reasons for these differences?

ROBERT COLES

*ROBERT COLES spent seven years following migrant workers north from Florida to gather material for the second volume—*Migrants, Sharecroppers, Mountaineers*—of his remarkable series of books,* Children of Crisis. *He learned about the workers' lives, he says, by visiting "certain homes week after week until it [had] come to pass that I [had] known certain families for many years." The sacrifice, patience, compassion, and discipline required for his massive project—a study of American children—transform the usual business of research into something saintly, magnificent.*

Coles's project began when he was stationed at Keesler Air Force Base in Biloxi, Mississippi. He was, he says, a "rather smug and all too self-satisfied child psychiatrist, just out of medical training." He was in the South at the beginning of the civil rights movement, and the scenes that he witnessed led him to abandon his plans to return to New England and to remain instead in the South to find out how children responded to social and political crisis. He began with standard psychiatric questions, such as "How did these children respond to stress?" but soon realized, he said, "that I was meeting families whose assumptions, hopes, fears, and expectations were quite definitely strange to me. I realized, too, how arbitrarily

I was fitting the lives of various individuals into my psychiatric categories—a useful practice under certain circumstances, but now, for me, a distinct hindrance. I was unwittingly setting severe, maybe crippling, limits on what I would allow myself to see, try to comprehend." He learned, through the children, to abandon his carefully rehearsed questions and to talk and listen. The stories he learned to tell are remarkable and moving, and his commentary on those stories, represented here by his remarks on the stories he has told of wealthy, privileged children, have an authority available to few writers. As Walker Percy once said of Coles, "like Freud, he is humble before the facts. . . . He treads a narrow path between theorizing and novelizing and emerges as what in fact he is: a physician, and a wise and gentle one. He is doctor to the worst of our ills."

Born in 1929, Coles graduated from Harvard in 1950 and earned an M.D. degree from Columbia University in 1954. He has published articles in the Atlantic Monthly, The New Yorker, *the* New Republic, *the* American Poetry Review, *and* Harper's, *and he has written more than thirty books. His multivolume work* Children of Crisis *won the Pulitzer Prize in 1973. "Entitlement" is one of the concluding chapters of Volume 5,* Privileged Ones.

Entitlement

The poor both are and are not alike. On the one hand they struggle against the same odds—hunger and malnutrition in the worst instances, or a marginal life that poses constant threats. Yet Eskimos do not regard their poverty in the same way that Appalachian yeomen do, or Chicanos in Texas or southern California. In the four volumes that have preceded this one° I have tried to show how the common social and economic vulnerability of the poor does not make for a uniform pattern of child-rearing. Historical precedents, cultural experiences, religious convictions exert their influence on parents and children, make boys and girls differ in all sorts of respects, depending on where they live and who their parents are. The same holds for the well-to-do or the rich. It won't do to talk of *the* affluent ones in America (never mind the world!). It won't do to say that in our upper-middle-class suburbs, or among our wealthy, one observes clear-cut, consistent psychological or cultural characteristics. Even in relatively homogeneous suburbs, there are substantial differences in home life, in

---

Coles is referring to the first four volumes of the series, *Children of Crisis: A Study of Courage and Fear; Migrants, Sharecroppers, Mountaineers; The South Goes North;* and *Eskimos, Chicanos, Indians.*

values taught, hobbies encouraged, beliefs advocated or virtually instilled.

But there are indeed distinct groups among the well-off—equivalent in their way to the various kinds of poor people. It is the obligation of someone who wants to know how children make sense of their lives—agricultural migrancy, Indian reservation life in the Southwest, the upper-income life of large homes amid ample acreage in rich towns or in wealthy urban enclaves—to document as faithfully as possible the way the common heritage of money and power affects the assumptions of individual boys and girls. Each child, however, is also influenced by certain social, racial, cultural, or religious traditions, or thoroughly idiosyncratic ones—a given *family's* tastes, sentiments, ideals, say. The issue is "class"; but the issue is not only "class."

Many of the influences, even some of the more idiosyncratic ones, that distinguish some children from others are themselves subject to side influences—a "rebound effect," one rather prosperous Illinois Mormon called it. He was anxious for me to know (just as he could not forget) that there was only so much his faith could resist. He took pains, constantly, to tell his children that he was not like his father; that he was not like his brother either, who lives in Salt Lake City and works for a bank. To live near Chicago and be a doctor, to be a Mormon living in a highly secular upper-middle-class world, was to be an exile. He felt stronger in his faith, but also weaker; he felt like his neighbors in many ways, but unlike them in critically important preferences and articles of faith.

What binds together a Mormon banker in Utah with his brother, or other coreligionists in Illinois or Massachusetts? What distinguishes such people, one from the other? Old New Orleans upper-class families are not in certain respects like families who live in, say, Wellesley Hills, Massachusetts, or Haverford, Pennsylvania, or up the hills outside San Antonio. There *are* resemblances, based on class, occupation, religion, common experiences, expectations, ideas conveyed to children. And yet, again, there are distinctions, shades of feeling and thinking, emphases of one sort or another—even within those families and well-to-do neighborhoods.

I use the word "entitlement" to describe what, perhaps, all quite well-off American families transmit to their children—an important psychological common denominator, I believe: an emotional expression, really, of those familiar, class-bound prerogatives, money and power. The word was given to me, amid much soul-searching, by the rather rich parents of a child I began to talk with almost two decades ago, in 1959. I have watched those parents become grandparents, seen what they described as "the responsibilities of entitlement" get handed down to a new generation. When the father, a lawyer and stockbroker from a prominent and quietly influential family, referred to the "entitlement" his children were growing up with, he had in mind a social rather than a psychological phenomenon: the various juries or committees that select the Mardi Gras participants in New Orleans's annual parade and celebration. He knew that his daughter was "entitled" to be invited here, to attend a dance there, to feel part of a carefully limited and sometimes self-important social scene.

He wanted, however, to go beyond that social fact; he wanted his children to feel obligated by how fortunate they were, and would no doubt always be, all things being equal—or unequal! He talked about what he had received from his parents and what he would give to his children, "automatically, without any thought," and what they too would pass on. The father was careful to distinguish between the social entitlement and "something else," a "something else" he couldn't quite define but knew he had to try to evoke if he were to be psychologically candid: "Our children have a good life ahead of them; and I think they know it now. I think they did when they were three or four, too. It's *entitlement,* that's what I call it. My wife didn't know what I was talking about when I first used the word. She thought it had something to do with our ancestry! Maybe it does! I don't mean to be snide. I just think our children grow up taking a lot for granted, and it can be good that they do, and it can be bad. It's like anything else, it all depends. I mean, you can have spoiled brats for children, or you can have kids who want to share what they have. I don't mean give away all their money! I mean be responsible, and try to live up to their ideals, and not just sit around wondering which island in the Caribbean to visit this year, and where to go next summer to get away from the heat and humidity here in New Orleans."

At the time he said no more. It was 1960, and I was interested mainly in what his son and his daughter thought about black children—and about the violence then being inflicted on a few black children brave enough and stubborn enough to walk past mobs into two elementary schools. But as months became years, I came back to that word "entitlement," especially because it was one I had heard years earlier, in Boston, when I was receiving my training in child psychiatry. "Narcissistic entitlement" was the phrase I had been taught to be familiar with, to use occasionally when speaking of a particular kind of "disturbed" child. The term could be used in place of more conventional, blunter ones that everyone else uses from time to time: a smug, self-satisfied child; or a child who thinks he (or she) owns the world, or will one day; or a self-centered child who expects a lot from just about everyone.

I recall a boy of eight I was treating in Boston, before I went South; my supervisor, a child psychoanalyst who had worked with a similar child for three years, and anticipated, alas, another year or two, at least, of thrice weekly office visits, told me that I was being naïvely hopeful, and a touch simpleminded, when I remarked upon the curiosity of the boy, his evident willingness to ask me questions about all sorts of persons, places, things—

and so his capacity for engagement with the world around him. Yes, she pointed out, there was indeed a measure of that, but it was best that *we* ask questions about the nature of *his* questions. As we did, they all came back to him—to quite specific experiences he had gone through and wanted to talk about. And he had told me that, actually; he never asked a question out of intellectual interest—rather, in his words, "because I like to know what might happen next to me."

It is hard to describe the special fearfulness and sadness such a child struggles with. He was not the "ordinary" child; he was quite troubled. And I suppose the parents of such children (even if those mothers and fathers have other, relatively solid children, psychologically speaking) must be disqualified as "normal" or "average." They may be like anyone else on the street; may be rather knowing, psychiatrically—able to sense something "wrong" with a child's "behavior" and go do something about it by seeking out a doctor. But the analyst-supervisor I was myself "seeing" once a week was convinced that there was a "special narcissism," she called it, that a certain kind of parent offers a child: "Narcissism is something we all struggle with; but some people have more of it than others, and some children come from homes that have so much that all the money and possessions, all the rugs and furniture and toys and vacations and savings accounts and insurance policies come crashing on the child's head. There is a shift from narcissism to narcissistic entitlement."

I wasn't sure exactly what she meant, or how the "shift" she had mentioned did indeed take place. I know, because she is someone I still discuss psychoanalytic theory with, that she was not sure herself what the exact dimensions were of that childhood journey. But she knew even then, before there were "fields" like "social psychiatry" or "community psychiatry," that at some point a family's psychology and psychopathology engage with its social and economic life; and that when a migrant child or a ghetto child has to contend with narcissism, it will take on a certain flavor (narcissistic despair, for instance); whereas for a child who lives in a big house and whose parents have a lot and want to give a lot to their offspring, "narcissistic entitlement" may well be a possibility. The child withdraws not only into himself or herself but, by extension, into a certain world of objects, habits, and rituals—the comfortable world of a room, a home, a way of life. The child has much, but wants and expects more—only to feel no great gratitude, but a desire for yet more: an inheritance the world is expected to provide. One's parents will oblige, as intermediaries. And if underneath there lie apprehension and gloom and, not least, a strain of gnawing worthlessness, that is of no matter to many children whose "narcissistic entitlement" becomes what psychoanalytic theorists refer to as a "character trait," rather than a "symptom" that prompts a visit to a doctor. That is, the child is regarded by everyone, psychiatrists included, as "normal," as "all right," or different, but not all *that* different. One doesn't send every cocksure, greedy, self-centered child to a child psychiatrist.

In many other well-to-do homes I've visited, parents have known in their bones what child psychiatrists think and wonder as they talk with their children. Will a certain child get too much—so much that he or she runs the danger of turning away from life, forsaking people for a life of passionate involvement with objects? Less ominously, might a mild tendency in that direction become especially evident when things get tough, psychologically, for one reason or another? Will the child be willing to reach for people, and get along with them, but always with certain limits on the involvement? Often when children are four, five, and six, parents who have felt able to offer them virtually anything begin to pull back, in concern if not outright horror. A son not only has become increasingly demanding or petulant; even when he is quiet he seems to be sitting on a throne of sorts—expecting things to happen, wondering with annoyance why they don't, reassuring himself that they will, or, if they haven't, shrugging his shoulders and waiting for the next event.

It was just such an impasse—not dramatic, but quite definite and worrisome—that prompted that New Orleans father to use the word "entitlement." He had himself been born to wealth, as will future generations of his family be, unless the American economic system changes drastically. But he was worried about what a lot of money can do to a person's "personality"; he uses that word as a layman, but he knows exactly what he has in mind. It isn't so much a matter of spoiling or indulging children; he is willing to let that happen, "within limits." But he knew precisely what those limits were: when the child begins to let his or her situation, the life that he or she lives, "go to the head." It is then that children begin "to act as if they have royal blood in them." And conservative though he is, for him each generation has to prove itself—not necessarily by finding new worlds to conquer or by becoming extraordinarily successful. He has wanted his children to show an interest in the world, to reach out and touch others, to develop their own initiatives, however circumscribed, undramatic, and conventional. It is those kinds of initiative he naturally finds appealing. He is rather satisfied with the life he was born to. He finds each day to be pleasant, interesting, and by his lights, quite useful. He has, however, worried at times that his children were taking *too* much for granted. When his young daughter, during a Mardi Gras season, kept *assuming* she would one day receive this honor and that honor—indeed, become a Mardi Gras queen—he realized that his notion of "entitlement" was not quite hers. *Noblesse oblige* requires a gesture toward others. Had a parent sensed the danger of what my supervisor referred to as a "shift" from "entitlement" to "narcissistic entitlement"?

He would not be the only parent to express such a concern to me in the course of my work. In homes where mothers and fathers profess no explicit reformist persuasions (to say the least!) they nevertheless worry about what happens to children who grow up surrounded by just about everything they want, virtually, on demand. And if much of the apprehension is conventional—that the child will become "spoiled"—there is an element of uneasiness that runs deeper. The parents may begin to regard spoiled behavior as but a symptom: "I don't mind if my children become a little spoiled. That's bound to happen. I worry that they will think that everything is coming to them; that they will grow up with the idea that if they're frustrated, or if they want something, then all they have to do is say a few words, and they'll have what they asked for. When they're like that, they've gone from spoiled to spoiled rotten—and beyond, to some state I don't even know how to describe."

When children are two and three they become increasingly conscious of what belongs to whom. They also become, usually, more and more willing and able to leave themselves behind, so to speak—reach out for objects as well as individuals. They develop their first friends, their first interests or regular and cherished activities. They learn too, most of them, a variety of restraints and frustrations. They must gain control of their bodies, manage without diapers, remember to empty their bladders before going to bed, and get up at night and do likewise in the bathroom rather than on the sheet and mattress. They must learn not to touch hot stoves; not to leave refrigerator doors open; not to spill things, break things, step on things; not to intrude on what belongs to others; not to confuse their prerogatives or possessions with the rights and property of parents, brothers and sisters, friends. At three and four, children from homes like those in New Orleans's Garden District have often started nursery school, have also started making visits to other homes or receiving visitors at their own homes. There are toys to share, games to play, a sandbox or a lawn or indeed a swimming pool or a paddock with its animals. All children have to struggle with themselves for the strength to offer as well as take, or to yield with tact and even a touch of gratitude what has been loaned rather than made an outright gift.

But for some children, a relative handful of the world's, such obligations and struggles are muted. Obviously it is possible for parents to have a lot of money yet avoid bringing up their children in such a way that they feel like members of a royal family. Yet even parents determined not to spoil their children often recognize what might be called the existential (as opposed to strictly psychological) aspects of their situation, and that of their children. A father may begin rather early on lecturing his children about the meaning of money; a mother may do her share by saying no, even when yes is so easy to say—but the child may well sense eventually what the parents know quite well: the difference between a voluntary posture and an utterly necessary one.

Such a child, by the age of five or six, has very definite notions of what is possible, even if not always permitted; possible because there is plenty of money that can be spent. That child, in conversation and without embarrassment or the kind of reticence and secretiveness that comes later, may reveal a substantial knowledge of economic affairs. A six-year-old girl in New Orleans knew that she would at twenty-one inherit a half a million dollars. She also knew that her father "only" gave her twenty-five cents a week—whereas some friends of hers received as much as a dollar. She was vexed; she asked her parents why they were so "strict." One friend had even used the word "stingy" for the parents. The father, in a matter-of-fact way, pointed out to the daughter that she did, after all, get "anything she really wants." Why, then, the need for an extravagant allowance? The girl was won over, told her friends thereafter that it was no matter to her whether she even received an allowance; the important point was the future and what it had to offer. The friends then checked back with their parents, who were rather alarmed—that such young children were talking so freely and openly about family financial matters.

As a result the girl learned from her friends that she had disclosed what ought to be kept firmly under wraps. She decided on the basis of such declarations that her friends may well be "comfortable," but they are not as rich as her parents are or as she will one day be. They in turn explained to her that she had gone beyond the bounds of available evidence. The friends may simply have been told to keep quiet about their family's monetary status—a good idea, the girl was reminded by her parents. The girl agreed, but was not really prepared at the time to follow such advice. She had heard her parents talk with *their* parents about money matters and had been told that it is best that she, too, gradually understand what her financial situation is and will be. That being the case, she wondered out loud why it wasn't appropriate for her to share what she had learned about her future prospects with those she considered good friends. Her parents could only repeat their conviction that certain matters are quite definitely and properly kept within the confines of the family.

Such conversations between young children and their parents help consolidate in boys and girls a conviction of present and future affluence. It obviously never occurs to these children that they won't have food at some point in the near or distant future. Nor do they ever really lack for anything. There are differences in amount, and lectures and sermons may accompany parental acts of generosity. But admonitions don't modify the quite shrewd appraisal children make of what they are heir to, and don't at all diminish the sense of entitlement.

In an Appalachian mine-owner's home, for instance, a boy of seven made the following comment in 1963, after his father's mine had suffered an explosion, killing two men and injuring seriously nine others: "I heard my mother saying she felt sorry for the families of the miners. I feel sorry for them, too. I hope the men who got hurt get better. I'm sure they will. My father has called in doctors from Lexington. He wants the best doctors in all Kentucky for those miners. Daddy says it was the miners' fault; they get careless, and the next thing you know, there's an explosion. It's too bad. I guess there are a lot of kids who are praying hard for their fathers. I wish God was nice to everyone. He's been very good to us. My Daddy says it's been hard work, running the mine and another one he has. It's just as hard to run a mine as it is to go down and dig the coal! I'm glad my father is the owner, though. I wouldn't want him to get killed or hurt bad down there, way underground. Daddy has given us a good life. We have a lot of fun coming up, he says, in the next few years. We're going on some trips. Daddy deserves his vacations. He says he's happy because he can keep us happy, and he does. If we want something real bad, we go tell him or Mum, and they oblige us almost all the time. That's what Daddy always says—that he's glad to oblige my sister and me!"

The father is not *always* "glad to oblige"; he can be quite stern at times, but the children have learned that his lectures have only a limited applicability to their life. Yes, there are restraints; not every request for money or a present is granted forthwith. On the other hand, their life is sufficiently comfortable to belie the parents' insistence on caution, lest there be nothing left. In fact, the lectures only seem to reinforce in the children a certain materialistic preoccupation. Having been told to make do with what they already have in such abundance, the boy and girl (and their counterparts in the homes I have visited in other parts of the United States) retreat to their respective rooms, get out their possessions, and begin to use them as well as simply gaze at them. The boy can be quite pointed and expressive about what he has—and is doing with what he has—at such moments: "I have my soldiers, and my trucks, and the tanks and the helicopters. I get them lined up. I build a fort. I have the blocks and the logs, and I make the fort strong. I have my helicopter pad. I make sure the pad is protected by tanks and some men with machine guns. Some terrorists might come and try to attack, and destroy the pad and the helicopter. It's best to keep a few planes in the air, to scout. You have to keep your eyes open, or there will be a surprise attack. I surround the fort with men, and I have these bushes and trees, and I put men behind them. And I have some men on horses."

He stops and looks at what he has done. He is rather proud of himself. He has thought at times of working toward a military career, but he knows that he "most likely" will follow in his father's footsteps. There is a profitable coal company to run and his father has told him that, in the boy's words, "coal has a big future now because there's an energy problem." That observation prompts him to worry about his fort. Does *it* have enough energy or might there one day be a shortage? No, he is sure that his fort will be able to manage successfully. There is a large stack of wood set aside in the stockade. As for the tanks, helicopters, airplanes, they will not lack fuel; there is an oil well nearby. And in the event that should give out, the boy is certain that oil can be flown in or, if necessary, a "secret pipeline" could be built, just in case some disaster should come upon the airfield–landing pad.

His sister has on some occasions become provocative, even truculent. She has asked him, after watching him "declare war" on an unseen enemy, why he always wins. He has replied that the answer is quite simple; he has the best army. She will occasionally express her misgivings: there might be, just *might* be, an army that could overcome his army, with its nineteenth-century fort and twentieth-century military hardware. The boy replies with scorn that his sister is being far too literal-minded. Anyway, America has never lost a war, he knows for sure, and he is an American and does not intend to lose one either. Nor has his father, when brought into the argument later, been anything but encouraging. True, Vietnam was "a mess"; but the country was never "really determined" to win—and maybe never should have involved itself in such a struggle, waged in "distant jungles." The sister has by then lost all interest in her younger (by one year) brother's "game."

The boy is not obsessed with the war game, either. He has many other opportunities to play—other games or, more personally, friends to have over, to go visit. When he plays the war game with them, however, there is invariably a battle of wits, a stalemate. The boy and his friends are tireless in the resourcefulness they summon to their encounters. If necessary, they find themselves in possession of atomic bombs, supersonic planes, surprise tunnels, magical weapons of all kinds, secret supply bases, hidden contingents of men. Eventually, they each declare the other "a winner." The boy realizes: "I know there has to be a losing side. My sister is right. You can't win all the time. But she doesn't like to lose, either. She's always saying her guinea pig is the prettiest, and she says she can ride her bike faster than anyone. I hope I'll get a five-speed bike soon; as soon as I'm a little taller, I'll get one. Then you can really go zoom, zoom down the roads. They say that when I'm grown up, we'll be landing on the moon all the time and we'll be landing on the planets—Mars, for sure. This country will do it! Maybe I could be an astronaut for a while, and then come back and help Daddy in his business. He says he may buy a couple more mines, and by the time I'm out of college, there will be a lot to do. He says I should plan to be a lawyer, because it really helps you, if you have a business, to know how to go to court and protect yourself. The unions want to interfere a lot, and Daddy has to fight them. He has to give some ground, but he's the boss, and they can't push too hard or he'll close up his mines. Then they'd all be out of work! And Daddy could hire some other miners. There are a lot of people who would be glad to get a job!"

So it goes: an abundance of energy for his fort and air force base and an abundance of workers for his father's mines. Abundance is his destiny, he has every reason to believe. He may even land on the stars. Certainly he has traveled widely in this country. He associates the seasons with travel, among other events. In winter, for instance, there is a trip South, to one or another Caribbean island. Winters can be long and hard in Appalachia, and a respite is invigorating—and "healthy." The boy watches his father exercise, hears his mother talk about certain foods, and remarks upon something else that has to do with his future: he may well live to be over a century old. Why not?

His parents are not health faddists, or unusually self-preoccupied: given exercise, a careful diet, and medical progress, one will do (in the father's words) "right well." As an additional boost to the family's collective health, a sauna has been installed, and the children are entranced with it. They also are preoccupied with their two dogs, and their other animals—the guinea pigs, hamsters, rabbits, chickens. There is always someone in the house, a maid, a handyman. Still, it is sad to say good-bye. Now, if the family owned a plane, the animals could come along on those trips!

The boy doesn't really believe that his father ever will own a Lear jet; yet, at moments he can imagine himself wrong. And he can construct a fantasy: suddenly an announcement, most likely at breakfast, of a "surprise." It is a familiar sequence. The boy has come to associate breakfast with good news. What is ahead for the day? When does a certain vacation start? During one breakfast the father announced that he had a surprise. The children were all ears. So was their mother; she knew of no forthcoming surprise. The father paused, waited for a bit of suspense to build up, then made his announcement: a new car—a red MG, a fast car that takes curves well and seats only two, in which he would take his wife and children for rides, one at a time.

Yet the boy had apparently been hoping for another kind of surprise: "I woke up and it was very funny, I remembered that I'd just had this dream. In it I was walking through the woods with Daddy, and all of a sudden there was an open field, and I looked, and I saw a hawk, and it was circling and circling. I like going hunting with Daddy, and I thought we were hunting. But when I looked at him, he didn't have his gun. Then he pointed at the hawk, and it was coming down. It landed ahead of us, and it was real strange—because the hawk turned into an airplane! I couldn't believe it. We went toward the plane, and Daddy said we could get a ride any time we wanted, because it was ours; he'd just bought it. That's when

I woke up, I think. I even forgot about the dream until I looked at my fort and the airplanes, and then I remembered the dream, and once I remembered it, I didn't forget it again."

Dreams evoke a social as well as psychological reality. Dreams show what a child can hope for, unashamedly expect. It so happens that among rich children one day's apparently fatuous, excessive fantasy or dream can turn into the next day's actuality. Four years after that boy had dreamed that his father owned a plane, the father got one. The boom of the 1970s in the coal fields made his father even richer. The boy was of course eager to go on flying trips; eager also to learn to fly. The family owned a horse farm by then, near Lexington, Kentucky, and when the boy and girl were not flying, they were riding. The girl learned to jump well, the boy to ride quite fast. At thirteen he dreamed (by day) of becoming an astronaut or of becoming the manager of his father's horse farm or of going to the Air Force Academy and afterward becoming a "supersonic pilot."

He would never become a commercial pilot, however; and his reasons were interesting: "I've gone on a lot of commercial flights, and there are a lot of people on board, and the pilot has to be nice to everyone, and he makes all these announcements about the seat belts, and stuff like that. My dad's pilot was in the air force, and then he flew commercial. He was glad to get out, though. He says you have to be like a waiter; you have to answer complaints from the customers and apologize to them, just because the ride gets bumpy. It's best to work for yourself, or work for another person, if you trust him and like him. If you go commercial, like our pilot says, you're a servant. You can't really speak your mind. I'd like to fly, but I'm worried about going into the air force. Our pilot says it can be fun, or it can be murder, depending on your superior officer. If I got a bad one, I guess I'd just quit. They can't keep you in forever against your will."

He has only confidence about the future, no real sense of danger. At times he talks (at thirteen) as if he could simultaneously hold down several jobs. He would run the family horse farm. He would take part in any number of races and hunts. He would also fly his own plane. He would learn how to parachute; he might even become a professional parachutist. He met one at a fair, and found the man not only brave, but "real nice to talk to." In more restrained (realistic?) moments, he forgets the horse farm, forgets airplanes or just plain air; he talks about law school—the place his father would like him to race to, land upon. When only an eighth-grade student he imagined himself, one day, owning an airplane, flying it back and forth from law school (at the University of Kentucky) to his father's horse farm, some fifty miles away.

He has never had any patience for lines, for traffic jams, for crowded stores. Many of the children I have worked with are similarly disposed; they do not like large groups of people in public places—in fact, have been taught the distinct value not only of privacy but the quiet that goes with being relatively alone. Some of the children are afraid of those crowds, can't imagine how it would be possible to survive them. Of course, what is strange, unknown, or portrayed as unattractive, uncomfortable, or just to be avoided as a nuisance can for a given child become a source of curiosity, even an event to be experienced at all costs. An eight-year-old girl who lived well outside Boston, even beyond its suburbs, on a farm, wanted desperately to go to the city and see Santa Claus—not because she believed in him, but because she wanted to see "those crowds" she had in fact seen on television. She got her wish, was excited at first, then quite disappointed, and ultimately made rather uncomfortable. She didn't like being jostled, shoved, pushed, and ignored when she protested. She was only too glad when her mother suggested that they had gone through quite enough. Yes, they had, the daughter agreed. Soon they were in a cab, then on a commuter train. The latter was going to be the limit for the girl thereafter; if she would venture into the world, the train would be its microcosm. She would travel by train to Boston, then turn right around and travel back—unless, of course, she were going to a restaurant or an art gallery or to her parents' club. In those places one is not overcome by people who shout, and step on the feet of others, and ignore any protests made.

A week after the girl had gone through her Boston "adventure" (as she had called the trip *before* she embarked upon it), each student in her third-grade class was asked to draw a picture in some way connected to the Christmas season, and the girl obliged eagerly. She drew Santa Claus standing beside a pile of packages, presents for the many children who stood near him. They blended into one another—a mob scene. Watching them but removed from them was one child, bigger and on a higher level—suspended in space, it seemed, and partially surrounded by a thin but visible line. The girl wrote on the bottom of the drawing "I saw Santa Claus." She made it quite clear what she had intended to portray: "He was standing there, handing out these gifts. They were all the same, I think, and they were plastic squirt guns for the boys and little dolls for the girls. I felt sorry for the kids. I asked my mother why kids wanted to push each other, just to get that junk. My mother said a lot of people just don't know any better. I was going to force my way up to that Santa Claus and tell him to stop being so dumb! My mother said he was probably a drunk, trying to make a few dollars, so he could spend it in a bar nearby that evening! I don't want to be in a store like that again. We went up to a balcony and watched, and then we got out of the place and came home. I told my mother that I didn't care if I ever went to Boston again. I have two friends, and they've never been in Boston, and they don't want to go there, except to ride through on the way to the airport."

She sounds at that moment more aloof, condescending, and downright snobbish than she ordinarily is. She spends some of her time with two or three girls who live on nearby "estates." Those girls don't see each other regularly, and each of them is quite able to be alone—in fact, rather as anxious to be by themselves, do things by themselves, as to be with one another and find things to work on together. Sometimes a day or two goes by with no formal arrangement to play. They meet in school, and that seems to be enough. Each girl has obligations—a horse to groom, a stall to work on. They are quite "self-sufficient," a word they have heard used repeatedly by their parents. Even within one's own social circle there is no point in surrendering to excessive gregariousness!

The girls meet by accident (or unacknowledged design) on various riding trails. On such daily expeditions one learns to be very much alone with one's thoughts. In the beginning they have to do with riding; but eventually they embrace the weather, the landscape, and, almost always, the child's body: "I think of my leg muscles, my hold on the horse. It's funny how you can forget a lot of your muscles until you mount that horse. Once up there you notice your feet and your knees and your hips, and you watch your arms and hands, and you think of your head and back—how straight are you sitting. It's your whole body that's on your mind, like the teacher says. It's a little like that with skiing, and a lot like that with ballet lessons; but for me, riding is when I'm most in touch with my body! And I'm also in touch with the horse's body. We're sort of one!"

Once up on the horse, riding, she is (by her own description) in her "own world." She has heard her mother use that expression. The mother is not boasting, or dismissing others who live in other worlds. The mother is describing, as does the child, a state of progressive withdrawal from people and, selectively, the familiar routines or objects of the environment, in favor of a mixture of reverie and disciplined activity. And when the girl, for one reason or another, is unable to ride, she misses not only the sport, but the state of mind that goes with riding.

Her mother is more explicit about what happens; she tells her daughter, at times, that she wants to "leave everything" and go riding. She tells her daughter that when she is on the horse, cantering across the field or trotting down a trail, she has a "feeling" that is "better than being on a plane." She finds that she can put everyone and everything into "perspective." Nothing seems impossible, burdensome, difficult. There are no distractions, nuisances, petty or boring details to attend to. One is not only away from it all, but above it all. And one is closer to one's "self." The mother talks about the "self" and the child does too. "It is strange," the girl comments, "because you forget yourself riding or skiing, but you also remember yourself the way you don't when you're just sitting around watching television or reading or playing in your room."

With none of the other American children I have worked with have I heard such a continuous and strong emphasis put on the "self." In fact, other children rarely if ever think about themselves in the way children of well-to-do and rich parents do—with insistence, regularity, and, not least, out of a learned sense of obligation. These privileged ones are children who live in homes with many mirrors. They have mirrors in their rooms, large mirrors in adjoining bathrooms. When they were three or four they were taught to use them; taught to wash their faces, brush their teeth, comb their hair. Personal appearance matters and becomes a central objective for such children. A boy of eight expresses his rebelliousness by clinging to sloppy clothes, but leaves the house every day for school in a neat and well-fitted uniform. A good number of these children wear them—shirts or sweaters with a school's name and/or insignia on them. Even when the child relaxes, comes home, and changes into "old" clothes, there is an air of decisiveness about the act—and certainly, the issue is one of choice: to wear *this,* or *that;* to look a particular way, in keeping with a particular mood, time of day, event.

The issue also is that of the "self"—its display, its possibilities, its cultivation and development, even the repeated use of the word. A ten-year-old boy who lives in the outermost part of Westchester County made this very clear. I had originally met him because his parents, both lawyers, were active in the civil rights movement. His father, a patrician Yankee, very much endorsed the students who went South in the early 1960s and, nearer to home, worked on behalf of integrated school up North. His own children, however, attended private schools—a source of anguish to both the father and the son, who do not lend themselves easily to a description that only emphasizes the hypocritical element in their lives.

The boy knew that he also *would* be (as opposed to wanted to be!) a lawyer. He was quick to perceive and acknowledge his situation, and as he did so he brought himself (his "self") right into the discussion: "I don't want to tell other kids what to do. I told my father I should be going to the public schools myself. Then I could say anything. Then I could ask why we don't have black kids with us in school. But you have to try to do what's best for your *own* life, even if you can't speak up for the black people. When I'm growing up, I'll be like my father; I'll help the black people all I can. It's this way: first you build *yourself* up. You learn all you can. Later, you can *give of yourself.* That's what Dad says: you can't help others until you've learned to help *yourself.* It's not that you're being selfish. People say you're selfish, if you're going to a private school and your parents have a lot of money. We had a maid here, and she wasn't right in the head. She lost her temper and told Dad that he's a phony, and he's out for *himself* and no one else, and the same goes for my sister and me. Then she quit. Daddy tried to get her to talk with us, but she wouldn't.

She said that's all we ever do—talk, talk. I told Daddy she was contradicting herself; because she told me a few weeks ago that I'm always doing something, and I should sit down and talk with her. But I didn't know what to say to her! I think she got angry with me because I was putting on my skis for cross-country skiing, and she said I had too much, that was my problem. I asked her where the regular skis were, and she said she wouldn't tell me, even if she knew! It's too bad, what happened to her.

"I feel sorry for her, though. Like my sister said, it's no fun to be a maid! The poor woman doesn't look very good. She weighs too much. She's only forty, my mother thinks, but she looks as if she's sixty, and is sick. She should take better care of herself. She said my sister and I make big messes in the bathroom. But that's because we *use* the bathroom! And her breath—God, it's terrible. She isn't as clean as she should be. My mother wanted to get her some deodorant, but we were afraid she'd just blow up at us. But she did anyway. So it didn't make any difference! Like my Dad said, it's too bad about her; she didn't know how to take care of herself and now she's thrown away this job, and she told my mother last year that it was the best one she'd ever had, so she's her own worst enemy. I wonder what she'll think when she looks at herself in the mirror and tries to figure out what to do next."

He was no budding egotist. If anything, he was less self-centered, at ten, than many other children of his community or others like it. He was willing to think about, at least, others less fortunate than himself—the maid, and black people in general. True, he would often repeat uncritically his father's words, or a version of them. But he was trying to respond to his father's wishes and beliefs as well as his words. It was impossible for him, no matter how compassionate his nature, to conceive of life as others live it—the maid, and yet, millions of children his age, who don't look in the mirror very often and may not even own one; who don't worry about what is worn, and how one looks, and what is said and how one sounds, and what is done (in the bathroom) and how one smells.

Sometimes minor details of life tell more than larger attitudes spoken and duly recorded by outside observers. A boy's fingernails, for instance; or his sister's skin—in each instance, a reflection of much more. Here is the boy from Westchester County, at eleven, talking about the new pair of scissors he has received from his father: "I like them. I didn't want my mother to clip my fingernails any longer. I'd rather take care of myself! I'll be shaving soon. I look forward to that! I've watched my father a lot. He showed me how to use the scissors and end up with nails that aren't too short and aren't too long. There's a kid in my class, he lets his nails get longer and longer and there's a lot of dirt under them, and you wonder how long they'll get, and then all of a sudden, one day, you notice that they've been cut off. His parents have got a divorce, and they have a maid taking care of him and his kid brother, and she runs the house and there's no one supervising her. You have to tell the help what to do, because if you don't, they forget and they don't live up to your standards, and they're acting as if they were back in their own homes."

So it happens—a boy's developing sense of himself as against a collective, amorphous "them." It is a "sense" that has both sociological and psychological dimensions to it. The former are perhaps more painful to spell out but also more readily apparent. The boy has learned that in the ghetto people live who don't use his parents' kind of judgment, and don't, either, have the same personal habits or concerns. The boy's sister has a similar kind of knowledge. At twelve she could be quite pointed: "We've had a couple of maids, and they don't know why I use my mother's Vaseline lotion on my arms and hands—and in winter on my face, too. They say I've got a wonderful complexion; but I don't think they know how to look real carefully at my skin—or their own either. Maybe they don't have the time. But I see them taking a 'break,' and what do they do? They go put on a prize show in the morning or a 'story' in the afternoon. I don't know how they can stand looking at that stuff! I've got a lot of chores. We're not spoiled here! I have to clean out the stalls and brush the horses carefully before we go riding. I have to pick up my room. My mother told me when I was real little, before I even was old enough to go to school, that she wasn't going to have me sitting and looking at television while the maid was straightening out my room. The same goes for outside the house; we have a gardener, but he's not allowed to come into the barn and help us with the animals.

"We had one maid, and she said we spent more time with the animals than she does with her children. I felt sad when she told me that. She has no understanding of what an animal needs. She was the one who was always telling me I was beautiful, and so I didn't need any lotion on my skin. I wanted to give her the lotion. She needs it. Her skin is in terrible shape. It's so dried and cracked. My mother says you can be poor and still know how to take care of yourself. It's not the money; it's the attitude you have toward yourself. If our maid stopped buying a lot of candy and potato chips, she could afford to get herself some skin lotion. And she wouldn't be so fat!"

A child has learned to distinguish between her own inclinations or preferences and those of another person—a whole category of people. This girl was, at the time, not quite an adolescent; for years, however, she had been prepared for that time, for adulthood as well—prepared by parents who not only wanted her to know how to use skin lotions, or choose "tasteful" lipstick, or shun anything but "natural" fingernail polish, or learn how to care for her hair and wash it, and pay attention to the scalp as well. Those parents wanted her to give an enormous amount of attention to *herself*—to her thoughts, which she has been taught are worthy of being spoken, and to her body, which is going to be, one day, "attractive." So she has been told by several maids—far too emphatically to suit the taste of her parents. They prefer a more understated, indirect approach. They remind the girl that she looks like her grandmother ("a handsome lady") or her aunt ("who was quite beautiful"). They let her know how graceful she is as a young dancing student, how agile and accomplished a rider she has become, how fast and accurate a game of tennis she has developed, even at her age. They smile at pictures of her smiling, applaud her once again when watching home movies. Her picture is on the mantle over the living room fireplace, on her father's desk, on her mother's desk, and is on her own desk, for that matter.

When she was six and seven she asked a lot of questions about herself. They were answered patiently, thoughtfully, and often with enthusiastic pride—a contrast indeed with many poor children, whose parents are tired, embittered, sad, or all too resigned to their fate, and hardly able to boast about the circumstances of life. The girl's questions occur to all children, rich or poor—are the banal inquiries we never quite stop asking ourselves: who am I, why am I here, whence do I come, and where am I going—the continuing preoccupations of philosophers, novelists, and painters. Children prefer the painters approach. They sometimes don't pay much attention to the answers to their questions. After all too verbal family meals they retire to a desk or table, draw pictures meant to suggest what life is and will be about. When the girl mentioned above wonders who she is or has questions about her future, she picks up crayons and draws herself with care and affection—on a horse, in a garden, high up in a tower, surveying the countryside.

In doing so she draws upon her concrete, day-to-day experiences. She also uses those experiences in order to suggest something larger about her particular life. Especially noteworthy is the care she and others like her take with themselves as they draw. So often poor children treat themselves cursorily; they quickly sketch a rather unflattering self-portrait. Sometimes they are unwilling to complete what they have begun—as if they are unsure of life itself. A migrant child once told me in a matter-of-fact way that he had no expectation of living beyond twenty. He was simply a child who knew the score. The children of doctors and lawyers and business executives have learned the score too. The girl mentioned above spends a half hour drawing herself, moves her eyes toward a mirror every once in a while to check on how she actually does look, and is eventually quite proud of what she has drawn. She also spends long periods of time looking at old photographs—of herself, her parents, her grandparents. Such observations and bits of anecdotal family history have become consolidated in the girl's mind. She regards herself—though she has learned to be affectingly modest—as a rather attractive person. No wonder she once posed herself, in a picture, beside a giant sunflower. She was in no way overshadowed by the flower; if anything, it adorned her own luminous presence.

When that girl became ill with chicken pox the anguish of her mental state was noticeable and instructive. She wanted to scratch the many lesions on her face and arms but was told, of course, by her parents that she must not. She heeded their advice. In the beginning she did scratch one pustule midway on her upper right arm. Her mother became quite upset. Before the mother could say a word, the child spoke up, acknowledged her awareness of the future implications of her deed. She had lost control, and she would suffer. Her description of that talk and of her later, more successful, bout with the disease, has struck me as a classic of sorts: "I don't want to look ugly. If I had scratched my face, like I did my right arm, I'd look a mess for life. I knew that. But I had *such* a bad case! The doctor said it was one of the worst he'd seen in the last few years. He told me he had seen even worse than mine, and I was sort of disappointed. I figured that I'd like to go through the biggest challenge, and come out on top!

"After a day or two, I began to wonder if I'd be able to survive! I got very weepy. I began to wonder whether I'd done anything wrong—to deserve this punishment. I couldn't look myself in the mirror. I didn't want to wash at all. I felt so dirty and horrible looking. I asked my brother and my parents not to look at me! My brother tried to kid me out of my mood. He came in with his Polaroid camera and said he'd take a picture of me, and I could keep it, and when I was over the disease, I could just laugh! Instead I started crying, right in front of him. He apologized.

"The worst part of the chicken pox was the waiting and the trying to keep control. My mother sat with me, and my Dad did too, when he got home. On the worst day, he offered to stay with me and not go to his office. I said no, I'd be all right. But he decided to stay anyway. He just sat there and read to me. We watched some television—the news and a cooking class. We talked a little. Dad kept telling me I was great, and not to worry; he was sure I was going to have a wonderful life, because I've got everything going for me. I told him 'not the chicken pox,' when he said that. But he just laughed and told me that the chicken pox would soon be a bad memory, and I'd forget about it completely in a couple of months. I'm not sure I ever will, though. I have this scar on my arm, and I'll always have it. My mother says no one will notice; but *I* do! She got angry the other day. She said I was worrying too much. But I've seen her worry a lot too. If a dress doesn't fit her, she sends it right back. She's always either on a diet or coming off one, or getting ready to go on one again. We have scales in every bathroom, and one in her bedroom. I told her I don't need to weigh myself and my brother doesn't; but she wants us to get in the habit, so we'll know later when to start being careful about food. She tells the maid to give us cookies only when she's not around; she doesn't want to be tempted. And her hair—well, that's 'a whole subject,' as my Daddy says. When he was with me that day, I asked him why Mom worries so much about her hair, and dyes it. Who cares if there's some gray in her hair! But Dad said that gray hair for Mom is like the chicken pox for me. I could see what he meant, but it's not exactly the same."

She did not for long insist upon the difference; she went along with her father's comparison. She did so not reluctantly, but with the detachment that goes with complete recovery—a feeling of remove from what was once painful. Her mother has always been regarded as a rather lovely woman; the girl was prepared to emphasize that fact in her mind, and associate her own present and future appearance with her mother's deserved reputation. The girl was also prepared to acknowledge quite candidly what a relatively severe case of a basically benign disease could do to her thoughts about herself: "I began to worry whether I really was as pretty as everyone had been saying. It was a mood; I'm over it now. I do have a few bad memories. Dad says they'll go. I hope so. I look at myself in the mirror and I'll suddenly be afraid that the chicken pox is coming back. I get scared. It's silly. I know I'm never going to get the chicken pox again!

"I wish I hadn't scratched that one place. It's such a small scar. But it gives me nightmares! I woke up the other night and my parents were in my room. I guess I'd been crying or shouting. In the morning my mother said I'd half-awakened, and I'd told them that a cat had been chasing me, and scratched me, and I was afraid there'd be a scar. I wonder a lot about the man I'll marry. Will he have brown hair or blond hair or black hair? My mother asked me if it makes any difference; I told her I like brown hair and green eyes, and I hope he'll be tall and thin. I wouldn't even want to go out once with a man who was overweight!"

This is no petty, superficial, half-witted, or empty-headed girl. She has gone to very good private schools—each of which has high academic standards and expectations. She can be serious, thoughtful, and idealistic—that is, worried about others less fortunate and hopeful that they somehow get to live better lives. As a child she can hardly be expected to come up with solutions for the world's various problems, but some of those problems do at times weigh upon her. Yet she can, all of a sudden, move from writing a composition about "world hunger" to discussing with her mother the virtues of various cosmetics or the appropriateness of certain dresses for one or another social occasion. She can also, rather disarmingly, stop thinking about "the troubles in America" her teacher has asked the class to write about, because her parakeet needs food or water, her two gerbils require new bedding, her alarm clock has to be set, her desk is cluttered and ought be straightened out, or her phone has rung. She has a room with its own demands and requirements, with a bureau mirror and one on the back of the door, a full-length mirror. Sometimes she gets tired of thinking of arithmetic problems and social problems, and spelling problems, of coming up with ideas meant to straighten out society.

The last word, incidentally, has two meanings for her. She started, at ten, dancing lessons. She was aware then that later on she would be going to parties, would become a debutante. Her mother plays down that word, debutante. Her mother is a New Englander who doesn't like "fuss," abhors elaborate, pretentious parties, the stuff of social climbing; but she also has a keen eye for who is acceptable to whom in her social circle, what name elicits deference, and whose "situation" is what mixture of "position" and "real wealth."

Those words are used discreetly, but they do not go unnoticed by a ten- or eleven-year-old child. The girl asks questions about her family, its origins and "place" in the social and economic system. "Our minister tells us to think of others, but it's hard, because I've never seen the poor. I gave half of some money I saved for Christmas to the starving people of Africa. Daddy said he was real proud of me. He gave me the money I'd contributed. He says that when I grow up I should marry a man who is kind and worries about other people, not just himself; that's the type of man who makes a good husband. I agree. It's best to marry someone who's pretty much like yourself, though. Otherwise you might run into trouble. He'll think one way, and you'll think another. There are a lot of divorces that take place. My parents have a lot of friends whose marriages aren't good. If you marry a person who thinks like you, and he has the same beliefs, then you have a better chance of staying married.

"When I leave this room and stay at a friend's, or when we go up skiing or down to our summer house, I get a funny feeling. I really miss my dolls and my bureau—the shells and dishes my parents have brought me when they have come back from trips. I have all kinds of shells, from all the Caribbean beaches. I have dishes and ashtrays from a lot of countries. I have posters; I love French posters. I hope I learn to speak French fluently. It's a beautiful language. It's strange, leaving your room and sleeping in a place that hasn't got much of anything that belongs to you, that's yours, that's *you*."

That last progression deserves respectful attention as a rather forceful, intelligent, and exact analysis of the complicated psychology of class-connected "narcissistic entitlement." She and others like her grow up surrounded by possessions, animate as well as inanimate. They have learned to live with them, to look after them, and to depend upon them for support. They have also learned to give of themselves to those "objects." When they leave for a winter or summer vacation they try to take some of their most treasured belongings with them, but often still experience a sense of emptiness or a feeling of being alone, isolated, bereft. Child psychiatrists use the expression "transitional object" to refer to a child's blanket or teddy bear or doll—taken to bed, carried around, held tight at the age of four, five, six.

Few children are unable to find those "transitional objects." I have seen the poorest of American children, living the most uprooted of lives, cling to a dirty old rag, a stick, a rock, the cheapest of plastic toys, often obtained secondhand, maybe from someone's trash barrel. Children of working-class parents or of so-called "middle-income" families seldom experience such sad desperation. On the other hand, many of those children share rooms with brothers and sisters and by no means assume that they are to be recipients of an apparently endless succession of gifts, vacations, pleasant surprises. In the homes of the rich, in contrast, the children almost invariably have their own rooms and the quantitative difference in their material acquisitions prompts a qualitative psychological difference: an enhanced expectation of what life has to offer, and with that, a strong inclination to build a sanctuary out of one's room and one's property. The girl is subtle but sharp and exact when she distinguishes between what belongs to her (a piece of property) and what has become hers—an existential psychological transformation. The next step is of course an ironic act of personal surrender: the object and the person merge somewhat—from "that's yours" to "that's *you*."

All children struggle when very young—starting at a little under a year, in fact—to distinguish between themselves and their parents. They begin to realize, at two and three, that it is *they* who exist—individuals who crawl and walk and make noises and talk. As they separate, to a degree, from their mothers, especially then, at two or three, they first know loneliness. Certainly, thereafter, for most children, there are reattachments to the mother, new attachments to other persons—and to things. But the child turns inward too upon occasion, makes an effort to find comfort and even pleasure in a newfound solitariness. Freud, at one point, referred to "the purified pleasure ego"—by which he meant a child's delight in the various excitements or satisfactions he or she can manage to find. I recall a four-year-old boy in one home I visited, not far from that of the girl quoted just above, who slid up and down a wonderfully solid, circular staircase, shouting me, me, me; he was in love with the dizzying speed, with the feeling of control and power he had—with himself.

Later on, at five and six, such a child becomes quite conscious of rights and wrongs, of what ought to be done to please parents and teachers, not to mention one's own developing conscience. Psychoanalysts describe the "idealized parent image"—the part of the child's mind that holds up examples, insists upon directions. The child absorbs from significant persons his or her notions of what matters and how he or she should in general be trying to live—and tries to go along. The "you" that the girl mentioned above at age ten—a summary, almost, of which belongings had become part of her "self"—was preceded by the earlier "you" comprehended at the age of six: "I'd like to do good in school, and learn to ski, and ride my bike fast, and get to make real tasty cookies with the maid, and then I'll be good, and people will say, she's doing everything she should be doing, and I'll say that to myself. When I'm finished brushing my teeth, they'll be clean, and my mother will soon be upstairs and check me out, and I'll say to myself: you're doing okay. And a few minutes later my mother says the same thing: 'You're doing okay!' "

That child has had ample opportunities—beyond using a toothbrush well—to prove herself, as well as find pleasure in competence. She has been taught tennis and swimming by coaches, cooking by a maid, riding by her mother. The girl has also learned how to draw and paint, play the piano, "do" ballet. She has gone abroad often, has mastered words, used her own passport. She has become acquainted with forms of etiquette, with new protocols. She knows when to defer, when to speak up. She knows how to recognize various songs, symphonies, operatic pieces. She knows how to walk the corridors of museums, recognize the work of certain artists. And too, she has acquired some of the psychological judgment good hostesses have: who is like whom, who belongs near whom at the table, who will be a "disaster" with whom. She used that word sometimes, when eleven and twelve, and in so doing revealed more than a "prepubescent" affinity for a way of talking, or a superficial cleverness about people. In fact, she was indicating something significant about her sense of *herself.*

One such "disaster" was her mother's much younger cousin, and the girl knew why: "She's sloppy. She's always been sloppy. She speaks sloppy. She had a harelip, and that was what ruined her. The parents didn't take her to the right doctor, and the girl became shy, and she didn't want to talk to anyone, and when she was a teenager she became even worse. She just stayed in her room a lot. Then she got religious, in a weird way. She was always praying. My mother says they should have sent her to a doctor. She decided to become a nun, I think. She wanted to convert and be a Catholic, and then be a nun. They talked her out of that. She came to life a little. She began to go out and meet people. Then she met this guy, and he was a music teacher, and he was poor, and they fell in love, and they wanted to get married. He was a disaster, my mother says. He could barely open his mouth, and he didn't know which fork to use, and he wore real funny clothes, and he had a bad complexion, and the worst case of dandruff my mother has ever seen. He just sat there, and it didn't even seem to bother him that he didn't talk. But my mother's cousin was a disaster, too. She was just an oddball, that's what. They got married, and my mother says they've been good for each other.

"They would be poor now, if it wasn't that my mother's aunt left them some money. I think they have enough to get by. We see them sometimes; they come to visit my grandmother. We have to keep a straight face. We can't laugh. That would be bad. You should feel sorry for people who aren't as fortunate as you are. If you don't, then you are rude and you don't have charity. If you're not nice to someone, you've lost. You sink down to the other person's level. That's what Daddy tells us, and he gets angry if we don't pay attention. He says we've got a responsibility to show good manners at all times. I'd never call someone a 'disaster' in front of him; at least while we're having supper. Sometimes he'll be having a drink, and then even he will call someone a fool or *no good;* that's *his* way of calling someone he knows and doesn't like a 'disaster.' "

In "Forms and Transformations of Narcissism" (*Journal of the American Psychoanalytic Association,* April, 1966), Heinz Kohut observes that the "form and content of the psychic representation of the idealized parent thus vary with the maturational stage of the child's cognitive apparatus." Then he adds, significantly, that the form and content "are also influenced by environmental factors that affect the choice of internalizations and their intensity." There may seem, at first glance, a considerable distance in substance if not tone between the child's reflections on her second cousin and a psychoanalyst's theoretical observations, addressed to his scholarly colleagues. But the psychiatrist is trying to formulate what the child is living through and occasionally able to comment upon. Even as a migrant child or ghetto child learns to feel weak and vulnerable, a child of well-off parents learns to feel, in many respects, confident. There are idiosyncratic variations, of course. One can be rich and psychotic, for instance, and instill fear, apprehension, and a sense of worthlessness in one's children. Yet even among the disturbed young children of well-to-do parents there are concerns and expectations that contrast profoundly with the notions of other children, from other backgrounds, possess about themselves. At a certain point in every child's life, as Dr. Kohut suggests, and as Freud repeatedly pointed out, culture and class became matters of a child's fantasy life and affect the tone of his or her self regard. The girl who wants to look a certain way, speak a certain way, who anticipates a certain way of life, and who derives personal strength and competence from the sense of herself she has learned to have, is a person whose "narcissism," whose "idealized parent image," has drawn upon many daily conversations and experiences, rewards and lessons.

At another point in his paper Dr. Kohut points out that our "ambitions and ideals" don't just appear out of nowhere. They have a psychological history, not to mention a social and economic background. He refers to their "preconscious correlates" and locates them (structurally speaking) in the "narcissistic self," whose various "ego ideals" have, of course, been acquired over countless intimate encounters—the family involvements that set the stage for a child's view of what "life" is going to be like. Dr. Kohut points out that ambitions do not always coincide with ideals. A child whose parents are poor or of working-class background may have heard a mother or father (or, rather often, a teacher) say that anyone can be President in this country, or rise to the top of a company, or become a doctor, a lawyer, a "success"—given "hard work." But the child has seen and heard much evidence to the contrary. The child has seen his or her parents curbed, scorned, exhausted, frustrated, embittered. The child has heard that "life" is no picnic, that wages don't keep up with prices, that the factory is laying off more and more people, including his or her father or mother. The child has heard, upon breaking a dish or a toy, upon failing to follow instructions, or falling short at school, that soon enough the difficulties and tensions of grown-up life will fall upon him or her. In contrast, privileged children, far fewer in number, are destined for quite another fate. In his own manner, Dr. Kohut approaches their lives; speaking of their "ambitions and ideals," he observes that "they are at times hard to distinguish, not only because ambitions are often disguised as ideals but also because there are indeed lucky moments in our lives, or lucky periods in the lives of the very fortunate, in which ambitions and ideals coincide."

For those "lucky," a sense of entitlement develops—the merger of what they have learned would be "ideal" and what they have actually experienced, into an ongoing attitude toward the world. Let others feel diminished, impeded, burdened; or let them long for a different kind of life, knowing all too clearly by the age of six or seven the difference between a castle in Spain and a ranch house in Levittown, or a ghetto tenement, or a tenant farmer's shack. For privileged children, there is every reason to feel entitlement. But let us not forget that entitlement is perfectly compatible with doubts, misgivings, despair. A child can feel—being realistic—entitled to a certain kind of life and yet have other reasons to be confused or hurt. Even schizophrenics experience the distinctions that have to do with class and caste, race and place of residence. The girl whose words I called upon above had her own thoughts, one day, about these theoretical issues of mental life—after she had heard, at the age of twelve, that her father was sick and required surgery: "I hope he'll be all right. It's serious, my mother told me. I can tell it is; Daddy hasn't been smiling much. He's been worried. He's been talking a lot about his insurance, and he took my brother and me to the bank, and he told us we'll be going there for the rest of our lives, or calling them up and asking them to send us over some money. He says that if we're careful, our children will have the same amount of money we have. It's best to use the interest and not the capital. The bank knows how to keep your money invested in the best stocks.

"Daddy will be all right. He's strong. He has the best doctor in the country; he's the best surgeon. I met him, and he was very nice. He gave my brother and me a book he'd written, about the seashore and the clams and oysters and lobsters you find in the water and the sand. He owns a lot of land by the ocean, and he's a marine biologist, my father says, besides being a surgeon. And he's an artist, too. I wouldn't mind being a doctor myself, but I don't know if I'd want to operate on anyone. The surgeon offered to show my brother and me how he operates; we could watch him—but not when he works on Daddy. My brother says yes, but I said no. I'd rather not be there,if anything goes wrong; then, when Daddy is being operated on, I'd worry even more.

"We'll be all right. My mother says everything will turn out good. Daddy may not be home for a couple of weeks, but we can go and see him all the time. We can eat with him in his room. It'll be like going out to a restaurant. He'll have television and his own phone. We can talk with him any time we want. He says he'll get a lot of reading done. He'll have a nice view from his room, and he'll get all the rest he'll need. Then, when he gets home, we're going away. Daddy says we'll be in Barbados for two weeks. He's promised to take us out of school. We'll get all our homework, and we won't fall back at all. My mother says it may turn out to be a blessing in disguise that Daddy got sick; he'll get a lot of rest, and he'll be much stronger. I hope so."

She was not about to acknowledge, even to herself, how worried she sensed her mother to be. But she (and her mother) had resources that very much ameliorated an anxious period of waiting. The dreaded outcome of the father's illness, a malignancy, did not materialize. All the money in the world could not have converted cancerous cells into normal ones. But during those days that preceded surgery the girl and her brother felt more hope than dread, and had quite valid sources of support for that hope. And during the father's convalescence, instead of hearing their mother and father lamenting bills, expressing worries about the loss of a job, or complaining about the "conditions" in the hospital, their time of trouble became for everyone concerned an opportunity for pleasure, relaxation, new initiatives and accomplishments. The girl and her brother ended up becoming scuba divers in the warm Caribbean water; went on motorcycle rides such as they had never had before; began to realize more exactly than ever how well-off their parents are and they as children are. "It all came out for the best," the girl said, weeks after her father was pronounced able to return to his work as a business executive. In a sense the words are a slogan of sorts, constantly kept in mind by her and others: life works out "for the best," mostly—and one has a right to conclude that if one has had ample confirming evidence.

For some of these children, the privileged life presents a danger of what clinicians have referred to as "secondary narcissism"—the "narcissistic entitlement" I mentioned at the beginning of this section. However, on the evidence of the privileged children I have come to know, I would emphasize the possibility that a feeling of "entitlement" may develop in a child without the potentially treacherous development of an excessively narcissistic tone. When a feeling of "entitlement" becomes "narcissistic," it has departed from what James Agee called "human actuality." Suppose the girl whose father had taken ill began, for her own reasons, to imagine that her father's illness would be associated with some extraordinary development: a call to the theater or television as a young actress; a medal of honor awarded by the school she attended; a party given her as an expression of her popularity. Suppose that girl, alternatively, expected the surgeon to cure her father, no matter *what* was discovered upon operating. Suppose that girl began crying constantly before her father entered the hospital; and did so petulantly, plaintively, as if less interested in her father's troubles than her own. At that point her narcissism would have taken its form from her private experiences, although the same child in other moments might lose her despairing self-centeredness. The point to emphasize is the mind's capacity to appreciate the reality of a certain kind of life. The mind can of course undercut a good thing, make a bad thing even worse, or make the best of it.

It is important that a privileged child's normal sense of "entitlement" be distinguished not only from pathological narcissism, but from the more common phenomenon known as being "spoiled." It is a matter of degree; "spoiled" children are self-centered all right, petulant and demanding—but not saddled with the grandiose illusions (or delusions) clinicians have in mind when using the phrase "narcissistic entitlement." The rich, the "well-to-do" are all too commonly charged with producing spoiled children. Yet one sees spoiled children everywhere, among the very poor as well as the inordinately rich. A child can be spoiled by a mother's attitude. What the child is "given" can be called excessive instinctual leeway or, in everyday words, however politicized in recent years, "permissive indulgence." I remember a migrant mother who knew precisely and uncannily what she was doing "wrong"—knew, indeed, to call it all "wrong." She told me one day that she had given birth to a particular child with more pain than usual and had been in lower spirits than ever before in her life during the first months of that child's life. When the baby began to notice the mother and the world, start crawling and separating himself from her, she felt a fierce desire within herself, expressed with unforgettable intensity, "to let that boy have anything he wants, anything he can lay his hands on." She was careful, for all her lack of education and her troubled spirits, to qualify herself. She moved quickly, immediately, from "anything he wants" to "anything he can lay his hands on." She knew that in the first or second year of life the child would have all he could do to reach and hold on to what he wanted.

But soon enough a child begins to see things that others have; on a rented, only half-working television set the migrant child saw a lot, and looked around the room and realized a lot. His was no blessed life! He continued, however, to want to take what little he could get. And of course children (or adults) can want things that are psychological in lieu of what is "material." They can become demanding, possessive, insistent, if allowed to be. They can compete with others for attention, push hard against others who try to assert themselves. They can make every effort to obtain center stage at all times. The migrant mother developed, deep within her hurt and sad self, a pride about her child and his stubborn, indulged, expropriative, loud-mouthed, and at times impossibly egotistical behavior.

He was the child who would shout and scream and swagger, shake his fists, really, at the wretched world he had been born to. No matter that such behavior, whether allowed or even encouraged, is hardly a guarantee of a future rise to success. On the contrary, a child of migrant parents who acts like that one is headed, quite likely, for future trouble. The mother knew that too. She knew that migrants are virtually peons; that they submit to endless demands and manipulations. Perhaps one of her children would be so "spoiled" that he would be utterly incapable of becoming a migrant or lasting as one for very long. She answered along those lines when her husband asked her why she doesn't spank the "spoiled one" as she does the other children.

He in turn mentioned the grim likelihood that the boy would not indeed last as a migrant. He would instead end up in jail—or soon dead. All right, better a last stand, the mother replied. But she knew that really there was no point to such a hope; it would never even come to that, because the boy would either learn to mind his manners, and submit to the only life he would most likely ever know, or go down not in defiant resistance but through the slow attrition of cheap wine and harmless side-of-the-road braggadoccio—the "maladjusted" migrant who works inefficiently, goes to the bars before and after work, dies in a car accident or drowns drunk in one of the hundreds of irrigation canals that crisscross the agricultural counties of Florida, where this particular family spent its winters.

The parallel with spoiled children of upper-income families is not so farfetched. In one of the first such families I came to know there was a girl who was described by both parents as "spoiled." At the time, I fear, I was ready to pronounce every child in New Orleans's Garden District spoiled.

Nevertheless, I soon began to realize that it wouldn't do to call one set of children spoiled, by virtue of their social and economic background—as against another set of children who were obviously less privileged. Though one meets among the poor any number of spoiled children, one also meets among the rich restrained, disciplined children; sometimes, even, boys and girls who have learned to be self-critical, even ascetic—anything but "spoiled" in the conventional sense of the word. True, one can find a touch and more of arrogance in those apparently Spartan boys and girls, who seem quite anxious to deny themselves all sorts of apparently accessible privileges. But one also finds in these children a consistent willingness to place serious and not always pleasant burdens on themselves. They often struck me, as I came to their homes fresh from visits with much poorer age-mates, as remarkably *less* spoiled: not so much whining or crying; fewer demands for candy or other sweets; even sometimes a relative indifference to toys, a disregard of television—so often demanded by the children I was seeing across the city, on the other side of the tracks.

Those children from prominent families appeared, even at the age of four or five, to put their energies in the service of "constructive" play or "useful" activities. They had begun to learn at two and three how important it was for them to do "right" as against "wrong"; to build rather than destroy; to concentrate their energies, devote them to particular tasks, which were to be finished rather than started and abandoned. They had, in some instances, even learned to take care of their own rooms—keep them neat, pick up after themselves, be conscious of what belongs where. Maids came to help, or lived with the family, but sometimes a particular boy or girl, as young as five or six, was a taskmaster to the maid rather than, certainly, a helpless or indulged child. And sometimes the maid herself became astonished by the example set by such children—and became their strong admirer.

A New Orleans black woman said to me in 1961: "I don't know how to figure out these rich, white kids. They're something! I used to think, before I took a job with this family, that the only difference between a rich kid and a poor kid is that the rich kid knows he has a lot of money and he grows up and he becomes spoiled rotten. That's what my mother told me; she took care of a white girl, and the girl was an only child, and her father owned a department store in McComb, Mississippi, and that girl thought she was God's special creature. My mother used to come home and tell us about the 'little princess'; but she turned out to be no good. She was so pampered she couldn't do a thing for herself. All she knew how to do was order people around. It's different with these two children here in New Orleans. I've never seen such a boy and such a girl. They think they're the best ones who ever lived—like that girl in McComb—but they don't behave like her. They're never asking me to do much of anything. They even ask if *they* can help *me!* They tell me that they want to know how to do everything. The girl says she wants to learn how to run the washing machine and the dishwasher. She says she wants to learn all my secret recipes. She says she'd like to give the best parties in the Garden District when she grows up, and she'd like to be able to give them without anyone's help. She says I could serve the food, but she would like to make it. The boy says he's going to be a lawyer and a banker, so he wants to know how much everything costs. He doesn't want to waste anything. He'll see me throw something away, and he wants to know why. I wish my own kids were like him!

"I wish my kids weren't so lazy; they don't care what's going on; they just want to play and play, and they waste a lot of food, and they break the toys I get them real fast. I even told my children I wish they could learn from these two children here. But these children here are special, and don't they know it! That's what being rich is: you know you're different from most people. These two kids are even more special, because they act as if they're going to be tops in everything, and they're pleased as can be with themselves, because there is nothing they can't do, and there's nothing they can't get, and there's nothing they can't win, and they're always showing off what they can do, and then before you can tell them how good they are, they're telling the same thing to themselves. It's confusing! They're not spoiled one bit, but oh, they have a high opinion of themselves!

"And I'll have to admit, there are times when I have the same high opinion of them! I'll look at them, and I'll say that they could be dropped on an island in the middle of a big ocean, and they'd know what to do, and if they didn't have anyone around to be pleased with them, they'd be all right because they'd be pleased with themselves! And it wouldn't take them long to know where to go and what to do on that island, because they are just so sure of themselves and so full of themselves that they always have their chins up, and they're happy, and they know where they're going, and they know what's ahead—that everything will come out fine in the end. When you have that kind of spirit in you, then you'll always get out of any jam you're in, and you'll always end up on top, because that's where you started, and that's where you believe you're going to end up, and if it's in your mind that it is like that, and it's *going* to be like that, and if you're willing to work hard, like these kids are, and if you're careful about everything, like they are, then you just *can't* lose, and don't these kids know it, I'll tell you!"

Actually the children she speaks of aren't as confident of themselves as she thinks, though she certainly has accurately conveyed their appearance. The kind of children she knows so well are extraordinarily privileged by virtue of background and money, are also intelligent and of attractive appearance; but those children have demons that occasionally urge them on, and their nature is not always easy to divine. Boys and girls may seem without anxiety or self-doubt at, say, eight or nine. Yet, there are moments of hesitation, if not apprehension. An eleven-year-old boy from a prominent and quite brilliant Massachusetts family (three generations of first-rate lawyers) told his teachers in an autobiographical composition about the vicissitudes of "entitlement": "I don't always do everything right. I'd like to be able to say I don't make any mistakes, but I do, and when I do, I feel bad. My father and mother say that if you train yourself, you can be right *almost* 100% of the time. Even they make mistakes, though. I like to be first in sports. I like to beat my brothers at skiing. But I don't always go down the slopes as fast as I could and I sometimes fall down. Last year I broke my leg. That was the first time I'd ever gone to a hospital and stayed there. It was my mother who reminded me that I'd been in the hospital for a week just after I was born! I'd forgotten! I was saying that I'd *never* been in the hospital overnight, and she corrected me.

"My great-grandfather is eighty-four, and he's in the best of health. It worries me that I have bad sinus trouble a lot of times after I get flu. I'd hate to be sick when I'm older. There's too much to do; if you get sick, you can't do much of anything, except stay home and rest. When I get a bad cold, I feel disappointed in myself. I don't think it's right to be easy on yourself. If you are, then you slip back, and you don't get a lot of the rewards in life. If you really work for the rewards, you'll get them."

His teachers have often given him that kind of platitude. In the fourth grade, for instance, his teacher had written on the blackboard (and kept it there for weeks): "Those who want something badly enough get it, provided they are willing to wait and work." The boy has been brought up to believe that it will be like that for him. He knows that others are not so lucky, but he hasn't really met those "others," and they don't cross his mind. What does occur to him sometimes is the need for constant exertion, lest he fail to "measure up." The expression is a family one, used repeatedly. No matter how difficult a task, no matter how frustrating it is for others, one "measures up" when one does it well. One "measures up" when one tries hard, succeeds. One measures up because one *must*. No allowance is made for any possible lack of ability or endowment. The assumption is that one has been "given a lot" (another family expression) and so a "return" is obligatory if justice is to be done. If one slackens or stumbles, one ought take oneself to task. The emphasis is on a quick and efficient moment of scrutiny followed by "a fast pickup," yet another admonitory injunction handed down.

Such counsel is not as callous or psychologically insensitive as it may sound—or even as it may have been *intended* to sound. The child who hears it gets briefly upset, but "a fast pickup" does indeed take place quite often. Again, it is a matter of feeling "entitled." A child who has been told repeatedly that all he or she needs to do is try hard does not feel inclined to allow himself or herself much skeptical self-examination. The point is to feel *entitled*—then act upon that feeling. The boy whose composition was just quoted from wrote again, apparently about his younger (aged five) brother: "I was watching my brother from my bedroom window. He was climbing up the fence we built for our corral. He got to the top, and then he just stood there and waved and shouted. No one was there. He was talking to himself. He was very happy. Then he would fall. He would be upset for a few seconds, but he would climb right back up again. Then he would be even happier! He was entitled to be happy. It is his fence, and he has learned to climb it, and stay up, and balance himself."

The little brother was indeed happy on top of the fence. He would talk to himself with obvious pleasure—tell nameless, invisible people that they are stupid and inadequate because, unlike him, they are unable to climb the fence and stay there and enjoy themselves. Yes, he was obviously talking to himself. He was also speaking to an earlier version of himself, to the boy of four who had wanted to climb that fence, wanted to get on top, and, just as important, stay there and enjoy the experience. Once he had succeeded, he enjoyed his new-found competence. He would practically never be curbed, humiliated, denied interesting or engaging occasions because of the "reality" of the world around him. Quite the contrary; there would be one inviting adventure after another over the months and years. One day, as a matter of fact, he ran across the field after he had shown himself able to climb a particular fence with ease—in search of a taller, slightly more precarious fence on the other side of the corral. And when that climb was "nothing" and the position of balance a giant bore, he predicted quite casually that he would never see a fence that he couldn't rather quickly master. His father did not want the boy to be completely unrealistic, however. To whistle in the dark, to assume that one can always triumph, is to be vulnerable—the weakness of the overconfident. One ought to have a great deal of drive and ambition, a conviction that the world will eventually be made to oblige—but only after a substantial effort.

It is absurd to say that all children whose parents make a certain amount of money or work at certain occupations, or live in a certain neighborhood, possess an attitude of mind (and an attitude toward the world) that might be sensibly tucked into the generalization referred to here as "entitlement." More than once I have insisted that each individual has his or her unique way of pulling together the various elements of mental life. I have wanted, however, to suggest a common manner of response toward life among children of a certain class and background. I realize that the particular word "entitlement" has complicated psychoanalytic implications or, for some, pejorative social or political implications, or indeed, for others, quite defensible and justifiable implications. For the children I have worked with, however, the word is simply a description of a certain actuality. There are both social and psychological dimensions to that actuality, and deep down these children know them rather well.

I have in mind especially the son of a powerful Florida grower. When the child was five he kept using the words "I'm entitled to." His parents were much annoyed. The father did not want his son using such a peremptory, self-important, demanding expression. He began interrupting the boy, telling him that he was not "entitled" to *anything,* that he must ask for what he wanted, and be grateful when he got it. The boy kept asking why, why. The father kept explaining—a litany of oughts and musts. The boy in turn fell back upon his considerable intelligence and powers of observation. He reminded his father of his own words: "If you earn something, you are entitled to keep it." Had not the boy "earned" the right to make his various requests—by trying to be "good" or "quiet"? Had not the father told him on a number of occasions that he was "coming along nicely," that he was "making his parents proud"?

The boy spoke up for himself in fits and starts, but he got his message across, because his father eventually settled for an ironic statement: "A boy who stands up for himself like that boy has—well, he's entitled to say every once in a while, that he's *entitled* to something!" It must be rather obvious—it was to the grower, for all his lack of interest in the plight of the hundreds of improverished migrants who worked his land so long and hard—that not every father can be grateful for his son's outspokenness, his young son's assumption that he was entitled to political freedom, social equality, economic privilege.

• • • • • • • • • • • •

QUESTIONS FOR A SECOND READING

1. Coles tells the stories of a number of children: the son of an Appalachian mine owner, an eight-year-old son from a Boston suburb, a boy and a girl from a family living in Westchester County. As you reread the essay, closely review what he has to say about one of these cases. What is there in his account that you can now—after you've read it a second time—identify as predictable, as evidence of Coles's particular method and bias, his way of looking at and interpreting, or reading, the evidence he gathers from his interviews? What, then, do you suppose he fails to see? or perhaps keeps secret? What didn't he look for that you think he might have? And, finally, what conclusions can you draw then about Coles's *method*—about what it both can and can't do?

2. Would you want to argue that any of these children is "sick" or "disturbed" or that somehow the child is not psychologically healthy? Which one? Where is the evidence? How do you read the evidence to draw this conclusion? What's the borderline between health and sickness in this case? Is Coles any help in making this distinction? Why or why not?

ASSIGNMENTS FOR WRITING

1. The key word in this chapter is, obviously, "entitlement," and Coles builds a variety of uses for it as the chapter proceeds. In a sense, Coles works out his analysis of these children by working out the possible uses of the term. At the end of the essay, he says

> More than once I have insisted that each individual has his or her unique way of pulling together the various elements of mental life. I have wanted, however, to suggest a common manner of response toward life among children of a certain class and background. I realize that the particular word "entitlement" has complicated psychoanalytic implications or, for some, pejorative social or political implications, or indeed, for others, quite defensible and justifiable implications. For the children I have worked with, however, the word is simply a description of a certain actuality. There are both social and psychological dimensions to that actuality, and deep down these children know them rather well.

   As you read Coles's argument, what are the social and psychological dimensions of "entitlement"? To explore what Coles's term "entitlement" might mean, write an essay that identifies as many varieties of social and psychological entitlement as Coles's chapter will justify. You should look at his uses of the term along with the cases they describe.

2. It is hard to read these case studies without thinking of your own life. Write an essay about the most significant differences between your experience as a child and the experiences of the children Coles discusses. How would you account for this difference—is it money? class? entitlement? some combination of factors? what?

MAKING CONNECTIONS

1. We might see "entitlements" as sets of expectations—psychological, social, economic. In Joyce Carol Oates's story, "Theft" (p. 353), Marya and Imogene come from different social classes and apparently have different expectations for themselves and for others. Write an essay in which you explain what these women expect and how their expectations determine who they are and how they act. Your job, in other words, is to study them the way Coles studies the children in "Entitlement." How, as a reader of Coles, might you tell their stories or explain their cases?

2. In "The Achievement of Desire" (p. 430), Richard Rodriguez points to his expectations about learning as a key element in his becoming who he is as an adult. Yet, he claims, he also had other expectations derived from his social class and family. And these various expectations were often in conflict with each other. Write an essay in which you discuss what Coles would call Rodriguez's "unique way of pulling together the various elements of mental life," making distinctions where you can between the social and psychological dimensions of his ways of thinking, speaking, and behaving. How, in other words, might Rodriguez's case be read from the perspective of Coles's essay, "Entitlement"? You might imagine that you are working alongside Coles, continuing a project he has begun.

THOMAS COTTLE AND STEPHEN KLINEBERG

THOMAS COTTLE was born in Chicago in 1937. He received his B.A. from Harvard University in 1959, then returned to his hometown to attend graduate school at the University of Chicago, eventually completing a Ph.D. in sociology in 1968. Once described as a "specialist in children's rights," Cottle is the author of a number of books on children, including Children in Jail *and* Black Children, White Dreams. *More recently, he has written about adults from a variety of Boston neighborhoods, all in an attempt to tell the stories of people whose lives would otherwise go unnoticed* (Private Lives and Public Accounts *and* The Present of Things Future: Explorations of Time in Human Experience). *Cottle is also a regular fixture on television; he has had a series of syndicated shows, including a children's show, "Hot Hero Sandwich," and shows for adults: "Up Close," "Soapbox," and "The Tom Cottle Show."*

As a writer, Cottle is at his best when he writes case studies like the study of the Grazianos here. Cottle begins these studies by collecting data—by spending as much time as he can with his subjects, even living with them for extended periods of time. In the end, however, what he does is to tell the story of people's lives and to do so as truthfully and accurately as he can. These case studies serve as the raw material from which social scientists make generalizations about people or society. Some critics have found his work patronizing—Sara Blackburn, for instance, writes, "We don't need more studies by experts, no matter how caring, of how bright, sensitive, and thus worthy of salvation are the victims of our political and social crimes." But Cottle is more often praised for his compassion, his sensitivity, and his concern for both the people he writes about and the ethical implications of his participation in their lives.

The Present of Things Future, *from which the Grazianos' case study is drawn, was cowritten with Stephen Klineberg (born 1940), a social psychologist who teaches at Rice University. Klineberg completed a Ph.D. in social psychology at Harvard University and his work has appeared in the* Journal of Personality and Social Psychology *and* The Key Reporter. *Cottle and Klineberg began with a general interest in the way people perceive and experience time. They have collaborated on a second book about this subject,* The Perception of Time. *Of* The Present of Things Future, *one critic wrote, "The authors make an excellent point of showing the social and cultural limitations which frequently profoundly influence anticipations of the future. An aspect of the study which may give rise to some controversy is the suggestion that the male and female may experience time quite differently."*

Ted and Ellie Graziano

I had been late arriving at the Grazianos' house on Poplar Street. Some unexpected traffic, which I had cursed, held me up, and that fact, coupled with the uncongenial design of Boston's streets, was enough to make me almost forty-five minutes behind schedule. Theodore Graziano, his good friends call him Mushy, had Tuesdays off from work and so the moments I could spend with him and his wife Eleanor together were precious. Normally, I would see one of them alone.

For about fifteen years, Ted Graziano has worked for a Boston newspaper. Starting as a stockroom boy (he was almost twenty-five at the time), he had worked his way up to where now, at thirty-nine, he was foreman of the shipping operation. Salaries had risen over the last years. Several threatened strikes and union pressure on management had brought his take-home pay to a level at which he could just about get by. The important thing for him was the security, a factor he had mentioned several times when we spoke in his office.

"This is not the time to be sitting on any gamble," he said as we began eating our sandwiches. "This is the time when the economy of the country demands that you get yourself a job that looks like it's got to hold out.

Doctors, lawyers, judges, they got it best. The working man, like always, he's going to be the first to get hit. Unemployment starts at the bottom and works its way up. It's like a disease that they can't find a cure for. You know it's out there and you just got to do the best you can to avoid getting it. Stay warm, eat good food . . ." He smiled at me, enjoying his humor. His strong hands held the sandwich he had made that morning. His black hair was thick, his forehead low, and only the thin lines around his eyes and mouth revealed his true age. It was hard to believe that Ted was approaching forty.

"Yeah, forty," Ted reflected when I raised the issue with him once. "I guess that means something. I still feel young though, and you know what they say about feeling your age."

"Yeah, I do. But I feel old."

"Maybe you ought to see a doctor," he laughed.

"Or stay away from young-feeling guys like you." I remember that particular remark. It had sounded patronizing, but he had enjoyed it. Still, the more I played out in my mind a conversation that might have ensued, the more patronizing it became. I think often, for example, that maybe the "good life" is working with one's hands, witnessing real accomplishment, and going home with no lingering thoughts about work until the next morning when you get up and repeat it. But that is precisely the point on which Ted Graziano had long ago put an end to my naïve notions.

"You take a job like this," he had said, waving his right arm about as if to take in the enormous shipping area, partitioned offices, and truck docks, "it's one helluvan operation. I got real responsibility here. You ask any man they got working here and they'll tell you about that responsibility. I tell you though, in the beginning, ten years ago or so, it was one helluva challenge. Couple nights there I got so damn excited with the prospect of it all I could barely sleep. Now, it's just another job to me. Plasterer gets up each morning and slops that shit on the walls; butcher goes cutting up his meat; I direct the newspaper business down here. It's a job, not much more. Every day you get a little excitement, but when you go to think about it day in and day out, it's routine. Man, there are times I'm working down here thinking about how nice it would be to be anywhere else. Sitting in the sun or taking care of people. Doing what you're doing, you know, walking around, talking to people. That'd be nice. I'd like that. But most of the time I have to take those thoughts and crush 'em up like little paper balls and throw 'em away." He shook his head from side to side, crumpling an imaginary sheet of paper in one of his hands. Then he looked back at me.

"Tell you what gets me—I know you're interested in this. It's the time thing. Two things about time I can tell you. First, is how slow it goes most of the time. Look there, once you start to use that word it just keeps coming back on you. Lots of ways you can use that word, though. Like wasting time. Boy, I must say that to the guys here twenty times a day." He had heard the word again and grinned. "Well, I ain't about to go commenting on my verbal skills. Wasting time is one thing, but it's not as important to me, really, as the way time passes so slowly most of the time. Clock seems to die on me every day. I'll be working and just check it out, then work long and hard and check it out again, and see only about fifteen minutes have passed when a good hour should have." He smiled. "You can't beat it. You just can't beat it." A feeling of resignation could be heard in his voice. The muscles of his powerful forearms moved slightly as he pulled his watch band higher on his wrist. "Here's the devil," he said. "Right here's our number one nemesis. Nothing I can do, it seems, to make the seconds go by any faster. 'Course, I'm sure that in a few years I'll be wishing I could slow the whole mess down."

"Yeah," I responded, "I guess lots of us know that feeling right now."

"Funny, I don't. Not yet anyway. Probably will pretty soon. Ain't getting younger just sitting here, but, like, you could say I'm still in the stage of life when I want time to speed up. You know, you could probably categorize people just by asking them, 'Do you want time to speed up or slow down?' I'll bet you'd discover some pretty interesting things. Of course, you'd have to take account of the fact that lots of times a person is doing things where he wants time to speed up or slow down. Still, I'll bet you'd find that lots of people feel the same way most of the time. Like me, I want it to speed up. It's true even when I'm home."

On another occasion, as we sat together on the concrete edge of the truck dock, with the last truck having departed and Ted ready to head for home, he offered another thought about his involvement with time. As usual, his tone with me was formal, for he never forgot that I was not one of his close friends.

"Maybe the worst part of the job is not that time passes slowly. The worst part of my life, really, is that I can see the whole thing laying out before me. See, if I were to tell you that the job is boring, monotonous, that wouldn't really capture the feelings I have when I think about it. And man, you *make* me think about it." He slapped my leg. "I always feel talking with you that I'm back in school writing one of those themes for an English teacher, and I'm trying my best to dig out the big words. Funny about that, too, that being back in school, 'cause like right now, trying to answer your questions, I want to give a good impression. . . ."

"Like getting a good grade?" I interrupted.

"Just like it. But there's more, too, because when I wrote those themes, or tried to write them," he smiled, "it was like I was talking to myself in a very deep and special way. This is all, now, different from working for a good grade. When you write, you know, you begin to know yourself in private. It's not like talking." I could see his thoughts beginning to overtake him. Perhaps he was saying that tenderness as well as anger can come out in writing. Hurt can, too, in ways that day-by-day encounters and friendships often do not allow.

"Anyway, let me get to this one thing. The rotten part of my job here is that everything is so predictable. I can see long, long stretches of time. Maybe the next ten, fifteen, twenty years. I can see them. Work and work, the same job. That's the monotonous part. If every day were the same, like it is, it would still be all right if I didn't ever have to wonder about how all the days string together. But it's the line of days, one after the other, each one repeating, and then the ability to be able to look down the road and see exactly what's coming. Jesus, that's, that's . . . Honest to God, man, it just about frightens me to death, because it means I can see the days leading right down to the end.

"You know you can't live every day of your life thinking only about that single day. That's part of the crap they feed you. You can't do it. You can't keep your mind from focusing on tomorrow and next week, next year. That's what I'm thinking about. You don't think that way in this life. You've got to think about the future. That's where the possibilities are. That's where anything that might be resembling hope is. This business of living day by day, even in a job like mine, can't make it. You can't make it that way. So now I got the problem of being born with a vision that looks down the road, way down the road, and being able to see everything that's coming. They got lots of guys, I'm sure, give their right eye to be able to see what's coming up for them. Well, I can see, and just being able to see is more of a curse than it is anything else. An evil curse. You know what I mean? You got this inborn thing that drives you to get yourself set for the future, right?"

I nodded yes. I thought, too, of the connection between one's images of the future and one's present mood. For when things go particularly well I am able to foresee the future—almost as if the sense of possibility cannot be contained by anything as finite as a future allotment of time.

"Yessir. Every man does," Ted went on. "But *you* don't know what's going to be. Today you talk with me and I tell you something. Tomorrow maybe you talk with Ellie or some kid and you don't know what they're up to. And in a week from now we may not even be seeing one another. You'll go get yourself another family or go do a story about something else. But you can be sure as hell I'll be right here. Two weeks vacation in July each year and then I'll be here. That gets to a guy, that knowing that you might be moving up, like I have, in an organization, and still you're not actually changing that much. I think that's why so many of us liked being in the army so much. Didn't anybody want to get killed naturally, but it *was* a change. Everything that led up to the army stopped once I got in, and what would come after no one could see. I thought about my future plenty then. Oh brother, we had a million conversations about the future. But no one could tell us the way it was going to be. The future was all a mystery. I remember, that was my word for it: 'the mysterious future.' It made you kind of scared. But now that I think about it, those little jittery feelings were exactly the feelings I needed to get me going. They give you a kind of push, a motivation. Now, my whole life is like a car running along a highway. Things going pretty smooth, no complaints, but pretty soon the scenery gets monotonous. So what do you think about? You think about the way it used to be, or maybe you start to wonder just how long it's going to be before your car runs out of gas." He stopped talking, although the movement of his face told me of the thoughts that preoccupied him.

My own thoughts, however, were turning to this method of inquiring about another person. Despite the care one takes, it is clear that many questions or concerns simply do not touch the lives of those with whom one speaks. Nonetheless, in response, they work hard at providing answers. And so those whose lives we may or may not gently invade transform disinterest or irrelevance into unpreparedness, and communicate to us that it is their fault and not ours that a gracious or beguiling response is not forthcoming.

For Ted, the subject of time was central and preoccupying. I had not fished for inquiries that might, somehow, conjoin his world with my own. I had, as they say, struck a chord, a reservoir he had not only wondered about, but seriously considered. I would hear his reflections on time again on the afternoon I reached the Graziano's forty-five minutes late. His orientation to the future, and what he meant by a transparent future, were not capricious notions for him. In particular, a temporal orientation predicated on personal experience was forming even in the midst of the random flow of those conversations that often seemed to me to be heading in no discernible direction.

Our home meetings took place in the kitchen, so I entered through the back door as the family members did. Alone in the house, Ted had been sitting in the kitchen reading the newspaper. Two glasses of milk and a cake covered with tin foil were on the kitchen table along with plates and forks. Early in our friendship, Eleanor Graziano had learned from Ted of my love for apple cakes and apple pies, and so something freshly baked regularly awaited my arrival. Today the smell in the kitchen was especially tantalizing. Ted watched me and grinned with pride. "Quite a lady, huh?"

"You better believe it," I replied.

"She'll be here in a minute. Something came up at her mother's. She left a note." Ted handed me a page from a calendar on which Ellie had written: "I will be back in a minute. Milk and cake are for you. I have not forgotten."

"Come on, let's eat the cake. I've been waiting for you dying with hunger here." Ted took great pleasure in cutting the cake and gently laying a piece on a plate. He reached over and placed a fork on the plate and then pushed one of the glasses of milk toward me. When I was taken care of, he prepared a piece, considerably smaller, for himself.

"So what do we talk about today, or shouldn't we say anything until Ellie gets here?" Ted asked, his mouth full of cake.

"Talk about anything you like, Mr. Graziano," I said. "I'm not listening anyway with this cake here."

"Eat it up. There's lots more where it came from. Your wife cooks, though, doesn't she?"

"Yes, she does."

"Well, then you aren't hurting too much." He sighed deeply, wiping some crumbs from his chin. "Lots of guys have it pretty bad. I told myself a long time ago, though, no wife of mine is going to work. Ever! No matter how bad it is, a man provides in his way, a woman in hers. Ellie doesn't need to go cleaning or secretarying, or work at the phone company like her girlfriends. We'll manage. Eight thousand years, and I'll have this house paid off, and when I die she'll be set up. She don't ever have to work if she don't want to. That's the way it's supposed to be. You agree?"

"Well, I guess I believe people have to work it out the way they want," I answered him. "Men live their way, women theirs."

"Now you're not going to tell me you're one of these liberation people, are you?" He smiled at me.

"Well, I guess in a way I am. Men and women, it seems to me, have to enhance one another, support each other to be what they want."

"Now, *that* I like. *That* I'll buy. That's all right. I like that enhancing business. You know, now that you mention it, that's maybe like my biggest gripe. I never did have anyone enhance my life. I can look back at it now, forty years next July, I can't see a person there anywhere enhanced me, helped me to get anything. Parents never gave a damn. When they died it made no difference in my life at all. No teachers ever cared about what I was doing in school. Priest couldn't have cared less about the whole group of us kids."

"You have Ellie," I said.

His eyes were closed slightly as several thoughts seem to touch him at once. "Yeah, I got Ellie, all right. Probably a good thing for me, too. But it's not really enhancement. That's not what I call the kind of support I'm talking about. A wife is a wife, she doesn't help you out there." He pointed in the direction of the kitchen window above the sink. "That's not what I mean."

"What is it then, Ted? Can you talk about it?"

"Let me get the words first." He paused, looking through his glass at the filmy layer of milk on the bottom. "The living day by day that women do is not what helps a man, or at least a man like me. There's a way a man has to get his whole life together. It's all got to fit somehow, make sense. You know what I mean?" He didn't wait for an answer. "It's got to be set up so that every move you make has some reason in a plan that you have to formulate somewhere along the line. It has to build toward something. Even when you're a little kid, people are asking you what you're going to be when you get older. I did the same thing with my kids. I remember holding Tony on my knee one night, I'll bet he wasn't six months old, and telling him about some of the things he might think about doing when he gets older. Now, here he is, what? Fifteen? He still doesn't know what he's going to do or be. But it doesn't make any difference, see, 'cause he knows he has to become something. That *I* put into his head, starting when he was six months. That's the important thing. He knows he's got to have a plan for when he gets older.

"My problem maybe was I never had one, really, although I did have this thing about making sure that you're living your life to prepare. That's about the only good thing my Dad ever did for me. He made me understand that you got to have something out there waiting for you, and that nothing is going to be out there unless you make the preparations, do the ground work, like they say."

"It makes sense to me."

"Sure. It's got to make sense to you 'cause you're a man. You know about these things. You may be richer than I am, I'll bet you are, too," he looked at me, "and you may have a more interesting job, which I know you do. I even told you once, remember?"

"Yes. In the shop."

"At the office, right," he corrected me.

"Office," I said quietly.

"But the important thing is that a man knows what it means to arrange for his life. That, no woman knows! That I know for sure." A melancholy feeling was taking the place of anger. "There's a kicker in it though, you know?"

"Which is?"

"Which is that a life that asks us to make sure that pasts and presents and futures fit together in some logical way has a price. You know, yourself, as time goes on it gets harder and harder to just live each day and get the most out of it. Can't be done. You don't live each day like that when you're a man. What you live is your work at the moment, your plans, what you call your prospects, *and* your regrets, what you should have done. You think about having bits of time back again to work with. You think how nice it would be to see what the future holds, even in a job like mine where I practically know how everything's going to turn out. Still, you'd like to take a little peek. Maybe just to know whether all those connections you're making are really sticking. You follow me?"

"Yes I do," I answered him.

"So you don't say the hell with what was and what will be. Like that song, what will be, will be. That's the way you think when you go out drinking. At least, that's the way it is for me. I go out and get a little in the bag," he started to smile. I smiled too, as I saw his face take on a look of pride. "That's when my future disappears and my past disappears and I got once and for all my present moment and nothing else, goddamn it, to be concerned about!" He shouted the words as he straightened up in the chair. "But now, I ask you, how long's a man with any self-respect going to run around in the bag? So you come home, and you sleep, and you drink coffee, and you make nice to your wife, and there you are the next day, thinking the same things all over again: how it all fits together, how you wish you could be young again, and how great it would be to know what the future's got waiting for you. And there you are, right back where you started, if you got any strength, that is."

"That's one helluvan analysis," I said, moving about in my chair and wishing, for the moment, to take a second piece of cake.

"Well, I don't know I'd call it an analysis, exactly," he said. "Nothing mysterious about what I've been saying. You keep your eye on the future. That's what men are for. You keep an eye on the future because the name of the game is that since you don't have much to say about dying, you have to fill in as many of the empty spaces out there as you can. You don't leave things to chance. Ellie always talks to me when I get in a huff about God or fate. 'Things will just happen,' she says all the time. 'Things are just going to happen.' Sure. They are. Lots of things are just going to happen. Like the roof might fall in on our heads, right here in the kitchen. But the odds aren't pure chance. The odds are against it because *I* fix the roof, *I* make certain things like that *won't* happen. That's what you do with the day. You fix things so that some things will happen and some things won't.

"The difference between Ellie and me is she waits. She waits for the roof to fall in. Then, when it happens, she does something. Or, she'll say, there's nothing I can do, so I shouldn't worry. What are you going to do? Men worry. They worry because they have to reorganize their lives to make the future better or safer or whatever they're after. Women bake cakes. You like her cake, she's pleased, that's enough for one day. Men worry too, because they have a plan which they have to put into operation." Ted rose from the table and went to the sink to wash his hands. I remembered being in this house one afternoon when the sink faucets were leaking and his temper, like my own on many occasions, had exploded. "No, now they see the operation taking place. Maybe it works, maybe it doesn't. The point is that with one part of their brain they're wondering what they could do *now* to make next week or next year work out better. They're starting new plans, if you know what I mean." He dried his hands on a blue towel that hung on the handle of the refrigerator door.

"Now with the other part of their brain," he resumed, seating himself opposite me, "they wonder what it would be like having the past back again so they might fix a few things, maybe play it all out a little differently. But what a man does that a woman doesn't have the faintest idea about is, that when he has the chance, I mean, *if* he had the chance to live it again, he's still working it around so that the present might be better. I should have gone this way rather than that way, he'll say. Do this instead of that."

"I think I do that myself."

"Sure you do. But you know what a woman does? She gets a chance to be young again, she'll just do it all over the same way. You ask Ellie. She'll tell you exactly what I'm telling you now. All the things from the past that she liked,she'll just do them all over again. And all the bad things too." He anticipated my question. "She'll just say you have to live through the good things and the bad things, or whatever that expression is. Take the good with the bad.

"You know what it's like, Tom? It's like football. There's a good reason why men like football. It's not just the violence. It's a man's game because it's played the way men think. Look what you got in football. First, you got competition. You got a chance to win or lose, and a man is practically born with the idea in his head that you got to win. Then, everybody's got a fair chance. But now here's the subtle part of that game. You have a game plan. Plan. See, there it is again. Now, this plan takes in your purpose, your goal, the way you're going to work it out. And you stick with it until you have to find a new one. And that's the point right there. You don't scrap a plan. A new plan simply means you have to find new patterns, new ways for things to stick together. And it's all leading up to something. Something you could practically predict. That's what football is. If you move here, I'll move there. You move here, I'll move there." He pushed his fingers against the table top, his right hand representing my team, his left hand representing his team. "You can make predictions. It's not a game of chance, like gambling. You know how something ought to work out. Here's another thing. What do they do when the game's over?"

"I don't know. They think about what's gone on."

"That's exactly right. They see the movies of the game, the replays like they call them. They use those films to change their plans and, in your words, to try to make the future come to pass in a different way." He paused. "Here, I got some more milk."

"That's a great metaphor, Ted. I've never thought of football in those terms. It's absolutely true."

"I guess I've been thinking about ways to carry our last discussion from the office forward a little bit. I can't say these things to Ellie. Of course, the kids don't want to hear about it. I talk with some of my friends, but, as you can imagine, not too many of them are as smart as you. I guess you know better than most of us how little schooling we all had. Our kids, I hope, will be different. Oops, I'm starting to sound like the old lady. Hoping instead of arranging."

"Well," I tried to assure him, "there's got to be a place for hope in the plan."

"Sure," he said with resignation, "of course there's a place for hope. But first you make preparations, then, whatever is left over that you can't control for, that falls over into the hope category. A fellow in my position ought to be able to say without fail, I can predict that my kids will go to college. I will get money somehow for them to go, whether it is good for them or not—and, believe me, I got lots of questions for you on that one—I can arrange the future for them. I don't need God or prayer, or hope. This is exactly what I'm talking about. I can arrange for all of this."

He rested his elbows on the table and held his hands up as though shaking a loaf of bread. "I can get all of this to happen. Fate's got no place in here. But baby, I'll tell you, sometimes it makes me wonder why we're here, and why we're doing what we're doing. You got to get out once in a while. I don't mean, don't misunderstand me, I don't mean just out of the house. . . ."

"I know what you mean."

"I mean out of the path of the ball, you know? Go this way for once, or that way, any way to break the monotony. Go backward or forward if that makes any difference. That's what I mean by getting out. In time!"

For a moment, Ted was silent. Then he resumed. "Prediction. That may be the key. Each man his own computer, able to see what's coming up at any point in his life. There are lots of guys who tell you that you can't go around predicting. They say it's bad luck. They're superstitious. Predict something good about your life and you'll see, something bad is always supposed to happen. That's what they say, anyway. Ellie goes along with this. Only God predicts, is probably what she'd tell you if you ever asked her about it. Now, don't get me wrong. You don't want to go around predicting. But predicting is like I was telling you before. It's like hope. It's part of what's left over. You have plans that you might like to see how they come out, but I'm not so sure you have to go around predicting. Still, like that football thing of ours, what'd you call it?"

"Game plan, you mean?"

"No, that other, like the picture I was describing."

"Metaphor?"

"Metaphor. Football metaphor." He seemed relieved. "I remember that from school. Similes and metaphors. Right?"

"Right."

"I never got straight which is which. Anyway, prediction. When you get to be a man they've got this future thing so pushed down your throat, the feeling of making a prediction just isn't so weird as it seems at first. Anything like a . . . technique that has to do with working out the future is something a man quickly gets used to. Not women. Hope's still the last resort though. Just like they say. When all else fails, maybe you better start praying. But when they say that all else fails, they mean that they've been working at something that isn't going to work now. You don't start with prayer. You may see those football players pray at the start of the game, like to get a little boost from the Good Lord. That's all right. Little superstition never killed anyone. God, Ellie better not hear me say that. They may be praying, but you and I know they've been practicing all week long. Not praying! Practicing! They've been getting themselves all set for Sunday. So if they make predictions, it's because they feel they have ways of fixing the outcomes. You get what I mean?

We had been speaking almost an hour when the back door opened, and Eleanor Graziano entered the kitchen. Her face was flushed and she was out of breath.

"Please, please excuse me. I'm so late. I went over to my mother's for a minute. I didn't even take my coat off and before you know it an hour's gone." I nodded to her and started to say something about my own lateness. Bracing herself in the doorway, she leaned down to remove her boots. "Did you find the cake?"

"Did we!" I replied.

"Was it all right?" she asked modestly.

I grinned at her. "Fair. It was fair, Ellie." She laughed and turned her face downward. Ted laughed too.

"A couple of jokesters I got here. Two little boys with no place to go and nothing to do but eat cake and get fat."

I couldn't resist: "Oh, you love it and you know it, Mrs. G."

"You I love," she laughed. "Mushy I'm not so sure about." Ted and I laughed again and looked at each other.

"You better be careful, wife, or I'll tell you what I've been telling Tom here for the last hour about *you*."

"Yeah, and what's that?" she asked her husband, throwing her boots in the back hallway.

"Oh," he started, "about people enhancing one another's lives. Game plans, you know, the usual." He winked at me.

"Game plans?" she asked "Football? Is that it?"

"That's it," I said.

"Not quite," Ted said.

"Then what is it?" she wanted to know.

"Sit down, Ellie. You and Tom talk. I'm going to the corner for cigars. When I come back we'll continue with this. It's time for a commercial."

"Commercial? Tom, will you please tell me what he's babbling about?"

"I will."

"Go on then," she said to her husband. "I've got a few things for Tom *you* don't have to know about."

"Yeah, like what?" Ted demanded.

Ellie was silent for a moment. Then she exploded the one word. "Hockey!"

The three of us roared with laughter.

Eleanor Graziano moved about the kitchen, looking into cabinets at canned goods, glasses, and plates.

"Will you stay for dinner?" she asked.

"No, I can't, Ellie, but I promise I will another time."

"Can't seem to find . . . don't tell me I forgot to get . . . if I don't make a list when I go to the store I'm dead. Can you beat this? I'm not forty yet and my mother, who is almost seventy, has a brain in better shape than mine."

"I doubt that."

"No, it's true," she protested without looking back. "So what do we speak about today? Are you still asking the same questions?"

"Same questions, I suppose."

"About working and living and everything, eh?"

"Yeah, that about covers it."

"Well, I don't know what else I can tell you. Mushy's the one with all the answers. There's nothing you could ask him that he wouldn't have an answer for. Everything. Everything he can find something to speak about. Some man, Mr. Graziano."

I watched her lay out supplies and utensils in preparation for making dinner. The counter tops were spotless, the sink empty of dishes and garbage, the faces of the cabinets glistening clean. It was all quite a change from the day when the Grazianos had moved into this house. Four years ago they lived in a four-room apartment less than a mile away. Then, suddenly, Ted had gotten it in his head to buy a house. Ellie argued that they couldn't afford it, but Ted was driven to buy, and with loans and arrangements at work, they managed to purchase this lovely three-bedroom home. Now they "could spread out," as Ellie said, finally admitting her delight. "The children can stay in the same school and we will live better. I'm closer to my mother, too. If we can just manage," she had sighed. "If we can just manage it will be a blessing, *the* blessing of my whole life."

Although Eleanor Chadwick had never known poverty as a child, she also had never imagined that her marriage to Teddy Graziano, "the Mushy man," would ever lead to a home and a kitchen glowing with warmth and pride like this one. Her father had been an elevator operator and starter during the day, a warehouse inspector four nights a week. He had lived his entire life in Boston. His salary allowed his wife and five children to live comfortably enough in a three-story walk-up apartment. A screened-in back porch opened out from the kitchen of that apartment, and on hot summer evenings the family gathered there feeling as cool as one could during a Boston summer. The view from the porch admittedly was rather uninteresting. "Who, after all, likes looking down an alley at a bunch of other apartment houses?" Ellie had said. "But it *was* cool up there. We enjoyed it together very much. That was ever so lovely, just to be together, even when it was so hot you thought you might die. They had a kid, I remember, who lived downstairs, who died of the heat. He just couldn't get enough cool air, the doctor said. So tragic. So tragic. He could have come up to our porch and saved his life. I suppose you could say I long to see my childhood again."

We had had this conversation about her childhood several years ago, on the very day, actually, that the Grazianos moved into their new home. Ellie and I had sat in the kitchen on cardboard boxes filled with supplies and clothes. "I would love to have those days back again," she said on that moving day. "Even before Mushy and all this. So many times I wish that tomorrow would be the beginning of a change, a sort of a change backward. It's not like you might think, that I fear getting older. I don't think I'm different from other people. But no one likes to grow old. When you have children they say it keeps you young. It's not true. Children age you. My, they age you. It's just that they don't give you any time to think about it. They got you running around all the time.

"No, it's just that wonderful feeling of worryless peace, childhood, being a little girl and having those long hours with my father. He was a delight to know. You would have liked him, Tom. I feel that very strongly. You two would have gotten on. 'Course, that's not saying too much, since Dad never had an enemy. He got on with everyone he ever knew. You know, in many ways, he was very much like Mushy; Mushy without the anger. Dad knew, for example, that he would never be rich, that he'd never achieve anything special or wonderful in his life. He knew lots of rich people, too, but I never heard him complain, or compare himself with someone else. The world was the way it was, and he was big enough to accept it. All of that, I'm sure, made for very peaceful living for the rest of us.

"Mushy's the same way, up to a point. I'm sure he feels that he's not going anywhere in his life, at his job, I mean, but he's not about to accept any of that. He wants to achieve something, to be able to show everybody, mostly himself, of course, that he's gotten something out of life. He'll always tell me that if next year's the same as this year, then he's been a failure. There's no other way. That kind of statement I never heard once from my father's mouth. Never once. For me, you see, that's the sign of a good man. If next year's the same as this one, then you thank God. You get down on your knees at night and you thank God that everybody is well, or still alive I should say, and that you have enough to eat, and a comfortable place to sleep. You know that everything is provided for. But Mushy doesn't want it that way. The comfortable things, of course, he wants. That he wants as much as anyone. Like, he wanted this house. . . ."

I remember Ellie looking about at the boxes and cartons and seeing in her face a look of "How are we ever going to get set up again? Why did we ever undertake this move and this severing of attachments?" I saw excitement, too, a controlled excitement as though one were not supposed to ask for such delicious treasures, but could nevertheless enjoy them if they came one's way.

"Well, I'm set here for life. This is it for me. I detest moving. I may be strange or peculiar, maybe I'm some kind of a mental or something, but I become attached to places. I get used to something very quickly and I don't ever want to change. You know something? I can feel in my hands the curtains we used to have in the apartment where I lived as a child. And the tables in the living room and the kitchen, too. That's how strong my memory is, so that must be how strong my attachment to things is. To people, too. It's sort of funny, though. It grieves me, it really does, that the good times are gone and by many, sad to say, forgotten. I think Mush is that way. Something good happens, like maybe a party. He likes it as much as anyone. But then, when it's over, that's sort of the end of it. Yesterday for him, even this morning, might just as well be a thousand years ago. Me, I'm so different from him it's hard to believe we could have gotten along as long as we have. Something important happens, it doesn't matter whether it's good or bad, I hang on to it. I don't ever want to let go. It's just like the house. I wanted to hang on to the old house. It has memories in it. That's what he doesn't understand. I love this, of course, but you give me the largest mansion you can find, a palace, and I'll sit in my bedroom, I mean bedrooms," she laughed, "and I'll be thinking of that little apartment I grew up in, and the porch and the summers, and all the rest of it."

She paused, looking at nothing in particular, screening a series of ideas before selecting one to present.

"You know that my mother will be seventy years old in March? That's even hard for me to believe. It's all so peculiar. I think peculiar's getting to be my favorite word. But it *is* hard for me to believe that she's that old. My mother is always forty. When I think of her she's just forty. She's in that old kitchen—God, that was some horrible place—working at making dinner, or cleaning out the stove, or peeling apples."

"And you're about ten?" I reasoned.

"Yes. I'm ten or eleven, watching my mother and admiring her very, very much. She was a beautiful woman, though no one could see that now. Beautiful, and blessed with endless energy, too. She's still got that, even now. But you know, what's funny is that when I think about her I'm not really remembering those years; I'm actually back there. I'm *really* ten, and she's *really* forty; that's the way it's always going to be. Neither one of us will ever change."

I could see in Ellie's face a sense of peace that bespoke the loveliness of those moments thirty years ago. "You see, I do become attached to places and to certain people and find myself hoping things never have to be any different than they are right now. I remember on many occasions as a child wishing that I didn't ever have to get any older. I even spoke to my mother about it. She always laughed at me. 'You're too young to be thinking about that,' is about all she could say to me then. Now I'm getting close to her age. Three years and I'll be forty myself, and I have a daughter and . . . well . . . life goes on."

That was a part of our conversation of almost four years ago. Now, as we waited together in the same kitchen for Ted to return, I know that we both felt a nostalgia, a longing for something, for the people of four years ago, for the people of our childhoods as well.

"You're pretty deep in thought, young man." Ellie surprised me. "Maybe *I* ought to be asking the questions today. Turn the tables on you." She was smiling.

"Yeah. I guess I was pretty deep into something there. I was remembering my own childhood, and also the discussion we had in here when you first moved. Remember that?"

"Yes." She strained to recover some of those earlier words. "Barely I do. About my childhood and the old place? Isn't that what we talked about once?"

"Yes. And your mother and father," I reminded her.

"Yes. I remember. My days as a little girl I certainly remember. I wonder what Mushy remembers of those days. I'll bet you very little. He sure likes to lock his past away. He thinks only of the future now. That's all. Every night in bed he's got another plan, another dream. Someday we're going to do this; someday we're going to do that. Trips, property, real estate, the kids going to college. This one's going to be a doctor; that one's going to be a nurse. I have to tell him, 'Mushy, it's 1970, not 1990. Let time pass already. You're living in an age that isn't even born yet.' Can you hear me saying that to him? 'Give the world a chance to do what it's going to do. What do you want the time to pass by so quickly for, anyway?'

"You know, I begin to think that people who don't have parents want the past to go away, or they avoid thinking about it, somehow, by doing all that planning and preparing. It's like today. I went by to bring my mother some groceries. Days like these it's hard for her to get around. So I brought over a few nothings, a little soup and some coffee. Bread. The usual." She blew out a long breath. "Anyway, when I saw my mother I couldn't help thinking how really old she looks. I see her regularly, almost every day because we live so close, so I can't see the changes taking place that easily. You need to stand back from it. But today, for some reason, maybe because I knew you were coming, I looked especially hard at her. And she's old! It frightens me. It actually begins to scare me. I'm not like my husband, with all his plans. I don't want it to be 1990. I don't want to be thinking about what's it all going to be like then, if we're still here. I don't want to go back, exactly, but I certainly don't want it to be 1990 or 1980 or whatever the king up there is thinking about at night. He wants it to be 1990, that's fine with me, but he can damn well get there without me. I'll just take my own sweet time about it." She ended by pulling extra hard on the tie of her apron strings.

"Ellie, what did you mean, you were thinking about your mother getting older because I was coming this afternoon?"

"I knew you'd ask me that."

"I knew you knew." We smiled at each other.

"Well, you get me thinking, somehow, about time, only I can't always find any complicated ideas in all of it. Time for me, like I told you once, is people. People get older, never younger. You reach a point in your life when you first begin to realize this and then you worry over it. Worry's maybe not the right word. But, you know, you feel bad that your little baby's grown up and is a big girl or boy, and that your mother really starts to look old. There's no denying it. I saw her today; it was almost like I was seeing her for the first time. She's an old lady now. She looks just like these old ladies you see wherever you go. When I was young, my brothers and sisters and me, we used to be playing somewhere and we would laugh at old men and women. I remember that like it was yesterday. When you're young you never think that you'll be one of those old people someday. You never do. You also don't think that much about your parents getting older. Older maybe, but not *that* old that you'd look at them and laugh. It's funny too, because I remember then, I still do it now, I thought about what it would be like when my parents died. Every child, I'm sure, thinks about things like that. But you don't think about them getting older or looking very old. Shriveled up and all, I mean. At least I didn't. Maybe I'm different. Oh, it's an awful thing to be talking about." She shook her head as if to be rid of these images.

"Well, anyway, just to finish, I make people my calendars, you might say. To see their faces is to see time. You can tell the date by looking at your mother's or your husband's face. You know what I mean? So today when my mother opened the door, I was flabbergasted. Your questions always make me think of the past, of my parents, and going to school, or whatever pops into my mind. I must have been thinking of my mother as a young woman. Forty or so. I think that's all I mean. You know, this is what you and I once talked about. My special way of not remembering, exactly, but of *being* the age of my memories. When they took place, I mean. That's what it was, I think. I'm not crazy, am I? I mean, this sort of thinking doesn't mean that I'm ready for the State Farm already, does it?"

"Well, it's either the State Farm or making apple cakes every day when I come."

"You want some more? Where did he put it, that miser? Funny, he's so busy planning he forgets to think that maybe you'd like some more cake."

"No thanks, I'm full."

"You're not," she said, "but I'm not one to force anybody."

For a while we sat together in silence. Often it feels awkward being in the house of someone with whom one shares intimate things, stories, memories and all. I feel that I should have questions ready at hand, for the other person may take my silence to mean that I'm not doing my job well. They're waiting for me, I tell myself, to keep the time filled and to take the lead. I started to rise from my chair. Through the window above the sink I saw Ted walking through a light rain. Ellie could not see him.

"Here he . . ." I started.

"I know one thing that makes me different from him." She had one last thought, one that Ted would hear later, but that I was meant to hear first. "I worry more than Mushy. I worry about what will happen. I worry there may not be ways to get things done as we want them to. But I don't worry about what I can't see, or about what's not here yet. What's more, and this is very important if you want to really understand us, is that I believe you must live with a belief in God. Some things you can't take care of yourself. Some things only God knows what to do with. Mushy thinks I'm nuts when I say this. So I've stopped saying it in front of him, and, for that matter, in front of the children when he's around. It drives him crazy. He worries, too, but for him it's that there won't be enough time to finish all the things he's planned to do. As for God, he's about as far from God as I am from, from, I don't know what. The President of the United States. It's not easy living with this disagreement either." I saw the top of Ted Graziano's head pass under the window.

"Don't think for one minute I'm telling you little petty businesses in our lives," Ellie continued. "I'm telling you the most important things. This is a very serious difference. We run, you might say, on different clocks. You know, like the East Coast and the West Coast. We're in the same country, speaking the same language most of the time, but we've got clocks inside of us that I'm sure not only run at different speeds, but, if it's possible, in different directions as well. That probably doesn't make any sense to you, but I think it sort of tells what I worry about quite a bit of the time." She hesitated again, although she had more to say. The back door flew open and Ted entered the kitchen.

"A man with cigars," he began, "is a man halfway to heaven." He slammed the door shut, and the latch chain smacked loudly against the glass pane. Shaking off the rain and stomping his feet dry, he was a man doing his best to announce his arrival.

I had turned my body to greet him. Beside me I heard Ellie say quietly: "Two separate clocks, each ticking its own sweet time, each heading off in a direction that would probably confuse the Almighty."

How and when the tension between Ted and Ellie grew to the proportions it would that rainy afternoon I cannot recall. I do know that their ordering of the world, the arrangements they had made with time itself, were now at stake, driving them toward some temporary conclusion, some partial settlement. Just beyond the boundaries of this extended moment lay a special and distinct instant when confrontation would switch off, and the flow of this one eruption would, like water, find a new bed in which to run. No death, no final stopping place, but a life marker, nonetheless; an instant colored with hatred, I suppose, and the anguish that life and people, circumstances and history, combine to create.

In this case, I was at the center of their tension, for I had not only asked the questions on which they had unloaded so many feelings, I had split them apart by speaking intimately with each of them. I knew things about each, they both believed, that they had not confided to each other. Mine was the easy position of being able to listen to someone's everyday world without having to share much of my own. It is that comfortable role of sharing compassion while hiding one's own conflicting or antagonistic attitudes. Ellie was right. People are themselves temporal units, delicate mechanisms in which the experience of duration and the capacity for knowing change, the sense of history and continuity, disruption and evolution are all curiously combined.

To be sure, we possess internal clocks, beating systems of all sorts. But the world that exists beyond us tampers with these systems, leaving us with a peculiar repertoire of rhythms and tempos that dominate our lives, or the style of our lives. And events like marriage and the birth of children cause us to feel a reverberation in these rhythms, as childhood experiences, reveries, and recollections seek to overcome the connections and adjustments that we have finally settled on.

Ellie was seated at the table across from me; Ted was standing in the doorway between the dining space and living room, pacing in and out of our vision, a machine rumbling its engines, dying to lurch forward and, with a deafening rage, be gone.

"You know, Ellie," he was saying, his anger rising, "that's probably where it all goes wrong, every time with every man and every woman."

"Where?" she asked. "Where does *what* go wrong?"

"There! You see, it's right there. That you even have to ask it is what I'm saying."

"I don't see the thread of it either, Ted," I said.

"Look. You and I may come from the same background," he pointed at his wife, "but there are times when we're so different it's almost laughable that we've made it this long."

"Are the kids upstairs?" Ellie questioned.

"Oh, the hell with the kids. Let 'em hear. What the hell's the difference if they hear? What do you want, children who don't know what's going on in their own house?"

"No, I don't." Ellie's voice sounded frightened.

"That's exactly what my parents always did. They tried to keep everything from us, as though we didn't know what was going on. Let 'em hear for once."

"I'm merely. . . ."

"Look, if you'd just let me say this already."

"I'm letting you say anything you want, Ted." Ellie and I watched him walk out of the kitchen, then return.

"You've never been able to understand what my life is made of," he went on. "I tell you my plans, my prospects of what might happen at work, I tell you my dreams. That is, I used to tell you my dreams. Little that you could care."

"I listen to every one of them."

"Listening isn't enough, goddamn it. It's like Tom here. He listens. But it isn't enough. You think my plans are nuts or that I live in the future somehow. Or that I got a lot of pipe dreams."

"I didn't say that."

"You do in your way. You ought to look and listen to yourself so you could see what I see. Here's a stranger comes in this house is more sympathetic to the way I want to work out my future than the woman I married. That's really a laugh. Now that really gets me."

"That's not fair, Ted," I said.

"I don't care about fair," he shot back. "We're way beyond talking about what's fair and what's not fair." Then to me: "I tell you things about my life, you don't come back with all the junk I have to hear from her."

"*Her* is still in this room," Ellie said sharply. "Why don't you speak a little to *her?*"

"I *am* speaking to you. Who the hell you think I'm speaking to? The man in the moon?"

"I thought you might have been speaking to him." She nodded at me.

"When I want to speak with him, I'll speak with him. This is *our* business."

"Hey, maybe I should go," I suggested.

"No sir, you sit right there," Ted insisted. "You want to know about us, you listen to this part too. Every day isn't so rosy. You stay around and see the seamy side, too."

"Ted," Ellie broke in, "you're sounding foolish."

"Oh shut up!" She didn't move. "You stay, Tom. I want you to hear. I work five hard days a week. I ain't got no good prospects for anything like lots of other guys. That newspaper goes under, I'm out a job. I'd like you, Mrs. Know-it-all, to tell me just exactly what I'm supposed to do then. Huh? You got this philosophy you take every day one at a time? Isn't that your usual speech?"

"That's my usual speech," Ellie responded with resignation.

"Yeah. That's it. That's a terrific philosophy. You know where I'd be with that philosophy running my life? Do you know? *Do* you?"

"No, I don't, Ted. Where would you be?"

"You don't care. What's the use?"

"I *do* care. I want to know."

"C'mon, Ted," I said, "we want to hear you."

"O.K. I'd be in the same job I had when I was eleven years old. I'd be delivering for that moron McCrackle or McCarver or whatever the hell his name was."

Ellie began to smile. "Mencken," she corrected him.

"Mencken. McCracken. What the hell's the difference? You don't understand what I'm saying anyway."

"That's not true," his wife answered him. "I do."

"Yeah? Then what am I saying?" He looked at her smugly.

"That if you hadn't had some dream or goal you wouldn't have gone beyond the life you knew as a little boy."

"That's exactly right. So what I'd like to learn from you is, if you understand that, how can you be so, so, I don't know what when it comes to listening to me?"

"I try to listen to you." Ellie's voice was kind.

"Maybe you do then. But our worlds are too different. You can't possibly understand what's in my head."

"I tell you what I believe in the best ways I can."

"That God . . . you mean that God stuff?"

"Yes," she said firmly. "That 'God stuff,' as you call it."

"That's where we part. I mean, that's where it all falls apart."

"Why? Where? What's falling apart, Ted?"

"Us. You, me. The whole thing. It falls apart. You rely on some set of beliefs that bring nothing." His anger, which had subsided, rose again. "God doesn't buy homes. God doesn't pay bills. Men do that. God doesn't provide! Love doesn't provide! You can go to church. . . ."

"I realize that."

"You can go to church every day of the week, my friend, but if I don't work, or you don't work, you don't eat. You ever hear of God throwing down food? Or clothes? Or homes? Does your friend God do *that?*"

"Of course not. That's not why people . . ."

"You see you're wrong there. I'm sorry to correct you, but that's exactly what all those poor slobs go there on Sunday for. They march off to church and give their last pennies to God and beg Him to give them food or shelter, or whatever the hell they ask for."

"I don't think that's what . . ."

"I'll tell you something else. That's exactly why they're poor."

"Who? Who's poor?" Ellie started. "What are you talking about?"

Ted bent over and pointed at her, all the while keeping his distance. "That's why the poor are poor!" he yelled at her. "Am I such a dummy that no one understands me any more? I thought I was being perfectly clear."

"Ted."

"C'mon, Ted," I joined in.

"Ted nothing," he came back. I made another gesture to leave. Ted came at me and grabbed my shoulder, pushing me back in the chair. "You want to think of me as a madman, go ahead. But you'll leave here only when I'm finished."

"C'mon, Ted," I tried again.

"No, *you* listen! Both of you. The reason the poor stay poor is because of what *you* believe," he pointed at Ellie.

"You mean *I'm* the cause of people being poor?" she asked sarcastically.

"That's exactly right. *You're* the cause. All this business of living day by day, of wanting God to solve problems, of not doing things until they actually happen, until they fall into your goddamn lap, *you* believe that, and that's why people like you don't get anywhere. People are making it in this country every day of their lives. You can still have a chance. But this business of laughing at someone 'cause he plans, or praying, that's the end. That's the living end. You hold on to your childhood; you've never let go of it; and we're married almost twenty years. You see your mother as much as you see your husband. I'd love to know what in the hell you two can find to talk about every day. That's something for you to study, Tom. If you *really* want to do an interesting study, that's what you should study: what Ellie and her mother find to talk about every day of every week of every month." Ellie had placed her head in her hands. She made no sound. "But you don't hear me complain about what portion of my salary goes to supporting her, do you?"

"No, I don't hear you complain," Ellie whispered.

"What'd you say?" Ted screamed at her.

She lifted her head and answered him more loudly: "I said, 'No, I don't hear you complain.' "

"No, I don't complain. I just shell out dough left and right for all those little things you bring her every day because that beautiful saint of a father of yours who loved everybody and everybody loved him, never planned, never dreamed. It ain't enough to be nice."

"Don't you dare speak about my father," Ellie said bitterly, staring at him.

"I'll speak about anyone I damn please. Who the hell's paying for this house anyway?"

"You don't have to speak about the dead."

"I'm not speaking about the dead. I'm speaking about poor people; people who think love and niceness and praying in a church are what matter. It's all a lot of *shit!* It's all a lot of shit! Your parents were *full* of shit!"

"Ted," she screamed at him. "Stop it!"

"And *my* parents were full of shit too. They all stunk! None of 'em knew what was going on. You know what they did? They led their lives day by day, minded their own business and decided if this is what history brought them, then that's the way it had to be. Destiny is what they call it. They just obeyed their destiny. You go ahead and look around at their children. Who's doing anything worthwhile? Huh? Who's trying to fight? Who's dreaming about the future and not about the past? Huh? You and your mother cause poverty. You sit together like mentals dreaming of the good old days when your father was alive, and none of you seems to give a rat's ass that you were poor."

"Ted, please." Ellie began to weep. My presence made it more difficult for her.

"Ted," I said, "I'm going to go."

"You're not going. I'm not done." We looked at Ellie. "Let her cry. She cries all the time. Maybe we should call her mother over and they could have a good cry together about the old days. Maybe we could make an invention and bring back the dead."

"You're a monster," Ellie sobbed.

"*I'm* the monster? Sure. Of course. *I'm* the monster, because I'm a little different from those idiots who run the church. I speak the truth. I tell you that you *waste* your life. All you have is yesterday and today. That's all all women have. Memories, tears, dreams, MOTHERS! You forget that I remember you as a child. I knew your family. They were doing nothing at all to escape their circumstances. You take a look at rich people someday. You know what they're doing? Right now? I'll tell you, and Tom will back me up, too." He continued to pace up and back across the room. "They're planning so many things for their lives they ain't got time to go to church. They got the lives of their kids planned and their kids' kids. You talk to some rich guy with his insurance policies and his trust funds. You ask them if they live day by day. They're an army, the rich. They march on the future and rip it up, eat it, and spit it out. That's what they do. They beat the future at its own game. Right, Tom? They're there before it. They don't wait to see how their kids are turning out. They put 'em in the best schools, like these finishing schools, so's they can make sure the kids will *have* to turn out right."

"I don't want to hear about the rich," I heard Ellie say.

"Of course you don't. No one wants to hear what really goes on in life. You'd rather believe your daddy's going to come home and give you presents."

"I told you about talking about my father."

"O.K. *My* father then. He came home. . . . When he was alive, he didn't do one goddamn thing to change his life. Not a goddamn thing. Ever! He was supposed to be a perfectly good guy. But he was like you, all caught up with this crap of taking each day one by one and making the best of it you can. You know what you get from that philosophy?"

"Oh, stop already. Please stop."

"Ted . . ." I shouted.

"You get windows over kitchen sinks like this one." I looked at him quizzically. "Windows over kitchen sinks," he repeated, nodding his head up and down. "The rich work to make their lives work out. Everything from their childhood on is bent toward fixing their lives and giving them security. You talk about the ability to make predictions? You should talk to the rich people like I do at work. They've got things figured out you wouldn't even be able to dream of. Believe me, I know. They think in enormous blocks of time. Not days. Not years, even. They're moving in decades, ten years, all the time left in this century. This ain't no nickel-and-dime stuff. It's all big business. Years at a time they take from the past and add onto the future. That's what their life is based on. Big business. Now, in this shitty little house which is about the best I'm ever going to be able to do, this woman here stands in front of a sink looking out the window all day worrying either about the weather, or whether it's daytime or nighttime. That's all women know. If it's daytime you make breakfast, if it's nighttime you make dinner. Bills, plans, what's going to become of us, they couldn't care less. Nighttime, daytime, all they want to know is what's in the cabinets to eat. Women and children. They're one and the same.

"So what do you want of me, Ted? What do you want of me?" Ellie's voice and tears were frightening to Ted. He moved back, disappearing into the dining area. "O.K., you're a big man, you're doing a great job here in front of us, putting on this big show, probably for Tom. You're doing fine. Now just what is it that you want? Just what do you want me and my mother and *your* children and *my* father to do? Why don't you answer that instead of carrying on here like a mental case. *You* answer, for once. What do *you* want? You want me to work? Is that it? You want the kids to stop going to school and go to work? Here, give me the phone. I'll call up the schools and pull the kids out. That's what you want, isn't it? C'mon, c'mon. Here, big man, give me the phone. Come on!" She held her open hand out in front of her. "HERE!" she screamed. Ted walked toward her.

"Stop it, goddamn it. The both of you." I heard myself yell.

"I'll give you," Ted was saying, "I'll give you the phone, across your fresh mouth is where I'll give you the phone."

"Go ahead," Ellie yelled. "You talk so much. Why don't you do something instead of babbling on like this, like some kind of an escapee from a mental hospital."

Ted's mouth closed; he nodded sarcastically. "Escapee from a mental. . . . This is what I have to take. Every day of my life. I am totally alone, making it possible for four human beings to lead their lives with a little dignity." His voice had quieted somewhat. "Four ungrateful human beings. I don't have a soul to talk to in this house. I see the way people are living. I see the way people are dying, and we're not getting any of it. Either one. I can't even afford to get us ground in the cemetery. Has that, Mrs. Big Mouth, ever crossed that brilliant brain of yours? Where, exactly, would you like them to put my corpse when I die if I don't arrange for a plot? Here? Would you like it in the kitchen maybe? Just where do the poor die? You ever think of that? That, too, is part of the future. Maybe that's what they mean by destiny. Huh? You ever think of that? I got to arrange for that too, pal.

"There's nothing for me to look forward to. I see the future that you and your mother and all those idiots you talk with at church pray to God to take care of you. I *see* the future. I'm already seventy years old and still at the Gazette, still lifting Sunday papers, still dragging my ass around that goddamn hole. You're praying, and I'm working to have enough money to buy a place, and a way to get rid of my body which, if you'd really care to know, was dead a long, long time ago. Let me give you a little lesson." He glared at the two of us before continuing.

"Let me give you both a bit of a lesson. You," he said, pointing to me, "will have to excuse me if I don't sound like some important professor from M.I.T. A man doesn't die when his heart stops. That's not the only death a man has got to look forward to. There are lots of deaths . . ."

"Like when your parents die?" Ellie quietly interrupted.

"NO!" he yelled at her. "Wrong again. Those are the deaths that women fall apart with. Men don't die at the sight of death. You talk to soldiers. They fight with hundreds, thousands of guys falling down all around 'em. No sir, women go to cemeteries and fall apart. Men hold women together because they know more about death than women. They know more about death because they work. They work every damn day of their lives and so they know what it is to reach a point where you can't go any further. Your own little progress is over. Dead. That's the death a man knows. The death of effort. How's that?" he questioned me. "The death of effort. You ever hear of the word incapacitated?" he asked his wife.

"Of course I did," Ellie answered.

"Of course I did," he mocked her in baby talk. "Of course you *didn't*, you mean. You can't know because women can't know the thought every day of your life of something happening and you're not able to work again. That's death, my friend." He glared at Ellie, assured that I, a man, would have to agree. "That's death."

"And women don't have that?" she inquired.

"No, women don't have that. Look at your mother. Someone else has to work so's she can eat. Someone else has to cook. Someone else has to wash up and clean and whatever you do. No sir, women don't have that. You don't know the feelings of these other deaths until you find yourself in a world where you don't have any choice; and you just stay at it, like it or not, knowing you better damn well stay healthy or a whole group of people are going to fall flat on their faces."

"You're talking through your hat," Ellie started. "How hard to you think it would be for all of us to go to work? We could make up the difference. Did *you*, Mr. Bright Ideas, ever think of *that?*"

"Many, many, many times," Ted replied softly. "Many times I've thought about what it would be like having your wife and children working while you sat around the house, sick or something. That, my friend, is another form of death. That may be the worst death of all. When women work it's a fill-in. They're a substitute, and brother, when they put in the substitutes it's because the first team either stinks or can't play. Or maybe," he smiled, " 'cause the first team's got a lead they'll never catch. If only it worked that way. If only I could ever get ahead of it, instead of always chasing, chasing, chasing . . ."

"What are you chasing, chasing, chasing?" Ellie asked, at last looking up. "Now that *is* a good question. What is it that you're always after that you can know all these *special* deaths that no one else seems to know anything about? Huh?"

"I'm chasing life!" he yelled back at her. "I'm chasing the rich and the government and my bosses and taxes and bills. That's what I'm chasing. I'm a drowning man. Look at me. I'm a drowning man, chasing after a breath. After air. Is that enough for you? I don't take life day by day and sit back and dream about the beautiful past. Anybody does that has already drowned. You chase, goddamn it. You chase your goals. You chase after the little that might possibly be coming your way. Like a fifty-dollar bonus for Christmas. *I* screw up, lady, and *you* don't get the money that you use to buy Christmas presents. You think bonuses just *come* to you? How do you think it works out there? That somebody just *gives* you things? Things come to you because you work your goddamn ass off, and what's more, and this no woman could ever know, you can work your ass off every day of your life, eight to six every day of your life, and end up with this!" He held his hand up, making a zero sign with his thumb and index finger. "Zero!" he yelled. "Nothing! You can work and work just like your father did and end up with nothing!"

"He was a happy man on the day he died."

"The hell he was. You don't know anything about your father. You ask your brother Milt about your father. You ask him just how happy he was in his life. He kept it from all of you. Ask your mother. She knows. Maybe now that you're a big girl she'll tell you some of the real facts of life. Go ask her when you see her tomorrow. Go tonight. Go now, for Christ's sake; it's been almost an hour since you've seen the old lady." He glanced up at the kitchen clock. I looked too and he caught me. "One more minute, then you can go too," he ordered me. "When you go there ask your mother about his drinking."

"Shut up, Ted." Ellie was angered and embarrassed. She looked at me. On several occasions we had spoken of her father's alcoholism, but the subject was not to be mentioned, apparently, when the three of us were together.

"I'm not supposed to be saying anything about that, eh? I'm supposed to keep my mouth shut so the world can think that everything around us and our beautiful childhoods was perfect? Well, I can't. You ask your mother about how many times your father died in his life before the Good Lord took him away. Ask her. She'll tell you ten thousand. Ten million. He died every night of his life. Every night he came home to that dump your family lived in, he died. You think it's easy for a man to look around every day at his life, where he worked, where he lives, and be reminded of what a failure he is and always will be? That's the death part, Ellie. And that's the part, reporter, you better write about if you want to understand us. The people like us. It's that double hit; that seeing every day of your life what you got and *knowing,* knowing like your own name, that it ain't ever going to get any better. That's what you live with, and that's what your father had in his mind and in his body every day of his life. That's why a man drinks. Believe me, I know. You keep it from your children just so long. But in this country, there isn't a man who fails and holds his head up. Any man who holds his head up after he loses is just trying to protect himself. No one likes a loser. That's why the rich can't stand us. That's why we moved here. Your home, my house, what we had together all those years were *prisons.* They were advertisements of how much we didn't have. You got any doubts about it, you just turn on the TV and see the way people are living, with their new cars and their boats, and their homes in the country. How many times a day they have to remind you of that, I'd like to know?"

For the first time, Ellie was nodding assent. I had seen her face show relief moments before when, unthinkingly, Ted had used the phrase, "the Good Lord took him away." Now she was her husband's wife, his woman, for at last the direction of his anguish had shifted, and it was America, the rich, social classes, me, that he attacked and held responsible for the perceptions of time that he nurtured. Finally she could feel that connection with a history and with a group of people who struggle precisely because the perceptions, attitudes, and ways of others were more powerful, more successful, perhaps, than they, cause them to struggle. No longer was it men against women; it was the poor against the rich, those who can, with a genuine sense of autonomy and possibility underwriting it, achieve with dignity, and those who must sweat out the work, the waiting, and the decisions of bosses for bonuses and a chance to move ahead slightly.

Ted stood, not exactly next to his wife, but closer to her, leaving me, still seated, the third person. Reflecting on his words, I sought a proper way to excuse myself. For minutes the three of us were silent. Ellie and I staring at the table top, Ted standing near us, motionless. I could hear him breathing, and I could feel my eyebrows rising and falling, as though something in me wanted to signal the two of them. We will all three of us go on from here, is what the silence meant to me. We will all face the forms of death, as Ted had said, that each of us faces, not every day perhaps, but often enough. And we will dream of a past, of homes perhaps where it is warm, and where everyone is content. We will know experiences that make us live moment by moment, for as long as each moment lasts, just as we will think up something for the future, a plan, a prediction, a style of ignoring it, almost as children generate some new idea for a game they have played before.

Ted broke the silence. His voice was even and resolute. "I want you to know, Tom, that you have my permission to write anything you want about this afternoon. All of it. I'm pretty sure Ellie feels the same way."

"I do. Yes, I do," Ellie said.

When I looked up at them they were already looking intently at me. "I appreciate that," I responded. "I don't ever know exactly what I'll be writing, of course."

"I don't know much about writing," Ted began. "I don't want to ever tell a man how to do his work if I don't know how to do that work better than that man. But I think it might just be good for you to take a shot at writing this. Don't worry about us. You go ahead and write what you feel you should. Call us about our meeting next week." That was all he said that afternoon.

Two feelings had come over me, two feelings as distinct as shaking hands with both Grazianos simultaneously, Ted's right hand in my right hand, Ellie's hand in my left hand. I felt, first, that I had been as moved by these two people as I had ever been by anyone or anything, and that because of this resonance deep inside me, our lives were now married. But I felt, too, a desire to make all three of us, through my writing, special and unforgettable; famous, I suppose. I was half-way home, driving through an angry rain that made visibility almost impossible, before the one word that swirled in my head finally came to rest: immortality.

In the end, the overriding dimension of time in human experience is the dimension of freedom. For freedom implies the right to embrace one's past, one's immediate experiences, and one's prospects as one chooses, all according to an equitable reality. Like the word "future," freedom implies possibility. When freedom is denied, therefore, a person's past, present, or future, or all three, may also be denied. And so a past is rejected, prospects are ruled outrageous, and a man and woman remain alone to suffer an anguish they are led to believe each has caused the other. In fact, it is a culture's power and the ways of social systems that sting human possibility and kill the belief in an honorable past, a tolerable present, and the prospect of a generous future.

. . . .

QUESTIONS FOR A SECOND READING

1. Ted locates his life in the future—at least he spends much of his time thinking about the future and preparing for it. When you go back to the essay, look at those passages (like the one on p. 147) where he talks about the

future. What does he say? If you were to take these passages as "keys" to understanding Ted and his view of the world, what would you notice? What would you be able to say?

2. Ted wants to be in control, or feels he has to be. What about Ellie? Review those sections of the essay where she talks about herself, about her beliefs, values, and actions. How does she see herself and her role in their relationship?
3. Reread the sections of the essay where Ted and Ellie offer metaphors for their relationship—the football game for Ted, and the clocks that run on different time for Ellie. What do the metaphors say about the way these two people understand themselves and their differences? What do they allow the Grazianos to see? What do they keep them from seeing? How might you extend these metaphors to serve your own analysis of these two people?

ASSIGNMENTS FOR WRITING

1. Ted Graziano realized that he and his wife have managed to keep their marriage together despite what he claims are profound differences. Write an essay in which you define the important differences between the Grazianos and explain what these might be said to represent (like the differences, for example, between two personality types, or between men and women of a particular generation, social class, or culture). If you take the Grazianos as a case for study, in other words, what generalizations might you make?
2. Write an essay explaining what you see as the most significant or revealing passage if you are interested in understanding Ted. What do you see in that passage that others might have missed? And what, then, can you say to help others understand Ted as you do?
3. Write an essay explaining what you see as the most significant or revealing passage if you are interested in understanding Ellie. What do you see in that passage that others might have missed? And what, then, can you say to help others understand Ellie as you do?

MAKING CONNECTIONS

1. Eric Nesterenko, in Studs Terkel's interview from *Working,* (p. 499), has a wife and three children, he's close to Ted Graziano in age, and he seems to come from the same working-class background as Ted. Yet these men have radically different outlooks, and they imagine quite different futures. How might you explain their differences? their different ways of seeing or imagining themselves? Write an essay in which you discuss the different ways they see themselves in relation to their pasts, their families, their jobs, or their futures, paying particular attention to the stories, metaphors, or im-

ages they use to define themselves or to "place" themselves as characters in their own story. Your essay should focus on the differences in the ways they represent themselves, but it should also try to explain these differences.

2. In the Raymond Carver story, "What We Talk about When We Talk about Love" (p. 76), a group sits around and talks about the things that matter to them. Ted and Ellie, too, talk to Cottle about their lives, hopes, and troubles (and they insist that he publish what they say for others to read). One question to ask of this case study is, "What do Ted and Ellie talk about when they talk about love?" Use the Carver story as a starting point for an essay about the Grazianos that addresses this question. In particular, pay attention to the differences in the two conversations. How, for example, are Ted and Ellie different in what they say and don't say from the people in Carver's story? To what would you attribute these differences?

ANNIE DILLARD

ANNIE DILLARD, when she went to live at Tinker Creek in Virginia's Blue Ridge mountains, kept a record of her life in the woods, Pilgrim at Tinker Creek. *The book opens with the following image:*

> *I used to have a cat, an old fighting tom, who would jump through the open window by my bed in the middle of the night and land on my chest. I'd half-awaken. He'd stick his skull under my nose and purr, stinking of urine and blood. Some nights he kneaded my bare chest with his front paws, powerfully, arching his back, as if sharpening his claws, or pummeling a mother for milk. And some mornings I'd wake in daylight and find my body covered with paw prints in blood; I looked as though I'd been painted with roses.*

There is a tough, clear edge to Dillard's nature writing that constantly shocks and surprises—even if the surprise is the surprise of recognition—and that elevates her work well beyond the cute sentimentality of most nature writing. She is often praised for the "clarity" or "honesty" of her vision, and it is true that she notices a remarkable range of natural events. Her great achievement, however, is as a writer. She once said in an interview that "nobody ever thinks a writer writes to write. They think it's because of the subject matter. They say you feel very deeply, when in fact you use your verbs very carefully. I mean, I feel deeply, but so does everybody." The difficulty with books about life in the woods is that we come to them convinced we already know what they will say. Dillard shows us that this is not necessarily true.

Dillard was born in Pittsburgh in 1945 and educated at Hollins College in Virginia. She won the Pulitzer Prize in 1974 for Pilgrim at Tinker Creek *and has published books of both poetry and essays, including* Teaching a Stone to Talk *and* Tickets for a Prayer Wheel. *She is currently working on a book about growing up in Pittsburgh and teaching at Wesleyan University in Connecticut.*

The Fixed

I

I have just learned to see praying mantis egg cases. Suddenly I see them everywhere; a tan oval of light catches my eye, or I notice a blob of thickness in a patch of slender weeds. As I write I can see the one I tied to the mock orange hedge outside my study window. It is over an inch long and shaped like a bell, or like the northern hemisphere of an egg cut through its equator. The full length of one of its long sides is affixed to a twig; the side that catches the light is perfectly flat. It has a dead straw, deadweed color, and a curious brittle texture, hard as varnish, but pitted minutely, like frozen foam. I carried it home this afternoon, holding it carefully by the twig, along with several others—they were light as air. I dropped one without missing it until I got home and made a count.

Within the week I've seen thirty or so of these egg cases in a rose-grown field on Tinker Mountain, and another thirty in weeds along Carvin's Creek. One was on a twig of tiny dogwood on the mud lawn of a newly built house. I think the mail-order houses sell them to gardeners at a dollar apiece. It beats spraying, because each case contains between one hundred twenty-five to three hundred fifty eggs. If the eggs survive ants, woodpeckers, and mice—and most do—then you get the fun of seeing the new mantises hatch, and the smug feeling of knowing, all summer long, that they're out there in your garden devouring gruesome numbers of fellow insects all nice and organically. When a mantis has crunched up the last shred of its victim, it cleans its smooth green face like a cat.

In late summer I often see a winged adult stalking the insects that swarm about my porch light. Its body is a clear, warm green; its naked, triangular head can revolve uncannily, so that I often see one twist its head to gaze at me as it were over its shoulder. When it strikes, it jerks so suddenly and with such a fearful clatter of raised wings, that even a hardened entomologist like J. Henri Fabre confessed to being startled witless every time.

Adult mantises eat more or less everything that breathes and is small enough to capture. They eat honeybees and butterflies, including monarch butterflies. People have actually seen them seize and devour garter snakes, mice, and even *hummingbirds.* Newly hatched mantises, on the other hand, eat small creatures like aphids and each other. When I was in elementary school, one of the teachers brought in a mantis egg case in a Mason jar. I watched the newly hatched mantises emerge and shed their skins; they were spidery and translucent, all over joints. They trailed from the egg case to the base of the Mason jar in a living bridge that looked like Arabic calligraphy, some baggling text from the Koran inscribed down the air by a fine hand. Over a period of several hours, during which time the teacher never summoned the nerve or the sense to release them, they ate each other until only two were left. Tiny legs were still kicking from the mouths of both. The two survivors grappled and sawed in the Mason jar; finally both died of injuries. I felt as though I myself should swallow the corpses, shutting my eyes and washing them down like jagged pills, so all that life wouldn't be lost.

When mantises hatch in the wild, however, they straggle about prettily, dodging ants, till all are lost in the grass. So it was in hopes of seeing an eventual hatch that I pocketed my jackknife this afternoon before I set out to walk. Now that I can see the egg cases, I'm embarrassed to realize how many I must have missed all along. I walked east through the Adams's woods to the cornfield, cutting three undamaged egg cases I found at the edge of the field. It was a clear, picturesque day, a February day without clouds, without emotion or spirit, like a beautiful woman with an empty face. In my fingers I carried the thorny stems from which the egg cases hung like roses; I switched the bouquet from hand to hand, warming the free hand in a pocket. Passing the house again, deciding not to fetch gloves, I walked north to the hill by the place where the steers come to drink from Tinker Creek. There in the weeds on the hill I found another eight egg cases. I was stunned—I cross this hill several times a week, and I always look for egg cases here, because it was here that I had once seen a mantis laying her eggs.

It was several years ago that I witnessed this extraordinary procedure, but I remember, and confess, an inescapable feeling that I was watching something not real and present, but a horrible nature movie, a "secrets-of-nature" short, beautifully photographed in full color, that I had to sit through unable to look anywhere else but at the dimly lighted EXIT signs along the walls, and that behind the scenes some amateur moviemaker was congratulating himself on having stumbled across this little wonder, or even on having contrived so natural a setting, as though the whole scene had been shot very carefully in a terrarium in someone's greenhouse.

I was ambling across this hill that day when I noticed a speak of pure white. The hill is eroded; the slope is a rutted wreck of red clay broken by grassy hillocks and low wild roses whose roots clasp a pittance of topsoil. I leaned to examine the white thing and saw a mass of bubbles like spittle. Then I saw something dark like an engorged leech rummaging over the spittle, and then I saw the praying mantis.

She was upside-down, clinging to a horizontal stem of wild rose by her feet which pointed to heaven. Her head was deep in dried grass. Her abdomen was swollen like a smashed finger; it tapered to a fleshy tip out of which bubbled a wet, whipped froth. I couldn't believe my eyes. I lay on the hill this way and that, my knees in thorns and my cheeks in clay, trying to see as well as I could. I poked near the female's head with a grass; she was clearly undisturbed, so I settled my nose an inch from that pulsing abdomen. It puffed like a concertina, it throbbed like a bellows; it roved, pumping, over the glistening, clabbered surface of the egg case testing and patting, thrusting and smoothing. It seemed to act so independently that I forgot the panting brown stick at the other end. The bubble creature seemed to have two eyes, a frantic little brain, and two busy, soft hands. It looked like a hideous, harried mother slicking up a fat daughter for a beauty pageant, touching her up, slobbering over her, patting and hemming and brushing and stoking.

The male was nowhere in sight. The female had probably eaten him. Fabre says that, at least in captivity, the female will mate with and devour up to seven males, whether she has laid her egg cases or not. The mating rites of mantises are well known: a chemical produced in the head of the male insect says, in effect, "No, don't go near her, you fool, she'll eat you alive." At the same time a chemical in his abdomen says, "Yes, by all means, now and forever yes."

While the male is making up what passes for his mind, the female tips the balance in her favor by eating his head. He mounts her. Fabre describes the mating, which sometimes lasts six hours, as follows: "The male, absorbed in the performance of his vital functions, holds the female in a tight embrace. But the wretch has no head; he has no neck; he has hardly a body. The other, with her muzzle turned over her shoulder continues very placidly to gnaw what remains of the gentle swain. And, all the time, that masculine stump, holding on firmly, goes on with the business! . . . I have seen it done with my own eyes and have not yet recovered from my astonishment."

I watched the egg-laying for over an hour. When I returned the next day, the mantis was gone. The white foam had hardened and browned to a dirty suds; then, and on subsequent days, I had trouble pinpointing the case, which was only an inch or so off the ground. I checked on it every week all winter long. In the spring the ants discovered it; every week I saw dozens of ants scrambling over the sides, unable to chew a way in. Later in the spring I climbed the hill every day, hoping to catch the hatch. The leaves of the trees had long since unfolded, the butterflies were out, and the robins' first broods were fledged; still the egg case hung silent and full on the stem. I read that I should wait for June, but still I visited the case every day. One morning at the beginning of June everything was gone. I couldn't find the lower thorn in the clump of three to which the egg case was fixed. I couldn't find the clump of three. Tracks ridged the clay, and I saw the lopped stems: somehow my neighbor had contrived to run a tractor-mower over that steep clay hill on which there grew nothing to mow but a few stubby thorns.

So. Today from this same hill I cut another three undamaged cases and carried them home with the others by their twigs. I also collected a suspiciously light cynthia moth cocoon. My fingers were stiff and red with cold, and my nose ran. I had forgotten the Law of the Wild, which is, "Carry Kleenex." At home I tied the twigs with their egg cases to various sunny bushes and trees in the yard. They're easy to find because I used white string; at any rate, I'm unlikely to mow my own trees. I hope the woodpeckers that come to the feeder don't find them, but I don't see how they'd get a purchase on them if they did.

Night is rising in the valley; the creek has been extinguished for an hour, and now only the naked tips of trees fire tapers into the sky like trails of sparks. The scene that was in the back of my brain all afternoon, obscurely, is beginning to rise from night's lagoon. It really has nothing to do with praying mantises. But this afternoon I threw tiny string lashings and hitches with frozen hands, gingerly, fearing to touch the egg cases even for a minute because I remembered the Polyphemus moth.

I have no intention of inflicting all my childhood memories on anyone. Far less do I want to excoriate my old teachers who, in their bungling, unforgettable way, exposed me to the natural world, a world covered in chitin, where implacable realities hold sway. The Polyphemus moth never made it to the past; it crawls in that crowded, pellucid pool at the lip of the great waterfall. It is as present as this blue desk and brazen lamp, as this blackened window before me in which I can no longer see even the white string that binds the egg case to the hedge, but only my own pale, astonished face.

Once, when I was ten or eleven years old, my friend Judy brought in a Polyphemus moth cocoon. It was January; there were doily snowflakes taped to the schoolroom panes. The teacher kept the cocoon in her desk all morning and brought it out when we were getting restless before recess. In a book we found what the adult moth would look like; it would be beautiful. With a wingspread of up to six inches, the Polyphemus is one of the few huge American silk moths, much larger than, say, a giant or tiger swallowtail butterfly. The moth's enormous wings are velveted in a rich, warm brown, and edged in bands of blue and pink delicate as a watercolor wash. A startling "eyespot," immense, and deep blue melding to an almost translucent yellow, luxuriates in the center of each hind wing. The effect is one of a masculine splendor foreign to the butterflies, a fragility unfurled to strength. The Polyphemus moth in the picture looked like a mighty wraith, a beating essence of the hardwood forest, alien-skinned and brown, with spread, blind eyes. This was the giant moth packed in the faded cocoon. We closed the book and turned to the cocoon. It was an oak leaf sewn into a plump oval bundle; Judy had found it loose in a pile of frozen leaves.

We passed the cocoon around; it was heavy. As we held it in our hands, the creature within warmed and squirmed. We were delighted, and wrapped it tighter in our fists. The pupa began to jerk violently, in heart-stopping knocks. Who's there? I can still feel those thumps, urgent through a muffling of spun silk and leaf, urgent through the swaddling of many years, against the curve of my palm. We kept passing it around. When it came to me again it was hot as a bun; it jumped half out of my hand. The teacher intervened. She put it, still heaving and banging, in the ubiquitous Mason jar.

It was coming. There was no stopping it now, January or not. One end of the cocoon dampened and gradually frayed in a furious battle. The whole cocoon twisted and slapped around in the bottom of the jar. The teacher fades, the classmates fade, I fade: I don't remember anything but that thing's struggle to be a moth or die trying. It emerged at last, a sodden crumple. It was a male; his long antennae were thickly plumed, as wide as his fat abdomen. His body was very thick, over an inch long, and deeply furred. A gray, furlike plush covered his head; a long, tan furlike hair hung from his wide thorax over his brown-furred, segmented abdomen. His multi-jointed legs, pale and powerful, were shaggy as a bear's. He stood still, but he breathed.

He couldn't spread his wings. There was no room. The chemical that coated his wings like varnish, stiffening them permanently, dried, and hardened his wings as they were. He was a monster in a Mason jar. Those huge wings stuck on his back in a torture of random pleats and folds, wrinkled as a dirty tissue, rigid as leather. They made a single nightmare clump still wracked with useless, frantic convulsions.

The next thing I remember, it was recess. The school was in Shadyside, a busy residential part of Pittsburgh. Everyone was playing dodgeball in the fenced playground or racing around the concrete schoolyard by the swings. Next to the playground a long delivery drive sloped downhill to the sidewalk and street. Someone—must have been the teacher—had let the moth out. I was standing in the driveway, alone, stock-still, but shivering. Someone had given the Polyphemus moth his freedom, and he was walking away.

He heaved himself down the asphalt driveway by infinite degrees, unwavering. His hideous crumpled wings lay glued and rucked on his back, perfectly still now, like a collapsed tent. The bell rang twice; I had to go. The moth was receding down the driveway, dragging on. I went; I ran inside. The Polyphemus moth is still crawling down the driveway, crawling down the driveway hunched, crawling down the driveway on six furred feet, forever.

Shading the glass with a hand, I can see how shadow has pooled in the valley. It washes up the sandstone cliffs on Tinker Mountain and obliterates them in a deluge; freshets of shadow leak into the sky. I am exhausted. In Pliny I read about the invention of clay modeling. A Sicyonian potter came to Corinth. There his daughter fell in love with a young man who had to make frequent long journeys away from the city. When he sat with her at home, she used to trace the outline of his shadow that a candle's light cast on the wall. Then, in his absence she worked over the profile, deepening it, so that she might enjoy his face, and remember. One day the father slapped some potter's clay over the gouged plaster; when the clay hardened he removed it, baked it, and "showed it abroad." The story ends here. Did the boy come back? What did the girl think of her father's dragging her lover all over town by the hair? What I really want to know is this: Is the shadow still there? If I went back and found the shadow of that face there on the wall by the fireplace, I'd rip down the house with my hands for that hunk.

The shadow's the thing. Outside shadows are blue, I read, because they are lighted by the blue sky and not the yellow sun. Their blueness bespeaks infinitesimal particles scattered down inestimable distance. Muslims, whose religion bans representational art as idolatrous, don't observe the rule strictly; but they do forbid sculpture, because it casts a shadow. So shadows define the real. If I no longer see shadows as "dark marks," as do the newly sighted, then I see them as making some sort of sense of the light. They give the light distance; they put it in its place. They inform my eyes of my location here, here O Israel, here in the world's flawed sculpture, here in the flickering shade of the nothingness between me and the light.

Now that shadow has dissolved the heavens' blue dome, I can see Andromeda again; I stand pressed to the window, rapt and shrunk in the galaxy's chill glare. "Nostalgia of the Infinite," di Chirico: cast shadows stream across the sunlit courtyard, gouging canyons. There is a sense in which shadows are actually cast, hurled with a power, cast as Ishmael was cast, *out,* with a flinging force. This is the blue strip running through creation, the icy roadside stream on whose banks the mantis mates, in whose unweighed waters the giant water bug sips frogs. Shadow Creek is the blue subterranean stream that chills Carvin's Creek and Tinker Creek; it cuts like ice under the ribs of the mountains, Tinker and Dead Man. Shadow Creek storms through limestone vaults under forests, or surfaces anywhere, damp, on the underside of a leaf. I wring it from rocks; it seeps into my cup. Chasms open at the glance of an eye; the ground parts like a wind-rent cloud over stars. Shadow Creek: on my least walk to the mailbox I may find myself knee-deep in its sucking, frigid pools. I must either wear rubber boots, or dance to keep warm.

II

Fish gotta swim and bird gotta fly; insects, it seems, gotta do one horrible thing after another. I never ask why of a vulture or shark, but I ask why of almost every insect I see. More than one insect—the possibility of fertile reproduction—is an assault on all human value, all hope of a reasonable god. Even that devout Frenchman, J. Henri Fabre, who devoted his entire life to the study of insects, cannot restrain a feeling of unholy revulsion. He describes a bee-eating wasp, the Philanthus, who has killed a honeybee. If the bee is heavy with honey, the wasp squeezes its crop "so as to make her disgorge the delicious syrup, which she drinks by licking the tongue which her unfortunate victim, in her death-agony, sticks out of her mouth at full length. . . . At the moment of some such horrible banquet, I have seen the Wasp, with her prey, seized by the Mantis: the bandit was rifled by another bandit. And here is an awful detail: while the Mantis held her transfixed under the points of the double saw and was already munching her belly, the Wasp continued to lick the honey of her Bee, unable to relinquish the delicious food even amid the terrors of death. Let us hasten to cast a veil over these horrors."

The remarkable thing about the world of insects, however, is precisely that there is no veil cast over these horrors. These are mysteries performed in broad daylight before our very eyes; we can see every detail, and yet they are still mysteries. If, as Heraclitus suggests, god, like an oracle, neither "declares nor hides, but sets forth by signs," then clearly I had better be scrying the signs. The earth devotes an overwhelming proportion of its energy to these buzzings and leaps in the grass, to these brittle gnawings and crawlings about. Theirs is the biggest wedge of the pie: Why? I ought to keep a giant water bug in an aquarium on my dresser, so I can think about it. We have brass candlesticks in our houses now; we ought to display praying mantises in our churches. Why do we turn from the insects in loathing? Our competitors are not only cold-blooded, and green- and yellow-blooded, but are also cased in a clacking horn. They lack the grace to go about as we do, softside-out to the wind and thorns. They have rigid eyes and brains strung down their backs. But they make up the bulk of our comrades-at-life, so I look to them for a glimmer of companionship.

When a grasshopper landed on my study window last summer, I looked at it for a long time. Its hard wing covers were short; its body was a dead waxen yellow, with black-green, indecipherable marks. Like all large insects, it gave me pause, plenty pause, with its hideous horizontal, multi-jointed mouthparts and intricate, mechanical-looking feet, all cups and spikes. I looked at its tapered, chitin-covered abdomen, plated and barred as a tank tread, and was about to turn away when I saw it breathe, puff puff, and I grew sympathetic. Yeah, I said, puff puff, isn't it? It jerked away with a buzz like a rasping file, audible through the pane, and continued to puff in the grass. So puff it is, and that's all there is; though I'm partial to honey myself.

Nature is, above all, profligate. Don't believe them when they tell you how economical and thrifty nature is, whose leaves return to the soil. Wouldn't it be cheaper to leave them on the tree in the first place? This deciduous business alone is a radical scheme, the brainchild of a deranged manic-depressive with limitless capital. Extravagance! Nature will try anything once. This is what the sign of the insects say. No form is too gruesome, no behavior too grotesque. If you're dealing with organic compounds, then let them combine. If it works, if it quickens, set it clacking in the grass; there's always room for one more; you ain't so handsome yourself. This is a spendthrift economy; though nothing is lost, all is spent.

That the insects have adapted is obvious. Their failures to adapt, however, are dazzling. It is hard to believe that nature is partial to such dimwittedness. Howard Ensign Evans tells of dragonflies trying to lay eggs on the shining hoods of cars. Other dragonflies seem to test a surface, to learn if it's really water, by dipping the tips of their abdomens in it. At the Los Angeles La Brea tar pits, they dip their abdomens into the reeking tar and get stuck. If by tremendous effort a dragonfly frees itself, Evans reports, it is apt to repeat the maneuver. Sometimes the tar pits glitter with the dry bodies of dead dragonflies.

J. Henri Fabre's pine processionaries speak to the same point. Although the new studies show that some insects can on occasion strike out into new territory, leaving instinct behind, still a blindered and blinkered enslavement to instinct is the rule, as the pine processionaries show. Pine processionaries are moth caterpillars with shiny black heads, who travel about at night in pine trees along a silken road of their own making. They straddle the road in a tight file, head to rear touching, and each caterpillar adds its thread to the original track first laid by the one who happens to lead the procession. Fabre interferes; he catches them on a daytime exploration approaching a circular track, the rim of a wide palm vase in his greenhouse. When the leader of the insect train completes a full circle, Fabre removes the caterpillars still climbing the vase and brushes away all extraneous silken tracks. Now he has a closed circuit of caterpillars, leaderless, trudging round his vase on a never-ending track. He wants to see how long it will take them to catch on. To his horror, they march not just an hour or so, but all day. When Fabre leaves the greenhouse at night, they are still tracing that wearying circle, although night is the time they usually feed.

In the chill of the next morning they are deadly still; when they rouse themselves, however, they resume what Fabre calls their "imbecility." They slog along all day, head to tail. The next night is bitterly cold; in the morning Fabre finds them slumped on the vase rim in two distinct clumps. When they line up again, they have two leaders, and the leaders in nature often explore to the sides of an already laid track. But the two ranks meet, and the entranced circle winds on. Fabre can't believe his eyes. The creatures have had neither water nor food nor rest; they are shelterless all day and all night long. Again the next night a hard frost numbs the caterpillars, who huddle in heaps. By chance the first one to wake is off the track; it strikes out in a new direction, and encounters the soil in the pot. Six others follow his track. Now the ones on the vase have a leader, because there is a gap in the rim. But they drag on stubbornly around their circle of hell. Soon the seven rebels, unable to eat the palm in the vase, follow their trail back to the rim of the pot and join the doomed march. The circle often breaks as starved or exhausted caterpillars stagger to a halt; but they soon breach the gap they leave, and no leaders emerge.

The next day a heat spell hits. The caterpillars lean far over the rim of the vase, exploring. At last one veers from the track. Followed by four others, it explores down the long side of the vase; there, next to the vase, Fabre has placed some pine needles for them to feed on. They ramble within nine inches of the pine needles, but, incredibly, wander upward to the rim and rejoin the dismal parade. For two more days the processionaries stagger on; at last they try the path laid down the vase by the last group. They venture out to new ground; they straggle at last to their nest. It has been seven days. Fabre himself, "already familiar with the abysmal stupidity of insects as a class whenever the least accident occurs," is nevertheless clearly oppressed by this new confirmation that the caterpillars lack "any gleam of intelligence in their benighted minds." "The caterpillars in distress," he concludes, "starved, shelterless, chilled with cold at night, cling obstinately to the silk ribbon covered hundreds of times, because they lack the rudimentary glimmers of reason which would advise them to abandon it."

I want out of this still air. What street-corner vendor wound the key on the backs of tin soldiers and abandoned them to the sidewalk, and crashings over the curb? Elijah mocked the prophets of Baal, who lay a bullock on a woodpile and begged Baal to consume it: "Cry aloud: for he is a god; either he is talking, or he is pursuing, or he is in a journey, or peradventure he sleepeth, and must be awaked." Cry aloud. It is the fixed that horrifies us, the fixed that assails us with the tremendous force of its mindlessness. The fixed is a Mason jar, and we can't beat it open. The prophets of Baal gashed themselves with knives and lancets, and the wood stayed wood. The fixed is the world without fire—dead flint, dead tinder, and nowhere a spark. It is motion without direction, force without power, the aimless procession of caterpillars round the rim of a vase, and I hate it because at any moment I myself might step to that charmed and glistening thread. Last spring in the flood I saw a brown cattail bob in the high muddy water of Carvin's Creek, up and down, side to side, a jerk a second. I went back the next day and nothing had changed; that empty twitching beat on in an endless, sickening tattoo. What geomancy reads what the windblown sand writes on the desert rock? I read that there all things live by a generous power and dance to a mighty tune; or I read there that all things are scattered and hurled, that our every arabesque and grand jeté is a frantic variation on our one free fall.

Two weeks ago, in the dark of night, I bundled up and quit the house for Tinker Creek. Long before I could actually see the creek, I heard it shooting the sandstone riffles with a chilled rush and splash. It has always been a happy thought to me that the creek runs on all night, new every minute, whether I wish it or know it or care, as a closed book on a shelf continues to whisper to itself its own inexhaustible tale. So many things have been shown me on these banks, so much light has illumined me by reflection here where the water comes down, that I can hardly believe that this grace never flags, that the pouring from ever-renewable sources is endless, impartial, and free. But that night Tinker Creek had vanished, usurped, and Shadow Creek blocked its banks. The nightcold pulsed in my bones. I stood on the frozen grass under the Osage orange. The night was moonless; the mountains loomed over the stars. By half looking away I could barely make out the gray line of foam at the riffles; the skin tightened over the corners of my mouth, and I blinked in the cold. That night the fact of the creek's running on in the dark—from high on the unseen side of Tinker Mountain, miles away—smacked sinister. Where was the old exhilaration? This dumb dead drop over rocks was a hideous parody of real natural life, warm and willful. It was senseless and horrifying; I turned away. The damned thing was flowing because it was *pushed.*

That was two weeks ago; tonight I don't know. Tonight the moon is full, and I wonder. I'm pleased with my day's "work," with the cocoon and egg cases hung on the hedge. Van Gogh found nerve to call this world "a study that didn't come off," but I'm not so sure. Where do I get my standards that I fancy the fixed world of insects doesn't meet? I'm tired of reading; I pick up a book and learn that "pieces of the leech's body can also swim." Take a deep breath, Elijah: light your pile. Van Gogh is utterly dead; the world may be fixed, but it never was broken. And shadow itself may resolve into beauty.

Once, when Tinker Creek had frozen inches thick at a wide part near the bridge, I found a pileated woodpecker in the sky by its giant shadow flapping blue on the white ice below. It flew under the neighborhood children's skates; it soared whole and wholly wild though they sliced its wings. I'd like a chunk of that shadow, a pane of freshwater ice to lug with me everywhere, fluttering huge under my arm, to use as the Eskimos did for a window on the world. Shadow is the blue patch where the light doesn't hit. It is mystery itself, and mystery is the ancients' ultima Thule, the modern explorers' Point of Relative Inaccessibility, that boreal point most distant from all known lands. There the twin oceans of beauty and horror meet. The great glaziers are calving. Ice that sifted to earth as snow in the time of Christ shears from the pack with a roar and crumbles to water. It could be that our instruments have not looked deeply enough. The RNA deep in the mantis's jaw is a beautiful ribbon. Did the crawling Polyphemus have in its watery heart one cell, and in that cell one special molecule, and in that molecule one hydrogen atom, and round that atom's nucleus one wild, distant electron that split showed a forest, swaying?

In lieu of a pinochle game, I'll walk a step before bed. No hesitation about gloves now; I swath myself in wool and down from head to foot, and step into the night.

The air bites my nose like pepper. I walk down the road, leap a ditch, and mount the hill where today I clipped the egg cases, where years ago I watched the female mantis frothing out foam. The rutted clay is frozen tonight in shards; its scarps loom in the slanting light like pressure ridges in ice under aurora. The light from the moon is awesome, full and wan. It's not the lustre of noonday it gives, but the lustre of elf-light, utterly lambent and utterly dreamed. I crash over clumps of brittle, hand-blown grass—and I stop still. The frozen twigs of the huge tulip poplar next to the hill clack in the cold like tinsnips.

I look to the sky. What do I know of deep space with its red giants and white dwarfs? I think of our own solar system, of the five mute moons of Uranus—Ariel, Umbriel, Titania, Oberon, Miranda—spinning in their fixed sleep of thralldom. These our actors, as I foretold you, were all spirits. At last I look to the moon; it hangs fixed and full in the east, enormously scrubbed and simple. Our own hometown ultima moon. It must have been a wonderful sight from there, when the olive continents cracked and spread, and the white ice rolled down and up like a window blind. My eyes feel cold when I blink; this is enough of a walk tonight. I lack the apparatus to feel a warmth that few have felt—but it's there. According to Arthur Koestler, Kepler felt the focused warmth when he was experimenting on something entirely different, using concave mirrors. Kepler wrote, "I was engaged in other experiments with mirrors, without thinking of the warmth; I involuntarily turned around to see whether somebody was breathing on my hand." It was warmth from the moon.

. . . .

QUESTIONS FOR A SECOND READING

1. This essay could be described as one person's efforts to learn to see the natural world around her. As you reread the essay, look for examples to illustrate this process of learning to see. What are the barriers? What are the necessary skills or arts? What are the key lessons? Locate one telling example you could use to address each of these questions.
2. In what way might the final section (the final three paragraphs) be viewed as a conclusion to this essay? And if the final section is a conclusion, what are the main sections that lead up to it and how are they linked?
3. Dillard's book, *Pilgrim at Tinker Creek,* has been variously described as a moving spiritual journey, a guidebook to the natural world of the eastern forests, and a storehouse of clichés and fuzzy thinking. As you reread "The Fixed," what examples might you bring forward to respond to these assertions?

ASSIGNMENTS FOR WRITING

1. This essay could be said to be about one person's efforts to learn to see the natural world. It begins, for example, "I have just learned to see praying mantis egg cases." Write an essay that examines the process of "learning to

see" as it is represented in Dillard's efforts. Work closely from what you see to be the significant examples in the chapter. What is involved in "learning to see?" What are the barriers? What are the key lessons? And why, so far as you are concerned, should anyone bother about such a thing in the first place?

2. Dillard says she went off to Tinker Creek in part to get away from the civilized world and in part to "witness" the world of nature. As you review the evidence in this chapter, what role did school or reading play in the process of witnessing nature? In what way, in other words, are those civilized activities necessary to Dillard's work in the woods? Build your essay from two or, at most, three specific examples from the text. What do her books (or her memories of books) allow her to do that she could not do for herself? And what, then, is the role she plays as a witness? On the basis of Dillard's example, what can you say about the best preparation for a person who wants to be able to see nature?

MAKING CONNECTIONS

1. Thomas Kuhn, in "The Historical Structure of Scientific Discovery" (p. 339), argues that discoveries have a "prehistory," a "posthistory," and an internal structure. Dillard is not a scientist, but one interesting question to ask of "The Fixed" is whether it does or does not record a discovery, something Dillard learned by looking, thinking, and writing about the natural world around her. Write an essay in which you apply Kuhn's terms and method of analysis to Dillard's chapter, treating her work as a systematic process. Discuss, that is, the prehistory and internal structure of her work (and speculate, if you like, about its possible posthistory).
2. Walker Percy, in his essay "The Loss of the Creature" (p. 394), offers several examples of people who have difficulty seeing the things around them: tourists at the Grand Canyon and in Mexico, a Falkland Islander spotting a dogfish on the beach, a student at Sarah Lawrence College. He talks about the various strategies people use to enable them to see what would otherwise remain hidden: looking over the shoulders of others, getting off the beaten track, apprenticing themselves to a master, using a dialectical method to "savor the familiar." Write an essay in which you place Dillard as an example in Percy's scheme. Where would she fit? How might you tell her story, briefly, in Percy's style? What would Percy notice in "The Fixed"? What might he say about the limits and possibilities of her attempts to see nature?

DOROTHY DINNERSTEIN

DOROTHY DINNERSTEIN, in The Mermaid and the Minotaur: Sexual Arrangement and Human Malaise *(1967) argues that members of a culture in which females do the bulk of early child-rearing are virtually doomed to misery. Because of this practice, men and women not only don't understand one another, they can't. Dinnerstein's unique fusion of Freudian psychology and feminist theory has been called "verbose," "repetitive," and "marred" as well as "relentlessly perceptive," "exciting," and "a landmark." The conflicting accounts are not surprising—a book that pushes hard on our standard assumptions about motherhood and family life can hardly be expected to produce indifference. In fact, Dinnerstein said that if her book succeeds in communicating its point, it will threaten and enrage its readers. "Part of why it has taken me so long to finish it is that I am threatened by it myself." If the prose of "Higamous-Hogamous" is sometimes difficult and confusing, Dinnerstein has admitted that this may be taken as an indication of how tough and unsettling a chapter it was for her to write in the first place.*

Dorothy Dinnerstein was born in Manhattan in 1923 and grew up mainly in the Bronx. After attending Brooklyn College, she received a Ph.D. in general psy-

chology in 1951 from the New School for Social Research. She has taught at Rutgers University, Newark, since 1959, most recently in the Institute for Cognitive Studies. Her new book, currently in progress, is called Sentience and Survival *and concerns "why people have trouble thinking about what they have to think about now if the world is to survive."*

Higamous-Hogamous

"Higamous hogamous, woman's monogamous.
Hogamous higamous, man is polygamous."
—FOLK RHYME

A central rule under a strikingly widespread range of conditions is, first, that men act sexually more possessive than women, and second, that women act less free than men to seek "selfish" sexual pleasure.

The reason for this rule can seem deceptively simple. Wherever we look common sense offers us glaringly visible explanations.[1] And the presence

[1]Men, for example, can bully women because, like males of other polygamous mammalian species, they are on the average stronger and heavier, and because the reduced mobility of females during pregnancy and lactation makes male protection advantageous—often essential—if young are to be born and suckled. (Indeed, the obstetrical complications induced by our shift to an upright posture . . . and the especially prolonged helplessness of our infants, have made this even truer for women than for their animal sisters.) The more powerful males in such a species are therefore in a position not only to monopolize the females by driving away competing males but also to enforce female consent to this arrangement: to ride herd, as for example stallions do, on their harems.

The relative scarcity of males is sometimes also seen as an explanation, though it is in fact not at all clear that scarcity itself is a major basis for one-sided erotic prerogative. (Even when the usual numerical asymmetry between the sexes is minor, the erotic one remains major, the important fact being that females are unevenly distributed among the available males. There are circumstances, moreover, in the human case at least, in which it is females who happen to be scarce: When this is so, we do not typically find them enjoying access to harems of jealously guarded males; on the contrary, they are shared—think of whorehouses in boom towns, or the Eskimo wife hospitably offered to the guest—at male initiative and under male guardianship. Still, shaky as it is, the scarcity explanation sounds simple enough to help lull common-sense curiosity about the real underpinnings of the higamous-hogamous rule.)

Overlaid on the obvious conditions that they share with other male animals, men have certain purely human reasons, and purely human means, for enforcing inequality of sexual privilege. These, too, are obvious: Only humans are mentally capable of being pained by the uncertainty of biological paternity, and therefore of trying to reduce this uncertainty by restricting female sex activity. Only humans embody traditions of sexual of these common-sense explanations—the existence of obvious *external* supports for the double-standard rule—makes it easy to overlook the presence of vital, but less obvious, *internal* supports. The rule will not be understood, or centrally changed, until people see that it rests not only on brute force, practical pressure, societal coercion, but also on something subtler and harder to defy: it is supported within each person on that stubborn wordless level of adult feeling which is continuous with infant feeling and with the emotional realm of early childhood.

The "practical" bases for asymmetric human sexual privilege have clearly started to crumble, and if advanced industrial civilization survives they will clearly crumble further.[2] What remains very much intact, however, is its deepest emotional basis: A central psychological asymmetry between the sexes, laid down in the first months, and consolidated in the first years, of life, is built into the primary-group arrangement that Washburn . . . describes as the "fundamental pattern . . . [of human] social organization." This central asymmetry, which drives men to insist on unilateral sexual prerogative and inclines women to consent to their insistence, will endure as a powerful force until the "fundamental pattern" is outgrown—until, that is, the female monopoly of child care is broken.

To see how this complex asymmetry develops and ramifies, one must examine it aspect by aspect. (And the necessity, I must warn the reader, makes a certain amount of repetition inevitable.) Let us look first at the special sexual possessiveness of men; then at the special muting of women's erotic impulsivity; and then at a third tendency which is—in our own culture at least—a close relative of these two: the tendency for sexual excitement to be more tightly tied to personal sentiment in women than in men.

---

coercion in a network of legal, educational, economic, and social practice. Only humans are purposeful enough to be plausibly suspected of having formed a deliberate conspiracy of the (male) strong to keep the (female) weak under control. (In recent feminist literature, Friedan's *The Feminine Mystique* and Millet's *Sexual Politics,* for example, offer vigorous, popular expressions of this suspicion.)

[2] As current technology advances and spreads, size and muscle, for example, have less and less to do with power to bully, and the physical hazards that have made males scarce become increasingly obsolescent. At the same time, less and less female energy needs to be devoted to childbearing. . . . Better birth control, moreover, and readier access to safe abortion will make doubt about biological paternity easier and easier to avoid. Meanwhile this kind of doubt is apt to become more bearable in any case as ties of blood become less and less dominant in determining the structure of enduring groups. In addition, our present legal, educational, and socioeconomic traditions, and our present means for enforcing them, will necessarily be melting down and reforming on a massive scale; one consequence will be that sex coercion will be less and less rigidly embedded in the old network of other societal arrangements that help make it feasible now.

My discussion here, and throughout the following chapters, is in one sense frankly ethnocentric; it is mainly couched, in its literal details, in terms of the nuclear family of contemporary white-middle-class America. *Its central points are meant, however, to be usefully translatable to any human situation in which women preside over life's first stages and men are at the same time present as emotionally significant figures for young children.*

Unilateral Sexual Possessiveness

The human male's tendency to claim one-sided access to a female, and the human female's tendency to consent to this claim, are rooted first of all in infancy, in the differing relationships of boy and girl to the parent[3] who has so far always dominated the beginning of life. On this initial set of differences another set is overlaid in early childhood. These two layers of experience (along with later ones) fuse, to be sure, in the formation of adult emotional proclivities; they are considered separately here only in order to help clarify their nature.

Roots in Infancy

At the outset, for the infant . . . it is in the relation with the mother that all joy is centered, and it is largely through body contact that this joy comes. Other people with a claim on the mother's intimate concern, and especially on her body, are resented competitors for a vital resource. Boy or girl, one wants her for oneself; on the most primitive level of feeling, one remains unreconciled to sharing her: To possess a woman (more precisely, to possess a creature of the kind who later, as our perceptions develop, turns out to belong to the category "woman") is under present conditions every child's early wish. What happens to this wish—which survives throughout life in what used to be called the heart—depends on whether its original object is later reincarnated partially inside, or primarily outside, one's own skin. And this later reincarnation, of course, is inevitably a different matter for the girl than for the boy.

As I pointed out above . . . the pleasure that lures animals into procreative activity has an additional function on the human level: it allows

[3]Or parental figure or figures. . . . Diffusion of the early maternal role among a number of women probably bears on the later intensity of the child's one-to-one emotional ties, and perhaps on the distinctness of personal individuation. What it does not bear on is our basic male-female arrangement. Review of ethnographic data re adult relations between the sexes in societies differing in *degree* of male contact with infants would clearly be helpful. But for the present discussion what matters is that women are in any case normally the *main* early parental figures.

us to relive some of the original life-giving delight of infancy. When the boy, as an adult, finds this delight in heterosexual lovemaking, he finds it outside himself, as before, in a female body. And if the inhabitant of this female body feels free to bestow its resources on a competitor, she is re-voking for him the situation in which mother, unbearably, did not belong to baby.

The girl grows up into a heterosexual situation significantly more complex. She has—at least partially—*become* the mother. She now lives in the female body that was once the vital source of nourishment, entertainment, reassurance. It is true, to be sure, that a man—despite his male physique—can provide for her, as she provides for him, a direct opportunity for reliving the original embrace. There are momentous physical facts to support this emotional opportunity:[4] he is corporeally large, warm, and strong, as the mother was; and his penis, taken into a yearning orifice of the body as the nipple once was taken, can provide a comparably miraculous joy. To the extent that he has this meaning for her, she is vulnerable to something like the simple, direct distress that he feels in the face of sexual competition. And yet their distress is not wholly the same. Hers is apt to be modulated in several ways.

First, despite the man's size, and his penis, the physical differences that are likely to exist between a man and the early mother—in shape and skin texture, in voice quality, gesture, rhythm—are important ones. His bodily presence typically cannot in itself call up the atmosphere of infancy for her in these respects so literally as hers can call it up for him. In the sense and to the extent that this is the case, his physical infidelity cannot revive the grief of infancy for her so graphically as hers can for him: its shock value for her is apt to be less concrete, more purely symbolic.

What may be more important, however, is the fact that even the *symbolic* shock value of the other's physical infidelity is far less absolute for her than for him. The mother-raised woman is likely to feel, more deeply than the mother-raised man, that she carries within herself a source of the magic early parental richness.[5] In this sense—even if not in others—she is more self-sufficient than the mother-raised man: what is inside oneself cannot be directly taken away by a rival.

The tranquillity that goes with this conviction typically rests, of course, on external confirmation of the woman's feeling of inner richness; she re-

---

[4]There are also, of course, momentous symbolic facts to support it. . . .

[5]Boys, too, identify with the first parent to some degree: we all know a few men who are more "motherly" than most women. But on the whole girls can probably do so more readily at the outset, even before they are aware of their own gender, because the mother is aware of it and acts accordingly. And surely it is easier for girls than for boys to maintain this identification later, when gender has become a salient category.

quires evidence that somebody else depends on access to what she has.[6] It is not unusual for her to accept a man's infidelities—even to enjoy them, for reasons discussed below—so long as she is sure he would be desolate to lose possession of her.[7] If this is how she feels, it is only by making him give her up altogether that a rival can shake the foundations of her confidence in herself as a being equipped with an internal supply of what is most basically needed. The fact that this attitude is far less usual in a man stems not just from the pressure of convention. More basically it stems from the mother-raised boy's sense that the original, most primitive source of life will always lie outside himself, that to be sure of reliable access to it he must have exclusive access to a woman.

Roots in Early Childhood

There is another way in which female-dominated childhood tends to make jealousy more complex for women than for men, less continuous with the infant's imperious, monolithic rage at maternal infidelity, less likely to arouse sharp impulses of self-assertion. To understand it, one must consider not only the relation between the preverbal infant and its mother, but also the shape of the small child's situation as it starts to enter a wider world. During this period, formal sex-role education—learning what is expected of a girl and of a boy—is of course going on. The importance of this process is by now well understood; it is a process that deserves, and is currently getting, detailed attention from writers oriented to the project of reorganizing our sexual arrangements. Here, however, we are concerned with a set of emotional facts whose significance is much less widely recognized, facts which have so far been discussed mainly in the conservative psychoanalytic spirit of understanding why things must be the way they are, not in the revolutionary psychoanalytic spirit of thinking out how they can be changed.

Under prevailing conditions the little girl, if she is to develop the early orientation to gender that will later allow her to feel heterosexual passion, must overcome an initial handicap. What is required of her is a central shift

---

[6]"As long as heee needs meee!" sings Nancy of her brutal lover in the musical version of *Oliver Twist*. Imagine a man singing this song!

[7]One of Isaac B. Singer's vivid stories depicts a long happy marriage in which the husband enjoys numerous affairs and the wife—secure in his affections, sure that she is central for him, pleased at his attractiveness to women and his adventurousness—accepts them. After many years, they become persuaded that the arrangement is unfair, and with his encouragement she takes a lover. At once and irrevocably, their deep-lying rapport is broken. Their home becomes a desert: she is devastated by his willingness to share her; he is devastated both by the coldness she now shows toward him and by the unexpectedly withering impact of the lover's presence on his own ardor toward her.

of erotic allegiance: It is to this shift that Freud and his students point, more unanimously than to the shaky theory of penis envy, as a basis for their working assumption that woman's sexual disadvantage is inevitable. (And in fact this assumption would be a wholly reasonable one, if female-dominated childhood were inevitable. There is nothing wrong with the logic behind it. The error is in its tacit initial premise.) The girl's original love, they remind us, was, like the boy's, a woman. Upon this prototypic erotic image, the image of man must be superimposed.

This emotional feat is typically in progress during the two- or three- to five-year-old period that Freud—naming it from the viewpoint of the boy—called Oedipal. During these years, the child's worldly awareness expands dramatically. The father becomes a more distinct figure, and as he does so it becomes clear that there are two sexes, with physical and social differences between them that are crucial for one's own present and future privileges, obligations, and opportunities. It becomes clear also that there exists a special and exclusive relation between the parents, the nature of which has sharp bearing on one's own place in the affections of each.[8]

"Oedipal" Jealousy. The little boy's concern about his own position in the relation with the two parents is apt to be focused mainly on the father's rival claim to the mother: She is the parent with whom the boy has been physically intimate from the outset, and to whom he is likely still to be much more attached, in this way, than to his newly vivid father; and now his growing awareness of bodily and social maleness tells him that she is a member of the sex for whose affections he is destined to compete with other males.

In the girl's case, this jealous concern about one's place with the parents is typically much more deeply two-edged. The father's animal allure is likely to be more powerful for her than it is for the boy. (This may be simply because he acts more seductive with her: he can treat her openly as an attractive little female; he is less free to flirt on an animal-poetic level with his son.[9] It may also be—we do not know—that even in the small

[8]Among us this tight childhood triangle—like the isolated, exclusive mother-infant pair—is more starkly drawn, less modulated by additional relations with other parental people, than is the case in the extended families in which most of the world's children grow up. . . . The emotional possibilities added by the presence of a number of adults, valuable as they are, have no basic bearing upon the species-wide erotic problems that underlie the double standard. Even in our own nuclear families, the stark triangle discussed here is usually complicated by the presence of siblings, again without changing the main lines of male-female stress engendered in female-dominated childhood. I simplify for the sake of brevity.

[9]He is less *free* because of the ban on overt expression of homoerotic attraction (an attraction whose self-evidently prominent place in the hierarchy of attractions that we can feel toward the world's creatures would quite probably, if it were not suppressed,

child some central neural basis for a specific interest in the opposite sex is already operating.) At the same time, the mother is for the girl, as for the boy, the parent around whom bodily-based tender passion was first organized. This means that for her, love of this kind is more evenly directed toward both parents than it is for the boy, and rivalry with the mother for the father's love is more evenly balanced against rivalry with the father for the mother's. The growing insight that this balance is scheduled to tip mainly in the father's direction is on some level wounding. To realize that one is a female, destined to compete with females for the erotic resources of males, is to discover that one is doomed to renounce one's first love.[10]

In the jealous woman, the emotional atmosphere of this childhood discovery is apt to be reactivated: She can feel at the same time pained by the other woman's access to the man and excited by the man's access to the other woman, through which she is offered vicarious reaccess to a female erotic figure. The eruption of this more or less buried early erotic interest can distract or humiliate or baffle her, taking the sharp edge off jealous anger. She may find herself helpless in the throes not only of masochistic satisfaction[11] at being forced to accept the painful presence of a rival but also of bisexual pleasure in simultaneous contact with a man and—vicariously—a woman.[12] (There are, of course, many women in whom no such feelings erupt, and whose jealousy is as fierce as any man's.)[13]

---

make it a lively part of every human life). If such a ban did not exist, he might in any case feel less sharply *interested* in flirting with his son than with his daughter; but so long as it does exist we cannot tell how great or how universal this possible difference in intensity of spontaneous interest might be.

Why this ban exists, and what the prospect of lifting it has to do with the prospect of change in male-female arrangements, is too large a question to be discussed in this book.

[10] More precisely, what the girl is expected to renounce—again because of the ban on overt homoerotic expression—is the passionate body-based component of her first love.

[11] Much of the qualitative difference between female and male masochism must stem not from physical sex differences, and not from the direct training of women to be submissive, but from female-dominated childhood. This (like the implications of what I am saying here for homosexuality) is too large a topic to be dealt with in the present volume. . . .

[12] An overt expression of this emotional possibility is active lovemaking between co-wives in a harem.

[13] The extent to which the sexually loved man himself represents for a woman the early mother, around whom passion and possessiveness are focused, varies enormously from case to case and depends upon a large number of emotional factors. (People, obviously, differ; my account is by necessity schematic and simplified.)

Another important variable is the strength of the woman's own sense of continuity with the early mother. If negative feeling toward her in infancy and just afterward was too strong, for instance, to permit the kind of identification with her that would make the woman feel herself now as a center of the primitive maternal richness, a rival would be less tolerable. Also, such a woman's homoerotic feeling could be as sternly buried as a man's—for different reasons—more typically is, and her jealously might therefore take on the special subterraneously fed rage that a man's sometimes does.

In the jealous man, two-edged feeling of this kind (though it does in fact often occur) is less typical. A certain degree of straightforward animal-poetic attraction toward the same-sex parent is likely to have been part of his, like the girl's, childhood Oedipal dilemma. The likelihood that this factor will later work to take the edge off heterosexual jealousy is less in his case, however, because his attraction to his father is apt to have differed in two crucial ways from the girl's attraction to her mother. One difference—to which I have referred just above from the father's point of view—is that the boy's erotic pull toward his father is apt to have been more ego-alien, less compatible with his own self-image and the expectations of the people around him, than the girl's toward her mother (which had to be accepted as an expression of the young child's still lively physical dependence on parental—a word that under prevailing conditions means maternal—care). Another, related, difference between these two early homoerotic pulls is that the onset of his was later. The father under present conditions tends to be a far less distinct figure than the mother until the child is verbal and mobile, and relatively knowledgeable and rational. The attraction to him is thus inevitably less primitive, more modulated from the beginning by the abstract considerations that language carries. It is an attraction, moreover, far less deeply tied up with sheer survival: bodily contact with him can be exhilarating and playful (he typically carries the child, and tosses it in the air), or threatening (he may administer corporal punishment, or show terrifying anger, or figure in violent sexual fantasies), but it does not ordinarily have to do, as contact with the mother does, with the basic maintenance of life.

What has been said above about the difference between the boy's "Oedipal" jealousy and the girl's, as these bear on one-sided male possessiveness in adult sex life, can be summed up as follows:

First, the young child's ties to its mother are earlier born, more continuous with the passions of helpless preverbal infancy, than those to its father. This means that in the mother-father-child triangle the heteroerotic side of the child's feeling has more primitive weight for the boy than for the girl, while the homoerotic side has more primitive weight for the girl than for the boy. The adult consequence of this difference is that a woman's heterosexual jealously is apt to be more deeply complicated than a man's by homoerotic excitement, her rage more blurred, her impulse to get rid of the intruder less pure.

Second, not only is the homoerotic side of the boy's feeling in this early triangle later born and less primitive than the girl's; it is also more disgraceful. The adult consequence is that even where homoerotic excitement *is* strong enough to complicate a man's heterosexual jealousy, this excitement is likelier to be suppressed, since it is too shameful to be admitted into awareness. Suppressed, erotic feeling toward a rival does not defuse jealous rage as it can when it comes closer to the surface of consciousness. Indeed, it is apt to have the opposite effect: suppressed, its energy can feed into the rage, making the latter even more primitive and self-righteous.

But the boy's relation to the parents contrasts with the girl's in a way that goes far beyond these intimate strains within the original threesome.

The "Oedipal" Dilemma and the Wider Human Realm. It is true that both son and daughter in these early years feel—and handle somewhat differently for the reasons discussed above—the pull between an old love and the possibility of adding a new one. A momentous additional difference between his case and hers, however, lies in the human-social nature of this new possibility, its implications for one's future place in the world beyond the parent-child triangle.

In the son's case, what is apt to be salient is that resentment of the father's claims upon the mother threatens to interfere with a crucial opportunity that is now opening before him: attachment to his newly interesting and powerful male parent represents solidarity with his own sex, a solidarity upon which much of his thrust toward worldly competence is starting to depend. His main task is to find a balance between two contrasting varieties of love, one that provides primitive emotional sustenance, and another that promises—if rivalry over the first can be handled—to offer membership in the wider community where prowess is displayed, enterprise planned, public event organized. His old tie to his mother starts at this point to be felt as an obstacle to new and more grown-up ties with his own sex. These are the ties upon which—in the world he is beginning to know, the world as it now is—the opportunity will rest to exercise some of his most important human capacities.

This new difficulty in the boy's relations with his mother is now likely to coalesce with certain longer-standing grievances, rooted in the inevitable frustrations of infancy, that had been part of his feeling for her from the beginning. . . . Together, these older and newer difficulties help form the basis for the eventual adult feeling that love for women must be kept in its place, not allowed to interfere with the vital ties between men.[14]

[14] Males in some other primate species also show a tendency toward the formation of strong all-male groups. This observation can tempt the observer to conclude (see, for example, Tiger's *Men in Groups*) that the segregation of women, their exclusion from public enterprise, the need of men to find sanctuary from them in each other's company, are somehow "built into" our gene composition; that these are tendencies handed down from our ancestors and for practical purposes permanent, since they are outgrowable (if at all) only through processes of physical evolution too slow and gradual to make any difference for contemporary life.

Yielding to this intellectual temptation means overlooking the distinctively human

Ideally, the little boy manages to find some provisional balance between the old, jealous, aggrieved erotic tug toward the mother and the new feeling of friendship with the father. Later on, he will have an opportunity to resolve this conflict more decisively. He will discover that authority over a woman or women is a mark of status, respected by men. This discovery will help him reconcile what were once competing wishes: the wish for secure access to certain essential emotional resources, which in his experience reside in females, and the wish to take part in certain essential human activities, which in the world he now enters are defined as male.[15]

What is reflected in man's unilateral possessiveness, then, is not only the original, monolithic infant wish for ownership of a woman but also a second, more equivocal feeling, rooted in early boyhood: that attachment to a woman is emotionally bearable, consistent with the solidarity among men which is part of maleness, only if she, and one's feelings toward her, remain under safe control.

For the girl, this aspect of the "Oedipal" conflict takes a different form and its resolution is likely to have the opposite outcome. To her, too, the father is an interesting, powerful figure through whom one reaches out toward the wider world. But he does not normally invite her, as he invites the boy, to follow him out into this fascinating world, and take on its challenges in recompense for the impossibility of owning the mother. Instead he offers the more direct recompense of a second erotic tie, excitingly, but no so sharply as in the boy's case, different from the first one. This second love at its outset valuably supplements the first (for the daughter, like the son, needs another relation to help her achieve perspective on the relation

---

psychological content of the human male impulse toward what ethologists call "bonding"; it means cherishing one's ignorance of the ways in which this impulse is shaped by tensions peculiar to the now mutable structure of family life in our own species—a species whose *continuity* with its animal relatives is savagely misinterpretable when looked at outside the framework of its *discontinuity* with these relatives.

(Yielding to this temptation also means, by the way, sidestepping the interesting question of just how *non*human forms of male "bonding" actually develop. Like all conclusions based on the concept of instinct—or on some more recent, equally opaque, new version of that concept—this one crushes, under the weight of a big impenetrable abstraction, the scientist's healthy impulse to ask questions about how, in detail, a particular form of behavior comes into being under the particular conditions in which it is observed.)

[15]It will occur to some readers at this point that these essential activities need not in fact be defined as male, and that if the public domain were open to mothers as well as to fathers one part, at least, of the situation I outline here might be deeply modified even if women did continue to dominate early child care. This mitigation of our trouble could come about, however, only if it were emotionally possible for mother-raised women and mother-raised men to take part freely and equally together in what are now male affairs. And unhappily, . . . this is just what mother-raised men and women cannot do.

with the mother). And in the girl's situation, the new love for man—unlike the boy's new love for man—is expected gradually to supplant the original love for woman. Her jealousy of the parents, as I said earlier, is more two-edged than the boy's; and at the same time, neither parent is likely to contest her erotic claim on the other as directly as the father contests the boy's claim on the mother.[16] All in all, then, she is under less urgent pressure than the boy is to find some clear-cut way of reconciling the second love with the first.

It will nevertheless turn out to be true in her case, as in the boy's, that ties to the opposite sex and solidarity with one's own sex will pull in opposite directions. But the nature of this pull—as she feels it in childhood, and as she acts on it later—is different for her than for him. For her the deepest obstacles to solidarity with one's own sex first appear not in the mother-father-baby triangle, where the boy first meets them, but in the deep ambivalence of the earlier mother-baby pair. Once the triangle forms, both the "truly masculine" boy and the "truly feminine" girl use its existence to help handle the formidable tensions inherent in the original pair. But they do so in contrasting ways; and the outcome is that women are on the whole far less able than men to balance dependence on each other against dependence on the opposite sex.[17]

When the father first emerges to offer the girl a tie that can supplement (and in part substitute for) the tie to the mother, he makes available to her

---

[16]The father, of course, sees his daughter as a much less threatening rival than his son. And the mother, for all the reasons under discussion here, is apt to show less heterosexual possessiveness than her husband does.

Indeed, in the triangle with her husband and daughter, the mother may well resent the man for his attractiveness to the little girl—who was once hers in the way she originally wanted her mother to be hers—more than she resents the little girl for her attractiveness to the man.

Recall the scene, in Bergman's film *The Virgin Spring,* in which a father and a mother try to understand the converging forces of evil responsible for their daughter's death. The mother confesses the hatred she felt toward her husband when she saw her daughter's love withdrawn from herself and turned to him. When a son goes off with his father, his mother's regret is more bearable; the father cannot replace her in a son's feelings as he can in a daughter's.

[17]The importance of achieving this kind of balance depends on how rigidly society is organized around gender distinctions. So far, these distinctions have been a structurally basic feature of social life. When they are not, the balance will cease to be a problem. But right now—when women need solidarity in groups that go beyond intimate family ties, to work on broad human projects that turn out to be mainly in their hands—it is a serious problem. To get beyond where we are right now we will have to surmount it. And to do so we will have to use the capacities for personal growth inherent in our traditionally mother-reared personalities. The liberation of those capacities depends, I think, on insight into *why* mother-reared people have the problems that they have.

a new way of handling—a way, that is, of sidestepping the task of resolving—the ambivalence at the heart of the infant-mother tie. What he offers is a fatefully tempting (pseudo) solution[18] to this central dilemma: positive feelings toward the mother are normally split off from negative ones in early life in order to preserve the possibility of feeling, at least sometimes, a sense of unqualified oneness with this central source of all that is good. What the girl can now do is transfer to the father—who starts out with a clean slate, so to speak, innocent of association with the inevitable griefs of infancy—much of the weight of these positive feelings, while leaving the negative ones mainly attached to their original object. She thus gains a less equivocal focus for her feelings of pure love, and feels freer to experience her grievances against her mother without fear of being cut off altogether from the ideal of wholehearted harmony with a magic, animally loved, parental being.[19]

This opportunity comes at a particularly timely point in her development since a new grievance against the mother is just adding itself to those already stored up: just as the boy, during this period, is learning that outside the family an arena exists in which he can exercise some central human capacities, the girl (who possesses these same capacities, and is too young to have been persuaded that she does not) also learns of this arena and begins at about the same time to grasp the strange fact that she is unwelcome to enter it. This misfortune she is apt to blame on her omnipotent mother, who has so far been responsible for every misfortune—as well as every delight—in her young life.[20] The father, if she is to become a "truly feminine" woman who contents herself with motherhood and the maintenance of family life, is typically absolved of blame for her exclusion from this vital extrafamilial arena. Indeed, he is all the more glamorous and newly needed because he provides the only access to it—vicarious

[18]This "solution" is not available to the boy, unless he takes a predominantly homoerotic stance. If he does so, however, he encounters other special complications: "escape" from unresolved ambivalence toward woman into romantic passion for man is an even less auspicious step for him than for the girl.

[19]She does not, of course, always use this opportunity. Other "solutions" are available: she can, for example, overidealize the mother, and/or project onto the father (with disruptive consequences for her later relations with men) most, or some, of the negative feelings. But I am focusing here on processes that lead to the traditional symbiotic emotional equilibrium that is thought of as heterosexual "adjustment."

[20]This is the core of truth in the Freudian statement that the girl blames her lack of a penis on the mother. All that is missing from the Freudian formulation is the insight that the value of the penis lies mainly not in its charm as a water toy, or in its magic erectile properties (of which the small girl, in our culture at least, is often ignorant), but rather in the social prerogatives it confers. (But this is a point that de Beauvoir has made so well that it surely needs no further belaboring.)

access[21]—that she can expect to have. He is glamorous also because the special compensation that she will be offered for keeping the home fires burning and forgoing the rewards of effort in the wide world—the compensation that lies in a certain kind of erotic attention, in exemption from certain risky challenges, in safety from certain possible humiliations[22]—is foreshadowed in the special homage that he has begun to express toward her as a little female: The deprivation for which she feels her mother is to blame is repaired, so far as it can be, by the father.

Early rage at the first parent, in other words, is typically used by the "masculine" boy during the Oedipal period to *consolidate* his tie with his own sex by establishing a principled independence, a more or less derogatory distance, from women. And it is typically used by the "feminine" girl in this same period to *loosen* her tie with her own sex by establishing a worshipful, dependent stance toward men. Just when that boy is learning to keep his feelings for the mother under control, that girl (precisely because her first emotional problems also centered on the mother) is learning to overidealize the father. This contrast, of course, heavily supports asymmetry of sexual privilege. For without comparably strong, well-defined ways of counterbalancing feelings for the opposite sex with a sense of human identity based on solidarity with each other, women are far less free than men to set their own terms in love.

The Nature of the Rule

In sum, then: Unilateral male sexual possessiveness rests on strong old feelings, both in men and in women. And so long as the care of the very young remains in female hands these feelings—in which echoes of infancy and of early childhood are fused—will persist.

---

[21] It is in fact a peculiarly privileged and societally significant vicarious access that he offers, an access upon which the stability of our present arrangements heavily rests. . . .

[22] There is another compensation which the reader might well expect to see included in this list of the future benefits foreshadowed in her relation with her father: the major prospect (heavily emphasized by psychoanalytic writers, and persuasively documented by cross-cultural observations such as those that Mead provides in *Male and Female*) of becoming herself a mother—the bodily creator, and all-providing possessor, of a magically delicious baby of her own.

I believe, however, that this is a murkier and more equivocal prospect than is generally acknowledged: the cherished-mistress facet of woman's status, implicit in the father's courtly homage, has less dirt and dislike in it than the maternal facet does. Also, the compensatory sense of future motherhood, insofar as it *is* positive, draws her closer to the mother as well as to the father (women are largely rivals in courtship, largely allies in childbearing and maternal concerns), and is therefore a neutral factor in her shift of positive feelings from the first parent toward the second.

But before turning to the next part of the higamous-hogamous rule, let me emphasize again the dual sense in which unilateral male possessiveness is in fact a "rule." What I have been offering is a *description* of psychological forces, rooted in mother-dominated childhood, which are widespread enough to make it possible for society to enforce a *prescription* about male and female adult behavior. When I say, for example, that a certain emotional situation, or frame of mind, "as a rule" characterizes father-emulating little boys, or jealous women, I am describing a tendency, a probability: there are many little boys, and many jealous women, whose experiences are quite different from the ones I describe. And it is very lucky that this is so, for if the tensions inherent in the "normal" human situation led uniformly to the same outcome for everyone we would have little hope of outgrowing what is maiming in our sexual arrangements. (See Box 1.) As a code of conventionally accepted comportment, on the other hand, the double standard of sexual possessiveness is a "rule" that, whether obeyed or defied, exerts some real coercive force on *every* person. (See Box 2.) To survive as this kind of rule, it need not have powerful emotional roots in all of us: just in most of us.

Box 1

My business here is to sketch out some broad generalizations about differences between men and women who have started out life under mainly female care, rather than to dwell on the many striking exceptions to these generalizations which quite obviously also exist. This is not, of course, because these exceptions seem to me negligible: their significance is clearly enough vital. It is because this significance cannot be appreciated until the diseased norm from which they deviate has been examined at its roots. In choosing this procedure, which relies on the reader's intellectual patience and good will, I knowingly run the risk that some feminists will accuse me, as they go along, of reinforcing socially oppressive sexual stereotypes; and that some antifeminists will feel free to misuse what I say to support their views. This risk is unavoidable. But it seems sensible to try to reduce misunderstanding at least a little by saying something at this point (now that the reader has an idea of what I am up to) about stereotyping in the perception of human group differences.

All group differences (even differences between nonhuman groups, like plants vs. animals, or edible vs. nonedible substances) tend to be oversimplified, absolutized, in everyday thought; irregularities, ambiguities, are smoothed over to save mental effort; our view of them is governed by principles of mental economy as inexorable as those that govern visual form perception, or the process of memorizing names and telephone numbers, or the learning of useful habits. Furthermore, in everyday thought about especially complex and emotionally charged situations, oversimplified generalizations are apt to be actively treasured, and exceptions to them purposefully underplayed.

This tendency can be so destructive socially that people who have seen some of its ugly consequences—for example, in the formation of racial and ethnic stereotypes—often angrily oppose the formulation of any group concepts whatsoever. But the fact is that we cannot orient ourselves to social reality without forming hosts of such concepts. They are indispensable;* the best we can do is to pay strenuously disciplined attention to their limitations. An important expression of such discipline is to keep in mind the presence and the meaning of exceptions to group generalizations.

This keeping in mind is especially relevant, and for most people especially difficult, in the case of generalizations about psychological sex differences. Men and women are not simply two separate groups (like Swedes and Italians, for instance) who happen to have differing distributions of certain traits, distributions which overlap so that some of each are apt to be damaged by social categorizations† which ignore the overlap. Men and women are on the contrary interlocked, symbiotically interdependent, groups; and many members of each, under prevailing conditions, keep pushing hard against the crippling constraints that membership forces upon all members of both. This makes instances of nonconformity to psychological generalizations about men and women peculiarly meaningful. Yet their very meaningfulness, the explosive societal significance of the fact that many people do not fit at all well into their assigned boxes, makes the people who do manage on the whole to stay in such boxes peculiarly unwilling to

*Think—to choose two minor examples—of a woman driver who feels safer picking up hitchhiking adolescents if they are girls rather than boys; or of a black driver who anticipates a pleasanter social encounter if he stops a black rather than a white passerby for local directions. Both drivers may be guessing wrong in a particular case, but neither is foolish: adolescent boys *do* commit more crimes than adolescent girls; whites *are* likelier than blacks to act tense or rude when approached by a black.

†Such as, for example, ethnic rules of thumb used by potential employers who might pigeonhole Italians into jobs requiring personal outgoingness and Swedes into jobs requiring polished attention to technical detail.

think about these nonconforming instances in a careful way. A human being who violates "rules of gender" is violating rules—prescriptive and descriptive—to which most others conform at real inner cost, and around which defensive fear and anger are therefore bound to be mobilized. Defensive fear and anger discourage strenuous intellectual activity.

What I hope readers will do, then, is try—despite the variety of emotional sore spots which a discussion like this one bumps into, and which make such an effort difficult—to keep in mind a fact upon which it would be dreary for me to keep dwelling as I go along: it is precisely the existence of many lively exceptions to the generalizations sketched out here (and of the deep human stresses around gender reflected in these exceptions) that makes it necessary and possible to solve the problem around which the sketch is centered. . . .

Also: if keeping the exceptions to my sketch in mind makes the sketch itself seem intolerably rough, I hope readers will ask themselves whether what really distresses them is the roughness of the sketch or (at least in part) the painfulness of the situation to which it points.

Box 2

There is a fact that can seem at first glance to belie the general statement about unilateral possessiveness made in this chapter: the fact that there are certain situations, both in our own and in other societies, in which the amicable sharing of women by mother-raised men is a well-established custom. But a closer look at such situations—at least as we meet them in our own cultural mainstream, where we do not need anthropologists to interpret them for us—makes it clear that their emotional atmosphere is wholly compatible with what this chapter describes as the underlying basis for the double sexual standard.

Among us, some women—probably the majority of those who are heterosexually active—are jealously owned by individual men.* And other women—a smaller number—are public property, available on

*Usually one per man, sometimes two. I suppose relatively few ordinary Americans manage to keep sole access to a wife and more than one mistress; if there are statistics, I have not seen them.

an auxiliary basis to men who also own private women (or could if they wanted to, or will when they are older). Gang bangs and fraternal excursions to whorehouses are traditions that express the emotional flavor of relations with these public women: they are shared not merely amicably but as a group affirmation of common maleness. There is of course no correspondingly recognized population of public men.†

The shared woman and the shared man are as a rule in directly contrasting situations. He can usually command fidelity from at least one of the women who share him, and his relation to her carries an element of triumphant vengeance against the early mother, who was unfaithful to her baby with the father and/or siblings while he depended for everything on her. (She shares him, as a rule, unwillingly; she may not know it, or she may be resigned to it; in any case it is not she, but he, who has decided that he must be shared.) The shared woman, on the other hand, usually has no claim on any man's fidelity. She is the captive and derogated mother, the dethroned tyrant, the defiled goddess, communally possessed in a spirit of ritual counterassertion against the sexual rivalries that weaken male solidarity. (Think, for instance, of the bizarre emotional familiarity one feels with the atmosphere of male sharing which pervades that disquieting fable *The Story of O.*) She is the mother whose son, putting away everyday childish feelings, ceremoniously abjures his wish to have her for himself in order to cement societally vital bonds with his brothers and father.

Both woman-sharing and man-sharing situations, in other words, are apt under the prevailing conditions to embody male rage at the early mother and female consent that she should be punished or dethroned. In submitting to *either* situation, the woman participates vi-

---

†Odd women here and there do make use of male whores, but this is a fringe phenomenon. It is not proverbially accepted as an expression of the client's irrepressible, girls-will-be-girls, forgivably naughty sexual high spirits; neither is it a traditional group escapade. It can also happen that women will mention a man to each other, with a certain glee, as a skillful and/or easily available sexual floater. This shows, to be sure, that a reversal of the usual pattern is not at all impossible; but what is interesting about it is that it happens so rarely.

The "private" woman who has outside affairs is somewhat less unusual; still, she is significantly rarer in our mainstream than the errant husband, and subject to much more extreme penalties if found out. And she is far less likely than the errant husband either to capture a private concubine or to take up with an amicably shared man (a whore or an "easy lay" whose name is passed around by her cronies).

cariously in the act of humiliating the mother, against whom she also has a grudge: she lends her person to this enterprise. And at the same time, since the humiliated mother is also herself, she has a chance to relive directly the situation of humiliated child, this time of her own accord.

I would be astonished if something of this atmosphere did not surround the sacred prostitute priestess, or the Eskimo wife whose husband hospitably shares her with his guests. (This is, needless to say, a hunch: its verification would be an anthropologist's task.) The ingredients of defilement and humiliation may be peculiar to our own puritanical, sado-masochistic culture. But it is hard to see how the purposeful sharing of woman by mother-raised men could fail to carry some flavor of ritual conquest over a deep-seated reluctance in the service of a higher purpose.

Woman-sharing ceremonies have another function too: They permit male homoerotic impulse some expression in a safe context of triumphant, harsh masculinity.‡ The cuckold is threatened by uncontrolable, uninvited, ego-alien upsurges of sexual feelings for the man with whom his wife has thrown him into vicarious contact. The participant in a gang bang voluntarily invokes this inner demon, releasing it into an arena fenced around with dramatic assertions of his intact initiative and his fearsome heterosexual prowess. And the gang bang, of course, is of interest here not as an aberration peculiar to juvenile delinquents and demoralized soldiers, but as the extreme expression of a male tendency that is quite normal in our culture: Ritualized verbal gang banging is so staple an ingredient of ordinary respectable man-to-man conversation that any objection to it is taken as a tasteless assault on an inoffensive form of pleasantry.

‡This they have in common with initiation ceremonies in which young males submit to the manhandling of older ones as the price of admission to the adult community. Indeed, initiation ceremonies and woman-sharing ceremonies have several functions in common.

The same is true for the rule—to which I now turn—that female erotic impulse must be curbed: It is a societal prescription, fed psychologically by an amalgam of very early and slightly later experience in enough mother-dominated childhoods to make it generally enforceable.

The Muting of Female Erotic Impulsivity

Roots in Infancy

Suppression of female sexual impulse has an obvious practical congruence with one-sided male possessiveness: a woman with a strong sexual will of her own may defy a man's wish to keep her for himself. But on the more covert emotional level that we are considering here, there is not only this practical, realistic concern; there is also a different, nonrational kind of fear, a deep fantasy-ridden resentment, directed against her impulsivity itself. Her own bodily pleasure in sex, independent of the pleasure she gives her partner, is the essential threatening fact. It is threatening, first of all, because it resonates with the distress of a very early discovery, a distress that antedates jealousy since it is felt while the infant is still too young to notice the existence of competitors for the mother's resources. This discovery is simply that the infant does not own or control the mother's body: because this body has needs and impulses of its own, its responsiveness to the infant's needs is never totally reliable. (A mother's milk, for example, may sometimes flow faster or slower than is comfortable for the infant. She may be sleepy, distracted, or sluggish when it wants to play; she may alarm it or disturb its peace with over-avid caresses.) The very same spontaneous, impulsive, autonomous erotic spirit in the first parent which—as the baby will later find out—allows her to turn at will to others makes her from the outset imperfectly subject to its desire even when they are alone.

The significance of this awareness on the infant's part goes far beyond the purely sexual matters now under discussion. Some broader consequences of the trouble we have in coming to terms with the early mother's inconveniently human autonomy are explored in Chapter 6.° And much of the rest of this book has to do with the trouble we have in handling the more general problem of which this autonomy of hers is just one manifestation: As Freud pointed out, the fact that human infants receive such nearly perfect care seduces them into fantasies which are inevitably crushed, fantasies of a world that automatically obeys, even anticipates, their wishes. The loss of this infant illusion of omnipotence—the discovery that circumstance is incompletely controllable, and that there exist centers of subjectivity, of desire and will, opposed or indifferent to one's own—is an original and basic human grief.

All of us, male and female, feel this grief. To some degree, it is irreparable. We manage in part to console ourselves for it indirectly, through

---

Chapter 6 Titled "Sometimes You Wonder If They're Human," examines why men would be inclined to say such a thing about women.

mastery, competence, enterprise: the new joy of successful activity is some compensation for the old joy of passive, effortless wish-fulfillment. This indirect way of handling the grief is central to the pathology of civilized life, a pathology to which our male-female arrangements contribute in a way that will be discussed in Chapters 7, 8, and 9.° At the same time, for the sexual situation with which we are concerned here, the important fact is that we also attempt to undo the grief *directly*. Indefatigably, we go on trying to recover what has been lost: We try it first-hand by seeking out situations in which we can reexperience personally, at least for a moment, the infant sense of omnipotence. And we try it second-hand by acting as nurturers, pleasure-givers, empathic wish-granters, by recreating the mother-infant atmosphere so as to relive vicariously some part of the lost delight.

In lovemaking, both man and woman make this direct attempt to repair the old loss. Each of them does so both first-hand, by taking bodily pleasure, and vicariously, by providing pleasure for the other person. But the balance tends not to be symmetrical. She is the one whose physique more closely resembles the physique of the first parent, and who is likely to have incorporated this parent's attitudes more deeply; he is therefore apt to be the one who can more literally relive the infant experience of fulfilling primitive wishes through unqualified access to another body. For her, the vicarious version of this reliving—providing the body through which the other's wishes are perfectly granted—is likely to be a more prominent feature of the interplay. If this symbiotic arrangement is to succeed, the woman's own sexual impulsivity must not be freely unleashed. Unleashed, it can disrupt the recreated harmony; it can revive—in a first-hand way for him and vicariously for her—the first intimations of isolated, nonomnipotent selfhood; it can reactivate in both of them the malaise that originated in the nursling's discovery of the mother's separate, uncontrollable subjective existence.[23]

Chapters 7, 8, and 9 Examine the roles men and women play (and are imagined to play) in the social world.

[23]There are also other, more specific, ways in which mother-dominated infancy makes for the stifling of female spontaneity in adult sex. Psychoanalytic workers infer, for example, that nurslings sometimes frighten themselves with fantasies about devouring their mothers. Having entertained this fantasy, the young cannibal is prey to a number of natural fears. One of these fears is that the mother is destroyed, or too damaged to take care of her baby. . . .

More relevant for sex, however, is the fear that the mother has corresponding intentions to eat her baby. A genitally demanding woman reactivates this fear. (A genitally demanding man who "uses her up" could also, in principle, reactivate it in a woman. But his body dissimilarity to the mother, and the fact that he is trying to push himself into the other person rather than suck the other person into himself, make the fear less literal for her. In any case, what matters is that man's fear can make coitus impossible, so woman is careful to avoid evoking it. Her fear merely results in frigidity, which need

The arrangement, of course, is an unstable one. Vicarious bliss has some advantages over direct bliss (imagination fills in gaps, glosses over blemishes), but no vigorous person willingly makes do with it as his or her whole portion. The infant in every adult wants pleasure unlimited and uninterrupted by the ebb and flow of another creature's impulses. On some level woman, like man, resents the other person's uncontrollable erotic rhythm. This resentment is softened in the mother-reared woman by her greater emotional access to vicarious delight. On the other hand, it is sharpened by the crucial physical fact that in coitus she is far more dependent on the man's erection than he is on her vaginal responsiveness. Men have doubtless always sensed the explosive potentialities of this fact: it feeds into their archetypal nightmare vision of the insatiable female, and deepens their feeling that the unleashing of woman's own erotic impulses would disturb the precarious heterosexual peace.

The independent sexual impulsivity of the female, then, is feared because it recalls the terrifying erotic independence of every baby's mother. To soothe the fear, we subordinate Eve's lust to Adam's, but this cure only makes the sickness worse: subordinated, Eve's lust is more frightening still.

Woman's sexuality is under doubly explosive pressure. Her physical situation in coitus, as compared with man's, has in it much more of the infant's dependence on an imperfectly reliable source of fulfillment. Yet it is she who must make reparation to him for what both endured as babies. Coital satiety (to be fucked as the baby would like to be fed: on demand and at the rate one chooses and as long as one wants) is for anatomic reasons a chancier[24] matter for her than for him; and in addition she is for social and emotional reasons less free to seek it out. Inevitably, like any other suppressed force, her sex impulses come to seem boundless, ominous. And inevitably, this makes it more urgent to suppress them.

---

not worry him unduly since it does not preclude coitus, or even conception; indeed, frigidity on her part can help to assuage anxiety on his.)

A related impulse—often acted upon by the nursling who has acquired teeth—is to hurt the mother by biting her. The archetypal "vagina dentata" myth (see Hays) embodies the sensible anxiety that she will bite back. Such anxiety, of course, is much less readily evoked by a quiet, passive woman than by an actively lustful one.

One thing women sense—or learn—is that they must avoid behavior which stirs up alarms of this kind in men.

[24]This chanciness in itself could tempt her to settle for the vicarious (mama) role in the you-be-mama-I'll-be-baby game instead of risking disappointment in pursuit of the direct (baby) one: combined with this temptation, the social and emotional pressures to accept the vicarious role are usually irresistible.

Roots in Early Childhood

The feelings discussed in the preceding section are primarily male feelings. Women share them only vicariously. But there are factors working to mute female lust that stem from a peculiarly female emotional situation. This situation takes shape not in infancy but in very early girlhood.

To repeat what I pointed out above in connection with sexual possessiveness, the mother-father-child triangle that Freud has called Oedipal is apt to arouse much more symmetrically balanced feelings in the girl than in the boy: since the homoerotic side of this triangle is older and more openly acceptable in her case than in his, she is not so purely the rival of the mother as the boy is the rival of the father. (Not only is her own jealousy more ambiguous than the boy's; her same-sex rival is herself more mildly, ambiguously jealous than the boy's is. The mother, to be sure, is an earlier, less rational authority, and in that sense a more formidable competitor than the father; still, competition with her is less apt to feel acutely risky since she is likely to feel less resentful than the father of the claims her child makes on her spouse.)

What is salient for the girl at this stage is not so much rivalry as another, more primitive problem: the realization that she must now, in some basic way, start to renounce, let go of, her first, life-giving love. To yield wholeheartedly to the charm of the opposite sex, she—unlike the boy—must shift a large portion of her early animal-poetic passion away from the parent to whom it was at first exclusively attached. The boy faces a clear crisis of nerve. She must handle a more diffuse, pervasive guilt, a vague sense of disloyalty, an ancient, primal fear of loss.

The sacrifice of sexual spontaneity, the curbing of sexual willfulness, that men will require of her in adult life can serve her own purposes, too, then: It can serve as a penance for this pervasive guilt. In turning toward man, but forgoing the vigorous pursuit of "selfish" body pleasure with him, she can achieve some of the heterosexual rapport that her love for her father taught her to want, and at the same time allay this primal fear of loss.

Woman's need for penance and her sense of primal loss are complicated, moreover, by the other large fact about the girl's Oedipal situation that was discussed above: the fact that the infidelity to her first love that began in this period typically went far deeper than her shift toward the second actually required. The sacrifice of full bodily pleasure with man, which I have heard described as "the gift to the mother,"[25] atones for something more than the partial desertion of her that the girl's growth toward heteroerotic susceptibility would in itself inevitably entail. What

[25] Annette Overby, personal communication.

the girl has been guilty of is lavishing upon her father—that is, upon man—not only the erotic recognition, and the warmth and trust, that he on his own could inspire in her, but also much of the physical affection and filial-romantic gratitude that would have remained attached to her mother—that is, to woman—if they had been integrated with the child's inevitable antagonisms toward her. What she has done is to give away to someone else love that a part of her knew belonged rightly to the mother, in order to spare herself an emotional effort that seemed—but was not really—unnecessary.[26] The result is that she has cut herself off from a continuity with her own early feeling, for which she now mourns. It is in part to propitiate her fantasy mother, to punish herself, and thereby to regain some of this inner continuity that she holds back the final force of her "selfish" carnal passion for man. She holds it back out of love for him too, out of unwillingness to alarm him and pleasure in acceding to his wishes; but also out of anger at herself and at him: anger at a gratuitous betrayal of her oldest root in life, a betrayal for which she was responsible but of which he (in the form of his original parental predecessor) was the instrument.

But feelings of guilt and loss connected with her first love are not the only preoccupations that work to take the edge off woman's sensual passion for man. She tends also to feel more preoccupied than he does, while they are making love, with the opportunity to achieve vicarious homoerotic contact, and in this way to steal back some of what life has taken away from her: she is apt to be busier than he is imagining herself in the other person's situation, more engrossed in the other person's access to her own body and thus less engrossed in her own access to the other person's body.[27] And in the meantime this holding back, this abstention from full use of the male body as a source of direct pleasure for herself, can also express another, related, feeling: a grudge against the male, her rival for her first, female, parent. The grudge is not normally strong enough to make him unattractive to her. But she can reconcile resentment and attraction by embracing him and at the same time vengefully using the embrace for an ulterior purpose: to get access to the mother again after all.

The mother-raised woman, then, submits to the mother-raised man's demand that she mute her own adult lust; and in submitting she consoles herself by betraying him and going back to her first, infant, love. She avenges herself on him by making him her instrument of re-access to what she has renounced. But it is a weak consolation and a poor revenge. For her re-access is only second-hand, and her old feelings of guilt and loss only

[26] Recognition of this fact is an important step toward solidarity among women (as well as toward freer, less grudging female enjoyment of male charms).

[27] There are other forces, too, that converge to push her into this vicarious position, that work to make her use herself as a mirror for other people's experience. . . .

feebly assuaged. What she is giving up is the right to use her body's sensuous capacities as directly, concretely, immediately as she did in the original embrace.

Sexual Excitement and Personal Sentiment

Closely related to the two aspects of the double standard of sexual behavior discussed above (at least in our own culture) is a third psychological sex difference: that carnal excitement tends to be more firmly tied to strong personal feeling in women than in men.

This tendency, like some others discussed just above, is supported by a fact that follows inexorably from our prevailing child-care arrangements: since the first parent is female, heteroerotic feeling has deeper roots in infancy for men than for women.

A Male Disability and a Female One

What these deeper roots mean is that in intimate relations between a man and a woman he is in one very important respect more vulnerable than she is: She can more readily re-evoke in him the unqualified, boundless, helpless passion of infancy. If he lets her, she can shatter his adult sense of power and control; she can bring out the soft, wild, naked baby in him.

Men try to handle this danger with the many kinds of sex-segregating institutions that they seem always and everywhere driven to create.[28] Secret societies, hunting trips, pool parlors, wars—all of these provide men with sanctuary from the impact of women, with refuges in which they can recuperate from the temptation to give way to ferocious, voracious dependence, and recover their feelings of competence, autonomy, dignity.

But they need other safeguards too. Short of avoiding women altogether, the best safeguard is to renounce the opportunity for deep feeling inherent in heterosexual love. One way to do this is to keep heterosexual love superficial, emotionally and physically. Another is to dissociate its physical from its emotional possibilities.

Woman is less vulnerable to this danger: In the sexual recapitulation of

---

[28] As I shall show in Chapters 6, 7, and 8, this male preference for all-male colleague groups has a number of other psychological determinants too, all of them rooted in the fact that women are the first parents. This root fact is of course mutable. But the preference is so fierce, and so hard for many people to imagine outgrowing, that theories are spun . . . to show that it must stem inexorably from something in our species' gene structure.

the infant-mother interplay, she has more of a sense than he does of embodying the powerful mother within herself; a greater part of her than of his reliving of the infant role is vicarious, through the other person. This makes her less afraid of being plunged back into the atmosphere of helpless infancy, and therefore typically better able to fuse intense emotional and intense physical intimacy.

Unfortunately, however, she is also typically less able to *separate* these two feelings when it would be appropriate to do so. Indeed, the gentlest hint that such separation may sometimes be appropriate is obnoxious to many women. To give way to bodily lust for a man without a sense of magical personal fusion with him seems to them unworthy, or dangerous, or degrading; incapacity to do this seems to them a mark of human dignity, rather than the disability which in fact it is. For this disability, there are many well-known practical reasons (women's economic and social dependence makes them emotionally clingy; sex is a more serious matter for them because it can make them pregnant; etc.). But there are also other reasons, less widely understood and at least as important.

I said above that a woman can assuage guilt about betraying her first, homoerotic, love in sex with a man by renouncing the pursuit of "selfish" bodily pleasure with him. But there is also another way for her to assuage this guilt: she can find that she is unable to give way to sensual delight except when romantic love—love shot through with the flavor of the original blissful mother-infant union—has flooded her being. This solution allows her to reap the joy of heterosexual carnality while keeping some magical, loyal connection to her earliest tie. (In her case, unlike his, the sense of catastrophic helplessness that return to the atmosphere of the old union can rekindle is kept within bounds by her own gender continuity, and her partner's gender discontinuity, with the first parent. And to the extent that she does feel painfully helpless with him, her pain . . . redresses for both of them an old imbalance: now it is mama who cries for baby and baby who lets mama cry.)

The hapless tendency of many women to melt into a feeling of emotional closeness with any man who manages to excite them sexually is related to still another factor: The mother, as a number of writers point out, is likely to experience a more effortless identification, a smoother communication, with a girl baby than with a boy baby. With him, there is more difference and separateness, more of a barrier to be bridged. This means that girls and boys are likely to be treated differently in the prototypic adult-infant situation in which bodily intimacy first occurs. The nature of this difference helps account for the differing degrees of ego-distinctness that they later bring to sex. The girl, as she did at the beginning, melts more easily into the personality of the person to whose flesh she is drawn. Infancy has not taught her, as surely as it has taught him, to feel simultaneously the boundaries of herself and the current between herself and what attracts her.

A Male "Solution"

For reasons that so far as I know remain to be explored, the degree to which men and women differ in their need and/or ability to dissociate personal love from sex feeling varies from one historical or cultural situation to another. (The present account does not explain this variation: clearly, it depends upon factors that have not been considered here.) But to the extent that it is in fact emotionally feasible for him to maintain such a dissociation, there is one further function, not yet mentioned, that it can always serve for a mother-raised man: It can help him to cope with the problem of ambivalence toward the first parent.

For this problem, as I have been pointing out, the Oedipal triangle offers the girl, but not the boy, a solution of sorts. (To repeat: she can dodge the work of healing the split between bad and good feelings toward the first parent by shifting a substantial portion of the magically good ones onto the second, so that her love for the opposite sex comes to be infused with the infant's grateful passion toward the mother while most of the hostile, derogatory attitudes remain attached to their original object.) The boy cannot use his father in this way without giving homoerotic attraction a dominant place in his love life. If woman is to remain for him the central human object of the passions most deeply rooted in life's beginnings, his relation to her must embrace, at a primitive level, *both* the worshipful and the derogatory, the grateful and the greedy, the affectionate and the hostile feeling toward the early mother.[29]

(Before going further, it seems best to stop and acknowledge a question that may well, by now, be irking the reader so seriously that a digression which articulates it—even an arbitrarily timed digression—will be felt as a relief: What makes me think that any conceivable child-care arrangement could magically dispel the problem of infantile ambivalence? What good would it do, after all, if fathers were as actively parental from the beginning as mothers and ambivalence therefore extended impartially to all our relations with people instead of focusing mainly on women? Trial readers of this chapter have asked this question with levels of indignation ranging

[29] Alternatively, he could transfer some of the *bad* feelings toward the father. But if he did this more than slightly, it could preclude the formation of any positive tie to his same-sex parent and handicap him as a member of the wider male community. The older, more life-essential tie to the mother can withstand more strain and remain in some important sense intact.

from gentle to vituperative. . . . If I were unaware of it, or had no clear idea what to say about it, indignation would indeed be justified. . . .)

To return, then, to our discussion of male heterosexual ambivalence: One way a man can handle this fundamental difficulty is to sort out the conflicting ingredients into two kinds of love, tender and sensual. Lust then carries all the angry, predatory impulses from which the protective, trusting side of his love for woman must be kept insulated. He may keep tender and sensual love separate by expressing them toward different women, or toward the same woman in different situations or moods. Or he may largely bury one side of his heteroerotic feeling, giving direct expression mainly to the other.

Another way he can handle the difficulty is to mute all animal-poetic feeling for other people. In this case, romantic and sexual interest play such a minor role in his life that women can remain the central object of such interest without causing any serious inner tumult. The result may or may not be a general constriction of the emotional flow between the man and his world. If not, what happens often enough to color the whole climate of history is that his passion can flow into work—that is, into the exercise of competence in the public domain—while his heteroerotic affection stays absent-minded and tepid, his sex life perfunctory. A man like this need not be literally polygamous: his wife is still apt to feel that he is "married" to his business, to the army, to the sea, to science as much as to her, or more so, while she is married only to him. A sex relation that he finds quite adequate to his needs is apt to leave her dissatisfied in one of two ways: Either it engages her deepest feelings, which she then finds unreciprocated, since his are engaged elsewhere; or it does not, in which case she feels centrally restless, her personal depths untapped, stagnating. It has often been pointed out that women depend lopsidedly on love for emotional fulfillment because they are barred from absorbing activity in the public domain. This is true. But it is also true that men can depend lopsidedly on participation in the public domain because they are stymied by love.[30]

[30]Freud, and more recently Marcuse and Brown, emphasize the malignancy . . . in the shift of energy away from erotic into "civilized" activity. But they are referring to the general taboo—in part societally imposed and in part intrapsychic—against direct expression of carnal feeling. What I am talking about here is a specific source of tension in the male-female tie, generated by our prevailing early-child-care arrangement, which works to shunt off into compulsive public activity some male passion that could be spent more appropriately and harmlessly in bed. The mid-1960s peace movement slogan "Make Love Not War" refers to this pathological shunting. But how many of the men who shouted it proved friendly to the sudden female demand for reexamination of our sexual status quo that soon followed?

Consequences for the Atmosphere Between the Sexes

The tendency of the sexes to differ in their ability to integrate, or separate, sensuality and sentiment has the same early origins, then, as the double standard. It also has the same worldly outcome. It originates in mother-dominated childhood and it contributes to the overall subordination of women. A woman's lust for a man is likely to tie her to him emotionally more closely than his lust ties him to her. Affection is likelier to keep her physically faithful to him than him to her. If he has a strong animal passion for her, his human loyalty and protectiveness may well be reserved mainly for another woman. If she is the one he tenderly loves, she may well have to make do with a sexual pittance. If he has not split off affection from lust—and sometimes even if he has—the chances are that he has muted both, turning most of his passion into realms from which she is excluded. His trouble fusing tender and sensual feeling, and her trouble separating them, enslaves and/or castrates her. She is typically dealing with a partner in some way heavily calloused, and he typically lives in an atmosphere of some kind of reproach: he is heartless; she nags and complains.[31]

The Upshot

The higamous-hogamous adult consequence of mother-dominated childhood maims both sexes. It makes women—for internal, not only external reasons—normally less able than men to defend their interests against rivals; or to give free rein to erotic impulse; or to enjoy sex (in the special way that it can be so enjoyed) without deep personal involvement. And at the same time, it makes men—for complementary internal reasons—normally less able than women to accept the fact that it is impossible wholly to monopolize the erotic interest of another person without crushing the untameable part of that person which makes her/him erotically interesting; or the fact that the other person's sexual impulses and rhythms are by no means automatically synchronized with one's own. It also makes them more frightened than women of the crucial realm of personal feeling to which sex offers access.

The maiming of men under higamous-hogamous conditions is in some respects more cruel than the maiming of women. The truth of emotional experience—their own and others—tends on the whole to be more threatening to them. As a result their freedom to feel emotional intimacy—with themselves and with others—tends on the whole to be more constricted,

[31] See Greer's *(The Female Eunuch)* and Firestone's *(The Dialectic of Sex)* recent portrayals of her castration and his heartlessness.

hemmed in by the massive denial which is necessary to keep so much truth at bay. And their physical sex pleasure—though wider-ranging than women's and much less likely to be plumb thwarted—is likelier to be impoverished by dissociation from deep personal feeling.

Nevertheless, both sexes see the double standard—quite correctly, I think—as more damaging to women. Men are on the whole content with it, and women on the whole pained by it, for the simple reason that it is women who bear the brunt of the crudest, most primitive constriction to which the double standard gives rise: Our sexual arrangements make for a head-on clash between a fact of human anatomy and the emotional constraints that stem inevitably from what Washburn calls the "fundamental pattern" imposed by evolutionary pressures "on the social organization of the human species."[32]

Anatomically, coitus offers a far less reliable guarantee of orgasm—or indeed of any intense direct local genital pleasure—to woman than to man. The first-hand coital pleasure of which she is capable more often requires conditions that must be purposefully sought out. Yet it is woman who has less liberty to conduct this kind of search: the societal and psychological constraints inherent in our "fundamental pattern" leave her less free than man to explore the erotic resources of a variety of partners, or even to affirm erotic impulse with any one partner. These constraints also make her less able to give way to simple physical delight without a sense of total self-surrender—a disability that further narrows her choice of partners, and makes her still more afraid of disrupting her rapport with any one partner by acting to intensify the delight, that is, by asserting her own sexual wishes.

The bodily bind in which this contradiction puts women—less leeway to pursue a primitive goal which is itself more elusive—is part (not the main part, but a vital part) of the reason why it is mainly women, not men, who are urging upon our species the terrifying task of reorganizing its technologically obsolete gender arrangements. As everyone on some level really understands, the issue at stake is not only freedom to seek out genital pleasure but something more as well: the sexual realm under dispute is a wildlife preserve in the civilized world, a refuge within which inarticulate, undomesticated private creative initiative is protected from extinction. (See Box 3.)

What the double standard hurts in women (to the extent that they genuinely, inwardly, bow to it) is the animal center of self-respect: the brute sense of bodily prerogative, of having a right to one's bodily feelings. A conviction that physical urges which one cannot help having are unjusti-

---

[32]This is just one of a number of such clashes. . . . It is the tension these inner frictions generate that makes our species' life keep growing and changing in the special way that it does.

Box 3

Women who act openly interested in getting more genital pleasure are suspected of wanting to take the bit in their teeth in a more general way too—that is, of threatening to overthrow the overall human dominance of men. And conversely women who do challenge the overall human dominance of men are suspected of being "frustrated"—that is, of wanting, or at least needing, more genital pleasure. Women are thus taunted into declaring themselves enchanted with their genital situation on pain of being branded emotionally unfeminine (bossy bitches, controlling, assaultive, selfish—in short, manlike—and hostile to the human dignity of actual men). And at the same time they are bullied into certifying themselves delighted with the prevailing male-female power relations on pain of being branded sexually unattractive (bitter bitches, incapable of getting and holding the love of a good man, unable to inspire the kind of phallic servicing that keeps truly beloved women content with their lot).

What everyone correctly senses is that if women are capable of more genital pleasure than they get now, and manage to find it, they will become more willful, less easily subordinated as people; and that, conversely, if they are capable of more human willfulness than they now show, and manage to win a real share of the worldly power now monopolized by men, they will become sexually more demanding. It is hard to tell which threat—the sexual or the wordly one—defenders of our old arrangement find more basically alarming.

fied, undignified, presumptuous, undercuts the deepest, oldest basis for a sense of worth; it contaminates the original wellspring of subjective autonomy. Fromm made this point very clearly when he argued, in *Man for Himself*, that socially imposed shame about the body serves the function of keeping people submissive to societal authority by weakening in them some inner core of individual authority.[33]

Antagonism to the body is not, of course, simply imposed by society. It does not stem solely from external constraints designed to foster social obedience. It is an attitude with deep spontaneous roots in the psycholog-

[33] This was his simpler, more sunny-minded reformulation of Freud's dark point, in *Civilization and Its Discontents*, about the sublimation of sexual into societally "useful" energy, a process which to Freud meant that the growth of civilization and its increasingly deadly character have been intrinsically inseparable.

ical situation of our species. . . . It is often used, moreover, to express not compliance, but defiance, independence, strength of will: fleshly ordeals such as fasting—and celibacy—are typically undertaken by humans in a spirit of willful, autonomous personal choice. But the burden of sensual self-abnegation imposed on women by the double standard is not undertaken in a willful spirit. It is passively accepted; and for this reason it does work as Fromm indicated that sensual self-abnegation can work: it helps make women in a special way humble, dependent, malleable.

The chronic bodily muting accepted by "feminine" women is the opposite of dramatic and self-assertive: it wholly lacks the brightness and clarity of a hunger strike or a religious vow of abstinence from sex. Occasionally women flare up a bit and use it vengefully, affirming it as a sign of their own moral superiority to, and power over, the abjectly lust-ridden male.[34] On the whole, however, the female burden of genital deprivation is carried meekly, invisibly. Sometimes it cripples real interest in sexual interaction, but often it does not: indeed, it can deepen a woman's need for the emotional rewards of carnal contact. What it most reliably cripples is human pride.

---

[34] "Idiots, all of them!" cackles Polly Peachum's old mother in the Brecht-Weill *Threepenny Opera.* She is singing a song of triumph over Mack the Knife, who can be trapped because he cannot resist the whorehouse. ("Because he knows what women do to him, he thrusts them well out of his way. He cries, 'I've mastered it, without half trying!' but comes the night and once again he's lying.") But she is singing in the dark. Mack enslaves "good" women more deeply and permanently than they can ever ensnare him: He is polygamous; they are monogamous. He has roots in rowdy male fellowship and in (criminal) enterprise; they brood about him, yearn for his return, and bicker with each other. As for "bad"—that is, shared—women, and the murderous, impotent rage that they feel in the face of man's contempt, think of Jenny Diver's "Black Freighter" song.

. . . .

QUESTIONS FOR A SECOND READING

1. As you reread this essay, look for sections that will help you sort out the specific applications of Dinnerstein's argument that there are "internal" as well as "external" supports to the double standard. The "roots" of adult behavior, she says, lie in an early primitive relationship between a child and the mother and father. The basic "structure" is this: the child bonds first with the mother and then with the father, and the bonding is different for a boy child than for a girl child because each identifies differently with the male and female parents. What is the early psychological history of the boy

child? What is the early psychological history of the girl child? What are the implications for each as adults?

2. As a writer, Dinnerstein has an elaborate system for adding material to the basic text in this chapter. There are both footnotes and boxes. Why, do you suppose? In what ways do these serve the writer? the reader? the subject? (And what do you suppose are the "roots" of the "rules" that govern *this* behavior?)

ASSIGNMENTS FOR WRITING

1. In her preface to *The Mermaid and the Minotaur,* Dinnerstein said that the book's method is "to appeal to the reader's own experience: if the result feels in any way enlightening, the argument is validated insofar as it can be." How *does* the argument "feel" if measured against your sense of your own experience? For this assignment, write an essay that examines the argument of "Higamous-Hogamous" in light of your experience. What feels right to you? What feels wrong? What examples can you bring forward to test what she says? And in what way could you say Dinnerstein's argument has enlightened you?
2. Dinnerstein claims that because of our child-rearing practices men are freer than women—freer to come and go, to invest in love and worldly affairs, to make history. What are the implications? Write an essay explaining what it means to be "freer" as Dinnerstein uses the word. Free from what? To do what? What might you find in your own experience to add to or to counter Dinnerstein's argument about men's and women's relative freedom?

MAKING CONNECTIONS

1. In the study of Ted and Ellie Graziano (p. 124), we run head-on into problems of freedom, control, and power. Ted and Ellie see things differently, including the roles of men and women. Write an essay in which you discuss how you think Dinnerstein might view the Grazianos and what is going on between them. What would Dinnerstein see as telling or important in the things the Grazianos say to each other and to Cottle? What do Ted and Ellie do to each other that Dinnerstein might consider problems? What beliefs, attitudes, and ideas do they hold that might stem from their having deep roots, as Dinnerstein calls them, in a culture of mother-raised children?

   Note: Your essay should not be considered an occasion to speculate about how the Grazianos were raised by their parents. Dinnerstein argues that certain problems are rooted in our culture's emphasis on mother-dominated childhoods. Your job is to look at the Grazianos as Dinnerstein might, to see how their difficulties can be explained in her terms.
2. Robert Coles, in his essay "Entitlement" (p. 89), develops a theory of how wealthy children learn to expect things from life. He calls these expectations

"entitlements" and tells a number of stories (from actual cases he studied) to support his arguments. He talks about both boys and girls, sometimes brothers and sisters. In a way, Dinnerstein's arguments are about entitlements, too; boys and girls learn to expect different things about themselves and their lives because of the way they are raised.

Write an essay in which you address the similarities and differences in Coles's and Dinnerstein's work on the forces shaping children's lives. Do their theories overlap? What might be their agreements? disagreements? What would Coles see and understand that Dinnerstein would miss? What would Dinnerstein see and understand that Coles would miss? How, for example, might Dinnerstein explain the difference between the girls and boys in Coles's study? And how would her explanation differ from Coles's?

RALPH WALDO EMERSON

RALPH WALDO EMERSON (1803–1882) is probably one of the most famous, most eloquent, and least read figures in American literature. He was a poet, a preacher, a visionary, and an itinerant lecturer; he left behind a remarkable series of essays, lectures, notebooks, and journals; and yet he is best known for his influence on those who followed him: Melville, Thoreau, Whitman, Dickinson, Frost, Hart Crane, and Wallace Stevens.

Textbooks most often introduce Emerson as the central figure in American transcendentalism. He does not, however, have to be read as a representative philosopher; to do so, in fact, violates his own feisty individualism and his struggle to stay free of schools of thought and the pressure of received opinion. He can be read for the pleasure of his unusual style of speaking and thinking and for the force of his immediate argument. The essay that follows, "The American Scholar," is about education, including university education, and it says some rather surprising things, including the following about the use of books (like the one you are reading right now): "Books are for the scholar's idle times," and "Meek young men grow up in libraries, believing it their duty to accept the views, which Cicero, which Locke, which Bacon, have given, forgetful that Cicero, Locke, and Bacon were only young men in libraries when they wrote these books." It is a shame to think that the only way to read Emerson is as an example of what people once *thought (and, in fact, it is wrong to think that in the nineteenth century most people thought or said such things). It is possible, alternatively, to read Emerson as a person with something to say to American scholars at today's colleges and universities.*

"The American Scholar" was presented as a lecture to the Harvard chapter of Phi Beta Kappa on August 31, 1837. It has been called "the most influential address ever made before an American college audience," and America's "intellectual Declaration of Independence." It was also called "misty, dreamy, and unintelligible." Emerson's prose is not orderly, straightforward, or systematic. It does not easily or quickly connect one thing to another but puts the responsibility in the hands of the reader—in your hands—which, according to one of the essay's arguments, is exactly where it belongs.

The American Scholar

An Oration
Delivered Before the Phi Beta Kappa Society,
at Cambridge, August 31, 1837

MR. PRESIDENT, AND GENTLEMEN,

I greet you on the re-commencement of our literary year. Our anniversary is one of hope, and, perhaps, not enough of labor. We do not meet for games of strength or skill, for the recitation of histories, tragedies and odes, like the ancient Greeks; for parliaments of love and poesy, like the Troubadours; nor for the advancement of science, like our contemporaries in the British and European capitals. Thus far, our holiday has been simply a friendly sign of the survival of the love of letters amongst a people too busy to give to letters any more. As such, it is precious as the sign of an indestructible instinct. Perhaps the time is already come, when it ought to be, and will be something else; when the sluggard intellect of this continent will look from under its iron lids and fill the postponed expectation of the world with something better than the exertions of mechanical skill. Our day of dependence, our long apprenticeship to the learning of other lands, draws to a close. The millions that around us are rushing into life, cannot always be fed on the sere remains of foreign harvests. Events, actions arise, that must be sung, that will sing themselves. Who can doubt that poetry will revive and lead in a new age, as the star in the constellation Harp which now flames in our zenith, astronomers announce, shall one day be the pole-star for a thousand years?

In the light of this hope, I accept the topic which not only usage, but the nature of our association, seem to prescribe to this day—the American Scholar. Year by year, we come up hither to read one more chapter of his biography. Let us inquire what light new days and events have thrown on his character, his duties, and his hopes.

It is one of those fables, which out of an unknown antiquity, convey an unlooked-for wisdom, that the gods, in the beginning, divided Man into men, that he might be more helpful to himself; just as the hand was divided into fingers, the better to answer its end.

The old fable covers a doctrine ever new and sublime; that there is One Man,—present to all particular men only partially, or through one faculty; and that you must take the whole society to find the whole man. Man is not a farmer, or a professor, or an engineer, but he is all. Man is priest, and scholar, and statesman, and producer, and soldier. In the *divided* or social state, these functions are parcelled out to individuals, each of whom aims to do his stint of the joint work, whilst each other performs his. The fable implies that the individual, to possess himself, must sometimes return from his own labor to embrace all the other laborers. But unfortunately, this original unit, this fountain of power, has been so distributed to multitudes, has been so minutely subdivided and peddled out, that it is spilled into drops, and cannot be gathered. The state of society is one in which the members have suffered amputation from the trunk, and strut about so many walking monsters,—a good finger, a neck, a stomach, an elbow, but never a man.

Man is thus metamorphosed into a thing, into many things. The planter, who is Man sent out into the field to gather food, is seldom cheered by any idea of the true dignity of his ministry. He sees his bushel and his cart, and nothing beyond, and sinks into the farmer, instead of Man on the farm. The tradesman scarcely ever gives an ideal worth to his work, but is ridden by the routine of his craft, and the soul is subject to dollars. The priest becomes a form; the attorney, a statute-book; the mechanic, a machine; the sailor, a rope of a ship.

In this distribution of functions, the scholar is the delegated intellect. In the right state, he is, *Man Thinking*. In the degenerate state, when the victim of society, he tends to become a mere thinker, or, still worse, the parrot of other men's thinking.

In this view of him, as Man Thinking, the whole theory of his office is contained. Him nature solicits, with all her placid, all her monitory pictures. Him the past instructs. Him the future invites. Is not, indeed, every man a student, and do not all things exist for the student's behoof? And, finally, is not the true scholar the only true master? But, as the old oracle said, "All things have two handles. Beware of the wrong one." In life, too often, the scholar errs with mankind and forfeits his privilege. Let us see him in his school, and consider him in reference to the main influences he receives.

I

The first in time and the first in importance of the influences upon the mind is that of nature. Every day, the sun; and, after sunset, night and her stars. Ever the winds blow; ever the grass grows. Every day, men and women, conversing, beholding and beholden. The scholar must needs stand wistful and admiring before this great spectacle. He must settle its value in his mind. What is nature to him? There is never a beginning, there is never an end to the inexplicable continuity of this web of God, but always circular power returning into itself. Therein it resembles his own spirit, whose beginning, whose ending he never can find—so entire, so boundless. Far, too, as her splendors shine, system on system shooting like rays, upward, downward, without centre, without circumference,—in the mass and in the particle nature hastens to render account of herself to the mind. Classification begins. To the young mind, every thing is individual, stands by itself. By and by, it finds how to join two things, and see in them one nature; then three, then three thousand; and so, tyrannized over by its own unifying instinct, it goes on trying things together, diminishing anomalies, discovering roots running under ground, whereby contrary and remote things cohere, and flower out from one stem. It presently learns, that, since the dawn of history, there has been a constant accumulation and classifying of facts. But what is classification but the perceiving that these objects are not chaotic, and are not foreign, but have a law which is also a law of the human mind? The astronomer discovers that geometry, a pure abstraction of the human mind, is the measure of planetary motion. The chemist finds proportions and intelligible method throughout matter: and science is nothing but the finding of analogy, identity in the most remote parts. The ambitious soul sits down before each refractory fact; one after another, reduces all strange constitutions, all new powers, to their class and their law, and goes on forever to animate the last fibre of organization, the outskirts of nature, by insight.

Thus to him, to this school-boy under the bending dome of day, is suggested, that he and it proceed from one root; one is leaf and one is flower; relation, sympathy, stirring in every vein. And what is that Root? Is not that the soul of his soul?—A thought too bold—a dream too wild. Yet when this spiritual light shall have revealed the law of more earthly natures,—when he has learned to worship the soul, and to see that the natural philosophy that now is, is only the first gropings of its gigantic hand, he shall look forward to an ever expanding knowledge as to a becoming creator. He shall see that nature is the opposite of the soul, answering to it part for part. One is seal, and one is print. Its beauty is the beauty of his own mind. Its laws are the laws of his own mind. Nature then becomes to him the measure of his attainments. So much of nature as he is ignorant of, so much of his own mind does he not yet possess. And, in fine, the ancient precept, "Know thyself," and the modern precept, "Study nature," becomes at last one maxim.

II

The next great influence into the spirit of the scholar, is, the mind of the Past,—in whatever form, whether of literature, of art, of institutions, that mind is inscribed. Books are the best type of the influence of the past, and perhaps we shall get at the truth—learn the amount of this influence more conveniently—by considering their value alone.

The theory of books is noble. The scholar of the first age received into him the world around; brooded thereon; gave it the new arrangement of his own mind, and uttered it again. It came into him—life; it went out from him—truth. It came to him—short-lived actions; it went out from him—immortal thoughts. It came to him—business; it went from him—poetry. It was—dead fact; now, it is quick thought. It can stand, and it can go. It now endures, it now flies, it now inspires. Precisely in proportion to the depth of mind from which it issued, so high does it soar, so long does it sing.

Or, I might say, it depends on how far the process had gone, of transmuting life into truth. In proportion to the completeness of the distillation, so will the purity and imperishableness of the product be. But none is quite perfect. As no air-pump can by any means make a perfect vacuum, so neither can any artist entirely exclude the conventional, the local, the perishable from his book, or write a book of pure thought that shall be as efficient, in all respects, to a remote posterity, as to contemporaries, or rather to the second age. Each age, it is found, must write its own books; or rather, each generation for the next succeeding. The books of an older period will not fit this.

Yet hence arises a grave mischief. The sacredness which attaches to the act of creation,—the act of thought,—is instantly transferred to the record. The poet chanting, was felt to be a divine man. Henceforth the chant is divine also. The writer was a just and wise spirit. Henceforward it is settled, the book is perfect; as love of the hero corrupts into worship of his statue. Instantly, the book becomes noxious. The guide is a tyrant. We sought a brother, and lo, a governor. The sluggish and perverted mind of the multitude, always slow to open to the incursions of Reason, having once so opened, having once received this book, stands upon it, and makes an outcry, if it is disparaged. Colleges are built on it. Books are written on it by thinkers, not by Man Thinking; by men of talent, that is, who start wrong, who set out from accepted dogmas, not from their own sight of principles. Meek young men grow up in libraries, believing it their duty to accept the views which Cicero, which Locke, which Bacon have given, forgetful that Cicero, Locke and Bacon were only young men in libraries when they wrote these books.

Hence, instead of Man Thinking, we have the bookworm. Hence, the book-learned class, who value books, as such; not as related to nature and the human constitution, but as making a sort of Third Estate with the world and the soul. Hence, the restorers of readings, the emendators, the bibliomaniacs of all degrees.

This is bad; this is worse than it seems. Books are the best of things, well used; abused, among the worst. What is the right use? What is the one end which all means go to effect? They are for nothing but to inspire. I had better never see a book than to be warped by its attraction clean out of my own orbit, and made a satellite instead of a system. The one thing in the world of value, is, the active soul,—the soul, free, sovereign, active. This every man is entitled to; this every man contains within him, although in almost all men, obstructed, and as yet unborn. The soul active sees absolute truth; and utters truth, or creates. In this action, it is genius; not the privilege of here and there a favorite, but the sound estate of every man. In its essence, it is progressive. The book, the college, the school of art, the institution of any kind, stop with some past utterance of genius. This is good, say they,—let us hold by this. They pin me down. They look backward and not forward. But genius always looks forward. The eyes of man are set in his forehead, not in his hindhead. Man hopes. Genius creates. To create,—to create,—is the proof of a divine presence. Whatever talents may be, if the man create not, the pure efflux of the Deity is not his:—cinders and smoke, there may be, but not yet flame. There are creative manners, there are creative actions, and creative words; manners, actions, words, that is, indicative of no custom or authority, but springing spontaneous from the mind's own sense of good and fair.

On the other part, instead of being its own seer, let it receive always from another mind its truth, though it were in torrents of light, without periods of solitude, inquest and self-recovery, and a fatal disservice is done. Genius is always sufficiently the enemy of genius by over-influence. The literature of every nation bear me witness. The English dramatic poets have Shakspearized now for two hundred years.

Undoubtedly there is a right way of reading,—so it be sternly subordinated. Man Thinking must not be subdued by his instruments. Books are for the scholar's idle times. When he can read God directly, the hour is too precious to be wasted in other men's transcripts of their readings. But when the intervals of darkness come, as come they must,—when the soul seeth not, when the sun is hid, and the stars withdraw their shining,—we repair to the lamps which were kindled by their ray to guide our steps to the East again, where the dawn is. We hear that we may speak. The Arabian proverb says, "A fig tree looking on a fig tree, becometh fruitful."

It is remarkable, the character of the pleasure we derive from the best books. They impress us ever with the conviction that one nature wrote and the same reads. We read the verses of one of the great English poets, of Chaucer, of Marvell, of Dryden, with the most modern joy,—with a pleasure, I mean, which is in great part caused by the abstraction of all *time* from their verses. There is some awe mixed with the joy of our surprise, when this poet, who lived in some past world, two or three hundred years ago, says that which lies close to my own soul, that which I also had well-nigh thought and said. But for the evidence thence afforded to the philosophical doctrine of the identity of all minds, we should suppose some pre-established harmony, some foresight of souls that were to be, and some preparation of stores for their future wants, like the fact observed in insects, who lay up food before death for the young grub they shall never see.

I would not be hurried by any love of system, by any exaggeration of instincts, to underrate the Book. We all know, that as the human body can be nourished on any food, though it were boiled grass and the broth of shoes, so the human mind can be fed by any knowledge. And great and heroic men have existed, who had almost no other information than by the printed page. I only would say, that it needs a strong head to bear that diet. One must be an inventor to read well. As the proverb says, "He that would bring home the wealth of the Indies, must carry out the wealth of the Indies." There is then creative reading, as well as creative writing. When the mind is braced by labor and invention, the page of whatever book we read becomes luminous with manifold allusion. Every sentence is doubly significant, and the sense of our author is as broad as the world. We then see, what is always true, that as the seer's hour of vision is short and rare among heavy days and months, so is its record, perchance, the least part of his volume. The discerning will read in his Plato or Shakespeare, only that least part,—only the authentic utterances of the oracle,—and all the rest he rejects, were it never so many times Plato's and Shakspeare's.

Of course, there is a portion of reading quite indispensable to a wise man. History and exact science he must learn by laborious reading. Colleges, in like manner, have their indispensable office,—to teach elements. But they can only highly serve us, when they aim not to drill, but to create;

when they gather from far every ray of various genius to their hospitable halls, and, by the concentrated fires, set the hearts of their youth on flame. Thought and knowledge are natures in which apparatus and pretension avail nothing. Gowns, and pecuniary foundations, though of towns of gold, can never countervail the least sentence or syllable of wit. Forget this, and our American colleges will recede in their public importance whilst they grow richer every year.

III

There goes in the world a notion that the scholar should be a recluse, a valetudinarian,—as unfit for any handiwork or public labor, as a penknife for an axe. The so-called "practical men" sneer at speculative men, as if, because they speculate or *see,* they could do nothing. I have heard it said that the clergy,—who are always more universally than any other class, the scholars of their day,—are addressed as women: that the rough, spontaneous conversation of men they do not hear, but only a mincing and diluted speech. They are often virtually disfranchised; and, indeed, there are advocates for their celibacy. As far as this is true of the studious classes, it is not just and wise. Action is with the scholar subordinate, but it is essential. Without it, he is not yet man. Without it, thought can never ripen into truth. Whilst the world hangs before the eye as a cloud of beauty, we cannot even see its beauty. Inaction is cowardice, but there can be no scholar without the heroic mind. The preamble of thought, the transition through which it passes from the unconscious to the conscious, is action. Only so much do I know, as I have lived. Instantly we know whose words are loaded with life, and whose not.

The world,—this shadow of the soul, or *other me,* lies wide around. Its attractions are the keys which unlock my thoughts and make me acquainted with myself. I run eagerly into the resounding tumult. I grasp the hands of those next to me, and take my place in the ring to suffer and to work, taught by an instinct that so shall the dumb abyss be vocal with speech. I pierce its order; I dissipate its fear; I dispose of it within the circuit of my expanding life. So much only of life as I know by experience, so much of the wilderness have I vanguished and planted, or so far have I extended my being, my dominion. I do not see how any man can afford, for the sake of his nerves and his nap, to spare any action in which he can partake. It is pearls and rubies to his discourse. Drudgery, calamity, exasperation, want, are instructers in eloquence and wisdom. The true scholar grudges every opportunity of action past by, as a loss of power.

It is the raw material out of which the intellect moulds her splendid products. A strange process too, this, by which experience is converted into thought, as a mulberry leaf is converted into satin. The manufacture goes forward at all hours.

The actions and events of our childhood and youth are now matters of calmest observation. They lie like fair pictures in the air. Not so with our recent actions,—with the business which we now have in hand. On this we are quite unable to speculate. Our affections as yet circulate through it. We no more feel or know it, than we feel the feet, or the hand, or the brain of our body. The new deed is yet a part of life,—remains for a time immersed in our unconscious life. In some contemplative hour, it detaches itself from the life like a ripe fruit, to become a thought of the mind. Instantly, it is raised, transfigures; the corruptible has put on incorruption. Always now it is an object of beauty, however, base its origin and neighborhood. Observe, too, the impossibility of antedating this act. In its grub state, it cannot fly, it cannot shine,—it is a dull grub. But suddenly, without observation, the selfsame thing unfurls beautiful wings, and is an angel of wisdom. So is there no fact, no event, in our private history, which shall not, sooner or later, lose its adhesive inert form, and astonish us by soaring from our body into the empyrean. Cradle and infancy, school and playground, the fear of boys, and dogs, and ferules, the love of little maids and berries, and many another fact that once filled the whole sky, are gone already; friend and relative, profession and party, town and country, nation and world, must also soar and sing.

Of course, he who has put forth his total strength in fit actions, has the richest return of wisdom. I will not shut myself out of this globe of action and transplant an oak into a flower pot, there to hunger and pine; nor trust the revenue of some single faculty, and exhaust one vein of thought, much like those Savoyards, who, getting their livelihood by carving shepherds, shepherdesses, and smoking Dutchmen, for all Europe, went out one day to the mountain to find stock, and discovered that they had whittled up the last of their pine trees. Authors we have in numbers, who have written out their vein, and who, moved by a commendable prudence, sail for Greece or Palestine, follow the trapper into the prairie, or ramble round Algiers to replenish their merchantable stock.

If it were only for a vocabulary the scholar would be covetous of action. Life is our dictionary. Years are well spent in country labors; in town—in the insight into trades and manufactures; in frank intercourse with many men and women; in science; in art; to the one end of mastering in all their facts a language, by which to illustrate and embody our perceptions. I learn immediately from any speaker how much he has already lived, through the poverty or the splendor of his speech. Life lies behind us as the quarry from whence we get tiles and copestones for the masonry of to-day. This is the way to learn grammar. Colleges and books only copy the language which the field and the work-yard made.

But the final value of action, like that of books, and better than books, is, that it is a resource. That great principle of Undulation in nature, that shows itself in the inspiring and expiring of the breath; in desire and satiety; in the ebb and flow of the sea, in day and night, in heat and cold, and as yet more deeply ingrained in every atom and every fluid, is known to us under the name of Polarity,—these "fits of easy transmission and reflection," as Newton called them, are the law of nature because they are the law of spirit.

The mind now thinks; now acts; and each fit reproduces the other. When the artist has exhausted his materials, when the fancy no longer paints, when thoughts are no longer apprehended, and books are a weariness,—he has always the resource *to live.* Character is higher than intellect. Thinking is the function. Living is the functionary. The stream retreats to its source. A great soul will be strong to live, as well as strong to think. Does he lack organ or medium to impart his truths? He can still fall back on this elemental force of living them. This is a total act. Thinking is a partial act. Let the grandeur of justice shine in his affairs. Let the beauty of affection cheer his lowly roof. Those "far from fame" who dwell and act with him, will feel the force of his constitution in the doings and passages of the day better than it can be measured by any public and designed display. Time shall teach him that the scholar loses no hour which the man lives. Herein he unfolds the sacred germ of his instinct, screened from influence. What is lost in seemliness is gained in strength. Not out of those on whom systems of education have exhausted their culture, comes the helpful giant to destroy the old or to build the new, but out of unhandselled savage nature, out of terrible Druids and Berserkirs, come at last Alfred and Shakspeare.

I hear therefore with joy whatever is beginning to be said of the dignity and necessity of labor to every citizen. There is virtue yet in the hoe and the spade, for learned as well as for unlearned hands. And labor is every where welcome; always we are invited to work; only be this limitation observed, that a man shall not for the sake of wider activity sacrifice any opinion to the popular judgments and modes of action.

I have now spoken of the education of the scholar by nature, by books, and by action. It remains to say somewhat of his duties.

They are such as become Man Thinking. They may all be comprised in self-trust. The office of the scholar is to cheer, to raise, and to guide men by showing them facts amidst appearances. He plies the slow, unhonored, and unpaid task of observation. Flamsteed and Herschel, in their glazed observatories, may catalogue the stars with the praise of all men, and, the results being splendid and useful, honor is sure. But he, in his private observatory, cataloguing obscure and nebulous stars of the human mind, which as yet no man has thought of as such,—watching days and months, sometimes, for a few facts; correcting still his old records;—must relinquish display and immediate fame. In the long period of his preparation, he must betray often an ignorance and shiftlessness in popular arts, incurring the disdain of the able who shoulder him aside. Long he must stammer in his speech; often forego the living for the dead. Worse yet, he must accept—how often! poverty and solitude. For the ease and pleasure of treading the old road, accepting the fashions, the education, the religion of society, he takes the cross of making his own, and, of course, the self-accusation, the faint heart, the frequent uncertainty and loss of time which are the nettles and tangling vines in the way of the self-relying and self-directed; and the state of virtual hostility in which he seems to stand to society, and especially to educated society. For all this loss and scorn, what offset? He is to find consolation in exercising the highest functions of human nature. He is one who raises himself from private considerations, and breathes and lives on public and illustrious thoughts. He is the world's eye. He is the world's heart. He is to resist the vulgar prosperity that retrogrades ever to barbarism, by preserving and communicating heroic sentiments, noble biographies, melodious verse, and the conclusions of history. Whatsoever oracles the human heart in all emergencies, in all solemn hours has uttered as its commentary on the world of actions,—these he shall receive and impart. And whatsoever new verdict Reason from her inviolable seat pronounces on the passing men and events of to-day,—this he shall hear and promulgate.

These being his functions, it becomes him to feel all confidence in himself, and to defer never to the popular cry. He and he only knows the world. The world of any moment is the merest appearance. Some great decorum, some fetish of a government, some ephemeral trade, or war, or man, is cried up by half mankind and cried down by the other half, as if all depended on this particular up or down. The odds are that the whole question is not worth the poorest thought which the scholar has lost in listening to the controversy. Let him not quit his belief that a popgun is a popgun, though the ancient and honorable of the earth affirm it to be the crack of doom. In silence, in steadiness, in severe abstraction, let him hold by himself; add observation to observation, patient of neglect, patient of reproach; and bide his own time,—happy enough if he can satisfy himself alone that this day he has seen something truly. Success treads on every right step. For the instinct is sure that prompts him to tell his brother what he thinks. He then learns that in going down into the secrets of his own mind, he has descended into the secrets of all minds. He learns that he who has mastered any law in his private thoughts, is master to that extent of all men whose language he speaks, and of all into whose language his own can be translated. The poet in utter solitude remembering his spontaneous thoughts and recording them, is found to have recorded that which men in crowded cities find true for them also. The orator distrusts at first the fitness of his frank confessions,—his want of knowledge of the persons he addresses,—until he finds that he is the complement of his hearers;—that they drink his words because he fulfils for them their own nature; the deeper he dives into his privatest secretest presentiment,—to his wonder he finds, this is the most acceptable, most public, and universally true. The people delight in it; the better part of every man feels, This is my music: this is myself.

In self-trust, all the virtues are comprehended. Free should the scholar be,—free and brave. Free even to the definition of freedom, "without any hindrance that does not arise out of his own constitution." Brave; for fear is a thing which a scholar by his very function puts behind him. Fear always springs from ignorance. It is a shame to him if his tranquillity, amid dangerous times, arise from the presumption that like children and women, his is a protected class; or if he seek a temporary peace by the diversion of his thoughts from politics or vexed questions, hiding his head like an ostrich in the flowering bushes, peeping into microscopes, and turning rhymes, as a boy whistles to keep his courage up. So is the danger a danger still: so is the fear worse. Manlike let him turn and face it. Let him look into its eye and search its nature, inspect its origin,—see the whelping of this lion,—which lies no great way back; he will then find in himself a perfect comprehension of its nature and extent; he will have made his hands meet on the other side, and can henceforth defy it, and pass on superior. The world is his who can see through its pretension. What deafness, what stone-blind custom, what overgrown error you behold, is there only by sufferance,—by your sufferance. See it to be a lie, and you have already dealt it its mortal blow.

Yes, we are the cowed,—we the trustless. It is a mischievous notion that we are come late into nature; that the world was finished a long time ago. As the world was plastic and fluid in the hands of God, so it is ever to so much of his attributes as we bring to it. To ignorance and sin, it is flint. They adapt themselves to it as they may; but in proportion as a man has anything in him divine, the firmament flows before him, and takes his signet and form. Not he is great who can alter matter, but he who can alter my state of mind. They are the kings of the world who give the color of their present thought to all nature and all art, and persuade men by the cheerful serenity of their carrying the matter, that this thing which they do, is the apple which the ages have desired to pluck, now at last ripe, and inviting nations to the harvest. The great man makes the great thing. Wherever Macdonald sits, there is the head of the table. Linnæus makes botany the most alluring of studies and wins it from the farmer and the herb-woman. Davy, chemistry: and Cuvier, fossils. The day is always his, who works in it with serenity and great aims. The unstable estimates of men crowd to him whose mind is filled with a truth, as the heaped waves of the Atlantic follow the moon.

For this self-trust, the reason is deeper than can be fathomed,—darker than can be enlightened. I might not carry with me the feeling of my audience in stating my own belief. But I have already shown the ground of my hope, in adverting to the doctrine that man is one. I believe man has been wronged: he has wronged himself. He has almost lost the light that can lead him back to his prerogatives. Men are become of no account. Men in history, men in the world of to-day are bugs, are spawn, and are called "the mass" and "the herd." In a century, in a millenium, one or two men; that is to say—one or two approximations to the right state of every man. All the rest behold in the hero or the poet their own green and crude being—ripened; yes, and are content to be less, so *that* may attain to its full stature. What a testimony—full of grandeur, full of pity, is borne to the demands of his own nature, by the poor clansman, the poor partisan, who rejoices in the glory of his chief. The poor and the low find some amends to their immense moral capacity, for their acquiescence in a political and social inferiority. They are content to be brushed like flies from the path of a great person, so that justice shall be done by him to that common nature which it is the dearest desire of all to see enlarged and glorified. They sun themselves in the great man's light, and feel it to be their own element. They cast the dignity of man from their downtrod selves upon the shoulders of a hero, and will perish to add one drop of blood to make that great heart beat, those giant sinews combat and conquer. He lives for us, and we live in him.

Men such as they are, very naturally seek money or power; and power because it is as good as money,—the "spoils," so called, "of office." And why not? for they aspire to the highest, and this, in their sleep-walking, they dream is highest. Wake them, and they shall quit the false good and leap to the true, and leave governments to clerks and desks. This revolution is to be wrought by the gradual domestication of the idea of Culture. The main enterprise of the world for splendor, for extent, is the upbuilding of a man. Here are the materials strown along the ground. The private life of one man shall be a more illustrious monarchy,—more formidable to its enemy, more sweet and serene in its influence to its friend, than any kingdom in history. For a man, rightly viewed, comprehendeth the particular natures of all men. Each philosopher, each bard, each actor, has only done for me, as by a delegate, what one day I can do for myself. The books which once we valued more than the apple of the eye, we have quite exhausted. What is that but saying that we have come up with the point of view which the universal mind took through the eyes of that one scribe; we have been that man, and have passed on. First, one; then, another; we drain all cisterns, and waxing greater by all these supplies, we crave a better and more abundant food. The man has never lived that can feed us ever. The human mind cannot be enshrined in a person who shall set a barrier on any one side to this unbounded, unboundable empire. It is one central fire which flaming now out of the lips of Etna, lightens the capes of Sicily; and now out of the throat of Vesuvius, illuminates the towers and vineyards of Naples. It is one light which beams out of a thousand stars. It is one soul which animates all men.

But I have dwelt perhaps tediously upon this abstraction of the Scholar. I ought not to delay longer to add what I have to say, of nearer reference to the time and to this country.

Historically, there is thought to be a difference in the ideas which predominate over successive epochs, and there are data for marking the genius of the Classic, of the Romantic, and now of the Reflective or Philosophical age. With the views I have intimated of the oneness or the identity of the mind through all individuals, I do not much dwell on these differences. In fact, I believe each individual passes through all three. The boy is a Greek; the youth, romantic; the adult, reflective. I deny not, however, that a revolution in the leading idea may be distinctly enough traced.

Our age is bewailed as the age of Introversion. Must that needs be evil? We, it seems, are critical. We are embarrassed with second thoughts. We cannot enjoy any thing for hankering to know whereof the pleasure consists. We are lined with eyes. We see with our feet. The time is infected with Hamlet's unhappiness,—

"Sicklied o'er with the pale cast of thought."

Is it so bad then? Sight is the last thing to be pitied. Would we be blind? Do we fear lest we should outsee nature and God, and drink truth dry? I look upon the discontent of the literary class as a mere announcement of the fact that they find themselves not in the state of mind of their fathers, and regret the coming state as untried; as a boy dreads the water before he has learned that he can swim. If there is any period one would desire to be born in,—is it not the age of Revolution; when the old and the new stand side by side, and admit of being compared; when the energies of all men are searched by fear and by hope; when the historic glories of the old, can be compensated by the rich possibilities of the new era? This time, like all times, is a very good one, if we but know what to do with it.

I read with joy some of the auspicious signs of the coming days as they glimmer already through poetry and art, through philosophy and science, through church and state.

One of these signs is the fact that the same movement which effected the elevation of what was called the lowest class in the state, assumed in literature a very marked and as benign an aspect. Instead of the sublime and beautiful, the near, the low, the common, was explored and poetized. That which had been negligently trodden under foot by those who were harnessing and provisioning themselves for long journeys into far countries, is suddenly found to be richer than all foreign parts. The literature of the poor, the feelings of the child, the philosophy of the street, the meaning of household life, are the topics of the time. It is a great stride. It is a sign—is it not? of new vigor, when the extremities are made active, when currents of warm life run into the hands and the feet. I ask not for the great, the remote, the romantic; what is doing in Italy or Arabia; what is Greek art, or Provencal Minstrelsy; I embrace the common, I explore and sit at the feet of the familiar, the low. Give me insight into to-day, and you may have the antique and future worlds. What would we really know the meaning of? The meal in the firkin; the milk in the pan; the ballad in the street; the news of the boat; the glance of the eye; the form and the gait of the body;—show me the ultimate reason of these matters;—show me the sublime presence of the highest spiritual cause lurking, as always it does lurk, in these suburbs and extremities of nature; let me see every trifle bristling with the polarity that ranges it instantly on an eternal law; and the shop, the plough, and the leger, refered to the like cause by which light undulates and poets sing;—and the world lies no longer a dull miscellany and lumber room, but has form and order; there is no trifle; there is no puzzle; but one design unites and animates the farthest pinnacle and the lowest trench.

This idea has inspired the genius of Goldsmith, Burns, Cowper, and, in a newer time, of Goethe, Wordsworth, and Carlyle. This idea they have differently followed and with various success. In contrast with their writing, the style of Pope, of Johnson, of Gibbon, looks cold and pedantic. This writing is blood-warm. Man is surprised to find that things near are not less beautiful and wondrous than things remote. The near explains the far. The drop is a small ocean. A man is related to all nature. This perception of the worth of the vulgar, is fruitful in discoveries. Goethe, in this very thing the most modern of the moderns, has shown us, as none ever did, the genius of the ancients.

There is one man of genius who has done much for this philosophy of life, whose literary value has never yet been rightly estimated;—I mean Emanuel Swedenborg. The most imaginative of men, yet writing with the precision of a mathematician, he endeavored to engraft a purely philosophical Ethics on the popular Christianity of his time. Such an attempt, of course, must have difficulty which no genius could surmount. But he saw and showed the connexion between nature and the affections of the soul. He pierced the emblematic or spiritual character of the visible, audible, tangible world. Especially did his shade-loving muse hover over and interpret the lower parts of nature; he showed the mysterious bond that allies moral evil to the foul material forms, and has given in epical parables a theory of insanity, of beasts, of unclean and fearful things.

Another sign of our times, also marked by an analogous political movement is, the new importance given to the single person. Every thing that tends to insulate the individual,—to surround him with barriers of natural respect, so that each man shall feel the world is his, and man shall treat with man as a sovereign state with a sovereign state;—tends to true union as well as greatness. "I learned," said the melancholy Pestalozzi, "that no man in God's wide earth is either willing or able to help any other man." Help must come from the bosom alone. The scholar is that man who must take up into himself all the ability of the time, all the contributions of the past, all the hopes of the future. He must be an university of knowledges. If there be one lesson more than another which should pierce his ear, it is, The world is nothing, the man is all; in yourself is the law of all nature, and you know not yet how a globule of sap ascends; in yourself lumbers the whole of Reason; it is for you to know all, it is for you to dare all. Mr. President and Gentlemen, this confidence in the unsearched might of man, belongs by all motives, by all prophecy, by all preparation, to the American Scholar. We have listened too long to the courtly muses of Europe. The spirit of the American freeman is already suspected to be timid, imitative, tame. Public and private avarice make the air we breathe thick and fat. The scholar is decent, indolent, complaisant. See already the tragic consequence. The mind of this country taught to aim at low objects, eats upon itself. There is no work for any but the decorous and the complaisant. Young men of the fairest promise, who begin life upon our shores, inflated by the mountain winds, shined upon by all the stars of God, find the earth below not in unison with these,—but are hindered from action by the disgust which the principles on which business is managed inspire, and turn drudges, or die of disgust,—some of them suicides. What is the remedy? They did not yet see, and thousands of young men as hopeful now crowding to the barriers for the career, do not yet see, that if the single man plant himself indomitably on his instincts, and there abide, the huge world will come round to him. Patience—patience;—with the shades of all the good and great for company; and for solace, the perspective of your own infinite life; and for work, the study and the communication of principles, the making those instincts prevalent, the conversion of the world. Is it not the chief disgrace in the world, not to be an unit;—not to be reckoned one character;—not to yield that peculiar fruit which each man was created to bear, but to be reckoned in the gross, in the hundred, or the thousand, of the party, the section, to which we belong; and our opinion predicted geographically, as the north, or the south. Not so, brothers and friends,—please God, ours shall not be so. We will walk on our own feet; we will work with our own hands; we will speak our own minds. The study of letters shall be no longer a name for pity, for doubt, and for sensual indulgence. The dread of man and the love of man shall be a wall of defence and a wreath of joy around all. A nation of men will for the first time exist, because each believes himself inspired by the Divine Soul which also inspires all men.

. . . .

QUESTIONS FOR A SECOND READING

1. At the end of his essay, Emerson says "If the single man plant himself indomitably on his instincts, and there abide, the huge world will come round to him." As you reread this essay, what do you come to understand about "instinct," as Emerson refers to it? Could you say, for example, that Emerson is arguing that every student should be free to do what he or she wants? If so, what role would teachers or writers play in a person's education? If not, what should a student do other than take notes, read carefully, and follow the rules?
2. The scholar in this essay is both a person who learns and a person who teaches. (The latter is described most fully in the section on the scholar's duties.) How does Emerson describe the best possible relationship between a scholar and his or her teachers? How does he describe the best possible relationship between the scholar and those he or she would teach? In what ways, if at all, would the scholar change as he or she moved from the role of student into the role of teacher?
3. In section I of the essay, Emerson charts the growth of a young person's mind and at the end concludes that, if all goes well, "Know Thyself" and "Study Nature" become "at last one maxim." What does he mean by this? It sounds lofty and pious, but if you take your own case or the case of a child you know well, how might you use section I to comment on current practices in American education? What would be your most useful and powerful examples?
4. In section II of the essay, Emerson talks about the relationship between the scholar and the "mind of the past" and, in particular, about the proper and improper uses of books. Books, he says, "are the best of things, well used; abused, among the worst." What do you suppose Emerson would say is the best use of this essay? As you read through the essay, what kind of reader does Emerson invite you to be? What would you have to do—specifically and at specific places—to be an "Emersonian" reader of Emerson?

ASSIGNMENTS FOR WRITING

1. Emerson says that in the three numbered sections of his essay he has "spoken of the education of the scholar by nature, by books, and by action." Let's say that you wanted to take Emerson as a guide and imagine an appropriate "Emersonian" curriculum or institution. Write an essay (cast, perhaps, as a position paper or an article for an alumni magazine) that uses "The American Scholar" to comment specifically on the curriculum at your own school. (It might be useful to go to your college catalogue, or whatever documents your school has prepared to explain its curriculum, to see what they have to say about the role of nature, books, and action in a person's education.)
2. Let's imagine Emerson himself as a teacher who wants to have his students read "The American Scholar" (perhaps along with some other selections from this anthology). What kind of assignment might he give? What, that is, would he ask you to *do* with the readings? What would he do as your teacher? Write an essay that considers both how, in practice, a modern teacher might encourage an Emersonian use of books and why, so far as you are concerned, a modern teacher might want to.

MAKING CONNECTIONS

1. Emerson speaks early in his essay about the importance of studying nature, although his way of speaking about this activity is at times puzzling and paradoxical. He says at one point

> The first in time and the first in importance of the influences upon the mind is that of nature. Every day the sun; and, after sunset, the night and her stars. Ever the winds blow; ever the grass grows. Every day, men and women, conversing, beholding and beholden. The scholar must needs stand wistful and admiring before this great spectacle. He must settle its value in his mind.

And, yet, at another he says

> To the young mind, every thing is individual, stands by itself. By and by, it finds how to join two things, and see in them one nature; then three, then three thousand; and so, tyrannized over by its own unifying instinct, it goes on tying things together, diminishing anomalies, discovering roots running under ground, whereby contrary and remote things cohere, and flower out from one stem.

It's hard to know how to reconcile the two stances here. In one the scholar stands wistful and admiring before a great spectacle; in the other the scholar connects this with that, following his or her own "tyrannical" unifying instinct. How is a person to stamp his or her order on nature and, at the same time, stand back and admire nature's variety?

When Annie Dillard goes off to live at Tinker Creek, a journey recorded in "The Fixed" (p. 155), she is working in a tradition that follows directly from Emerson and his student, Thoreau; that is, she is seriously following this injunction to study nature. Write an essay in which you use Dillard as an example to test and examine what Emerson says about the process and value of *studying* nature. If you look at Dillard as a case in point, as an example of what it means to "study nature," what is the relation between her seeing something and the thing she sees? Or, more generally, what is the good of studying nature? Is she or is she not doing what Emerson says we should do?

Note: Here is a way to begin this assignment. Take one specific example from "The Fixed," one that you think best shows Dillard as a student of nature. If you work solely from that example, how might you make sense out of the (often mysterious) final paragraph in section I of "The American Scholar" (where Emerson says, for example, that the scholar "shall see that nature is the opposite of his soul, answering to it part for part. One is seal, and one is print").

2. Both Emerson, in "The American Scholar," and Paulo Freire, in "The 'Banking' Concept of Education" (p. 238), seem to be arguing for freedom or for a form of education that allows students to be free. If we grant that this is common ground, it may be interesting to consider the significant differences in their arguments. Write an essay in which you compare Emerson's and Freire's account of the ideal education. What does "freedom" come to mean for each? And what does this freedom have to do with knowledge or truth, or whatever it is that a student is supposed to gain by an education?

STANLEY FISH

STANLEY FISH was born in Providence, Rhode Island, in 1938. He is the author of several books, including John Skelton's Poetry, Self-Consuming Artifacts: The Experience of Seventeenth-Century Literature, *and* Surprised by Sin: The Reader in Paradise Lost. *He is presently William Kenan, Jr., Professor of English at Johns Hopkins University in Baltimore.*

Fish is one of this country's most influential and provocative literary critics. His writing is witty, bold, and straightforward; and he seems to delight in controversy. Fish once said, in fact, that his only responsibility as a critic was to be interesting, not to be right. (He later took this statement back—although not the part about being interesting.)

The essay included here, "How to Recognize a Poem When You See One," is from a series of lectures he gave at Kenyon College in Ohio in 1979. Fish said that he found the event exhilarating and exhausting and that "apparently, some of the same feelings were shared by the audience, for in an editorial written for the college newspaper (entitled, 'Fish Baits Audience'*) generous praise of my 'intellectual skill' was qualified by the observation that, needless to say, 'it was not always the skill of a gentleman.' "*

In his recent work, Fish does not write about individual literary texts and what they mean but about reading itself—about how such texts are read or how they might be read. He begins with the assumption that "good" readers can read the same work and not agree on what it says. When two people read the same story but interpret it differently, Fish would argue, this does not necessarily mean that one reader "got it" and that the other didn't, but that different people read differently—they "make" the story into different stories when they read. The question Fish asks, then, is whether this means that any text can mean anything that anyone says it means—whether meaning is so unstable that a story could be said to have an infinite number of meanings and that no one, not even an English teacher, can tell right from wrong.

The following essay is from a book titled Is There a Text In This Class? *The title comes from a question asked by a student at Johns Hopkins. Her professor responded, "Yes; it's the* Norton Anthology of Literature,*" to which the student responded, "No, no. I mean in this class do we believe in poems and things, or is it just us?" "How To Recognize a Poem When You See One" addresses the question of whether there are such things as poems or whether readers make them up as they go along.*

How to Recognize a Poem When You See One

In the summer of 1971 I was teaching two courses under the joint auspices of the Linguistic Institute of America and the English Department of the State University of New York at Buffalo. I taught these courses in the morning and in the same room. At 9:30 I would meet a group of students who were interested in the relationship between linguistics and literary criticism. Our nominal subject was stylistics but our concerns were finally theoretical and extended to the presuppositions and assumptions which underlie both linguistic and literary practice. At 11:00 these students were replaced by another group whose concerns were exclusively literary and were in fact confined to English religious poetry of the seventeenth century. These students had been learning how to identify Christian symbols and how to recognize typological patterns and how to move from the observation of these symbols and patterns to the specification of a poetic intention that was usually didactic or homiletic. On the day I am thinking about, the only connection between the two classes was an assignment given to the first which was still on the blackboard at the beginning of the second. It read:

Jacobs–Rosenbaum
Levin
Thorne
Hayes
Ohman (?)

I am sure that many of you will have already recognized the names on this list, but for the sake of the record, allow me to identify them. Roderick Jacobs and Peter Rosenbaum are two linguists who have coauthored a number of textbooks and coedited a number of anthologies. Samuel Levin is a linguist who was one of the first to apply the operations of transformational grammar to literary texts. J. P. Thorne is a linguist at Edinburgh who, like Levin, was attempting to extend the rules of transformational grammar to the notorious irregularities of poetic language. Curtis Hayes is a linguist who was then using transformational grammar in order to establish an objective basis for his intuitive impression that the language of Gibbon's *Rise and Fall of the Roman Empire* is more complex than the language of Hemingway's novels. And Richard Ohmann is the literary critic who, more than any other, was responsible for introducing the vocabulary of transformational grammar to the literary community. Ohmann's name was spelled as you see it here because I could not remember whether it contained one or two n's. In other words, the question mark in parenthesis signified nothing more than a faulty memory and a desire on my part to appear scrupulous. The fact that the names appeared in a list that was arranged vertically, and that Levin, Thorne, and Hayes formed a column that was more or less centered in relation to the paired names of Jacobs and Rosenbaum, was similarly accidental and was evidence only of a certain compulsiveness if, indeed, it was evidence of anything at all.

In the time between the two classes I made only one change. I drew a frame around the assignment and wrote on the top of that frame "p. 43." When the members of the second class filed in I told them that what they saw on the blackboard was a religious poem of the kind they had been studying and I asked them to interpret it. Immediately they began to perform in a manner that, for reasons which will become clear, was more or less predictable. The first student to speak pointed out that the poem was probably a hieroglyph, although he was not sure whether it was in the shape of a cross or an altar. This question was set aside as the other students, following his lead, began to concentrate on individual words, interrupting each other with suggestions that came so quickly that they seemed spontaneous. The first line of the poem (the very order of events assumed the already constituted status of the object) received the most attention: Jacobs was explicated as a reference to Jacob's ladder, traditionally allegorized as a figure for the Christian ascent to heaven. In this poem, however, or so my students told me, the means of ascent is not a ladder but a tree, a rose tree or rosenbaum. This was seen to be an obvious reference to the Virgin Mary who was often characterized as a rose without thorns, itself an emblem of the immaculate conception. At this point the poem appeared to the students to be operating in the familiar manner of an iconographic riddle. It at once posed the question, "How is it that a man can climb to heaven by means of a rose tree?" and directed the reader to the inevitable answer: by the fruit of that tree, the fruit of Mary's womb, Jesus. Once this interpretation was established it received support from, and conferred significance on, the word "thorne," which could only be an allusion to the crown of thorns, a symbol of the trial suffered by Jesus and of the price he paid to save us all. It was only a short step (really no step at all) from this insight to the recognition of Levin as a double reference, first to the tribe of Levi, of whose priestly function Christ was the fulfillment, and second to the unleavened bread carried by the children of Israel on their exodus from Egypt, the place of sin, and in response to the call of Moses, perhaps the most familiar of the old testament types of Christ. The final word of the poem was given at least three complementary readings: it could be "omen," especially since so much of the poem is concerned with foreshadowing and prophecy; it could be Oh Man, since it is man's story as it intersects with the divine plan that is the poem's subject; and it could, of course, be simply "amen," the proper conclusion to a poem celebrating the love and mercy shown by a God who gave his only begotten son so that we may live.

In addition to specifying significances for the words of the poem and relating those significances to one another, the students began to discern larger structural patterns. It was noted that of the six names in the poem three—Jacobs, Rosenbaum, and Levin—are Hebrew, two—Thorne and Hayes—are Christian, and one—Ohman—is ambiguous, the ambiguity being marked in the poem itself (as the phrase goes) by the question mark in parenthesis. This division was seen as a reflection of the basic distinction between the old dispensation and the new, the law of sin and the law of love. That distinction, however, is blurred and finally dissolved by the typological perspective which invests the old testament events and heroes with new testament meanings. The structure of the poem, my students concluded, is therefore a double one, establishing and undermining its basic pattern (Hebrew vs. Christian) at the same time. In this context there is finally no pressure to resolve the ambiguity of Ohman since the two possible readings—the name is Hebrew, the name is Christian—are both authorized by the reconciling presence in the poem of Jesus Christ. Finally, I must report that one student took to counting letters and found, to no one's surprise, that the most prominent letters in the poem were S, O, N.

Some of you will have noticed that I have not yet said anything about

Hayes. This is because of all the words in the poem it proved the most recalcitrant to interpretation, a fact not without consequence, but one which I will set aside for the moment since I am less interested in the details of the exercise than in the ability of my students to perform it. What is the source of that ability? How is it that they were able to do what they did? What is it that they did? These questions are important because they bear directly on a question often asked in literary theory, What are the distinguishing features of literary language? Or, to put the matter more colloquially, How do you recognize a poem when you see one? The commonsense answer, to which many literary critics and linguists are committed, is that the act of recognition is triggered by the observable presence of distinguishing features. That is, you know a poem when you see one because its language displays the characteristics that you know to be proper to poems. This, however, is a model that quite obviously does not fit the present example. My students did not proceed from the noting of distinguishing features to the recognition that they were confronted by a poem; rather, it was the act of recognition that came first—they knew in advance that they were dealing with a poem—and the distinguishing features then followed.

In other words, acts of recognition, rather than being triggered by formal characteristics, are their source. It is not that the presence of poetic qualities compels a certain kind of attention but that the paying of a certain kind of attention results in the emergence of poetic qualities. As soon as my students were aware that it was poetry they were seeking, they began to look with poetry-seeing eyes, that is, with eyes that saw everything in relation to the properties they knew poems to possess. They knew, for example (because they were told by their teachers), that poems are (or are supposed to be) more densely and intricately organized than ordinary communications; and that knowledge translated itself into a willingness—one might even say a determination—to see connections between one word and another and between every word and the poem's central insight. Moreover, the assumption that there *is* a central insight is itself poetry-specific, and presided over its own realization. Having assumed that the collection of words before them was unified by an informing purpose (because unifying purposes are what poems have), my students proceeded to find one and to formulate it. It was in the light of that purpose (now assumed) that significances for the individual words began to suggest themselves, significances which then fleshed out the assumption that had generated them in the first place. Thus the meanings of the words and the interpretation in which those words were seen to be embedded emerged together, as a consequence of the operations my students began to perform once they were told that this was a poem.

It was almost as if they were following a recipe—if it's a poem do this, if it's a poem, see it that way—and indeed definitions of poetry *are* recipes, for by directing readers as to what to look for in a poem, they instruct them in ways of looking that will produce what they expect to see. If your definition of poetry tells you that the language of poetry is complex, you will scrutinize the language of something identified as a poem in such a way as to bring out the complexity you know to be "there." You will, for example, be on the look-out for latent ambiguities; you will attend to the presence of alliterative and consonantal patterns (there will always be some), and you will try to make something of them (you will always succeed); you will search for meanings that subvert, or exist in a tension with the meanings that first present themselves; and if these operations fail to produce the anticipated complexity, you will even propose a significance for the words that are *not* there, because, as everyone knows, everything about a poem, including its omissions, is significant. Nor, as you do these things, will you have any sense of performing in a willful manner, for you will only be doing what you learned to do in the course of becoming a skilled reader of poetry. Skilled reading is usually thought to be a matter of discerning what is there, but if the example of my students can be generalized, it is a matter of knowing how to *produce* what can thereafter be said to be there. Interpretation is not the art of construing but the art of constructing. Interpreters do not decode poems; they make them.

To many, this will be a distressing conclusion, and there are a number of arguments that could be mounted in order to forestall it. One might point out that the circumstances of my students' performance were special. After all, they had been concerned exclusively with religious poetry for some weeks, and therefore would be uniquely vulnerable to the deception I had practiced on them and uniquely equipped to impose religious themes and patterns on words innocent of either. I must report, however, that I have duplicated this experiment any number of times at nine or ten universities in three countries, and the results are always the same, even when the participants know from the beginning that what they are looking at was originally an assignment. Of course this very fact could itself be turned into an objection: doesn't the reproducibility of the exercise prove that there is something about these words that leads everyone to perform in the same way? Isn't it just a happy accident that names like Thorne and Jacobs have counterparts or near counterparts in biblical names and symbols? And wouldn't my students have been unable to do what they did if the assignment I gave to the first class had been made up of different names? The answer to all of these questions is no. Given a firm belief that they were confronted by a religious poem, my students would have been able to turn any list of names into the kind of poem we have before us now, because they would have read the names within the assumption that they were informed with Christian significances. (This is nothing more than a literary analogue to Augustine's rule of faith.) You can test this assertion by replacing Jacobs-Rosenbaum, Levin, Thorne, Hayes, and Ohman with names drawn from the faculty of Kenyon College—Temple, Jordan, Seymour, Daniels, Star, Church. I will not exhaust my time or your patience by performing a full-dress analysis, which would involve, of course, the relation between those who saw the River Jordan and those who saw *more* by seeing the Star of Bethlehem, thus fulfilling the prophecy by which the temple of Jerusalem was replaced by the inner temple or church built up in the heart of every Christian. Suffice it to say that it could easily be done (you can take the poem home and do it yourself) and that the shape of its doing would be constrained not by the names but by the interpretive assumptions that gave them a significance even before they were seen. This would be true even if there were no names on the list, if the paper or blackboard were blank; the blankness would present no problem to the interpreter, who would immediately see in it the void out of which God created the earth, or the abyss into which unregenerate sinners fall, or, in the best of all possible poems, both.

Even so, one might reply, all you've done is demonstrate how an interpretation, if it is prosecuted with sufficient vigor, can impose itself on material which has its own proper shape. Basically, at the ground level, in the first place, when all is said and done, "Jacobs-Rosenbaum Levin Thorne Hayes Ohman(?)" is an assignment; it is only a trick that allows you to transform it into a poem, and when the effects of the trick have worn off, it will return to its natural form and be seen as an assignment once again. This is a powerful argument because it seems at once to give interpretation its due (as an act of the will) and to maintain the independence of that on which interpretation works. It allows us, in short, to preserve our commonsense intuition that interpretation must be interpretation of *something*. Unfortunately, the argument will not hold because the assignment we all see is no less the product of interpretation than the poem into which it was turned. That is, it requires just as much work, and work of the same kind, to see this as an assignment as it does to see it as a poem. If this seems counterintuitive, it is only because the work required to see it as an assignment is work we have already done, in the course of acquiring the huge amount of background knowledge that enables you and me to function in the academic world. In order to know what an assignment is, that is, in order to know what to do with something identified as an assignment, you must first know what a class is (know that it isn't an economic grouping) and know that classes meet at specified times for so many weeks, and that one's performance in a class is largely a matter of performing between classes.

Think for a moment of how you would explain this last to someone who did not already know it. "Well," you might say, "a class is a group situation in which a number of people are instructed by an informed person in a particular subject." (Of course the notion of "subject" will itself require explication.) "An assignment is something you do when you're not in class." "Oh, I see," your interlocutor might respond, "an assignment is something you do to take your mind off what you've been doing in class." "No, an assignment is a part of a class." "But how can that be if you only do it when the class is not meeting?" Now it would be possible, finally, to answer that question, but only by enlarging the horizons of your explanation to include the very concept of a university, what it is one might be doing there, why one might be doing it instead of doing a thousand other things, and so on. For most of us these matters do not require explanation, and indeed, it is hard for us to imagine someone for whom they do; but that is because our tacit knowledge of what it means to move around in academic life was acquired so gradually and so long ago that it doesn't seem like knowledge at all (and therefore something someone else might *not* know) but a part of the world. You might think that when you're on campus (a phrase that itself requires volumes) that you are simply walking around on the two legs God gave you; but your walking is informed by an internalized awareness of institutional goals and practices, of norms of behavior, of lists of do's and don't's, of invisible lines and the dangers of crossing them; and, as a result, you see everything as *already* organized in relation to those same goals and practices. It would never occur to you, for example, to wonder if the people pouring out of that building are fleeing from a fire; you *know* that they are exiting from a class (what could be more obvious?) and you know that because your perception of their action occurs within a knowledge of what people in a university could possibly be doing and the reasons they could have for doing it (going to the next class, going back to the dorm, meeting someone in the student union). It is within that same knowledge that an assignment becomes intelligible so that it appears to you immediately as an obligation, as a set of directions, as something with parts, some of which may be more significant than others. That is, it is a proper question to ask of an assignment whether some of its parts might be omitted or slighted, whereas readers of poetry know that no part of a poem can be slighted (the rule is "everything counts") and they do not rest until every part has been given a significance.

In a way this amounts to no more than saying what everyone already knows: poems and assignments are different, but my point is that the differences are a result of the different interpretive operations we perform and not of something inherent in one or the other. An assignment no more compels its own recognition than does a poem; rather, as in the case of a poem, the shape of an assignment emerges when someone looks at something identified as one with assignment-seeing eyes, that is, with eyes which are capable of seeing the words as already embedded within the institutional structure that makes it possible for assignments to have a sense. The ability to see, and therefore to make, an assignment is no less a learned ability than the ability to see, and therefore to make, a poem. Both are constructed artifacts, the products and not the producers of interpretation, and while the differences between them are real, they are interpretive and do not have their source in some bedrock level of objectivity.

Of course one might want to argue that there is a bedrock level at which these names constitute neither an assignment nor a poem but are merely a list. But that argument too falls because a list is no more a natural object—one that wears its meaning on its face and can be recognized by anyone—than an assignment or a poem. In order to see a list, one must already be equipped with the concepts of seriality, hierarchy, subordination, and so on, and while these are by no mean esoteric concepts and seem available to almost everyone, they are nonetheless learned, and if there were someone who had not learned them, he or she would not be able to see a list. The next recourse is to descend still lower (in the direction of atoms) and to claim objectivity for letters, paper, graphite, black marks on white spaces, and so on; but these entities too have palpability and shape only because of the assumption of some or other system of intelligibility, and they are therefore just as available to a deconstructive dissolution as are poems, assignments, and lists.

The conclusion, therefore, is that all objects are made and not found, and that they are made by the interpretive strategies we set in motion. This does not, however, commit me to subjectivity because the means by which they are made are social and conventional. That is, the "you" who does the interpretive work that puts poems and assignments and lists into the world is a communal you and not an isolated individual. No one of us wakes up in the morning and (in French fashion) reinvents poetry or thinks up a new educational system or decides to reject seriality in favor of some other, wholly original, form of organization. We do not do these things because we could not do them, because the mental operations we can perform are limited by the institutions in which we are *already* embedded. These institutions precede us, and it is only by inhabiting them, or being inhabited by them, that we have access to the public and conventional senses they make. Thus while it is true to say that we create poetry (and assignments and lists), we create it through interpretive strategies that are finally not our own but have their source in a publicly available system of intelligibility. Insofar as the system (in this case a literary system) constrains us, it also fashions us, furnishing us with categories of understanding, with which we in turn fashion the entities to which we can then point. In short, to the list of made or constructed objects we must add ourselves, for we no less than the poems and assignments we see are the products of social and cultural patterns of thought.

To put the matter in this way is to see that the opposition between objectivity and subjectivity is a false one because neither exists in the pure form that would give the opposition its point. This is precisely illustrated by my anecdote in which we do *not* have free-standing readers in a relationship of perceptual adequacy or inadequacy to an equally free-standing text. Rather, we have readers whose consciousnesses are constituted by a set of conventional notions which when put into operation constitute in turn a conventional, and conventionally seen, object. My students could do what they did, and do it in unison, because as members of a literary community they knew what a poem was (their knowledge was public), and that knowledge led them to look in such a way as to populate the landscape with what they knew to be poems.

Of course poems are not the only objects that are constituted in unison by shared ways of seeing. Every object or event that becomes available within an institutional setting can be so characterized. I am thinking, for example, of something that happened in my classroom just the other day. While I was in the course of vigorously making a point, one of my students, William Newlin by name, was just as vigorously waving his hand. When I asked the other members of the class what it was that Mr. Newlin was doing, they all answered that he was seeking permission to speak. I then asked them how they knew that. The immediate reply was that it was obvious; what else could he be thought to be doing? The meaning of his gesture, in other words, was right there on its surface, available for reading by anyone who had the eyes to see. That meaning, however, would not have been available to someone without any knowledge of what was involved in being a student. Such a person might have thought that Mr. Newlin was pointing to the fluorescent lights hanging from the ceiling, or calling our attention to some object that was about to fall ("the sky is falling," "the sky is falling"). And if the someone in question were a child of elementary or middle-school age, Mr. Newlin might well have been seen as seeking permission not to speak but to go to the bathroom, an interpretation or reading that would never occur to a student at Johns Hopkins or any other institution of "higher learning" (and how would we explain to the uninitiated the meaning of *that* phrase).

The point is the one I have made so many times before: it is neither the case that the significance of Mr. Newlin's gesture is imprinted on its surface where it need only be read off, or that the construction put on the gesture by everyone in the room was individual and idiosyncratic. Rather, the source of our interpretive unanimity was a structure of interests and understood goals, a structure whose categories so filled our individual consciousnesses that they were rendered as one, immediately investing phenomena with the significance they *must* have, given the already-in-place assumptions about what someone could possibly be intending (by word or gesture) in a classroom. By seeing Mr. Newlin's raised hand with a single shaping eye, we were demonstrating what Harvey Sacks has characterized as "the fine power of a culture. It does not, so to speak, merely fill brains in roughly the same way, it fills them so that they are alike in fine detail."[1] The occasion of Sacks's observation was the ability of his hearers to understand a sequence of two sentences—"The baby cried. The mommy picked it up."—exactly as he did (assuming, for example that "the 'mommy' who picks up the 'baby' is the mommy of that baby"), despite the fact that alternative ways of understanding were demonstrably possible. That is, the mommy of the second sentence could well have been the mommy of some other baby, and it need not even have been a baby that this "floating" mommy was picking up. One is tempted to say that in the absence of a specific context we are authorized to take the words literally, which is what Sacks's hearers do; but as Sacks observes, it is within the assumption of a context—one so deeply assumed that we are unaware of it—that the words acquire what seems to be their literal meaning. There is nothing *in the words* that tells Sacks and his hearers how to relate the mommy and the baby of this story, just as there is nothing *in the form* of Mr. Newlin's gesture that tells his fellow students how to determine its significance. In both cases the determination (of relation and significance) is the work of categories of organization—the family, being a student—that are from the very first giving shape and value to what is heard and seen.

Indeed, these categories are the very shape of seeing itself, in that we are not to imagine a perceptual ground more basic than the one they afford. That is, we are not to imagine a moment when my students "simply see" a physical configuration of atoms and *then* assign that configuration a significance, according to the situation they happen to be in. To be in the situation (this or any other) is to "see" with the eyes of its interests, its goals, its understood practices, values, and norms, and so to be conferring significance *by* seeing, not after it. The categories of my students' vision are the categories by which they understand themselves to be functioning as students (what Sacks might term "doing studenting"), and objects will appear to them in forms related to that way of functioning rather than in some objective or preinterpretive form. (This is true even when an object is seen as not related, since nonrelation is not a pure but a differential category—the specification of something by enumerating what it is not; in short, nonrelation is merely one form of relation, and its perception is always situation-specific.)

Of course, if someone who was not functioning as a student was to walk into my classroom, he might very well see Mr. Newlin's raised hand

[1] "On the Analysability of Stories by Children," in *Ethnomethodology*, ed. Roy Turner (Baltimore: Penguin, 1974), p. 218.

(and "raised hand" is already an interpretation-laden description) in some other way, as evidence of a disease, as the salute of a political follower, as a muscle-improving exercise, as an attempt to kill flies; but he would always see it in *some* way, and never as purely physical data waiting for his interpretation. And, moreover, the way of seeing, whatever it was, would never be individual or idiosyncratic, since its source would always be the institutional structure of which the "see-er" was an extending agent. This is what Sacks means when he says that a culture fills brains "so that they are alike in fine detail"; it fills them so that no one's interpretive acts are exclusively his own but fall to him by virtue of his position in some socially organized environment and are therefore always shared and public. It follows, then, that the fear of solipsism, of the imposition by the unconstrained self of its own prejudices, is unfounded because the self does not exist apart from the communal or conventional categories of thought that enable its operations (of thinking, seeing, reading). Once one realizes that the conceptions that fill consciousness, including any conception of its own status, are culturally derived, the very notion of an unconstrained self, of a consciousness wholly and dangerously free, becomes incomprehensible.

But without the notion of the unconstrained self, the arguments of Hirsch, Abrams, and the other proponents of objective interpretation are deprived of their urgency. They are afraid that in the absence of the controls afforded by a normative system of meanings, the self will simply substitute its own meanings for the meanings (usually identified with the intentions of the author) that texts bring with them, the meanings that texts *"have"*; however, if the self is conceived of not as an independent entity but as a social construct whose operations are delimited by the systems of intelligibility that inform it, then the meanings it confers on texts are not its own but have their source in the interpretive community (or communities) of which it is a function. Moreover, these meanings will be neither subjective nor objective, at least in the terms assumed by those who argue within the traditional framework: they will not be objective because they will always have been the product of a point of view rather than having been simply "read off"; and they will not be subjective because that point of view will always be social or institutional. Or by the same reasoning one could say that they are *both* subjective and objective: they are subjective because they inhere in a particular point of view and are therefore not universal; and they are objective because the point of view that delivers them is public and conventional rather than individual or unique.

To put the matter in either way is to see how unhelpful the terms "subjective" and "objective" finally are. Rather than facilitating inquiry, they close it down, by deciding in advance what shape inquiry can possibly take. Specifically, they assume, without being aware that it is an assumption and therefore open to challenge, the very distinction I have been putting into question, the distinction between interpreters and the objects they interpret. That distinction in turn assumes that interpreters and their objects are two different kinds of *a*contextual entities, and within these twin assumptions the issue can only be one of control: will texts be allowed to constrain their own interpretation or will irresponsible interpreters be allowed to obscure and overwhelm texts. In the spectacle that ensues, the spectacle of Anglo-American critical controversy, texts and selves fight it out in the persons of their respective champions, Abrams, Hirsch, Reichert, Graff on the one hand, Holland, Bleich, Slatoff, and (in some characterizations of him) Barthes° on the other. But if selves are constituted by the ways of thinking and seeing that inhere in social organizations, and if these constituted selves in turn constitute texts according to these same ways, then there can be no adversary relationship between text and self because they are the necessarily related products of the same cognitive possibilities. A text cannot be overwhelmed by an irresponsible reader and one need not worry about protecting the purity of a text from a reader's idiosyncracies. It is only the distinction between subject and object that gives rise to these urgencies, and once the distinction is blurred they simply fall away. One can respond with a cheerful yes to the question "Do readers make meanings?" and commit oneself to very little because it would be equally true to say that meanings, in the form of culturally derived interpretive categories, make readers.

Indeed, many things look rather different once the subject-object dichotomy is eliminated as the assumed framework within which critical discussion occurs. Problems disappear, not because they have been solved but because they are shown never to have been problems in the first place. Abrams, for example, wonders how, in the absence of a normative system of stable meanings, two people could ever agree on the interpretation of a work or even of a sentence; but the difficulty is only a difficulty if the two (or more) people are thought of as isolated individuals whose agreement must be compelled by something external to them. (There is something of the police state in Abrams's vision, complete with posted rules and boundaries, watchdogs to enforce them, procedures for identifying their violators as criminals.) But if the understandings of the people in question are informed by the same notions of what counts as a fact, of what is central, peripheral, and worthy of being noticed—in short, by the same interpretive principles—then agreement between them will be assured, and its source will not be a text that enforces its own perception but a way of perceiving that results in the emergence to those who share it (or those whom it shares)

Abrams, Hirsch, Reichert, Graff . . . , Holland, Bleich, Slatoff, and . . . Barthes Central figures in the critical controversy over whether meanings should properly be said to reside in texts or in readers.

of the same text. That text might be a poem, as it was in the case of those who first "saw" "Jacobs-Rosenbaum Levin Hayes Thorne Ohman(?)," or a hand, as it is every day in a thousand classrooms; but whatever it is, the shape and meaning it appears immediately to have will be the "ongoing accomplishment"[2] of those who agree to produce it.

[2] A phrase used by the ethnomethodologists to characterize the interpretive activities that create and maintain the features of everyday life. See, for example, Don H. Zimmerman, "Fact as a Practical Accomplishment," in *Ethnomethodology*, pp. 128–143.

QUESTIONS FOR A SECOND READING

1. Fish devotes part of this essay to talking about the experience of being a student. He talks, for example, about students "doing studenting" and seeing what they have been taught to see. Does this sound right to you? Does his account of a student's experience seem consistent with your experience, as you understand it? As you reread the essay, think about where and how Fish might be said to have it right or to have it wrong when he talks about the student's experience of the classroom.
2. Surely Fish had several stories to tell when he told this story about what he did in class. In fact, it is safe to say that he had an audience in mind beyond the teachers and students who gathered together to hear him at Kenyon College. He alludes, for example, to people who have a "fear of solipsism" or who are "afraid" of the absence of those controls "afforded by a normative system of meaning." Fish is addressing the special concerns of a special community of literary theorists, but you don't have to know the issues (or share their way of speaking) to read Fish's essay. It is interesting, however, to imagine who these people are and what they argue about. As you read through the essay for a second time, see what conclusions you can draw about this specialized audience. What does Fish expect that they will see in the story he tells? What does he assume will please them, or impress them, or make them nervous? How do you think their questions or concerns are similar to or different from your own? (What points in the essay, for example, make you nervous? or impressed? or pleased?)

ASSIGNMENTS FOR WRITING

1. Fish seems quite pleased to tell the story that he tells, and he seems quite happy with what his students do with the "poem" on the blackboard. It's not just that he is pleased with his performance as a teacher (although that

pleasure is there), but that the story he tells nicely reveals a basic truth about learning or about all classrooms where students are expected to interpret phenomena—books, artifacts, experiments, human behavior—as members of an interpretive community. Fish's unusual example enables us to see something we would otherwise miss in our own routine experience. At least that is part of the argument of the essay.

Choose a single class period from your recent experience that you could hold up for comparison. Choose carefully, since a class with few points of connection will leave you with little to say. Write an essay in which you tell the story of this class period, and tell it from Fish's point of view. You could imagine, for example, that you are part of his team, doing field work to test his argument. Does your example seem to demonstrate the validity of Fish's argument? Does it suggest a modification of his argument or a different perspective altogether?

2. Fish tells the story of Mr. Newlin's raised hand as a way of summarizing or recapitulating the story of his class and the "poem." Mr. Newlin's raised hand could be a sign that Mr. Newlin has to go to the bathroom, or that the light is falling from the ceiling, or that he is catching flies. It only "obviously" means that Mr. Newlin has something to say to a teacher to those who see through those eyes (who share a "structure of interests and understood goals . . .").

   Write an essay in which you tell a similar anecdote, one about an everyday sight that has a significance obvious to everyone who sees it, but that could also be interpreted in other ways. In your essay you should examine several possible interpretations, speculate on why the "community" sees one but not the others, and discuss the consequences of this single, shaping vision. You should, wherever possible, use Fish's key terms or phrases and try to see through his eyes, at least initially, since this will give you a way of working out some of the more difficult theoretical parts of his argument.

MAKING CONNECTIONS

1. "Undoubtedly there is a right way of reading," says Emerson in "The American Scholar" (p. 203), "so it be sternly subordinated." Both Emerson and Fish are concerned with how students read, with the limits and possibilities of those acts of reading, and with the role of reading in a general education.

   Let's imagine that two experimental schools have been designed on Fishian and Emersonian principles. We'll call them Emerson University and Fish University.

   What differences would there be in the way students are taught to read (or in the way readings might be assigned) at each school? What would instructors do? How, for example, might they use some of the essays in this book? What would students be asked to do?

   What differences would there be in introductory courses? in courses for seniors? What assumptions would teachers make at each school about the link between introductory and advanced work?

Write an essay in which you report on the differences between these two programs of study. You could imagine that you are preparing a comparative study for an article on these two experimental schools.

2. Walker Percy, in "The Loss of the Creature" (p. 393) argues that "a student who has the desire to get at a dogfish or a Shakespeare sonnet may have the greatest difficulty in salvaging the creature itself from the educational package in which it is presented." Fish's anecdote seems to provide an almost classic case for Percy. You could say that this teacher took a dogfish, put it on the desk in a Shakespeare class, and his students turned it into a sonnet. Fish says, "Skilled reading is usually thought to be a matter of discerning what is there, but if the example of my students can be generalized, it is a matter of knowing how to *produce* what can thereafter be said to be there. Interpretation is not the art of construing but the art of constructing."

   How would Percy read Fish's account of his poetry class? What would he notice? What would he say? And if Percy's greatest hope is that students can find a way of rescuing their specimens from the "educational package," what might he offer as an alternative for those students whose accomplishments Fish finds so comfortably predictable? Write an essay in which you "read" Fish's anecdote about the poetry class from the point of view of Percy's "The Loss of the Creature." You can imagine that you are carrying on Percy's work and applying his methods and ideas to the case of Fish and his students.

PAULO FREIRE

PAULO FREIRE (pronounce it "Fr-air-ah" unless you can make a Portugese "r") is one of the most influential radical educators of our world. A native of Recife, Brazil, he spent most of his early career working in poverty-stricken areas of his homeland, developing methods for teaching illiterate adults to read and write and (as he would say) to think critically and, thereby, to take power over their own lives. Because he has created a classroom where teachers and students have equal power and equal dignity, his work has stood as a model for educators around the world. It led also to sixteen years of exile after the military coup in Brazil in 1964. During that time he taught in Europe and in the United States and worked for the Allende government in Chile, training the teachers whose job it would be to bring modern agricultural methods to the peasants.

Freire was born in 1921. He has worked with the adult education programs of UNESCO, the Chilean Institute of Agrarian Reform, and the World Council of Churches. He is now professor of educational philosophy at the Catholic University of São Paulo. He is the author of Education for Critical Consciousness, The Politics of Education, *and* The Pedagogy of the Oppressed *(from which the following essay is drawn).*

For Freire, education is not an objective process, if by objective we mean "neutral" or "without bias or prejudice." Because teachers could be said to have something that their students lack, it is impossible to have a "neutral" classroom; and when teachers present a subject to their students, they also present a point of view on that subject. The choice, according to Freire, is fairly simple: teachers either work "for the liberation of the people—their humanization—or for their domestication, their domination." The practice of teaching, however, is anything but simple. According to Freire, a teacher's most crucial skill is his or her ability to assist students' struggle to gain control over the conditions of their lives, and this means helping them not only to know but "to know that they know."

The "Banking" Concept of Education

A careful analysis of the teacher-student relationship at any level, inside or outside the school, reveals its fundamentally *narrative* character. This relationship involves a narrating Subject (the teacher) and patient, listening objects (the students). The contents, whether values or empirical dimensions of reality, tend in the process of being narrated to become lifeless and petrified. Education is suffering from narration sickness.

The teacher talks about reality as if it were motionless, static, compartmentalized, and predictable. Or else he expounds on a topic completely alien to the existential experience of the students. His task is to "fill" the students with the contents of his narration—contents which are detached from reality, disconnected from the totality that engendered them and could give them significance. Words are emptied of their concreteness and become a hollow, alienated, and alienating verbosity.

The outstanding characteristic of this narrative education, then, is the sonority of words, not their transforming power. "Four times four is sixteen; the capital of Pará is Belém." The student records, memorizes, and repeats these phrases without perceiving what four times four really means, or realizing the true significance of "capital" in the affirmation "the capital of Pará is Belém," that is, what Belém means for Pará and what Pará means for Brazil.

Narration (with the teacher as narrator) leads the students to memorize mechanically the narrated content. Worse yet, it turns them into "containers," into "receptacles" to be "filled" by the teacher. The more completely he fills the receptacles, the better a teacher he is. The more meekly the receptacles permit themselves to be filled, the better students they are.

Education thus becomes an act of depositing, in which the students are the depositories and the teacher is the depositor. Instead of communicating, the teacher issues communiqués and makes deposits which the students patiently receive, memorize, and repeat. This is the "banking" concept of education, in which the scope of action allowed to the students extends only as far as receiving, filing, and storing the deposits. They do, it is true, have the opportunity to become collectors or cataloguers of the things they store. But in the last analysis, it is men themselves who are filed away through the lack of creativity, transformation, and knowledge in this (at best) misguided system. For apart from inquiry, apart from the praxis, men cannot be truly human. Knowledge emerges only through invention and reinvention, through the restless, impatient, continuing, hopeful inquiry men pursue in the world, with the world, and with each other.

In the banking concept of education, knowledge is a gift bestowed by those who consider themselves knowledgeable upon those whom they consider to know nothing. Projecting an absolute ignorance onto others, a characteristic of the ideology of oppression, negates education and knowledge as processes of inquiry. The teacher presents himself to his students as their necessary opposite; by considering their ignorance absolute, he justifies his own existence. The students, alienated like the slave in the Hegelian dialectic, accept their ignorance as justifying the teacher's existence—but, unlike the slave, they never discover that they educate the teacher.

The *raison d'être* of libertarian education, on the other hand, lies in its drive towards reconciliation. Education must begin with the solution of the teacher-student contradiction, by reconciling the poles of the contradiction so that both are simultaneously teachers *and* students.

This solution is not (nor can it be) found in the banking concept. On the contrary, banking education maintains and even stimulates the contradiction through the following attitudes and practices, which mirror oppressive society as a whole:

a. the teacher teaches and the students are taught;
b. the teacher knows everything and the students know nothing;
c. the teacher thinks and the students are thought about;
d. the teacher talks and the students listen—meekly;
e. the teacher disciplines and the students are disciplined;
f. the teacher chooses and enforces his choice, and the students comply;
g. the teacher acts and the students have the illusion of acting through the action of the teacher;
h. the teacher chooses the program content, and the students (who were not consulted) adapt to it;
i. the teacher confuses the authority of knowledge with his own profes-

sional authority, which he sets in opposition to the freedom of the students;

j. the teacher is the Subject of the learning process, while the pupils are mere objects.

It is not surprising that the banking concept of education regards men as adaptable, manageable beings. The more students work at storing the deposits entrusted to them, the less they develop the critical consciousness which would result from their intervention in the world as transformers of that world. The more completely they accept the passive role imposed on them, the more they tend simply to adapt to the world as it is and to the fragmented view of reality deposited in them.

The capability of banking education to minimize or annul the students' creative power and to stimulate their credulity serves the interests of the oppressors, who care neither to have the world revealed nor to see it transformed. The oppressors use their "humanitarianism" to preserve a profitable situation. Thus they react almost instinctively against any experiment in education which stimulates the critical faculties and is not content with a partial view of reality but always seeks out the ties which link one point to another and one problem to another.

Indeed, the interests of the oppressors lie in "changing the consciousness of the oppressed, not the situation which oppresses them";[1] for the more the oppressed can be led to adapt to that situation, the more easily they can be dominated. To achieve this end, the oppressors use the banking concept of education in conjunction with a paternalistic social action apparatus, within which the oppressed receive the euphemistic title of "welfare recipients." They are treated as individual cases, as marginal men who deviate from the general configuration of a "good, organized, and just" society. The oppressed are regarded as the pathology of the healthy society, which must therefore adjust these "incompetent and lazy" folk to its own patterns by changing their mentality. These marginals need to be "integrated," "incorporated" into the healthy society that they have "foresaken."

The truth is, however, that the oppressed are not "marginals," are not men living "outside" society. They have always been "inside"—inside the structure which made them "beings for others." The solution is not to "integrate" them into the structure of oppression, but to transform that structure so that they can become "beings for themselves." Such transformation, of course, would undermine the oppressors' purposes; hence their

[1]Simone de Beauvoir, *La Pensée de Droite, Aujord'hui* (Paris); ST, *El Pensamiento político de la Derecha* (Buenos Aires, 1963), p. 34.

utilization of the banking concept of education to avoid the threat of student *conscientização*.°

The banking approach to adult education, for example, will never propose to students that they critically consider reality. It will deal instead with such vital questions as whether Roger gave green grass to the goat, and insist upon the importance of learning that, on the contrary, *R*oger gave green grass to the *r*abbit. The "humanism" of the banking approach masks the effort to turn men into automatons—the very negation of their ontological vocation to be more fully human.

Those who use the banking approach, knowingly or unknowingly (for there are innumerable well-intentioned bank-clerk teachers who do not realize that they are serving only to dehumanize), fail to perceive that the deposits themselves contain contradictions about reality. But, sooner or later, these contradictions may lead formerly passive students to turn against their domestication and the attempt to domesticate reality. They may discover through existential experience that their present way of life is irreconcilable with their vocation to become fully human. They may perceive through their relations with reality that reality is really a *process*, undergoing constant transformation. If men are searchers and their ontological vocation is humanization, sooner or later they may perceive the contradiction in which banking education seeks to maintain them, and then engage themselves in the struggle for their liberation.

But the humanist, revolutionary educator cannot wait for this possibility to materialize. From the outset, his efforts must coincide with those of the students to engage in critical thinking and the quest for mutual humanization. His efforts must be imbued with a profound trust in men and their creative power. To achieve this, he must be a partner of the students in his relations with them.

The banking concept does not admit to such partnership—and necessarily so. To resolve the teacher-student contradiction, to exchange the role of depositor, prescriber, domesticator, for the role of student among students would be to undermine the power of oppression and serve the cause of liberation.

Implicit in the banking concept is the assumption of a dichotomy between man and the world: man is merely *in* the world, not *with* the world or with others; man is spectator, not re-creator. In this view, man is not a conscious being *(corpo consciente)*; he is rather the possessor of *a* consciousness: an empty "mind" passively open to the reception of deposits of real-

---

conscientização According to Freire's translator, "The term *conscientizacao* refers to learning to perceive social, political, and economic contradictions, and to take action against the oppressive elements of reality."

ity from the world outside. For example, my desk, my books, my coffee cup, all the objects before me—as bits of the world which surrounds me—would be "inside" me, exactly as I am inside my study right now. This view makes no distinction between being accessible to consciousness and entering consciousness. The distinction, however, is essential: the objects which surround me are simply accessible to my consciousness, not located within it. I am aware of them, but they are not inside me.

It follows logically from the banking notion of consciousness that the educator's role is to regulate the way the world "enters into" the students. His task is to organize a process which already occurs spontaneously, to "fill" the students by making deposits of information which he considers to constitute true knowledge.[2] And since men "receive" the world as passive entities, education should make them more passive still, and adapt them to the world. The educated man is the adapted man, because he is better "fit" for the world. Translated into practice, this concept is well suited to the purposes of the oppressors, whose tranquility rests on how well men fit the world the oppressors have created, and how little they question it.

The more completely the majority adapt to the purposes which the dominant minority prescribe for them (thereby depriving them of the right to their own purposes), the more easily the minority can continue to prescribe. The theory and practice of banking education serve this end quite efficiently. Verbalistic lessons, reading requirements,[3] the methods for evaluating "knowledge," the distance between the teacher and the taught, the criteria for promotion: everything in this ready-to-wear approach serves to obviate thinking.

The bank-clerk educator does not realize that there is no true security in his hypertrophied role, that one must seek to live *with* others in solidarity. One cannot impose oneself, nor even merely co-exist with one's students. Solidarity requires true communication, and the concept by which such an educator is guided fears and proscribes communication.

Yet only through communication can human life hold meaning. The teacher's thinking is authenticated only by the authenticity of the students' thinking. The teacher cannot think for his students, nor can he impose his thought on them. Authentic thinking, thinking that is concerned about *reality*, does not take place in ivory tower isolation, but only in commu-

---

[2]This concept corresponds to what Sartre calles the "digestive" or "nutritive" concept of education, in which knowledge is "fed" by the teacher to the students to "fill them out." See Jean-Paul Sartre, "Une idée fundamentale de la phénomenologie de Husserl: L'intentionalité," *Situations I* (Paris, 1947).

[3]For example, some professors specify in their reading lists that a book should be read from pages 10 to 15—and do this to "help" their students!

nication. If it is true that thought has meaning only when generated by action upon the world, the subordination of students to teachers becomes impossible.

Because banking education begins with a false understanding of men as objects, it cannot promote the development of what Fromm calls "biophily," but instead produces its opposite: "necrophily."

> While life is characterized by growth in a structured, functional manner, the necrophilous person loves all that does not grow, all that is mechanical. The necrophilous person is driven by the desire to transform the organic into the inorganic, to approach life mechanically, as if all living persons were things. . . . Memory, rather than experience; having, rather than being, is what counts. The necrophilous person can relate to an object—a flower or a person—only if he possesses it; hence a threat to his possession is a threat to himself; if he loses possession he loses contact with the world. . . . He loves control, and in the act of controlling he kills life.[4]

Oppression—overwhelming control—is necrophilic; it is nourished by love of death, not life. The banking concept of education, which serves the interests of oppression, is also necrophilic. Based on a mechanistic, static, naturalistic, spatialized view of consciousness, it transforms students into receiving objects. It attempts to control thinking and action, leads men to adjust to the world, and inhibits their creative power.

When their efforts to act responsibly are frustrated, when they find themselves unable to use their faculties, men suffer. "The suffering due to impotence is rooted in the very fact that the human equilibrium has been disturbed."[5] But the inability to act which causes men's anguish also causes them to reject their impotence, by attempting

> . . . to restore [their] capacity to act. But can [they], and how? One way is to submit to and identify with a person or group having power. By this symbolic participation in another person's life, [men have] the illusion of acting, when in reality [they] only submit to and become part of those who act.[6]

Populist manifestations perhaps best exemplify this type of behavior by the oppressed, who, by identifying with charismatic leaders, come to feel that they themselves are active and effective. The rebellion they express as they emerge in the historical process is motivated by that desire to act

---

[4] Eric Fromm, *The Heart of Man* (New York, 1966), p. 41.
[5] *Ibid.*, p. 31.
[6] *Ibid.*

effectively. The dominant elites consider the remedy to be more domination and repression, carried out in the name of freedom, order, and social peace (that is, the peace of the elites). Thus they can condemn—logically, from their point of view—"the violence of a strike by workers and [can] call upon the state in the same breath to use violence in putting down the strike."[7]

Education as the exercise of domination stimulates the credulity of students, with the ideological intent (often not perceived by educators) of indoctrinating them to adapt to the world of oppression. This accusation is not made in the naïve hope that the dominant elites will thereby simply abandon the practice. Its objective is to call the attention of true humanists to the fact that they cannot use banking educational methods in the pursuit of liberation, for they would only negate that very pursuit. Nor may a revolutionary society inherit these methods from an oppressor society. The revolutionary society which practices banking education is either misguided or mistrusting of men. In either event, it is threatened by the specter of reaction.

Unfortunately, those who espouse the cause of liberation are themselves surrounded and influenced by the climate which generates the banking concept, and often do not perceive its true significance or its dehumanizing power. Paradoxically, then, they utilize this same instrument of alienation in what they consider an effort to liberate. Indeed, some "revolutionaries" brand as "innocents," "dreamers," or even "reactionaries" those who would challenge this educational practice. But one does not liberate men by alienating them. Authentic liberation—the process of humanization—is not another deposit to be made in men. Liberation is a praxis: the action and reflection of men upon their world in order to transform it. Those truly committed to the cause of liberation can accept neither the mechanistic concept of consciousness as an empty vessel to be filled, nor the use of banking methods of domination (propaganda, slogans—deposits) in the name of the liberation.

Those truly committed to liberation must reject the banking concept in its entirety, adopting instead a concept of men as conscious beings, and consciousness as consciousness intent upon the world. They must abandon the educational goal of deposit-making and replace it with the posing of the problems of men in their relations with the world. "Problem-posing" education, responding to the essence of consciousness—*intentionality*—rejects communiqués and embodies communications. It epitomizes the special characteristic of consciousness: being *conscious of*, not only as intent on objects but as turned in upon itself in a Jasperian "split"—consciousness as consciousness *of* consciousness.

---

[7] Reinhold Niebuhr, *Moral Man and Immoral Society* (New York, 1960), p. 130.

Liberating education consists in acts of cognition, not transferrals of information. It is a learning situation in which the cognizable object (far from being the end of the cognitive act) intermediates the cognitive actors—teacher on the one hand and students on the other. Accordingly, the practice of problem-posing education entails at the outset that the teacher-student contradiction be resolved. Dialogical relations—indispensable to the capacity of cognitive actors to cooperate in perceiving the same cognizable object—are otherwise impossible.

Indeed, problem-posing education, which breaks with the vertical patterns characteristic of banking education, can fulfill its function as the practice of freedom only if it can overcome the above contradiction. Through dialogue, the teacher-of-the students and the students-of-the-teacher cease to exist and a new term emerges: teacher-student with students-teacher. The teacher is no longer merely the-one-who-teaches, but one who is himself taught in dialogue with the students, who in turn while being taught also teach. They become jointly responsible for a process in which all grow. In this process, arguments based on "authority" are no longer valid; in order to function, authority must be *on the side of* freedom, not *against* it. Here, no one teaches another, nor is anyone self-taught. Men teach each other, mediated by the world, by the cognizable objects which in banking education are "owned" by the teacher.

The banking concept (with its tendency to dichotomize everything) distinguishes two stages in the action of the educator. During the first he cognizes a cognizable object while he prepares his lessons in his study or his laboratory; during the second, he expounds to his students about that object. The students are not called upon to know, but to memorize the contents narrated by the teacher. Nor do the students practice any act of cognition, since the object towards which that act should be directed is the property of the teacher rather than a medium evoking the critical reflection of both teacher and students. Hence in the name of the "preservation of culture and knowledge" we have a system which achieves neither true knowledge nor true culture.

The problem-posing method does not dichotomize the activity of the teacher-student: he is not "cognitive" at one point and "narrative" at another. He is always "cognitive," whether preparing a project or engaging in dialogue with the students. He does not regard cognizable objects as his private property, but as the object of reflection by himself and the students. In this way, the problem-posing educator constantly re-forms his reflections in the reflection of the students. The students—no longer docile listeners—are now critical co-investigators in dialogue with the teacher. The teacher presents the material to the students for their consideration, and re-considers his earlier considerations as the students express their own. The role of the problem-posing educator is to create, together with the students, the conditions under which knowledge at the level of the *doxa* is superseded by true knowledge, at the level of the *logos*.

Whereas banking education anesthetizes and inhibits creative power, problem-posing education involves a constant unveiling of reality. The former attempts to maintain the *submersion* of consciousness; the latter strives for the *emergence* of consciousness and *critical intervention* in reality.

Students, as they are increasingly posed with problems relating to themselves in the world and with the world, will feel increasingly challenged and obliged to respond to that challenge. Because they apprehend the challenge as interrelated to other problems within a total context, not as a theoretical question, the resulting comprehension tends to be increasingly critical and thus constantly less alienated. Their response to the challenge evokes new challenges, followed by new understandings; and gradually the students come to regard themselves as committed.

Education as the practice of freedom—as opposed to education as the practice of domination—denies that man is abstract, isolated, independent, and unattached to the world; it also denies that the world exists as a reality apart from men. Authentic reflection considers neither abstract man nor the world without men, but men in their relations with the world. In these relations consciousness and world are simultaneous: consciousness neither precedes the world nor follows it.

> La conscience et le monde sont donnés d'un même coup: extérieur par essence à la conscience, le monde est, par essence relatif à elle.[8]

In one of our culture circles in Chile, the group was discussing . . . the anthropological concept of culture. In the midst of the discussion, a peasant who by banking standards was completely ignorant said: "Now I see that without man there is no world." When the educator responded: "Let's say, for the sake of argument, that all the men on earth were to die, but that the earth itself remained, together with trees, birds, animals, rivers, seas, the stars . . . wouldn't all this be a world?"

"Oh, no," the peasant replied emphatically. "There would be no one to say: 'This is a world'."

The peasant wished to express the idea that there would be lacking the consciousness of the world which necessarily implies the world of consciousness. *I* cannot exist without a *not-I*. In turn, the *not-I* depends on that existence. The world which brings consciousness into existence be-

[8]Sartre, *op. cit.*, p. 32. [The passage is obscure but could be read as "Consciousness and the world are given at one and the same time: the exterior world as it enters consciousness is relative to our ways of seeing and understanding that world." Editors' note.]

comes the world of that consciousness. Hence, the previously cited affirmation of Sartre: *"La conscience et le monde sont dormés d'un même coup."*

As men, simultaneously reflecting on themselves and on the world, increase the scope of their preception, they begin to direct their observations towards previously inconspicuous phenomena:

> In perception properly so-called, as an explicit awareness [*Gewahren*], I am turned towards the object, to the paper, for instance. I apprehend it as being this here and now. The apprehension is a singling out, every object having a background in experience. Around and about the paper lie books, pencils, ink-well, and so forth, and these in a certain sense are also "perceived," perceptually there, in the "field of intuition"; but whilst I was turned towards the paper there was no turning in their direction, nor any apprehending of them, not even in a secondary sense. They appeared and yet were not singled out, were not posited on their own account. Every perception of a thing has such a zone of background intuitions or background awareness, if "intuiting" already includes the state of being turned towards, and this also is a "conscious experience," or more briefly a "consciousness of" all indeed that in point of fact lies in the co-perceived objective background.[9]

That which had existed objectively but had not been perceived in its deeper implications (if indeed it was perceived at all) begins to "stand out," assuming the character of a problem and therefore of challenge. Thus, men begin to single out elements from their "background awarenesses" and to reflect upon them. These elements are now objects of men's consideration, and, as such, objects of their action and cognition.

In problem-posing education, men develop their power to perceive critically *the way they exist* in the world *with which* and *in which* they find themselves; they come to see the world not as a static reality, but as a reality in process, in transformation. Although the dialectical relations of men with the world exist independently of how these relations are perceived (or whether or not they are perceived at all), it is also true that the form of action men adopt is to a large extent a function of how they perceive themselves in the world. Hence, the teacher-student and the students-teachers reflect simultaneously on themselves and the world without dichotomizing this reflection from action, and thus establish an authentic form of thought and action.

Once again, the two educational concepts and practices under analysis

[9] Edmund Husserl, *Ideas—General Introduction to Pure Phenomenology* (London, 1969), pp. 105–106.

come into conflict. Banking education (for obvious reasons) attempts, by mythicizing reality, to conceal certain facts which explain the way men exist in the world; problem-posing education sets itself the task of demythologizing. Banking education resists dialogue; problem-posing education regards dialogue as indispensable to the act of cognition which unveils reality. Banking education treats students as objects of assistance; problem-posing education makes them critical thinkers. Banking education inhibits creativity and domesticates (although it cannot completely destroy) the *intentionality* of consciousness by isolating consciousness from the world, thereby denying men their ontological and historical vocation of becoming more fully human. Problem-posing education bases itself on creativity and stimulates true reflection and action upon reality, thereby responding to the vocation of men as beings who are authentic only when engaged in inquiry and creative transformation. In sum: banking theory and practice, as immobilizing and fixating forces, fail to acknowledge men as historical beings; problem-posing theory and practice take man's historicity as their starting point.

Problem-posing education affirms men as beings in the process of *becoming*—as unfinished, uncompleted beings in and with a likewise unfinished reality. Indeed, in contrast to other animals who are unfinished, but not historical, men know themselves to be unfinished; they are aware of their incompletion. In this incompletion and this awareness lie the very roots of education as an exclusively human manifestation. The unfinished character of men and the transformational character of reality necessitate that education be an ongoing activity.

Education is thus constantly remade in the praxis. In order to *be,* it must *become.* Its "duration" (in the Bergsonian meaning of the word) is found in the interplay of the opposites *permanence* and *change.* The banking method emphasizes permanence and becomes reactionary; problem-posing education—which accepts neither a "well-be-haved" present nor a predetermined future—roots itself in the dynamic present and becomes revolutionary.

Problem-posing education is revolutionary futurity. Hence it is prophetic (and, as such, hopeful). Hence, it corresponds to the historical nature of man. Hence, it affirms men as beings who transcend themselves, who move forward and look head, for whom immobility represents a fatal threat, for whom looking at the past must only be a means of understanding more clearly what and who they are so that they can more wisely build a future. Hence, it identifies with the movement which engages men as beings aware of their incompletion—an historical movement which has its point of departure, its Subjects and its objective.

The point of departure of the movement lies in men themselves. But since men do not exist apart from the world, apart from reality, the movement must begin with the men-world relationship. Accordingly, the point of departure must always be with men in the "here and now," which constitutes the situation within which they are submerged, from which they emerge, and in which they intervene. Only by starting from this situation—which determines their perception of it—can they begin to move. To do this authentically they must perceive their state not as fated and unalterable, but merely as limiting—and therefore challenging.

Whereas the banking method directly or indirectly reinforces men's fatalistic perception of their situation, the problem-posing method presents this very situation to them as a problem. As the situation becomes the object of their cognition, the naïve or magical perception which produced their fatalism gives way to perception which is able to perceive itself even as it perceives reality, and can thus be critically objective about that reality.

A deepened consciousness of their situation leads men to apprehend that situation as an historical reality susceptible of transformation. Resignation gives way to the drive for transformation and inquiry, over which men feel themselves to be in control. If men, as historical beings necessarily engaged with other men in a movement of inquiry, did not control that movement, it would be (and is) a violation of men's humanity. Any situation in which some men prevent others from engaging in the process of inquiry is one of violence. The means used are not important; to alienate men from their own decision-making is to change them into objects.

This movement of inquiry must be directed towards humanization—man's historical vocation. The pursuit of full humanity, however, cannot be carried out in isolation or individualism, but only in fellowship and solidarity; therefore it cannot unfold in the antagonistic relations between oppressors and oppressed. No one can be authentically human while he prevents others from being so. Attempting *to be more* human, individualistically, leads to *having more*, egotistically: a form of dehumanization. Not that it is not fundamental *to have* in order *to be* human. Precisely because it *is* necessary, some men's *having* must not be allowed to constitute an obstacle to others' *having*, must not consolidate the power of the former to crush the latter.

Problem-posing education, as a humanist and liberating praxis, posits as fundamental that men subjected to domination must fight for their emancipation. To that end, it enables teachers and students to become Subjects of the educational process by overcoming authoritarianism and an alienating intellectualism; it also enables men to overcome their false perception of reality. The world—no longer something to be described with deceptive words—becomes the object of that transforming action by men which results in their humanization.

Problem-posing education does not and cannot serve the interests of the oppressor. No oppressive order could permit the oppressed to begin to question: Why? While only a revolutionary society can carry out this education in systematic terms, the revolutionary leaders need not take full power before they can employ the method. In the revolutionary process, the leaders cannot utilize the banking method as an interim measure, justified on grounds of expediency, with the intention of *later* behaving in a genuinely revolutionary fashion. They must be revolutionary—that is to say, dialogical—from the outset.

. . . .

QUESTIONS FOR A SECOND READING

1. While Freire speaks powerfully about the politics of the classroom, he provides few examples of actual classroom situations. As you go back through the essay, try to ground (or to test) what he says with examples of your own. What would take place in a "problem-posing" class in English, history, psychology, or math? What is an "authentic form of thought and action"? How might you describe what Freire refers to as "reflection"? What example can you give of a time when you were "conscious of consciousness" and it made a difference to you with your school work?

   You might also look for moments when Freire does provide examples of his own. On pages 241–242, for example, Freire makes the distinction between a student's role as a "spectator" and as a "re-creator" by referring to his own relationship to the objects on his desk. How might you explain this distinction? Or, how might you use the example of his books and coffee cup to explain the distinction he makes between "being accessible to consciousness" and "entering consciousness"?
2. Freire uses two terms drawn from Marxist literature: *praxis* and *alienation*. From the way these words are used in the essay, how would you define them? And how might they be applied to the study of education?
3. A writer can be thought of as a teacher and a reader as a student. If you think of Freire as your teacher in this essay, does he enact his own principles? Does he speak to you as though he were making deposits in a bank? Or is there a way in which the essay allows for dialogue? Look for sections in the essay you could use to talk about the role Freire casts you in as a reader.

WRITING ASSIGNMENTS

1. Surely all of us, anyone who has made it through twelve years of formal education, can think of a class, or an occasion outside of class, to serve as a quick example of what Freire calls the "banking" concept of education, where

students were turned into "containers" to be "filled" by their teachers. If Freire is to be useful to you, however, he must do more than enable you to call up quick examples. He should allow you to say more than that a teacher once treated you like a container or that a teacher once gave you your freedom.

Write an essay that centers on a rich and illustrative incident from your own experience (perhaps, but not necessarily, from your experience in school), and read it (that is, interpret it) as Freire would. You will need to tell a story from your own experience but also to comment on it—to see it and understand it as though you were continuing or extending Freire's work. You should be sure to choose an incident with some substance to it. You will need to be able to provide important details: things that were said and done, perhaps the exact wording of an assignment, a textbook, or a teacher's comments.

Freire would not want you to work passively or mechanically however, as though you were following orders. He would want you to make your own mark on the work he has begun. Use your example, in other words, as a way of testing and examining what Freire says, particularly those passages that you find difficult or obscure.

2. Problem-posing education, according to Freire, "sets itself the task of demythologizing"; it "stimulates true reflection and action"; it allows students to be "engaged in inquiry and creative transformation." These are grand and powerful phrases, and it is interesting to consider what they might mean if applied to the work of a course in reading and writing.

   If the object for study were Freire's essay, "The 'Banking' Concept of Education," what would Freire (or a teacher determined to adapt his practices) ask students to *do* with the essay? What writing assignment might he set for his students? Prepare that assignment, or a set of questions or guidelines or instructions (or whatever) that Freire might prepare for his class.

   Once you've prepared the writing assignment, go on and write the essay that you think would best fulfill it. And, once you've completed the essay, go on, finally, to write the teacher's comments on it—to write what you think Freire, or a teacher following his example, might write on a piece of student work.

MAKING CONNECTIONS

1. Freire says

> Students, as they are increasingly posed with problems relating to themselves in the world and with the world, will feel increasingly challenged and obliged to respond to that challenge. Because they apprehend the challenge as interrelated to other problems within a total context, not as a theoretical question, the resulting comprehension tends to be increasingly critical and thus constantly less alienated.

Students learn to do this, Freire says, through dialogue with their teachers. Freire could be said to serve as your first teacher here. He has raised the issue for you and given you some language you can use to frame questions and to imagine the possibilities of response.

Using one of the essays in this book as a starting point, pose a problem that challenges you and makes you feel obliged to respond, a problem that, in Freire's terms, relates to you "in the world and with the world." This is a chance for you, in other words, to pose a Freirian question and then to write a Freirian essay, all as an exercise in the practice of freedom.

When you are done, you might reread what you have written to see how it resembles or differs from what you are used to writing. What are the indications that you are working with greater freedom? If you find evidence of alienation or "domination," to what would you attribute it and what, then, might you do next to overcome it?

2. Freire writes about the distribution of power and authority in the classroom and argues that education too often alienates individuals from their own historical situation. Richard Rodriguez, in "The Achievement of Desire" (p. 430) writes about his education as a process of difficult but necessary alienation from his home, his childhood, and his family. And he writes about power—about the power that he gained and lost as he became increasingly successful as a student.

   Both Freire and Rodriguez write about education as a central event in the shaping of an adult life. It is interesting to imagine what they might have to say to each other. Write a dialogue between Freire and Rodriguez in which they discuss what Rodriguez has written in "The Achievement of Desire." What would they have to say to each other? What questions would they ask? How would they respond to one another in the give-and-take of conversation?

   Note: This should be a dialogue, not a debate. Your speakers are trying to learn something about each other and about education. They are not trying to win points or convince a jury.

SIGMUND FREUD

SIGMUND FREUD (1856–1939) is clearly one of the great investigators of our age, setting the pattern for all our examinations—serious and popular—into personality and behavior and giving new force to our suspicion that things are not as they appear to be. Few writers can claim a greater influence on the way we think and speak of ourselves. Indeed, as Harold Bloom said, "in a sense we are all Freudians, whether we want to be or not." Without him we couldn't contemplate our unconscious wishes, our repressed desires, our sibling rivalries, or our Freudian slips. When we explain our friends' fears or desires in terms of personality traits that they do not see or cannot face, we are mimicking the more disciplined form of analysis that Freud developed to treat his patients.

Freud was born in Freiberg, Moravia (now Czechoslovakia), but moved to Vienna as a child. He studied medicine at the University of Vienna. He began his career doing conventional work on nervous disorders, but revolutionized the treatment of mental illness by developing the technique of psychoanalysis. On the now-famous couch in his office in Vienna, Freud's patients spoke of their dreams, fears, and desires. This record of unconscious life, Freud argued, would explain conscious behavior. Freud continued to teach and practice in Vienna until forced by the Nazis to flee to London in 1938. He died a year later.

The Freud represented in these chapters from Totem and Taboo *is not Freud the psychoanalyst, however. This book is not about individual patients but about all of us, about what Dorothy Dinnerstein calls "the pathology of our organized social life." Freud begins with a basic paradox: the things we fear are often also the things we desire, and the things we desire are often also the things we fear. Our emotions are ambivalent, in other words. Freud asks why this is true; he considers the human history of this ambivalence and speculates on the degree to which we create the very situations that disturb us.* Totem and Taboo *was first published in 1913 and is felt by many to be a major steppingstone in the development of Freud's later argument (in* Civilization and Its Discontents*) that civilized society makes it impossible for anyone to have a healthy balanced unconscious life.*

In making his case for the range of Freud's influence, Bloom (a Professor of Humanities at Yale University) also said that "Freud's universal and comprehensive theory of the mind probably will outlive the psychoanalytical therapy, and seems already to have placed him with Plato and Montaigne and Shakespeare rather than with the scientists he overtly aspired to emulate." Freud's accounts of our collective past and our unconscious lives are some of the great fictions of our time. The following selections are presented as evidence of Freud the essayist, the storyteller or myth-maker, not Freud the scientist. The argument he presents is an interpretation. It is not self-evidently or scientifically "true," but offers a bold, imaginative representation of the evolution of culture and its relation to individual personalities.

The chapter that follows begins with a general discussion of taboo and then, in section 3, turns to a lengthy discussion of examples. You can assume, then, that problems or mysteries in the opening two sections will be cleared up in section 3. And Freud stops now and then to give you a summary of where he thinks he has gone and what he thinks he has done. One of the charms of Freud's prose (some would say one of the frustrations) is that Freud works on his subject while he is writing. It is not at all uncommon for him to get sidetracked or lost, to announce that he has seemingly backed himself into an impossible contradiction. You should not read a piece like this, in other words, expecting to know exactly where you are at every minute. It can be a great pleasure to watch Freud at work, even if you don't follow every turn or make every connection. If need be, you will have plenty of time to go back and review difficult sections later.

Taboo and the Ambivalence of Emotions

1

Taboo is a Polynesian word, the translation of which provides difficulties for us because we no longer possess the idea which it connotes. It was still current with the ancient Romans: their word "sacer" was the same as the taboo of the Polynesians. The ἄγος of the Greeks and the Kodaush of the Hebrews must also have signified the same thing which the Polynesians express through their word taboo and what many races in America, Africa (Madagascar), North and Central Asia express through analogous designations.

For us the meaning of taboo branches off into two opposite directions. On the one hand it means to us, sacred, consecrated: but on the other hand it means, uncanny, dangerous, forbidden, and unclean. The opposite for taboo is designated in Polynesian by the word *noa* and signifies something ordinary and generally accessible. Thus something like the concept of reserve inheres in taboo; taboo expresses itself essentially in prohibitions and restrictions. Our combination of "holy dred" would often express the meaning of taboo.

The taboo restrictions are different from religious or moral prohibitions They are not traced to a commandment of a god, but really they themselves impose their own prohibitions; they are differentiated from moral prohibitions by failing to be included in a system which declares abstinences in general to be necessary and gives reasons for this necessity. The taboo prohibitions lack all justification and are of unknown origin. Though incomprehensible to us they are taken as a matter of course by those who are under their dominance.

Wundt[1] calls taboo the oldest unwritten code of law of humanity. It is generally assumed that taboo is older than the gods and goes back to the prereligious age. . . .

2

He who approaches the problem of taboo from the field of psychoanalysis, which is concerned with the study of the unconscious part of the individual's psychic life, needs but a moment's reflection to realize that these phenomena are by no means foreign to him. He knows people who

[1]*Voelkerpsychologie*, II. Band: *Mythus und Religion*, 1906, II, p. 308.

have individually created such taboo prohibitions for themselves, which they follow as strictly as savages observe the taboos common to their tribe or society. If he were not accustomed to call these individuals "compulsion neurotics" he would find the term "taboo disease" quite appropriate for their malady. Psychoanalytic investigation has taught him the clinical etiology and the essential part of the psychological mechanism of this compulsion disease, so that he cannot resist applying what he has learnt there to explain corresponding manifestations in folk psychology.

There is one warning to which we shall have to give heed in making this attempt. The similarity between taboo and compulsion disease may be purely superficial, holding good only for the manifestations of both without extending into their deeper characteristics. Nature loves to use identical forms in the most widely different biological connections as, for instance, for coral stems and plants and even for certain crystals or for the formation of certain chemical precipitates. Assuredly would it be both premature and unprofitable to base conclusions relating to inner relationships upon the correspondence of merely mechanical conditions. We shall bear this warning in mind without, however, giving up our intended comparison on account of the possibility of such confusions.

The first and most striking correspondence between the compulsion prohibitions of neurotics and taboo lies in the fact that the origin of these prohibitions is just as unmotivated and enigmatic. They have appeared at some time or other and must now be retained on account of an unconquerable anxiety. An external threat of punishment is superfluous, because an inner certainty (a conscience) exists that violation will be followed by unbearable disaster. The very most that compulsion patients can tell us is the vague premonition that some person of their environment will suffer harm if they should violate the prohibition. Of what the harm is to consist is not known, and this inadequate information is more likely to be obtained during the later discussions of the expiatory and defensive actions than when the prohibitions themselves are being discussed.

As in the case of taboo, the nucleus of the neurotic prohibition is the act of touching, whence we derive the name "touching phobia" or *délire de toucher*. The prohibition extends not only to direct contact with the body but also to the figurative use of the phrase as "to come into contact" or "be in touch with some one or something." Anything that leads the thoughts to what is prohibited and thus calls forth mental contact is just as much prohibited as immediate bodily contact; this same extension is also found in taboo.

Some prohibitions are easily understood from their purpose but others strike us as incomprehensible, foolish, and senseless. We designate such commands as "ceremonials" and we find that taboo customs show the same variations.

Obsessive prohibitions possess an extraordinary capacity for displacement; they make use of almost any form of connection to extend from one object to another and then in turn make this new object "impossible," as one of my patients aptly puts it. This impossibility finally lays an embargo upon the whole world. The compulsion neurotics act as if the "impossible" persons and things were the carriers of a dangerous contagion which is ready to displace itself through contact to all neighbouring things. We have already emphasized the same characteristics of contagion and transference in the description of taboo prohibitions. We also know that any one, who has violated a taboo by touching something which is taboo, becomes taboo himself, and no one may come into contact with him.

I shall put side by side two examples of transference or, to use a better term, displacement, one from the life of the Maori, and the other from my observation of a woman suffering from a compulsion neurosis:

"For a similar reason a Maori chief would not blow on a fire with his mouth; for his sacred breath would communicate its sanctity to the fire, which would pass it on to the meat in the pot, which would pass it on to the man who ate the meat which was in the pot, which stood on the fire, which was breathed on by the chief; so that the eater, infected by the chief's breath conveyed through these intermediaries, would surely die."[2]

My patient demanded that a utensil which her husband had purchased and brought home should be removed lest it make the place where she lived impossible. For she had heard that this object was bought in a store which was situated, let us say, in Stag Street. But as the word "stag" was the name of a friend now in a distant city, whom she had known in her youth under her maiden name and whom she now found "impossible," that name was taboo, and the object bought in Vienna was just as taboo as this friend with whom she did not want to come in contact.

Compulsion prohibitions, like taboo prohibitions, entail the most extraordinary renunciations and restrictions of life, but a part of these can be removed by carrying out certain acts which now also must be done because they have acquired a compulsive character (obsessive acts); there is no doubt that these acts are in the nature of penances, expiations, defense reactions, and purifications. The most common of these obsessive acts is washing with water (washing obsession). A part of the taboo prohibitions can also be replaced in this way, that is to say, their violation can be made good through such a "ceremonial," and here too lustration through water is the preferred way.

Let us now summarize the points in which the correspondence between taboo customs and the symptoms of compulsion neurosis are most clearly

---

[2]Frazer, *The Golden Bough,* II: *Taboo and the Perils of the Soul,* 1911, p. 136.

manifested: 1. In the lack of motivation of the commandments, 2. in their enforcement through an inner need, 3. in their capacity for displacement and in the danger of contagion from what is prohibited, 4. and in the causation of ceremonial actions and commandments which emanate from the forbidden.

However, psychoanalysis has made us familiar with the clinical history as well as the psychic mechanism of compulsion neurosis. Thus, the history of a typical case of touching phobia reads as follows: In the very beginning, during the early period of childhood, the person manifested a strong pleasure in touching himself, the object of which was much more specialized than one would be inclined to suspect. Presently the carrying out of this very pleasurable act of touching was opposed by a prohibition from without.[3] The prohibition was accepted because it was supported by strong inner forces;[4] it proved to be stronger than the impulse which wanted to manifest itself through this act of touching. But due to the primitive psychic constitution of the child this prohibition did not succeed in abolishing the impulse. Its only success lay in repressing the impulse (the pleasure of touching) and banishing it into the unconscious. Both the prohibition and the impulse remained; the impulse because it had only been repressed and not abolished, the prohibition, because if it had ceased, the impulse would have broken through into consciousness and would have been carried out. An unsolved situation, a psychic fixation, had thus been created and now everything else emanated from the continued conflict between prohibition and impulse.

The main characteristic of the psychic constellation which has thus gone under fixation lies in what one might call the ambivalent behaviour[5] of the individual to the object, or rather to an action regarding it. The individual constantly wants to carry out this action (the act of touching), he sees in it the highest pleasure, but he may not carry it out, and he even abominates it. The opposition between these two streams cannot be easily adjusted because—there is no other way to express it—they are so localized in the psychic life that they cannot meet. The prohibition becomes fully conscious, while the surviving pleasure of touching remains unconscious, the person knowing nothing about it. If this psychological factor did not exist the ambivalence could neither maintain itself so long nor lead to such subsequent manifestations.

In the clinical history of the case we have emphasized the appearance of the prohibition in early childhood as the determining factor, but for the further elaboration of the neurosis this rôle is played by the repression

[3]Both the pleasure and the prohibition referred to touching one's own genitals.

[4]The relation to beloved persons who impose the prohibition.

[5]To use an excellent term coined by Bleuler.

which appears at this age. On account of the repression which has taken place, which is connected with forgetting (amnesia), the motivation of the prohibition that has become conscious remains unknown, and all attempts to unravel it intellectually must fail, as the point of attack cannot be found. The prohibition owes its strength—its compulsive character—to its association with its unknown counterpart, the hidden and unabated pleasure, that is to say, to an inner need into which conscious insight is lacking. The transferability and reproductive power of the prohibition reflect a process which harmonizes with the unconscious pleasure and is very much facilitated through the psychological determinants of the unconscious. The pleasure of the impulse constantly undergoes displacement in order to escape the blocking which it encounters and seeks to acquire surrogates for the forbidden in the form of substitutive objects and actions. For the same reason the prohibition also wanders and spreads to the new aims of the proscribed impulse. Every new advance of the repressed libido is answered by the prohibition with a new severity. The mutual inhibition of these two contending forces creates a need for discharge and for lessening the existing tension, in which we may recognize the motivation for the compulsive acts. In the neurosis there are distinctly acts of compromise which on the one hand may be regarded as proofs of remorse and efforts to expiate and similar actions; but on the other hand they are at the same time substitutive actions which recompense the impulse for what has been forbidden. It is a law of neurotic diseases that these obsessive acts serve the impulse more and more and come nearer and nearer to the original and forbidden act.

We may now make the attempt to study taboo as if it were of the same nature as the compulsive prohibitions of our patients. It must naturally be clearly understood that many of the taboo prohibitions which we shall study are already secondary, displaced and distorted, so that we shall have to be satisfied if we can shed some light upon the earliest and most important taboo prohibitions. We must also remember that the differences in the situation of the savage and of the neurotic may be important enough to exclude complete correspondence and prevent a point by point transfer from one to the other such as would be possible if we were dealing with exact copies.

First of all it must be said that it is useless to question savages as to the real motivation of their prohibitions or as to the genesis of taboo. According to our assumption they must be incapable of telling us anything about it since this motivation is "unconscious" to them. But following the model of the compulsive prohibition we shall construct the history of taboo as follows: Taboos are very ancient prohibitions which at one time were forced upon a generation of primitive people from without, that is, they probably were forcibly impressed upon them by an earlier generation. These prohibitions concerned actions for which there existed a strong desire. The prohibitions maintained themselves from generation to generation, perhaps only as the result of a tradition set up by paternal and social authority. But in later generations they have perhaps already become "organized" as a piece of inherited psychic property. Whether there are such "innate ideas" or whether these have brought about the fixation of the taboo by themselves or by cooperating with education no one could decide in the particular case in question. The persistence of taboo teaches, however, one thing, namely, that the original pleasure to do the forbidden still continues among taboo races. They therefore assume an *ambivalent attitude* toward their taboo prohibitions; in their unconscious they would like nothing better than to transgress them but they are also afraid to do it; they are afraid just because they would like to transgress, and the fear is stronger than the pleasure. But in every individual of the race the desire for it is unconscious, just as in the neurotic.

The oldest and most important taboo prohibitions are the two basic laws of *totemism:* namely, not to kill the totem animal, and to avoid sexual intercourse with totem companions of the other sex.

It would, therefore, seem that these must have been the oldest and strongest desires of mankind. We cannot understand this and therefore we cannot use these examples to test our assumptions as long as the meaning and the origin of the totemic system is so wholly unknown to us. But the very wording of these taboos and the fact that they occur together will remind any one who knows the results of the psychoanalytic investigation of individuals, of something quite definite which psychoanalysts call the central point on the infantile wish life and the nucleus of the later neurosis.

All other varieties of taboo phenomena which have led to the attempted classifications noted above become unified if we sum them up in the following sentence: The basis of taboo is a forbidden action for which there exists a strong inclination in the unconscious.

We know, without understanding it, that whoever does what is prohibited and violates the taboo, becomes himself taboo. But how can we connect this fact with the other, namely that taboo adheres not only to persons who have done what is prohibited, but also to persons who are in exceptional circumstances, as well as to these circumstances themselves and impersonal things? What can this dangerous attribute be which always remains the same under all the different conditions? Only one thing, namely, the propensity to arouse the ambivalence of man and to tempt him to violate the prohibition.

An individual, who has violated a taboo, becomes himself taboo because he has the dangerous property of tempting others to follow his example. He arouses envy; why should he be allowed to do what is prohibited to others? He is therefore really *contagious,* in so far as every example incites to imitation and, therefore, he himself must be avoided.

But a person may become permanently or temporarily taboo without having violated any taboos, for the simple reason that he is in a condition which has the property of inciting the forbidden desires of others and of awakening the ambivalent conflict in them. Most of the exceptional positions and conditions have this character and possess this dangerous power. The king or chieftain arouses envy of his prerogatives; everybody would perhaps like to be king. The dead, the newly born, and women when they are incapacitated, all act as incitements because of their peculiar helplessness, while the individual who has just reached sexual maturity tempts through the promise of a new pleasure. Therefore, all these persons and all these conditions are taboo, for one must not yield to the temptations which they offer.

Now, too, we understand why the forces inherent in the "mana" of various persons can neutralize one another so that the mana of one individual can partly cancel that of the other. The taboo of a king is too strong for his subject because the social difference between them is too great. But a minister, for example, can become the harmless mediator between them. Translated from the language of taboo into the language of normal psychology this means: the subject who shrinks from the tremendous temptation which contact with the king creates for him can brook the intercourse of an official, whom he does not have to envy so much and whose position perhaps seems attainable to him. The minister, on his part, can moderate his envy of the king by taking into consideration the power that has been granted to him. Thus, smaller differences in the magic power that lead to temptation are less to be feared than exceptionally big differences.

It is equally clear how the violation of certain taboo prohibitions becomes a social danger which must be punished or expiated by all the members of society lest it harm them all. This danger really exists if we substitute the known impulses for the unconscious desires. It consists in the possibility of imitation, as a result of which society would soon be dissolved. If the others did not punish the violation they would perforce become aware that they want to imitate the evil doer.

Though the secret meaning of a taboo prohibition cannot possibly be of so special a nature as in the case of a neurosis, we must not be astonished to find that touching plays a similar rôle in taboo prohibition as in the *délire de toucher*. To touch is the beginning of every act of possession, of every attempt to make use of a person or thing.

We have interpreted the power of contagion which inheres in the taboo as the property of leading into temptation, and of inciting to imitation. This does not seem to be in accord with the fact that the contagiousness of the taboo is above all manifested in the transference to objects which thus themselves become carriers of the taboo.

This transferability of the taboo reflects what is found in the neurosis, namely, the constant tendency of the unconscious impulse to become displaced through associative channels upon new objects. Our attention is thus drawn to the fact that the dangerous magic power of the mana corresponds to two real faculties, the capacity of reminding man of his forbidden wishes, and the apparently more important one of tempting him to violate the prohibition in the service of these wishes. Both functions reunite into one, however, if we assume it to be in accord with a primitive psychic life that with the awakening of a memory of a forbidden action there should also be combined the awakening of the tendency to carry out the action. Memory and temptation then again coincide. We must also admit that if the example of a person who has violated a prohibition leads another to the same action, the disobedience of the prohibition has been transmitted like a contagion, just as the taboo is transferred from a person to an object, and from this to another.

If the violation of a taboo can be condoned through expiation or penance, which means, of course, a *renunciation* of a possession or a liberty, we have the proof that the observance of a taboo regulation was itself a renunciation of something really wished for. The omission of one renunciation is cancelled through a renunciation at some other point. This would lead us to conclude that, as far as taboo ceremonials are concerned, penance is more primitive than purification.

Let us now summarize what understanding we have gained of taboo through its comparison with the compulsive prohibition of the neurotic. Taboo is a very primitive prohibition imposed from without (by an authority) and directed against the strongest desires of man. The desire to violate it continues in the unconscious; persons who obey the taboo have an ambivalent feeling toward what is affected by the taboo. The magic power attributed to taboo goes back to its ability to lead man into temptation; it behaves like a contagion, because the example is contagious, and because the prohibited desire becomes displaced in the unconscious upon something else. The expiation for the violation of a taboo through a renunciation proves that a renunciation is at the basis of the observance of the taboo.

3

We may ask what we have gained from the comparison of taboo with compulsion neurosis and what value can be claimed for the interpretation we have given on the basis of this comparison? Our interpretation is evidently of no value unless it affords an advantage not to be had in any other way and unless it affords a better understanding of taboo than was otherwise possible. We might claim that we have already given proof of its usefulness in what has been said above; but we shall have to try to strengthen our proof by continuing the explanation of taboo prohibitions and customs in detail.

But we can avail ourselves of another method. We can shape our investigation so as to ascertain whether a part of the assumptions which we have transferred from the neurosis to the taboo, or the conclusions at which we have thereby arrived can be demonstrated directly in the phenomena of taboo. We must decide, however, what we want to look for. The assertion concerning the genesis of taboo, namely, that it was derived from a primitive prohibition which was once imposed from without, cannot of course, be proved. We shall therefore seek to confirm those psychological conditions for taboo with which we have become acquainted in the case of compulsion neurosis. How did we gain our knowledge of these psychological factors in the case of neurosis? Through the analytical study of the symptoms, especially the compulsive actions, the defense reactions and the obsessive commands. These mechanisms gave every indication of having been derived from *ambivalent* impulses or tendencies, they either represented simultaneously the wish and counter-wish or they served preponderantly one of the two contrary tendencies. If we should now succeed in showing that ambivalence, *i.e.*, the sway of contrary tendencies, exists also in the case of taboo regulations or if we should find among taboo mechanisms some which like neurotic obsessions give simultaneous expression to both currents, we would have established what is practically the most important point in the psychological correspondence between taboo and compulsion neurosis.

We have already mentioned that the two fundamental taboo prohibitions are inaccessible to our analysis because they belong to totemism; another part of the taboo rules is of secondary origin and cannot be used for our purpose. For among these races taboo has become the general form of law giving and has helped to promote social tendencies which are certainly younger than taboo itself, as for instance, the taboos imposed by chiefs and priests to insure their property and privileges. But there still remains a large group of laws which we may undertake to investigate. Among these I lay stress on those taboos which are attached (*a*) to enemies, (*b*) to chiefs, and (*c*) to the dead; the material for our investigation is taken from the excellent collection of J. G. Frazer in his great work, *The Golden Bough.*[6]

The Treatment of Enemies

Inclined as we may have been to ascribe to savage and semisavage races uninhibited and remorseless cruelty towards their enemies, it is of great interest to us to learn that with them, too, the killing of a person compels the observation of a series of rules which are associated with taboo customs. These rules are easily brought under four groups; they demand

[6]Third Edition, Part II: *Taboo and the Perils of the Soul,* 1911.

1. reconciliation with the slain enemy, 2. restrictions, 3. actions of expiation, and purifications of the manslayer, and 4. certain ceremonial rites. The incomplete reports do not allow us to decide with certainty how general or how isolated such taboo customs may be among these races, but this is a matter of indifference as far as our interest in these occurrences is concerned. Still, it may be assumed that we are dealing with widespread customs and not with isolated peculiarities.

The reconciliation customs practised on the island of Timor, after a victorious band of warriors has returned with the severed heads of the vanquished enemy, are especially significant because the leader of the expedition is subject to heavy additional restrictions. "At the solemn entry of the victors, sacrifices are made to conciliate the souls of the enemy; otherwise one would have to expect harm to come to the victors. A dance is given and a song is sung in which the slain enemy is mourned and his forgiveness is implored; 'Be not angry,' they say, 'because your head is here with us; had we been less lucky, our heads might have been exposed in your village. We have offered the sacrifice to appease you. Your spirit may now rest and leave us at peace. Why were you our enemy? Would it not have been better that we should remain friends? Then your blood would not have been spilt and your head would not have been cut off.' "[7]

Similar customs are found among the Palu in Celebes; the Gallas sacrifice to the spirits of their dead enemies before they return to their home villages.[8]

Other races have found methods of making friends, guardians, and protectors out of their former enemies after they are dead. This consists in the tender treatment of the severed heads, of which many wild tribes of Borneo boast. When the See-Dayaks of Sarawak bring home a head from a war expedition, they treat it for months with the greatest kindness and courtesy and address it with the most endearing names in their language. The best morsels from their meals are put into its mouth, together with titbits and cigars. The dead enemy is repeatedly entreated to hate his former friends and to bestow his love upon his new hosts because he has now become one of them. It would be a great mistake to think that any derision is attached to this treatment, horrible though it may seem to us.[9]

Observers have been struck by the mourning for the enemy after he is slain and scalped, among several of the wild tribes of North America. When a Choctaw had killed an enemy he began a month's mourning during which he submitted himself to serious restrictions. The Dakota Indians mourned

[7] Frazer, *l.c.*, p. 166.

[8] Paulitschke, *Ethnography of North-east Africa*.

[9] Frazer, *Adonis, Attis, Osiris*, p. 248, 1907; referring to Hugh Low, *Sarawak* (London, 1848).

in the same way. One authority mentions that the Osaga Indians after mourning for their own dead mourned for their foes as if they had been friends.[10]

Before proceeding to the other classes of taboo customs for the treatment of enemies, we must define our position in regard to a pertinent objection. Both Frazer as well as other authorities may well be quoted against us to show that the motive for these rules of reconciliation is quite simple and has nothing to do with "ambivalence." These races are dominated by a superstitious fear of the spirits of the slain, a fear which was also familiar to classical antiquity, and which the great British dramatist brought upon the stage in the hallucinations of Macbeth and Richard the Third. From this superstition all the reconciliation rules as well as the restrictions and expiations which we shall discuss later can be logically deduced; moreover, the ceremonies included in the fourth group also argue for this interpretation, since the only explanation of which they admit is the effort to drive away the spirits of the slain which pursue the manslayers.[11] Besides, the savages themselves directly admit their fear for the spirits of their slain foes and trace back the taboo customs under discussion to this fear.

This objection is certainly pertinent and if it were adequate as well we would gladly spare ourselves the trouble of our attempt to find a further explanation. We postpone the consideration of this objection until later and for the present merely contrast it to the interpretation derived from our previous discussion of taboo. All these rules of taboo lead us to conclude that other impulses besides those that are merely hostile find expression in the behaviour towards enemies. We see in them manifestations of repentance, of regard for the enemy, and of a bad conscience for having slain him. It seems that the commandment, Thou shalt not slay, which could not be violated without punishment, existed also among these savages, long before any legislation was received from the hands of a god.

We now return to the remaining classes of taboo rules. The *restrictions* laid upon the victorious manslayer are usually frequent and are mostly of a serious nature. In Timor (compare the reconciliation customs mentioned above) the leader of the expedition cannot return to his house under any circumstances. A special hut is erected for him in which he spends two months engaged in the observance of various rules of purification. During this period he may not see his wife or nourish himself; another person must put his food in his mouth.[12] Among some Dayak tribes warriors re-

---

[10] J. O. Dorsay, see Frazer, *Taboo*, etc., p. 181.

[11] Frazer, *Taboo*, pp. 166–174. These ceremonies consist of hitting shields, shouting, bellowing and making noises with various instruments, etc.

[12] Frazer, *Taboo*, p. 166, referring to S. Mueller, *Reisen en Onderzoekingen in den Indischen Archipel.* (Amsterdam, 1857).

turning from a successful expedition must remain sequestered for several days and abstain from certain foods; they may not touch iron and must remain away from their wives. In Logea, an island near New Guinea, men who have killed an enemy or have taken part in the killing, lock themselves up in their houses for a week. They avoid every intercourse with their wives and friends, they do not touch their victuals with their hands, and live on nothing but vegetable foods which are cooked for them in special dishes. As a reason for this last restriction it is alleged that they must smell the blood of the slain, otherwise they would sicken and die. Among the Toaripi- or Motumotu-tribes in New Guinea a manslayer must not approach his wife and must not touch his food with his fingers. A second person must feed him with special food. This continues until the next new moon.

I avoid the complete enumeration of all the cases of restrictions of the victorious slayer mentioned by Frazer, and emphasize only such cases in which the character of taboo is especially noticeable or where the restriction appears in connection with expiation, purification, and ceremonial.

Among the Monumbos in New Guinea a man who has killed an enemy in combat becomes "unclean," the same word being employed which is applied to women during menstruation or confinement. For a considerable period he is not allowed to leave the men's club-house, while the inhabitants of his village gather about him and celebrate his victory with songs and dances. He must not touch any one, not even his wife and children; if he did so they would be afflicted with boils. He finally becomes clean through washing and other ceremonies.

Among the Natchez in North America young warriors who had procured their first scalp were bound for six months to the observance of certain renunciations. They were not allowed to sleep with their wives or to eat meat, and received only fish and maize pudding as nourishment. When a Choctaw had killed and scalped an enemy he began a period of mourning for one month, during which he was not allowed to comb his hair. When his head itched he was not allowed to scratch it with his hand but used a small stick for this purpose.

After a Pima Indian had killed an Apache he had to submit himself to severe ceremonies of purification and expiation. During a fasting period of sixteen days he was not allowed to touch meat or salt, to look at a fire, or to speak to any one. He lived alone in the woods, where he was waited upon by an old woman who brought him a small allowance of food; he often bathed in the nearest river, and carried a lump of clay on his head as a sign of mourning. On the seventeenth day there took place a public ceremony through which he and his weapons were solemnly purified. As the Pima Indians took the manslayer taboo much more seriously than their enemies, and, unlike them, did not postpone expiation and purification until the end of the expedition, their prowess in war suffered very much through their moral severity, or what might be called their piety. In spite of their extraordinary bravery they proved to be unsatisfactory allies to the Americans in their wars against the Apaches.

The detail and variations of these expiatory and purifying ceremonies after the killed of an enemy would be most interesting for purposes of a more searching study, but I need not enumerate any more of them here because they cannot furnish us with any new points of view. I might mention that the temporary or permanent isolation of the professional executioner, which was manifested up to our time, is a case in point. The position of the "free-holder" in mediæval society really conveys a good idea of the "taboo" of savages.[13]

The current explanation of all these rules of reconciliation, restriction, expiation, and purification, combines two principles, namely the extension of the taboo of the dead to everything that has come into contact with him, and the fear of the spirit of the slain. In what combination these two elements are to explain the ceremonial, whether they are to be considered as of equal value or whether one of them is primary and the other secondary, and which one, is nowhere stated, nor would this be an easy matter to decide. In contradiction to all this we emphasize the unity which our interpretation gains by deducing all these rules from the ambivalence of the emotion of savages towards their enemies.

The Taboo of Rulers

The behaviour of primitive races towards their chiefs, kings, and priests, is controlled by two principles which seem rather to supplement than to contradict each other. They must both be guarded and be guarded against.[14]

Both objects are accomplished through innumerable rules of taboo. Why one must guard against rulers is already known to us; because they are the bearers of that mysterious and dangerous magic power which communicates itself by contact, like an electric charge, bringing death and destruction to any one not protected by a similar charge. All direct or indirect contact with this dangerous sacredness is therefore avoided, and where it cannot be avoided a ceremonial has been found to ward off the dreaded consequences. The Nubas in East Africa, for instance, believe that they must die if they enter the house of their priest-king, but that they escape this danger if, on entering, they bare the left shoulder and induce the king to touch it with his hand. Thus we have the remarkable case of the king's

[13] For these examples see Frazer, *Taboo*, pp. 165–170, "Manslayers Tabooed."

[14] Frazer, *Taboo*, p. 132. "He must not only be guarded, he must also be guarded against."

touch becoming the healing and protective measure against the very dangers that arise from contact with the king; but it is probably a question of the healing power of the intentional touching on the king's part in contradistinction to the danger of touching him, in other words, of the opposition between passivity and activity towards the king.

Where the healing power of the royal touch is concerned we do not have to look for examples among savages. In comparatively recent times the kings of England exercised this power upon scrofula, whence it was called "The King's Evil." Neither Queen Elizabeth nor any of her successors renounced this part of the royal prerogative. Charles I is said to have healed a hundred sufferers at one time, in the year 1633. Under his dissolute son Charles II, after the great English revolution had passed, royal healings of scrofula attained their greatest vogue.

This king is said to have touched close to a hundred thousand victims of scrofula in the course of his reign. The crush of those seeking to be cured used to be so great that on one occasion six or seven patients suffered death by suffocation instead of being healed. The skeptical king of Orange, William III, who became king of England after the banishment of the Stuarts, refused to exercise the spell; on the one occasion when he consented to practise the touch, he did so with words: "May God give you better health and more sense."[15]

The following account will bear witness to the terrible effect of touching by virtue of which a person, even though unintentionally, becomes active against his king or against what belongs to him. A chief of high rank and great holiness in New Zealand happened to leave the remains of his meal by the roadside. A young slave came along, a strong healthy fellow, who saw what was left over and started to eat it. Hardly had he finished when a horrified spectator informed him of his offence in eating the meal of the chief. The man had been a strong, brave warrior, but as soon as he heard this he collapsed and was afflicted by terrible convulsions, from which he died towards sunset of the following day.[16] A Maori woman ate a certain fruit and then learned that it came from a place on which there was a taboo. She cried out that the spirit of the chief whom she had thus offended would surely kill her. This incident occurred in the afternoon, and on the next day at twelve o'clock she was dead.[17] The tinder box of a Maori chief once cost several persons their lives. The chief had lost it, and those who found it used it to light their pipes. When they learned whose property the tinder box was they all died of fright.[18]

[15] Frazer, *The Magic Art*, I, p. 368.
[16] *Old New Zealand*, by a Pakeha Maori (London, 1884), see Frazer, *Taboo*, p. 135.
[17] W. Brown, *New Zealand and Its Aborigines* (London, 1845) Frazer, *l.c.*
[18] Frazer, *l.c.*

It is hardly astonishing that the need was felt to isolate dangerous persons like chiefs and priests, by building a wall around them which made them inaccessible to others. We surmise that this wall, which originally was constructed out of taboo rules, still exists to-day in the form of court ceremony.

But probably the greater part of this taboo of the rulers cannot be traced back to the need of guarding against them. The other point of view in the treatment of privileged persons, the need of guarding them from dangers with which they are threatened, has had a distinct share in the creation of taboo and therefore of the origin of court etiquette.

The necessity of guarding the king from every conceivable danger arises from his great importance for the weal and woe of his subjects. Strictly speaking, he is a person who regulates the course of the world; his people have to thank him not only for rain and sunshine, which allow the fruit of the earth to grow, but also for the wind which brings the ships to their shores and for the solid ground on which they set their feet.[19]

These savage kings are endowed with a wealth of power and an ability to bestow happiness which only gods possess; certainly in later stages of civilization none but the most servile courtiers would play the hypocrite to the extent of crediting their sovereigns with the possession of attributes similar to these.

It seems like an obvious contradiction that persons of such perfection of power should themselves require the greatest care to guard them against threatening dangers, but this is not the only contradiction revealed in the treatment of royal persons on the part of savages. These races consider it necessary to watch over their kings to see that they use their powers in the right way; they are by no means sure of their good intentions or of their conscientiousness. A strain of mistrust is mingled with the motivation of the taboo rules for the king. "The idea that early kingdoms are despotisms," says Frazer,[20] "in which the people exist only for the sovereign, is wholly inapplicable to the monarchies we are considering. On the contrary, the sovereign in them exists only for his subjects; his life is only valuable so long as he discharges the duties of his position by ordering the course of nature for his people's benefit. So soon as he fails to do so, the care, the devotion, the religious homage which they had hitherto lavished on him cease and are changed into hatred and contempt; he is ignominiously dismissed and may be thankful if he escapes with his life. Worshipped as a god one day, he is killed as a criminal the next. But in this changed behaviour of the people there is nothing capricious or inconsis-

[19] Frazer, *Taboo, The Burden of Royalty*, p. 7.
[20] *l.c.*, p. 7.

tent. On the contrary, their conduct is quite consistent. If their king is their god he is, or should be, also their preserver; and if he will not preserve them he must make room for another who will. So long, however, as he answers their expectations, there is no limit to the care which they take of him, and which they compel him to take of himself. A king of this sort lives hedged in by ceremonious etiquette, a network of prohibitions and observances, of which the intention is not to contribute to his dignity, much less to his comfort, but to restrain him from conduct which by disturbing the harmony of nature, might involve himself, his people and the universe in one common catastrophe. Far from adding to his comfort, these observances, by trammelling his every act, annihilate his freedom and often render the very life, which it is their object to preserve, a burden and sorrow to him."

One of the most glaring examples of thus fettering and paralysing a holy ruler through taboo ceremonial seems to have been reached in the life routine of the Mikado of Japan, as it existed in earlier centuries. A description which is now over two hundred years old[21] relates: "He thinks that it would be very prejudicial to his dignity and holiness to touch the ground with his feet; for this reason when he intends to go anywhere, he must be carried thither on men's shoulders. Much less will they suffer that he should expose his sacred person to the open air, and the sun is not thought worthy to shine on his head. There is such a holiness ascribed to all the parts of his body that he dares to cut off neither his hair, nor his beard, nor his nails. However, lest he should grow too dirty, they may clean him in the night when he is asleep; because they say that what is taken from his body at that time, hath been stolen from him, and that such a theft does not prejudice his holiness or dignity. In ancient times, he was obliged to sit on the throne for some hours every morning, with the imperial crown on his head; but to sit altogether like a statue without stirring either hands or feet, head or eyes, nor indeed any part of his body, because by this means it was thought that he could preserve peace and tranquillity in his empire; for if unfortunately, he turned himself on one side or other, or if he looked a good while towards any part of his dominion, it was apprehended that war, famine, fire or some other great misfortune was near at hand to desolate the country."

Some of the taboos to which barbarian kings are subject vividly recall the restrictions placed on murderers. On Shark Point at Cape Padron in Lower Guinea (West Africa), a priest-king called Kukulù lives alone in a woods. He is not allowed to touch a woman or to leave his house and cannot even rise out of his chair, in which he must sleep in a sitting posi-

[21] Kaempfer, *History of Japan*, see in Frazer, *l.c.*, p. 3.

tion. If he should lie down the wind would cease and shipping would be disturbed. It is his function to keep storms in check, and in general, to see to an even, healthy condition of the atmosphere.[22] The more powerful a king of Loango is, says Bastian, the more taboos he must observe. The heir to the throne is also bound to them from childhood on; they accumulate about him while he is growing up, and by the time of his accession he is suffocated by them.

Our interest in the matter does not require us to take up more space to describe more fully the taboos that cling to royal and priestly dignity. We merely add that restrictions as to freedom of movement and diet play the main rôle among them. But two examples of taboo ceremonial taken from civilized nations,and therefore from much higher stages of culture, will indicate to what an extent association with these privileged persons tends to preserve ancient customs.

The *flamen Dialis,* the high-priest of Jupiter in Rome, had to observe an extraordinarily large number of taboo rules. He was not allowed to ride, to see a horse or an armed man, to wear a ring that was not broken, to have a knot in his garments, to touch wheat flour or leaven, or even to mention by name a goat, a dog, raw meat, beans, and ivy; his hair could only be cut by a free man and with a bronze knife, his hair combings and nail parings had to be buried under a lucky tree; he could not touch the dead, go into the open with bare head, and similar prohibitions. His wife, the *flaminica,* also had her own prohibitions: she was not allowed to ascend more than three steps on a certain kind of stairs and on certain holidays she could not comb her hair; the leather for her shoes could not be taken from any animal that had died a natural death but only from one that had been slaughtered or sacrificed; when she heard thunder she was unclean until she made an expiatory sacrifice.[23]

The old kings of Ireland were subject to a series of very curious restrictions, the observance of which was expected to bring every blessing to the country while their violation entailed every form of evil. The complete description of these taboos is given in the *Book of Rights,* of which the oldest manuscript copies bear the dates 1390 and 1418. The prohibitions are very detailed and concern certain activities at specified places and times; in some cities, for instance, the king cannot stay on a certain day of the week, while at some specified hour this or that river may not be crossed, or again there is a plain on which he cannot camp a full nine days, etc.[24]

Among many savage races the severity of the taboo restrictions for the

[22] Bastian, *The German Expedition to the Coast of Loango* (Jena 1874), cited by Frazer, *l.c.*, p. 5.

[23] Frazer, *l.c.*, p. 13.

[24] Frazer, *l.c.*, p. 11.

priest-kings has had results of historic importance which are especially interesting from our point of view. The honour of being a priest-king ceased to be desirable; the person in line for the succession often used every means to escape it. Thus, in Cambodia, where there is a fire and water king, it is often necessary to use force to compel the successor to accept the honour. On Niue or Savage Island, a coral island in the Pacific Ocean, monarchy actually came to an end because nobody was willing to undertake the responsible and dangerous office. In some parts of West Africa a general council is held after the death of the king to determine upon the successor. The man on whom the choice falls is seized, tied, and kept in custody in the fetish house until he has declared himself willing to accept the crown. Sometimes the presumptive successor to the throne finds ways and means to avoid the intended honour; thus it is related of a certain chief that he used to go armed day and night and resist by force every attempt to place him on the throne.[25] Among the Negroes of Sierra Leone the resistance against accepting the kingly honour was so great that most of the tribes were compelled to make strangers their kings.

Frazer makes these conditions responsible for the fact that in the development of history a separation of the original priest-kingship into a spiritual and secular power finally took place. Kings, crushed by the power of their holiness, became incapable of exercising their power over real things and had to leave this to inferior but executive persons who were willing to renounce the honours of royal dignity. From these there grew up the secular rulers, while the spiritual over-lordship, which was now of no practical importance, was left to the former taboo kings. It is well known to what extent this hypothesis finds confirmation in the history of old Japan.

A survey of the picture of the relations of primitive peoples to their rulers gives rise to the expectation that our advance from description to psychoanalytic understanding will not be difficult. These relations are granted great privileges which are practically cancelled by taboo prohibitions in regard to other privileges. They are privileged persons, they can do or enjoy what is withheld from the rest through taboo. But in contrast to this freedom they are restricted by other taboos which do not affect the ordinary individual. Here, therefore, is the first contrast, which amounts almost to a contradiction, between an excess of freedom and an excess of restriction as applied to the same persons. They are credited with extraordinary magic powers, and contact with their person or their property is therefore feared, while on the other hand the most beneficial effect is expected from these contacts. This seems to be a second and an especially glaring contradiction; but we have already learned that it is only apparent.

[25] A. Bastian, *The German Expedition to the Coast of Loango,* cited by Frazer, *l.c.,* p. 18.

The king's touch, exercised by him with benevolent intention heals and protects; it is only when a common man touches the king or his royal effects that the contact becomes dangerous, and this is probably because the act may recall aggressive tendencies. Another contradiction which is not so easily solved is expressed in the fact that great power over the processes of nature is ascribed to the ruler and yet the obligation is felt to guard him with especial care against threatening dangers, as if his own power, which can do so much, were incapable of accomplishing this. A further difficulty in the relation arises because there is no confidence that the ruler will use his tremendous power to the advantage of his subjects as well as for his own protection; he is therefore distrusted and surveillance over him is considered to be justified. The taboo etiquette, to which the life of the king is subject, simultaneously serves all these objects of exercising a tutelage over the king, of guarding him against dangers and of guarding his subjects against danger which he brings to them.

We are inclined to give the following explanation of the complicated and contradictory relation of the primitive peoples to their rulers. Through superstition as well as through other motives, various tendencies find expression in the treatment of kings, each of which is developed to the extreme without regard to the other. As a result of this, contradictions arise at which the intellect of savages takes no more offence than a highly civilized person would as long as it is only a question of religious matters or of "loyalty."

That would be so far so good; but the psychoanalytic technique may enable us to penetrate more deeply into the matter and to add something about the nature of these various tendencies. If we subject the facts as stated to analysis, just as if they formed the symptoms of a neurosis, our first attention would be directed to the excess of anxious worry which is said to be the cause of the taboo ceremonial. The concurrence of such excessive tenderness is very common in the neurosis and especially in the compulsion neurosis upon which we are drawing primarily for our comparison. We now thoroughly understand the origin of this tenderness. It occurs wherever, besides the predominant tenderness, there exists a contrary but unconscious stream of hostility, that is to say wherever the typical case of an ambivalent affective attitude is realized. The hostility is then cried down by an excessive increase of tenderness which is expressed as anxiety and becomes compulsive because otherwise it would not suffice for its task of keeping the unconscious opposition in a state of repression. Every psychoanalyst knows how infallible this anxious excess of tenderness can be resolved even under the most improbable circumstances, as for instance, when it appears between mother and child, or in the case of affectionate married people. Applied to the treatment of privileged persons this theory of an ambivalent feeling would reveal that their veneration, their very deification, is opposed in the unconscious by an intense hostile tendency, so that, as we had expected, the situation of an ambivalent feeling is here realized. The distrust which certainly seems to contribute to the motivation of the royal taboo, would be another direct manifestation of the same unconscious hostility. Indeed the ultimate issues of this conflict show such a diversity among different races that we would not be at a loss for examples in which the proof of such hostility would be much easier. We learn from Frazer[26] that the savage Timmes of Sierra Leone reserve the right to administer a beating to their elected king on the evening before his coronation, and that they make use of this constitutional right with such thoroughness that the unhappy ruler sometimes does not long survive his accession to the throne; for this reason the leaders of the race have made it a rule to elect some man against whom they have a particular grudge. Nevertheless, even in such glaring cases the hostility is not acknowledged as such, but is expressed as if it were a ceremonial.

Another trait in the attitude of primitive races towards their rulers recalls a mechanism which is universally present in mental disturbances and is openly revealed in the so-called delusions of persecution. Here the importance of a particular person is extraordinarily heightened and his omnipotence is raised to the improbable in order to make it easier to attribute to him the responsibility for everything painful which happens to the patient. Savages really do not act differently towards their rulers when they ascribe to them power over rain and shine, wind and weather, and then dethrone or kill them because nature has disappointed their expectation of a good hunt or a ripe harvest. The prototype which the paranoiac reconstructs in his persecution mania, is found in the relation of the child to its father. Such omnipotence is regularly attributed to the father in the imagination of the son, and distrust of the father has been shown to be intimately connected with the highest esteem for him. When a paranoiac names a person of his acquaintance as his "persecutor," he thereby elevates him to the paternal succession and brings him under conditions which enable him to make him responsible for all the misfortune which he experiences. Thus this second analogy between the savage and the neurotic may allow us to surmise how much in the relation of the savage to his ruler arises from the infantile attitude of the child to its father.

But the strongest support for our point of view, which seeks to compare taboo prohibitions with neurotic symptoms, is to be found in the taboo ceremonial itself, the significance of which for the status of kinship has already been the subject of our previous discussion. This ceremonial unmistakably reveals its double meaning and its origin from ambivalent ten-

[26] *l.c.*, p. 18, citing Zwefel et Monstier, *Voyage aux Sources du Niger*, 1880.

dencies if only we are willing to assume that the effects it produces are those which it intended from the very beginning. It not only distinguishes kings and elevates them above all ordinary mortals, but it also makes their life a torture and an unbearable burden and forces them into a thraldom which is far worse than that of their subjects. It would thus be the correct counterpart to the compulsive action of the neurosis, in which the suppressed impulse and the impulse which suppresses it meet in mutual and simultaneous satisfaction. The compulsive action is nominally a protection against the forbidden action; but we would say that actually it is a repetition of what is forbidden. The word "nominally" is here applied to the conscious whereas the word "actually" applies to the unconscious instance of the psychic life. Thus also the taboo ceremonial of kings is nominally an expression of the highest veneration and a means of guarding them; actually it is the punishment for their elevation, the revenge which their subjects take upon them. The experiences which Cervantes makes Sancho Panza undergo as governor of his island have evidently made him recognize this interpretation of courtly ceremonial as the only correct one. It is very possible that this point would be corroborated if we could induce kings and rulers of today to express themselves on this point.

Why the emotional attitude towards rulers should contain such a strong unconscious share of hostility is a very interesting problem which, however, exceeds the scope of this book. We have already referred to the infantile father-complex; we may add that an investigation of the early history of kingship would bring the decisive explanations. Frazer has an impressive discussion of the theory that the first kings were strangers who, after a short reign, were destined to be sacrificed at solemn festivals as representatives of the deity; but Frazer himself does not consider his facts altogether convincing.[27] Christian myths are said to have been still influenced by the after-effects of this evolution of kings.

The Taboo of the Dead

We know that the dead are mighty rulers: we may be surprised to learn that they are regarded as enemies.

Among most primitive people the taboo of the dead displays, if we may keep to our infection analogy, a peculiar virulence. It manifests itself in the first place, in the consequences which result from contact with the dead, and in the treatment of the mourners for the dead. Among the Maori any one who had touched a corpse or who had taken part in its interment, became extremely unclean and was almost cut off from intercourse with

[27] Frazer, *The Magic Art and the Evolution of Kings*, 2 vols., 1911 (*The Golden Bough*).

his fellow beings; he was, as we say, boycotted. He could not enter a house or approach persons or objects without infecting them with the same properties. He could not even touch his food with his own hands, which were now unclean and therefore quite useless to him. His food was put on the ground and he had no alternative except to seize it as best he could, with his lips and teeth, while he held his hands behind on his back. Occasionally he could be fed by another person who helped him to his food with outstretched arms so as not to touch the unfortunate one himself, but this assistant was then in turn subjected to almost equally oppressive restrictions. Almost every village contained some altogether disreputable individual, ostracized by society, whose wretched existence depended upon people's charity. This creature alone was allowed within arm's length of a person who had fulfilled the last duty towards the deceased. But as soon as the period of segregation was over and the person rendered unclean through the corpse could again mingle with his fellow-beings, all the dishes which he had used during the dangerous period were broken and all his clothing was thrown away.

The taboo customs after bodily contact with the dead are the same all over Polynesia, in Melanesia, and in a part of Africa; their most constant feature is the prohibition against handling one's food and the consequent necessity of being fed by somebody else. It is noteworthy that in Polynesia, or perhaps only in Hawaii,[28] priest-kings were subject to the same restrictions during the exercise of holy functions. In the taboo of the dead on the Island of Tonga the abatement and gradual abolition of the prohibitions through the individual's own taboo power are clearly shown. A person who touched the corpse of a dead chieftan was unclean for ten months; but if he was himself a chief, he was unclean for only three, four, or five months, according to the rank of the deceased; if it was the corpse of the idolized head-chief even the greatest chiefs become taboo for ten months. These savages are so certain that any one who violates these taboo rules must become seriously ill and die, that according to the opinion of an observer, they have never yet dared to convince themselves of the contrary.[29]

The taboo restrictions imposed upon persons whose contact with the dead is to be understood in the transferred sense, namely the mourning relatives such as widows and widowers, are essentially the same as those mentioned above, but they are of greater interest for the point we are trying to make. In the rules hitherto mentioned we see only the typical expression of the virulence and power of diffusion of the taboo; in those about to be cited we catch a gleam of the motives, including both the ostensible

[28]Frazer, *Taboo*, p. 148, etc.

[29]W. Mariner, *The Natives of the Tonga Islands*, 1818, see Frazer, *l.c.*, p. 140.

ones and those which may be regarded as the underlying and genuine ones.

Among the Shuswap in British Columbia widows and widowers have to remain segregated during their period of mourning; they must not use their hands to touch the body or the head and all utensils used by them must not be used by any one else. No hunter will want to approach the hut in which such mourners live, for that would bring misfortune; if the shadow of one of the mourners should fall on him he would become ill. The mourners sleep on thorn bushes, with which they also surround their beds. This last precaution is meant to keep off the spirit of the deceased; plainer still is the reported custom of other North American tribes where the widow, after the death of her husband, has to wear a kind of trousers of dried grass in order to make herself inaccessible to the approach of the spirit. Thus it is quite obvious that touching "in the transferred sense" is after all understood only as bodily contact, since the spirit of the deceased does not leave his kin and does not desist from "hovering about them," during the period of mourning.

Among the Agutainos, who live on Palawan, one of the Philippine Islands, a widow may not leave her hut for the first seven or eight days after her husband's death, except at night, when she need not expect encounters. Whoever sees her is in danger of immediate death and therefore she herself warns others of her approach by hitting the trees with a wooden stick with every step she takes; these trees all wither. Another observation explains the nature of the danger inherent in a widow. In the district of Mekeo, British New Guinea, a widower forfeits all civil rights and lives like an outlaw. He may not tend a garden, or show himself in public, or enter the village or go on the street. He slinks about like an animal, in the high grass or in the bushes, and must hide in a thicket if he sees anybody, especially a woman, approaching. This last hint makes it easy for us to trace back the danger of the widower or widow to the danger of temptation. The husband who has lost his wife must evade the desire for a substitute; the widow has to contend with the same wish, and besides this, she may arouse the desire of other men because she is without a master. Every such satisfaction through a substitute runs contrary to the intention of mourning and would cause the anger of the spirit to flare up.[30]

One of the most surprising, but at the same time one of the most instructive taboo customs of mourning among primitive races is the prohibition against pronouncing the *name* of the deceased. This is very wide-

[30] The same patient whose "impossibilities" I have correlated with taboo (see above, p. 257) acknowledged that she always became indignant when she met anybody on the street who dressed in mourning. "Such people should be forbidden to go out!" she said.

spread, and has been subject to many modifications with important consequences.

Aside from the Australians and the Polynesians, who usually show us taboo customs in their best state of preservation, we also find this prohibition among races so far apart and unrelated to each other as the Samojedes in Siberia and the Todas in South India, the Mongolians of Tartary and the Tuaregs of the Sahara, the Aino of Japan and the Akamba and Nandi in Central Africa, the Tinguanes in the Philippines and the inhabitants of the Nikobari Islands and of Madagascar and Borneo.[31] Among some of these races the prohibition and its consequences hold good only for the period of mourning while in others it remains permanent; but in all cases it seems to diminish with the lapse of time after the death.

The avoidance of the name of the deceased is as a rule kept up with extraordinary severity. Thus, among many South American tribes, it is considered the gravest insult to the survivors to pronounce the name of the deceased in their presence, and the penalty set for it is no less than that for the slaying itself.[32] At first it is not easy to guess why the mention of the name should be so abominated, but the dangers associated with it have called into being a whole series of interesting and important expedients to avoid this. Thus the Masai in Africa have hit upon the evasion of changing the name of the deceased immediately upon his death; he may now be mentioned without dread by this new name, while all the prohibitions remain attached to the old name. It seems to be assumed that the ghost does not know his new name and will not find it out. The Australian tribes on Adelaide and Encounter Bay are so consistently cautious that when a death occurs almost every person who has the same name as the deceased or a very similar one, exchanges it for another. Sometimes by a further extension of the same idea as seen among several tribes in Victoria and in North America all the relatives of the deceased change their names regardless of whether their names resemble the name of the deceased in sound. Among the Guaycuru in Paraguay the chief used to give new names to all the members of the tribe, on such sad occasions, which they then remembered as if they had always had them.[33]

Furthermore, if the deceased had the same name as an animal or object, etc., some of the races just enumerated thought it necessary to give these animals and objects new names, in order not to be reminded of the deceased when they mentioned them. Through this there must have resulted a never ceasing change of vocabulary, which caused a good deal of difficulty for the missionaries, especially where the interdiction upon a name

---

[31] Frazer, *l.c.*, p. 353.

[32] Frazer, *l.c.*, p. 352, etc.

[33] Frazer, *l.c.*, p. 357, citing an old Spanish observer, 1732.

was permanent. In the seven years which the missionary Dobrizhofer spent among the Abipons in Paraguay, the name for jaguar was changed three times and the words for crocodile, thorns, and animal slaughter underwent a similar fate.[34] But the dread of pronouncing a name which has belonged to a deceased person extends also to the mention of everything in which the deceased had any part, and a further important result of this process of suppression is that these races have no tradition or any historical reminiscences, so that we encounter the greatest difficulties in investigating their past history. Among a number of these primitive races compensating customs have also been established in order to re-awaken the names of the deceased after a long period of mourning; they are bestowed upon children who were regarded as reincarnations of the dead.

The strangeness of this taboo on names diminishes if we bear in mind that the savage looks upon his name as an essential part and an important possession of his personality, and that he ascribes the full significance of things to words. Our children do the same, as I have shown elsewhere, and therefore they are never satisfied with accepting a meaningless verbal similarity, but consistently conclude that when two things have identical names a deeper correspondence between them must exist. Numerous peculiarities of normal behaviour may lead civilized man to conclude that he too is not yet as far removed as he thinks from attributing the importance of things to mere names and feeling that his name has become peculiarly identified with his person. This is corroborated by psychoanalytic experiences, where there is much occasion to point out the importance of names in unconscious thought activity.[35] As was to be expected, the compulsion neurotics behave just like savages in regard to names. They show the full "complex sensitiveness" towards the utterance and hearing of special words (as do also other neurotics) and derive a good many, often serious, inhibitions from their treatment of their own name. One of these taboo patients whom I knew, had adopted the avoidance of writing down her name for fear that it might get into somebody's hands who thus would come into possession of a piece of her personality. In her frenzied faithfulness, which she needed to protect herself against the temptations of her phantasy, she had created for herself the commandment, "not to give away anything of her personality." To this belonged first of all her name, then by further application her handwriting, so that she finally gave up writing.

Thus it no longer seems strange to us that savages should consider a dead person's name as a part of his personality and that it should be subjected to the same taboo as the deceased. Calling a dead person by name can also be traced back to contact with him, so that we can turn our atten-

[34] Frazer, *l.c.*, p. 360.
[35] Stekel, *Abraham*.

tion to the more inclusive problem of why this contact is visited with such a severe taboo.

The nearest explanation would point to the natural horror which a corpse inspires, especially in view of the changes so soon noticeable after death. Mourning for a dead person must also be considered as a sufficient motive for everything which has reference to him. But horror of the corpse evidently does not cover all the details of taboo rules, and mourning can never explain to us why the mention of the dead is a severe insult to his survivors. On the contrary, mourning loves to preoccupy itself with the deceased, to elaborate his memory, and preserve it for the longest possible time. Something besides mourning must be made responsible for the peculiarities of taboo customs, something which evidently serves a different purpose. It is this very taboo on names which reveals this still unknown motive, and if the customs did not tell us about it we would find it out from the statements of the mourning savages themselves.

For they do not conceal the fact that they fear the presence and the return of the spirit of a dead person; they practise a host of ceremonies to keep him off and banish him.[36] They look upon the mention of his name as a conjuration which must result in his immediate presence.[37] They, therefore, consistently do everything to avoid conjuring and awakening a dead person. They disguise themselves in order that the spirit may not recognize them,[38] they distort either his name or their own, and become infuriated when a ruthless stranger incites the spirit against his survivors by mentioning his name. We can hardly avoid the conclusion that they suffer, according to Wundt's expression, from the fear of "his soul now turned into a demon."[39]

With this understanding we approach Wundt's conception who, as we have heard, sees the nature of taboo in the fear of demons.

The assumption which this theory makes, namely, that immediately after death the beloved member of a family becomes a demon, from whom the survivors have nothing but hostility to expect, so that they must protect themselves by every means from his evil desires, is so peculiar that our first impulse is not to believe it. Yet almost all competent authors agree as to this interpretation of primitive races. Westermarck,[40] who, in my opin-

---

[36] Frazer, *l.c.*, p. 353, cites the Tuaregs of the Sahara as an example of such an acknowledgment.

[37] Perhaps this condition is to be added: as long as any part of his physical remains exist. Frazer, *l.c.*, p. 372.

[38] *On the Nikobar Islands*, Frazer, *l.c.*, p. 382.

[39] Wundt, *Religion and Myth*, Vol. II, p. 49.

[40] *The Origin and Development of Moral Conceptions*, see section entitled "Attitude Towards the Dead," Vol. II, p. 424. Both the notes and the text show an abundance of corroborating and often very characteristic testimony, *e.g.*, the Maori believed that "the nearest

ion, gives altogether too little consideration to taboo, makes this statement: "On the whole facts lead me to conclude that the dead are more frequently regarded as enemies than as friends and that Jevons and Grant Allen are wrong in their assertion that it was formerly believed that the malevolence of the dead was as a rule directed only against strangers, while they were paternally concerned about the life and welfare of their descendants and the members of their clan."

R. Kleinpaul has written an impressive book in which he makes use of the remnants of the old belief in souls among civilized races to show the relation between the living and the dead.[41] According to him too, this relation culminates in the conviction that the dead, thirsting for blood, draw the living after them. The living did not feel themselves safe from the persecutions of the dead until a body of water had been put between them. That is why it was preferred to bury the dead on islands or to bring them to the other side of a river: the expressions "here" and "beyond" originated in this way. Later moderation has restricted the malevolence of the dead to those categories where a peculiar right to feel rancour had to be admitted, such as the murdered who pursue their murderer as evil spirits, and those who, like brides, had died with their longings unsatisfied. Kleinpaul believes that originally, however, the dead were all vampires, who bore ill-will towards the living, and strove to harm them and deprive them of life. It was the corpse that first furnished the conception of an evil spirit.

The hypothesis that those whom we love best turn into demons after death obviously allows us to put a further question. What prompted primitive races to ascribe such a change of sentiment to the beloved dead? Why did they make demons out of them? According to Westermarck this question is easily answered.[42] "As death is usually considered the worst calamity that can overtake man, it is believed that the deceased are very dissatisfied with their lot. Primitive races believe that death comes only through being slain, whether by violence or by magic, and this is considered already sufficient reason for the soul to be vindictive and irritable. The soul presumably envies the living and longs for the company of its former kin; we can therefore understand that the soul should seek to kill them with diseases in order to be reunited with them. . . .

". . . A further explanation of the malevolence ascribed to souls lies in

---

and most beloved relatives changed their nature after death and bore ill-will even to their former favourites." The Austral Negroes believe that every dead person is for a long time malevolent; the closer the relationship the greater the fear. The Central Eskimos are dominated by the idea that the dead come to rest very late and that at first they are to be feared as mischievous spirits who frequently hover about the village to spread illness, death, and other evils. (Boas.)

[41] R. Kleinpaul: *The Living and the Dead in Folklore, Religion and Myth*, 1898.

[42] *l.c.*, p. 426.

the instinctive fear of them, which is itself the result of the fear of death."

Our study of psychoneurotic disturbances points to a more comprehensive explanation, which includes that of Westermarck.

When a wife loses her husband, or a daughter her mother, it not infrequently happens that the survivor is afflicted with tormenting scruples, called "obsessive reproaches" which raise the question whether she herself has not been guilty through carelessness or neglect, of the death of the beloved person. No recalling of the care with which she nursed the invalid, or direct refutation of the asserted guilt can put an end to the torture, which is the pathological expression of mourning and which in time slowly subsides. Psychoanalytic investigation of such cases has made us acquainted with the secret mainsprings of this affliction. We have ascertained that these obsessive reproaches are in a certain sense justified and therefore are immune to refutation or objections. Not that the mourner has really been guilty of the death or that she has really been careless, as the obsessive reproach asserts; but still there was something in her, a wish of which she herself was aware, which was not displeased with the fact that death came, and which would have brought it about sooner had it been strong enough. The reproach now reacts against this unconscious wish after the death of the beloved person. Such hostility, hidden in the unconscious behind tender love, exists in almost all cases of intensive emotional allegiance to a particular person, indeed it represents the classic case, the prototype of the ambivalence of human emotions. There is always more or less of this ambivalence in everybody's disposition; normally it is not strong enough to give rise to the obsessive reproaches we have described. But where there is abundant predisposition for it, it manifests itself in the relation to those we love most, precisely where you would least expect it. The disposition to compulsion neurosis which we have so often taken for comparison with taboo problems, is distinguished by a particularly high degree of this original ambivalence of emotions.

We now know how to explain the supposed demonism of recently departed souls and the necessity of being protected against their hostility through taboo rules. By assuming a similar high degree of ambivalence in the emotional life of primitive races such as psychoanalysis ascribes to persons suffering from compulsion neurosis, it becomes comprehensible that the same kind of reaction against the hostility latent in the unconscious behind the obsessive reproaches of the neurotic should also be necessary here after the painful loss had occurred. But this hostility, which is painfully felt in the unconscious in the form of satisfaction with the demise, experiences a different fate in the case of primitive man: the defence against it is accomplished by displacement upon the object of hostility, namely, the dead. We call this defence process, frequent both in normal and diseased psychic life, a *projection*. The survivor will deny that he has ever entertained hostile impulses toward the beloved dead; but now the soul of the deceased entertains them and will try to give vent to them during the entire period of mourning. In spite of the successful defence through projection, the punitive and remorseful character of this emotional reaction manifests itself in being afraid, in self-imposed renunciations and in subjection to restrictions which are partly disguised as protective measures against the hostile demon. Thus we find again that taboo has grown out of the soil of an ambivalent emotional attitude. The taboo of the dead also originates from the opposition between the conscious grief and the unconscious satisfaction at death. If this is the origin of the resentment of spirits it is self-evident that just the nearest and formerly most beloved survivors have to fear it most.

As in neurotic symptoms, the taboo regulations also evince opposite feelings. Their restrictive character expresses mourning, while they also betray very clearly what they are trying to conceal, namely, the hostility towards the dead, which is now motivated as self-defence. We have learnt to understand part of the taboo regulations as temptation fears. A dead person is defenceless, which must act as an incitement to satisfy hostile desires entertained against him; this temptation has to be opposed by the prohibition.

But Westermarck is right in not admitting any difference in the savage's conception between those who have died by violence and those who have died a natural death. As will be shown later, in the unconscious mode of thinking even a natural death is perceived as murder; the person was killed by evil wishes. Any one interested in the origin and meaning of dreams dealing with the death of dear relatives such as parents and brothers and sisters will find that the same feeling of ambivalence is responsible for the fact that the dreamer, the child, and the savage all have the same attitude towards the dead.[43]

A little while ago we challenged Wundt's conception, which explains the nature of taboo through the fear of demons, and yet we have just agreed with the explanation which traces back the taboo of the dead to a fear of the soul of the dead after it has turned into a demon. This seems like a contradiction, but it will not be difficult for us to explain it. It is true that we have accepted the idea of demons, but we know that this assumption is not something final which psychology cannot resolve into further elements. We have, as it were, exposed the demons by recognizing them as mere projections of hostile feelings which the survivor entertains toward the dead.

The double feeling—tenderness and hostility—against the deceased,

[43]See: Freud *The Interpretation of Dreams.*

which we consider well founded, endeavours to assert itself at the time of bereavement as mourning and satisfaction. A conflict must ensue between these contrary feelings, and as one of them, namely the hostility, is altogether or for the greater part unconscious, the conflict cannot result in a conscious difference in the form of hostility or tenderness as, for instance, when we forgive an injury inflicted upon us by some one we love. The process usually adjusts itself through a special psychic mechanism, which is designated in psychoanalysis as *projection.* This unknown hostility, of which we are ignorant and of which we do not wish to know, is projected from our inner perception into the outer world and is thereby detached from our own person and attributed to the other. Not we, the survivors, rejoice because we are rid of the deceased, on the contrary, we mourn for him; but now, curiously enough, he has become an evil demon who would rejoice in our misfortune and who seeks our death. The survivors must now defend themselves against this evil enemy; they are freed from inner oppression, but they have only succeeded in exchanging it for an affliction from without.

It is not to be denied that this process of projection, which turns the dead into malevolent enemies, finds some support in the real hostilities of the dead which the survivors remember and with which they really can reproach the dead. These hostilities are harshness, the desire to dominate, injustice, and whatever else forms the background of even the most tender relations between men. But the process cannot be so simple that this factor alone could explain the origin of demons by projection. The offences of the dead certainly motivate in part the hostility of the survivors, but they would have been ineffective if they had not given rise to this hostility and the occasion of death would surely be the least suitable occasion for awakening the memory of the reproaches which justly could have been brought against the deceased. We cannot dispense with the unconscious hostility as the constant and really impelling motive. This hostile tendency towards those nearest and dearest could remain latent during their lifetime, that is to say, it could avoid betraying itself to consciousness either directly or indirectly through any substitutive formation. However, when the person who was simultaneously loved and hated died, this was no longer possible, and the conflict became acute. The mourning originating from the enhanced tenderness, became on the one hand more intolerant of the latent hostility, while on the other hand it could not tolerate that the latter should not give origin to a feeling of pure gratification. Thus there came about the repression of the unconscious hostility through projection, and the formation of the ceremonial in which fear of punishment of demons finds expression. With the termination of the period of mourning, the conflict also loses its acuteness so that the taboo of the dead can be abated or sink into oblivion.

4

Having thus explained the basis on which the very instructive taboo of the dead has grown up, we must not miss the opportunity of adding a few observations which may become important for the understanding to taboo in general.

The projection of unconscious hostility upon demons in the taboo of the dead is only a single example from a whole series of processes to which we must grant the greatest influence in the formation of primitive psychic life. In the foregoing case the mechanism of projection is used to settle an emotional conflict; it serves the same purpose in a large number of psychic situations which lead to neuroses. But projection is not specially created for the purpose of defence, it also comes into being where there are no conflicts. The projection of inner perceptions to the outside is a primitive mechanism which, for instance, also influences our sense-perceptions, so that it normally has the greatest share in shaping our outer world. Under conditions that have not yet been sufficiently determined even inner perceptions of ideational and emotional processes are projected outwardly, like sense perceptions, and are used to shape the outer world, whereas they ought to remain in the inner world. This is perhaps genetically connected with the fact that the function of attention was originally directed not towards the inner world, but to the stimuli streaming in from the outer world, and only received reports of pleasure and pain from the endo-psychic processes. Only with the development of the language of abstract thought through the association of sensory remnants of word representations with inner processes, did the latter gradually become capable of perception. Before this took place primitive man had developed a picture of the outer world through the outward projection of inner perceptions, which we, with our reinforced conscious perception, must now translate back into psychology.

The projection of their own evil impulses upon demons is only a part of what has become the world system ("Weltanschauung") of primitive man which we shall discuss later as "animalism." We shall then have to ascertain the psychological nature of such a system formation and the points of support which we shall find in the analysis of these system formations will again bring us face to face with the neurosis. For the present we merely wish to suggest that the "secondary elaboration" of the dream content is the prototype of all these system formations.[44] And let us not forget that beginning at the stage of system formation there are two origins for every

[44] See: *The Interpretation of Dreams.*

act judged by consciousness, namely the systematic, and the real but unconscious origin.[45]

Wundt[46] remarks that "among the influences which myth everywhere ascribes to demons the evil ones preponderate, so that according to the religions of races evil demons are evidently older than good demons." Now it is quite possible that the whole conception of demons was derived from the extremely important relation to the dead. In the further course of human development the ambivalence inherent in this relation then manifested itself by allowing two altogether contrary psychic formations to issue from the same root, namely, the fear of demons and of *ghosts*, and the reverence for ancestors.[47] Nothing testifies so much to the influence of mourning on the origin of belief in demons as the fact that demons were always taken to be the spirits of persons not long dead. Mourning has a very distinct psychic task to perform, namely, to detach the memories and expectations of the survivors from the dead. When this work is accomplished the grief, and with it the remorse and reproach, lessens, and therefore also the fear of the demon. But the very spirits which at first were feared as demons now serve a friendlier purpose; they are revered as ancestors and appealed to for help in times of distress.

If we survey the relation of survivors to the dead through the course of the ages, it is very evident that the ambivalent feeling has extraordinarily abated. We now find it easy to suppress whatever unconscious hostility towards the dead there may still exist without any special psychic effort on our part. Where formerly satisfied hate and painful tenderness struggled with each other, we now find piety, which appears like a cicatrice and demands: *De mortuis nil nisi bonum.*° Only neurotics still blur the mourning for the loss of their dear ones with attacks of compulsive reproaches which psychoanalysis reveals as the old ambivalent emotional feeling. How this change was brought about, and to what extent constitutional changes and real improvement of familiar relations share in causing the abatement of the ambivalent feeling, need not be discussed here. But this example would lead us to assume *that the psychic impulses of primitive man possessed a higher degree of ambivalence than is found at present among civilized human beings. With the decline of this ambivalence the taboo, as the compromise symptom of the ambiv-*

De mortuis nil nisi bonum Of the dead (say) nothing but good.

[45]The projection creations of primitive man resemble the personifications through which the poet projects his warring impulses out of himself, as separated individuals.

[46]*Myth and Religion*, p. 129.

[47]In the psychoanalysis of neurotic persons who suffer, or have suffered, in their childhood from the fear of ghosts, it is often not difficult to expose these ghosts as the parents. Compare also in this connection the communication of P. Haeberlin, *Sexual Ghosts* (*Sexual Problems*, Feb. 1912), where it is a question of another erotically accentuated person, but where the father was dead.

alent conflict, also slowly disappeared. Neurotics who are compelled to reproduce this conflict, together with the taboo resulting from it, may be said to have brought with them an atavistic remnant in the form of an archaic constitution the compensation of which in the interest of cultural demands entails the most prodigious psychic efforts on their part.

At this point we may recall the confusing information which Wundt offered us about the double meaning of the word taboo, namely, holy and unclean (see above). It was supposed that originally the word taboo did not yet mean holy and unclean but signified something demonic, something which may not be touched, thus emphasizing a characteristic common to both extremes of the later conception; this persistent common trait proves, however, that an original correspondence existed between what was holy and what was unclean, which only later became differentiated.

In contrast to this, our discussion readily shows that the double meaning in question belonged to the word taboo from the very beginning and that it serves to designate a definite ambivalence as well as everything which has come into existence on the basis of this ambivalence. Taboo is itself an ambivalent word and by way of supplement we may add that the established meaning of this word might of itself have allowed us to guess what we have found as the result of extensive investigation, namely, that the taboo prohibition is to be explained as the result of an emotional ambivalence. A study of the oldest languages has taught us that at one time there were many such words which included their own contrasts so that they were in a certain sense ambivalent, though perhaps not exactly in the same sense as the word taboo.[48] Slight vocal modifications of this primitive word containing two opposite meanings later served to create a separate linguistic expression for the two opposites originally united in one word.

The word taboo has had a different fate; with the diminished importance of the ambivalence which it connotes, it has itself disappeared, or rather, the words analogous to it have vanished from the vocabulary. In a later connection I hope to be able to show that a tangible historic change is probably concealed behind the fate of this conception; that the word at first was associated with definite human relations which were characterized by great emotional ambivalence from which it expanded to other analogous relations.

Unless we are mistaken, the understanding of taboo also throws light upon the nature and origin of *conscience.* Without stretching ideas we can speak of a taboo conscience and a taboo sense of guilt after the violation of a taboo. Taboo conscience is probably the oldest form in which we meet the phenomenon of conscience.

---

[48] Compare my article on Abel's *Gegensinn der Urwort* in the *Jahrbuch für tische und Psychopathologische Forschungen,* Bd. II, 1910.

For what is "conscience"? According to linguistic testimony it belongs to what we know most surely; in some languages its meaning is hardly to be distinguished from consciousness.

Conscience is the inner perception of objections to definite wish impulses that exist in us; but the emphasis is put upon the fact that this rejection does not have to depend on anything else, that it is sure of itself. This becomes even plainer in the case of a guilty conscience, where we become aware of the inner condemnation of such acts which realized some of our definite wish impulses. Confirmation seems superfluous here; whoever has a conscience must feel in himself the justification of the condemnation, and the reproach for the accomplished action. But this same character is evinced by the attitude of savages towards taboo. Taboo is a command of conscience, the violation of which causes a terrible sense of guilt which is as self-evident as its origin is unknown.[49]

It is, therefore, probable that conscience also originates on the basis of an ambivalent feeling from quite definite human relations which contain this ambivalence. It probably originates under conditions which are in force both for taboo and the compulsion neurosis, that is, one component of the two contrasting feelings is unconscious and is kept repressed by the compulsive domination of the other component. This is confirmed by many things which we have learned from our analysis of neurosis. In the first place the character of compulsion neurotics shows a predominant trait of painful conscientiousness which is a symptom of reaction against the temptation which lurks in the unconscious, and which develops into the highest degrees of guilty conscience as their illness grows worse. Indeed, one may venture the assertion that if the origin of guilty conscience could not be discovered through compulsion neurotic patients, there would be no prospect of ever discovering it. This task is successfully solved in the case of the individual neurotic, and we are confident of finding a similar solution in the case of races.

In the second place we cannot help noticing that the sense of guilt contains much of the nature of anxiety; without hesitation it may be described as "conscience phobia." But fear points to unconscious sources. The psychology of the neuroses taught us that when wish feelings undergo repression their libido becomes transformed into anxiety. In addition we must bear in mind that the sense of guilt also contains something unknown and unconscious, namely the motivation for the rejection. The character of anxiety in the sense of guilt corresponds to this unknown quantity.

---

[49] It is an interesting parallel that the sense of guilt resulting from the violation of a taboo is in no way diminished if the violation took place unwittingly (see examples above), and that even in the Greek myth the guilt of Oedipus is not cancelled by the fact that it was incurred without his knowledge and will and even against them.

If taboo expresses itself mainly in prohibitions it may well be considered self-evident, without remote proof from the analogy with neurosis that it is based on a positive, desireful impulse. For what nobody desires to do does not have to be forbidden, and certainly whatever is expressly forbidden must be an object of desire. If we applied this plausible theory to primitive races we would have to conclude that among their strongest temptations were desires to kill their kings and priests, to commit incest, to abuse their dead and the like. That is not very probable. And if we should apply the same theory to those cases in which we ourselves seem to hear the voice of conscience most clearly we would arouse the greatest contradiction. For there we would assert with the utmost certainty that we did not feel the slightest temptation to violate any of these commandments, as for example,the commandment: Thou shalt not kill, and that we felt nothing but repugnance at the very idea.

But if we grant the testimony of our conscience the importance it claims, then the prohibition—the taboo as well as our moral prohibitions—becomes superfluous, while the existence of a conscience, in turn, remains unexplained and the connection between conscience, taboo and neurosis disappears. The net result of this would then be our present state of understanding unless we view the problem psychoanalytically.

But if we take into account the following results of psychoanalysis, our understanding of the problem is greatly advanced. The analysis of dreams of normal individuals has shown that our own temptation to kill others is stronger and more frequent than we had suspected and that it produces psychic effects even where it does not reveal itself to our consciousness. And when we have learnt that the obsessive rules of certain neurotics are nothing but measures of self-reassurance and self-punishment erected against the reinforced impulse to commit murder, we can return with fresh appreciation to our previous hypothesis that every prohibition must conceal a desire. We can then assume that this desire to murder actually exists and that the taboo as well as the moral prohibition are psychologically by no means superfluous but are, on the contrary, explained and justified through our ambivalent attitude towards the impulse to slay.

The nature of this ambivalent relation so often emphasized as fundamental, namely, that the positive underlying desire is unconscious, opens the possibility of showing further connections and explaining further problems. The psychic processes in the unconscious are not entirely identical with those known to us from our conscious psychic life, but have the benefit of certain notable liberties of which the latter are deprived. An unconscious impulse need not have originated where we find it expressed; it can spring from an entirely different place and may originally have referred to other persons and relations, but through the mechanism of *displacement*, it reaches the point where it comes to our notice. Thanks to the indestructibility of unconscious processes and their inaccessibility to correction, the impulse may be saved over from earlier times to which it was adapted to later periods and conditions in which its manifestations must necessarily seem foreign. These are all only hints, but a careful elaboration of them would show how important they may become for the understanding of the development of civilization.

In closing these discussions we do not want to neglect to make an observation that will be of use for later investigations. Even if we insist upon the essential similarity between taboo and moral prohibitions, we do not dispute that a psychological difference must exist between them. A change in the relations of the fundamental ambivalence can be the only reason why the prohibition no longer appears in the form of a taboo.

In the analytical consideration of taboo phenomena we have hitherto allowed ourselves to be guided by their demonstrable agreements with compulsion neurosis; but as taboo is not a neurosis but a social creation we are also confronted with the task of showing wherein lies the essential difference between the neurosis and a product of culture like the taboo.

Here again, I will take a single fact as my starting point. Primitive races fear a punishment for the violation of a taboo, usually a serious disease or death. This punishment threatens only him who has been guilty of the violation. It is different with the compulsion neurosis. If the patient wants to do something that is forbidden to him he does not fear punishment for himself, but for another person. The person is usually indefinite, but, by means of analysis, is easily recognized as someone very near and dear to the patient. The neurotic therefore acts as if he were altruistic, while primitive man seems egotistical. Only if retribution fails to overtake the taboo violator spontaneously does a collective feeling awaken among savages that they are all threatened through the sacrilege, and they hasten to inflict the omitted punishment themselves. It is easy for us to explain the mechanism of this solidarity. It is a question of fear of the contagious example, the temptation to imitate, that is to say, of the capacity of the taboo to infect. If some one has succeeded in satisfying the repressed desire, the same desire must manifest itself in all his companions; hence, in order to keep down this temptation, this envied individual must be despoiled of the fruit of his daring. Not infrequently the punishment gives the executors themselves an opportunity to commit the same sacrilegious act by justifying it as an expiation. This is really one of the fundamentals of the human code of punishment which rightly presumes the same forbidden impulses in the criminal and in the members of society who avenge his offence.

Psychoanalysis here confirms what the pious were wont to say, that we are all miserable sinners. How then shall we explain the unexpected nobility of the neurosis which fears nothing for itself and everything for the beloved person?

Psychoanalytic investigation shows that this nobility is not primary. Originally, that is to say at the beginning of the disease, the threat of punishment pertained to one's own person; in every case the fear was for one's own life; the fear of death being only later displaced upon another beloved person. The process is somewhat complicated but we have a complete grasp of it. An evil impulse—a death wish—towards the beloved person is always at the basis of the formation of a prohibition. This is repressed through a prohibition, and the prohibition is connected with a certain act which by displacement usually substitutes the hostile for the beloved person, and the execution of this act is threatened with the penalty of death. But the process goes further and the original wish for the death of the beloved other person is then replaced by fear for his death. The tender altruistic trait of the neurosis therefore merely *compensates* for the opposite attitude of brutal egotism which is at the basis of it. If we designate as social these emotional impulses which are determined through regard for another person who is not taken as a sexual object, we can emphasize the withdrawal of these social factors as an essential feature of the neurosis, which is later disguised through over-compensation.

Without lingering over the origin of these social impulses and their relation to other fundamental impulses of man, we will bring out the second main characteristic of the neurosis by means of another example. The form in which taboo manifests itself has the greatest similarity to the touching phobia of neurotics, the *délire de toucher*. As a matter of fact this neurosis is regularly concerned with the prohibition of sexual touching and psychoanalysis has quite generally shown that the motive power which is deflected and displaced in the neurosis is of sexual origin. In taboo the forbidden contact has evidently not only sexual significance but rather the more general one of attack, of acquisition and of personal assertion. If it is prohibited to touch the chief or something that was in contact with him it means that an inhibition should be imposed upon the same impulse which on other occasions expresses itself in suspicious surveillance of the chief and even in physical ill-treatment of him before his coronation (see above). *Thus the preponderance of sexual components of the impulse over the social components is the determining factor of the neurosis.* But the social impulses themselves came into being through the union of egotistical and erotic components into special entities.

From this single example of a comparison between taboo and compulsion neurosis it is already possible to guess the relation between individual forms of the neurosis and the creations of culture, and in what respect the study of the psychology of the neurosis is important for the understanding of the development of culture.

In one way the neuroses show a striking and far-reaching correspondence with the great social productions of art, religion and philosophy, while again they seem like distortions of them. We may say that hysteria is a caricature of an artistic creation, a compulsion neurosis, a caricature of a religion, and a paranoiac delusion a caricature of a philosophic system. In the last analysis this deviation goes back to the fact that the neuroses are asocial formations; they seek to accomplish by private means what arose in society through collective labour. In analysing the impulse of the neuroses one learns that motive powers of sexual origin exercise the determining influence in them, while the corresponding cultural creations rest upon social impulses and on such as have issued from the combination of egotistical and sexual components. It seems that the sexual need is not capable of uniting men in the same way as the demands of self-preservation; sexual satisfaction is in the first place the private concern of the individual.

Genetically the asocial nature of the neurosis springs from its original tendency to flee from a dissatisfying reality to a more pleasurable world of phantasy. This real world which neurotics shun is dominated by the society of human beings and by the institutions created by them; the estrangement from reality is at the same time a withdrawal from human companionship. . . .

In closing this study, which has been carried out in extremely condensed form, I want to state the conclusion that the beginnings of religion, ethics, society, and art meet in the Œdipus complex. This is in entire accord with the findings of psychoanalysis, namely, that the nucleus of all neuroses as far as our present knowledge of them goes is the Œdipus complex. It comes as a great surprise to me that these problems of racial psychology can also be solved through a single concrete instance, such as the relation to the father. Perhaps another psychological problem must be included here. We have so frequently had occasion to show the ambivalence of emotions in its real sense, that is to say the coincidence of love and hate towards the same object, at the root of important cultural formations. We know nothing about the origin of this ambivalence. It may be assumed to be a fundamental phenomenon of our emotional life. But the other possibility seems to me also worthy of consideration: that ambivalence, originally foreign to our emotional life, was acquired by mankind from the father complex,[50] where psychoanalytic investigation of the individual today still reveals the strongest expression of it.[51]

---

[50] That is to say, the parent complex.

[51] I am used to being misunderstood and therefore do not think it superfluous to state clearly that in giving these deductions I am by no means oblivious of the complex nature of the phenomena which give rise to them; the only claim made is that a new factor has been added to the already known or still unrecognized origins of religion, morality, and society, which was furnished through psychoanalytic experience. The syn-

Before closing we must take into account that the remarkable convergence reached in these illustrations, pointing to a single inclusive relation, ought not to blind us to the uncertainties of our assumptions and to the difficulties of our conclusions. Of these difficulties I will point out only two which must have forced themselves upon many readers.

In the first place it can hardly have escaped any one that we base everything upon the assumption of a psyche of the mass in which psychic processes occur as in the psychic life of the individual. Moreover, we let the sense of guilt for a deed survive for thousands of years, remaining effective in generations which could not have known anything of this deed. We allow an emotional process such as might have arisen among generations of sons that had been ill-treated by their fathers, to continue to new generations which had escaped such treatment by the very removal of the father. These seem indeed to be weighty objections and any other explanation which can avoid such assumptions would seem to merit preference.

But further consideration shows that we ourselves do not have to carry the whole responsibility for such daring. Without the assumption of a mass psyche, or a continuity in the emotional life of mankind which permits us to disregard the interruptions of psychic acts through the transgression of individuals, social psychology could not exist at all. If psychic processes of one generation did not continue in the next, if each had to acquire its attitude towards life afresh, there would be no progress in this field and almost no development. We are now confronted by two new questions: how much can be attributed to this psychic continuity within the series of generations, and what ways and means does a generation use to transfer its psychic states to the next generation? I do not claim that these problems have been sufficiently explained or that direct communication and tradition, of which one immediately thinks, are adequate for the task. Social psychology is in general little concerned with the manner in which the required continuity in the psychic life of succeeding generations is established. A part of the task seems to be performed by the inheritance of psychic dispositions which, however, need certain incentives in the individual life in order to become effective. This may be the meaning of the poet's words: Strive to possess yourself of what you have inherited from your ancestors. The problem would appear more difficult if we could admit that there are psychic impulses which can be so completely suppressed that they leave no traces whatsoever behind them. But that does not exist. The greatest suppression must leave room for distorted substitutions and

---

thesis of the whole explanation must be left to another. But it is in the nature of this new contribution that it could play none other than the central role in such a synthesis, although it will be necessary to overcome great affective resistances before such importance will be conceded to it.

their resulting reactions. But in that case we may assume that no generation is capable of concealing its more important psychic processes from the next. For psychoanalysis has taught us that in his unconscious psychic activity every person possesses an apparatus which enables him to interpret the reactions of others, that is to say, to straighten out the distortions which the other person has affected in the expression of his feelings. By this method of unconscious understanding of all customs, ceremonies, and laws which the original relation to the primal father had left behind, later generations may also have succeeded in taking over this legacy of feelings.

There is another objection which the analytic method of thought itself might raise.

We have interpreted the first rules of morality and moral restrictions of primitive society as reactions to a deed which gave the authors of it the conception of crime. They regretted this deed and decided that it should not be repeated and that its execution must bring no gain. This creative sense of guilt has not become extinct with us. We find its asocial effects in neurotics producing new rules of morality and continued restrictions, in expiation for misdeeds committed, or as precautions against misdeeds to be committed. But when we examine these neurotics for the deeds which have called forth such reactions, we are disappointed. We do not find deeds, but only impulses and feelings which sought evil but which were restrained from carrying it out. Only psychic realities and not actual ones are at the basis of the neurotics' sense of guilt. It is characteristic of the neurosis to put a psychic reality above an actual one and to react as seriously to thoughts as the normal person reacts only towards realities.

May it not be true that the case was somewhat the same with primitive men? We are justified in ascribing to them an extraordinary overvaluation of their psychic acts as a partial manifestation of their narcistic organization. According to this the mere impulses of hostility towards the father and the existence of the wish phantasy to kill and devour him may have sufficed to bring about the moral reaction which has created totemism and taboo. We should thus escape the necessity of tracing back the beginning of our cultural possession, of which we rightly are so proud, to a horrible crime which wounds all our feelings. The causal connection, which stretches from that beginning to the present time, would not be impaired, for the psychic reality would be of sufficient importance to account for all those consequences. It may be agreed that a change has really taken place in the form of society from the father horde to the brother clan. This is a strong argument, but it is not conclusive. The change might have been accomplished in a less violent manner and still have conditioned the appearance of the moral reaction. As long as the pressure of the primal father was felt, the hostile feelings against him were justified and repentance at these feelings had to wait for another opportunity. Of as little validity is the second objection, that everything derived from the ambivalent relation to the father, namely taboos, and rules of sacrifice is characterized by the highest seriousness and by complete reality. The ceremonials and inhibitions of compulsion neurotics exhibit this characteristic too and yet they go back to a merely psychic reality, to resolution and not to execution. We must beware of introducing the contempt for what is merely thought or wished which characterizes our sober world where there are only material values, into the world of primitive man and the neurotic, which is full of inner riches only.

We face a decision here which is really not easy. But let us begin by acknowledging that the difference which may seem fundamental to others does not, in our judgment, touch the most important part of the subject. If wishes and impulses have the full value of fact for primitive man, it is for us to follow such a conception intelligently instead of correcting it according to our standard. But in that case we must scrutinize more closely the prototype of the neurosis itself which is responsible for having raised this doubt. It is not true that compulsion neurotics, who today are under the pressure of over-scrupulousness, defend themselves only against the psychic reality of temptations and punish themselves for impulses which they have only felt. A piece of historic reality is also involved; in their childhood these persons had nothing but evil impulses and as far as their childish impotence permitted they put them into action. Each of these over-good persons had a period of badness in his childhood, and a perverse phase as a fore-runner and a premise of the latter over-morality. The analogy between primitive men and neurotics is therefore much more fundamentally established if we assume that with the former, too, the psychic reality, concerning whose structure there is no doubt, originally coincided with the actual reality, and that primitive men really did what according to all testimony they intended to do.

But we must not let our judgment about primitive men be influenced too far by the analogy with neurotics. Differences must also be taken into account. Of course the sharp division between thinking and doing as we draw it does not exist either with savages or with neurotics. But the neurotic is above all inhibited in his actions; with him the thought is a complete substitute for the deed. Primitive man is not inhibited, the thought is directly converted into the deed, the deed is for him, so to speak, rather a substitute for the thought, and for that reason I think we may well assume in the case we are discussing, though without vouching for the absolute certainty of the decision, that "In the beginning was the deed."

• • • • • • • • • • • • •

QUESTIONS FOR A SECOND READING

1. Early in the selection, Freud makes it clear that he intends to compare taboo to "compulsion neurosis," a specific kind of anxious behavior. As you reread, pay close attention to the sections where he elaborates on this comparison. What is compulsion neurosis? How is it like and unlike taboo? How does a person come to be a compulsive neurotic? to hold a taboo? What behaviors might one expect from both compulsive neurotics and those who hold taboos? Finally, what is accomplished by comparing "normal" people and neurotics?
2. Throughout this reading, Freud refers to the unconscious as if it were a tangible thing or place. He says such things as "in the unconscious they [the people he's talking about] would like nothing better than to transgress them [their ambivalent attitudes] but they are afraid to do it." He also attributes qualities or states of being to the unconscious. It *projects, defends,* and *represses.* When you reread, look for such descriptions of the unconscious. Freud seems to want you to think of the unconscious as another person inside you or as a place you sometimes inhabit. Who is this person? What is this place like? What does the unconscious do? Where does it come from? What does it project, defend, and repress? And how is the unconscious different from what people usually talk about when they talk about consciousness and conscience?

ASSIGNMENTS FOR WRITING

1. Write an essay that defines, according to Freud, taboo and the ambivalence of emotions. What, in other words, does it mean to be a person who observes a taboo and, consequently, has ambivalent emotions? Use some of Freud's examples in your paper, but see if you can go on to say more about them than he does.
2. Freud tells three different kinds of stories—about the treatment of enemies, rulers, and the dead—to make and support his points about taboo. For this assignment, make a list of what you consider taboos in present-day American culture. Settle on one you would like to write about and prepare an essay in which you describe the taboo and explain how it works—explain, that is, the ambivalent emotions associated with it.

   Although this is a theoretical problem, you should make it concrete by working with examples (the way Freud does with his three kinds of stories). You will have more to say if you write about situations and people you know well. Ask yourself how the taboo is acted out: What is the prohibition involved? Whom does it affect? What problems does it solve and create? What are the mixed emotions associated with it? How are they expressed? What might be responsible for the taboo?

MAKING CONNECTIONS

1. Freud claims that "in the case of taboo, the nucleus of the neurotic prohibition is the act of touching, whence we derive the name 'touching phobia.' . . . The prohibition extends not only to direct contact with the body but also to the figurative use of the phrase as 'to come into contact' or 'be in touch with some one or something.' " Marya, one of the main characters in the Joyce Carol Oates story "Theft" (p. 353), can't stand to be touched, yet she is preoccupied with the experience of touching other people and their things. On a double date with her friend Imogene, she bolts from Matthew when he tries to hold her, and later, when Imogene and Marya fight, she shouts, "Don't you touch me! What do you mean, touching *me!*" Before this, she withdraws when Imogene clasps her hands after a play, and she admits that her reputation as an intellectual protects her from others, keeps her at a distance. There are other instances of her withdrawing from contact with others, yet she "touches" strangers all the time, even through her impulsive stealing.

   As you read the Oates story, ask yourself what is happening with Marya. Your assignment is to write an essay showing how Freud might explain Marya's problem.

   Read through the story once, then go back to the story after you've read it and do a more detailed, specific reading of Marya's behavior to develop a more complete picture of why she behaves the way she does. And to imagine her problem through Freud's eyes, you'll need to have a strong understanding of the ideas expressed in his essay. This means you will want to reread it, paying attention to what Freud says about touching, using that as a basis for imagining what he might say about Marya.

2. In Saul Bellow's story, "A Silver Dish" (p. 22), we meet Woody Selbst's father, Morris. We enter the story with a question about Morris's death: "What do you do about death—in this case, the death of an old father? If you're a modern person, sixty years of age, and a man who's been around, like Woody Selbst, what do you do?"

   For this assignment, your job is to see the story through Freud's eyes, through his discussion of taboos concerning the dead. Morris's death might be seen as a struggle for Woody, and Bellow's story might be read as another example of a study of the taboo of the dead.

   Write an essay showing how Freud might interpret the story of Woody Selbst. You will want to read the Bellow story at least twice, once to grasp the story as a whole and a second time to devote special attention to Woody's reaction to his father's death. You will also want to reread the section of the Freud essay titled "The Taboo of the Dead." As you reread the story, pay particular attention to the things Woody says or does that would interest Freud. What are his ambivalent feelings? Where is evidence of a taboo? If you are working in Freud's spirit, what conclusions might you draw from this case?

CLIFFORD GEERTZ

CLIFFORD GEERTZ was born in San Francisco in 1929 and, after two years in the U.S. Navy Reserve earned a B.A. from Antioch College and a Ph.D. from Harvard. A Fellow of the National Academy of Science, the American Academy of Arts and Sciences, and the American Philosophical Society, Geertz has been a professor in the department of social science of the Institute for Advanced Study in Princeton, New Jersey, since 1970. He has written several books (mostly anthropological studies of Third World cultures) and published two collections of essays, Interpretation of Cultures *and* Local Knowledge. Interpretation of Cultures, *from which the following essay is drawn, became a classic and won for Geertz the rare distinction of being an academic whose scholarly work is eagerly read by people outside his academic discipline, even outside the academic community altogether.*

"Deep Play" was first presented at a Paris conference organized by Geertz, the literary critic Paul de Man, and the American Academy of Arts and Sciences. The purpose of the conference was to bring together scholars from various academic departments (in the humanities, the social sciences, and the natural sciences) to see if they could find a way of talking to each other and, in doing so, to find a common ground to their work. The conference planners believed that there was *a common*

ground, that all of these scholars were bound together by their participation in what they called the "systematic study of meaningful forms." This is a grand phrase, but Geertz's essay clearly demonstrates what work of this sort requires of an anthropologist. The essay begins with a story, an anecdote, and the story Geertz tells is as open to your interpretation as it is to anyone else's. What follows, however, are Geertz's attempts to interpret the story he has told, first this way and then that. As you watch him work—finding patterns, making comparisons, drawing on the theories of experts, proposing theories of his own—you are offered a demonstration of how he finds meaningful forms and then sets out to study them systematically.

"Deep Play," in fact, was sent out as a model for all prospective conference participants, since it was a paper that showed not only what its author knew about his subject (cockfights in Bali) but what he knew about the methods and procedures that gave him access to his subject. It is a witty and sometimes dazzling essay with a wonderful story to tell—a story of both a Balinese cockfight and an anthropologist trying to write about and understand people whose culture seems, at first, so very different from his own.

Deep Play: Notes on the Balinese Cockfight

The Raid

Early in April of 1958, my wife and I arrived, malarial and diffident, in a Balinese village we intended, as anthropologists, to study. A small place, about five hundred people, and relatively remote, it was its own world. We were intruders, professional ones, and the villagers dealt with us as Balinese seem always to deal with people not part of their life who yet press themselves upon them: as though we were not there. For them, and to a degree for ourselves, we were nonpersons, specters, invisible men.

We moved into an extended family compound (that had been arranged before through the provincial government) belonging to one of the four major factions in village life. But except for our landlord and the village chief, whose cousin and brother-in-law he was, everyone ignored us in a way only a Balinese can do. As we wandered around, uncertain, wistful, eager to please, people seemed to look right through us with a gaze focused several yards behind us on some more actual stone or tree. Almost nobody greeted us; but nobody scowled or said anything unpleasant to us either, which would have been almost as satisfactory. If we ventured to approach someone (something one is powerfully inhibited from doing in such an atmosphere), he moved, negligently but definitively, away. If, seated or leaning against a wall, we had him trapped, he said nothing at all, or mumbled what for the Balinese is the ultimate nonword—"yes." The indifference, of course, was studied; the villagers were watching every move we made and they had an enormous amount of quite accurate information about who we were and what we were going to be doing. But they acted as if we simply did not exist, which, in fact, as this behavior was designed to inform us, we did not, or anyway not yet.

This is, as I say, general in Bali. Everywhere else I have been in Indonesia, and more latterly in Morocco, when I have gone into a new village people have poured out from all sides to take a very close look at me, and, often, an all-too-probing feel as well. In Balinese villages, at least those away from the tourist circuit, nothing happens at all. People go on pounding, chatting, making offerings, staring into space, carrying baskets about while one drifts around feeling vaguely disembodied. And the same thing is true on the individual level. When you first meet a Balinese, he seems virtually not to relate to you at all; he is, in the term Gregory Bateson and Margaret Mead made famous, "away."[1] Then—in a day, a week, a month (with some people the magic moment never comes)—he decides, for reasons I have never been quite able to fathom, that you *are* real, and then he becomes a warm, gay, sensitive, sympathetic, though, being Balinese, always precisely controlled person. You have crossed, somehow, some moral or metaphysical shadow line. Though you are not exactly taken as a Balinese (one has to be born to that), you are at least regarded as a human being rather than a cloud or a gust of wind. The whole complexion of your relationship dramatically changes to, in the majority of cases, a gentle, almost affectionate one—a low-keyed, rather playful, rather mannered, rather bemused geniality.

My wife and I were still very much in the gust of wind stage, a most frustrating, and even, as you soon begin to doubt whether you are really real after all, unnerving one, when, ten days or so after our arrival, a large cockfight was held in the public square to raise money for a new school.

Now, a few special occasions aside, cockfights are illegal in Bali under the Republic (as, for not altogether unrelated reasons, they were under the Dutch), largely as a result of the pretensions to puritanism radical nationalism tends to bring with it. The elite, which is not itself so very puritan, worries about the poor, ignorant peasant gambling all his money away, about what foreigners will think, about the waste of time better devoted to building up the country. It sees cockfighting as "primitive," "backward," "unprogressive," and generally unbecoming an ambitious nation. And, as with those other embarrassments—opium smoking, begging, or uncovered breasts—it seeks, rather unsystematically, to put a stop to it.

Of course, like drinking during prohibition or, today, smoking marihuana, cockfights, being a part of "The Balinese Way of Life," nonetheless go on happening, and with extraordinary frequency. And, like prohibition or marihuana, from time to time the police (who, in 1958 at least, were almost all not Balinese but Javanese) feel called upon to make a raid, confiscate the cocks and spurs, fine a few people, and even now and then expose some of them in the tropical sun for a day as object lessons which never, somehow, get learned, even though occasionally, quite occasionally, the object dies.

As a result, the fights are usually held in a secluded corner of a village in semisecrecy, a fact which tends to slow the action a little—not very much, but the Balinese do not care to have it slowed at all. In this case, however, perhaps because they were raising money for a school that the government was unable to give them, perhaps because raids had been few recently, perhaps, as I gathered from subsequent discussion, there was a notion that the necessary bribes had been paid, they thought they could take a chance on the central square and draw a larger and more enthusiastic crowd without attracting the attention of the law.

They were wrong. In the midst of the third match, with hundreds of people, including, still transparent, myself and my wife, fused into a single body around the ring, a superorganism in the literal sense, a truck full of policemen armed with machine guns roared up. Amid great screeching cries of "pulisi! pulisi!" from the crowd, the policemen jumped out, and, springing into the center of the ring, began to swing their guns around like gangsters in a motion picture, though not going so far as actually to fire them. The superorganism came instantly apart as its components scattered in all directions. People raced down the road, disappeared head first over walls, scrambled under platforms, folded themselves behind wicker screens, scuttled up coconut trees. Cocks armed with steel spurs sharp enough to cut off a finger or run a hole through a foot were running wildly around. Everything was dust and panic.

On the established anthropological principle, When in Rome, my wife and I decided, only slightly less instantaneously than everyone else, that the thing to do was run too. We ran down the main village street, northward, away from where we were living, for we were on that side of the ring. About half-way down another fugitive ducked suddenly into a compound—his own, it turned out—and we, seeing nothing ahead of us but rice fields, open country, and a very high volcano, followed him. As the three of us came tumbling into the courtyard, his wife, who had apparently been through this sort of thing before, whipped out a table, a tablecloth, three chairs, and three cups of tea, and we all, without any explicit communication whatsoever, sat down, commenced to sip tea, and sought to compose ourselves.

A few moments later, one of the policemen marched importantly into the yard, looking for the village chief. (The chief had not only been at the fight, he had arranged it. When the truck drove up he ran to the river, stripped off his sarong, and plunged in so he could say, when at length they found him sitting there pouring water over his head, that he had been away bathing when the whole affair had occurred and was ignorant of it. They did not believe him and fined him three hundred rupiah, which the village raised collectively.) Seeing my wife and I, "White Men," there in the yard, the policeman performed a classic double take. When he found his voice again he asked, approximately, what in the devil did we think we were doing there. Our host of five minutes leaped instantly to our defense, producing an impassioned description of who and what we were, so detailed and so accurate that it was my turn, having barely communicated with a living human being save my landlord and the village chief for more than a week, to be astonished. We had a perfect right to be there, he said, looking the Javanese upstart in the eye. We were American professors; the government had cleared us; we were there to study culture; we were going to write a book to tell Americans about Bali. And we had all been there drinking tea and talking about cultural matters all afternoon and did not know anything about any cockfight. Moreover, we had not seen the village chief all day, he must have gone to town. The policeman retreated in rather total disarray. And, after a decent interval, bewildered but relieved to have survived and stayed out of jail, so did we.

The next morning the village was a completely different world for us. Not only were we no longer invisible, we were suddenly the center of all attention, the object of a great outpouring of warmth, interest, and, most especially, amusement. Everyone in the village knew we had fled like everyone else. They asked us about it again and again (I must have told the story, small detail by small detail, fifty times by the end of the day), gently, affectionately, but quite insistently teasing us: "Why didn't you just stand there and tell the police who you were?" "Why didn't you just say you were only watching and not betting?" "Were you really afraid of those little guns?" As always, kinesthetically minded and, even when fleeing for their lives (or, as happened eight years later, surrendering them), the world's most poised people, they gleefully mimicked, also over and over again, our graceless style of running and what they claimed were our panic-stricken facial expressions. But above all, everyone was extremely pleased and even more surprised that we had not simply "pulled out our papers" (they knew about those too) and asserted our Distinguished Visitor status, but had instead demonstrated our solidarity with what were now our co-villagers. (What we had actually demonstrated was our cowardice, but there is fellowship in that too.) Even the Brahmana priest, an old, grave, half-way-to-Heaven type who because of its associations with the underworld would never be involved, even distantly, in a cockfight, and was difficult to approach even to other Balinese, had us called into his courtyard to ask us about what had happened, chuckling happily at the sheer extraordinariness of it all.

In Bali, to be teased is to be accepted. It was the turning point so far as our relationship to the community was concerned, and we were quite literally "in." The whole village opened up to us, probably more than it ever would have otherwise (I might actually never have gotten to that priest, and our accidental host became one of my best informants), and certainly very much faster. Getting caught, or almost caught, in a vice raid is perhaps not a very generalizable recipe for achieving that mysterious necessity of anthropological field work, rapport, but for me it worked very well. It led to a sudden and unusually complete acceptance into a society extremely difficult for outsiders to penetrate. It gave me the kind of immediate, inside-view grasp of an aspect of "peasant mentality" that anthropologists not fortunate enough to flee headlong with their subjects from armed authorities normally do not get. And, perhaps most important of all, for the other things might have come in other ways, it put me very quickly on to a combination emotional explosion, status war, and philosophical drama of central significance to the society whose inner nature I desired to understand. By the time I left I had spent about as much time looking into cockfights as into witchcraft, irrigation, caste, or marriage.

Of Cocks and Men

Bali, mainly because it is Bali, is a well-studied place. Its mythology, art, ritual, social organization, patterns of child rearing, forms of law, even styles of trance, have all been microscopically examined for traces of that elusive substance Jane Belo called "The Balinese Temper."[2] But, aside from a few passing remarks, the cockfight has barely been noticed, although as a popular obsession of consuming power it is at least as important a revelation of what being a Balinese "is really like" as these more celebrated phenomena.[3] As much of America surfaces in a ball park, on a golf links, at a race track, or around a poker table, much of Bali surfaces in a cock ring. For it is only apparently cocks that are fighting there. Actually, it is men.

To anyone who has been in Bali any length of time, the deep psychological identification of Balinese men with their cocks is unmistakable. The double entendre here is deliberate. It works in exactly the same way in Balinese as it does in English, even to producing the same tired jokes, strained puns, and uninventive obscenities. Bateson and Mead have even suggested that, in line with the Balinese conception of the body as a set of separately animated parts, cocks are viewed as detachable, self-operating penises, ambulant genitals with a life of their own.[4] And while I do not have the kind of unconscious material either to confirm or disconfirm this intriguing notion, the fact that they are masculine symbols *par excellence* is about as indubitable, and to the Balinese about as evident, as the fact that water runs downhill.

The language of everyday moralism is shot through, on the male side of it, with roosterish imagery. *Sabung*, the word for cock (and one which appears in inscriptions as early as A.D. 922), is used metaphorically to mean "hero," "warrior," "champion," "man of parts," "political candidate," "bachelor," "dandy," "lady-killer," or "tough guy." A pompous man whose behavior presumes above his station is compared to a tailless cock who struts about as though he had a large, spectacular one. A desperate man who makes a last, irrational effort to extricate himself from an impossible situation is likened to a dying cock who makes one final lunge at his tormentor to drag him along to a common destruction. A stingy man, who promises much, gives little, and begrudges that is compared to a cock which, held by the tail, leaps at another without in fact engaging him. A marriageable young man still shy with the opposite sex or someone in a new job anxious to make a good impression is called "a fighting cock caged for the first time."[5] Court trials, wars, political contests, inheritance disputes, and street arguments are all compared to cockfights.[6] Even the very island itself is perceived from its shape as a small, proud cock, poised, neck extended, back taut, tail raised, in eternal challenge to large, feckless, shapeless Java.[7]

But the intimacy of men with their cocks is more than metaphorical. Balinese men, or anyway a large majority of Balinese men, spend an enormous amount of time with their favorites, grooming them, feeding them, discussing them, trying them out against one another, or just gazing at them with a mixture of rapt admiration and dreamy self-absorbtion. Whenever you see a group of Balinese men squatting idly in the council shed or along the road in their hips down, shoulders forward, knees up fashion, half or more of them will have a rooster in his hands, holding it between his thighs, bouncing it gently up and down to strengthen its legs, ruffling its feathers with abstract sensuality, pushing it out against a neighbor's rooster to rouse its spirit, withdrawing it toward his loins to calm it again. Now and then, to get a feel for another bird, a man will fiddle this way with someone else's cock for a while, but usually by moving around to squat in place behind it, rather than just having it passed across to him as though it were merely an animal.

In the houseyard, the high-walled enclosures where the people live, fighting cocks are kept in wicker cages, moved frequently about so as to maintain the optimum balance of sun and shade. They are fed a special diet, which varies somewhat according to individual theories but which is mostly maize, sifted for impurities with far more care than it is when mere humans are going to eat it and offered to the animal kernel by kernel. Red pepper is stuffed down their beaks and up their anuses to give them spirit. They are bathed in the same ceremonial preparation of tepid water, medicinal herbs, flowers, and onions in which infants are bathed, and for a prize cock just about as often. Their combs are cropped, their plumage dressed, their spurs trimmed, their legs massaged, and they are inspected for flaws with the squinted concentration of a diamond merchant. A man who has a passion for cocks, an enthusiast in the literal sense of the term, can spend most of his life with them, and even those, the overwhelming majority, whose passion though intense has not entirely run away with them, can and do spend what seems not only to an outsider, but also to themselves, an inordinate amount of time with them. "I am cock crazy," my landlord, a quite ordinary *afficionado* by Balinese standards, used to moan as he went to move another cage, give another bath, or conduct another feeding. "We're all cock crazy."

The madness has some less visible dimensions, however, because although it is true that cocks are symbolic expressions or magnifications of their owner's self, the narcissistic male ego writ out in Aesopian terms, they are also expressions—and rather more immediate ones—of what the Balinese regard as the direct inversion, aesthetically, morally, and metaphysically, of human status: animality.

The Balinese revulsion against any behavior regarded as animal-like can hardly be overstressed. Babies are not allowed to crawl for that reason. Incest, though hardly approved, is a much less horrifying crime than bestiality. (The appropriate punishment for the second is death by drowning, for the first being forced to live like an animal.)[8] Most demons are represented—in sculpture, dance, ritual, myth—in some real or fantastic animal form. The main puberty rite consists in filing the child's teeth so they will not look like animal fangs. Not only defecation but eating is regarded as a disgusting, almost obscene activity, to be conducted hurriedly and privately, because of its association with animality. Even falling down or any form of clumsiness is considered to be bad for these reasons. Aside from cocks and a few domestic animals—oxen, ducks—of no emotional significance, the Balinese are aversive to animals, and treat their large number of dogs not merely callously but with a phobic cruelty. In identifying with his cock, the Balinese man is identifying not just with his ideal self, or even his penis, but also, and at the same time, with what he most fears, hates, and ambivalence being what it is, is fascinated by—The Powers of Darkness.

The connection of cocks and cockfighting with such Powers, with the animalistic demons that threaten constantly to invade the small, cleared off space in which the Balinese have so carefully built their lives and devour its inhabitants, is quite explicit. A cockfight, any cockfight, is in the first instance a blood sacrifice offered, with the appropriate chants and oblations, to the demons in order to pacify their ravenous, cannibal hunger. No temple festival should be conducted until one is made. (If it is omitted someone will inevitably fall into a trance and command with the voice of an angered spirit that the oversight be immediately corrected.) Collective responses to natural evils—illness, crop failure, volcanic eruptions—almost always involve them. And that famous holiday in Bali, The Day of Silence *(Njepi),* when everyone sits silent and immobile all day long in order to avoid contact with a sudden influx of demons chased momentarily out of hell, is preceded the previous day by large-scale cockfights (in this case legal) in almost every village on the island.

In the cockfight, man and beast, good and evil, ego and id, the creative power of aroused masculinity and the destructive power of loosened animality fuse in a bloody drama of hatred, cruelty, violence, and death. It is little wonder that when, as is the invariable rule, the owner of the winning cock takes the carcass of the loser—often torn limb from limb by its enraged owner—home to eat, he does so with a mixture of social embarrassment, moral satisfaction, aesthetic disgust, and cannibal joy. Or that a man who has lost an important fight is sometimes driven to wreck his family shrines and curse the gods, an act of metaphysical (and social) suicide. Or that in seeking earthly analogues for heaven and hell the Balinese compare the former to the mood of a man whose cock has just won, the latter to that of a man whose cock has just lost.

The Fight

Cockfights *(tetadjen; sabungan)* are held in a ring about fifty feet square. Usually they begin toward late afternoon and run three or four hours until sunset. About nine or ten separate matches *(sehet)* comprise a program. Each match is precisely like the others in general pattern: there is no main match, no connection between individual matches, no variation in their format, and each is arranged on a completely ad hoc basis. After a fight has ended and the emotional debris is cleaned away—the bets paid, the curses cursed, the carcasses possessed—seven, eight, perhaps even a dozen men slip negligently into the ring with a cock and seek to find there a logical opponent for it. This process, which rarely takes less than ten minutes, and often a good deal longer, is conducted in a very subdued, oblique, even dissembling manner. Those not immediately involved give it at best but disguised, sidelong attention; those who, embarrassedly, are, attempt to pretend somehow that the whole thing is not really happening.

A match made, the other hopefuls retire with the same deliberate indifference, and the selected cocks have their spurs *(tadji)* affixed—razor-sharp, pointed steel swords, four of five inches long. This is a delicate job which only a small proportion of men, a half-dozen or so in most villages, know how to do properly. The man who attaches the spurs also provides them, and if the rooster he assists wins its owner awards him the spur-leg of the victim. The spurs are affixed by winding a long length of string around the foot of the spur and the leg of the cock. For reasons I shall come to presently, it is done somewhat differently from case to case, and is an obsessively deliberate affair. The lore about spurs is extensive—they are sharpened only at eclipses and the dark of the moon, should be kept out of the sight of women, and so forth. And they are handled, both in use and out, with the same curious combination of fussiness and sensuality the Balinese direct toward ritual objects generally.

The spurs affixed, the two cocks are placed by their handlers (who may or may not be their owners) facing one another in the center of the ring.[9] A coconut pierced with a small hole is placed in a pail of water, in which it takes about twenty-one seconds to sink, a period known as a *tjeng* and marked at beginning and end by the beating of a slit gong. During these twenty-one seconds the handlers *(pengangkeb)* are not permitted to touch their roosters. If, as sometimes happens, the animals have not fought during this time, they are picked up, fluffed, pulled, prodded, and otherwise insulted, and put back in the center of the ring and the process begins again. Sometimes they refuse to fight at all, or one keeps running away, in which case they are imprisoned together under a wicker cage, which usually gets them engaged.

Most of the time, in any case, the cocks fly almost immediately at one another in a wing-beating, head-thrusting, leg-kicking explosion of animal fury so pure, so absolute, and in its own way so beautiful, as to be almost abstract, a Platonic concept of hate. Within moments one or the other drives home a solid blow with his spur. The handler whose cock has delivered the blow immediately picks it up so that it will not get a return blow, for if he does not the match is likely to end in a mutually mortal tie as the two birds wildly hack each other to pieces. This is particularly true if, as often happens, the spur sticks in its victim's body, for then the aggressor is at the mercy of his wounded foe.

With the birds again in the hands of their handlers, the coconut is now sunk three times after which the cock which has landed the blow must be set down to show that he is firm, a fact he demonstrates by wandering idly around the ring for a coconut sink. The coconut is then sunk twice more and the fight must recommence.

During this interval, slightly over two minutes, the handler of the wounded cock has been working frantically over it, like a trainer patching a mauled boxer between rounds, to get it in shape for a last, desperate try for victory. He blows in its mouth, putting the whole chicken head in his own mouth and sucking and blowing, fluffs it, stuffs its wounds with various sorts of medicines, and generally tries anything he can think of to arouse the last ounce of spirit which may be hidden somewhere within it. By the time he is forced to put it back down he is usually drenched in chicken blood, but, as in prize fighting, a good handler is worth his weight in gold. Some of them can virtually make the dead walk, at least long enough for the second and final round.

In the climactic battle (if there is one; sometimes the wounded cock simply expires in the handler's hands or immediately as it is placed down again), the cock who landed the first blow usually proceeds to finish off his weakened opponent. But this is far from an inevitable outcome, for if a cock can walk he can fight, and if he can fight, he can kill, and what counts is which cock expires first. If the wounded one can get a stab in and stagger on until the other drops, he is the official winner, even if he himself topples over an instant later.

Surrounding all this melodrama—which the crowd packed tight around the ring follows in near silence, moving their bodies in kinesthetic sympathy with the movement of the animals, cheering their champions on with wordless hand motions, shiftings of the shoulders, turnings of the head, falling back *en masse* as the cock with the murderous spurs careens toward one side of the ring (it is said that spectators sometimes lose eyes and fingers from being too attentive), surging forward again as they glance off toward another—is a vast body of extraordinarily elaborate and precisely detailed rules.

These rules, together with the developed lore of cocks and cockfighting which accompanies them, are written down in palm leaf manuscripts *(lontar; rontal)* passed on from generation to generation as part of the general legal and cultural tradition of the villages. At a fight, the umpire *(saja komong; djuru kembar)*—the man who manages the coconut—is in charge of their application and his authority is absolute. I have never seen an umpire's judgment questioned on any subject, even by the more despondent losers, nor have I ever heard, even in private, a charge of unfairness directed against one, or, for that matter, complaints about umpires in general. Only exceptionally well-trusted, solid, and, given the complexity of the code, knowledgeable citizens perform this job, and in fact men will bring their cocks only to fights presided over by such men. It is also the umpire to whom accusations of cheating, which, though rare in the extreme, occasionally arise, are referred; and it is he who in the not infrequent cases where the cocks expire virtually together decides which (if either, for, though the Balinese do not care for such an outcome, there can be ties) went first. Likened to a judge, a king, a priest, and a policeman, he is all of these, and under his assured direction the animal passion of the fight proceeds within the civic certainty of the law. In the dozens of cockfights I saw in Bali, I never once saw an altercation about rules. Indeed, I never saw an open altercation, other than those between cocks, at all.

This crosswise doubleness of an event which, taken as a fact of nature, is rage untrammeled and, taken as a fact of culture, is form perfected, defines the cockfight as a sociological entity. A cockfight is what, searching for a name for something not vertebrate enough to be called a group and not structureless enough to be called a crowd, Erving Goffman has called a "focused gathering"—a set of persons engrossed in a common flow of activity and relating to one another in terms of that flow.[10] Such gatherings meet and disperse; the participants in them fluctuate; the activity that focuses them is discreet—a particulate process that reoccurs rather than a continuous one that endures. They take their form from the situation that evokes them, the floor on which they are placed, as Goffman puts it; but it is a form, and an articulate one, nonetheless. For the situation, the floor is itself created, in jury deliberations, surgical operations, block meetings, sit-ins, cockfights, by the cultural preoccupations—here, as we shall see, the celebration of status rivalry—which not only specify the focus but, assembling actors and arranging scenery, bring it actually into being.

In classical times (that is to say, prior to the Dutch invasion of 1908), when there were no bureaucrats around to improve popular morality, the staging of a cockfight was an explicitly societal matter. Bringing a cock to an important fight was, for an adult male, a compulsory duty of citizenship; taxation of fights, which were usually held on market day, was a major source of public revenue; patronage of the art was a stated responsibility of princes; and the cock ring, or *wantilan,* stood in the center of the village near those other monuments of Balinese civility—the council house, the origin temple, the marketplace, the signal tower, and the banyan tree. Today, a few special occasions aside, the newer rectitude makes so open a statement of the connection between the excitements of collective life and those of blood sport impossible, but, less directly expressed, the connection itself remains intimate and intact. To expose it, however, it is necessary to turn to the aspect of cockfighting around which all the others pivot, and through which they exercise their force, an aspect I have thus far studiously ignored. I mean, of course, the gambling.

Odds and Even Money

The Balinese never do anything in a simple way that they can contrive to do in a complicated one, and to this generalization cockfight wagering is no exception.

In the first place, there are two sorts of bets, or *toh.*[11] There is the single axial bet in the center between the principals *(toh ketengah),* and there is the cloud of peripheral ones around the ring between members of the audience *(toh kesasi).* The first is typically large; the second typically small. The first is collective, involving coalitions of bettors clustering around the owner; the second is individual, man to man. The first is a matter of deliberate, very quiet, almost furtive arrangement by the coalition members and the umpire huddled like conspirators in the center of the ring; the second is a matter of impulsive shouting, public offers, and public acceptances by the excited throng around its edges. And most curiously, and as we shall see most revealingly, *where the first is always, without exception, even money, the second, equally without exception, is never such.* What is a fair coin in the center is a biased one on the side.

The center bet is the official one, hedged in again with a webwork of rules, and is made between the two cock owners, with the umpire as overseer and public witness.[12] This bet, which, as I say, is always relatively and sometimes very large, is never raised simply by the owner in whose name it is made, but by him together with four or five, sometimes seven or eight, allies—kin, village mates, neighbors, close friends. He may, if he is not especially well-to-do, not even be the major contributor, though, if only to show that he is not involved in any chicanery, he must be a significant one.

Of the fifty-seven matches for which I have exact and reliable data on the center bet, the range is from fifteen ringgits to five hundred, with a mean at eighty-five and with the distribution being rather noticeably trimodal: small fights (15 ringgits either side of 35) accounting for about 45 percent of the total number; medium ones (20 ringgits either side of 70) for about 25 percent; and large (75 ringgits either side of 175) for about 20 percent, with a few very small and very large ones out at the extremes. In a society where the normal daily wage of a manual laborer—a brickmaker, an ordinary farmworker, a market porter—was about three ringgits a day, and considering the fact that fights were held on the average about every two-and-a-half days in the immediate area I studied, this is clearly serious gambling, even if the bets are pooled rather than individual efforts.

The side bets are, however, something else altogether. Rather than the solemn, legalistic pactmaking of the center, wagering takes place rather in the fashion in which the stock exchange used to work when it was out on the curb. There is a fixed and known odds paradigm which runs in a continuous series from ten-to-nine at the short end to two-to-one at the long: 10-9, 9-8, 8-7, 7-6, 6-5, 5-4, 4-3, 3-2, 2-1. The man who wishes to back the *underdog cock* (leaving aside how favorites, *kebut*, and underdogs, *ngai*, are established for the moment) shouts the short-side number indicating the odds he wants *to be given.* That is, if he shouts *gasal*, "five," he wants the underdog at five-to-four (or, for him, four-to-five); if he shouts "four," he wants it at four-to-three (again, he putting up the "three"), if "nine," at nine-to-eight, and so on. A man backing the favorite, and thus considering giving odds if he can get them short enough, indicates the fact by crying out the color-type of that cock—"brown," "speckled," or whatever.[13]

As odds-takers (backers of the underdog) and odds-givers (backers of the favorite) sweep the crowd with their shouts, they begin to focus in on one another as potential betting pairs, often from far across the ring. The taker tries to shout the giver into longer odds, the giver to shout the taker into shorter ones.[14] The taker, who is the wooer in this situation, will signal how large a bet he wishes to make at the odds he is shouting by holding a number of fingers up in front of his face and vigorously waving them. If the giver, the wooed, replies in kind, the bet is made; if he does not, they unlock gazes and the search goes on.

The side betting, which takes place after the center bet has been made and its size announced, consists then in a rising crescendo of shouts as backers of the underdog offer their propositions to anyone who will accept them, while those who are backing the favorite but do not like the price being offered, shout equally frenetically the color of the cock to show they too are desperate to bet but want shorter odds.

Almost always odds-calling, which tends to be very consensual in that at any one time almost all callers are calling the same thing, starts off toward the long end of the range—five-to-four or four-to-three—and then moves, also consensually, toward the short end with greater or lesser speed and to a greater or lesser degree. Men crying "five" and finding themselves answered only with cries of "brown" start crying "six," either drawing the other callers fairly quickly with them or retiring from the scene as their too-generous offers are snapped up. If the change is made and partners are still scarce, the procedure is repeated in a move to "seven," and so on, only rarely, and in the very largest fights, reaching the ultimate "nine" or "ten" levels. Occasionally, if the cocks are clearly mismatched, there may be no upward movement at all, or even a movement down the scale to four-to-three, three-to-two, very, very rarely two-to-one, a shift which is accompanied by a declining number of bets as a shift upward is accompanied by an increasing number. But the general pattern is for the betting to move a shorter or longer distance up the scale toward the, for sidebets, nonexistent pole of even money, with the overwhelming majority of bets falling in the four-to-three to eight-to-seven range.[15]

As the moment for the release of the cocks by the handlers approaches, the screaming, at least in a match where the center bet is large, reaches almost frenzied proportions as the remaining unfulfilled bettors try desperately to find a last minute partner at a price they can live with. (Where the center bet is small, the opposite tends to occur: betting dies off, trailing into silence, as odds lengthen and people lose interest.) In a large-bet, well-made match—the kind of match the Balinese regard as "real cockfighting"— the mob scene quality, the sense that sheer chaos is about to break loose, with all those waving, shouting, pushing, clambering men is quite strong, an effect which is only heightened by the intense stillness that falls with instant suddenness, rather as if someone had turned off the current, when the slit gong sounds, the cocks are put down, and the battle begins.

When it ends, anywhere from fifteen seconds to five minutes later, *all bets are immediately paid.* There are absolutely no IOU's, at least to a betting opponent. One may, of course, borrow from a friend before offering or accepting a wager, but to offer or accept it you must have the money already in hand and, if you lose, you must pay it on the spot, before the next match begins. This is an iron rule, and as I have never heard of a disputed umpire's decision (though doubtless there must sometimes be some), I have also never heard of a welshed bet, perhaps because in a worked-up cockfight crowd the consequences might be, as they are reported to be sometimes for cheaters, drastic and immediate.

It is, in any case, this formal assymetry between balanced center bets and unbalanced side ones that poses the critical analytical problem for a theory which sees cockfight wagering as the link connecting the fight to the wider world of Balinese culture. It also suggests the way to go about solving it and demonstrating the link.

The first point that needs to be made in this connection is that the higher the center bet, the more likely the match will in actual fact be an even one. Simple considerations of rationality suggest that. If you are betting fifteen ringgits on a cock, you might be willing to go along with even money even if you feel your animal somewhat the less promising. But if you are betting five hundred you are very, very likely to be loathe to do so. Thus, in large-bet fights, which of course involve the better animals, tremendous care is taken to see that the cocks are about as evenly matched as to size, general condition, pugnacity, and so on as is humanly possible. The different ways of adjusting the spurs of the animals are often employed to secure this. If one cock seems stronger, an agreement will be made to position his spur at a slightly less advantageous angle—a kind of handicapping, at which spur affixers are, so it is said, extremely skilled. More care will be taken, too, to employ skillful handlers and to match them exactly as to abilities.

In short, in a large-bet fight the pressure to make the match a genuinely fifty-fifty proposition is enormous, and is consciously felt as such. For medium fights the pressure is somewhat less, and for small ones less yet, though there is always an effort to make things at least approximately equal, for even at fifteen ringgits (five days work) no one wants to make an even money bet in a clearly unfavorable situation. And, again, what statistics I have tend to bear this out. In my fifty-seven matches, the favorite won thirty-three times over-all, the underdog twenty-four, a 1.4 to 1 ratio. But if one splits the figures at sixty ringgits center bets, the ratios turn out to be 1.1 to 1 (twelve favorites, eleven underdogs) for those above this line, and 1.6 to 1 (twenty-one and thirteen) for those below it. Or, if you take the extremes, for very large fights, those with center bets over a hundred ringgits the ratio is 1 to 1 (seven and seven); for very small fights, those under forty ringgits, it is 1.9 to 1 (nineteen and ten).[16]

Now, from this proposition—that the higher the center bet the more exactly a fifty-fifty proposition the cockfight is—two things more or less immediately follow: (1) the higher the center bet, the greater is the pull on the side betting toward the short-odds end of the wagering spectrum and vice versa; (2) the higher the center bet, the greater the volume of side betting and vice versa.

The logic is similar in both cases. The closer the fight is in fact to even money, the less attractive the long end of the odds will appear and, therefore, the shorter it must be if there are to be takers. That this is the case is apparent from mere inspection, from the Balinese's own analysis of the matter, and from what more systematic observations I was able to collect. Given the difficulty of making precise and complete recordings of side betting, this argument is hard to cast in numerical form, but in all my cases the odds-giver, odds-taker consensual point, a quite pronounced minimax saddle where the bulk (at a guess, two-thirds to three-quarters in most cases) of the bets are actually made, was three or four points further along the scale toward the shorter end for the large-center-bet fights than for the small ones, with medium ones generally in between. In detail, the fit is not, of course, exact, but the general pattern is quite consistent: the power of the center bet to pull the side bets toward its own even-money pattern is directly proportional to its size, because its size is directly proportional to the degree to which the cocks are in fact evenly matched. As for the volume question, total wagering is greater in large-center-bet fights because such fights are considered more "interesting" not only in the sense that they are less predictable, but, more crucially, that more is at stake in them—in terms of money, in terms of the quality of the cocks, and consequently, as we shall see, in terms of social prestige.[17]

The paradox of fair coin in the middle, biased coin on the outside is thus a merely apparent one. The two betting systems, though formally incongruent, are not really contradictory to one another, but part of a single larger system in which the center bet is, so to speak, the "center of gravity," drawing, the larger it is the more so, the outside bets toward the short-odds end of the scale. The center bet thus "makes the game," or perhaps better, defines it, signals what, following a notion of Jeremy Bentham's, I am going to call its "depth."

The Balinese attempt to create an interesting, if you will, "deep," match by making the center bet as large as possible so that the cocks matched will be as equal and as fine as possible, and the outcome, thus, as unpredictable as possible. They do not always succeed. Nearly half the matches are relatively trivial, relatively uninteresting—in my borrowed terminology, "shallow"—affairs. But that fact no more argues against my interpretation than the fact that most painters, poets, and playwrights are mediocre argues against the view that artistic effort is directed toward profundity and, with a certain frequency, approximates it. The image of artistic technique is indeed exact: the center bet is a means, a device, for creating "interesting," "deep" matches, *not* the reason, or at least not the main reason, *why* they are interesting, the source of their fascination, the substance of their depth. The question why such matches are interesting—indeed, for the Balinese, exquisitely absorbing—takes us out of the realm of formal concerns into more broadly sociological and social-psychological ones, and to a less purely economic idea of what "depth" in gaming amounts to.[18]

Playing with Fire

Bentham's concept of "deep play" is found in his *The Theory of Legislation.*[19] By it he means play in which the stakes are so high that it is, from his utilitarian standpoint, irrational for men to engage in it at all. If a man whose fortune is a thousand pounds (or ringgits) wages five hundred of it on an even bet, the marginal utility of the pound he stands to win is clearly less than the marginal disutility of the one he stands to lose. In genuine deep play, this is the case for both parties. They are both in over their heads. Having come together in search of pleasure they have entered into a relationship which will bring the participants, considered collectively, net pain rather than net pleasure. Bentham's conclusion was, therefore, that deep play was immoral from the first principles and, a typical step for him, should be prevented legally.

But more interesting than the ethical problem, at least for our concerns here, is that despite the logical force of Bentham's analysis men do engage in such play, both passionately and often, and even in the face of law's revenge. For Bentham and those who think as he does (nowadays mainly lawyers, economists, and a few psychiatrists), the explanation is, as I have said, that such men are irrational—addicts, fetishists, children, fools, savages, who need only to be protected against themselves. But for the Balinese, though naturally they do not formulate it in so many words, the explanation lies in the fact that in such play money is less a measure of utility, had or expected, than it is a symbol of moral import, perceived or imposed.

It is, in fact, in shallow games, ones in which smaller amounts of money are involved, that increments and decrements of cash are more nearly synonyms for utility and disutility, in the ordinary, unexpanded sense—for pleasure and pain, happiness and unhappiness. In deep ones, where the amounts of money are great, much more is at stake than material gain: namely, esteem, honor, dignity, respect—in a word, though in Bali a profoundly freighted word, status.[20] It is at stake symbolically, for (a few cases of ruined addict gamblers aside) no one's status is actually altered by the outcome of a cockfight; it is only, and that momentarily, affirmed or insulted. But for the Balinese, for whom nothing is more pleasurable than an affront obliquely delivered or more painful than one obliquely received—particularly when mutual acquaintances, undeceived by surfaces, are watching—such appraisive drama is deep indeed.

This, I must stress immediately, is *not* to say that the money does not matter, or that the Balinese is no more concerned about losing five hundred ringgits than fifteen. Such a conclusion would be absurd. It is because money *does,* in this hardly unmaterialistic society, matter and matter very much that the more of it one risks the more of a lot of other things, such as one's pride, one's poise, one's dispassion, one's masculinity, one also risks, again only momentarily but again very publicly as well. In deep cockfights an owner and his collaborators, and, as we shall see, to a lesser but still quite real extent also their backers on the outside, put their money where their status is.

It is in large part *because* the marginal disutility of loss is so great at the higher levels of betting that to engage in such betting is to lay one's public self, allusively and metaphorically, through the medium of one's cock, on the line. And though to a Benthamite this might seem merely to increase the irrationality of the enterprise that much further, to the Balinese what it mainly increases is the meaningfulness of it all. And as (to follow Weber rather than Bentham) the imposition of meaning on life is the major end and primary condition of human existence, that access of significance more than compensates for the economic costs involved.[21] Actually, given the even-money quality of the larger matches, important changes in material fortune among those who regularly participate in them seem virtually nonexistent, because matters more or less even out over the long run. It is, actually, in the smaller, shallow fights, where one finds the handful of more pure, addict-type gamblers involved—those who *are* in it mainly for the money—that "real" changes in social position, largely downward, are affected. Men of this sort, plungers, are highly dispraised by "true cockfighters" as fools who do not understand what the sport is all about, vulgarians who simply miss the point of it all. They are, these addicts, regarded as fair game for the genuine enthusiasts, those who do understand, to take a little money away from, something that is easy enough to do by luring them, through the force of their greed, into irrational bets on mismatched cocks. Most of them do indeed manage to ruin themselves in a remarkably short time, but there always seems to be one or two of them around, pawning their land and selling their clothes in order to bet, at any particular time.[22]

This graduated correlation of "status gambling" with deeper fights and, inversely, "money gambling" with shallower ones is in fact quite general. Bettors themselves form a sociomoral hierarchy in these terms. As noted earlier, at most cockfights there are, around the very edges of the cockfight area, a large number of mindless, sheer-chance type gambling games (roulette, dice throw, coin-spin, pea-under-the-shell) operated by concessionaires. Only women, children, adolescents, and various other sorts of people who do not (or not yet) fight cocks—the extremely poor, the socially despised, the personally idiosyncratic—play at these games, at, of course, penny ante levels. Cockfighting men would be ashamed to go anywhere near them. Slightly above these people in standing are those who, though they do not themselves fight cocks, bet on the smaller matches around the edges. Next, there are those who fight cocks in small, or occasionally medium matches, but have not the status to join in the large ones, though they may bet from time to time on the side in those. And finally, there are those, the really substantial members of the community, the solid citizenry around whom local life revolves, who fight in the larger fights and bet on them around the side. The focusing element in these focused gatherings, these men generally dominate and define the sport as they dominate and define the society. When a Balinese male talks, in that almost venerative way, about "the true cockfighter," the *bebatoh* ("bettor") or *djuru kurung* ("cage keeper"), it is this sort of person, not those who bring the mentality of the pea-and-shell game into the quite different, inappropriate context of the cockfight, the driven gambler (*potét,* a word which has the secondary meaning of thief or reprobate), and the wistful hanger-on, that they mean. For such a man, what is really going on in a match is something rather close to an *affaire d'honneur* (though, with the Balinese talent for practical fantasy, the blood that is spilled is only figuratively human) than to the stupid, mechanical crank of a slot machine.

What makes Balinese cockfighting deep is thus not money in itself, but what, the more of it that is involved the more so, money causes to happen: the migration of the Balinese status hierarchy into the body of the cockfight. Psychologically an Aesopian representation of the ideal/demonic, rather narcissistic, male self, sociologically it is an equally Aesopian representation of the complex fields of tension set up by the controlled, muted, ceremonial, but for all that deeply felt, interaction of those selves in the context of everyday life. The cocks may be surrogates for their owners' personalities, animal mirrors of psychic form, but the cockfight is—or more exactly, deliberately is made to be—a simulation of the social matrix, the involved system of crosscutting, overlapping, highly corporate groups—

villages, kingroups, irrigation societies, temple congregations, "castes"—in which its devotees live.[23] And as prestige, the necessity to affirm it, defend it, celebrate it, justify it, and just plain bask in it (but not, given the strongly ascriptive character of Balinese stratification, to seek it), is perhaps the central driving force in the society, so also—ambulant penises, blood sacrifices, and monetary exchanges aside—is it of the cockfight. This apparent amusement and seeming sport is, to take another phrase from Erving Goffman, "a status bloodbath."[24]

The easiest way to make this clear, and at least to some degree to demonstrate it, is to invoke the village whose cockfighting activities I observed the closest—the one in which the raid occurred and from which my statistical data are taken.

As all Balinese villages, this one—Tihingan, in the Klungkung region of southeast Bali—is intricately organized, a labyrinth of alliances and oppositions. But, unlike many, two sorts of corporate groups, which are also status groups, particularly stand out, and we may concentrate on them, in a part-for-whole way, without undue distortion.

First, the village is dominated by four large, patrilineal, partly endogamous descent groups which are constantly vying with one another and from the major factions in the village. Sometimes they group two and two, or rather the two larger ones versus the two smaller ones plus all the unaffiliated people; sometimes they operate independently. There are also subfactions within them, subfactions within the subfactions, and so on to rather fine levels of distinction. And second, there is the village itself, almost entirely endogamous, which is opposed to all the other villages round about in its cockfight circuit (which, as explained, is the market region), but which also forms alliances with certain of these neighbors against certain others in various supra-village political and social contexts. The exact situation is thus, as everywhere in Bali, quite distinctive; but the general pattern of a tiered hierarchy of status rivalries between highly corporate but various based groupings (and, thus, between the members of them) is entirely general.

Consider, then, as support of the general thesis that the cockfight, and especially the deep cockfight, is fundamentally a dramatization of status concerns, the following facts, which to avoid extended ethnographic description I will simply pronounce to be facts—though the concrete evidence-examples, statements, and numbers that could be brought to bear in support of them is both extensive and unmistakable:

1. A man virtually never bets against a cock owned by a member of his own kingroup. Usually he will feel obliged to bet for it, the more so the closer the kin tie and the deeper the fight. If he is certain in his mind that it will not win, he may just not bet at all, particularly if it is

only a second cousin's bird or if the fight is a shallow one. But as a rule he will feel he must support it and, in deep games, nearly always does. Thus the great majority of the people calling "five" or "speckled" so demonstratively are expressing their allegiance to their kinsman, not their evaluation of his bird, their understanding of probability theory, or even their hopes of unearned income.

2. This principle is extended logically. If your kingroup is not involved you will support an allied kingroup against an unallied one in the same way, and so on through the very involved networks of alliances which, as I say, make up this, as any other, Balinese village.
3. So, too, for the village as a whole. If an outsider cock is fighting any cock from your village you will tend to support the local one. If, what is a rare circumstance but occurs every now and then, a cock from outside your cockfight circuit is fighting one inside it you will also tend to support the "home bird."
4. Cocks which come from any distance are almost always favorites, for the theory is the man would not have dared to bring it if it was not a good cock, the more so the further he has come. His followers are, of course, obliged to support him, and when the more grand-scale legal cockfights are held (on holidays, and so on) the people of the village take what they regard to be the best cocks in the village, regardless of ownership, and go off to support them, although they will almost certainly have to give odds on them and to make large bets to show that they are not a cheapskate village. Actually, such "away games," though infrequent, tend to mend the ruptures between village members that the constantly occurring "home games," where village factions are opposed rather than united, exacerbate.
5. Almost all matches are sociologically relevant. You seldom get two outsider cocks fighting, or two cocks with no particular group backing, or with group backing which is mutually unrelated in any clear way. When you do get them, the game is very shallow, betting very slow, and the whole thing very dull, with no one save the immediate principals and an addict gambler or two at all interested.
6. By the same token, you rarely get two cocks from the same group, even more rarely from the same subfaction, and virtually never from the same sub-subfaction (which would be in most cases one extended family) fighting. Similarly, in outside village fights two members of the village will rarely fight against one another, even though, as bitter rivals, they would do so with enthusiasm on their home grounds.
7. On the individual level, people involved in an institutionalized hostility relationship, called *puik,* in which they do not speak or otherwise have anything to do with each other (the causes of this formal breaking of relations are many: wife-capture, inheritance arguments, political

differences) will bet very heavily, sometimes almost maniacally, against one another in what is a frank and direct attack on the very masculinity, the ultimate ground of his status, of the opponent.

8. The center bet coalition is, in all but the shallowest games, *always* made up by structural allies—no "outside money" is involved. What is "outside" depends upon the context, of course, but given it, no outside money is mixed in with the main bet; if the principals cannot raise it, it is not made. The center bet, again especially in deeper games, is thus the most direct and open expression of social opposition, which is one of the reasons why both it and match making are surrounded by such an air of unease, furtiveness, embarrassment, and so on.
9. The rule about borrowing money—that you may borrow *for* a bet but not *in* one—stems (and the Balinese are quite conscious of this) from similar considerations: you are never at the *economic* mercy of your enemy that way. Gambling debts, which can get quite large on a rather short-term basis, are always to friends, never to enemies, structurally speaking.
10. When two cocks are structurally irrelevant or neutral so far as *you* are concerned (though, as mentioned, they almost never are to each other) you do not even ask a relative or a friend whom he is betting on, because if you know how he is betting and he knows you know, and you go the other way, it will lead to strain. This rule is explicit and rigid; fairly elaborate, even rather artificial precautions are taken to avoid breaking it. At the very least you must pretend not to notice what he is doing, and he what you are doing.
11. There is a special word for betting against the grain, which is also the word for "pardon me" *(mpura)*. It is considered a bad thing to do, though if the center bet is small it is sometimes all right as long as you do not do it too often. But the larger the bet and the more frequently you do it, the more the "pardon me" tack will lead to social disruption.
12. In fact, the institutionalized hostility relation, *puik*, is often formally initiated (though its causes always lie elsewhere) by such a "a pardon me" bet in a deep fight, putting the symbolic fat in the fire. Similarly, the end of such a relationship and resumption of normal social intercourse is often signalized (but, again, not actually brought about) by one or the other of the enemies supporting the other's bird.
13. In sticky, cross-loyalty situations, of which in this extraordinarily complex social system there are of course many, where a man is caught between two more or less equally balanced loyalties, he tends to wander off for a cup of coffee or something to avoid having to bet, a form of behavior reminiscent of that of American voters in similar situations.[25]
14. The people involved in the center bet are, especially in deep fights,

virtually always leading members of their group—kinship, village, or whatever. Further, those who bet on the side (including these people) are, as I have already remarked, the more established members of the village—the solid citizens. Cockfighting is for those who are involved in the everyday politics of prestige as well, not for youth, women, subordinates, and so forth.

15. So far as money is concerned, the explicitly expressed attitude toward it is that it is a secondary matter. It is not, as I have said, of no importance; Balinese are no happier to lose several weeks' income than anyone else. But they mainly look on the monetary aspects of the cockfight as self-balancing, a matter of just moving money around, circulating it among a fairly well-defined group of serious cockfighters. The really important wins and losses are seen mostly in other terms, and the general attitude toward wagering is not any hope of cleaning up, of making a killing (addict gamblers again excepted), but that of the horseplayer's prayer: "O, God, please let me break even." In prestige terms, however, you do not want to break even, but, in a momentary, punctuate sort of way, win utterly. The talk (which goes on all the time) is about fights against such-and-such a cock of So-and-So which your cock demolished, not on how much you won, a fact people, even for large bets, rarely remember for any length of time, though they will remember the day they did in Pan Loh's finest cock for years.

16. You must bet on cocks of your own group aside from mere loyalty considerations, for if you do not people generally will say, "What! Is he too proud for the likes of us? Does he have to go to Java or Den Pasar [the capital town] to bet, he is such an important man?" Thus there is a general pressure to bet not only to show that you are important locally, but that you are not so important that you look down on everyone else as unfit even to be rivals. Similarly, home team people must bet against outside cocks or the outsiders will accuse it—a serious charge—of just collecting entry fees and not really being interested in cockfighting, as well as again being arrogant and insulting.

17. Finally, the Balinese peasants themselves are quite aware of all this and can and, at least to an ethnographer, do state most of it in approximately the same terms as I have. Fighting cocks, almost every Balinese I have ever discussed the subject with has said, is like playing with fire only not getting burned. You activate village and kingroup rivalries and hostilities, but in "play" form, coming dangerously and entrancingly close to the expression of open and direct interpersonal and intergroup aggression (something which, again, almost never happens in the normal course of ordinary life), but not quite, because, after all, it is "only a cockfight."

More observations of this sort could be advanced, but perhaps the general point is, if not made, at least well-delineated, and the whole argument thus far can be usefully summarized in a formal paradigm:

THE MORE A MATCH IS . . .

1. Between near status equals (and/or personal enemies)
2. Between high status individuals

THE DEEPER THE MATCH.

THE DEEPER THE MATCH . . .

1. The closer the identification of cock and man (or: more properly, the deeper the match the more the man will advance his best, most closely-identified-with cock).
2. The finer the cocks involved and the more exactly they will be matched.
3. The greater the emotion that will be involved and the more the general absorbtion in the match.
4. The higher the individual bets center and outside, the shorter the outside bet odds will tend to be, and the more betting there will be overall.
5. The less an "economic" and the more a "status" view of gaming will be involved, and the "solider" the citizens who will be gaming.[26]

Inverse arguments hold for the shallower the fight, culminating, in a reversed-signs sense, in the coin-spinning and dice-throwing amusements. For deep fights there are no absolute upper limits, though there are of course practical ones, and there are a great many legend-like tales of great Duel-in-the-Sun combats between lords and princes in classical times (for cockfighting has always been as much an elite concern as a popular one), far deeper than anything anyone, even aristocrats, could produce today anywhere in Bali.

Indeed, one of the great culture heroes of Bali is a prince, called after his passion for the sport, "The Cockfighter," who happened to be away at a very deep cockfight with a neighboring prince when the whole of his family—father, brothers, wives, sisters—were assassinated by commoner usurpers. Thus spared, he returned to dispatch the upstarts, regain the throne, reconstitute the Balinese high tradition, and build its most powerful, glorious, and prosperous state. Along with everything else that the Balinese see in fighting cocks—themselves, their social order, abstract hatred, masculinity, demonic power—they also see the archetype of status virtue, the arrogant, resolute, honor-mad player with real fire, the ksatria prince.[27]

Feathers, Blood, Crowds, and Money

"Poetry makes nothing happen," Auden says in his elegy of Yeats, "it survives in the valley of its saying . . . a way of happening, a mouth." The cockfight too, in this colloquial sense, makes nothing happen. Men go on allegorically humiliating one another and being allegorically humiliated by one another, day after day, glorying quietly in the experience if they have triumphed, crushed only slightly more openly by it if they have not. *But no one's status really changes.* You cannot ascend the status ladder by winning cockfights; you cannot, as an individual, really ascend it at all. Nor can you descend it that way.[28] All you can do is enjoy and savor, or suffer and withstand, the concocted sensation of drastic and momentary movement along an aesthetic semblance of that ladder, a kind of behind-the-mirror status jump which has the look of mobility without its actuality.

As any art form—for that, finally, is what we are dealing with—the cockfight renders ordinary, everyday experience comprehensible by presenting it in terms of acts and objects which have had their practical consequences removed and been reduced (or, if you prefer, raised) to the level of sheer appearances, where their meaning can be more powerfully articulated and more exactly perceived. The cockfight is "really real" only to the cocks—it does not kill anyone, castrate anyone, reduce anyone to animal status, alter the hierarchical relations among people, nor refashion the hierarchy; it does not even redistribute income in any significant way. What it does is what, for other peoples with other temperaments and other conventions, *Lear* and *Crime and Punishment* do; it catches up these themes—death, masculinity, rage, pride, loss, beneficence, chance—and, ordering them into an encompassing structure, presents them in such a way as to throw into relief a particular view of their essential nature. It puts a construction on them, makes them, to those historically positioned to appreciate the construction, meaningful—visible, tangible, graspable—"real," in an ideational sense. An image, fiction, a model, a metaphor, the cockfight is a means of expression; its function is neither to assuage social passions nor to heighten them (though, in its play-with-fire way, it does a bit of both), but, in a medium of feathers, blood, crowds, and money, to display them.

The question of how it is that we perceive qualities in things—paintings, books, melodies, plays—that we do not feel we can assert literally to be there has come, in recent years, into the very center of aesthetic theory.[29] Neither the sentiments of the artist, which remain his, nor those of the audience, which remain theirs, can account for the agitation of one painting or the serenity of another. We attribute grandeur, wit, despair, exuberance to strings of sounds; lightness, energy, violence, fluidity to blocks of stone. Novels are said to have strength, buildings eloquence, plays momentum, ballets repose. In this realm of eccentric predicates, to say that the cockfight, in its perfected cases at least, is "disquietful" does not seem at all unnatural, merely, as I have just denied it practical consequence, somewhat puzzling.

The disquietfulness arises, "somehow," out of a conjunction of three attributes of the fight: its immediate dramatic shape; its metaphoric content; and its social context. A cultural figure against a social ground, the fight is at once a convulsive surge of animal hatred, a mock war of symbolical selves, and a formal simulation of status tensions, and its aesthetic power derives from its capacity to force together these diverse realities. The reason it is disquietful is not that it has material effects (it has some, but they are minor); the reason that it is disquietful is that, joining pride to selfhood, selfhood to cocks, and cocks to destruction, it brings to imaginative realization a dimension of Balinese experience normally well-obscured from view. The transfer of a sense of gravity into what is in itself a rather blank and unvarious spectacle, a commotion of beating wings and throbbing legs, is effected by interpreting it as expressive of something unsettling in the way its authors and audience live, or, even more ominously, what they are.

As a dramatic shape, the fight displays a characteristic that does not seem so remarkable until one realizes that it does not have to be there: a radically atomistical structure.[30] Each match is a world unto itself, a particulate burst of form. There is the match making, there is the betting, there is the fight, there is the result—utter triumph and utter defeat—and there is the hurried, embarrassed passing of money. The loser is not consoled. People drift away from him, look through him, leave him to assimilate his momentary descent into nonbeing, reset his face, and return, scarless and intact, to the fray. Nor are winners congratulated, or events rehashed; once a match is ended the crowd's attention turns totally to the next, with no looking back. A shadow of the experience no doubt remains with the principals, perhaps even with some of the witnesses, of a deep fight, as it remains with us when we leave the theater after seeing a powerful play well-performed; but it quite soon fades to become at most a schematic memory—a diffuse glow or an abstract shudder—and usually not even that. Any expressive form lives only in its own present—the one it itself creates. But, here, that present is severed into a string of flashes, some more bright than others, but all of them disconnected, aesthetic quanta. Whatever the cockfight says, it says in spurts.

But, as I have argued lengthily elsewhere, the Balinese live in spurts.[31] Their life, as they arrange it and perceive it, is less a flow, a directional movement out of the past, through the present, toward the future than an on-off pulsation of meaning and vacuity, an arhythmic alternation of short periods when "something" (that is, something significant) is happening and equally short ones where "nothing" (that is, nothing much) is—between what they themselves call "full" and "empty" times, or, in another idiom, "junctures" and "holes." In focusing activity down to a burning-glass dot, the cockfight is merely being Balinese in the same way in which everything from the monadic encounters of everyday life, through the changing pointillism of *gamelan* music, to the visiting-day-of-the-gods temple celebrations are. It is not an imitation of the punctuateness of Balinese social life, nor a depiction of it, nor even an expression of it; it is an example of it, carefully prepared.[32]

If one dimension of the cockfight's structure, its lack of temporal directionality, makes it seem a typical segment of the general social life, however, the other, its flat-out, head-to-head (or spur-to-spur) aggressiveness, makes it seem a contradiction, a reversal, even a subversion of it. In the normal course of things, the Balinese are shy to the point of obsessivenesss of open conflict. Oblique, cautious, subdued, controlled, masters of indirection and dissimulation—what they call *alus,* "polished," "smooth,"—they rarely face what they can turn away from, rarely resist what they can evade. But here they portray themselves as wild and murderous, manic explosions of instinctual cruelty. A powerful rendering of life as the Balinese most deeply do not want it (to adapt a phrase Frye has used of Gloucester's blinding) is set in the context of a sample of it as they do in fact have it.[33] And, because the context suggests that the rendering, if less than a straightforward description is nonetheless more than an idle fancy, it is here that the disquietfulness—the disquietfulness of the *fight,* not (or, anyway, not necessarily) its patrons, who seem in fact rather thoroughly to enjoy it—emerges. The slaughter in the cock ring is not a depiction of how things literally are among men, but, what is almost worse, of how, from a particular angle, they imaginatively are.[34]

The angle, of course, is stratificatory. What, as we have already seen, the cockfight talks most forcibly about is status relationships, and what it says about them is that they are matters of life and death. That prestige is a profoundly serious business is apparent everywhere one looks in Bali—in the village, the family, the economy, the state. A peculiar fusion of Polynesian title ranks and Hindu castes, the hierarchy of pride is the moral backbone of the society. But only in the cockfight are the sentiments upon which that hierarchy rests revealed in their natural colors. Enveloped elsewhere in a haze of etiquette, a thick cloud of euphemism and ceremony, gesture and allusion, they are here expressed in only the thinnest disguise of an animal mask, a mask which in fact demonstrates them far more effectively than it conceals them. Jealousy is as much a part of Bali as poise, envy as grace, brutality as charm; but without the cockfight the Balinese would have a much less certain understanding of them, which is, presumably, why they value it so highly.

Any expressive form works (when it works) by disarranging semantic contexts in such a way that properties conventionally ascribed to certain things are unconventionally ascribed to others, which are then seen actually to possess them. To call the wind a cripple, as Stevens does, to fix tone and manipulate timbre, as Schoenberg does, or, closer to our case, to picture an art critic as a dissolute bear, as Hogarth does, is to cross conceptual wires; the established conjunctions between objects and their qualities are altered and phenomena—fall weather, melodic shape, or cultural journalism—are clothed in signifiers which normally point to other referents.[35] Similarly, to connect—and connect, and connect—the collision of roosters with the devisiveness of status is to invite a transfer of perceptions from the former to the latter, a transfer which is at once a description and a judgment. (Logically, the transfer could, of course, as well go the other way; but, like most of the rest of us, the Balinese are a great deal more interested in understanding men than they are in understanding cocks.)

What sets the cockfight apart from the ordinary course of life, lifts it from the realm of everyday practical affairs, and surrounds it with an aura of enlarged importance is not, as functionalist sociology would have it, that it reinforces status discriminations (such reinforcement is hardly necessary in a society where every act proclaims them), but that it provides a metasocial commentary upon the whole matter of assorting human beings into fixed hierarchical ranks and then organizing the major part of collective existence around that assortment. Its function, if you want to call it that, is interpretive: it is a Balinese reading of Balinese experience; a story they tell themselves about themselves.

Saying Something of Something

To put the matter this way is to engage in a bit of metaphorical refocusing of one's own, for it shifts the analysis of cultural forms from an endeavor in general parallel to dissecting an organism, diagnosing a symptom, deciphering a code, or ordering a system—the dominant analogies in contemporary anthropology—to one in general parallel with penetrating a literary text. If one takes the cockfight, or any other collectively sustained symbolic structure, as a means of "saying something of something" (to invoke a famous Aristotelian tag), then one is faced with a problem not in social mechanics but social semantics.[36] For the anthropologist, whose concern is with formulating sociological principles, not with promoting or appreciating cockfights, the question is, what does one learn about such principles from examining culture as an assemblage of texts?

Such an extension of the notion of a text beyond written material, and even beyond verbal, is, though metaphorical, not, of course, all that novel. The *interpretatio naturae* tradition of the middle ages, which, culminating in

Spinoza, attempted to read nature as Scripture, the Nietszchean effort to treat value systems as glosses on the will to power (or the Marxian one to treat them as glosses on property relations), and the Freudian replacement of the enigmatic text of the manifest dream with the plain one of the latent, all offer precedents, if not equally recommendable ones.[37] But the idea remains theoretically undeveloped; and the more profound corollary, so far as anthropology is concerned, that cultural forms can be treated as texts, as imaginative works built out of social materials, has yet to be systematically exploited.[38]

In the case at hand, to treat the cockfight as a text is to bring out a feature of it (in my opinion, the central feature of it) that treating it as a rite or a pastime, the two most obvious alternatives, would tend to obscure: its use of emotion for cognitive ends. What the cockfight says it says in a vocabulary of sentiment—the thrill of risk, the despair of loss, the pleasure of triumph. Yet what it says is not merely that risk is exciting, loss depressing, or triumph gratifying, banal tautologies of affect, but that it is of these emotions, thus exampled, that society is built and individuals put together. Attending cockfights and participating in them is, for the Balinese, a kind of sentimental education. What he learns there is what his culture's ethos and his private sensibility (or, anyway, certain aspects of them) look like when spelled out externally in a collective text; that the two are near enough alike to be articulated in the symbolics of a single such text; and—the disquieting part—that the text in which this revelation is accomplished consists of a chicken hacking another mindlessly to bits.

Every people, the proverb has it, loves its own form of violence. The cockfight is the Balinese reflection on theirs: on its look, its uses, its force, its fascination. Drawing on almost every level of Balinese experience, it brings together themes—animal savagery, male narcissism, opponent gambling, status rivalry, mass excitement, blood sacrifice—whose main connection is their involvement with rage and the fear of rage, and, binding them into a set of rules which at once contains them and allows them play, builds a symbolic structure in which, over and over again, the reality of their inner affiliation can be intelligibly felt. If, to quote Northrop Frye again, we go to see *Macbeth* to learn what a man feels like after he has gained a kingdom and lost his soul, Balinese go to cockfights to find out what a man, usually composed, aloof, almost obsessively self-absorbed, a kind of moral autocosm, feels like when, attacked, tormented, challenged, insulted, and driven in result to the extremes of fury, he has totally triumphed or been brought totally low. The whole passage, as it takes us back to Aristotle (though to the *Poetics* rather than the *Hermeneutics*), is worth quotation:

> But the poet [as opposed to the historian], Aristotle says, never makes any real statements at all, certainly no particular or

> specific ones. The poet's job is not to tell you what happened, but what happens: not what did take place, but the kind of thing that always does take place. He gives you the typical, recurring, or what Aristotle calls universal event. You wouldn't go to *Macbeth* to learn about the history of Scotland—you go to it to learn what a man feels like after he's gained a kingdom and lost his soul. When you meet such a character as Micawber in Dickens, you don't feel that there must have been a man Dickens knew who was exactly like this: you feel that there's a bit of Micawber in almost everybody you know, including yourself. Our impressions of human life are picked up one by one, and remain for most of us loose and disorganized. But we constantly find things in literature that suddenly co-ordinate and bring into focus a great many such impressions, and this is part of what Aristotle means by the typical or universal human event.[39]

It is this kind of bringing of assorted experiences of everyday life to focus that the cockfight, set aside from that life as "only a game" and reconnected to it as "more than a game," accomplishes, and so creates what, better than typical or universal, could be called a paradigmatic human event—that is, one that tells us less what happens than the kind of thing that would happen if, as is not the case, life were art and could be as freely shaped by styles of feeling as *Macbeth* and *David Copperfield* are.

Enacted and reenacted, so far without end, the cockfight enables the Balinese, as, read and reread, *Macbeth* enables us, to see a dimension of his own subjectivity. As he watches fight after fight, with the active watching of an owner and a bettor (for cockfighting has no more interest as a pure spectator sport than croquet or dog racing do), he grows familiar with it and what it has to say to him, must as the attentive listener to string quartets or the absorbed viewer of still lifes grows slowly more familiar with them in a way which opens his subjectivity to himself.[40]

Yet, because—in another of those paradoxes, along with painted feelings and unconsequenced acts, which haunt aesthetics—that subjectivity does not properly exist until it is thus organized, art forms generate and regenerate the very subjectivity they pretend only to display. Quartets, still lifes, and cockfights are not merely reflections of a preexisting sensibility analogically represented; they are positive agents in the creation and maintenance of such a sensibility. If we see ourselves as a pack of Micawbers it is from reading too much Dickens (if we see ourselves as unillusioned realists, it is from reading too little); and similarly for Balinese, cocks, and cockfights. It is in such a way, coloring experience with the light they cast it in, rather than through whatever material effects they may have, that the arts play their role, as arts, in social life.[41]

In the cockfight, then, the Balinese forms and discovers his temperament and his society's temper at the same time. Or, more exactly, he forms and discovers a particular face of them. Not only are there a great many other cultural texts providing commentaries on status hierarchy and self-regard in Bali, but there are a great many other critical sectors of Balinese life besides the stratificatory and the agonistic that receive such commentary. The ceremony consecrating a Brahmana priest, a matter of breath control, postural immobility, and vacant concentration upon the depths of being, displays a radically different, but to the Balinese equally real, property of social hierarchy—its reach toward the numinous transcendent. Set not in the matrix of the kinetic emotionality of animals, but in that of the static passionlessness of divine mentality, it expresses tranquility not disquiet. The mass festivals at the village temples, which mobilize the whole local population in elaborate hostings of visiting gods—songs, dances, compliments, gifts—assert the spiritual unity of village mates against their status inequality and project a mood of amity and trust.[42] The cockfight is not the master key to Balinese life, any more than bullfighting is to Spanish. What it says about that life is not unqualified nor even unchallenged by what other equally eloquent cultural statements say about it. But there is nothing more surprising in this than in the fact that Racine and Molière were contemporaries, or that the same people who arrange chrysanthemums cast swords.[43]

The culture of a people is an ensemble of texts, themselves ensembles, which the anthropologist strains to read over the shoulders of those to whom they properly belong. There are enormous difficulties in such an enterprise, methodological pitfalls to make a Freudian quake, and some moral perplexities as well. Nor is it the only way that symbolic forms can be sociologically handled. Functionalism lives, and so does psychologism. But to regard such forms as "saying something of something," and saying it to somebody, is at least to open up the possibility of an analysis which attends to their substance rather than to reductive formulas professing to account for them.

As in more familiar exercises in close reading, one can start anywhere in a culture's repertoire of forms and end up anywhere else. One can stay, as I have here, within a single, more or less bounded form and circle steadily within it. One can move between forms in search of broader unities or informing contrasts. One can even compare forms from different cultures to define their character in reciprocal relief. But whatever the level at which one operates, and however intricately, the guiding principle is the same: societies, like lives, contain their own interpretations. One has only to learn how to gain access to them.

References

[1] Gregory Bateson and Margaret Mead, *Balinese Character: A Photographic Analysis* (New York: New York Academy of Sciences, 1942), p. 68.

[2] Jane Belo, "The Balinese Temper," in Jane Belo, ed., *Traditional Balinese Culture* (New York: Columbia University Press, 1970; originally published in 1935), pp. 85–110.

[3] The best discussion of cockfighting is again Bateson and Mead's (*Balinese Character*, pp. 24–25, 140), but it, too, is general and abbreviated.

[4] *Ibid.*, pp. 25–26. The cockfight is unusual within Balinese culture in being a single-sex public activity from which the other sex is totally and expressly excluded. Sexual differentiation is culturally extremely played down in Bali and most activities, formal and informal, involve the participation of men and women on equal ground, commonly as linked couples. From religion, to politics, to economics, to kinship, to dress, Bali is a rather "uni-sex" society, a fact both its customs and its symbolism clearly express. Even in contexts where women do not in fact play much of a role—music, painting, certain agricultural activities—their absence, which is only relative in any case, is more a mere matter of fact than socially enforced. To this general pattern, the cockfight, entirely of, by, and for men (women—at least *Balinese* women—do not even watch), is the most striking exception.

[5] Christiaan Hooykaas, *The Lay of the Jaya Prana* (London, 1958), p. 39. The lay has a stanza (no. 17) with the reluctant bridegroom use. Jaya Prana, the subject of a Balinese Uriah myth, responds to the lord who has offered him the loveliest of six hundred servant girls: "Godly King, my Lord and Master / I beg you, give me leave to go / such things are not yet in my mind; / like a fighting cock encaged / indeed I am on my mettle / I am alone / as yet the flame has not been fanned."

[6] For these, see V. E. Korn, *Het Adatrecht van Bali*, 2d ed. ('S-Gravenhage: G. Naeff, 1932), index under *toh.*

[7] There is indeed a legend to the effect that the separation of Java and Bali is due to the action of a powerful Javanese religious figure who wished to protect himself against a Balinese culture hero (the ancestor of two Ksatria castes) who was a passionate cockfighting gambler. See Christiaan Hooykaas, *Agama Tirtha* (Amsterdam: Noord-Hollandsche, 1964), p. 184.

[8] An incestuous couple is forced to wear pig yokes over their necks and crawl to a pig trough and eat with their mouths there. On this, see Jane Belo, "Customs Pertaining to Twins in Bali," in Belo, ed., *Traditional Balinese Culture*, p. 49; on the abhorence of animality generally, Bateson and Mead, *Balinese Character*, p. 22.

[9] Except for unimportant, small-bet fights (on the question of fight "importance," see below) spur affixing is usually done by someone other than the owner. Whether the owner handles his own cock or not more or less depends on how skilled he is at it, a consideration whose importance is again relative to the importance of the fight. When spur affixers and cock handlers are someone other than the owner, they are almost always a close relative—a brother or cousin—or a very intimate friend of his. They are thus almost extensions of his personality, as the fact that all three will refer to the cock as "mine," say "I" fought So-and-So, and so on, demonstrates. Also, owner-handler-affixer triads tend to be fairly fixed, though individuals may participate in several and often exchange roles within a given one.

[10] Erving Goffman, *Encounters: Two Studies in the Sociology of Interaction* (Indianapolis: Bobbs-Merrill, 1961), pp. 9–10.

[11] This word, which literally means an indelible stain or mark, as in a birthmark or a vein in a stone, is used as well for a deposit in a court case, for a pawn, for security offered in a loan, for a stand-in for someone else in a legal or ceremonial context, for an

earnest advanced in a business deal, for a sign placed in a field to indicate its ownership is in dispute, and for the status of an unfaithful wife from whose lover her husband must gain satisfaction or surrender her to him. See Korn, *Het Adatrecht van Bali;* Theodoor Pigeaud, *Javaans-Nederlands Handwoordenbock* (Groningen: Wolters, 1938); H. H. Juynboll, *Oudjavaansche-Nederlandsche Woordenlijst* (Leiden: Brill, 1923).

[12]The center bet must be advanced in cash by both parties prior to the actual fight. The umpire holds the stakes until the decision is rendered and then awards them to the winner, avoiding, among other things, the intense embarrassment both winner and loser would feel if the latter had to pay off personally following his defeat. About 10 per cent of the winner's receipts are subtracted for the umpire's share and that of the fight sponsors.

[13]Actually, the typing of cocks, which is extremely elaborate (I have collected more than twenty classes, certainly not a complete list), is not based on color alone, but on a series of independent, interacting, dimensions, which include, beside color, size, bone thickness, plumage, and temperament. (But *not* pedigree. The Balinese do not breed cocks to any significant extent, nor, so far as I have been able to discover, have they ever done so. The *asil,* or jungle cock, which is the basic fighting strain everywhere the sport is found, is native to southern Asia, and one can buy a good example in the chicken section of almost any Balinese market for anywhere from four or five ringgits up to fifty or more.) The color element is merely the one normally used as the type name, except when the two cocks of different types—as on principle they must be—have the same color, in which case a secondary indication from one of the other dimensions ("large speckled" v. "small speckled," etc.) is added. The types are coordinated with various cosmological ideas which help shape the making of matches, so that, for example, you fight a small, headstrong, speckled brown-on-white cock with flat-lying feathers and thin legs from the east side of the ring on a certain day of the complex Balinese calendar, and a large, cautious, all-black cock with tufted feathers and stubby legs from the north side on another day, and so on. All this is again recorded in palm-leaf manuscripts and endlessly discussed by the Balinese (who do not all have identical systems), and full-scale componential-cum-symbolic analysis of cock classifications would be extremely valuable both as an adjunct to the description of the cockfight and in itself. But my data on the subject, though extensive and varied, do not seem to be complete and systematic enough to attempt such an analysis here. For Balinese cosmological ideas more generally see Belo, ed., *Traditional Balinese Culture,* and J. L. Swellengrebel, ed., *Bali: Studies in Life, Thought, and Ritual* (The Hague: W. van Hoeve, 1960); for calendrical ones, Clifford Geertz, *Person, Time, and Conduct in Bali: An Essay in Cultural Analysis* (New Haven: Southeast Asia Studies, Yale University, 1966), pp. 45–53.

[14]For purposes of ethnographic completeness, it should be noted that it is possible for the man backing the favorite—the odds-giver—to make a bet in which he wins if his cock wins or there is a tie, a slight shortening of the odds (I do not have enough cases to be exact, but ties seem to occur about once every fifteen or twenty matches). He indicates his wish to do this by shouting *sapih* ("tie") rather than the cock-type, but such bets are in fact infrequent.

[15]The precise dynamics of the movement of the betting is one of the most intriguing, most complicated, and, given the hectic conditions under which it occurs, most difficult to study, aspects of the fight. Motion picture recording plus multiple observers would probably be necessary to deal with it effectively. Even impressionistically—the only approach open to a lone ethnographer caught in the middle of all this—it is clear that certain men lead both in determining the favorite (that is, making the opening cock-type calls which always initiate the process) and in directing the movement of the odds, these "opinion leaders" being the more accomplished cockfighters-cum-solid-citizens to be dis-

cussed below. If these men begin to change their calls, others follow; if they begin to make bets, so do others and—though there is always a large number of frustrated bettors crying for shorter or longer odds to the end—the movement more or less ceases. But a detailed understanding of the whole process awaits what, alas, it is not very likely ever to get: a decision theorist armed with precise observations of individual behavior.

[16]Assuming only binomial variability, the departure from a fifty-fifty expectation in the sixty ringgits and below case is 1.38 standard deviations, or (in a one direction test) an eight in one hundred possibility by chance alone; for the below forty ringgits case it is 1.65 standard deviations, or about five in one hundred. The fact that these departures though real are not extreme merely indicates, again, that even in the smaller fights the tendency to match cocks at least reasonably evenly persists. It is a matter of relative relaxation of the pressures toward equalization, not their elimination. The tendency for high-bet contests to be coin-flip propositions is, of course, even more striking, and suggests the Balinese know quite well what they are about.

[17]The reduction in wagering in smaller fights (which, of course, feeds on itself; one of the reasons people find small fights uninteresting is that there is less wagering in them, and contrariwise for large ones) takes place in three mutually reinforcing ways. First, there is a simple withdrawal of interest as people wander off to have a cup of coffee or chat with a friend. Second, the Balinese do not mathematically reduce odds, but bet directly in terms of stated odds as such. Thus, for a nine-to-eight bet, one man wagers nine ringgits, the other eight; for five-to-four, one wagers five, the other four. For any given currency unit, like the ringgit, therefore, 6.3 times as much money is involved in a ten-to-nine bet as in a two-to-one bet, for example, and, as noted, in small fights betting settles toward the longer end. Finally, the bets which are made tend to be one- rather than two-, three-, or in some of the very largest fights, four- or five-finger ones. (The fingers indicate the *multiples* of the stated bet odds at issue, not absolute figures. Two fingers in a six-to-five situation means a man wants to wager ten ringgits on the underdog against twelve, three in an eight-to-seven situation, twenty-one against twenty-four, and so on.)

[18]Besides wagering there are other economic aspects of the cockfight, especially its very close connection with the local market system which, though secondary both to its motivation and to its function, are not without importance. Cockfights are open events to which anyone who wishes may come, sometimes from quite distant areas, but well over 90 per cent, probably over 95, are very local affairs, and the locality concerned is defined not by the village, nor even by the administrative district, but by the rural market system. Bali has a three-day market week with the familiar "solar-system" type rotation. Though the markets themselves have never been very highly developed, small morning affairs in a village square, it is the microregion such rotation rather generally marks out—ten or twenty square miles, seven or eight neighboring villages (which in contemporary Bali is usually going to mean anywhere from five to ten or eleven thousand people) from which the core of any cockfight audience, indeed virtually all of it, will come. Most of the fights are in fact organized and sponsored by small combines of petty rural merchants under the general premise, very strongly held by them and indeed by all Balinese, that cockfights are good for trade because "they get money out of the house, they make it circulate." Stalls selling various sorts of things as well as assorted sheer-chance gambling games (see below) are set up around the edge of the area so that this even takes on the quality of a small fair. This connection of cockfighting with markets and market sellers is very old, as, among other things, their conjunction in inscriptions (Roelof Goris, *Prasasti Bali,* 2 vols. [Bandung: N. V. Masa Baru, 1954]) indicates. Trade has followed the cock for centuries in rural Bali and the sport has been one of the main agencies of the island's monetization.

[19]The phrase is found in the Hildreth translation, International Liberty of Psychology, 1931, note to p. 106; see L. L. Fuller, *The Morality of Law* (New Haven: Yale University Press, 1964), pp. 6ff.

[20]Of course, even in Bentham, utility is not normally confined as a concept to monetary losses and gains, and my argument here might be more carefully put in terms of a denial that for the Balinese, as for any people, utility (pleasure, happiness . . .) is merely identifiable with wealth. But such terminological problems are in any case secondary to the essential point: the cockfight is not roulette.

[21]Max Weber, *The Sociology of Religion* (Boston: Beacon Press, 1963). There is nothing specifically Balinese, of course, about deepening significance with money, as Whyte's description of corner boys in a working-class district of Boston demonstrates: "Gambling plays an important role in the lives of Cornerville people. Whatever game the corner boys play, they nearly always bet on the outcome. When there is nothing at stake, the game is not considered a real contest. This does not mean that the financial element is all-important. I have frequently heard men say that the honor of winning was much more important than the money at stake. The corner boys consider playing for money the real test of skill and, unless a man performs well when money is at stake, he is not considered a good competitor." W. F. Whyte, *Street Corner Society*, 2d ed. (Chicago: University of Chicago Press, 1955), p. 140.

[22]The extremes to which this madness is conceived on occasion to go—and the fact that it is considered madness—is demonstrated by the Balinese folktale *I Tuhung Kuning.* A gambler becomes so deranged by his passion that, leaving on a trip, he orders his pregnant wife to take care of the prospective newborn if it is a boy but to feed it as meat to his fighting cocks if it is a girl. The mother gives birth to a girl, but rather than giving the child to the cocks she gives them a large rat and conceals the girl with her own mother. When the husband returns the cocks, crowing a jingle, inform him of the deception and, furious, he sets out to kill the child. A goddess descends from heaven and takes the girl up to the skies with her. The cocks die from the food given them, the owner's sanity is restored, the goddess brings the girl back to the father who reunites him with his wife. The story is given as "Geel Komkommertje" in Jacoba Hooykaas-van Leeuwen Boomkamp, *Sprookjes en Verhalen van Bali* ('S-Gravenhage: Van Hoeve, 1956), pp. 19–25.

[23]For a fuller description of Balinese rural social structure, see Clifford Geertz, "Form and Variation in Balinese Village Structure," *American Anthropologist*, 61 (1959), 94–108; "Tihingan, A Balinese Village," in R. M. Koentjaraningrat, *Villages in Indonesia* (Ithaca: Cornell University Press, 1967), pp. 210–243; and, though it is a bit off the norm as Balinese villages go, V. E. Korn, *De Dorpsrepubliek tnganan Pagringsingan* (Santpoort [Netherlands]: C. A. Mees, 1933).

[24]Goffman, *Encounters*, p. 78.

[25]B. R. Berelson, P. F. Lazersfeld, and W. N. McPhee, *Voting: A Study of Opinion Formation in a Presidential Campaign* (Chicago: University of Chicago Press, 1954).

[26]As this is a formal paradigm, it is intended to display the logical, not the causal, structure of cockfighting. Just which of these considerations leads to which, in what order, and by what mechanisms, is another matter—one I have attempted to shed some light on in the general discussion.

[27]In another of Hooykaas-van Leeuwen Boomkamp's folk tales ("De Gast," *Sprookies en Verhalen van Bali*, pp. 172–180), a low caste *Sudra*, a generous pious, and carefree man who is also an accomplished cock fighter, loses, despite his accomplishment, fight after fight until he is not only out of money but down to his last cock. He does not despair, however—"I bet," he says, "upon the Unseen World."

His wife, a good and hard-working woman, knowing how much he enjoys cockfighting, gives him her last "rainy day" money to go and bet. But, filled with misgivings due to his run of ill luck, he leaves his own cock at home and bets merely on the side. He soon loses all but a coin or two and repairs to a food stand for a snack, where he meets a decrepit, odorous, and generally unappetizing older beggar leaning on a staff. The old man asks for food, and the hero spends his last coins to buy him some. The old man then asks to pass the night with the hero, which the hero gladly invites him to do. As there is no food in the house, however, the hero tells his wife to kill the last cock for dinner. When the old man discovers this fact, he tells the hero he has three cocks in his own mountain hut and says the hero may have one of them for fighting. He also asks for the hero's son to accompany him as a servant, and, after the son agrees, this is done.

The old man turns out to be Siva and, thus, to live in a great palace in the sky, though the hero does not know this. In time, the hero decides to visit his son and collect the promised cock. Lifted up into Siva's presence, he is given the choice of three cocks. The first crows: "I have beaten fifteen opponents." The second crows, "I have beaten twenty-five opponents." The third crows, "I have beaten the King." "That one, the third, is my choice," says the hero, and returns with it to earth.

When he arrives at the cockfight, he is asked for an entry fee and replies, "I have no money; I will pay after my cock has won." As he is known never to win, he is let in because the king, who is there fighting, dislikes him and hopes to enslave him when he loses and cannot pay off. In order to insure that this happens, the king matches his finest cock against the hero's. When the cocks are placed down, the hero's flees, and the crowd, led by the arrogant king, hoots in laughter. The hero's cock then flies at the king himself, killing him with a spur stab in the throat. The hero flees. His house is encircled by the king's men. The cock changes into a Garuda, the great mythic bird of Indic legend, and carries the hero and his wife to safety in the heavens.

When the people see this, they make the hero king and his wife queen and they return as such to earth. Later his son, released by Siva, also returns and the hero-king announces his intention to enter a hermitage. ("I will fight no more cockfights. I have bet on the Unseen and won.") He enters the hermitage and his son becomes king.

[28] Addict gamblers are really less declassed (for their status is, as everyone else's, inherited) than merely impoverished and personally disgraced. The most prominent addict gambler in my cockfight circuit was actually a very high caste *satria* who sold off most of his considerable lands to support his habit. Though everyone privately regarded him as a fool and worse (some, more charitable, regarded him as sick), he was publicly treated with the elaborate deference and politeness due his rank. On the independence of personal reputation and public status in Bali, see Geertz, *Person, Time, and Conduct,* pp. 28–35.

[29] For four, somewhat variant treatments, see Susanne Langer, *Feeling and Form* (New York: Scribners, 1953); Richard Wollheim, *Art and Its Objects* (New York: Harper and Row, 1968); Nelson Goodman, *Languages of Art* (Indianapolis: Bobbs-Merrill, 1968); Maurice Merleau-Ponty, "The Eye and the Mind," in his, *The Primacy of Perception* (Evanston: Northwestern University Press, 1964), pp. 159–190.

[30] British cockfights (the sport was banned there in 1840) indeed seem to have lacked it, and to have generated, therefore, a quite different family of shapes. Most British fights were "mains," in which a preagreed number of cocks were aligned into two teams and fought serially. Score was kept and wagering took place both on the individual matches and on the main as a whole. There were also "battle Royales," both in England and on the Continent, in which a large number of cocks were let loose at once with the one left standing at the end the victor. And in Wales, the so-called "Welsh main" followed an elimination pattern, along the lines of a present-day tennis tournament, winners proceeding to the next round. As a genre, the cockfight has perhaps less compositional

flexibility than, say, Latin comedy, but it is not entirely without any. On cockfighting more generally, see Arch Ruport, *The Act of Cockfighting* (New York: Devin-Adair, 1949); G. R. Scott, *History of Cockfighting* (1957); and Lawrence Fitz-Barnard, *Fighting Sports* (London: Odhams Press, 1921).

[31] *Person, Time, and Conduct,* esp. pp. 42ff. I am, however, not the first person to have argued it: see G. Bateson, "Bali, the Value System of a Steady State," and "An Old Temple and a New Myth," in Belo, ed., *Traditional Balinese Culture,* pp. 384–402 and 111–136.

[32] For the necessity of distinguishing among "description," "representation," "exemplification," and "expression" (and the irrelevance of "imitation" to all of them), as modes of symbolic reference, see Goodman, *Languages of Art,* pp. 6–10, 45–91, 225–241.

[33] Northrop Frye, *The Educated Imagination* (Bloomington: University of Indiana Press, 1964), p. 99.

[34] There are two other Balinese values and disvalues which, connected with punctuate temporality on the one hand and unbridled aggressiveness on the other, reinforce the sense that the cockfight is at once continuous with ordinary social life and a direct negation of it: what the Balinese call *ramé,* and what they call *paling. Ramé* means crowded, noisy, and active, and is a highly sought after social state: crowded markets, mass festivals, busy streets are all *ramé,* as, of course, is, in the extreme, a cockfight. *Ramé* is what happens in the "full" times (its opposite, *sepi,* "quiet," is what happens in the "empty" ones). *Paling* is social vertigo, the dizzy, disoriented, lost, turned around feeling one gets when one's place in the coordinates of social space is not clear, and it is tremendously disfavored, immensely anxiety-producing state. Balinese regard the exact maintenance of spatial orientation ("not to know where north is" is to be crazy), balance, decorum, status relationships, and so forth, as fundamental to ordered life *(krama)* and *paling,* the sort of whirling confusion of position the scrambling cocks exemplify as its profoundest enemy and contradiction. On *ramé,* see Bateson and Mead, *Balinese Character,* pp. 3, 64; on *paling, ibid.,* p. 11, and Belo, ed., *Traditional Balinese Culture,* pp. 90ff.

[35] The Stevens reference is to his "The Motive for Metaphor," ("You like it under the trees in autumn,/Because everything is half dead./The wind moves like a cripple among the leaves/And repeats words without meaning"); the Schoenberg reference is to the third of his *Five Orchestral Pieces* (Opus 16), and is borrowed from H. H. Drager, "The Concept of 'Tonal Body,' " in Susanne Langer, ed., *Reflections of Art* (New York: Oxford University Press, 1961), p. 174. On Hogarth, and on this whole problem—there called "multiple matrix matching"—see E. H. Gombrich, "The Use of Art for the Study of Symbols," in James Hogg, ed., *Psychology and the Visual Arts* (Baltimore: Penguin Books, 1969), pp. 149–170. The more usual term for this sort of semantic alchemy is "metaphorical transfer," and good technical discussions of it can be found in M. Black, *Models and Metaphors* (Ithaca: Cornell University Press, 1962), pp. 25ff; Goodman, *Language as Art,* pp. 44ff; and W. Percy, "Metaphor as Mistake," *Sewanee Review,* 66 (1958), 78–99.

[36] The tag is from the second book of the *Organon, On Interpretation.* For a discussion of it, and for the whole argument for freeing "the notion of text . . . from the notion of scripture or writing," and constructing, thus, a general hermeneutics, see Paul Ricoeur, *Freud and Philosophy* (New Haven: Yale University Press, 1970), pp. 20ff.

[37] *Ibid.*

[38] Lévi-Strauss's "structuralism" might seem an exception. But it is only an apparent one, for, rather than taking myths, totem rites, marriage rules, or whatever as texts to interpret, Lévi-Strauss takes them as ciphers to solve, which is very much not the same thing. He does not seek to understand symbolic forms in terms of how they function in concrete situations to organize perceptions (meanings, emotions, concepts, attitudes); he seeks to understand them entirely in terms of their internal structure, *indépendent de tout*

sujet, de tout objet, et de toute contexte. For my own view of this approach—that is suggestive and indefensible—see Clifford Geertz, "The Cerebral Savage: On the Work of Lévi-Strauss," *Encounter,* 48 (1967), 25–32.

[39]Frye, *The Educated Imagination,* pp. 63–64.

[40]The use of the, to Europeans, "natural" visual idiom for perception—"see," "watches," and so forth—is more than usually misleading here, for the fact that, as mentioned earlier, Balinese follow the progress of the fight as much (perhaps, as fighting cocks are actually rather hard to see except as blurs of motion, more) with their bodies as with their eyes, moving their limbs, heads, and trunks in gestural mimicry of the cocks' maneuvers, means that much of the individual's experience of the fight is kinesthetic rather than visual. If ever there was an example of Kenneth Burke's definition of a symbolic act as "the dancing of an attitude" (*The Philosophy of Literary Form,* rev. ed. [New York: Vintage Books, 1957], p. 9) the cockfight is it. On the enormous role of kinesthetic perception in Balinese life, Bateson and Mean, *Balinese Character,* pp. 84–88; on the active nature of aesthetic perception in general, Goodman, *Language of Art,* pp. 241–244.

[41]All this coupling of the occidental great with the oriental lowly will doubtless disturb certain sorts of aestheticians as the earlier effort of anthropologists to speak of Christianity and totemism in the same breath disturbed certain sorts of theologians. But as ontological questions are (or should be) bracketed in the sociology of religion, judgmental ones are (or should be) bracketed in the sociology of art. In any case, the attempt to deprovincialize the concept of art is but part of the general anthropological conspiracy to deprovincialize all important social concepts—marriage, religion, law, rationality—and though this is a threat to aesthetic theories which regard certain works of art as beyond the reach of sociological analysis, it is no threat to the conviction, for which Robert Graves claims to have been reprimanded at his Cambridge tripos, that some poems are better than others.

[42]For the consecration ceremony, see V. E. Korn, "The Consecration of the Priest," in Swellengrebel, ed., *Bali,* pp. 131–154; for (somewhat exaggerated) village communion, Roelof Goris, "The Religious Character of the Balinese Village," *ibid.,* pp. 79–100.

[43]That what the cockfight has to say about Bali is not altogether without perception and the disquiet it expresses about the general pattern of Balinese life is not wholly without reason is attested by the fact that in two weeks of December, 1965, during the upheavals following the unsuccessful coup in Djakarta, between forty and eighty thousand Balinese (in a population of about two million) were killed, largely by one another—the worst outburst in the country. (John Hughes, *Indonesian Upheaval* [New York: McKay, 1967], pp. 173–183. Hughes's figures are, of course, rather casual estimates, but they are not the most extreme.) This is not to say, of course, that the killings were caused by the cockfight, could have been predicted on the basis of it, or were some sort of enlarged version of it with real people in the place of the cocks—all of which is nonsense. It is merely to say that if one looks at Bali not just through the medium of its dances, its shadowplays, its sculpture, and its girls, but—as the Balinese themselves do—also through the medium of its cockfight, the fact that the massacre occurred seems, if no less appealing, less like a contradiction to the laws of nature. As more than one real Gloucester has discovered, sometimes people actually get life precisely as they most deeply do not want it.

• • • • • • • • • • • • •

QUESTIONS FOR A SECOND READING

1. Geertz says that the cockfight provides a "commentary upon the whole matter of sorting human beings into fixed hierarchical ranks and then organizing the major parts of collective existence around that assortment." The cockfights don't reinforce the patterns of Balinese life; they comment on them. Perhaps the first question to ask as you go back to the essay is, "What is that commentary?" What do the cockfights say? And what don't they say?
2. "Deep Play: Notes on the Balinese Cockfight" is divided into seven sections. As you reread the essay, pay attention to the connections between these sections and the differences in the way they are written and in what they propose to do (some, for example, tell stories, some use numbers, some have more footnotes than others).

   What is the logic or system that makes one section follow another? Do you see the subtitles as seven headings on a topic outline? The last two sections are perhaps the most difficult to read and understand. They also make repeated reference to literary texts. Why? What is Geertz doing here?

   If you look at the differences in the style or method of each section, what might they be said to represent? If each is evident of something Geertz, as an anthropologist, knows how to do, what, in each case, is he doing? What is his expertise? And why, in each case, would it require this particular style of writing?
3. Throughout the essay Geertz is working very hard to *do* something with what he observed in Bali. (There are "enormous difficulties in such an enterprise," he says.) He is also, however, working hard *not* to do some things. (He doesn't want to be a "formalist," for example.) As you read the essay for the second time, look for passages that help you specifically define what it is Geertz wants to do and what it is he wants to be sure not to do.

ASSIGNMENTS FOR WRITING

1. If this essay were your only evidence, how might you describe the work of an anthropologist? What do anthropologists do and how do they do what they do? Write an essay in which you look at "Deep Play" section by section, describing on the basis of each what it is that an anthropologist must be able to do. In each case, you have the chance to watch Geertz at work. (Your essay, then, might well have sections that correspond to Geertz's.) When you have worked through them all, write a final section that discusses how these various skills or arts fit together to define the expertise of someone like Geertz.

2. Geertz says that "the culture of a people is an ensemble of texts, themselves ensembles, which the anthropologist strains to read over the shoulders of those to whom they properly belong." Anthropologists are expert at "reading" in this way. One of the interesting things about being a student is that you get to (or you have to) act like an expert even though, properly speaking, you are not. Write an essay in which you prepare a Geertzian "reading" of some part of our culture you know well (sorority rush, window-shopping in a shopping mall, studying in the library, decorating a dorm room, whatever). Ideally, you should go out and observe the behavior you are studying, examining it and taking notes with your project in mind. You should imagine that you are working in Geertz's spirit, imitating his method and style and carrying out work that he has begun.

MAKING CONNECTIONS

1. Geertz was trained as an anthropologist and Robert Coles (p. 88) was trained as a child psychiatrist. Both, however, went off to foreign territory (and you should work with the assumption that the world of wealthy children was foreign to Coles) to study the people and to learn what they could about who they were, how they saw the world, and why they acted as they did.

   Write an essay in which you explore and describe the different methods of these two scholars. What do they notice? What do they do with what they notice? And what can you say, then, about the possibilities and limitations of each method of analysis?

2. In "The Loss of the Creature" (p. 394), Walker Percy writes about tourists (actually several different kinds of tourists) and the difficulty they have seeing what lies before them. Properly speaking, anthropologists are not tourists. There is a scholarly purpose to their travel, and presumably they have learned or developed the strategies necessary to get beyond the preformed "symbolic complexes" which would keep them from seeing the place or the people they have traveled to study. Geertz is an expert, in other words, not just any "layman seer of sights."

   In his travels to Bali, Geertz seems to get just what he wants. He gets both the authentic experience and a complex understanding of that experience. If you read "Deep Play" from the perspective of Percy's essay, however, it is interesting to ask whether Percy would say that this was the case, and it is interesting to ask how Percy would characterize the "strategies" that define Geertz's approach to his subject.

   Write an essay in which you place Geertz in the context of Percy's tourists—not all of them, but the two or three whose stories seem most interesting when placed alongside Geertz's. The purpose of your essay should be to determine whether or not Geertz has solved the problem Percy defines for the tourist in "The Loss of the Creature."

THOMAS KUHN

THOMAS KUHN was once referred to by Clifford Geertz as an "all-purpose subversive," a man responsible for one of the "shaking originalities" of our century. It is an apt description. His work has not only revised our way of understanding scientific progress, it has given us a new way of looking at progress in any academic discipline or communal enterprise.

The key term in Kuhn's theory (and the most controversial term) is "paradigm." According to Kuhn, scientists work within a common paradigm when they work with a shared storehouse of examples, a shared set of theories to explain those examples, and a shared set of procedures to look at new ones. Essentially, these scientists have all had the same training; they all read the same journals, share the same goals, adhere to the same principles, and conduct their work in a similar fashion.

Kuhn argues that scientists can happily and profitably work within a paradigm (astronomers can go to the observatory and assume that it is their job to look at the stars in pretty much the same way as all other astronomers). Something significant and dramatic occurs, however, when a scientist steps outside the paradigm, when the old examples and explanations no longer hold, and scientists suddenly see the world in a fundamentally different way (as when the sun, rather than the earth, was recognized as the center of our planetary system). Kuhn presents this argument in his book The Structure of Scientific Revolutions, *but part of the argument is nicely summarized in an earlier paper of his, "The Historical Structure of Scientific Discovery," first published in the journal* Science.

Kuhn was born in 1922 in Cincinnati and attended Harvard University, graduating summa cum laude in physics in 1943. He earned his Ph.D., also at Harvard, six years later. A Guggenheim fellow in 1954–55, Kuhn worked for the U.S. Office of Scientific Research and Development before teaching at the University of California at Berkeley, at Princeton, and at MIT. Kuhn was trained as a physicist but now works in the history of science, a field that originally attracted him when he noticed how different science looked to an historian, someone looking in from the outside.

The Historical Structure of Scientific Discovery

My object in this article is to isolate and illuminate one small part of what I take to be a continuing historiographic revolution in the study of science. The structure of scientific discovery is my particular topic, and I can best approach it by pointing out that the subject itself may well seem extraordinarily odd. Both scientists and, until quite recently, historians have ordinarily viewed discovery as the sort of event which, though it may have preconditions and surely has consequences, is itself without internal structure. Rather than being seen as a complex development extended both in space and time, discovering something has usually seemed to be a unitary event, one which, like seeing something, happens to an individual at a specific time and place.

This view of the nature of discovery has, I suspect, deep roots in the nature of the scientific community. One of the few historical elements recurrent in the textbooks from which the prospective scientist learns his field is the attribution of particular natural phenomena to the historical personages who first discovered them. As a result of this and other aspects of their training, discovery becomes for many scientists an important goal. To make a discovery is to achieve one of the closest approximations to a property right that the scientific career affords. Professional prestige is often closely associated with these acquisitions.[1] Small wonder, then, that acrimonious disputes about priority and independence in discovery have often marred the normally placid tenor of scientific communication. Even less wonder that many historians of science have seen the individual discovery as an appropriate unit with which to measure scientific progress and have devoted much time and skill to determining what man made which discovery at what point in time. If the study of discovery has a surprise to offer, it is only that, despite the immense energy and ingenuity expended upon it, neither polemic nor painstaking scholarship has often succeeded in pinpointing the time and place at which a given discovery could properly be said to have "been made."

That failure, both of argument and of research, suggests the thesis that I now wish to develop. Many scientific discoveries, particularly the most interesting and important, are not the sort of event about which the questions "Where?" and, more particularly, "When?" can appropriately be asked. Even if all conceivable data were at hand, those questions would not regularly possess answers. That we are persistently driven to ask them nonetheless is symptomatic of a fundamental inappropriateness in our image of discovery. That inappropriateness is here my main concern, but I approach it by considering first the historical problem presented by the attempt to date and to place a major class of fundamental discoveries.

The troublesome class consists of those discoveries—including oxygen, the electric current, X rays, and the electron—which could not be predicted from accepted theory in advance and which therefore caught the assembled profession by surprise. That kind of discovery will shortly be my exclusive concern, but it will help first to note that there is another sort and one which presents very few of the same problems. Into this second class of discoveries fall the neutrino, radio waves, and the elements which filled empty places in the periodic table. The existence of all these objects had been predicted from theory before they were discovered, and the men who made the discoveries therefore knew from the start what to look for. That foreknowledge did not make their task less demanding or less interesting, but it did provide criteria which told them when their goal had been reached.[2] As a result, there have been few priority debates over discoveries

[1] For a brilliant discussion of these points, see R. K. Merton, "Priorities in Scientific Discovery: A Chapter in the Sociology of Science," *American Sociological Review* 22 (1957): 635. Also very relevant, though it did not appear until this article had been prepared, is F. Reif, "The Competitive World of the Pure Scientist," *Science* 134 (1961): 1957.

[2] Not all discoveries fall so neatly as the preceding into one or the other of my two classes. For example, Anderson's work on the positron was done in complete ignorance of Dirac's theory from which the new particle's existence had already been very nearly predicted. On the other hand, the immediately succeeding work by Blackett and Occhialini made full use of Dirac's theory and therefore exploited experiment more fully and

of this second sort, and only a paucity of data can prevent the historian from ascribing them to a particular time and place. Those facts help to isolate the difficulties we encounter as we return to the troublesome discoveries of the first class. In the cases that most concern us here there are no benchmarks to inform either the scientist or the historian when the job of discovery has been done.

As an illustration of this fundamental problem and its consequences, consider first the discovery of oxygen. Because it has repeatedly been studied, often with exemplary care and skill, that discovery is unlikely to offer any purely factual surprises. Therefore it is particularly well suited to clarify points of principle.[3] At least three scientists—Carl Scheele, Joseph Priestley, and Antoine Lavoisier—have a legitimate claim to this discovery, and polemicists have occasionally entered the same claim for Pierre Bayen.[4] Scheele's work, though it was almost certainly completed before the relevant researches of Priestley and Lavoisier, was not made public until their work was well known.[5] Therefore it had no apparent causal role, and I shall simplify my story by omitting it.[6] Instead, I pick up the main route

---

constructed a more forceful case for the positron's existence than Anderson had been able to do. On this subject see N. R. Hanson, "Discovering the Positron," *British Journal for the Philosophy of Science* 12 (1961): 194; 12 (1962): 299. Hanson suggests several of the points developed here. I am much indebted to Professor Hanson for a preprint of this material.

[3] I have developed a less familiar example from the same viewpoint in "The Caloric Theory of Adiabatic Compression," *Isis* 49 (1958): 132. A closely similar analysis of the emergence of a new theory is included in the early pages of my essay "Energy Conservation as an Example of Simultaneous Discovery," in *Critical Problems in the History of Science*, ed. M. Clagett (Madison: University of Wisconsin Press, 1959), pp. 321–56 (pp. 66–104 above). Reference to these papers may add depth and detail to the following discussion.

[4] The still classic discussion of the discovery of oxygen is A. N. Meldrum, *The Eighteenth Century Revolution in Science: The First Phase* (Calcutta, 1930), chap. 5. A more convenient and generally quite reliable discussion is included in J. B. Conant, *The Overthrow of the Phlogiston Theory: The Chemical Revolution of 1775–1789*, Harvard Case Histories in Experimental Science, case 2 (Cambridge: Harvard University Press, 1950). A recent and indispensable review which includes an account of the development of the priority controversy, is M. Daumas, *Lavoisier, théoricien et expérimentateur* (Paris, 1955), chaps. 2 and 3. H. Guerlac has added much significant detail to our knowledge of the early relations between Priestley and Lavoisier in his "Joseph Priestley's First Papers on Gases and Their Reception in France," *Journal of the History of Medicine* 12 (1957): 1 and in his very recent monograph, *Lavoisier: The Crucial Year* (Ithaca: Cornell University Press, 1961). For Scheele see J. R. Partington, *A Short History of Chemistry*. 2d ed. (London, 1951), pp. 104–09.

[5] For the dating of Scheele's work, see A. E. Nordenskjöld, *Carl Wilhelm Scheele, Nachgelassene Briefe und Aufzeichnungen* (Stockholm, 1892).

[6] U. Bocklund ("A Lost Letter from Scheele to Lavoisier," *Lychnos*, 1957–58, pp. 39–62) argues that Scheele communicated his discovery of oxygen to Lavoisier in a letter of

to the discovery of oxygen with the work of Bayen, who, sometime before March 1774, discovered that red precipitate of mercury (HgO) could, by heating, be made to yield a gas. That aeriform product Bayen identified as fixed air (CO_2), a substance made familiar to most pneumatic chemists by the earlier work of Joseph Black.[7] A variety of other substances were known to yield the same gas.

At the beginning of August 1774, a few months after Bayen's work had appeared, Joseph Priestley repeated the experiment, though probably independently. Priestly, however, observed that the gaseous product would support combustion and therefore changed the identification. For him the gas obtained on heating red precipitate was nitrous air (N_2O), a substance that he had himself discovered more than two years before.[8] Later in the same month Priestley made a trip to Paris and there informed Lavoisier of the new reaction. The latter repeated the experiment once more, both in November 1775 and in February 1774. But, because he used tests somewhat more elaborate than Priestley's, Lavoisier again changed the identification. For him, as of May 1775, the gas released by red precipitate was neither fixed air nor nitrous air. Instead, it was "[atmospheric] air itself entire without alteration . . . even to the point that . . . it comes out more pure."[9] Meanwhile, however, Priestley had also been at work, and, before the beginning of March 1775, he, too, had concluded that the gas must be "common air." Until this point all of the men who had produced a gas from red precipitate of mercury had identified it with some previously known species.[10]

The remainder of this story of discovery is briefly told. During March 1775 Priestley discovered that his gas was in several respects very much

30 Sept. 1774. Certainly the letter is important, and it clearly demonstrates that Scheele was ahead of both Priestley and Lavoisier at the time it was written. But I think the letter is not quite so candid as Bocklund supposes, and I fail to see how Lavoisier could have drawn the discovery of oxygen from it. Scheele describes a procedure for reconstituting common air, not for producing a new gas, and that, as we shall see, is almost the same information that Lavoisier received from Priestley at about the same time. In any case, there is no evidence that Lavoisier performed the sort of experiment that Scheele suggested.

[7] P. Bayen, "Essai d'expériences chymiques, faites sur quelques précipités de mercure, dans la vue de découvrir leur nature, Seconde partie," *Observations sur la physique* 3 (1774): 280–95, particularly pp. 289–91.

[8] J. B. Conant, *The Overthrow of the Phlogiston Theory,* pp. 34–40.

[9] Ibid., p. 23. A useful translation of the full text is available in Conant.

[10] For simplicity I use the term *red precipitate* throughout. Actually, Bayen used the precipitate; Priestley used both the precipitate and the oxide produced by direct calcination of mercury; and Lavoisier used only the latter. The difference is not without importance, for it was not unequivocally clear to chemists that the two substances were identical.

"better" than common air, and he therefore reidentified the gas once more, this time calling it "dephlogisticated air," that is, atmospheric air deprived of its normal complement of phlogiston.° This conclusion Priestley published in the *Philosophical Transactions*, and it was apparently that publication which led Lavoisier to reexamine his own results.[11] The reexamination began during February 1776 and within a year had led Lavoisier to the conclusion that the gas was actually a separable component of the atmospheric air which both he and Priestley had previously thought of as homogeneous. With this point reached, with the gas recognized as an irreducibly distinct species, we may conclude that the discovery of oxygen had been completed.

But to return to my initial question, when shall we say that oxygen was discovered and what criteria shall we use in answering that question? If discovering oxygen is simply holding an impure sample in one's hands, then the gas had been "discovered" in antiquity by the first man who ever bottled atmospheric air. Undoubtedly, for an experimental criterion, we must at least require a relatively pure sample like that obtained by Priestley in August 1774. But during 1774 Priestley was unaware that he had discovered anything except a new way to produce a relatively familiar species. Throughout that year his "discovery" is scarcely distinguishable from the one made earlier by Bayen, and neither case is quite distinct from that of the Reverend Stephen Hales, who had obtained the same gas more than forty years before.[12] Apparently to discover something one must also be aware of the discovery and know as well what it is that one has discovered.

But, that being the case, how much must one know? Had Priestley come close enough when he identified the gas as nitrous air? If not, was either he or Lavoisier significantly closer when he changed the identification to common air? And what are we to say about Priestley's next identification, the one made in March 1775? Dephlogisticated air is still not oxygen or even, for the phlogistic chemist, a quite unexpected sort of gas. Rather it is a particularly pure atmospheric air. Presumably, then, we wait for Lavoisier's work in 1776 and 1777, work which led him not merely to isolate the gas but to see what it was. Yet even that decision can be questioned, for in 1777 and to the end of his life Lavoisier insisted that oxygen was an

---

Phlogiston Was once believed to be the element that caused combustion and that was given off by anything burning.

[11] There has been some doubt about Priestley's having influenced Lavoisier's thinking at this point, but, when the latter returned to experimenting with the gas in February 1776, he recorded in his notebooks that he had obtained "l'air dephlogistique de M. Priestley" (M. Daumas, *Lavoisier*, p. 36).

[12] J. R. Partington, *A Short History of Chemistry*, p. 91.

atomic "principle of acidity" and that oxygen *gas* was formed only when that "principle" united with caloric, the matter of heat.[13] Shall we therefore say that oxygen had not yet been discovered in 1777? Some may be tempted to do so. But the principle of acidity was not banished from chemistry until after 1810 and caloric lingered on until the 1860s. Oxygen had, however, become a standard chemical substance long before either of those dates. Furthermore, what is perhaps the key point, it would probably have gained that status on the basis of Priestley's work alone without benefit of Lavoisier's still partial reinterpretation.

I conclude that we need a new vocabulary and new concepts for analyzing events like the discovery of oxygen. Though undoubtedly correct, the sentence "Oxygen was discovered" misleads by suggesting that discovering something is a single simple act unequivocally attributable, if only we knew enough, to an individual and an instant in time. When the discovery is unexpected, however, the latter attribution is always impossible and the former often is as well. Ignoring Scheele, we can, for example, safely say that oxygen had not been discovered before 1774; probably we would also insist that it had been discovered by 1777 or shortly thereafter. But within those limits any attempt to date the discovery or to attribute it to an individual must inevitably be arbitrary. Furthermore, it must be arbitrary just because discovering a new sort of phenomenon is necessarily a complex process which involves recognizing both *that* something is and *what* it is. Observation and conceptualization, fact and the assimilation of fact to theory, are inseparably linked in the discovery of scientific novelty. Inevitably, that process extends over time and may often involve a number of people. Only for discoveries in my second category—those whose nature is known in advance—can discovering *that* and discovering *what* occur together and in an instant.

Two last, simpler, and far briefer examples will simultaneously show how typical the case of oxygen is and also prepare the way for a somewhat more precise conclusion. On the night of 13 March 1781, the astronomer William Herschel made the following entry in his journal: "In the quartile near Zeta Tauri . . . is a curious either nebulous star or perhaps a comet."[14] That entry is generally said to record the discovery of the planet Uranus, but it cannot quite have done that. Between 1690 and Herschel's observation in 1781 the same object had been seen and recorded at least seventeen times by men who took it to be a star. Herschel differed from them only in supposing that, because in his telescope it appeared especially large, it

[13] For the traditional elements in Lavoisier's interpretations of chemical reactions, see H. Metzger, *La philosophie de la matière chez Lavoisier* (Paris, 1935), and Daumas, *Lavoisier*, chap. 7.

[14] P. Doig, *A Concise History of Astronomy* (London: Chapman, 1950), pp. 115–16.

might actually be a *comet!* Two additional observations on 17 and 19 March confirmed that suspicion by showing that the object he had observed moved among the stars. As a result, astronomers throughout Europe were informed of the discovery, and the mathematicians among them began to compute the new comet's orbit. Only several months later, after all those attempts had repeatedly failed to square with observation, did the astronomer Lexell suggest that the object observed by Herschel might be a planet. And only when additional computations, using a planet's rather than a comet's orbit, proved reconcilable with observation was that suggestion generally accepted. At what point during 1781 do we want to say that the planet Uranus was discovered? And are we entirely and unequivocally clear that it was Herschel rather than Lexell who discovered it?

Or consider still more briefly the story of the discovery of X rays, a story which opens on the day in 1895 when the physicist Roentgen interrupted a well-precedented investigation of cathode rays because he noticed that a barium platinocyanide screen far from his shielded apparatus glowed when the discharge was in process.[15] Additional investigations—they required seven hectic weeks during which Roentgen rarely left the laboratory—indicated that the cause of the glow traveled in straight lines from the cathode ray tube, that the radiation cast shadows, that it could not be deflected by a magnet, and much else besides. Before announcing his discovery Roentgen had convinced himself that his effect was not due to cathode rays themselves but to a new form of radiation with at least some similarity to light. Once again the question suggests itself: When shall we say that X rays were actually discovered? Not, in any case, at the first instant, when all that had been noted was a glowing screen. At least one other investigator had seen that glow and, to his subsequent chagrin, discovered nothing at all. Nor, it is almost as clear, can the moment of discovery be pushed back to a point during the last week of investigation. By that time Roentgen was exploring the properties of the new radiation he had *already* discovered. We may have to settle for the remark that X rays emerged in Würzburg between 8 November and 28 December 1895.

The characteristics shared by these examples are, I think, common to all the episodes by which unanticipated novelties become subjects for scientific attention. I therefore conclude these brief remarks by discussing three such common characteristics, ones which may help to provide a framework for the further study of the extended episodes we customarily call "discoveries."

In the first place, notice that all three of our discoveries—oxygen, Uranus, and X rays—began with the experimental or observational isolation

[15]L. W. Taylor, *Physics, the Pioneer Science* (Boston: Houghton Mifflin Co., 1941), p. 790.

of an anomaly, that is, with nature's failure to conform entirely to expectation. Notice, further, that the process by which that anomaly was educed displays simultaneously the apparently incompatible characteristics of the inevitable and the accidental. In the case of X rays, the anomalous glow which provided Roentgen's first clue was clearly the result of an accidental disposition of his apparatus. But by 1895 cathode rays were a normal subject for research all over Europe; that research quite regularly juxtaposed cathode-ray tubes with sensitive screens and films; as a result, Roentgen's accident was almost certain to occur elsewhere, as in fact it had. Those remarks, however, should make Roentgen's case look very much like those of Herschel and Priestley. Herschel first observed his oversized and thus anomalous star in the course of a prolonged survey of the northern heavens. That survey was, except for the magnification provided by Herschel's instruments, precisely of the sort that had repeatedly been carried through before and that had occasionally resulted in prior observations of Uranus. And Priestley, too—when he isolated the gas that behaved almost but not quite like nitrous air and then almost but not quite like common air—was seeing something unintended and wrong in the outcome of a sort of experiment for which there was much European precedent and which had more than once before led to the production of the new gas.

These features suggest the existence of two normal requisites for the beginning of an episode of discovery. The first, which throughout this paper I have largely taken for granted, is the individual skill, wit, or genius to recognize that something has gone wrong in ways that may prove consequential. Not any and every scientist would have noted that no unrecorded star should be so large, that the screen ought not to have glowed, that nitrous air should not have supported life. But that requisite presupposes another which is less frequently taken for granted. Whatever the level of genius available to observe them, anomalies do not emerge from the normal course of scientific research until both instruments and concepts have developed sufficiently to make their emergence likely and to make the anomaly which results recognizable as a violation of expectation.[16] To say that an unexpected discovery begins only when scientists know well both how their instruments and how nature should behave. What distinguished Priestley, who saw an anomaly, from Hales, who did not, is largely the considerable articulation of pneumatic techniques and expectations that had come into being during the four decades which sep-

[16]Though the point cannot be argued here, the conditions which make the emergence of anomaly likely and those which make anomaly recognizable are to a very great extent the same. That fact may help us understand the extraordinarily large amount of simultaneous discovery in the sciences.

arate their two isolations of oxygen.[17] The very number of claimants indicates that after 1770 the discovery could not have been postponed for long.

The role of anomaly is the first of the characteristics shared by our three examples. A second can be considered more briefly, for it has provided the main theme for the body of my text. Though awareness of anomaly marks the beginning of a discovery, it marks only the beginning. What necessarily follows, if anything at all is to be discovered, is a more or less extended period during which the individual and often many members of his group struggle to make the anomaly lawlike. Invariably that period demands additional observation or experimentation as well as repeated cogitation. While it continues, scientists repeatedly revise their expectations, usually their instrumental standards, and sometimes their most fundamental theories as well. In this sense discoveries have a proper internal history as well as prehistory and a posthistory. Furthermore, within the rather vaguely delimited interval of internal history, there is no single moment or day which the historian, however complete his data, can identify as the point at which the discovery was made. Often, when several individuals are involved, it is even impossible unequivocally to identify any one of them as the discoverer.

Finally, turning to the third of these selected common characteristics, note briefly what happens as the period of discovery draws to a close. A full discussion of that question would require additional evidence and a separate paper, for I have had little to say about the aftermath of discovery in the body of my text. Nevertheless, the topic must not be entirely neglected, for it is in part a corollary of what has already been said.

Discoveries are often described as mere additions or increments to the growing stockpile of scientific knowledge, and that description has helped make the unit discovery seem a significant measure of progress. I suggest, however, that it is fully appropriate only to those discoveries which, like the elements that filled missing places in the periodic table, were anticipated and sought in advance and which therefore demanded no adjustment, adaptation, and assimilation from the profession. Though the sorts of discoveries we have here been examining are undoubtedly additions to scientific knowledge, they are also something more. In a sense that I can now develop only in part, they also react back upon what has previously been known, providing a new view of some previously familiar objects and simultaneously changing the way in which even some traditional parts of science are practiced. Those in whose area of special competence the new phenomenon falls often see both the world and their work differently as

[17] A useful sketch of the development of pneumatic chemistry is included in Partington, *A Short History of Chemistry*, chap. 6.

they emerge from the extended struggle with anomaly which constitutes the discovery of that phenomenon.

William Herschel, for example, when he increased by one the time-honored number of planetary bodies, taught astronomers to see new things when they looked at the familiar heavens even with instruments more traditional than his own. That change in the vision of astronomers must be a principal reason why, in the half century after the discovery of Uranus, twenty additional circumsolar bodies were added to the traditional seven.[18] A similar transformation is even clearer in the aftermath of Roentgen's work. In the first place, established techniques for cathode-ray research had to be changed, for scientists found they had failed to control a relevant variable. Those changes included both the redesign of old apparatus and revised ways of asking old questions. In addition, those scientists most concerned experienced the same transformation of vision that we have just noted in the aftermath of the discovery of Uranus. X rays were the first new sort of radiation discovered since infrared and ultraviolet at the beginning of the century. But within less than a decade after Roentgen's work, four more were disclosed by the new scientific sensitivity (for example, to fogged photographic plates) and by some of the new instrumental techniques that had resulted from Roentgen's work and its assimilation.[19]

Very often these transformations in the established techniques of scientific practice prove even more important than the incremental knowledge provided by the discovery itself. That could at least be argued in the cases of Uranus and of X rays; in the case of my third example, oxygen, it is categorically clear. Like the work of Herschel and Roentgen, that of Priestley and Lavoisier taught scientists to view old situations in new ways. Therefore, as we might anticipate, oxygen was not the only new chemical species to be identified in the aftermath of their work. But, in the case of oxygen, the readjustments demanded by assimilation were so profound

---

[18] R. Wolf, *Geschichte der Astronomie* (Munich, 1877), pp. 513–15, 683–93. The prephotographic discoveries of the asteroids is often seen as an effect of the invention of Bode's law. But that law cannot be the full explanation and may not even have played a large part. Piazzi's discovery of Ceres, in 1801, was made in ignorance of the current speculation about a missing planet in the "hole" between Mars and Jupiter. Instead, like Herschel, Piazzi was engaged on a star survey. More important, Bode's law was old by 1800 (ibid., p. 683), but only one man before that date seems to have thought it worthwhile to look for another planet. Finally, Bode's law, by itself, could only suggest the utility of looking for additional planets; it did not tell astronomers where to look. Clearly, however, the drive to look for additional planets dates from Herschel's work on Uranus.

[19] For α-, β-, and γ-radiation, discovery of which dates from 1896, see Taylor, *Physics*, pp. 800–804. For the fourth new form of radiation, N rays, see D. J. S. Price, *Science Since Babylon* (New Haven: Yale University Press, 1961), pp. 84–89. That N rays were ultimately the source of a scientific scandal does not make them less revealing of the scientific community's state of mind.

that they played an integral and essential role—though they were not by themselves the cause—in the gigantic upheaval of chemical theory and practice which has since been known as the chemical revolution. I do not suggest that every unanticipated discovery has consequences for science so deep and so far-reaching as those which followed the discovery of oxygen. But I do suggest that every such discovery demands, from those most concerned, the sorts of readjustment that, when they are more obvious, we equate with scientific revolution. It is, I believe, just because they demand readjustments like these that the process of discovery is necessarily and inevitably one that shows structure and that therefore extends in time.

. . . .

QUESTIONS FOR A SECOND READING

1. In his essay, Kuhn says that "we need a new vocabulary and new concepts for analyzing events like the discovery of oxygen." As you read back through the essay, what might be the key term of this "new vocabulary," and what are the key concepts?
2. Kuhn says that the sentence, "Oxygen was discovered," though undoubtedly correct, "misleads by suggesting that discovering something is a single simple act unequivocably attributable, if only we knew enough, to an individual and an instant in time." The phrase "if only we knew enough" calls attention to the kind of knowledge historians of the old school used to think they had to aspire to in order to write the history of science. What did those historians believe they had to know? How would you characterize that kind of knowledge? And what kind of knowledge, then, do Kuhn and historians of his school believe they should have? As you reread the essay, look for passages that will help you to distinguish between these two schools of historians.

ASSIGNMENTS FOR WRITING

1. Kuhn's essay presents some interesting problems for a general reader. It's not a particularly difficult essay to understand—the examples are not overly technical or arcane, and the terms, with few exceptions, are drawn from the general language of academic discussion. It would take considerable effort and training, however, to be able to look critically at Kuhn's examples—to look at what he does with the discovery of oxygen, to see what else he might have done or what he was unable to do. Furthermore, few of us have ready access to instances of advanced scientific experimentation and discov-

ery that we could use to test or to apply Kuhn's theory of the "internal structure" of scientific discovery.

If you can't work with Kuhn's examples, however, you can work with his terms, terms that can be put to work to examine discoveries drawn from your own immediate repertoire of examples. Write an essay that describes and analyzes a discovery whose "history" you know well. This need not be a "scientific" discovery, but it should be a discovery of some consequence to you personally. In Kuhn's terms, it should be a discovery that gave you a "new view" of something familiar, something you had taken for granted, and that caused you to readjust your way of thinking. This "discovery" may have occurred in school (even in the science lab), but it may also have occurred at home, on the streets, or in sports. The point of your essay should be to describe this event and then, as though you were doing a Kuhnian analysis, to analyze its "historical structure."

2. Kuhn says that all three of the discoveries he studied began with an anomaly, with "nature's failure to conform entirely to expectation." Phrases like this are often used to describe the experience of reading, where a reader moves along expecting to hear the sorts of things one usually hears but then is surprised by what a writer does and has to readjust his view of what the author is saying.

   Write an essay in which you tell a story of reading, the history of your experience as a reader with this essay or with one of the other essays in this book. Your primary responsibility is to be a good historian—to tell a story that is rich in detail and rich in understanding. You are writing this history, however, to see the degree to which Kuhn's approach to understanding scientific discovery can be usefully applied to the study of the process of reading. You should use his terms and methods where you can, and where they do not seem appropriate, think about why they don't work and what you need to put in their place.

MAKING CONNECTIONS

1. In his essay, Kuhn talks about William Herschel and the discovery of Uranus. In "When We Dead Awaken" (p. 412), and in the poem "Planetarium" contained in that essay, Adrienne Rich writes about Caroline Herschel, his sister. Both Rich and Kuhn, we could say, are writing histories of these figures. Write an essay in which you discuss what you see to be the interesting difference (or differences) between the goals and methods of these two historians. Both Rich and Kuhn have explicitly stated goals, to be sure, but you should work as well from the evidence of what they actually do when they write about these figures (and you should say what you can about *why* they do what they do). You want to be sure to draw examples, that is, from their *actual* practice.
2. Kuhn provides a way of seeing and describing the "internal structure" of a discovery. He also provides a way of seeing and talking about the relation

of a scientist to the community within which he or she works—the community of scientists who share a particular way of seeing and talking about the subjects they study.

Kuhn's terms and methods could be used to study Clifford Geertz's essay, "Deep Play: Notes on the Balinese Cockfight" (p. 299). While it would be hard to say that Geertz "discovered" the Balinese cockfight, it is possible to say that he discovered a way of describing and interpreting it. Geertz also places his work in the context of the work of others, some of whom are working anthropologists, but some of whom are not. He does this through references in the essay itself, but also in his footnotes. There is an ample record, in other words, of the scholarly community within which Geertz was working.

Write an essay in which you give a Kuhnian reading of Geertz's essay. What, in other words, might Kuhn say if he were studying and describing Geertz's work with the Balinese cockfight? How might he describe the historical structure of Geertz's discovery?

JOYCE CAROL OATES

JOYCE CAROL OATES (born 1938) began publishing her fiction as an undergraduate at Syracuse University, winning the Mademoiselle *college fiction award for her story "In The Old World" in 1959. She has since published almost forty books of fiction, poetry, and literary criticism—an extraordinary record. Along the way, she completed an M.A. at the University of Wisconsin and began a career as a teacher, teaching at the University of Detroit, the University of Windsor, Ontario, and Princeton, among others. She once said, "I'm always working. . . . Writing is much more interesting to me than eating or sleeping." In Oates's case, one is inclined to believe that this may in fact be true.*

Even though the evidence might indicate that writing comes naturally to her, Oates has said that failure is what writing continually teaches: "The writer, however battered a veteran, can't have any real faith . . . in his stamina (let alone his theoretical 'gift') to get through the ordeal. . . . One is frequently asked whether the process becomes easier with the passage of time, and the reply is obvious—Nothing gets easier with the passage of time, not even the passing of time." Oates writes, she says, in "flurries" and then works and reworks her stories into shape. This process of revision sometimes goes on even after a work has been published.

The version of "Theft" Oates offered for this volume, for example, differs from the version we first read in Northwest Review. *And the story reappears in her recent novel,* Marya: A Life *(1986). "The pleasure* is *the rewriting," Oates once said. "The first sentence can't be written until the final sentence is written. . . . The completion of any work automatically necessitates its revisioning. The same is true with reading, of course."*

Theft

The semester Marya became acquainted with Imogene Skillman, a thief suddenly appeared in Maynard House, where Marya was rooming in her sophomore year at Port Oriskany: striking at odd, inspired, daring hours, sometimes in the early morning when a girl was out of her room and showering in the bathroom just down the corridor, sometimes late at night when some of the girls sat in the kitchen, drinking coffee, their voices kept low so that the resident adviser would not hear. (The kitchen was supposed to close officially at midnight. Maynard House itself "closed" at midnight—there were curfews in those days, in the women's residences.) A wristwatch stolen from one room, seven dollars from another, a physics textbook from yet another . . . the thief was clearly one of the residents, one of the twenty-six girls who roomed in the house, but no one knew who it was; no one wanted to speculate too freely. Naturally there were wild rumors, cruel rumors. Marya once heard the tail end of a conversation in which her own name—"Knauer"—was mentioned. She had brushed by, her expression neutral, stony. She wanted the girls to know she had heard—she scorned even confronting them.

One Saturday morning in November Marya returned to her room after having been gone less than five minutes—she'd run downstairs to check the mail, though she rarely received letters—to see, with a sickening pang, that the door was ajar.

Her wallet had been taken from her leather bag, which she'd left carelessly in sight, tossed on top of her bed.

Her lips shaped empty, angry prayers—Oh God please *no*—but of course it was too late. She felt faint, sickened. She had just cashed a check for forty-five dollars—a week's part-time wages from the university library—and she'd had time to spend only a few dollars; she needed the money badly. "No," she said aloud, baffled, chagrined. "God damn it, *no*."

Someone stood in the opened doorway behind her saying Marya? Is something wrong? but Marya paid her no notice. She was opening the drawers of her bureau one by one; she saw, disgusted, frightened, that the thief had been there too—rooting around in Marya's woollen socks and sweaters and frayed underwear. And her fountain pen was gone. She kept it in the top drawer of the bureau, a prize of her own, a handsome black Parker pen with a thick nub . . . now it was gone.

She had to resist the impulse to yank the drawer out and throw it to the floor—to yank all the drawers out—to give herself up to rage. A flame seemed to pass through her, white-hot, scalding. It was so unfair: she needed that money, every penny of that money, she'd worked in the library in that flickering fluorescent light until she staggered with exhaustion, and even then she'd been forced to beg her supervisor to allow her a few more hours. Her scholarships were only for tuition; she needed that money. And the pen—she could never replace the pen.

It was too much: something in her chest gave way: she burst into tears like an overgrown child. She had never heard such great gulping ugly sobs. And the girl in the doorway—Phyllis, whose room was across the hall—shy, timid, sweet-faced Phyllis—actually tried to hold her in her arms and comfort her. It's so unfair, it's so unfair, Marya wept, what am I going to *do*. . . .

Eventually the wallet was returned to Marya, having been found in a trash can up the street. Nothing was missing but the money, as it turned out: nothing but the money! Marya thought savagely. The wallet itself—simulated crocodile, black, with a fancy brass snap—now looked despoiled, worn, contemptible. It had been a present from Emmett two years before and she supposed she'd had it long enough.

She examined it critically inside and out. She wondered what the thief had thought. Marya Knauer's things, Marya Knauer's "personal" possessions: were they worth stealing, really?

For weeks afterward Marya dreaded returning to her room. Though she was careful to lock the door all the time now it always seemed, when she stepped inside, that someone had been there . . . that something was out of place. Sometimes when she was halfway up the long steep hill to Stafford Hall she turned impulsively and ran back to her dormitory seven blocks away, to see if she'd remembered to lock the door. You're breaking down, aren't you, she mocked herself as she ran, her heart pumping, perspiration itching beneath her arms,—this is how it begins, isn't it: cracking up.

In the early years of the century Maynard House must have been impressive: a small Victorian mansion with high handsome windows, a wide veranda rimmed with elaborate fretwork, a cupola, a half-dozen fireplaces, walnut paneling in several of the downstairs rooms. But now it had become dim and shabby. The outside needed painting; the wallpaper in most of the rooms was discolored. Because it was so far from the main campus, and because its rooms were so cramped (Marya could stand at her full height on only one side of her room, the ceiling on the other slanted so steeply) it was one of the lowest priced residences for women. The girls who roomed there were all scholarship students like Marya, and, like Marya, uneasily preoccupied with studies, grades, part-time employment, finances of a minute and degrading nature. They were perhaps not so humorless and unattractive as Maynard House's reputation would have it, but they did share a superficial family resemblance—they might have been cousins, grimly energetic, easily distracted, a little vain (for they *were* scholarship winners after all, competition for these scholarships was intense throughout the state), badly frightened at the prospect of failure. They were susceptible to tears at odd unprovoked moments, to eating binges, to outbursts of temper; several, including Marya, were capable of keeping their doors closed for days on end and speaking to no one when they did appear.

Before the theft Marya had rather liked Maynard House; she prized her cubbyhole of a room because it was *hers;* because in fact she could lock the door for days on end. The standard university furniture didn't displease her—the same minimal bed, desk, chair, bureau, bedside table, lamp in each room—and the sloped ceiling gave the room a cavelike, warmly intimate air, especially at night when only her desk lamp was burning. Though she couldn't really afford it Marya had bought a woven rug for the floor—Aztec colors, even more fierce than those in hers and Alice's rug at home—and a new lampshade edged with a festive gold braid; she had bought a Chagall print for ninety-eight cents (marked down because it was slightly shopworn) at the University Store. The walls were decorated with unframed charcoal drawings she had done, sketches of imaginary people, a few glowering self-portraits: when she was too tense or excited to sleep after hours of studying, or after having taken an exam, she took up a stick of charcoal and did whatever it seemed to wish to do—her fingers empowered with a curious sort of energy, twitchy, sporadic, often quite surprising. From the room's walls smudged and shadowy variants of her own sober face contemplated her. Strong cheekbones, dark eyes, thick dark censorious brows. . . . She had made the portraits uglier than she supposed she really was; that provided some comfort, it might be said to have been a reverse vanity. Who is *that?* one of the girls on the floor once asked, staring at Marya's own image,—is it a man?—a woman?

Marya prized her aloneness, her monastic isolation at the top of the house, tucked away in a corner. She could stay up all night if she wished, she could skip breakfast if she wished, she could fall into bed after her morning classes and sleep a heavy drugged sleep for much of the afternoon; and no one knew or cared. It seemed extraordinary to her now that for so many years—for all of her lifetime, in fact—she had had to submit to the routine schedule of Wilma's household: going to bed when she wasn't sleepy, getting up when the others did, eating meals with them, living her life as if it were nothing more than an extension of theirs. She loved to read for pleasure once her own assignments were completed: the reading she did late at night acquired an aura, a value, a mysterious sort of enchantment, that did not usually belong to daylight. It was illicit, precious beyond estimation. It seemed to her at such times that she was capable of slipping out of her own consciousness and into that of the writer's . . . into the very rhythms of another's prose. Bodiless, weightless, utterly absorbed, she traversed the landscape of another's mind and found it like her own yet totally unlike—surprising and jarring her, enticing her, leading her on. It was a secret process yet it was not criminal or forbidden—she made her way with the stealth of the thief, elated, subdued, through another's imagination, risking no harm, no punishment. The later the hour and the more exhausted she was, the greater, oddly, her powers of concentration; nothing in her resisted, nothing stood aside to doubt or ridicule; the books she read greedily seemed to take life through her, by way of her, with virtually no exertion of her own. It scarcely seemed to matter what she read, or whom—Nietzsche, William James, the Brontës, Wallace Stevens, Virginia Woolf, Stendhal, the early Greek philosophers—the experience of reading was electrifying, utterly mesmerizing, beyond anything she could recall from the past. She'd been, she thought severely, a superficial person in the past—how could anything that belonged to Innisfail, to those years, matter?

A writer's authentic self, she thought, lay in his writing and not in his life; it was the landscape of the imagination that endured, that was really real. Mere life was the husk, the actor's performance, negligible in the long run. . . . How could it be anything more than the vehicle by which certain works of art were transcribed. . . ? The thought frightened her, exhilarated her. She climbed out of her bed and leaned out her window as far as she could, her hair whipping in the wind. For long vacant minutes she stared at the sky; her vision absorbed without recording the illuminated water tower two miles north of the campus, the flickering red lights of a radio station, the passage of clouds blown livid across the moon. Standing in her bare feet, shivering, her head fairly ringing with fatigue and her eyes filling with tears, she thought her happiness almost too exquisite to be borne.

The first time Imogene Skillman climbed, uninvited, to Marya's room at the top of the old mansion, she stood in the doorway and exclaimed in her low throaty amused voice, "So *this* is where you hide out! . . . this depressing little hole."

Imogene was standing with her hands on her hips, her cheeks flushed, her eyes moving restlessly about. Why, Marya's room was a former maid's room, wasn't it, partitioned off from the others on the floor; and it had only that one window—no wonder the air was stale and close; and that insufferable Chagall print!—wasn't Marya aware that everyone on campus had one? And it was a poor reproduction at that. Then Imogene noticed the charcoal sketches; she came closer to investigate; she said, after a long moment, "At least these are interesting, I wouldn't mind owning one or two of them myself."

Marya had been taken by surprise, sitting at her desk, a book opened before her; she hadn't the presence of mind to invite Imogene in, or to tell her to go away.

"So this is where Marya Knauer lives," Imogene said slowly. Her eyes were a pellucid blue, blank and innocent as china. "All alone, of course. Who would *you* have roomed with—?"

The loss of the money and the Parker fountain pen was so upsetting to Marya, and so bitterly ironic, partly because Marya herself had become a casual thief.

She thought, I deserve this.

She thought, I will never steal anything again.

Alice had led her on silly little shoplifting expeditions in Woolworth's: plastic combs, spools of thread, lipsticks, useless items (hairnets, thumbtacks) pilfered for the sheer fun of it. Once, years ago, when she was visiting Bonnie Michalak, she made her way stealthily into Mrs. Michalak's bedroom and took—what had it been?—a button, a thimble, two or three pennies?—from the top of her dresser. A tube of much-used scarlet lipstick from the locker of a high school friend; a card-sized plastic calendar (an advertisement from a stationer's in town) from Mr. Schwilk's desk; stray nickels and dimes, quarters, fifty-cent pieces. . . . One of her prizes, acquired with great daring and trepidation, was a (fake) ruby ring belonging to someone's older sister, which Marya had found beneath carelessly folded clothing in a stall in the women's bathroom at Wolf's Head Lake; but had never dared to wear. The thefts were always impulsive and rather pointless. Marya saw her trembling hand dart out, saw the fingers close . . . and in that instant, wasn't the object hers?

There was a moment when an item passed over from belonging to another person to belonging to Marya; that moment interested her greatly. She felt excitement, near-panic, elation. A sense of having triumphed, in however petty a fashion.

(It had come to seem to her in retrospect that she'd stolen Father Shearing's wristwatch. She seemed to recall . . . unless it was a particularly vivid dream . . . she seemed to recall slipping the watch from his table into her bookbag, that old worn soiled bookbag she's had for years. Father Shearing was asleep in his cranked-up bed. Though perhaps not . . . perhaps he was watching her all along through his eyelashes. Marya? Dear Marya? A common thief?)

Since coming to Port Oriskany she felt the impulse more frequently but she knew enough to resist. It was a childish habit, she thought, disgusted,—it wasn't even genuine theft, intelligently committed. Presumably she wanted to transgress; even to be punished; she *wanted* to be sinful.

Odd, Marya thought uneasily, that no one has ever caught me. When I haven't seemed to care. When I haven't seemed to have *tried*.

It happened that, in her classes, she found herself gazing at certain individuals, and at their belongings, day after day, week after week. What began as simple curiosity gradually shaded into intense interest. She might find herself, for instance, staring at a boy's spiral notebook in a lecture class . . . plotting a way to getting it for herself, leafing through it, seeing what he'd written. (For this boy, like Marya, was a daydreamer; an elaborate and tireless doodler, not without talent.) There was an antique opal ring belonging to a girl in her English literature class: the girl herself had waist-long brown hair, straight and coarse, and Marya couldn't judge whether she was striking, and very good-looking, or really quite repulsive. (Marya's own hair was growing long again—long and wavy and unruly—but it would never be that length again; the ends simply broke off.) Many of the students at Port Oriskany were from well-to-do families, evidently, judging from their clothes and belongings: Marya's eye moved upon hand-tooled leather bags, and boots, and wristwatches, and earrings, and coats (suede, leather, fur-trimmed, camel's hair) half in scorn and half in envy. She did not want to steal these items, she did not *want* these items, yet, still, her gaze drifted onto them time and again, helplessly. . . .

She studied faces too, when she could. Profiles. That blonde girl in her political science class, for instance: smooth clear creamy skin, china-blue mocking eyes, a flawless nose, mouth: long hair falling over one shoulder. Knee-high leather boots, kid gloves, a handsome camel's hair coat, a blue cashmere muffler that hadn't been cleaned in some time. An engagement ring with a large square-cut diamond. . . . But it was the girl's other pieces of jewelry that drew Marya's interest. Sometimes she wore a big silver ring with a turquoise stone; and a long sporty necklace made of copper coins; and a succession of earrings in her pierced ears—gold loops that swung and caught the light, tiny iridescent-black stones, ceramic disks in which gold-burnished reds and blues flashed. Marya stared and stared, her heart quickening with—was it envy?—but envy of precisely what? It could not have been these expensive trinkets she coveted.

Imogene Skillman was a theatre arts major; she belonged to one of the sororities on Masefield Avenue; Marya had even been able to discover that she was from Laurel Park, Long Island, and that she was engaged to a law student who had graduated from Port Oriskany several years ago. After she became acquainted with Imogene she would have been deeply humiliated if Imogene had known how much Marya knew of her beforehand. Not only her background, and her interest in acting, but that big leather bag, those boots, the silver ring, the ceramic earrings. . . .

It might have been Imogene's presence in class that inspired Marya to speak as she frequently did; answering their professor's questions in such detail, in such self-consciously structured sentences. (Marya thought of herself as shy, but, as it turned out, she could often speak at length if required—she became, suddenly, articulate and emphatic—even somewhat combative. The tenor of her voice caused people to turn around in their seats and often surprised, when it did not disconcert, her professors.) It wasn't that she spoke her mind—she rarely offered opinions—it seemed to her necessary to consider as many sides of an issue as possible, as many relevant points, presenting her case slowly and clearly and forcefully, showing no sign of the nervousness she felt. It was not simply that most of her professors solicited serious discussion—gave evidence, in fact, of being greatly dependent upon it to fill up fifty minutes of class time—or even that (so Marya reasoned, calculated) her precious grade might depend upon such contributions; she really became caught up in the subjects themselves. Conflicting theories of representative democracy, property rights, civil disobedience . . . the ethics of propaganda . . . revolution and counter-revolution . . . whether in fact terrorism might ever be justified. . . . Even when it seemed, as it sometimes did, that Marya's concern for these issues went beyond that of the professor's, she made her point; she felt a grudging approval throughout the room; and Imogene Skillman turned languidly in her seat to stare at her.

One afternoon Imogene left behind a little handwoven purse that must have slipped out of her leather bag. Marya snatched it up as if it were a prize. She followed after Imogene—followed her out of the building—that tall blond girl in the camel's hair coat—striding along, laughing, in a high-spirited conversation with her friends. Marya approached her and handed her the purse, saying only, "You dropped this," in a neutral voice; she turned away without waiting for Imogene's startled thanks.

Afterward she felt both elated and unaccountably fatigued. As if she had experienced some powerful drain on her energy. As if, having returned Imogene's little purse to her, she now regretted having done so; and wondered if she had been a fool.

Marya's friendship with Imogene Skillman began, as it was to end, with a puzzling abruptness.

One day Imogene simply appeared beside Marya on one of the campus paths, asking if she was walking this way?—and falling comfortably in step with her. It was done as easily and as effortlessly as if they were old friends; as if Imogene had been reading Marya's most secret thoughts.

She began by flattering her, telling her she said "interesting" things in class; that she seemed to be the only person their professor really listened to. Then, almost coyly: "I should confess that it's your voice that really intrigues me. What if—so I ask myself, I'm always trying things on other people!—what if *she* was playing Hedda—Hedda Gabler—with that remarkable voice—and not mine—*mine* is so reedy—I've heard myself on tape and can barely stop from gagging. And there's something about your manner too—also your chin—when you speak—it looks as if you're gritting your teeth but you *are* making yourself perfectly audible, don't be offended! The thing is, I'm doing Hedda myself, I can't help but be jealous of how you might do her in my place though it's all *my* imagination of course. Are you free for lunch? No? Yes? We could have it at my sorority—no, better out—it's not so claustrophobic, out. We'll have to hurry, though, Marya, is it?—I have a class at one I don't *dare* cut again."

It gave Marya a feeling of distinct uneasiness, afterward, to think that Imogene had pursued *her*. Or, rather, that Imogene must have imagined herself the pursuer; and kept up for weeks the more active, the more charitably outgoing and inquisitive, of their two roles. (During their first conversation, for instance, Marya found herself stammering and blushing as she tried to answer Imogene's questions—Where are you from, what are you studying, where do you live on campus, what do you *think* of this place, isn't it disappointing?—put in so candid and ingenuous a manner, with that wide blue-eyed stare, Marya felt compelled to reply. She also felt vaguely criminal, guilty—as if she'd somehow drawn Imogene to her by the very intensity of her own interest, without Imogene's conscious knowledge.)

If Imogene reached out in friendship, at the beginning, Marya naturally drew back. She shared the Knauers' peasant shrewdness, or was it mean-spiritedness: what does this person want from *me*, why on earth would this person seek out *me?* It was mysterious, puzzling, disconcerting. Imogene was so pretty, so popular and self-assured, a dominant campus personality; Marya had only a scattering of friends—friendly acquaintances, really. She hadn't, as she rather coolly explained to Imogene, time for "wasting" on people.

She also disapproved of Imogene's public manner, her air of flippancy, carelessness. In fact Imogene was quite intelligent—her swiftness of thought, her skill at repartee, made that clear—but she played at seeming otherwise, to Marya's surprise and annoyance. Imogene was always *Imogene,* always *on.* She was a master of sudden dramatic reversals: sunny warmth that shaded into chilling mockery; low-voiced serious conversations, on religion, perhaps (Imogene was an agnostic who feared, she said, lapsing into Anglicanism—it ran in her family), that deteriorated into wisecracks and bawdy jokes simply because one of her theatre friends appeared. While Marya was too reserved to ask Imogene about herself, Imogene was pitiless in her interrogation of Marya, once the formality of their first meeting was out of the way. Has your family *always* lived in that part of the state, do you mean your father was really a *miner,* how old were you when he died, how old were you when your mother died, do you keep in touch with your high school friends, are you happy here, are you in love with anyone, have you ever been in love, are you a virgin, do you have any plans for this summer, what will you do after graduation?—what do you think your *life* will be? Marya was dazed, disoriented. She answered as succinctly and curtly as she dared, never really telling the truth, yet not precisely lying; she had the idea that Imogene could detect a lie; she'd heard her challenge others when she doubted the sincerity of what they said. Half-truths went down very well, however. Half-truths, Marya had begun to think, were so much more reasonable—so much more convincing—than whole truths.

For surely brazen golden-haired Imogene Skillman didn't really want to know the truth about Marya's family—her father's death (of a heart attack, aged thirty-nine, wasn't that a possibility?—having had rheumatic fever, let's say, as a boy); her mother's disappearance that was, at least poetically, a kind of death too (automobile accident, Marya ten at the time, no one to blame). Marya was flattered, as who would not be, by Imogene's intense *interest* and *sympathy* ("You seem to have had such a hard life. . . .") but she was shrewd enough to know she must not push her friend's generosity of spirit too far: it was one thing to be moved, another thing to be repulsed.

So she was sparing with the truth. A little truth goes a long way, she thought, not knowing if the remark was an old folk saying, or something she'd coined herself.

She told herself that she resented Imogene's manner, her assumption of an easygoing informality that was all one-sided, or nearly; at the same time it couldn't be denied that Marya Knauer visibly brightened in Imogene Skillman's presence. She saw with satisfaction how Imogene's friends—meeting them in the student union, in the pub, in the restaurants and coffee shops along Fairfield Street—watched them with curiosity, and must have wondered who Imogene's new friend was.

Marya Knauer: but who is *she?*—where did Imogene pick up *her?*

Marya smiled cynically to herself, thinking that she understood at last the gratification a man must feel, in public, in the company of a beautiful woman. Better, really, than being the beautiful woman yourself.

They would have quarrelled, everything would have gone abrasive and sour immediately, if Marya hadn't chosen (consciously, deliberately) to admire Imogene's boldness, rather than to be insulted by it. (*Are you happy, are you lonely, have you even been in love, are you a virgin?*—no one had ever dared ask Marya such questions. The Knauers were reticent, prudish, about such things as personal feelings: Wilma might haul off and slap her, and call her a little shit, but she'd have been convulsed with embarrassment to ask Marya if she was happy or unhappy, if she loved anyone, if, maybe, she knew how Wilma loved *her*. Just as Lee and Everard might quarrel, and Lee might dare to tell his brawny hot-tempered father to go to hell, but he'd never have asked him—he'd never have even imagined asking him—how much money he made in a year, how much he had in the bank, what the property was worth, did he have a will, did he guess that, well, Lee sort of looked up to *him*, loved *him*, despite all these fights?)

Marya speculated that she'd come a great distance from Innisfail and the Canal Road—light-years, really, not two hundred miles—and she had to be careful, cautious, about speaking in the local idiom.

Imogene was nearly as tall as Marya, and her gold-gleaming hair and ebullient manner made her seem taller. Beside her, Marya knew herself shabby, undramatic, unattractive; it was not *her* prerogative to take offense, to recoil from her friend's extreme interest. After all—were so very many people interested in her, here in Port Oriskany? Did anyone really care if she lied, or told the truth, or invented ingenious half-truths. . . ? In any case, despite Imogene's high spirits, there was usually something harried about her. She hadn't studied enough for an exam, play rehearsals were going badly, she'd had an upsetting telephone call from home the night before, what in Christ's name was she to *do?* . . . Marya noted that beautiful white-toothed smile marred by tiny tics of vexation. Imogene was always turning the diamond ring round and round her finger, impatiently; she fussed with her earrings and hair; she was always late, always running—her coat unbuttoned and flapping about her, her tread heavy. Her eyes sometimes filled with tears that were, or were not, genuine.

Even her agitation, Marya saw, was enviable. There are certain modes of unhappiness with far more style than happiness.

Imogene insisted that Marya accompany her to a coffee shop on Fairfield—pretentiously called a coffee "house"—where all her friends gathered. These were her *real* friends, apart from her sorority sisters and her fraternity admirers. Marya steeled herself against their critical amused eyes; she didn't want to be one of their subjects for mimicry. (They did devastating imitations of their professors and even of one another—Marya had to admit, laughing, that they were really quite good. If only she'd known such people back in Innisfail!—in high school!—she might have been less singled out for disapproval; she might have been less lonely.)

Marya made certain that she gave her opinions in a quick flat unhesitating voice, since opinions tenuously offered were usually rejected. If she chose to talk with these people at all she made sure that she talked fast, so that she wouldn't be interrupted. (They were always interrupting one another, Imogene included.) With her excellent memory Marya could, if required, quote passages from the most difficult texts; her vocabulary blossomed wonderfully in the presence of a critical, slightly hostile audience she knew she *must* impress. (For Imogene prided herself on Marya Knauer's brilliance, Mary Knauer's knowledge and wit. Yes, that's right, she would murmur, laughing, nudging Marya in the ribs, go on, go *on,* you're absolutely right—you've got them now!) And Marya smoked cigarettes with the others, and drank endless cups of bitter black coffee, and flushed with pleasure when things went well . . . though she was wasting a great deal of time these days, wasn't she? . . . and wasn't time the precious element that would carry her along to her salvation?

The coffee shop was several blocks from the University's great stone archway, a tunnellike place devoid of obvious charm, where tables were crowded together and framed photographs of old, vanished athletes lined the walls. Everyone—Imogene's "everyone"—drifted there to escape from their living residences, and to sit for hours, talking loudly and importantly, about Strindberg, or Whitman, or Yeats, or the surrealists, or Prufrock, or Artaud, or *Ulysses,* or the Grand Inquisitor; or campus politics (who was in, who was out); or the theatre department (comprised half of geniuses and saints, half of losers). Marya soon saw that several of the boys were in love with Imogene, however roughly they sometimes treated her. She didn't care to learn their names but of course she did anyway—Scott, and Andy, and Matthew (who took a nettlesome sort of dislike to Marya); there was a dark ferret-faced mathematics student named Brian whose manner was broadly theatrical and whose eyeglasses flashed with witty malice. The other girls in the group were attractive enough, in fact quite striking, but they were no match for Imogene when she was most herself.

Of course the love, even the puppyish affection, went unrequited. Imogene was engaged—the diamond ring was always in sight, glittering and winking; Imogene occasionally made reference to someone named Richard, whose opinion she seemed to value highly. (What is Imogene's fiancé like, Marya asked one of the girls, and was told he was "quiet"—"watchful"—that Imogene behaved a little differently around him; she was quieter herself.)

One wintry day when Marya should have been elsewhere she sat with Imogene's friends in a booth at the smoky rear of the coffee house, half-listening to their animated talk, wondering why Imogene cared so much for them. Her mind drifted loose; she found herself examining one of the photographs on the wall close by. It was sepia-tinted, and very old: the 1899 University rowing team. Beside it was a photograph of the 1902 football team. How young those smiling athletes must have felt, as the century turned, Marya thought. It must have seemed to them . . . *theirs.*

She was too lazy to excuse herself and leave. She was too jealous of Imogene. No, it was simply that her head ached; she hadn't slept well the night before and wouldn't sleep well tonight. . . . Another rowing team. Hopeful young men, standing so straight and tall; their costumes slightly comical; their haircuts bizarre. An air of team spirit, hearty optimism, doom. Marya swallowed hard, feeling suddenly strange. She really should leave . . . She really shouldn't be here. . . .

Time had been a nourishing stream, a veritable sea, for those young men. Like fish they'd swum in it without questioning it—without knowing it was the element that sustained them and gave them life. And then it had unaccountably withdrawn and left them exposed . . . Forever youthful in those old photographs, in their outdated costumes; long since aged, dead, disposed of.

Marya thought in a panic that she must leave; she must return to her room and lock the door.

But when she rose Imogene lay a hand on her arm and asked irritably what was wrong, why was she always jumping up and down: couldn't she for Christ's sake sit *still?*

The vehemence of Imogene's response struck them all, it was in such disproportion to Marya's behavior. Marya herself was too rushed, too frightened, to take offense. She murmured, "Good-bye, Imogene," without looking at her; and escaped.

It was that night, not long before curfew, that Imogene dropped by for the first time at Maynard House. She rapped on Marya's door, poked her head in, seemed to fill the doorway, chattering brightly as if nothing were wrong; as if they'd parted amiably. Of course she *was* rather rude about the room—Marya hadn't realized it must have been a maid's room, in the house's earliest incarnation—but her rudeness as always passed by rather casually, in a sort of golden blue. She looked so pretty, flushed with cold, her eyes inordinately damp. . . .

Tell me about these drawings, she said,—I didn't know you were an artist. These are *good.*

But Marya wasn't in a mood for idle conversation. She said indifferently that she *wasn't* an artist; she was a student.

But Imogene insisted she was an artist. Because the sketches were so rough, unfinished, yet they caught the eye, there was something unnerving about them. "Do you see yourself like this, though?—Marya?" Imogene asked almost wistfully. "So stern and ugly?—it *isn't* you, is it?"

"It isn't anyone," Marya said. "It's a few charcoal strokes on old paper."

She was highly excited that Imogene Skillman had come to her room: had anyone on the floor noticed?—had the girl downstairs at the desk, on telephone duty, noticed? At the same time she wished her gone, it was an intrusion into her privacy, insufferable. She had never invited Imogene to visit her—she never would.

"So this is where you live," Imogene said, drawing a deep breath. Her eyes darted mercilessly about; she would miss nothing, forget nothing. "You're alone and you don't mind, that's *just* like you. You have a whole other life, a sort of secret life, don't you," she said, with a queer pouting downward turn of her lips.

Friendship, Marya speculated in her journal,—the most enigmatic of all relationships.

In a sense it flourished unbidden; in another, it had to be cultivated, nurtured, sometimes even forced into existence. Though she was tirelessly active in most aspects of her life she'd always been quite passive when it came to friendship. She hadn't time, she told herself; she hadn't energy for something so . . . ephemeral.

Nothing was worthwhile, really worthwhile, except studying; getting high grades; and her own reading, her own work. Sometimes Marya found herself idly contemplating a young man—in one of her classes, in the library; sometimes, like most of her female classmates, she contemplated one or another of her male professors. But she didn't want a lover, not even a romance. To cultivate romance, Marya thought, you had to give over a great deal of time for daydreaming: she hadn't time to waste on *that*.

Since the first month of her freshman year Marya had acquired a reputation for being brilliant—the word wasn't hers but Imogene's: Do you know everyone thinks you're brilliant, everyone is afraid of you?—and it struck Marya as felicitous, a sort of glass barrier that would keep other people at a distance. . . . And then again she sometimes looked up from her reading, and noted that hours had passed; where was she and what was she doing to herself? (Had someone called her? Whispered her name? Marya, Marya. . . . You little savage, Marya. . . .) Suddenly she ached with the desire to see Wilma, and Everard; and her brothers; even Lee. She felt as if she must leave this airless little cubbyhole of a room—take a Greyhound bus to Innisfail—see that house on the Canal Road—sit at the kitchen table with the others—tell them she loved them, she loved them and couldn't help herself: what was happening?

Great handfuls of her life were being stolen from her and she would never be able to retrieve them.

To counteract Imogene Skillman's importance in her life, Marya made it a point to be friendly—if not, precisely, to *become friends*—with a number of Maynard House girls. She frequently ate meals with them in the dining hall a few blocks away, though she was inclined (yes, it was rude) to bring along a book or two just in case. And if the conversation went nowhere Marya would murmur, Do you mind?—I have so much reading to do.

Of course they didn't mind. Catherine or Phyllis or Sally or Diane. They too were scholarship students; they too were frightened, driven.

(Though Marya knew they discussed her behind her back. She was the only girl in the house with a straight-A average and they were waiting . . . were they perhaps hoping? . . . for her to slip down a notch or two. They were afraid of her sarcasm, her razorish wit. Then again, wasn't she sometimes very funny?—If you liked that sort of humor. As for the sorority girl Imogene Skillman: what did Marya see in *her?*—what did *she* see in Marya? It was also likely, wasn't it, that Marya was the house thief? For the thief still walked off with things sporadically. These were mean, pointless thefts—a letter from a mailbox, another textbook, a single angora glove, an inexpensive locket on a tarnished silver chain. Pack-rat sort of thievery, unworthy, in fact, of any girl who roomed in Maynard.)

When Marya told Imogene about the thief and the money she'd lost, Imogene said indifferently that there was a great deal of stealing on campus, and worse things too (this, with a sly twist of her lips), but no one wanted to talk about it; the student newspaper (the editors were all friends of hers, she knew such things) was forever being censored. For instance, last year a girl committed suicide by slashing her wrists in one of the off-campus senior houses and the paper wasn't allowed to publish the news, not even to *hint* at it, and the local newspaper didn't run anything either, it was all a sort of totalitarian kingergarten state, the university. As for theft: "*I've* never stolen anything in my life," Imogene said, smiling, brooding, "because why would I want anything that somebody else has already had?—something second-hand, used?"

Your friend Imogene, people began to say.

Your friend Imogene: she dropped by at noon, left this note for you.

Marya's pulses rang with pleasure, simple gratitude. She was flattered but—well, rather doubtful. Did she even *like* Imogene? Were they really friends? In a sense she liked one or two of the girls in Maynard better than she liked Imogene. Phyllis, for instance, a mathematics major, very sharp, very bright, though almost painfully shy; and a chunky farm girl named Diane from a tiny settlement north of Shaheen Falls, precociously matronly, with thick glasses and a heavy tread on the stairs and a perpetual odor of unwashed flesh, ill-laundered clothes. . . . But Diane was bright, very bright; Marya thought privately that here was her real competition at Port Oriskany, encased in baby fat, blinking through those thick lenses. (The residence buzzed with the rumor, however, that Diane was doing mysteriously poorly in her courses, had she a secret grief?—an unstated terror?) Marya certainly liked Phyllis and Diane, she recognized them as superior individuals, really much nicer, much kinder, than Imogene. Yet she had to admit it would not have deeply troubled her if she never saw them again. And the loss of Imogene would have been a powerful blow.

She went twice to see the production of *Hedda Gabler* in which Imogene starred. For she really did star, it was a one-woman show. That hard slightly drawling slightly nasal voice, that mercurial manner (cruel, seductive, mock-sweet, languid, genuinely anguished by turns), certain odd tricks and mannerisms (the way she held her jaw, for instance: had she pilfered that from Marya?)—Imogene was *really* quite good; really a success. And they'd made her up to look even more beautiful on stage than she looked in life: her golden hair in a heavy Victorian twist, her cheeks subtly rouged, her eyes enormous. Only in the tense sparring scene with Judge Brack, when Hedda was forced to confront a personality as strong as her own, did Imogene's acting falter: her voice went strident, her manner became too broadly erotic.

Marya thought, slightly dazed,—Is she really talented? Is there some basis for her reputation, after all?

Backstage, Marya didn't care to compete for Imogene's attention; let the others hug and kiss her and shriek congratulations if they wished. It was all exaggerated, florid, embarrassing . . . so much emotion, such a *display*: . . . And Imogene looked wild, frenzied, her elaborate makeup now rather clownish, seen at close quarters. "Here's Marya," she announced, "—Marya will tell the truth—here's Marya—shut up, you idiots!—she'll tell the truth—*was* I any good, Marya?—*was* I really Hedda?" She pushed past her friends and gripped Marya's hands, staring at her with great shining painted eyes. She smelled of greasepaint and powder and perspiration; it seemed to Marya that Imogene towered over her.

"Of course you were good," Marya said flatly. "You know you were good."

Imogene gripped her hands tighter, her manner was feverish, outsized. "What are you saying?—you didn't care for the performance? It wasn't right? I failed?"

"Don't be ridiculous," Marya said, embarrassed, trying to pull away. "You don't need me to assess you, in any case. You *know* you were—"

"You didn't like it! Did you!"

"—you were perfect."

"Perfect!" Imogene said in a hoarse stage voice, "—but that doesn't sound like one of your words, Marya—you don't *mean* it."

It was some seconds before Marya, her face burning with embarrassment and resentment, could extricate her hands from Imogene's desperate grip. No, she couldn't come to the cast party; she had to get back to work. And yes, yes, for Christ's sake, *yes*—Imogene had been "perfect": or nearly.

Friendship, Marya wrote in her journal, her heart pounding with rage,—play-acting of an amateur type.

Friendship, she wrote,—a puzzle that demands too much of the imagination.

So she withdrew from Imogene, tried even to stop thinking about her, looking for her on campus. (That blue muffler, that camel's hair coat. And she had a new coat too: Icelandic shearling, with a black fur collar.) She threw herself into her work with more passion than before. Exams were upon her, papers were due, she felt the challenge with a sort of eager dread, an actual greed, knowing she could do well even if she didn't work hard; and she intended to work very, very hard. Even if she got sick, even if her eyes went bad.

Hour after hour of reading, taking notes, writing, rewriting. In her room, the lamp burning through the night; in one or another of her secret places in the library; in a corner of an old brick mansion a quarter-mile away that had been converted into the music school, where she might read and scribble notes and daydream, her heartbeat underscored by the muffled sounds of pianos, horns, violins, cellos, flutes, from the rows of practice rooms. The sounds—the various musics—were all rather harmonious, heard like this, in secret. Marya thought, closing her eyes: If you could only *be* music.

At the same time she had her job in the library, her ill-paid job, a drain on her time and spirit, a terrible necessity. She explained that she'd lost her entire paycheck—the money had been stolen out of her wallet—she *must* be allowed to work a little longer, to clock a few more hours each week. She intended (so she explained to her supervisor) to make up the loss she's suffered by disciplining herself severely, spending no extra money if she could avoid it. She *must* be allowed a few hours extra work. . . . (The Parker pen could never be replaced, of course. As for the money: Marya washed her hair now once a week, and reasoned that she did not really need toothpaste, why did anyone *need* toothpaste?—she was sparing with her toiletries in general, and, if she could, used other girls', left in the third floor bathroom. She was always coming upon lost ballpoint pens, lost notebooks, even loose change; she could appropriate—lovely word, "appropriate"—cheap mimeograph paper from a supply room in the library; sometimes she even found half-empty packs of cigarettes—though her newest resolution was to stop smoking, since she resented every penny spent on so foolish a habit. Her puritan spirit blazed; she thought it an emblem of her purity, that the waistbands of her skirts were now too loose, her underwear was a size too large.)

After an evening of working in the library—her pay was approximately $1 an hour—she hurried home to Maynard, exhausted, yet exhilarated, eager to get to her schoolwork. Once she nearly fainted running up the stairs and Diane, who happened to be nearby, insisted that she come into her room for a few minutes. You look terrible, she said in awe—almost as bad as I do. But Marya brushed her aside, Marya hadn't time. She was light-headed from the stairs, that was all.

One night Imogene telephoned just before the switchboard was to close. What the hell was wrong, Imogene demanded, was Marya angry at her? She hurried out of class before Imogene could say two words to her—she never came down to Fairfield Street any longer—was she secretly in love?—was she working longer hours at the library?—would she like to come to dinner sometime this week, at the sorority?—or next week, before Christmas break?

Yes, thought Marya, bathed in gratitude, in golden splendor, "No," she said aloud, quietly, chastely, "—but thank you very much."

Schopenhauer, Dickens, Marx, Euripides. Oscar Wilde. Henry Adams. Sir Thomas More. Thomas Hobbes. And Shakespeare—of course. She read, she took notes, she daydreamed. It sometimes disturbed her that virtually nothing of what she read had been written by women (except Jane Austen, dear perennial Jane, *so* feminine!) but in her arrogance she told herself *she* would change all that.

Is this how it begins, she wondered, half-amused. Breaking down. Cracking up.

Why breaking *down* . . . but cracking *up*. . . ?

Her long periods of intense concentration began to be punctuated by bouts of directionless daydreaming, sudden explosions of *feeling*. At such times Shakespeare was too dangerous to be read closely—Hamlet whispered truths too cruel to be borne, every word in *Lear* hooked in flesh and could not be dislodged. As for Wilde, Hobbes, Schopenhauer . . . even cynicism, Marya saw, can't save you.

At such times she went for walks along Masefield Avenue, past the enormous sorority and fraternity houses. They too were converted mansions but had retained much of their original glamor and stateliness. Imogene's, for instance, boasted pretentious white columns, four of them, in mock-Southern Colonial style. The cryptic Greek letters on the portico struck an especially garish and irrelevant note. What did such symbols mean, what did it mean (so Marya wondered, not quite bitterly) to be *clubbable*—?

In the winter twilight, in the cold, these outsized houses appeared especially warm and secretive; every window of their several storeys blazed. Marya thought, Why don't I feel anything, can't I even feel envy. . . ? But the sororities were crudely discriminatory (one was exclusively for Catholic girls, another exclusively for Jewish girls, the sixteen others had quotas for Catholics and blackballed all Jews who dared cross their threshold: the procedure was that blunt, that childish). Dues and fees were absurdly high, beyond the inflated price for room and board; the meetings involved pseudoreligious "Greek" rituals (handshakes, secret passwords, special prayers). Imogene complained constantly, was always cutting activities and being fined ($10 fine for missing a singing rehearsal!—the very thought made Marya shiver in disbelief), always mocking the alumns, those well-to-do matrons with too much time on their hands. Such assholes, all of them, Imogene said loftily, such *pretentious* assholes. It was part of Imogene's charm that she could be both contemptuous of pretension and marvelously—shamelessly—pretentious herself.

Time is the element in which we exist, Marya noted solemnly in her journal,—We are either borne along by it, or drowned in it.

It occurred to her with a chilling certitude that *every moment not consciously devoted to her work* was an error, a blunder. As if you can kill time, Thoreau said, without injuring Eternity.

Lying drowsily and luxuriously in bed after she'd wakened . . . conversations with most people, or, indeed *all* people . . . spending too long in the shower, or cleaning her room, or staring out the window, or eating three meals a day (unless of course she brought along a book to read) . . . daydreaming and brooding about Innisfail, or the Canal Road, or that wretched little tarpaper-roofed shanty near Shaheen Falls that had been her parents' house . . . crying over the past (though in fact she rarely cried these days) as if the past were somehow present. In high school she had been quite an athlete, especially at basketball and field hockey; in college she hadn't time, hadn't the slightest interest. It pleased her that she always received grades of A but at the same time she wondered,—Are these *really* significant grades, do I *really* know anything?—or is Port Oriskany one of the backwaters of the world, where nothing, even "excellence," greatly matters? She needed high grades in order to get into graduate school, however; beyond that she didn't allow herself to think. Though perhaps she wouldn't go to graduate school at all . . . perhaps she would try to write . . . her great problem being not that she hadn't anything to write about but that she had too much.

Unwisely, once, she confided in Imogene that she halfway feared to write anything that wasn't academic or scholarly or firmly rooted in the real world: once she began she wouldn't be able to stop: she was afraid of sinking too deep into her own head, cracking up, becoming lost.

Imogene said it once that Marya was just the type to be excessive, she needed reining in. "I know the symptoms," she said severely. Anyway, what good would academic success—or any kind of success—do her, if she destroyed her health?

"*You're* concerned about my health?" Marya asked incredulously.

"Of course. Yes, I *am*. Why shouldn't I be," Imogene said, "—aren't I a friend of yours?"

Marya stared at her, unable to reply. It struck her as wildly incongruous that Imogene Skillman, with her own penchant for abusing her health (she drank too much at fraternity parties, she stayed up all night doing hectic last-minute work) should be worrying about Marya.

"Aren't I a friend of yours?" Imogene asked less certainly. "Don't I have the right . . . ?"

Marya turned away with an indifferent murmur, perhaps because she was so touched.

"My health isn't of any use to me," she said, "if I don't get anything accomplished. If I fail."

Of course it was possible, Marya saw, to ruin one's health and fail anyway.

Several of her fellow residents in Maynard House were doing poorly in their courses, despite their high intelligence and the goading terror that energized them. One of them was Phyllis, who was failing an advanced calculus class; another, a chronically withdrawn and depressed girl named Mary, a physics major, whose deeply shadowed eyes and pale grainy skin, as well as her very name, struck a superstitious chord of dread in Marya—she avoided her as much as possible, and had the idea that Mary avoided *her*.

The University piously preached an ethic of knowledge for its own sake—knowledge and beauty being identical—the "entire person" was to be educated, not simply the mind; but of course it acted swiftly and pragmatically upon another ethic entirely. Performance was all, the grade-point average *was* everything. Marya, no idealist, saw that this was sound and just; but she felt an impatient sort of pity for those who fell by the wayside, or who, like the scholarship girls, in not being *best*, were to be judged *worthless*, and sent back home. (Anything below a B was failing for them.) She wanted only to be best, to be outstanding, to be . . . defined to herself as extraordinary . . . for, apart from being extraordinary, had she any essence at all?

The second semester of her freshman year she had come close to losing her perfect grade-point average. Unwisely, she signed up for a course in religion, having been attracted to the books on the syllabus and the supplementary reading list (the *Upanishads;* the *Bhagavad-Gītā;* the *Bible;* the *Koran; Hymns of the Rigveda;* books on Gnosticism, and Taoism, and medieval Christianity, and the Christian heresies, and animism, magic, witchcraft, Renaissance ideas of Platonic love). It was all very promising, very heady stuff; quite the antidote to the catechismal Catholicism in which Marya no longer believed, and for which she had increasingly less tolerance. The professor, however, turned out to be an ebullient balding popinjay who lectured from old notes in a florid and self-dramatizing style, presenting ideas in a melange clearly thrown together from others' books and articles. He wanted nothing more than these ideas (which were fairly simple, not at all metaphysical or troubling) given back to him on papers and examinations; and he did not encourage questions from the class. Marya would surely have done well—she transcribed notes faultlessly, even when contemptuous of their content—but she could not resist sitting in stony silence and refusing to laugh when the professor embarked upon one or another of his jocular anecdotes. It was a classroom mannerism of his, almost a sort of tic, that each time he alluded to something female he lowered his voice and added, as if off the cuff, a wry observation, meant not so much to be insulting as to be mildly teasing. He was a popular lecturer, well-liked by most, not taken seriously by the better students; even the girls laughed at his jokes, being grateful, as students are, for something—anything—to laugh at. Marya alone sat with her arms folded, her brow furrowed, staring. It was not until some years later that she realized, uncomfortably, how she must have appeared to that silly perspiring man—a sort of gorgon in the midst of his amiable little sea of admirers.

So it happened that, though Marya's grades for the course were all A's, the grade posted for her final examination was C; and the final grade for the course—a humiliating B+.

Marya was stunned, Marya was sickened—she would have had to reach back to her childhood—or to the night of that going-away party—for an episode of equal mortification. That it was petty made it all the more mortifying.

I can forget this insult and forget him, Marya instructed herself,—or I can go to him and protest. To forget it seemed in a way noble, even Christian; to go to the man's office and humble herself in trying to get the grade raised (for she knew very well she hadn't written a C exam) somehow childish, degrading.

Of course she ran up to his office; made an appointment to see him; and, after a few minutes' clucking and fretting (he pretended she had failed to answer the last question, she hadn't handed in both examination booklets, but there the second booklet was, at the bottom of a heap of papers—ah, what a surprise!), he consented to raise the grade to A. And smiled roguishly at her, as if she had been caught out in mischief, or some sort of deception; for which he was forgiving her. "You seem like a rather grim young woman," he said, "you never smile—you look so *preoccupied*." Marya stared at his swinging foot. He was a satyrish middle-aged man, red-brown tufts of hair in his ears, a paunch straining against his shirt front, a strangely vulnerable smile; a totally mediocre personality in every way—vain, uncertain, vindictive—yet Marya could see why others liked him; he was predictable, safe, probably decent enough. But she hated him. She simply wished him dead.

He continued as if not wanting to release her, waiting for her smile of blushing gratitude and her meek *thank you*—which assuredly was not going to come; he said again, teasing, "Are you *always* such an ungiving young woman, Miss Knauer?"—and Marya swallowed hard, and fixed her dark loathing stare on him, and said: "My mother is sick. She's been sick all semester. I know I shouldn't think about it so much . . . I shouldn't depress other people . . . but sometimes I can't help it. She isn't expected to live much longer, the cancer has metastasized to the brain. . . . I'm sorry if I offended you."

He stared at her; then began to stammer his apologies, rising from his desk, flushing deeply—the very image of chagrin and repentance. In an instant the entire atmosphere between them changed. He was sorry, he murmured, so very sorry . . . of course he couldn't have known. . . .

A minute later Marya was striding down the corridor, her pulses beating hot, in triumph. In her coat pocket was the black fountain pen she had lifted from the man's cluttered desk.

An expensive pen, as it turned out. A Parker, with a squarish blunt nub, and the engraved initials E. W. S.

Marya used the pen to take notes in her journal, signing her name repeatedly, hypnotically: *Marya, Marya Knauer, Marya Marya Marya Marya Knauer,* a name that eventually seemed to have been signed by someone else, a stranger.

The shame of having humbled herself before that ignorant man had been erased by the shame—what should have been shame—of theft.

So Marya speculated, thinking of that curious episode in her life. Eventually the pen ran out of ink and she didn't indulge herself in buying more—it was so old-fashioned a practice, a luxury she couldn't afford.

Phyllis began staying out late, violating curfew, returning to the residence drunk, dishevelled, tearful, angry—she couldn't stand the four walls of her room any longer, she told Marya; she couldn't stand shutting the door upon herself.

One night she didn't return at all. It was said afterward that she had been picked up by Port Oriskany police, wandering downtown, miles away, dazed and only partly clothed in the bitter cold—the temperature had gone as low as −5°F. She was taken at once to the emergency room of the city hospital; her parents, who lived upstate, were called; they came immediately the next morning to take her back home. No one at Maynard House was ever to see her again.

All the girls in the residence talked of Phyllis, somewhat dazed themselves, frightened. How quickly it had happened—how quickly Phyllis had disappeared. Marya was plied with questions about Phyllis (how many subjects she was failing, who were the boys she'd gone out with) but Marya didn't know; Marya grew vague, sullen.

And then the waters close over your head. —This phrase ran through Marya's mind repeatedly.

They talked about Phyllis for two or three days, then forgot her.

The following Saturday, however, Phyllis's mother and older sister arrived to pack up her things, clean out her room, fill out a half-dozen university forms. The resident advisor accompanied them; they looked confused, nervous, rather lost. Both women had Phyllis's pale blond limp hair, her rather small, narrow face. How is Phyllis, some of the girls asked, smiling, cautious, and Mrs. Myer said without looking at anyone, Oh Phyllis is fine, resting and eating and sleeping right again, sleeping good hours, she said, half-reproachfully, as if sleeping right hadn't been possible in Maynard House; and they were all to blame. Marya asked whether she might be returning second semester. No, not that soon, Mrs. Myer said quickly. She and the silent older sister were emptying drawers, packing suitcases briskly. Marya helped with Phyllis's books and papers, which lay in an untidy heap on her desk and on the floor surrounding the desk. There were dust balls everywhere. A great cobweb in which the dessicated corpses of insects hung, including that of the spider itself. Stiffened crumpled Kleenex wadded into balls, everywhere underfoot. An odor of grime and despair. . . . Marya discovered a calculus bluebook slashed heavily in red with a grade of D.; a five-page paper on a subject that made no sense to her—Ring theory?—with a blunt red grade of F. It seemed to Marya that Phyllis was far more real now, more present, than she had been in the past . . . even when she'd tried to comfort Marya by taking her in her arms.

Marya supposed she had been Phyllis's closest friend at Port Oriskany. Yet Phyllis's mother and sister hadn't known her name, had no message for her . . . clearly Phyllis had never mentioned her to them at all. It was disappointing, sobering.

And the waters close over your head, Marya thought.

Then something remarkable happened: Marya rose from Phyllis's closet, a pile of books in her arms, her hair in her face, when she happened to see Mrs. Myer dumping loose items out of a drawer into a suitcase: a comb, ballpoint pens, coins, loose pieces of jewelry,—and her black fountain pen. *The* pen, unmistakable.

My God, Marya whispered.

No one heard. Marya stood rooted to the spot, staring, watching as her prize disappeared into Phyllis's suitcase, hidden now by a miscellany of socks and underwear. *The* pen—the emblem of her humiliation and triumph—disappearing forever.

It wasn't until months later that someone in Maynard made the observation that the thefts seemed to have stopped. . . . Since Phyllis moved out. . . . And the rest of the girls (they were at breakfast, eight or ten of them at a table) took it up, amazed, reluctant, wondering. Was it possible . . . *Phyllis* . . . ?

Marya said quietly that they shouldn't say such things since it couldn't be proved; that constituted slander.

Wednesday dinner, a "formal" dinner, in Imogene's sorority house, and Marya is seated beside Imogene, self-conscious, unnaturally shy, eating her food without tasting it. She *can* appreciate the thick slabs of roast beef, the small perfectly cooked parsley potatoes, the handsome gilt-edged china, the white linen tablecloth ("Oh it's Portuguese—from Portugal"), the crystal water goblets, the numerous tall candles, the silvery-green silk wallpaper, the house mother's poised social chatter at the head table . . . and the girls' stylized animation, their collective stylized beauty. For they *are* beautiful, without exception; as unlike the girls of Maynard House as one species is unlike another.

Imogene Skillman, in this dazzling context, isn't Marya's friend; she is clearly a sorority girl; even wearing her pin with its tiny diamonds and rubies just above her left breast. Her high delicate laughter echoes that of the others' . . . she isn't going to laugh coarsely here, or say anything witty and obscene . . . she can be a little mischievous, just a little cutting, at best. Marya notes how refined her table manners have become for the occasion; how practiced she is at passing things about, summoning one of the houseboys for assistance without quite looking at him. (The houseboy in his white uniform!—one of a subdued and faintly embarrassed little squadron of four or five boys, he turns out to be an acquaintance of Marya's from her Shakespeare class, who resolutely avoids her eye throughout the prolonged meal.)

Marya makes little effort to take part in the table's conversation, which swings from campus topics to vacation plans—Miami Beach, Sarasota, Bermuda, the Barbados, Trinidad, Switzerland ("for skiing"). Where are you going, Imogene asks Marya brightly, and Marya, with a pinched little smile, says she will spend a few days at home, then return to school; she has work to do that must be done here. And Imogene's friends gaze upon her with faint neutral smiles. Is this the one Imogene boasted of, who is so intelligent and so well-spoken. . . ? So *witty*. . . ?

For days Marya has been anticipating this dinner, half in dread and half in simple childish excitement. She feared being ravenous with hunger and eating too much out of anxiety; she feared having no appetite at all. But everything is remote, detached, impersonal. Everything is taking place at a little distance from her. A mistake, my coming here, she thinks,—my being invited. But she doesn't feel any great nervousness or discomfort. Like the uniformed houseboys who stand with such unnatural stiffness near the doorway to the kitchen, Marya is simply waiting for the meal to end.

She finds herself thinking of friendship, in the past tense. Phyllis, and Diane, and one or two others at Maynard; and, back in Innisfail, Bonnie Michalak, Erma Dietz. She *might* have been a close friend to any of these girls but of course she wasn't, isn't. As for Imogene—she knows she is disappointing Imogene but she can't seem to force herself to care. She halfway resents Imogene for having invited her—for having made a fool out of *herself*, in bringing Marya Knauer to dinner.

How pretty you look, Imogene said, very nearly puzzled, when Marya arrived at six-thirty,—what have you *done* to yourself?

Marya flushed with annoyance; then laughed; with such exuberance that Imogene laughed with her. For it *was* amusing, wasn't it?—Marya Knauer with her hair attractively up in a sort of French twist; Marya Knauer with her lips reddened, and her eyebrows plucked ("pruned," she might have said), Marya Knauer in a green-striped jersey dress that fitted her almost perfectly. A formal dinner meant high heels and stockings, which Marya detested; but she was wearing them nonetheless. And all for Imogene.

Yet now, seated beside Imogene, she pays very little attention to her friend's chatter; she feels subdued, saddened; thinking instead of old friendships, old half-friendships, that year or so during which she'd imagined herself extraordinary, because it had seemed that Emmett Schroeder loved her. She had not loved him—she wasn't capable, she supposed, of loving anyone—but she had certainly basked in the sunny intensity of *his* love: she'd lapped it up eagerly, thirstily (so she very nearly saw herself, a dog lapping water) as if convinced that it had something to do with her. And now Imogene's friendship, which she knows she cannot keep for very long . . . Imogene who has a reputation for being as recklessly improvident with her female friends as with her male friends. . . . Why make the effort, Marya reasons, when all that matters in life is one's personal accomplishment? Work, success, that numbing grade-point average . . . that promise of a future, any future. . . .

While Imogene and several of the others are discussing (animatedly, severely) a sorority sister not present, Marya studies her face covertly; recalls an odd remark Imogene made some weeks ago. The measure of a person's love for you is the depth of his hurt at your betrayal: *that's* the only way you can know how much, or how little, you matter.

Imogene's face had fairly glowed in excited triumph, as she told Marya this bit of wisdom. Marya thought,—She knows from experience, the bitch. She knows her own value.

Imogene is telling a silly convoluted story about a dear friend of hers (it turns out to be Matthew, devoted Matthew) who "helped" her with her term paper on Chekhov: she'd given him a messy batch of notes, he was kind enough to "arrange" them and "expand upon them" and "shape them into an 'A' paper." He's a saint, Imogene says sighing, laughing,—so sweet and so patient; so pathetic, really. But now Imogene is worried ("terrified") that their professor will call her into his office and interrogate her on her own paper, which she hadn't had time to read in its entirety; it was thirty pages long and heavy with footnotes. The girls assure her that if he marked it "A" it *is* an "A"; he'd never ask to see it again. Yes, says Imogene, opening her eyes wide,—but wait until he reads my final exam, and I say these ridiculous things about Chekhov!

Part of this is play-acting, Marya knows, because Imogene is quite intelligent enough, on the subject of Chekhov or anything else connected with drama; so Marya says, though not loudly enough for the entire table to hear: "That wasn't a very kind thing for *you* to do, was it?—and not very honest either."

Imogene chooses not to hear the tone of Marya's remark; she says gaily: "Oh you mean leading poor Matt on? Making him think—? But otherwise he wouldn't have written so *well,* there wouldn't have been so many impressive *footnotes.*"

Marya doesn't reply. Marya draws her thumbnail hard against the linen tablecloth, making a secret indentation.

Imogene says, making a joke of it: "Marya's such a puritan—I know better than to ask help of *her.*"

Marya doesn't rise to the bait; the conversation shifts onto other topics; in another fifteen minutes the lengthy dinner is over.

"You aren't going home immediately, are you?" Imogene says, surprised. She is smiling but there are strain lines around her mouth. "Come upstairs to my room for a while. Come *on,* we haven't had a chance to talk."

"Thank you for everything," says Marya. "But I really have to leave. I'm pressed for time these days. . . ."

"You *are* angry?—about that silly Matthew?" Imogene says.

Marya shrugs her shoulders, turns indifferently away.

"Well—are *you* so honest?" Imogene cries.

Marya gets her coat from the closet, her face burning. (Are *you* so honest! *You!*) Imogene is apologizing, talking of other things, laughing, while Marya thinks calmly that she will never see Imogene Skillman again.

"There's no reason why you shouldn't take this coat, it's a perfectly good coat," Imogene said in her "serious" voice—frank, level, unemphatic. "I don't want it any longer because I have so many coats, I never get to wear it and it *is* perfectly lovely, it shouldn't just hang in the closet. . . . Anyway here it is; I think it would look wonderful on you."

Marya stared at the coat. It was the camel's hair she had long admired. Pleasantly scratchy beneath her fingers, belted in back, with a beautiful silky-beige lining: she estimated it would have cost $250 or more, new. And it was almost new.

(Marya's coat, bought two or three years before in Innisfail, had cost $45 on sale.)

Imogene insisted, and Marya tried on the coat, flicking her hair out from inside the collar, studying herself critically in Imogene's full-length mirror. Imogene was saying, "If you're worrying that people will know it's my coat—it *was* my coat—don't: camel's hair coats all look alike. Except they don't look like wool imitations."

Marya met Imogene's frank blue gaze in the mirror. "What about your parents, your mother?—won't someone wonder where the coat has gone?"

Imogene puckered her forehead quizzically. "What business is it of theirs?" she asked. "It's *my* coat. My things are mine, I do what I want with them."

Marya muttered that she just couldn't *take* the coat, and Imogene scolded her for talking with her jaw clenched, and Marya protested in a louder voice, yet still faintly, weakly. . . . "It's a beautiful coat," she said. She was thinking: It's too good for me. I can't accept and I can't refuse and I hate Imogene for this humiliation.

Imogene brought the episode to an end by saying rather coldly: "You'll hurt my feelings, Knauer, if you refuse it. If you're weighing your pride against mine, don't bother—mine is far, far more of a burden."

"So you are—Marya," Mrs. Skillman said in an ambiguous voice (warm? amused? doubtful?) in the drab front parlor of Maynard House, as Marya approached. She and Mr. Skillman and Imogene were taking Marya out to dinner, downtown at the Statler Chop House, one of the area's legendary good restaurants. "We've heard so much about you from Imogene," Mrs. Skillman said, "I think we were expecting someone more. . . ."

"Oh Mother, what on earth—!" Imogene laughed sharply.

". . . I was going to say *taller,* perhaps *older,*" Mrs. Skillman said, clearly annoyed by her daughter's interruption.

Marya shook hands with both the Skillmans and saw to her relief that they appeared to be friendly well-intentioned people, attractive enough, surely, and very well-dressed, but nothing like their striking daughter. *She* might have been their daughter, brunette and subdued. (Except she hadn't dared wear the camel's hair coat, as Imogene had wanted. She was wearing her old plaid wool and her serviceable rubberized boots.)

In their presence Imogene was a subtly different person. Rather more disingenuous, childlike, sweet. Now and then at dinner Marya heard a certain self-mocking tone in her friend's voice ("am I playing this scene correctly?—how is it going down?") but neither of the Skillmans took notice; and perhaps it was Marya's imagination anyway.

Then, near the end of the meal, Imogene got suddenly high on white wine and said of her father's business: "It's a sophisticated form of theft."

She giggled; no one else laughed; Marya kept her expression carefully blank.

". . . I mean it *is,* you know . . . it's indirect. . . . 'Savings and Loans' . . . and half the clients blacks who want their Dee-troit cars financed," Imogene said.

"Imogene, you aren't funny," Mrs. Skillman said.

"She's just teasing," Mr. Skillman said. "My little girl likes to tease."

"I do like to tease, don't I?—Marya knows," Imogene said, nudging her. Then, as if returning to her earlier sobriety, she said: *"I never mean a word of what I say and everybody knows it."*

The subject leapt to Imogene's negligence about writing letters, or even telephoning home. "If we try to call," Mrs. Skillman said, "the line at the residence is busy for hours; and when we finally get through you aren't in; you're *never* in. And you never return our calls. . . ."

Imogene said carelessly that her sorority sisters were bad at taking down messages. Most of them were assholes, actually—

"Imogene!" Mrs. Skillman said.

"Oh Mother you know they *are,*" Imogene said in a childlike voice.

After an awkward pause Mr. Skillman asked about Richard: Richard had evidently telephoned *them,* asking if something was wrong with Imogene because he couldn't get through to her either. "Your mother and I were hoping there wasn't some sort of . . . misunderstanding between you."

Imogene murmured that there weren't any misunderstandings at all between them.

"He seemed to think . . . to wonder . . ." Mrs. Skillman said. "That is, as long as we were driving up to visit. . . ."

Imogene finished off her glass of white wine and closed her eyes ecstatically. She said: "I really don't care to discuss my private matters in a restaurant. —Anyway Marya is here: why don't we talk about something lofty and intellectual? *She's* taking a philosophy course—if she can't tell us the meaning of life no one can."

"You and Richard haven't quarrelled, have you?" Mrs. Skillman said.

Imogene raised her left hand and showed the diamond ring to her mother, saying: "*Please* don't worry, I haven't given it back, it's safe." To Marya she said lightly: "Mother would be mortified if Dickie demanded it back. It's somebody's old dead socialite *grandmother's.*"

"Imogene," Mr. Skillman said, his voice edged with impatience, "you really shouldn't tease so much. I've just read that teasing is a form of aggression . . . did you know that?"

"Not that I'd give it back if Dickie *did* demand it," Imogene laughed. "It's mine, I've earned it, let him *sue* to get it back—right, Marya?—he's going to be a hotshot lawyer after all. Let him *practice.*"

Everyone, including Marya, laughed as if Imogene had said something unusually witty; and Imogene, in the cool voice she used to summon the houseboys at her sorority, asked a passing waiter for more wine.

Richard.

"Dickie."

Am I jealous of someone called "Dickie," Marya wondered, lying sprawled and slovenly across her bed. She was doing rough, impatient charcoal sketches of imaginary faces—beetle-browed, glowering, defiantly ugly—that inevitably turned out to be forms of her own.

In Imogene's cluttered room on the second floor of the baronial sorority house Marya had come upon, to her astonishment, copies of *Bride* magazine. She leafed through them, jeering, while Imogene hid her face in laughing protestation. Wedding gowns! Satin and pearls! Veils made of antique lace! Orange blossoms! Shoes covered in white silk! And what is this, Marya said, flapping the pages in Imogene's direction,—a wedding-cake bridegroom to go with it all?—standing a little out of the range of the camera's focus, amiable and blurred.

"Ah, but you'll have to be a bridesmaid," Imogene said dryly. "Or a maid of honor."

Imogene showed her snapshots of the legendary Richard, flicking them like playing cards. Marya saw that, yes, Richard was a handsome young man—dark strong features, a slightly heavy chin, intelligent eyes. He was demanding, perhaps; an excellent match for Imogene. But it was difficult, Marya thought, to believe that the person in the snapshots—*this* person, standing with his hands on his hips, his hair lifting in the wind—would be capable of loving Imogene as much as she required being loved.

Imogene threw herself across her bed, lay on her back, let her long hair dangle to the floor. Her belly was stretched flat; her pelvic bones protruded. She smoothed her shirt across her abdomen with long nervous fingers. ". . . The first time I came with him," she said hesitantly, but with a breathy laugh, "it wasn't . . . you know . . . it wasn't with him inside me, the way you're supposed to . . . I was afraid of that then, I thought I might get pregnant. And he was so big, I thought he'd hurt me, they're *very* big compared to . . . compared to us. The first time it worked for me he was, well, you know, kissing me there . . . he'd gotten all crazy and wild and I couldn't stop him, and I never thought I would let anyone do that . . . I'd *heard* about that . . . because . . . oh Marya, am I embarrassing you? . . . because afterward," she said, laughing shrilly, "they only want to kiss you: and it's disgusting."

She rolled over amidst the tumble of things strewn on her bed and hid her face from Marya.

After a long time she said, her breath labored, her face still turned away: "Am I embarrassing you?"

Marya's throat and chest were so constricted, she couldn't reply.

A Marya Knauer anecdote, told by Imogene with peals of cruel ribald laughter. . . .

Imogene insisted that Marya accompany her on a date, yes a "date," an actual "date" (though it was generally thought that Marya shunned men because she imagined they weren't *serious* enough). Her escort was Matthew Fein, of all people—Matthew who had seemed to dislike Marya but who in fact (so Imogene revealed) had simply been afraid of her.

"Afraid of me?—you're being ridiculous," Marya said. She hardly knew whether to be hurt or flattered.

"Of course he's afraid of you, or was," Imogene said. "And my poor sorority sisters!—they told me afterward they'd never seen such eyes as yours—taking them all in and condemning them! *Those* assholes!"

It would be an ordinary evening, Imogene promised, no need to dress up, no *need* for the high-heels-stockings routine, though it was perfectly all right (so Imogene said innocently) if Marya wanted to comb her hair. Imogene's date for the evening was a senior in business administration and advertising whose name Marya never caught, or purposefully declined to hear. They drove out to a suburban mall to see a movie—in fact it was a pretentious French "film"—and then they went to a local Italian restaurant where everyone, excepting of course Marya, drank too much; and then they drove to the water-tower hill where numerous other cars were parked, their headlights off. Marya stiffened. Matthew had not yet touched her but she knew that he would be kissing her in another minute; and she had no idea of how to escape gracefully.

". . . Few minutes?" Imogene murmured from the front seat.

She was sending them away!—Marya saw with disbelief that, by the time she and Matthew climbed out of the car, Imogene and her date were locked in a ravenous embrace. One would have thought the two of them lovers; one would have thought them at least fond of each other. Marya's heart was beating frantically. That bitch! That bitch! Marya worried that she might suffocate—she couldn't seem to catch her breath.

Matthew took her cold unresisting hand. He slipped his arm around her shoulders.

They were meant to stroll for a few minutes along the darkened path, to contemplate, perhaps, the view of Port Oriskany below, all sparkling winking lights. A romantic sight, no doubt. Beautiful in its way. Matthew was saying something rather forced—making a joke of some kind—about the French movie?—about Imogene's reckless behavior?—but Marya interrupted. "Isn't she supposed to be engaged?" she asked. "Yes, I suppose so," Matthew said in resignation, "but she does this all the time. It's just Imogene." "She does this all the *time?*" Marya said, "but why—?" Matthew laughed uncomfortably. He was not quite Marya's height and his dark eyes shied away from hers. "I don't know," he said defensively, "—as I said, it's just Imogene, it's her business. Why shouldn't she do what she wants to do? Don't be angry with *me.*"

He was nervous yet keenly excited; Marya sensed his sexual agitation. Behind them, parked along the gravelled drive, were lovers' cars, one after another; from this distance, the car in which Imogene and her "date" were pawing at each other was undistinguishable from the others.

"You might not approve," Matthew said, his voice edged now with an air of authority, "—but Imogene is a free soul, she does what she wants, I don't suppose she actually *lies* to her fiancé. He'd have to allow her some freedom, you know, or she'd break off the engagement."

"You know a lot about her," Marya said.

"Imogene is a close friend of mine, we've worked together . . . I was stage manager for *Hedda Gabler,* don't you remember?"

"It's all so . . . trivial," Marya said slowly. "So degrading."

"What do you mean?"

"Oh—this."

"This—?"

Marya indicated the cars parked along the drive. Her expression was contemptuous.

"You take an awfully superior attitude, don't you," Matthew said, with an attempt at jocular irony. He tightened his arm around her shoulders; he drew nearer. Marya could hear his quickened breathing.

Is this idiot really going to kiss me, Marya wondered. Her heart was still beating heavily; she could see Imogene's profile, the cameo-clear outline of her face, illuminated for an instant as the headlights were extinguished. Then she moved into the young man's embrace, she kissed him, slid her arms around his neck. . . .

"Does she make love with them?" Marya asked.

"Them—?"

"Different boys. Men. One week after another."

"I don't know," Matthew said resentfully. "I suppose so—if she wants to."

"I thought *you* were in love with her," Marya said mockingly.

"We're just friends," Matthew said, offended.

"Oh no," said Marya, "—everyone knows you're in *love* with her."

Matthew drew away from Marya and walked beside her without speaking. There was nothing for them to do, suddenly; not a thing left to say. It was still March and quite cold. Their footsteps sounded dully on the crusted snow. Marya thought, The various ways we seek out our humiliations. . . .

After a few minutes Matthew said something conciliatory about the night, the stars, the city lights, "infinity," certain remarks of Pascal's; but Marya made no effort to listen. She kept seeing Imogene kissing that near-stranger, Imogene locking her arms about his neck *as if he mattered. As if they were lovers.*

She was going to observe aloud, cynically, that making love was as good a way as any of passing the time, if you hadn't anything better to do, when Matthew, brave Matthew, turned to her and took hold of her shoulders and tried to kiss her. It was a desperate gesture—his breath smelled of sweet red wine—but Marya would have none of it. She shoved him roughly in the chest.

"Marya, for Christ's sake grow up," Matthew said angrily. "You're a big girl now—"

"Why should you *kiss* me?" Marya said, equally angry, "—when you don't even *like* me? When you know I don't like you in the slightest, when we haven't anything to say to each other, when we're just waiting for the evening to get finished!—in fact we've been made fools of, both of us. And now you want to kiss me," she said, jeering, "—just for something to do."

He began to protest but Marya dismissed him with a derisory wave of her hand. She was going to walk back to the residence, she said; she was through with them all. Especially Imogene.

Matthew followed along behind her for a few minutes, trying to talk her into coming back to the car. It was almost midnight, he said; the campus was two miles away; what if something happened to her. . . . Marya ignored him and walked faster, descending the hill past a slow stream of cars that were ascending it, their headlights blinding her eyes. She lowered her head, tried to hide her face, her hands thrust deep in the pockets of her camel's hair coat. At first she was furious—almost sick with fury—her head rang with accusations against Imogene—but the cold still night air was so invigorating, so wonderfully cleansing, she felt quite good by the time she got to Maynard House, not very long after midnight. She felt *very* good.

Next day, Sunday, Imogene stood at the downstairs desk ringing Marya's buzzer repeatedly, one two three four, one two three four, and then one long rude ring, until Marya appeared at the top of the stairs, her hair in a towel. "Who the hell—?" she called down. She and Imogene stared at each other. Then Imogene said contemptuously, "Here's your purse, you left your purse in the car, Knauer. D'you know, Knauer, your behavior is getting eccentric, it isn't even amusing, just what if something had happened to you last night—walking back here all alone—a college girl, in some of those neighborhoods!—don't you think Lyle and Matt and I would feel responsible? But *you*," she said, her voice rising, "—*you* haven't the slightest sense of—of responsibility to other people—"

"Just leave the purse," Marya said, leaning over the bannister. "Leave it and go back to screwing what's-his-name—that's *your* responsibility—"

"Go screw yourself!" Imogene shouted. "Go fuck yourself!"

"Go fuck *yourself!*" Marya shouted.

As the stories sifted back to Marya, over a period of a week or ten days, they became increasingly disturbing, ugly.

In one version Marya Knauer had been almost attacked—that is, raped—in a black neighborhood near the foot of Tower Hill; and had run back to her residence hall, hysterical and sobbing. It was an even graver insult that her purse had been taken from her—her purse and all her money.

In another version, Marya was so panicked at being simply touched by her date (she was a virgin, she was frigid, she'd never been kissed before) that she ran from the car, hysterical and panting . . . ran all the way back to campus. The boy was a blind date, someone in drama, or maybe business administration, it was all a total surprise to him that Marya Knauer was so . . . crazy.

In a third improbable version it was Imogene Skillman's fiancé who offered to take Marya back to the residence, because she was so upset—having a breakdown of some kind—and when they were halfway there she threw herself on him in the car *while he was actually driving*. And then, ashamed, she opened the car door and jumped out *while the car was still in motion*.

"It's Imogene," Marya said, licking her numbed lips. "She's making these things up . . . Why is she *doing* this to me. . . !"

There were vague rumors too that Marya had borrowed small sums of money from Imogene. And items of clothing as well—the camel's hair coat, for instance. (Because she hadn't a coat of her own. Because her coat had literally gone to shreds. Because she was so *poor,* a scholarship student from the hills, practically a *hillbilly. . . .*) As far as she was concerned, Imogene was reported saying, Marya Knauer could keep the coat if she was that desperate. Imogene no longer wanted it back.

Marya telephoned Imogene and accused her of telling lies, of telling slanderous tales. "Do you think I don't know who's behind this?" Marya cried. But Imogene hung up at once: Imogene was too wise to reply.

Marya began to see how people watched her . . . smiling covertly as she passed. They were pitying, yet merciless. They knew. Marya Knauer with all her pretensions, Marya Knauer who had made a fool of herself with another girl's fiancé, Marya Knauer who was cracking up. . . .

In the fluorescent-lit dining hall she sat alone in an alcove, eating quickly, her head bowed; it was too much trouble to remove her plates and glass of water from the tray. Two boys passed near and she heard them laugh softly. . . . *That* the one? There? one of them whispered. She turned back to her book (*. . . the thought of suicide is a strong consolation, one can get through many a bad night with it*) but the print danced crazily in her eyes.

"Do you think I don't know who's behind this,—who's responsible?" Marya asked aloud, in anguish, in the privacy of her room. She tried to lock her door from the inside—as if there were any danger of being interrupted, invaded—but the doors in Maynard, as in university housing generally, did not lock in that direction.

At about this time Marya was notified that a short story she had submitted to a national competition had placed first; and, not long afterward—within a week or ten days, in fact—she learned that another story, sent out blindly and naively to a distinguished literary magazine, was accepted for publication.

She thought of telephoning Wilma and Everard . . . she thought of telephoning Imogene . . . of running along the corridors of Maynard House, knocking on doors, sharing her good news. But her elation was tempered almost at once by a kind of sickened dread—she was going to be unequal to the task of whatever it was (so her panicked thoughts raced, veered) she might be expected to do.

Lately her "serious" writing frightened her. Not just the content itself—though the content was often wild, disturbing, unanticipated—but the emotional and psychological strain it involved. She could write all night long, sprawled across her bed, taking notes, drafting out sketches and scenes, narrating a story she seemed to be hearing in a kind of trance; she could write until her hand ached and her eyes filled with tears and she felt that another pulsebeat would push her over the brink—into despair, into madness, into sheer extinction. Nothing is worth this, she told herself very early one morning, nothing can be worth this, she thought, staring at herself in the mirror of the third floor bathroom,—a ghastly hollow-eyed death's head of a face, hardly recognizable as Marya, as a girl of nineteen.

Give up. Don't risk it. *Don't* risk it.

So she cautioned herself, so she gave and took warning. There was another kind of writing—highly conscious, cerebral, critical, discursive—which she found far easier; far less dangerous. She was praised for it lavishly, given the highest grades, the most splendid sort of encouragement. She should plan, her professors said, to go on to graduate school . . . they would advise her, help her get placed, help her make her way. . . . Don't risk this, she told herself, the waters will suck you down and close over your head: I know the symptoms.

And she did, she did. As if she had lived a previous life and could recall vividly the anguish of . . . whatever it was that might happen.

One windy morning at the end of March she saw Imogene Skillman walking with several of her friends. Imogene in sunglasses, her hair blowing wild, her laughter shrill and childish. Imogene in tight-fitting jeans and a bulky white ski sweater, overlong in the sleeves. That slatternly waifish affect. . . . Marya stood watching. Staring. Poor Marya Knauer, staring. Why did you lie about me! she wanted to cry. Why did you betray me! But she stood silent, paralyzed, watching. No doubt a figure of pathos—or of comedy—her snarled black hair blowing wild as Imogene's, her skin grainy and sallow.

Of course Imogene saw her; but Imogene's eyes were discreetly hidden by the dark-tinted glasses. No need for her to give any sign of recognition. No need.

Marya wrote Imogene a muddled little note, the first week in April.

Things aren't going well for me, I missed a philosophy exam & have no excuse & can't make myself lie. I don't know . . . am I unhappy (is it that simple?) or am I coming down with some sort of exotic illness (is it that simple?) Why don't you drop by & see me sometime . . . or I could come over there & see you. . . .

Yet she felt a revulsion for Imogene; she *really* disliked her. That lazy drunken dip of her head, her lipstick smeared across her face, sliding her arms around the neck of . . . whoever it had been: kissing open-mouthed, simulating passion. Would you two let us alone for a few minutes, Imogene drawled,—Would you two like to go for a stroll, for a few minutes?

I'll come over there, Marya wrote, *and strangle you with that pretentious braid of yours.*

In all she wrote a dozen notes, some by hand and some on the typewriter. But she sent only the first ("why don't you drop by & see me sometime . . . or I could come over there & see you"), not expecting, and not receiving, an answer.

What is fictitious in a friendship, Marya pondered, and what is "real": the world outside the head, the world *inside:* but whose world?—from whose point of view?

If Imogene died. . . .

If Imogene were dying. . . .

She wouldn't lift a hand to prevent that death!—so she thought.

At the same time she quizzed herself about how to respond, should Imogene really ask her to be a bridesmaid. (She had declined being a bridesmaid at Alice's wedding; but then she had the excuse of schoolwork, distance.) Imogene's wedding was going to be a costly affair held in Long Beach, New York sometime the following year. The bridesmaid's dress, the shoes . . . the shoes alone . . . would be staggeringly expensive.

I can't afford it, Marya would say.

I can't afford *you*.

Though they hadn't any classes together this semester Marya learned that Imogene had been absent from one of her lectures for three days running. So she simply went, one rainy April afternoon, to Imogene's residence—to that absurd white-columned "house" on Masefield Avenue—and rapped hard on Imogene's door; and let herself in before Imogene could call out sleepily, who is it. . . ?

The shades were crookedly drawn. Clothes and towels and books were strewn about. Imogene lay half-undressed on the bed with the quilted spread pulled over her; the room smelled of something acrid and medicinal.

"Oh Marya," Imogene said guiltily.

"Are you sick?" Marya asked.

They had both spoken at the same time.

". . . a headache, cramps, nothing worth mentioning," Imogene said hoarsely. ". . . the tail-end of this shitty flu that's been going around."

Marya stood with her hands on her hips, regarding Imogene in bed. Imogene's skin looked oddly coarse, her hair lay in spent greasy tangles on the pillow, spilling off the edge of the bed; her body was flat, curiously immobile. Without makeup she looked both young and rather ravaged. "If you're really sick, if you need a doctor, your sorority sisters will see to it," Marya said half-mockingly.

"I'm not really sick," said Imogene at once. "I'm resting."

After a long pause Marya said, as if incidentally: "You told so many lies about me."

Imogene coughed feebly. "They weren't exactly *lies,* there was an essence. . . ."

"They were lies," Marya said. "I wanted to strangle you."

Imogene lay without moving, her hands flat on her stomach. She said in a childish vague voice: "Oh nobody believed anything, it was just . . . talk . . . spinning tales. . . . You know, thinking 'What if' . . . that sort of thing. Anyway there was an *essence* that was true."

Marya was pacing about the room, the balls of her feet springy, the tendons of her calves strained. "I don't intend to let you destroy me," she said softly. "I don't even intend to do poorly in my courses." She brushed her hair out of her face and half-smiled at Imogene—a flash of hatred. "You won't make me lose my perfect record," she said.

"Won't I," said Imogene.

Marya laughed. She said: "But why did you concoct a story about your fiancé and me?—you know I've never even met him; I don't have any interest in meeting him."

"Yes you do," Imogene said, a little sharply. "You're jealous of him—of him and me."

"You're angry that I'm not jealous *enough,*" Marya said. "Do you think I'd want to sleep with your precious 'Dickie'?"

"You think so goddam fucking highly of yourself, don't you," Imogene said, sitting up, adjusting a pillow impatiently behind her. "*You* can't be cracked open, can you?—a nut that can't be cracked," she said, laughing, yawning. "A tight little virgin, I suppose. And Catholic too!—what a joke! Very very proud of yourself."

"Why didn't you talk to me on the phone, why didn't you answer my note?" Marya asked quietly.

"Why did you avoid me on campus?"

"Avoid you when?"

"Why do you always look the other way?"

"Look the other way *when—?*"

"All the time."

Marya was striking her hands, her fists, lightly together. She drew a deep shaky breath. "As for the coat—you *gave* me the coat. Your precious Salvation Army gesture. You *gave* me the coat, you *forced* it on me."

"Oh Knauer, nobody forces anything on *you,*" Imogene said, sneering. "What bullshit—!"

"I want to know why you've been spreading lies about me and ridiculing me behind my back," Marya said levelly.

Imogene pulled at her hair in a lazy, mawkishly theatrical gesture. "Hey. Did I tell you. I'm transferring out of here next year," she said. "I'm going to school somewhere in New York, N.Y.U. probably. The drama courses are too *restrained* here, there's too much crap about *tradition.* . . ."

"I said I want to know *why.*"

"Oh for Christ's sweet sake what are you talking about!" Imogene cried.

"I'm sick, my head is spinning, if you don't leave me alone I'm going to puke all over everything. I haven't been to a class in two weeks and I don't give a damn but I refuse to give *you* the satisfaction. . . . Transfer to New York, Marya, why don't you: you know you think you're too good for us *here*."

Marya stared at her, trembling. She had a vision of running at her friend and pummelling her with her fists—the two of them fighting, clawing, grunting in silence.

"Your jealousy, your morbid possessiveness. . . ." Imogene was saying wildly, her eyes wide, ". . . the way you sat in judgment on my parents . . . my poor father trying so hard to be *nice* to you, to be *kind*, because he felt *sorry* for you . . . and my mother too. . . . 'Is she one of your strays and misfits?' Mother said, 'another one of that gang that will turn on you'. . . . As for my sorority sisters. . . ."

Marya said slowly, groping: "And what about you? You're spoiled, you're vicious. . . . And you don't even act that well: people here baby you, lie to you, tell you the kind of crap you want to hear."

At this Imogene threw herself back against the flattened pillows, laughing, half-sobbing. "Yes," she said. "Good. Now leave me alone."

"Do you think they tell you anything else?—anything else but crap?" Marya said carelessly, "—people who are in love with you? People who don't even know who you *are?*"

Imogene pawed at the bedspread and pulled it roughly over herself. She lay very still but Marya could hear her labored breath. ". . . I took some aspirin before you came in, I want to sleep, maybe you'd better let me alone. I think you'd better let me alone."

She closed her eyes, she waved Marya away with a languid gesture.

"Good-bye, Marya!" she whispered.

On the sidewalk outside the house Marya took out the earrings boldly to examine them.

The Aztec ones, the barbarian-princess ones, bronze and red and blue, burnished, gleaming. . . . Marya had seen her hand reach out to take them but she did not remember *taking* them from the room.

She tossed them in the palm of her hand as she strode along Masefield Avenue, smiling, grinning. No one, she thought in triumph, can keep me from my perfect record.

She went that day to an earring shop down on Fairfield Street; asked to have her ears pierced and Imogene's splendid earrings inserted. But the proprietor told her that wasn't the procedure; first, gold studs are inserted . . . then, after a few weeks, when the wounds are healed. . . .

No, Marya insisted, put in *these*. I don't have time to waste.

But there was the danger of infection, she was told. Everything has to be germ-free, antiseptic. . . .

"I don't give a damn about that," Marya said fiercely. "These earrings *are* gold. Put antiseptic on *them*. . . . Just pierce my ears and put them in and I'll pay you and that's all."

"Do you have five dollars?" the young man said curtly.

Crossing the quadrangle between Stafford Hall and the chapel one cold May afternoon, Marya caught sight of Imogene approaching her. It had been approximately two weeks since the theft of the earrings—two weeks during which Marya had worn the earrings everywhere, for everyone to see, to comment upon, to admire. She and Imogene had frequently noticed each other, usually at a distance, though once in rather close quarters on a crowded stairway; and Marya had been amused at Imogene's shocked expression: and the clumsy way she'd turned aside, pretending she hadn't seen Marya and Marya's new earrings.

Not a very good actress after all, Marya thought.

Now, however, Imogene was approaching her head-on, though her movements were rather forced, wooden. Marya didn't slacken her pace; she was headed for the library. She wore her raincoat half-unbuttoned, her head was bare, her hair loose, the earrings swung heavily as she walked, tugged at her earlobes. (Yes, her earlobes *were* sore. Probably infected, Marya thought indifferently, waking in the night to small stabs of pain.)

Imogene's face was dead white, and not very attractive. Something horsy about that face, after all, Marya thought. Her mouth was strained, and the tendons in her neck were clearly visible as, suddenly, she ran at Marya. She was screaming something about "hillbilly bitch"—"thief"— She grabbed at Marya's left ear, she would have ripped the earring out of Marya's flesh, but Marya was too quick for her: she knew instinctively what Imogene would try to do.

She struck Imogene's hand aside, and gave her a violent shove; Imogene slapped her hard across the face; Marya slapped *her*. "You bitch!" Imogene cried. "You won't get away with this! *I know you!*"

All their books had fallen to the sidewalk, Imogene's leather bag was tripping her up, passers-by stopped to stare, incredulous. What a sight, Imogene Skillman and Marya Knauer fighting, in front of the chapel,—both in blue jeans, both livid with rage. Marya was shouting, "Don't you touch me, you! What do you mean, touching *me!*" She was the better fighter, crouching with her knees bent, like a man, swinging at Imogene, striking her on the jaw. Not a slap but an actual punch: Marya's fist was unerring.

The blow was a powerful one, for Marya struck from the shoulder. Imogene's head snapped back—blood appeared on her mouth—she staggered backward and swayed, almost lost her balance. "Oh Marya," she said.

Marya snatched up her things and turned away. Her long fast stride and the set of her shoulders, the set of her head, must have indicated confidence; angry assurance; but in fact she was badly shaken . . . it was some time before she could catch her breath. When she turned to look back Imogene was sitting on the ground and a small crowd had gathered around her. You'll be all right, Marya thought, someone will always take care of *you*.

After that, very little happened.

Marya kept the earrings, though her ears *were* infected and she had to give up wearing them; Imogene Skillman never approached her again, never pressed charges; nor did anyone dare bring the subject up to either of the girls.

Marya's record remained perfect but Imogene did poorly at the end of the semester, failing two subjects; and, in place of transferring to another university she quit college altogether.

That fall, Marya learned that Imogene was living in New York City. She had broken off her engagement over the summer; she had joined a troupe of semiprofessional actors, and lived in an apartment off St. Mark's Square. It was said that she had a small role in an off-Broadway play scheduled to open sometime that winter but Marya never learned the title of the play, or when, precisely, it opened; or how successful it was.

• • • • • • • • • • • • • • • •

QUESTIONS FOR A SECOND READING

1. Go back over the variety of thefts in this story (and not all of them Marya's): outright thefts, supposed or imagined thefts, and metaphorical thefts (where something other than property could be said to be "stolen"). If we are getting Marya's view of the world in this story, what is it? Why would "theft" be a good term for describing what goes on in that world? What can you conclude from this about Marya's sense of her relations to other people? about the way she sees the connections between people and things?
2. How would you explain the relationship between Marya and Imogene? Is there a difference between how you would explain it and how the story *would have you* explain it? That is, what does Oates offer as the key terms and key moments in the story, and what do *you* see as the key terms and key moments?

ASSIGNMENTS FOR WRITING

1. The narrator of this story says, "There was a moment when an item passed over from belonging to another person to belonging to Marya; that moment interested her greatly." Why do you suppose this moment interests Marya? How does this fit with your sense of her personality? And how, then, would you explain why she steals? For this assignment, write an essay explaining why you think Marya steals. What's her problem, and how might you account for it?
2. Reading, for Marya, at times was "a secret process yet it was not criminal or forbidden—she made her way with the stealth of the thief, elated, subdued, through another's imagination, risking no harm, no punishment." Look back over the sections of the story that give you access to Marya's intellectual life and her success as a student. What connections can you make with her life as a thief? In an essay, explore how her successful intellectual performance as a student could be related to her thievery. As you read the story, what are the points of the comparison?

MAKING CONNECTIONS

1. The stories by Bellow ("A Silver Dish," p. 22) and Oates deal with theft. People take things, and things are taken from them. For this assignment, you need to think about theft as something more than the act of stealing. Ask yourself what the thefts in the Bellow and Oates stories might stand for, what they might represent. How, in other words, might one use the *metaphor* of theft to talk about people, their pasts and presents, and the culture they live in? Write an essay in which you discuss "Theft" and "A Silver Dish" and what the thefts in these stories allow you to understand about the people involved and their relationships to each other. (Don't misunderstand—stealing is bad, but that's not the point. This question isn't about actual acts of stealing but what stealing—as something people do and have done to them—might represent.)
2. Richard Rodriguez, in "The Achievement of Desire" (p. 430), talks about his schooling as the process of becoming a "scholarship boy." He borrows the term (or takes it, as he takes many things, from his teachers) and uses it to analyze his experience as a student. If you look at Marya the way Rodriguez looks at himself, do you think the term (or its equivalent, "scholarship girl") applies to her? If you consider Rodriguez as a student like Marya, as a person fascinated with that "moment when an item passed over from belonging to another person to belonging" to him, a person not beyond stealing but not quite a thief either, what can you say to explain his relationship to others? to the culture around him? Write an essay in which you discuss Rodriguez and Marya as examples of people who have a similar response to the experience of growing up, entering the world, and becoming educated.

WALKER PERCY

WALKER PERCY, in his mid-40s, after a life of relative obscurity and after a career as, he said, a "failed physician," wrote his first novel, The Moviegoer. *It won the National Book Award for fiction in 1962, and Percy emerged as one of this country's leading novelists. Little in his background would have predicted such a career.*

After graduating from Columbia University's medical school in 1941, Percy (born 1916) went to work at Bellevue Hospital in New York City. He soon contracted tuberculosis from performing autopsies on derelicts and was sent to a sanitorium to recover, where, as he said, "I was in bed so much, alone so much, that I had nothing to do but read and think. I began to question everything I had once believed." He returned to medicine briefly but suffered a relapse and during his long recovery began "to make reading a full-time occupation." He left medicine, but not until 1954, almost a decade later, did he publish his first essay, "Symbol as Need."

The essays that followed, including "The Loss of the Creature," all dealt with the relationships between language and understanding or belief, and they were all published in obscure academic journals. In the later essays, Percy seemed to turn away from academic forms of argument and to depend more and more on stories or anecdotes from daily life—to write, in fact, as a storyteller and to be wary of abstraction or explanation. Robert Coles has said that it was Percy's failure to find a form that would reach a larger audience that led him to try his hand at a novel. You will notice in the essay that follows that Percy delights in piling example upon example; he never seems to settle down to a topic sentence, or any sentence for that matter that sums everything up and makes the examples superfluous.

Percy's novels include The Moviegoer, Lancelot, *and* Love in the Ruins. *He has published two books of essays:* The Message in the Bottle: How Queer Man Is, How Queer Language Is, and What One Has to Do with the Other *and* Lost in the Cosmos: The Last Self-Help Book.

The Loss of the Creature

I

Every explorer names his island Formosa, beautiful. To him it is beautiful because, being first, he has access to it and can see it for what it is. But to no one else is it ever as beautiful—except the rare man who manages to recover it, who knows that it has to be recovered.

Garcia López de Cárdenas discovered the Grand Canyon and was amazed at the sight. It can be imagined: One crosses miles of desert, breaks through the mesquite, and there it is at one's feet. Later the government set the place aside as a national park, hoping to pass along to millions the experience of Cárdenas. Does not one see the same sight from the Bright Angel Lodge that Cárdenas saw?

The assumption is that the Grand Canyon is a remarkably interesting and beautiful place and that if it had a certain value *P* for Cárdenas, the same value *P* may be transmitted to any number of sightseers—just as Banting's discovery of insulin can be transmitted to any number of diabetics. A counterinfluence is at work, however, and it would be nearer the truth to say that if the place is seen by a million sightseers, a single sightseer does not receive value *P* but a millionth part of value *P*.

It is assumed that since the Grand Canyon has the fixed interest value *P*, tours can be organized for any number of people. A man in Boston decides to spend his vacation at the Grand Canyon. He visits his travel bureau, looks at the folder, signs up for a two-week tour. He and his family take the tour, see the Grand Canyon, and return to Boston. May we say that this man has seen the Grand Canyon? Possibly he has. But it is more likely that what he has done is the one sure way not to see the canyon.

Why is it almost impossible to gaze directly at the Grand Canyon under these circumstances and see it for what it is—as one picks up a strange object from one's back yard and gazes directly at it? It is almost impossible because the Grand Canyon, the thing as it is, has been appropriated by the symbolic complex which has already been formed in the sightseer's mind. Seeing the canyon under approved circumstances is seeing the symbolic complex head on. The thing is no longer the thing as it confronted the Spaniard; it is rather that which has already been formulated—by picture postcard, geography book, tourist folders, and the words *Grand Canyon*. As a result of this preformulation, the source of the sightseer's pleasure undergoes a shift. Where the wonder and delight of the Spaniard arose from his penetration of the thing itself, from a progressive discovery of depths, patterns, colors, shadows, etc., now the sightseer measures his satisfaction *by the degree to which the canyon conforms to the preformed complex.* If it does so, if it looks just like the postcard, he is pleased; he might even say, "Why it is every bit as beautiful as a picture postcard!" He feels he has not been cheated. But if it does not conform, if the colors are somber, he will not be able to see it directly; he will only be conscious of the disparity between what it is and what it is supposed to be. He will say later that he was unlucky in not being there at the right time. The highest point, the term of the sightseer's satisfaction, is not the sovereign discovery of the thing before him; it is rather the measuring up of the thing to the criterion of the preformed symbolic complex.

Seeing the canyon is made even more difficult by what the sightseer does when the moment arrives, when sovereign knower confronts the thing to be known. Instead of looking at it, he photographs it. There is no confrontation at all. At the end of forty years of preformulation and with the Grand Canyon yawning at his feet, what does he do? He waives his right of seeing and knowing and records symbols for the next forty years. For him there is no present; there is only the past of what has been formulated and seen and the future of what has been formulated and not seen. The present is surrendered to the past and the future.

The sightseer may be aware that something is wrong. He may simply be bored; or he may be conscious of the difficulty: that the great thing yawning at his feet somehow eludes him. The harder he looks at it, the less he can see. It eludes everybody. The tourist cannot see it; the bellboy at the Angel Lodge cannot see it: for him it is only one side of the space he lives in, like one wall of a room; to the ranger it is a tissue of everyday signs relevant to his own prospects—the blue haze down there means that he will probably get rained on during the donkey ride.

How can the sightseer recover the Grand Canyon? He can recover it in any number of ways, all sharing in common the stratagem of avoiding the approved confrontation of the tour and the Park Service.

It may be recovered by leaving the beaten track. The tourist leaves the tour, camps in the back country. He arises before dawn and approaches the South Rim through a wild terrain where there are no trails and no railed-in lookout points. In other words, he sees the canyon by avoiding all the facilities for seeing the canyon. If the benevolent Park Service hears about this fellow and thinks he has a good idea and places the following notice in the Bright Angel Lodge: *Consult ranger for information on getting off the beaten track*—the end result will only be the closing of another access to the canyon.

It may be recovered by a dialectical movement which brings one back to the beaten track but at a level above it. For example, after a lifetime of avoiding the beaten track and guided tours, a man may deliberately seek out the most beaten track of all, the most commonplace tour imaginable: he may visit the canyon by a Greyhound tour in the company of a party from Terre Haute—just as a man who has lived in New York all his life may visit the Statute of Liberty. (Such dialectical savorings of the familiar as the familiar are, of course, a favorite stratagem of *The New Yorker* magazine.) The thing is recovered from familiarity by means of an exercise in familiarity. Our complex friend stands behind the fellow tourists at the Bright Angel Lodge and sees the canyon through them and their predicament, their picture taking and busy disregard. In a sense, he exploits his fellow tourists; he stands on their shoulders to see the canyon.

Such a man is far more advanced in the dialectic than the sightseer who is trying to get off the beaten track—getting up at dawn and approaching the canyon through the mesquite. This strategem is, in fact, for our complex man the weariest, most beaten track of all.

It may be recovered as a consequence of a breakdown of the symbolic machinery by which the experts present the experience to the consumer. A family visits the canyon in the usual way. But shortly after their arrival, the park is closed by an outbreak of typhus in the south. They have the canyon to themselves. What do they mean when they tell the home folks of their good luck: "We had the whole place to ourselves"? How does one see the thing better when the others are absent? Is looking like sucking: the more lookers, the less there is to see? They could hardly answer, but by saying this they testify to a state of affairs which is considerably more complex than the simple statement of the schoolbook about the Spaniard and the millions who followed him. It is a state in which there is a complex distribution of sovereignty, of zoning.

It may be recovered in a time of national disaster. The Bright Angel Lodge is converted into a rest home, a function that has nothing to do with the canyon a few yards away. A wounded man is brought in. He regains consciousness; there outside his window is the canyon.

The most extreme case of access by privilege conferred by disaster is the Huxleyan novel of the adventures of the surviving remnant after the great wars of the twentieth century. An expedition from Australia lands in Southern California and heads east. They stumble across the Bright Angel Lodge, now fallen into ruins. The trails are grown over, the guard rails fallen away, the dime telescope at Battleship Point rusted. But there is the canyon, exposed at last. Exposed by what? By the decay of those facilities which were designed to help the sightseer.

This dialectic of sightseeing cannot be taken into account by planners, for the object of the dialectic is nothing other than the subversion of the efforts of the planners.

The dialectic is not known to objective theorists, psychologists, and the like. Yet it is quite well known in the fantasy-consciousness of the popular arts. The devices by which the museum exhibit, the Grand Canyon, the ordinary thing, is recovered have long since been stumbled upon. A movie shows a man visiting the Grand Canyon. But the moviemaker knows something the planner does not know. He knows that one cannot take the sight frontally. The canyon must be approached by the stratagems we have mentioned: the Inside Track, the Familiar Revisited, the Accidental Encounter. Who is the stranger at the Bright Angel Lodge? Is he the ordinary tourist from Terre Haute that he makes himself out to be? He is not. He has another objective in mind, to revenge his wronged brother, counterespionage, etc. By virtue of the fact that he has other fish to fry, he may take a stroll along the rim after supper and then we can see the canyon through him. The movie accomplishes its purpose by concealing it. Overtly the characters (the American family marooned by typhus) and we the onlookers experience pity for the sufferers, and the family experience anxiety for themselves; covertly and in truth they are the happiest of people and we are happy through them, for we have the canyon to ourselves. The movie cashes in on the recovery of sovereignty through disaster. Not only is the canyon now accessible to the remnant: the members of the remnant are now accessible to each other; a whole new ensemble of relations becomes possible—friendship, love, hatred, clandestine sexual adventures. In a movie when a man sits next to a woman on a bus, it is necessary either that the bus break down or that the woman lose her memory. (The question occurs to one: Do you imagine there are sightseers who see sights just as they are supposed to? a family who live in Terre Haute, who decide to take the canyon tour, who go there, see it, enjoy it immensely, and go home content? a family who are entirely innocent of all the barriers, zones, losses of sovereignty I have been talking about? Wouldn't most people be sorry if Battleship Point fell into the canyon, carrying all one's fellow passengers to their death, leaving one alone on the South Rim? I cannot answer this. Perhaps there are such people. Certainly a great many American families would swear they had no such problems, that they came, saw, and went away happy. Yet it is just these families who would be happiest if they had gotten the Inside Track and been among the surviving remnant.)

It is now apparent that as between the many measures which may be taken to overcome the opacity, the boredom, of the direct confrontation of the thing or creature in its citadel of symbolic investiture, some are less authentic than others. That is to say, some stratagems obviously serve other purposes than that of providing access to being—for example, various unconscious motivations which it is not necessary to go into here.

Let us take an example in which the recovery of being is ambiguous, where it may under the same circumstances contain both authentic and unauthentic components. An American couple, we will say, drives down into Mexico. They see the usual sights and have a fair time of it. Yet they are never without the sense of missing something. Although Taxco and Cuernavaca are interesting and picturesque as advertised, they fall short of "it." What do the couple have in mind by "it"? What do they really hope for? What sort of experience could they have in Mexico so that upon their return, they would feel that "it" had happened? We have a clue: Their hope has something to do with their own role as tourists in a foreign country and the way in which they conceive this role. It has something to do with other American tourists. Certainly they feel that they are very far from "it" when, after traveling five thousand miles, they arrive at the plaza in Guanajuato only to find themselves surrounded by a dozen other couples from the Midwest.

Already we may distinguish authentic and unauthentic elements. First, we see the problem the couple faces and we understand their efforts to surmount it. The problem is to find an "unspoiled" place. "Unspoiled" does not mean only that a place is left physically intact; it means also that it is not encrusted by renown and by the familiar (as in Taxco), that it has not been discovered by others. We understand that the couple really want to get at the place and enjoy it. Yet at the same time we wonder if there is not something wrong in their dislike of their compatriots. Does access to the place require the exclusion of others?

Let us see what happens.

The couple decide to drive from Guanajuato to Mexico City. On the way they get lost. After hours on a rocky mountain road, they find themselves in a tiny valley not even marked on the map. There they discover an Indian village. Some sort of religious festival is going on. It is apparently a corn dance in supplication of the rain god.

The couple know at once that this is "it." They are entranced. They spend several days in the village, observing the Indians and being themselves observed with friendly curiosity.

Now may we not say that the sightseers have at last come face to face with an authentic sight, a sight which is charming, quaint, picturesque, unspoiled, and that they see the sight and come away rewarded? Possibly this may occur. Yet it is more likely that what happens is a far cry indeed from an immediate encounter with being, that the experience, while masquerading as such, is in truth a rather desperate impersonation. I use the word *desperate* advisedly to signify an actual loss of hope.

The clue to the spuriousness of their enjoyment of the village and the festival is a certain restiveness in the sightseers themselves. It is given expression by their repeated exclamations that "this is too good to be true," and by their anxiety that it may not prove to be so perfect, and finally by their downright relief at leaving the valley and having the experience in the bag, so to speak—that is, safely embalmed in memory and movie film.

What is the source of their anxiety during the visit? Does it not mean that the couple are looking at the place with a certain standard of performance in mind? Are they like Fabre, who gazed at the world about him with wonder, letting it be what it is; or are they not like the overanxious mother who sees her child as one performing, now doing badly, now doing well? The village is their child and their love for it is an anxious love because they are afraid that at any moment it might fail them.

We have another clue in their subsequent remark to an ethnologist friend. "How we wished you had been there with us! What a perfect goldmine of folkways! Every minute we would say to each other, if only you were here! You must return with us." This surely testifies to a generosity of spirit, a willingness to share their experience with others, not at all like their feelings toward their fellow Iowans on the plaza at Guanajuato!

I am afraid this is not the case at all. It is true that they longed for their ethnologist friend, but it was for an entirely different reason. They wanted him, not to share their experience, but to certify their experience as genuine.

"This is it" and "Now we are really living" do not necessarily refer to the sovereign encounter of the person with the sight that enlivens the mind and gladdens the heart. It means that now at last we are having the acceptable experience. The present experience is always measured by a prototype, the "it" of their dreams. "Now I am really living" means that now I am filling the role of sightseer and the sight is living up to the prototype of sights. This quaint and picturesque village is measured by a Platonic ideal of the Quaint and the Picturesque.

Hence their anxiety during the encounter. For at any minute something could go wrong. A fellow Iowan might emerge from a 'dobe hut; the chief might show them his Sears catalogue. (If the failures are "wrong" enough, as these are, they might still be turned to account as rueful conversation pieces: "There we were expecting the chief to bring us a churinga and he shows up with a Sears catalogue!") They have snatched victory from disaster, but their experience always runs the danger of failure.

They need the ethnologist to certify their experience as genuine. This is borne out by their behavior when the three of them return for the next corn dance. During the dance, the couple do not watch the goings-on; instead they watch the ethnologist! Their highest hope is that their friend should find the dance interesting. And if he should show signs of true absorption, an interest in the goings-on so powerful that he becomes oblivious of his friends—then their cup is full. "Didn't we tell you?" they say at last. What they want from him is not ethnological explanations; all they want is his approval.

What has taken place is a radical loss of sovereignty over that which is as much theirs as it is the ethnologist's. The fault does not lie with the ethnologist. He has no wish to stake a claim to the village; in fact, he desires the opposite: he will bore his friends to death by telling them about the village and the meaning of the folkways. A degree of sovereignty has been surrendered by the couple. It is the nature of the loss, moreover, that they are not aware of the loss, beyond a certain uneasiness. (Even if they read this and admitted it, it would be very difficult for them to bridge the gap in their confrontation of the world. Their consciousness of the corn dance cannot escape their consciousness of their consciousness, so that with the onset of the first direct enjoyment, their higher consciousness pounces and certifies: "Now you are doing it! Now you are really living!" and, in certifying the experience, sets it at nought.)

Their basic placement in the world is such that they recognize a priority of title of the expert over his particular department of being. The whole horizon of being is staked out by "them," the experts. The highest satisfaction of the sightseer (not merely the tourist but any layman seer of sights) is that his sight should be certified as genuine. The worst of this impoverishment is that there is no sense of impoverishment. The surrender of title is so complete that it never even occurs to one to reassert title. A poor man may envy the rich man, but the sightseer does not envy the expert. When a caste system becomes absolute, envy disappears. Yet the caste of layman-expert is not the fault of the expert. It is due altogether to the eager surrender of sovereignty by the layman so that he may take up the role not of the person but of the consumer.

I do not refer only to the special relation of layman to theorist. I refer to the general situation in which sovereignty is surrendered to a class of privileged knowers, whether these be theorists or artists. A reader may surrender sovereignty over that which has been written about, just as a consumer may surrender sovereignty over a thing which has been theorized about. The consumer is content to receive an experience just as it has been presented to him by theorists and planners. The reader may also be content to judge life by whether it has or has not been formulated by those who know and write about life. A young man goes to France. He too has a fair time of it, sees the sights, enjoys the food. On his last day, in fact as he sits in a restaurant in Le Havre waiting for his boat, something happens. A group of French students in the restaurant get into an impassioned argument over a recent play. A riot takes place. Madame la concierge joins in, swinging her mop at the rioters. Our young American is transported. This is "it." And he had almost left France without seeing "it"!

But the young man's delight is ambiguous. On the one hand, it is a pleasure for him to encounter the same Gallic temperament he had heard about from Puccini and Rolland. But on the other hand, the source of his pleasure testifies to a certain alienation. For the young man is actually barred from a direct encounter with anything French excepting only that which has been set forth, authenticated by Puccini and Rolland—those who know. If he had encountered the restaurant scene without reading Hemingway, without knowing that the performance was so typically, charmingly French, he would not have been delighted. He would only have been anxious at seeing things get out of hand. The source of his delight is the sanction of those who know.

This loss of sovereignty is not a marginal process, as might appear from my example of estranged sightseers. It is a generalized surrender of the horizon to those experts within whose competence a particular segment of the horizon is thought to lie. Kwakiutls are surrendered to Franz Boas; decaying Southern mansions are surrendered to Faulkner and Tennessee Williams. So that, although it is by no means the intention of the expert to expropriate sovereignty—in fact he would not even know what sovereignty meant in this context—the danger of theory and consumption is a seduction and deprivation of the consumer.

In the New Mexican desert, natives occasionally come across strange-looking artifacts which have fallen from the skies and which are stenciled: *Return to U.S. Experimental Project, Alamogordo. Reward.* The finder returns the object and is rewarded. He knows nothing of the nature of the object he has found and does not care to know. The sole role of the native, the highest role he can play, is that of finder and returner of the mysterious equipment.

The same is true of the layman's relation to *natural* objects in a modern technical society. No matter what the object or event is, whether it is a star, a swallow, a Kwakiutl, a "psychological phenomenon," the layman who confronts it does not confront it as a sovereign person, as Crusoe confronts a seashell he finds on the beach. The highest role he can conceive himself as playing is to be able to recognize the title of the object, to return it to the appropriate expert and have it certified as a genuine find. He does not even permit himself to see the thing—as Gerald Hopkins could see a rock or a cloud or a field. If anyone asks him why he doesn't look, he may reply that he didn't take that subject in college (or he hasn't read Faulkner).

This loss of sovereignty extends even to oneself. There is the neurotic who asks nothing more of his doctor than that his symptoms should prove interesting. When all else fails, the poor fellow has nothing to offer but his own neurosis. But even this is sufficient if only the doctor will show interest when he says, "Last night I had a curious sort of dream; perhaps it will be significant to one who knows about such things. It seems I was standing in a sort of alley—" (I have nothing else to offer you but my own unhappiness. Please say that it, at least, measures up, that it is a *proper* sort of unhappiness.)

II

A young Falkland Islander walking along a beach and spying a dead dogfish and going to work on it with his jackknife has, in a fashion wholly unprovided in modern educational theory, a great advantage over the Scarsdale high-school pupil who finds the dogfish on his laboratory desk. Similarly the citizen of Huxley's *Brave New World* who stumbles across a volume of Shakespeare in some vine-grown ruins and squats on a potsherd to read it is in a fairer way of getting at a sonnet than the Harvard sophomore taking English Poetry II.

The educator whose business it is to teach students biology or poetry is unaware of a whole ensemble of relations which exist between the student and the dogfish and between the student and the Shakespeare sonnet. To put it bluntly: A student who has the desire to get at a dogfish or a Shakespeare sonnet may have the greatest difficulty in salvaging the creature itself from the educational package in which it is presented. The great difficulty is that he is not aware that there is a difficulty; surely, he thinks, in such a fine classroom, with such a fine textbook, the sonnet must come across! What's wrong with me?

The sonnet and the dogfish are obscured by two different processes. The sonnet is obscured by the symbolic package which is formulated not by the sonnet itself but by the *media* through which the sonnet is transmitted, the media which the educators believe for some reason to be transparent. The new textbook, the type, the smell of the page, the classroom, the aluminum windows and the winter sky, the personality of Miss Hawkins—these media which are supposed to transmit the sonnet may only succeed in transmitting themselves. It is only the hardiest and cleverest of students who can salvage the sonnet from this many-tissued package. It is only the rarest student who knows that the sonnet must be salvaged from the package. (The educator is well aware that something is wrong, that there is a fatal gap between the student's learning and the student's life: The student reads the poem, appears to understand it, and gives all the answers. But what does he recall if he should happen to read a Shakespeare sonnet twenty years later? Does he recall the poem or does he recall the smell of the page and the smell of Miss Hawkins?)

One might object, pointing out that Huxley's citizen reading his sonnet in the ruins and the Falkland Islander looking at his dogfish on the beach also receive them in a certain package. Yes, but the difference lies in the fundamental placement of the student in the world, a placement which makes it possible to extract the thing from the package. The pupil at Scarsdale High sees himself placed as a consumer receiving an experience-package; but the Falkland Islander exploring his dogfish is a person exercising the sovereign right of a person in his lordship and mastery of creation. He too could use an instructor and a book and a technique, but he would use them as his subordinates, just as he uses his jackknife. The biology student does not use his scalpel as an instrument; he uses it as a magic wand! Since it is a "scientific instrument," it should do "scientific things."

The dogfish is concealed in the same symbolic package as the sonnet. But the dogfish suffers an additional loss. As a consequence of this double deprivation, the Sarah Lawrence student who scores A in zoology is apt to know very little about a dogfish. She is twice removed from the dogfish, once by the symbolic complex by which the dogfish is concealed, once again by the spoliation of the dogfish by theory which renders it invisible. Through no fault of zoology instructors, it is nevertheless a fact that the zoology laboratory at Sarah Lawrence College is one of the few places in the world where it is all but impossible to see a dogfish.

The dogfish, the tree, the seashell, the American Negro, the dream, are rendered invisible by a shift of reality from concrete thing to theory which Whitehead has called the fallacy of misplaced concreteness. It is the mistaking of an idea, a principle, an abstraction, for the real. As a consequence of the shift, the "specimen" is seen as less real than the theory of the specimen. As Kierkegaard said, once a person is seen as a specimen of a race or a species, at that very moment he ceases to be an individual. Then there are no more individuals but only specimens.

To illustrate: A student enters a laboratory which, in the pragmatic view, offers the student the optimum conditions under which an educational experience may be had. In the existential view, however—that view of the student in which he is regarded not as a receptacle of experience but as a knowing being whose peculiar property it is to see himself as being in a certain situation—the modern laboratory could not have been more effectively designed to conceal the dogfish forever.

The student comes to his desk. On it, neatly arranged by his instructor, he finds his laboratory manual, a dissecting board, instruments, and a mimeographed list:

Exercise 22: Materials
1 dissecting board
1 scalpel
1 forceps
1 probe
1 bottle india ink and syringe
1 specimen of *Squalus acanthias*

The clue to the situation in which the student finds himself is to be found in the last item: 1 specimen of *Squalus acanthias.*

The phrase *specimen of* expresses in the most succinct way imaginable the radical character of the loss of being which has occurred under his very nose. To refer to the dogfish, the unique concrete existent before him, as a "specimen of *Squalus acanthias*" reveals by its grammar the spoliation of the dogfish by the theoretical method. This phrase, *specimen of,* example of, instance of, indicates the ontological status of the individual creature in the eyes of the theorist. The dogfish itself is seen as a rather shabby expression of an ideal reality, the species *Squalus acanthias.* The result is the radical devaluation of the individual dogfish. (The *reductio ad absurdum* of Whitehead's shift is Toynbee's employment of it in his historical method. If a gram of NaCl is referred to by the chemist as a "sample of" NaCl, one may think of it as such and not much is missed by the oversight of the act of being of this particular pinch of salt, but when the Jews and the Jewish religion are understood as—in Toynbee's favorite phrase—a "classical example of" such and such a kind of *Voelkerwanderung,* we begin to suspect that something is being left out.)

If we look into the ways in which the student can recover the dogfish (or the sonnet), we will see that they have in common the stratagem of avoiding the educator's direct presentation of the object as a lesson to be learned and restoring access to sonnet and dogfish as beings to be known, reasserting the sovereignty of knower over known.

In truth, the biography of scientists and poets is usually the story of the discovery of the indirect approach, the circumvention of the educator's presentation—the young man who was sent to the *Technikum* and on his way fell into the habit of loitering in book stores and reading poetry; or the young man dutifully attending law school who on the way became curious about the comings and goings of ants. One remembers the scene in *The*

Heart Is a Lonely Hunter where the girl hides in the bushes to hear the Capehart in the big house play Beethoven. Perhaps she was the lucky one after all. Think of the unhappy souls inside, who see the record, worry about scratches, and most of all worry about whether they are *getting it*, whether they are bona fide music lovers. What is the best way to hear Beethoven: sitting in a proper silence around the Capehart or eavesdropping from an azalea bush?

However it may come about, we notice two traits of the second situation: (1) an openness of the thing before one—instead of being an exercise to be learned according to an approved mode, it is a garden of delights which beckons to one; (2) a sovereignty of the knower—instead of being a consumer of a prepared experience, I am a sovereign wayfarer, a wanderer in the neighborhood of being who stumbles into the garden.

One can think of two sorts of circumstances through which the thing may be restored to the person. (There is always, of course, the direct recovery: A student may simply be strong enough, brave enough, clever enough to take the dogfish and the sonnet by storm, to wrest control of it from the educators and the educational package.) First by ordeal: The Bomb falls; when the young man recovers consciousness in the shambles of the biology laboratory, there not ten inches from his nose lies the dogfish. Now all at once he can see it, directly and without let, just as the exile or the prisoner or the sick man sees the sparrow at his window in all its inexhaustibility; just as the commuter who has had a heart attack sees his own hand for the first time. In these cases, the simulacrum of everydayness and of consumption has been destroyed by disaster; in the case of the bomb, literally destroyed. Secondly, by apprenticeship to a great man: One day a great biologist walks into the laboratory; he stops in front of our student's desk; he leans over, picks up the dogfish, and, ignoring instruments and procedure, probes with a broken fingernail into the little carcass. "Now here is a curious business," he says, ignoring also the proper jargon of the specialty. "Look here how this little duct reverses its direction and drops into the pelvis. Now if you would look into a coelacanth, you would see that it—" And all at once the student can see. The technician and the sophomore who loves his textbooks are always offended by the genuine research man because the latter is usually a little vague and always humble before the thing; he doesn't have much use for the equipment or the jargon. Whereas the technician is never vague and never humble before the thing; he holds the thing disposed of by the principle, the formula, the textbook outline; and he thinks a great deal of equipment and jargon.

But since neither of these methods of recovering the dogfish is pedagogically feasible—perhaps the great man even less so than the Bomb—I wish to propose the following educational technique which should prove equally effective for Harvard and Shreveport High School. I propose that English poetry and biology should be taught as usual, but that at irregular intervals, poetry students should find dogfishes on their desks and biology students should find Shakespeare sonnets on their dissection boards. I am serious in declaring that a Sarah Lawrence English major who began poking about in a dogfish with a bobby pin would learn more in thirty minutes than a biology major in a whole semester; and that the latter upon reading on her dissecting board

> That time of year Thou may'st in me behold
> When yellow leaves, or none, or few, do hang
> Upon those boughs which shake against the cold—
> Bare ruin'd choirs where late the sweet birds sang.

might catch fire at the beauty of it.

The situation of the tourist at the Grand Canyon and the biology student are special cases of a predicament in which everyone finds himself in a modern technical society—a society, that is, in which there is a division between expert and layman, planner and consumer, in which experts and planners take special measures to teach and edify the consumer. The measures taken are measures appropriate to the consumer: The expert and the planner *know* and *plan,* but the consumer *needs* and *experiences.*

There is a double deprivation. First, the thing is lost through its packaging. The very means by which the thing is presented for consumption, the very techniques by which the thing is made available as an item of need-satisfaction, these very means operate to remove the thing from the sovereignty of the knower. A loss of title occurs. The measures which the museum curator takes to present the thing to the public are self-liquidating. The upshot of the curator's efforts are not that everyone can see the exhibit but that no one can see it. The curator protests: Why are they so indifferent? Why do they even deface the exhibit? Don't they know it is theirs? But it is not theirs. It is his, the curator's. By the most exclusive sort of zoning, the museum exhibit, the park oak tree, is part of an ensemble, a package, which is almost impenetrable to them. The archaeologist who puts his find in a museum so that everyone can see it accomplishes the reverse of his expectations. The result of his action is that no one can see it now but the archaeologist. He would have done better to keep it in his pocket and show it now and then to strangers.

The tourist who carves his initials in a public place, which is theoretically "his" in the first place, has good reasons for doing so, reasons which the exhibitor and planner know nothing about. He does so because in his role of consumer of an experience (a "recreational experience" to satisfy a "recreational need") he knows that he is disinherited. He is deprived of his title over being. He knows very well that he is in a very special sort of zone in which his only rights are the rights of a consumer. He moves like a ghost through schoolroom, city streets, trains, parks, movies. He carves his initials as a last desperate measure to escape his ghostly role of consumer. He is saying in effect: I am not a ghost after all; I am a sovereign person. And he establishes title the only way remaining to him, by staking his claim over one square inch of wood or stone.

Does this mean that we should get rid of museums? No, but it means that the sightseer should be prepared to enter into a struggle to recover a sight from a museum.

The second loss is the spoliation of the thing, the tree, the rock, the swallow, by the layman's misunderstanding of scientific theory. He believes that the thing is *disposed of* by theory, that it stands in the Platonic relation of being a *specimen of* such and such an underlying principle. In the transmission of scientific theory from theorist to layman, the expectation of the theorist is reversed. Instead of the marvels of the universe being made available to the public, the universe is disposed of by theory. The loss of sovereignty takes this form: As a result of the science of botany, trees are not made available to every man. On the contrary. The tree loses its proper density and mystery as a concrete existent and, as merely another *specimen of* a species, becomes itself nugatory.

Does this mean that there is no use taking biology at Harvard and Shreveport High? No, but it means that the student should know what a fight he has on his hands to rescue the specimen from the educational package. The educator is only partly to blame. For there is nothing the educator can do to provide for this need of the student. Everything the educator does only succeeds in becoming, for the student, part of the educational package. The highest role of the educator is the maieutic role of Socrates: to help the student come to himself not as a consumer of experience but as a sovereign individual.

The thing is twice lost to the consumer. First, sovereignty is lost: It is theirs, not his. Second, it is radically devalued by theory. This is a loss which has been brought about by science but through no fault of the scientist and through no fault of scientific theory. The loss has come about as a consequence of the seduction of the layman by science. The layman will be seduced as long as he regards beings as consumer items to be experienced rather than prizes to be won, and as long as he waives his sovereign rights as a person and accepts his role of consumer as the highest estate to which the layman can aspire.

As Mounier said, the person is not something one can study and provide for; he is something one struggles for. But unless he also struggles for himself, unless he knows that there is a struggle, he is going to be just what the planners think he is.

• • • • • • • • • • • • •

QUESTIONS FOR A SECOND READING

1. Percy's essay proceeds by adding example to example, one after another. If all the examples were meant to illustrate the same thing, the same general point or idea, then one would most likely have been enough. The rest would have been redundant. It makes sense, then, to assume that each example gives a different view of what Percy is saying, that each modifies the others, or qualifies them, or adds a piece that was otherwise lacking. It's as though Percy needed one more to get it right or to figure out what was missing along the way. As you read back through the essay, pay particular attention to the *differences* between the examples (between the various tourists going to the Grand Canyon, or between the tourists at the Grand Canyon and the tourists in Mexico). Also note the logic or system that leads from one to the next. What progress of thought is represented by the movement from one example to another, or from tourists to students?
2. The essay is filled with talk about "loss"—the loss of sovereignty, the loss of the creature—but it is resolutely ambiguous about what it is that we have lost. As you work your way back through the essay, note the passages that describe what we are missing. Are we to believe that Cárdenas actually had it—that he had no preconceived notions when he saw the Grand Canyon? And why is this loss such a matter of concern? What difference does it make whether or not we have "the creature" or not? How would a person's life be any different if there wasn't any loss? any sense of loss?

ASSIGNMENTS FOR WRITING

1. Percy tells several stories—some of them quite good stories—but it is often hard to know just what he is getting at, just what point it is he is trying to make. If he's making an argument, it's not the sort of argument that is easy to summarize. And if the stories (or anecdotes, perhaps) are meant to serve as examples, they are not the sort of examples that lead directly to a single, general conclusion or that serve to clarify a point or support an obvious thesis. In fact, at the very moment when you expect Percy to come forward and pull things together, he offers yet another story, as though another example, rather than any general statement, would get you closer to what he is saying.

   There are, at the same time, terms and phrases in this essay to suggest that this is an essay with a point to make. Percy talks, for example, about "the loss of sovereignty," "symbolic packages," "consumers of experience," and "dialectic," and it seems safe to say that these terms and phrases are meant to name or comment on key scenes, situations, or characters in the examples.

For this assignment, tell a story of your own, a story that is suggested by the stories Percy tells—perhaps a story about a time you went looking for something or at something, or about a time when you did or did not find a dogfish in your Shakespeare class. You should imagine that you are carrying out a project that Walker Percy has begun, a project that has you looking back at your own experience through the lens of "The Loss of the Creature," noticing what Percy would notice and following the paths that he would find interesting. Try to bring the terms that Percy uses—like "sovereign," "consumer," "expert," and "dialectic"—to bear on the story you have to tell. Feel free to imitate Percy's style and method in your essay.

2. Percy charts several routes to the Grand Canyon: you can take the packaged tour, you can get off the beaten track, you can wait for a disaster, you can follow the "dialectical movement which brings one back to the beaten track but at a level above it." This last path (or strategem), he says, is for the complex traveler: "Our complex friend stands behind his fellow tourists at the Bright Angel Lodge and sees the canyon through them and their predicament, their picture taking and busy disregard. In a sense, he exploits his fellow tourists; he stands on their shoulders to see the canyon."

   The complex traveler sees the Grand Canyon through the example of the common tourists with "their predicament, their picture taking and busy disregard." He "stands on their shoulders" to see the canyon. The distinction between complex and common approaches is an important one in the essay. It is interesting to imagine how the distinction could be put to work to define ways of reading.

   Suppose that you read "The Loss of the Creature" as a common reader. What would you see? What would you identify as key sections of the text? What would you miss? What would you say about what you see?

   If you think of yourself, now, as a complex reader, modelled after any of Percy's more complex tourists or students, what would you see? What would you identify as key sections of the text? What would you miss? What would you say about what you see?

   For this assignment, write an essay with three sections. You may number them, if you choose. The first section should represent the work of a common reader with "The Loss of the Creature," and the second should represent the work of a complex reader. The third section should look back and comment on the previous two. In particular, you might address these questions: Why might a person prefer one reading over the other? What is to be gained or lost with both?

MAKING CONNECTIONS

1. In "The Loss of the Creature," Percy writes about tourists and the difficulty they have seeing that which lies before them. In "Deep Play: Notes on the Balinese Cockfight" (p. 299) Clifford Geertz tells the story of his travels in Bali. Anthropologists, properly speaking, are not tourists. There is a schol-

arly purpose to their travel and, presumably, they have learned or developed the strategies necessary to get beyond the preformed "symbolic complex" that would keep them from seeing the place or the people they have traveled to study. They are experts, in other words, not common sightseers.

In his travels to Bali, Geertz seems to get just what he wants. He gets both the authentic experience and a complex understanding of that experience. If you read "Deep Play" from the perspective of Percy's essay, however, it is interesting to ask whether Percy would say that this was the case (whether Percy might say that Geertz has gone as far as one can go after Cárdenas), and it is interesting to ask how Percy would characterize the "strategies" that define Geertz's approach to his subject.

Write an essay in which you place Geertz in the context of Percy's tourists (not all of them, but two or three whose stories seem most interesting when placed alongside Geertz's). The purpose of your essay is offer a Percian reading of Geertz's essay—to study his text, that is, in light of the terms and methods Percy has established in "The Loss of the Creature."

2. Annie Dillard's experience studying insects in "The Fixed" (p. 155) lies outside the range of examples in "The Loss of the Creature." Dillard has a formal education, unlike the Falkland Islander, but she has gone off to the woods—she is not working in the context of an educational institution, like the student in the biology laboratory. The question to ask is whether Dillard's writing—the way she talks about insects—provides an example of a person whose "approach" or "strategem" has allowed her to recover either her subject or her own "sovereignty."

   Dillard provides an interesting case, then, for a person who wants to extend the range of Percy's analysis. Write an essay in which you place Dillard in the context of Percy's students. The purpose of your essay is to offer a Percian reading of Dillard's work—to study her text, that is, as though you were continuing and testing the work Percy has begun in "The Loss of the Creature."

ADRIENNE RICH

ADRIENNE RICH (b. 1929) once said that whatever she knows, she wants to "know it in [her] own nerves." As a writer, Rich found it necessary to acknowledge her anger at both the oppression of women and her immediate experience of that oppression. She needed to find the "anger that is creative." "Until I could tap into that very rich ocean," she said, "I think that my work was constrained in certain ways. There's this fear of anger in women, which is partly because we've been told it was always destructive, it was always unseemly, and unwomanly, and monstrous."

Rich's poetry combines passion and anger with a "yen for order." She wrote her first book of poems, A Change of World, *while an undergraduate at Radcliffe College. The book won the 1951 Yale Younger Poets Award and a generous introduction from W. H. Auden, who was one of the judges. Her subsequent works, which include* The Diamond Cutters, Snapshots of A Daughter-in-Law, Necessities of Life, Leaflets, The Will to Change, *and* Diving into the Wreck *show an increasing concern for the political and psychological consequences of life in a patriarchal society. When offered the National Book Award for* Diving into the Wreck *(1974), Rich refused the award as an individual but accepted it, in a statement written with two other nominees—Audre Lorde and Alice Walker (whose essay "In Search of Our Mothers' Gardens" appears on p. 508)—in the name of all women:*

> *We . . . together accept this award in the name of all the women whose voices have gone and still go unheard in a patriarchal world, and in the name of those who, like us, have been tolerated as token women in this culture, often at great cost and in great pain. . . . We dedicate this occasion to the struggle for self-determination of all women, of every color, identification or derived class . . . the women who will understand what we are doing here and those who will not understand yet; the silent women whose voices have been denied us, the articulate women who have given us the strength to do our work.*

After graduating from Radcliffe in 1951, Rich married and raised three sons. One of her prose collections, Of Woman Born: Motherhood as Experience and Institution, *treats her experience as both mother and daughter with eloquence, even as it calls for the destruction of motherhood as an institution. Rich has published eleven books of poetry and two collections of prose. She has taught at Columbia, Brandeis, Swarthmore, and at the City College of New York.*

When We Dead Awaken: Writing as Re-Vision[1]

The Modern Language Association is both marketplace and funeral parlor for the professional study of Western literature in North America. Like all gatherings of the professions, it has been and remains a "procession of the sons of educated men" (Virginia Woolf): a congeries of old-boys' networks, academicians rehearsing their numb canons in sessions dedicated to the literature of white males, junior scholars under the lash of "publish or perish" delivering papers in the bizarrely lit drawing-rooms of immense hotels: a ritual competition veering between cynicism and desperation.

However, in the interstices of these gentlemanly rites (or, in Mary Daly's words, on the boundaries of this patriarchal space),[2] *some feminist scholars, teachers, and graduate students, joined by feminist writers, editors, and publishers, have for a*

[1] As Rich explains, this essay—written in 1971—was first published in 1972 and then included in her volume *On Lies, Secrets, and Silence* (1978). At that time she added the introductory note reprinted here, as well as some notes, identified as "*A. R., 1978.*" [Editor's note in the Norton edition.]

[2] Mary Daly, *Beyond God the Father* (Boston: Beacon, 1971), pp. 40–41.

decade been creating more subversive occasions, challenging the sacredness of the gentlemanly canon, sharing the rediscovery of buried works by women, asking women's questions, bringing literary history and criticism back to life in both senses. The Commission of the Status of Women in the Profession was formed in 1969, and held its first public event in 1970. In 1971 the Commission asked Ellen Peck Killoh, Tillie Olsen, Elaine Reuben, and myself, with Elaine Hedges as moderator, to talk on "The Woman Writer in the Twentieth Century." The essay that follows was written for that forum, and later published, along with the other papers from the forum and workshops, in an issue of College English *edited by Elaine Hedges ("Women Writing and Teaching," vol. 34, no. 1, October 1972). With a few revisions, mainly updating, it was reprinted in* American Poets in 1976, *edited by William Heyen (New York: Bobbs-Merrill, 1976). That later text is the one published here.*

The challenge flung by feminists at the accepted literary canon, at the methods of teaching it, and at the biased and astigmatic view of male "literary scholarship," has not diminished in the decade since the first Women's Forum; it has become broadened and intensified more recently by the challenges of black and lesbian feminists pointing out that feminist literary criticism itself has overlooked or held back from examining the work of black women and lesbians. The dynamic between a political vision and the demand for a fresh vision of literature is clear: without a growing feminist movement, the first inroads of feminist scholarship could not have been made; without the sharpening of a black feminist consciousness, black women's writing would have been left in limbo between misogynist black male critics and white feminists still struggling to unearth a white women's tradition; without an articulate lesbian/feminist movement, lesbian writing would still be lying in that closet where many of us used to sit reading forbidden books "in a bad light."

Much, much more is yet to be done; and university curricula have of course changed very little as a result of all this. What *is* changing is the availability of knowledge, of vital texts, the visible effects on women's lives of seeing, hearing our wordless or negated experience affirmed and pursued further in language.

Ibsen's *When We Dead Awaken* is a play about the use that the male artist and thinker—in the process of creating culture as we know it—has made of women, in his life and in his work; and about a woman's slow struggling awakening to the use to which her life has been put. Bernard Shaw wrote in 1900 of this play:

> [Ibsen] shows us that no degradation ever devized or permitted is as disastrous as this degradation; that through it women can die into luxuries for men and yet can kill them; that men

> and women are becoming conscious of this; and that what remains to be seen as perhaps the most interesting of all imminent social developments is what will happen "when we dead awaken."[3]

It's exhilarating to be alive in a time of awakening consciousness; it can also be confusing, disorienting, and painful. This awakening of dead or sleeping consciousness has already affected the lives of millions of women, even those who don't know it yet. It is also affecting the lives of men, even those who deny its claims upon them. The argument will go on whether an oppressive economic class system is responsible for the oppressive nature of male/female relations, or whether, in fact, patriarchy—the domination of males—is the original model of oppression on which all others are based. But in the last few years the women's movement has drawn inescapable and illuminating connections between our sexual lives and our political institutions. The sleepwalkers are coming awake, and for the first time this awakening has a collective reality; it is no longer such a lonely thing to open one's eyes.

Re-vision—the act of looking back, of seeing with fresh eyes, of entering an old text from a new critical direction—is for women more than a chapter in cultural history: it is an act of survival. Until we can understand the assumptions in which we are drenched we cannot know ourselves. And this drive to self-knowledge, for women, is more than a search for identity: it is part of our refusal of the self-destructiveness of male-dominated society. A radical critique of literature, feminist in its impulse, would take the work first of all as a clue to how we live, how we have been living, how we have been led to imagine ourselves, how our language has trapped as well as liberated us, how the very act of naming has been till now a male prerogative, and how we can begin to see and name—and therefore live—afresh. A change in the concept of sexual identity is essential if we are not going to see the old political order reassert itself in every new revolution. We need to know the writing of the past, and know it differently than we have ever known it; not to pass on a tradition but to break its hold over us.

For writers, and at this moment for women writers in particular, there is the challenge and promise of a whole new psychic geography to be explored. But there is also a difficult and dangerous walking on the ice, as we try to find language and images for the consciousness we are just coming into, and with little in the past to support us. I want to talk about some aspect of this difficulty and this danger.

---

[3]G. B. Shaw, *The Quintessence of Ibsenism* (New York: Hill & Wang, 1922), p. 139.

Jane Harrison, the great classical anthropologist, wrote in 1914 in a letter to her friend Gilbert Murray:

> By the by, about "Women," it has bothered me often—why do women never want to write poetry about Man as a sex—why is Woman a dream and a terror to man and not the other way around? . . . Is it mere convention and propriety, or something deeper?[4]

I think Jane Harrison's question cuts deep into the myth-making tradition, the romantic tradition; deep into what women and men have been to each other; and deep into the psyche of the woman writer. Thinking about that question, I began thinking of the work of two twentieth-century women poets, Sylvia Plath and Diane Wakoski. It strikes me that in the work of both Man appears as, if not a dream, a fascination and a terror; and that the source of the fascination and the terror is, simply, Man's power—to dominate, tyrannize, choose, or reject the woman. The charisma of Man seems to come purely from his power over her and his control of the world by force, not from anything fertile or life-giving in him. And, in the work of both these poets, it is finally the woman's sense of *herself*—embattled, possessed—that gives the poetry its dynamic charge, its rhythms of struggle, need, will, and female energy. Until recently this female anger and this furious awareness of the Man's power over her were not available materials to the female poet, who tended to write of Love as the source of her suffering, and to view that victimization by Love as an almost inevitable fate. Or, like Marianne Moore and Elizabeth Bishop, she kept sexuality at a measured and chiseled distance in her poems.

One answer to Jane Harrison's question has to be that historically men and women have played very different parts in each others' lives. Where woman has been a luxury for man, and has served as the painter's model and the poet's muse, but also as comforter, nurse, cook, bearer of his seed, secretarial assistant, and copyist of manuscripts, man has played a quite different role for the female artist. Henry James repeats an incident which the writer Prosper Mérimée described, of how, while he was living with George Sand,

> he once opened his eyes, in the raw winter dawn, to see his companion, in a dressing-gown, on her knees before the domestic hearth, a candle-stick beside her and a red *madras* round her head, making bravely, with her own hands the fire that was to enable her to sit down betimes to urgent pen and paper. The story represents him as having felt that the spec-

[4] J. G. Stewart, *Jane Ellen Harrison: A Portrait from Letters* (London: Merlin, 1959), p. 140.

> tacle chilled his ardor and tried his taste; her appearance was unfortunate, her occupation an inconsequence, and her industry a reproof—the result of all which was a lively irritation and an early rupture.[5]

The specter of this kind of male judgment, along with the misnaming and thwarting of her needs by a culture controlled by males, has created problems for the woman writer: problems of contact with herself, problems of language and style, problems of energy and survival.

In rereading Virginia Woolf's *A Room of One's Own* (1929) for the first time in some years, I was astonished at the sense of effort, of pains taken, of dogged tentativeness, in the tone of that essay. And I recognized that tone. I had heard it often enough, in myself and in other women. It is the tone of a woman almost in touch with her anger, who is determined not to appear angry, who is *willing* herself to be calm, detached, and even charming in a roomful of men where things have been said which are attacks on her very integrity. Virginia Woolf is addressing an audience of women, but she is acutely conscious—as she always was—of being overheard by men: by Morgan and Lytton and Maynard Keynes and for that matter by her father, Leslie Stephen.[6] She drew the language out into an exacerbated thread in her determination to have her own sensibility yet protect it from those masculine presences. Only at rare moments in that essay do you hear the passion in her voice; she was trying to sound as cool as Jane Austen, as Olympian as Shakespeare, because that is the way the men of the culture thought a writer should sound.

No male writer has written primarily or even largely for women, or with the sense of women's criticism as a consideration when he chooses his materials, his theme, his language. But to a lesser or greater extent, every woman writer has written for men even when, like Virginia Woolf, she was supposed to be addressing women. If we have come to the point when this balance might begin to change, when women can stop being haunted, not only by "convention and propriety" but by internalized fears of being and saying themselves, then it is an extraordinary moment for the woman writer—and reader.

---

[5] Henry James, "Notes on Novelists," in *Selected Literary Criticism of Henry James*, Morris Shapira, ed. (London: Heinemann, 1963), pp. 157–58.

[6] *A. R., 1978:* This intuition of mine was corroborated when, early in 1978, I read the correspondence between Woolf and Dame Ethel Smyth (Henry W. and Albert A. Berg Collection, The New York Public Library, Astor, Lenox and Tilden Foundations); in a letter dated June 8, 1933, Woolf speaks of having kept her own personality out of *A Room of One's Own* lest she not be taken seriously: ". . . how personal, so will they say, rubbing their hands with glee, women always are; *I even hear them as I write.*" (Italics mine.)

I have hesitated to do what I am going to do now, which is to use myself as an illustration. For one thing, it's a lot easier and less dangerous to talk about other women writers. But there is something else. Like Virginia Woolf, I am aware of the women who are not with us here because they are washing the dishes and looking after the children. Nearly fifty years after she spoke, that fact remains largely unchanged. And I am thinking also of women whom she left out of the picture altogether—women who are washing other people's dishes and caring for other people's children, not to mention women who went on the streets last night in order to feed their children. We seem to be special women here, we have liked to think of ourselves as special, and we have known that men would tolerate, even romanticize us as special, as long as our words and actions didn't threaten their privilege of tolerating or rejecting us and our work according to *their* ideas of what a special woman ought to be. An important insight of the radical women's movement has been how divisive and how ultimately destructive is this myth of the special woman, who is also the token woman. Every one of us here in this room has had great luck—we are teachers, writers, academicians; our own gifts could not have been enough, for we all know women whose gifts are buried or aborted. Our struggles can have meaning and our privileges—however precarious under patriarchy—can be justified only if they can help to change the lives of women whose gifts—and whose very being—continue to be thwarted and silenced.

My own luck was being born white and middle-class into a house full of books, with a father who encouraged me to read and write. So for about twenty years I wrote for a particular man, who criticized and praised me and made me feel I was indeed "special." The obverse side of this, of course, was that I tried for a long time to please him, or rather, not to displease him. And then of course there were other men—writers, teachers—the Man, who was not a terror or a dream but a a literary master and a master in other ways less easy to acknowledge. And there were all those poems about women, written by men: it seemed to be a given that men wrote poems and women frequently inhabited them. These women were almost always beautiful, but threatened with the loss of beauty, the loss of youth—the fate worse than death. Or, they were beautiful and died young, like Lucy and Lenore. Or, the woman was like Maud Gonne, cruel and disastrously mistaken, and the poem reproached her because she had refused to become a luxury for the poet.

A lot is being said today about the influence that the myths and images of women have on all of us who are products of culture. I think it has been a peculiar confusion to the girl or woman who tries to write because she is peculiarly susceptible to language. She goes to poetry or fiction looking for *her* way of being in the world, since she too has been putting words and images together; she is looking eagerly for guides, maps, possibilities; and over and over in the "words' masculine persuasive force" of literature she comes up against something that negates everything she is about: she meets the image of Woman in books written by men. She finds a terror and a dream, she finds a beautiful pale face, she finds La Belle Dame Sans Merci, she finds Juliet or Tess or Salomé, but precisely what she does not find is that absorbed, drudging, puzzled, sometimes inspired creature, herself, who sits at a desk trying to put words together.

So what does she do? What did I do? I read the older women poets with their peculiar keenness and ambivalence: Sappho, Christina Rossetti, Emily Dickinson, Elinor Wylie, Edna Millay, H. D. I discovered that the woman poet most admired at the time (by men) was Marianne Moore, who was maidenly, elegant, intellectual, discreet. But even in reading these women I was looking in them for the same things I had found in the poetry of men, because I wanted women poets to be the equals of men, and to be equal was still confused with sounding the same.

I know that my style was formed first by male poets: by the men I was reading as an undergraduate—Frost, Dylan Thomas, Donne, Auden, MacNeice, Stevens, Yeats. What I chiefly learned from them was craft.[7] But poems are like dreams: in them you put what you don't know you know. Looking back at poems I wrote before I was twenty-one, I'm startled because beneath the conscious craft are glimpses of the split I even then experienced between the girl who wrote poems, who defined herself in writing poems, and the girl who was to define herself by her relationships with men. "Aunt Jennifer's Tigers" (1951), written while I was a student, looks with deliberate detachment at this split.

> Aunt Jennifer's tigers stride across a screen,
> Bright topaz denizens of a world of green.
> They do not fear the men beneath the tree;
> They pace in sleek chivalric certainty.
>
> Aunt Jennifer's fingers fluttering through her wool
> Find even the ivory needle hard to pull.
> The massive weight of Uncle's wedding band
> Sits heavily upon Aunt Jennifer's hand.
>
> When Aunt is dead, her terrified hands will lie
> Still ringed with ordeals she was mastered by.
> The tigers in the panel that she made
> Will go on striding, proud and unafraid.

---

[7] *A. R., 1978:* Yet I spent months, at sixteen, memorizing and writing imitations of Millay's sonnets; and in notebooks of that period I find what are obviously attempts to imitate Dickinson's metrics and verbal compression. I knew H. D. only through anthologized lyrics; her epic poetry was not then available to me.

In writing this poem, composed and apparently cool as it is, I thought I was creating a portrait of an imaginary woman. But this woman suffers from the opposition of her imagination, worked out in tapestry, and her lifestyle, "ringed with ordeals she was mastered by." It was important to me that Aunt Jennifer was a person as distinct from myself as possible—distanced by the formalism of the poem, by its objective, observant tone—even by putting the woman in a different generation.

In those years formalism was part of the strategy—like asbestos gloves, it allowed me to handle materials I couldn't pick up barehanded. A later strategy was to use the persona of a man, as I did in "The Loser" (1958):

A man thinks of the woman he once loved: first, after her wedding, and then nearly a decade later.

I
I kissed you, bride and lost, and went
home from that bourgeois sacrament,
your cheek still tasting cold upon
my lips that gave you benison
with all the swagger that they knew—
as losers somehow learn to do.

Your wedding made my eyes ache; soon
the world would be worse off for one
more golden apple dropped to ground
without the least protesting sound,
and you would windfall lie, and we
forget your shimmer on the tree.

Beauty is always wasted: if
not Mignon's song sung to the deaf,
at all events to the unmoved.
A face like yours cannot be loved
long or seriously enough.
Almost, we seem to hold it off.

II
Well, you are tougher than I thought.
Now when the wash with ice hangs taut
this morning of St. Valentine,
I see you strip the squeaking line,
your body weighed against the load,
and all my groans can do no good.

Because you are still beautiful,
though squared and stiffened by the pull
of what nine windy years have done.
You have three daughters, lost a son.

I see all your intelligence
flung into that unwearied stance.

My envy is of no avail.
I turn my head and wish him well
who chafed your beauty into use
and lives forever in a house
lit by the friction of your mind.
You stagger in against the wind.

I finished college, published my first book by a fluke, as it seemed to me, and broke off a love affair. I took a job, lived alone, went on writing, fell in love. I was young, full of energy, and the book seemed to mean that others agreed I was a poet. Because I was also determined to prove that as a woman poet I could also have what was then defined as a "full" woman's life, I plunged in my early twenties into marriage and had three children before I was thirty. There was nothing overt in the environment to warn me: these were the fifties, and in reaction to the earlier wave of feminism, middle-class women were making careers of domestic perfection, working to send their husbands through professional schools, then retiring to raise large families. People were moving out to the suburbs, technology was going to be the answer to everything, even sex; the family was in its glory. Life was extremely private; women were isolated from each other by the loyalties of marriage. I have a sense that women didn't talk to each other much in the fifties—not about their secret emptinesses, their frustrations. I went on trying to write; my second book and first child appeared in the same month. But by the time that book came out I was already dissatisfied with those poems, which seemed to me mere exercises for poems I hadn't written. The book was praised, however, for its "gracefulness"; I had a marriage and a child. If there were doubts, if there were periods of null depression or active despairing, these could only mean that I was ungrateful, insatiable, perhaps a monster.

About the time my third child was born, I felt that I had either to consider myself a failed woman and a failed poet, or to try to find some synthesis by which to understand what was happening to me. What frightened me most was the sense of drift, of being pulled along on a current which called itself my destiny, but in which I seemed to be losing touch with whoever I had been, with the girl who had experienced her own will and energy almost ecstatically at times, walking around a city or riding a train at night or typing in a student room. In a poem about my grandmother I wrote (of myself): "A young girl, thought sleeping, is certified dead" ("Halfway"). I was writing very little, partly from fatigue, that female fatigue of suppressed anger and loss of contact with my own being; partly from the discontinuity of female life with its attention to small chores, errands, work that others constantly undo, small children's constant needs. What I did write was unconvincing to me; my anger and frustration were hard to acknowledge in or out of poems because in fact I cared a great deal about my husband and my children. Trying to look back and understand that time I have tried to analyze the real nature of the conflict. Most, if not all, human lives are full of fantasy—passive day-dreaming which need not be acted on. But to write poetry or fiction, or even to think well, is not to fantasize, or to put fantasies on paper. For a poem to coalesce, for a character or an action to take shape, there has to be an imaginative transformation of reality which is no way passive. And a certain freedom of the mind is needed—freedom to press on, to enter the currents of your thought like a glider pilot, knowing that your motion can be sustained, that the buoyancy of your attention will not be suddenly snatched away. Moreover, if the imagination is to transcend and transform experience it has to question, to challenge, to conceive of alternatives, perhaps to the very life you are living at that moment. You have to be free to play around with the notion that day might be night, love might be hate; nothing can be too sacred for the imagination to turn into its opposite or to call experimentally by another name. For writing is renaming. Now, to be maternally with small children all day in the old way, to be with a man in the old way of marriage, requires a holding-back, a putting-aside of that imaginative activity, and demands instead a kind of conservatism. I want to make it clear that I am *not* saying that in order to write well, or think well, it is necessary to become unavailable to others, or to become a devouring ego. This has been the myth of the masculine artist and thinker; and I do not accept it. But to be a female human being trying to fulfill traditional female functions in a traditional way *is* in direct conflict with the subversive function of the imagination. The word traditional is important here. There must be ways, and we will be finding out more and more about them, in which the energy of creation and the energy of relation can be united. But in those years I always felt the conflict as a failure of love in myself. I had thought I was choosing a full life: the life available to most men, in which sexuality, work, and parenthood could coexist. But I felt, at twenty-nine, guilt toward the people closest to me, and guilty toward my own being.

I wanted, then, more than anything, the one thing of which there was never enough: time to think, time to write. The fifties and early sixties were years of rapid revelations: the sit-ins and marches in the South, the Bay of Pigs, the early antiwar movement, raised large questions—questions for which the masculine world of the academy around me seemed to have expert and fluent answers. But I needed to think for myself—about pacifism and dissent and violence, about poetry and society, and about my own relationship to all these things. For about ten years I was reading in fierce snatches, scribbling in notebooks, writing poetry in fragments; I was looking desperately for clues, because if there were no clues then I thought I might be insane. I wrote in a notebook about this time:

> Paralyzed by the sense that there exists a mesh of relationships—e.g., between my anger at the children, my sensual life, pacifism, sex (I mean sex in its broadest significance, not merely sexual desire)—an interconnectedness which, if I could see it, make it valid, would give me back myself, make it possible to function lucidly and passionately. Yet I grope in and out among these dark webs.

I think I began at this point to feel that politics was not something "out there" but something "in here" and of the essence of my condition.

In the late fifties I was able to write, for the first time, directly about experiencing myself as a woman. The poem was jotted in fragments during children's naps, brief hours in a library, or at 3:00 A.M. after rising with a wakeful child. I despaired of doing any continuous work at this time. Yet I began to feel that my fragments and scraps had a common consciousness and a common theme, one which I would have been very unwilling to put on paper at an earlier time because I had been taught that poetry should be "universal," which meant, of course, nonfemale. Until then I had tried very much *not* to identify myself as a female poet. Over two years I wrote a ten-part poem called "Snapshots of a Daughter-in-Law" (1958–1960), in a longer looser mode than I'd ever trusted myself with before. It was an extraordinary relief to write that poem. It strikes me now as too literary, too dependent on allusion; I hadn't found the courage yet to do without authorities, or even to use the pronoun "I"—the woman in the poem is always "she." One section of it, No. 2, concerns a woman who thinks she is going mad; she is haunted by voices telling her to resist and rebel, voices which she can hear but not obey.

> 2.
> Banging the coffee-pot into the sink
> she hears the angels chiding, and looks out
> past the raked gardens to the sloppy sky.
> Only a week since They said: *Have no patience.*
>
> The next time it was: *Be insatiable.*
> Then: *Save yourself; others you cannot save.*
> Sometimes she's let the tapstream scald her arm,
> a match burn to her thumbnail,
>
> or held her hand above the kettle's snout
> right in the woolly steam. They are probably angels,
> since nothing hurts her anymore, except
> each morning's grit blowing into her eyes.

The poem "Orion," written five years later, is a poem of reconnection with a part of myself I had felt I was losing—the active principle, the energetic imagination, the "half-brother" whom I projected, as I had for many years, into the constellation Orion. It's no accident that the words "cold and egotistical" appear in this poem, and are applied to myself.

Far back when I went zig-zagging
through tamarack pastures
you were my genius, you
my cast-iron Viking, my helmed
lion-heart king in prison.
Years later now you're young

my fierce half-brother, staring
down from that simplified west
your breast open, your belt dragged down
by an oldfashioned thing, a sword
the last bravado you won't give over
though it weighs you down as you stride

and the stars in it are dim
and maybe have stopped burning.
But you burn, and I know it;
as I throw back my head to take you in
an old transfusion happens again:
divine astronomy is nothing to it.

Indoors I bruise and blunder,
break faith, leave ill enough
alone, a dead child born in the dark.
Night cracks up over the chimney,
pieces of time, frozen geodes
come showering down in the grate.

A man reaches behind my eyes
and finds them empty
a woman's head turns away
from my head in the mirror
children are dying my death
and eating crumbs of my life.

Pity is not your forte.
Calmly you ache up there
pinned aloft in your crow's nest,
my speechless pirate!
You take it all for granted
and when I look you back

it's with a starlike eye
shooting its cold and egotistical spear

where it can do least damage.
Breathe deep! No hurt, no pardon
out here in the cold with you
you with your back to the wall.

The choice still seemed to be between "love"—womanly, maternal love, altruistic love—a love defined and ruled by the weight of an entire culture; and egotism—a force directed by men into creation, achievement, ambition, often at the expense of others, but justifiably so. For weren't they men, and wasn't that their destiny as womanly, selfless love was ours? We know now that the alternatives are false ones—that the word "love" is itself in need of re-vision.

There is a companion poem to "Orion," written three years later, in which at last the woman in the poem and the woman writing the poem become the same person. It is called "Planetarium," and it was written after a visit to a real planetarium, where I read an account of the work of Caroline Herschel, the astronomer, who worked with her brother William, but whose name remained obscure, as his did not.

Thinking of Caroline Herschel, 1750–1848,
astronomer, sister of William; and others

A woman in the shape of a monster
a monster in the shape of a woman
the skies are full of them

a woman   "in the snow
among the Clocks and instruments
or measuring the ground with poles"

in her 98 years to discover
8 comets

she whom the moon ruled
like us
levitating into the night sky
riding the polished lenses

Galaxies of women, there
doing penance for impetuousness
ribs chilled
in those spaces   of the mind

An eye,
  "virile, precise and absolutely certain"
  from the mad webs of Uranisborg
                                        encountering the NOVA

every impulse of light exploding
from the core
as life flies out of us

    Tycho whispering at last
    "Let me not seem to have lived in vain"

What we see, we see
and seeing is changing

the light that shrivels a mountain
and leaves a man alive

Heartbeat of the pulsar
heart sweating through my body

The radio impulse
pouring in from Taurus

    I am bombarded yet   I stand

I have been standing all my life in the
direct path of a battery of signals
the most accurately transmitted most
untranslateable language in the universe
I am a galactic cloud so deep   so invo-
luted that a light wave could take 15
years to travel through me   And has
taken   I am an instrument in the shape
of a woman trying to translate pulsations
into images   for the relief of the body
and the reconstruction of the mind.

In closing I want to tell you about a dream I had last summer. I dreamed I was asked to read my poetry at a mass women's meeting, but when I began to read, what came out were the lyrics of a blues song. I share this dream with you because it seemed to me to say something about the problems and the future of the woman writer, and probably of women in general. The awakening of consciousness is not like the crossing of a frontier—one step and you are in another country. Much of woman's poetry has been of the nature of the blues song: a cry of pain, of victimization, or a lyric of seduction.[8] And today, much poetry by women—and prose for that matter—is charged with anger. I think we need to go through that anger, and we will betray our own reality if we try, as Virginia Woolf was trying, for an objectivity, a detachment, that would make us sound more like Jane

[8] *A. R., 1978:* When I dreamed that dream, was I wholly ignorant of the tradition of Bessie Smith and other women's blues lyrics which transcended victimization to sing of resistance and independence?

Austen or Shakespeare. We know more than Jane Austen or Shakespeare knew: more than Jane Austen because our lives are more complex, more than Shakespeare because we know more about the lives of women—Jane Austen and Virginia Woolf included.

Both the victimization and the anger experienced by women are real, and have real sources, everywhere in the environment, built into society, language, the structures of thought. They will go on being tapped and explored by poets, among others. We can neither deny them, nor will we rest there. A new generation of women poets is already working out of the psychic energy released when women begin to move out towards what the feminist philosopher Mary Daly has described as the "new space" on the boundaries of patriarchy.[9] Women are speaking to and of women in these poems, out of a newly released courage to name, to love each other, to share risk and grief and celebration.

To the eye of a feminist, the work of Western male poets now writing reveals a deep, fatalistic pessimism as to the possibilities of change, whether societal or personal, along with a familiar and threadbare use of women (and nature) as redemptive on the one hand, threatening on the other; and a new tide of phallocentric sadism and overt woman-hating which matches the sexual brutality of recent films. "Political" poetry by men remains stranded amid the struggles for power among male groups; in condemning U.S. imperialism or the Chilean junta the poet can claim to speak for the oppressed while remaining, as male, part of a system of sexual oppression. The enemy is always outside the self, the struggle somewhere else. The mood of isolation, self-pity, and self-imitation that pervades "nonpolitical" poetry suggests that a profound change in masculine consciousness will have to precede any new male poetic—or other—inspiration. The creative energy of patriarchy is fast running out; what remains is its self-generating energy for destruction. As women, we have our work cut out for us.

---

[9] Mary Daly, *Beyond God the Father: Towards a Philosophy of Women's Liberation* (Boston: Beacon, 1973).

. . . .

QUESTIONS FOR A SECOND READING

1. Toward the end of the essay, Rich says

> And today, much poetry by women—and prose for that matter—is charged with anger. I think we need to go through that anger, and we will betray our own reality if we try, as Virginia Woolf was trying,

> for an objectivity, a detachment, that would make us sound more like Jane Austen or Shakespeare.

Would you say this essay is charged with anger? (This is not the same question as "Is Rich angry?" The former asks about the essay, the latter about Rich herself.)

Both "victimization" and "the anger experienced by women," Rich says, are "built into society, language, the structures of thought." Where in the structure or language of this essay do you find evidence of victimization or anger? One of the essay's arguments is that women must learn to see the old forms of language as traps and to develop new forms to better serve women's experience. See if you can use this essay as an example to test what she says. As you reread the essay, look for places that will allow you to talk about Rich's anger—or, perhaps, her detachment or her victimization. Is she trapped by the language available to her? Does she write like a victim? If not, what would you point to as signs of her freedom?

2. It is a rare pleasure to hear a poet talk in detail about her work. As you read back through the essay, pay particular attention to what Rich notices in her poems. What *does* she notice? What does she say about what she notices? What does this allow you to say about poems or the making of poems? What does it allow you to say about the responsibilities of a reader?

ASSIGNMENTS FOR WRITING

1. Rich says

> For a poem to coalesce, for a character or an action to take shape, there has to be an imaginative transformation of reality which is no way passive. . . . Moreover, if the imagination is to transcend and transform experience it has to question, to challenge, to conceive of alternatives, perhaps to the very life you are living at that moment. You have to be free to play around with the notion that day might be night, love might be hate; nothing can be too sacred for the imagination to turn into its opposite or to call experimentally by another name. For writing is re-naming.

This is powerful language, and it is interesting to imagine how it might work for a person trying to read and understand one of Rich's poems. For this assignment, choose one of the poems Rich includes in the essay and write an essay of your own that considers the poem as an act of "re-naming." What is transformed into what? And to what end? Or to what consequence? What can you say about the poem as an act of imagination?

2. In "When We Dead Awaken," Rich chooses several of her poems to represent stages in her history as a poet. Write an essay describing what you consider to be the most significant pattern of change in Rich's poems. When you are done, compare your account to Rich's account of the changes she sees in her own work. Does your account agree with hers? On what points?

Note: You will need, in your essay, to make very careful and precise use of examples drawn from the poems and from Rich's discussion of those poems.

MAKING CONNECTIONS

1. In speaking of the last poem she presents, "Planetarium," Rich says, "at last the woman in the poem and the woman writing the poem became the same person." "Orion" however, was also written in the first person (in the voice of a woman, that is, who says "Indoors I bruise and blunder") and the one prior to that, section 2 from "Snapshots of a Daughter-in-Law," speaks through the point of view of a woman (a woman who, according to Rich, represented at least a part of herself). It seems reasonable to say that the achievement in "Planetarium" marks a crucial or difficult next step for the poet, but it is not so easy to say what that step was or why it was important. And Rich leaves that last poem, in fact, to stand on its own, with no direct commentary on her part.

   Write a paper in which you explain the poet's achievement as she moves from "Snapshots" to "Planetarium" by comparing her (as either a similar or different case) to the figure of the art critic in "Ways of Seeing" (p. 48) or to the figure of the scientist in "The Historical Structure of Scientific Discovery" (p. 339). Both the critic and the scientist make or fail to make "important next steps." Berger and Kuhn provide terms you can use to name and understand that process of intellectual development, its difficulties, achievements, and consequences. Using a figure from one of these essays as a point of reference can give you a way of thinking about Adrienne Rich and the development represented by the movement from "Snapshots" to "Orion" to "Planetarium."

2. Gloria Steinem's "Ruth's Song" (p. 472), Alice Walker's "In Search of Our Mothers' Gardens" (p. 508), and Rich's "When We Dead Awaken" all make strong statements about the situation of women and about the importance of looking to the past to better understand the present and provide options for the future. The essays have certain similarities, but it is also interesting to consider their differences. Write an essay in which you examine the interesting differences among these three essays; consider the essays as three forms of feminist thought, three different ways of thinking critically about the situation of women.

RICHARD RODRIGUEZ

RICHARD RODRIGUEZ, the son of Mexican immigrants, was born in San Francisco in 1944. He grew up in Sacramento, where he attended Catholic schools before going on to Stanford University, Columbia University, the Warburg Institute in London, and the University of California at Berkeley, eventually completing a Ph.D. in English Renaissance literature. His essays have been published in Saturday Review, The American Scholar, Change, *and elsewhere. He now lives in San Francisco and works as a lecturer, educational consultant, and free-lance writer.*

In his book of autobiographical essays, Hunger of Memory*—which the* Christian Science Monitor *called "beautifully written, wrung from a sore heart"—Rodriguez tells the story of his education, paying particular attention to both the meaning of his success as a student and, as he said, "its consequent price—the loss." Rodriguez's loss is represented most powerfully by his increased alienation from his parents and the decrease of intimate exchanges in family life. His parents' primary language was Spanish; his, once he became eager for success in school, was English. But the barrier was not only a language barrier. Rodriguez discovered that the interests he developed at school and through his reading were interests he did* *not share with those at home—in fact, his desire to speak of them tended to threaten and humiliate his mother and father.*

This separation, Rodriguez argues, is a necessary part of every person's development, even though not everyone experiences it so dramatically. We must leave home and familiar ways of speaking and understanding in order to participate in public life. On these grounds, Rodriguez has been a strong voice against bilingual education, arguing that classes conducted in Spanish will only reinforce Spanish-speaking students' separateness from mainstream American life.

The selection that follows, Chapter 2 of Hunger of Memory, *deals with Rodriguez's experiences in school. If, he said, "because of my schooling I had grown culturally separated from my parents, my education finally had given me ways of speaking and caring about that fact." This essay is a record of how he came to understand the changes in his life. A reviewer writing in the* Atlantic Monthly *concluded that* Hunger of Memory *will survive in our literature "not because of some forgotten public issues that once bisected Richard Rodriguez's life, but because his history of that life has something to say about what it means to be American . . . and what it means to be human."*

The Achievement of Desire

I stand in the ghetto classroom—"the guest speaker"—attempting to lecture on the mystery of the sounds of our words to rows of diffident students. "Don't you hear it? Listen! The music of our words. *'Sumer is i-cumen in. . . .'* And songs on the car radio. We need Aretha Franklin's voice to fill plain words with music—her life." In the face of their empty stares, I try to create an enthusiasm. But the girls in the back row turn to watch some boy passing outside. There are flutters of smiles, waves. And someone's mouth elongates heavy, silent words through the barrier of glass. Silent words—the lips straining to shape each voiceless syllable: *"Meet meee late errr."* By the door, the instructor smiles at me, apparently hoping that I will be able to spark some enthusiasm in the class. But only one student seems to be listening. A girl, maybe fourteen. In this gray room her eyes shine with ambition. She keeps nodding and nodding at all that I say; she even takes notes. And each time I ask a question, she jerks up and down in her desk like a marionette, while her hand waves over the bowed heads of her classmates. It is myself (as a boy) I see as she faces me now (a man in my thirties).

The boy who first entered a classroom barely able to speak English, twenty years later concluded his studies in the stately quiet of the reading room in the British Museum. Thus with one sentence I can summarize my academic career. It will be harder to summarize what sort of life connects the boy to the man.

With every award, each graduation from one level of education to the next, people I'd meet would congratulate me. Their refrain always the same: "Your parents must be very proud." Sometimes then they'd ask me how I managed it—my "success." (How?) After a while, I had several quick answers to give in reply. I'd admit, for one thing, that I went to an excellent grammar school. (My earliest teachers, the nuns, made my success their ambition.) And my brother and both my sisters were very good students. (They often brought home the shiny school trophies I came to want.) And my mother and father always encouraged me. (At every graduation they were behind the stunning flash of the camera when I turned to look at the crowd.)

As important as these factors were, however, they account inadequately for my academic advance. Nor do they suggest what an odd success I managed. For although I was a very good student, I was also a very bad student. I was a "scholarship boy," a certain kind of scholarship boy. Always successful, I was always unconfident. Exhilarated by my progress. Sad. I became the prized student—anxious and eager to learn. Too eager, too anxious—an imitative and unoriginal pupil. My brother and two sisters enjoyed the advantages I did, and they grew to be as successful as I, but none of them ever seemed so anxious about their schooling. A second-grade student, I was the one who came home and corrected the "simple" grammatical mistakes of our parents. ("Two negatives make a positive.") Proudly I announced—to my family's startled silence—that a teacher had said I was losing all trace of a Spanish accent. I was oddly annoyed when I was unable to get parental help with a homework assignment. The night my father tried to help me with an arithmetic exercise, he kept reading the instructions, each time more deliberately, until I pried the textbook out of his hands, saying, "I'll try to figure it out some more by myself."

When I reached the third grade, I outgrew such behavior. I became more tactful, careful to keep separate the two very different worlds of my day. But then, with ever-increasing intensity, I devoted myself to my studies. I became bookish, puzzling to all my family. Ambition set me apart. When my brother saw me struggling home with stacks of library books, he would laugh, shouting: "Hey, Four Eyes!" My father opened a closet one day and was startled to find me inside, reading a novel. My mother would find me reading when I was supposed to be asleep or helping around the house or playing outside. In a voice angry or worried or just curious, she'd ask: "What do you see in your books?" It became the family's joke.

When I was called and wouldn't reply, someone would say I must be hiding under my bed with a book.

(How did I manage my success?)

What I am about to say to you has taken me more than twenty years to admit: *A primary reason for my success in the classroom was that I couldn't forget that schooling was changing me and separating me from the life I enjoyed before becoming a student.* That simple realization! For years I never spoke to anyone about it. Never mentioned a thing to my family or my teachers or classmates. From a very early age, I understood enough, just enough about my classroom experiences to keep what I knew repressed, hidden beneath layers of embarrassment. Not until my last months as a graduate student, nearly thirty years old, was it possible for me to think much about the reasons for my academic success. Only then. At the end of my schooling, I needed to determine how far I had moved from my past. The adult finally confronted, and now must publicly say, what the child shuddered from knowing and could never admit to himself or to those many faces that smiled at his every success. ("Your parents must be very proud. . . .")

I

At the end, in the British Museum (too distracted to finish my dissertation) for weeks I read, speed-read, books by modern educational theorists, only to find infrequent and slight mention of students like me. (Much more is written about the more typical case, the lower-class student who barely is helped by his schooling.) Then one day, leafing through Richard Hoggart's *The Uses of Literacy,* I found, in his description of the scholarship boy, myself. For the first time I realized that there were other students like me, and so I was able to frame the meaning of my academic success, its consequent price—the loss.

Hoggart's description is distinguished, at least initially, by deep understanding. What he grasps very well is that the scholarship boy must move between environments, his home and the classroom, which are at cultural extremes, opposed. With his family, the boy has the intense pleasure of intimacy, the family's consolation in feeling public alienation. Lavish emotions texture home life. *Then,* at school, the instruction bids him to trust lonely reason primarily. Immediate needs set the pace of his parents' lives. From his mother and father the boy learns to trust spontaneity and nonrational ways of knowing. *Then,* at school, there is mental calm. Teachers emphasize the value of a reflectiveness that opens a space between thinking and immediate action.

Years of schooling must pass before the boy will be able to sketch the cultural differences in his day as abstractly as this. But he senses those differences early. Perhaps as early as the night he brings home an assignment from school and finds the house too noisy for study.

> He has to be more and more alone, if he is going to "get on." He will have, probably unconsciously, to oppose the ethos of the hearth, the intense gregariousness of the working-class family group. Since everything centres upon the living-room, there is unlikely to be a room of his own; the bedrooms are cold and inhospitable, and to warm them or the front room, if there is one, would not only be expensive, but would require an imaginative leap—out of the tradition—which most families are not capable of making. There is a corner of the living room table. On the other side Mother is ironing, the wireless is on, someone is singing a snatch of song or Father says intermittently whatever comes into his head. The boy has to cut himself off mentally, so as to do his homework, as well as he can.[1]

The next day, the lesson is as apparent at school. There are even rows of desks. Discussion is ordered. The boy must rehearse his thoughts and raise his hand before speaking out in a loud voice to an audience of classmates. And there is time enough, and silence, to think about ideas (big ideas) never considered at home by his parents.

Not for the working-class child alone is adjustment to the classroom difficult. Good schooling requires that any student alter early childhood habits. But the working-class child is usually least prepared for the change. And, unlike many middle-class children, he goes home and sees in his parents a way of life not only different but starkly opposed to that of the classroom. (He enters the house and hears his parents talking in ways his teachers discourage.)

Without extraordinary determination and the great assistance of others—at home and at school—there is little chance for success. Typically most working-class children are barely changed by the classroom. The exception succeeds. The relative few become scholarship students. Of these, Richard Hoggart estimates, most manage a fairly graceful transition. Somehow they learn to live in the two very different worlds of their day. There are some others, however, those Hoggart pejoratively terms "scholarship boys," for whom success comes with special anxiety. Scholarship boy: good student, troubled son. The child is "moderately endowed," intellectually mediocre, Hoggart supposes—though it may be more pertinent to note the

---

[1] All quotations in this essay are from Richard Hoggart, *The Uses of Literacy* (London: Chatto and Windus, 1957), chapter 10. [Author's note]

special qualities of temperament in the child. High-strung child. Brooding. Sensitive. Haunted by the knowledge that one *chooses* to become a student. (Education is not an inevitable or natural step in growing up). Here is a child who cannot forget that his academic success distances him from a life he loved, even from his own memory of himself.

Initially, he wavers, balances allegiance. ("The boy is himself [until he reaches, say, the upper forms] very much of *both* the worlds of home and school. He is enormously obedient to the dictates of the world of school, but emotionally still strongly wants to continue as part of the family circle.") Gradually, necessarily, the balance is lost. The boy needs to spend more and more time studying, each night enclosing himself in the silence permitted and required by intense concentration. He takes his first step toward academic success, away from his family.

From the very first days, through the years following, it will be with his parents—the figures of lost authority, the persons toward whom he feels deepest love—that the change will be most powerfully measured. A separation will unravel between them. Advancing in his studies, the boy notices that his mother and father have not changed as much as he. Rather, when he sees them, they often remind him of the person he once was and the life he earlier shared with them. He realizes what some Romantics also know when they praise the working class for the capacity for human closeness, qualities of passion and spontaneity, that the rest of us experience in like measure only in the earliest part of our youth. For the Romantic, this doesn't make working-class life childish. Working-class life challenges precisely because it is an *adult* way of life.

The scholarship boy reaches a different conclusion. He cannot afford to admire his parents. (How could he and still pursue such a contrary life?) He permits himself embarrassment at their lack of education. And to evade nostalgia for the life he has lost, he concentrates on the benefits education will bestow upon him. He becomes especially ambitious. Without the support of old certainties and consolations, almost mechanically, he assumes the procedures and doctrines of the classroom. The kind of allegiance the young student might have given his mother and father only days earlier, he transfers to the teacher, the new figure of authority. "[The scholarship boy] tends to make a father-figure of his form-master," Hoggart observes.

But Hoggart's calm prose only makes me recall the urgency with which I came to idolize my grammar school teachers. I began by imitating their accents, using their diction, trusting their every direction. The very first facts they dispensed, I grasped with awe. Any book they told me to read, I read—then waited for them to tell me which books I enjoyed. Their every casual opinion I came to adopt and to trumpet when I returned home. I stayed after school "to help"—to get my teacher's undivided attention. It was the nun's encouragement that mattered most to me. (She understood exactly what—my parents never seemed to appraise so well—all my achievements entailed.) Memory gently caressed each word of praise bestowed in the classroom so that compliments teachers paid me years ago come quickly to mind even today.

The enthusiasm I felt in second-grade classes I flaunted before both my parents. The docile, obedient student came home a shrill and precocious son who insisted on correcting and teaching his parents with the remark: "My teacher told us. . . ."

I intended to hurt my mother and father. I was still angry at them for having encouraged me toward classroom English. But gradually this anger was exhausted, replaced by guilt as school grew more and more attractive to me. I grew increasingly successful, a talkative student. My hand was raised in the classroom; I yearned to answer any question. At home, life was less noisy than it had been. (I spoke to classmates and teachers more often each day than to family members.) Quiet at home, I sat with my papers for hours each night. I never forgot that schooling had irretrievably changed my family's life. That knowledge, however, did not weaken ambition. Instead, it strengthened resolve. Those times I remembered the loss of my past with regret, I quickly reminded myself of all the things my teachers could give me. (They could make me an educated man.) I tightened my grip on pencil and books. I evaded nostalgia. Tried hard to forget. But one does not forget by trying to forget. One only remembers. I remembered too well that education had changed my family's life. I would not have become a scholarship boy had I not so often remembered.

Once she was sure that her children knew English, my mother would tell us, "You should keep up your Spanish." Voices playfully groaned in response. "*¡Pochos!*" my mother would tease. I listened silently.

After a while, I grew more calm at home. I developed tact. A fourth-grade student, I was no longer the show-off in front of my parents. I became a conventionally dutiful son, politely affectionate, cheerful enough, even—for reasons beyond choosing—my father's favorite. And much about my family life was easy then, comfortable, happy in the rhythm of our living together: hearing my father getting ready for work; eating the breakfast my mother had made me; looking up from a novel to hear my brother or one of my sisters playing with friends in the backyard; in winter, coming upon the house all lighted up after dark.

But withheld from my mother and father was any mention of what most mattered to me: the extraordinary experience of first-learning. Late afternoon: In the midst of preparing dinner, my mother would come up behind me while I was trying to read. Her head just over mine, her breath warmly scented with food. "What are you reading?" Or, "Tell me all about your new courses." I would barely respond, "Just the usual things, nothing special." (A half smile, then silence. Her head moving back in the silence. Silence! Instead of the flood of intimate sounds that had once flowed smoothly between us, there was this silence.) After dinner, I would rush to a bedroom with papers and books. As often as possible, I resisted parental pleas to "save lights" by coming to the kitchen to work. I kept so much, so often, to myself. Sad. Enthusiastic. Troubled by the excitement of coming upon new ideas. Eager. Fascinated by the promising texture of a brand-new book. I hoarded the pleasures of learning. Alone for hours. Enthralled. Nervous. I rarely looked away from my books—or back on my memories. Nights when relatives visited and the front rooms were warmed by Spanish sounds, I slipped quietly out of the house.

It mattered that education was changing me. It never ceased to matter. My brother and sisters would giggle at our mother's mispronounced words. They'd correct her gently. My mother laughed girlishly one night, trying not to pronounce *sheep* as *ship*. From a distance I listened sullenly. From that distance, pretending not to notice on another occasion, I saw my father looking at the title pages of my library books. That was the scene on my mind when I walked home with a fourth-grade companion and heard him say that his parents read to him every night. (A strange-sounding book—*Winnie the Pooh*.) Immediately, I wanted to know, "What is it like?" My companion, however, thought I wanted to know about the plot of the book. Another day, my mother surprised me by asking for a "nice" book to read. "Something not too hard you think I might like." Carefully I chose one, Willa Cather's *My Ántonia*. But when, several weeks later, I happened to see it next to her bed unread except for the first few pages, I was furious and suddenly wanted to cry. I grabbed up the book and took it back to my room and placed it in its place, alphabetically on my shelf.

"Your parents must be very proud of you." People began to say that to me about the time I was in sixth grade. To answer affirmatively, I'd smile. Shyly I'd smile, never betraying my sense of the irony: I was not proud of my mother and father. I was embarrassed by their lack of education. It was not that I ever thought they were stupid, though stupidly I took for granted their enormous native intelligence. Simply, what mattered to me was that they were not like my teachers.

But, "Why didn't you tell us about the award?" my mother demanded, her frown weakened by pride. At the grammar school ceremony several weeks after, her eyes were brighter than the trophy I'd won. Pushing back the hair from my forehead, she whispered that I had "shown" the *gringos*. A few minutes later, I heard my father speak to my teacher and felt ashamed of his labored, accented words. Then guilty for the shame. I felt such contrary feelings. (There is no simple road-map through the heart of the scholarship boy.) My teacher was so soft-spoken and her words were edged sharp and clean. I admired her until it seemed to me that she spoke too carefully. Sensing that she was condescending to them, I became nervous. Resentful. Protective. I tried to move my parents away. "You both must be very proud of Richard," the nun said. They responded quickly. (They were proud.) "We are proud of all our children." Then this afterthought: "They sure didn't get their brains from us." They all laughed. I smiled.

Tightening the irony into a knot was the knowledge that my parents were always behind me. They made success possible. They evened the path. They sent their children to parochial schools because the nuns "teach better." They paid a tuition they couldn't afford. They spoke English to us.

For their children my parents wanted chances they never had—an easier way. It saddened my mother to learn that some relatives forced their children to start working right after high school. To *her* children she would say, "Get all the education you can." In schooling she recognized the key to job advancement. And with the remark she remembered her past.

As a girl new to America my mother had been awarded a high school diploma by teachers too careless or busy to notice that she hardly spoke English. On her own, she determined to learn how to type. That skill got her jobs typing envelopes in letter shops, and it encouraged in her an optimism about the possibility of advancement. (Each morning when her sisters put on uniforms, she chose a bright-colored dress.) The years of young womanhood passed, and her typing speed increased. She also became an excellent speller of words she mispronounced. "And I've never been to college," she'd say, smiling, when her children asked her to spell words they were too lazy to look up in a dictionary.

Typing, however, was dead-end work. Finally frustrating. When her youngest child started high school, my mother got a full-time office job once again. (Her paycheck combined with my father's to make us—in fact—what we had already become in our imagination of ourselves—middle class.) She worked then for the (California) state government in numbered civil service positions secured by examinations. The old ambition of her youth was rekindled. During the lunch hour, she consulted bulletin boards for announcements of openings. One day she saw mention of something called an "anti-poverty agency." A typing job. A glamorous job, part of the governor's staff. "A knowledge of Spanish required." Without hesitation she applied and became nervous only when the job was suddenly hers.

"Everyone comes to work all dressed up," she reported at night. And didn't need to say more than that her co-workers wouldn't let her answer the phones. She was only a typist, after all, albeit a very fast typist. And an excellent speller. One morning there was a letter to be sent to a Washington cabinet officer. On the dictating tape, a voice referred to urban guerrillas. My mother typed (the wrong word, correctly): "gorillas." The mistake horrified the anti-poverty bureaucrats who shortly after arranged to have her returned to her previous position. She would go no further. So she willed her ambition to her children. "Get all the education you can; with an education you can do anything." (With a good education *she* could have done anything.)

When I was in high school, I admitted to my mother that I planned to become a teacher someday. That seemed to please her. But I never tried to explain that it was not the occupation of teaching I yearned for as much as it was something more elusive: I wanted to *be* like my teachers, to possess their knowledge, to assume their authority, their confidence, even to assume a teacher's persona.

In contrast to my mother, my father never verbally encouraged his children's academic success. Nor did he often praise us. My mother had to remind him to "say something" to one of his children who scored some academic success. But whereas my mother saw in education the opportunity for job advancement, my father recognized that education provided an even more startling possibility: It could enable a person to escape from a life of mere labor.

In Mexico, orphaned when he was eight, my father left school to work as an "apprentice" for an uncle. Twelve years later, he left Mexico in frustration and arrived in America. He had great expectations then of becoming an engineer. ("Work for my hands and my head.") He knew a Catholic priest who promised to get him money enough to study full time for a high school diploma. But the promises came to nothing. Instead there was a dark succession of warehouse, cannery, and factory jobs. After work he went to night school along with my mother. A year, two passed. Nothing much changed, except that fatigue worked its way into the bone; then everything changed. He didn't talk anymore of becoming an engineer. He stayed outside on the steps of the school while my mother went inside to learn typing and shorthand.

By the time I was born, my father worked at "clean" jobs. For a time he was a janitor at a fancy department store. ("Easy work; the machines do it all.") Later he became a dental technician. ("Simple.") But by then he was pessimistic about the ultimate meaning of work and the possibility of ever escaping its claims. In some of my earliest memories of him, my father already seems aged by fatigue. (He has never really grown old like my mother.) From boyhood to manhood, I have remembered him in a single image: seated, asleep on the sofa, his head thrown back in a hideous corpselike grin, the evening newspaper spread out before him. "But look at all you've accomplished," his best friend said to him once. My father said nothing. Only smiled.

It was my father who laughed when I claimed to be tired by reading and writing. It was he who teased me for having soft hands. (He seemed to sense that some great achievement of leisure was implied by my papers and books.) It was my father who became angry while watching on television some woman at the Miss America contest tell the announcer that she was going to college. ("Majoring in fine arts.") "College!" he snarled. He despised the trivialization of higher education, the inflated grades and cheapened diplomas, the half education that so often passed as mass education in my generation.

It was my father again who wondered why I didn't display my awards on the wall of my bedroom. He said he liked to go to doctors' offices and see their certificates and degrees on the wall. ("Nice.") My citations from school got left in closets at home. The gleaming figure astride one of my trophies was broken, wingless, after hitting the ground. My medals were placed in a jar of loose change. And when I lost my high school diploma, my father found it as it was about to be thrown out with the trash. Without telling me, he put it away with his own things for safekeeping.

These memories slammed together at the instant of hearing that refrain familiar to all scholarship students: "Your parents must be proud. . . ." Yes, my parents were proud. I knew it. But my parents regarded my progress with more than mere pride. They endured my early precocious behavior—but with what private anger and humiliation? As their children got older and would come home to challenge ideas both of them held, they argued before submitting to the force of logic or superior factual evidence with the disclaimer, "It's what we were taught in our time to believe." These discussions ended abruptly, though my mother remembered them on other occasions when she complained that our "big ideas" were going to our heads. More acute was her complaint that the family wasn't close anymore, like some others she knew. Why weren't we close, "more in the Mexican style"? Everyone is so private, she added. And she mimicked the yes and no answers she got in reply to her questions. Why didn't we talk more? (My father never asked.) I never said.

I was the first in my family who asked to leave home when it came time to go to college. I had been admitted to Stanford, one hundred miles away. My departure would only make physically apparent the separation that had occurred long before. But it was going too far. In the months preceding my leaving, I heard the question my mother never asked except indirectly. In the hot kitchen, tired at the end of her workday, she demanded to know, "Why aren't the colleges here in Sacramento good enough for you? They are for your brother and sister." In the middle of a car ride, not turning to face me, she wondered, "Why do you need to go so far away?" Late at night, ironing, she said with disgust, "Why do you have to put us through this big expense? You know your scholarship will never cover it all." But when September came there was a rush to get everything ready. In a bedroom that last night I packed the big brown valise, and my mother sat nearby sewing initials onto the clothes I would take. And she said no more about my leaving.

Months later, two weeks of Christmas vacation: The first hours home were the hardest. ("What's new?") My parents and I sat in the kitchen for a conversation. (But, lacking the same words to develop our sentences and to shape our interests, what was there to say? What could I tell them of the term paper I had just finished on the "universality of Shakespeare's appeal"?) I mentioned only small, obvious things: my dormitory life; week-end trips I had taken; random events. They responded with news of their own. (One was almost grateful for a family crisis about which there was much to discuss.) We tried to make our conversation seem like more than an interview.

II

From an early age I knew that my mother and father could read and write both Spanish and English. I had observed my father making his way through what, I now suppose, must have been income tax forms. On other occasions I waited apprehensively while my mother read onion-paper letters airmailed from Mexico with news of a relative's illness or death. For both my parents, however, reading was something done out of necessity and as quickly as possible. Never did I see either of them read an entire book. Nor did I see them read for pleasure. Their reading consisted of work manuals, prayer books, newspaper, recipes.

Richard Hoggart imagines how, at home,

> . . . [The scholarship boy] sees strewn around, and reads regularly himself, magazines which are never mentioned at school, which seem not to belong to the world to which the school introduces him; at school he hears about and reads books never mentioned at home. When he brings those books into the house they do not take their place with other books which the family are reading, for often there are none or almost none; his books look, rather, like strange tools.

In our house each school year would begin with my mother's careful instruction: "Don't write in your books so we can sell them at the end of the year." The remark was echoed in public by my teachers, but only in part: "Boys and girls, don't write in your books. You must learn to treat them with great care and respect."

OPEN THE DOORS OF YOUR MIND WITH BOOKS, read the red and white poster over the nun's desk in early September. It soon was apparent to me that reading was the classroom's central activity. Each course had its own book. And the information gathered from a book was unquestioned. READ TO LEARN, the sign on the wall advised in December. I privately wondered: What was the connection between reading and learning? Did one learn something only by reading it? Was an idea only an idea if it could be written down? In June, CONSIDER BOOKS YOUR BEST FRIENDS. Friends? Reading was, at best, only a chore. I needed to look up whole paragraphs of words in a dictionary. Lines of type were dizzying, the eye having to move slowly across the page, then down, and across. . . . The sentences of the first books I read were cooly impersonal. Toned hard. What most bothered me, however, was the isolation reading required. To console myself for the loneliness I'd feel when I read, I tried reading in a very soft voice. Until: "Who is doing all that talking to his neighbor?" Shortly after, remedial reading classes were arranged for me with a very old nun.

At the end of each school day, for nearly six months, I would meet with her in the tiny room that served as the school's library but was actually only a storeroom for used textbooks and a vast collection of *National Geographics*. Everything about our sessions pleased me: the smallness of the room; the noise of the janitor's broom hitting the edge of the long hallway outside the door; the green of the sun, lighting the wall; and the old woman's face blurred white with a beard. Most of the time we took turns. I began with my elementary text. Sentences of astonishing simplicity seemed to me lifeless and drab: "The boys ran from the rain . . . She wanted to sing . . . The kite rose in the blue." Then the old nun would read from her favorite books, usually biographies of early American presidents. Playfully she ran through complex sentences, calling the words alive with her voice, making it seem that the author somehow was speaking directly to me. I smiled just to listen to her. I sat there and sensed for the very first time some possibility of fellowship between a reader and a writer, a communication, never *intimate* like that I heard spoken words at home convey, but one nonetheless *personal*.

One day the nun concluded a session by asking me why I was so reluctant to read by myself. I tried to explain; said something about the way written words made me feel all alone—almost, I wanted to add but didn't, as when I spoke to myself in a room just emptied of furniture. She studied my face as I spoke; she seemed to be watching more than listening. In an uneventful voice she replied that I had nothing to fear. Didn't I realize that reading would open up whole new worlds? A book could open doors for me. It could introduce me to people and show me places I never imagined existed. She gestured toward the bookshelves. (Bare-breasted African women danced, and the shiny hubcaps of automobiles on the back covers of the *Geographic* gleamed in my mind.) I listened with respect. But her words were not very influential. I was thinking then of another consequence of literacy, one I was too shy to admit but nonetheless trusted. Books were going to make me "educated." *That* confidence enabled me, several months later, to overcome my fear of the silence.

In fourth grade I embarked upon a grandiose reading program. "Give me the names of important books," I would say to startled teachers. They soon found out that I had in mind "adult books." I ignored their suggestion of anything I suspected was written for children. (Not until I was in college, as a result, did I read *Huckleberry Finn* or *Alice's Adventures in Wonderland.*) Instead, I read *The Scarlet Letter* and Franklin's *Autobiography.* And whatever I read I read for extra credit. Each time I finished a book, I reported the achievement to a teacher and basked in the praise my effort earned. Despite my best efforts, however, there seemed to be more and more books I needed to read. At the library I would literally tremble as I came upon whole shelves of books I hadn't read. So I read and I read and I read: *Great Expectations;* all the short stories of Kipling; *The Babe Ruth Story;* the entire first volume of the *Encyclopedia Britannica* (A–ANSTEY); the *Iliad; Moby Dick; Gone with the Wind; The Good Earth; Ramona; Forever Amber; The Lives of the Saints; Crime and Punishment; The Pearl. . . .* Librarians who initially frowned when I checked out the maximum ten books at a time started saving books they thought I might like. Teachers would say to the rest of the class, "I only wish the rest of you took reading as seriously as Richard obviously does."

But at home I would hear my mother wondering, "What do you see in your books?" (Was reading a hobby like her knitting? Was so much reading even healthy for a boy? Was it the sign of "brains"? Or was it just a convenient excuse for not helping about the house on Saturday mornings?) Always, "What do you see . . . ?"

What *did* I see in my books? I had the idea that they were crucial for my academic success, though I couldn't have said exactly how or why. In the sixth I simply concluded that what gave a book its value was some major idea or theme it contained. If that core essence could be mined and memorized, I would become learned like my teachers. I decided to record in a notebook the themes of the books that I read. After reading *Robinson Crusoe,* I wrote that its theme was "the value of learning to live by oneself." When I completed *Wuthering Heights,* I noted the danger of "letting emotions get out of control." Rereading these brief moralistic appraisals usually left me disheartened. I couldn't believe that they were really the source of reading's value. But for many more years, they constituted the only means I had of describing to myself the educational value of books.

In spite of my earnestness, I found reading a pleasurable activity. I came to enjoy the lonely good company of books. Early on weekday mornings, I'd read in my bed. I'd feel a mysterious comfort then, reading in the dawn quiet—the blue-gray silence interrupted by the occasional churning of the refrigerator motor a few rooms away or the more distant sounds of a city bus beginning its run. On weekends I'd go to the public library to read, surrounded by old men and women. Or, if the weather was fine, I would take my books to the park and read in the shade of a tree. A warm summer evening was my favorite reading time. Neighbors would leave for vacation and I would water their lawns. I would sit through the twilight on the front porches or in backyards, reading to the cool, whirling sounds of the sprinklers.

I also had favorite writers. But often those writers I enjoyed most I was least able to value. When I read William Saroyan's *The Human Comedy,* I was immediately pleased by the narrator's warmth and the charm of his story. But as quickly I became suspicious. A book so enjoyable to read couldn't be very "important." Another summer I determined to read all the novels of Dickens. Reading his fat novels, I loved the feeling I got—after the first hundred pages—of being at home in a fictional world where I knew the names of the characters and cared about what was going to happen to them. And it bothered me that I was forced away at the conclusion, when the fiction closed tight, like a fortune-teller's fist—the futures of all the major characters neatly resolved. I never knew how to take such feelings seriously, however. Nor did I suspect that these experiences could be part of a novel's meaning. Still, there were pleasures to sustain me after I'd finish my books. Carrying a volume back to the library, I would be pleased by its weight. I'd run my fingers along the edge of the pages and marvel at the breadth of my achievement. Around my room, growing stacks of paperback books reenforced my assurance..

I entered high school having read hundreds of books. My habit of reading made me a confident speaker and writer of English. Reading also enabled me to sense something of the shape, the major concerns, of Western thought. (I was able to say something about Dante and Descartes and Engels and James Baldwin in my high school term papers.) In these various ways, books brought me academic success as I hoped that they would. But I was not a good reader. Merely bookish, I lacked a point of view when I read. Rather, I read in order to acquire a point of view. I vacuumed books for epigrams, scraps of information, ideas, themes—anything to fill the hollow within me and make me feel educated. When one of my teachers suggested to his drowsy tenth-grade English class that a person could not have a "complicated idea" until he had read at least two thousand books, I heard the remark without detecting either its irony or its very complicated truth. I merely determined to compile a list of all the books I had ever read. Harsh with myself, I included only once a title I might have read several times. (How, after all, could one read a book more than once?) And I included only those books over a hundred pages in length. (Could anything shorter be a book?)

There was yet another high school list I compiled. One day I came across a newspaper article about the retirement of an English professor at a nearby state college. The article was accompanied by a list of the "hundred most important books of Western Civilization." "More than anything else in my life," the professor told the reporter with finality, "these books have made me all that I am." That was the kind of remark I couldn't ignore. I clipped out the list and kept it for the several months it took me to read all of the titles. Most books, of course, I barely understood. While reading Plato's *Republic,* for instance, I needed to keep looking at the book jacket comments to remind myself what the text was about. Nevertheless, with the special patience and superstition of a scholarship boy, I looked at every word of the text. And by the time I reached the last word, relieved, I convinced myself that I had read *The Republic.* In a ceremony of great pride, I solemnly crossed Plato off my list.

III

The scholarship boy pleases most when he is young—the working-class child struggling for academic success. To his teachers, he offers great satisfaction; his success is their proudest achievement. Many other persons offer to help him. A businessman learns the boy's story and promises to underwrite part of the cost of his college education. A woman leaves him her entire library of several hundred books when she moves. His progress is featured in a newspaper article. Many people seem happy for him. They marvel. "How did you manage so fast?" From all sides, there is lavish praise and encouragement.

In his grammar school classroom, however, the boy already makes students around him uneasy. They scorn his desire to succeed. They scorn him for constantly wanting the teacher's attention and praise. "Kiss Ass," they call him when his hand swings up in response to every question he hears. Later, when he makes it to college, no one will mock him aloud. But he detects annoyance on the faces of some students and even some teachers who watch him. It puzzles him often. In college, then in graduate school, he behaves much as he always has. If anything is different about him it is that he dares to anticipate the successful conclusion of his studies. At last he feels that he belongs in the classroom, and this is exactly the source of the dissatisfaction he causes. To many persons around him, he appears too much the academic. There may be some things about him that recall his beginnings—his shabby clothes; his persistent poverty; or his dark skin (in those cases when it symbolizes his parents' disadvantaged condition)—but they only make clear how far he has moved from his past. He has used education to remake himself.

It bothers his fellow academics to face this. They will not say why exactly. (They sneer.) But their expectations become obvious when they are disappointed. They expect—they want—a student less changed by his schooling. If the scholarship boy, from a past so distant from the classroom, could remain in some basic way unchanged, he would be able to prove that it is possible for anyone to become educated without basically changing from the person one was.

Here is no fabulous hero, no idealized scholar-worker. The scholarship boy does not straddle, cannot reconcile, the two great opposing cultures of his life. His success is unromantic and plain. He sits in the classroom and offers those sitting beside him no calming reassurance about their own lives. He sits in the seminar room—a man with brown skin, the son of working-class Mexican immigrant parents. (Addressing the professor at the head of the table, his voice catches with nervousness.) There is no trace of his parents' in his speech. Instead he approximates the accents of teachers and classmates. Coming from *him* those sounds seem suddenly odd. Odd too is the effect produced when *he* uses academic jargon—bubbles at the tip of his tongue: "*Topos* . . . negative capability . . . vegetation imagery in Shakespearean comedy." He lifts an opinion from Coleridge, takes something else from Frye or Empson or Leavis. He even repeats exactly his professor's earlier comment. All his ideas are clearly borrowed. He seems to have no thought of his own. He chatters while his listeners smile—their look one of disdain.

When he is older and thus when so little of the person he was survives, the scholarship boy makes only too apparent his profound lack of *self*-confidence. This is the conventional assessment that even Richard Hoggart repeats:

> [The scholarship boy] tends to over-stress the importance of examinations, of the piling-up of knowledge and of received opinions. He discovers a technique of apparent learning, of the acquiring of facts rather than of the handling and use of facts. He learns how to receive a purely literate education, one using only a small part of the personality and challenging only a limited area of his being. He begins to see life as a ladder, as a permanent examination with some praise and some further exhortation at each stage. He becomes an expert imbiber and doler-out; his competence will vary, but will rarely be accompanied by genuine enthusiasms. He rarely feels the reality of knowledge, of other men's thoughts and imaginings, on his own pulses. . . . He has something of the blinkered pony about him. . . .

But this is criticism more accurate than fair. The scholarship boy is a very bad student. He is the great mimic; a collector of thoughts, not a thinker; the very last person in class who ever feels obliged to have an opinion of his own. In large part, however, the reason he is such a bad student is because he realizes more often and more acutely than most other students—than Hoggart himself—that education requires radical self-reformation. As a very young boy, regarding his parents, as he struggles with an early homework assignment, he knows this too well. That is why he lacks self-assurance. He does not forget that the classroom is responsible for remaking him. He relies on his teacher, depends on all that he hears in the classroom and reads in his books. He becomes in every obvious way the worst student, a dummy mouthing the opinions of others. But he would not be so bad—nor would he become so successful, a *scholarship* boy—if he did not accurately perceive that the best synonym for primary "education" is "imitation."

Those who would take seriously the boy's success—and his failure—would be forced to realize how great is the change any academic undergoes, how far one must move from one's past. It is easiest to ignore such considerations. So little is said about the scholarship boy in pages and pages of educational literature. Nothing is said of the silence that comes to separate the boy from his parents. Instead, one hears proposals for increasing the self-esteem of students and encouraging early intellectual independence. Paragraphs glitter with a constellation of terms like *creativity* and *originality.* (Ignored altogether is the function of imitation in a student's life.) Radical educationalists meanwhile complain that ghetto schools "oppress" students by trying to mold them, stifling native characteristics. The truer critique would be just the reverse: not that schools change ghetto students too much, but that while they might promote the occasional scholarship student, they change most students barely at all.

From the story of the scholarship boy there is no specific pedagogy to glean. There is, however, a much larger lesson. His story makes clear that education is a long, unglamorous, even demeaning process—*a nurturing never natural to the person one was before one entered a classroom.* At once different from most other students, the scholarship boy is also the archetypal "good student." He exaggerates the difficulty of being a student, but his exaggeration reveals a general predicament. Others are changed by their schooling as much as he. They too must re-form themselves. They must develop the skill of memory long before they become truly critical thinkers. And when they read Plato for the first several times, it will be with awe more than deep comprehension.

The impact of schooling on the scholarship boy is only more apparent to the boy himself and to others. Finally, although he may be laughable—a blinkered pony—the boy will not let his critics forget their own change. He ends up too much like them. When he speaks, they hear themselves echoed. In his pedantry, they trace their own. His ambitions are theirs. If his failure were singular, they might readily pity him. But he is more troubling than that. They would not scorn him if this were not so.

IV

Like me, Hoggart's imagined scholarship boy spends most of his years in the classroom afraid to long for his past. Only at the very end of his schooling does the boy-man become nostalgic. In this sudden change of heart, Richard Hoggart notes:

> He longs for the membership he lost, "he pines for some Nameless Eden where he never was." The nostalgia is the stronger and the more ambiguous because he is really "in quest of his own absconded self yet scared to find it." He both wants to go back and yet thinks he has gone beyond his class, feels himself weighted with knowledge of his own and their situation, which hereafter forbids him the simpler pleasures of his father and mother. . . .

According to Hoggart, the scholarship boy grows nostalgic because he remains the uncertain scholar, bright enough to have moved from his past, yet unable to feel easy, a part of a community of academics.

This analysis, however, only partially suggests what happened to me in my last year as a graduate student. When I traveled to London to write a dissertation on English Renaissance literature, I was finally confident of membership in a "community of scholars." But the pleasure that confidence gave me faded rapidly. After only two or three months in the reading room of the British Museum, it became clear that I had joined a lonely community. Around me each day were dour faces eclipsed by large piles of books. There were the regulars, like the old couple who arrived every morning, each holding a loop of the shopping bag which contained all their notes. And there was the historian who chattered madly to herself. ("Oh dear! Oh! Now, what's this? What? Oh, my!") There were also the faces of young men and women worn by long study. And everywhere eyes turned away the moment our glance accidentally met. Some persons I sat beside day after day, yet we passed silently at the end of the day, strangers. Still, we were united by a common respect for the written word and for scholarship. We did form a union, though one in which we remained distant from one another.

More profound and unsettling was the bond I recognized with those writers whose books I consulted. Whenever I opened a text that hadn't been used for years, I realized that my special interests and skills united me to a mere handful of academics. We formed an exclusive—eccentric!—society, separated from others who would never care or be able to share our concerns. (The pages I turned were stiff like layers of dead skin.) I began to wonder: Who, beside my dissertation director and a few faculty members, would ever read what I wrote? And: Was my dissertation much more than an act of social withdrawal? These questions went unanswered in the silence of the Museum reading room. They remained to trouble me after I'd leave the library each afternoon and feel myself shy—unsteady, speaking simple sentences at the grocer's or the butcher's on my way back to my bed-sitter.

Meanwhile my file cards accumulated. A professional, I knew exactly how to search a book for pertinent information. I could quickly assess and summarize the usability of the many books I consulted. But whenever I started to write, I knew too much (and not enough) to be able to write anything but sentences that were overly cautious, timid, strained brittle under the heavy weight of footnotes and qualifications. I seemed unable to dare a passionate statement. I felt drawn by professionalism to the edge of sterility, capable of no more than pedantic, lifeless, unassailable prose.

Then nostalgia began.

After years spent unwilling to admit its attractions, I gestured nostalgically toward the past. I yearned for that time when I had not been so alone. I became impatient with books. I wanted experience more immediate. I feared the library's silence. I silently scorned the gray, timid faces around me. I grew to hate the growing pages of my dissertation on genre and Renaissance literature. (In my mind I heard relatives laughing as they tried to make sense of its title.) I wanted something—I couldn't say exactly what. I told myself that I wanted a more passionate life. And a life less thoughtful. And above all, I wanted to be less alone. One day I heard some Spanish academics whispering back and forth to each other, and their sounds seemed ghostly voices recalling my life. Yearning became preoccupation then. Boyhood memories beckoned, flooded my mind. (Laughing intimate voices. Bounding up the front steps of the porch. A sudden embrace inside the door.)

For weeks after, I turned to books by educational experts. I needed to learn how far I had moved from my past—to determine how fast I would be able to recover something of it once again. But I found little. Only a chapter in a book by Richard Hoggart. . . . I left the reading room and the circle of faces.

I came home. After the year in England, I spent three summer months living with my mother and father, relieved by how easy it was to be home. It no longer seemed very important to me that we had little to say. I felt easy sitting and eating and walking with them. I watched them, nevertheless, looking for evidence of those elastic, sturdy strands that bind generations in a web of inheritance. I thought as I watched my mother one night: Of course a friend had been right when she told me that I gestured and laughed just like my mother. Another time I saw for myself: My father's eyes were much like my own, constantly watchful.

But after the early relief, this return, came suspicion, nagging until I realized that I had not neatly sidestepped the impact of schooling. My desire to do so was precisely the measure of how much I remained an academic. *Negatively* (for that is how this idea first occurred to me): My need to think so much and so abstractly about my parents and our relationship was in itself an indication of my long education. My father and mother did not pass their time thinking about the cultural meanings of their experience. It was I who described their daily lives with airy ideas. And yet, *positively:* The ability to consider experience so abstractly allowed me to shape into desire what would otherwise have remained indefinite, meaningless longing in the British Museum. If, because of my schooling, I had grown culturally separated from my parents, my education finally had given me ways of speaking and caring about that fact.

My best teachers in college and graduate school, years before, had tried to prepare me for this conclusion, I think, when they discussed texts of aristocratic pastoral literature. Faithfully, I wrote down all that they said. I memorized it: "The praise of the unlettered by the highly educated is one of the primary themes of 'elitist' literature." But, "the importance of the praise given the unsolitary, richly passionate and spontaneous life is that it simultaneously reflects the value of a reflective life." I heard it all. But there was no way for any of it to mean very much to me. I was a scholarship boy at the time, busily laddering my way up the rungs of education. To pass an examination, I copied down exactly what my teachers told me. It would require many more years of schooling (an inevitable miseducation) in which I came to trust the silence of reading and the habit of abstracting from immediate experience—moving away from a life of closeness and immediacy I remembered with my parents, growing older—before I turned unafraid to desire the past, and thereby achieved what had eluded me for so long—the end of education.

• • • • • • • • • • • • •

QUESTIONS FOR A SECOND READING

1. In *Hunger of Memory*, the book from which "The Achievement of Desire" is drawn, Rodriguez says several times that the story he tells, although it is very much his story, is also a story of our common experience—growing up, leaving home, becoming educated, entering the world. When you reread this essay, look particularly for sections or passages you might bring forward as evidence that this is, in fact, an essay which can give you a way of looking at your own life, and not just his. To what degree *is* his story the story of our common experience?

2. At the end of the essay, Rodriguez says

> It would require many more years of schooling (an inevitable miseducation) in which I came to trust the silence of reading and the habit of abstracting from immediate experience—moving away from a life of closeness and immediacy I remembered with my parents, growing older—before I turned unafraid to desire the past, and thereby achieved what had eluded me for so long—the end of education.

What, as you reread this essay is the "end of education"? And what does that end (that goal? stopping point?) have to do with "miseducation," "the silence of reading," "the habit of abstracting from immediate experience," and "desiring the past"?

ASSIGNMENTS FOR WRITING

1. You could look at the relationship between Richard Rodriguez and Richard Hoggart as a case study of the relation of a reader to a writer or a student to a teacher. Look closely at Rodriguez's references to Hoggart's book, *The Uses of Literacy*, and at the way Rodriguez made use of that book to name and describe his own experience as a student. What did he find in the book? How did he use it? How does he use it in his own writing?

   Write an essay in which you discuss Rodriguez's use of Hoggart's *The Uses of Literacy*. How, for example, would you compare Rodriguez's version of the "scholarship boy" with Hoggart's? (At one point, Rodriguez says that Hoggart's account is "more accurate than fair." What might he have meant by that?) And what kind of reader is the Rodriguez who is writing "The Achievement of Desire"—is he still a "scholarship boy," or is that description no longer appropriate?

   Note: You might begin your research with what may seem to be a purely technical matter, examining how Rodriguez handles quotations and works Hoggart's words into paragraphs of his own. On the basis of Rodriguez's use of quoted passages, how would you describe the relationship between Hoggart's words and Rodriguez's? Who has the greater authority? Who is the expert, and under what conditions? What "rules" might Rodriguez be said to follow or to break? Do you see any change in the course of the essay in how Rodriguez uses block quotations? in how he comments on them?

2. Rodriguez insists that his story is also everyone's story. Take an episode from your life, one that seems in some way similar to one of the episodes in "The Achievement of Desire," and cast it into a shorter version of Rodriguez's essay. Your job here is to look at your experience in Rodriguez's terms, which means thinking the way he does, noticing what he would notice, interpreting details in a similar fashion, using his key terms, seeing through his point of view; it could also mean imitating his style of writing, doing whatever it is you see him doing characteristically while he writes. Imitation, Rodriguez argues, is not necessarily a bad thing; it can, in fact, be one of the powerful ways in which a person learns.

MAKING CONNECTIONS

1. Paulo Freire, in "The 'Banking' Concept of Education" (p. 238), discusses the political implications of the relations between teachers and students. Some forms of schooling, he says, can give students control over their lives, but most schooling teaches students only to submit to domination by others. If you look closely at the history of Rodriguez's schooling and if you do so from the perspective of Freire's essay, what do you see? Write an essay describing how Freire might analyze Rodriguez's education. How would he see the process as it unfolds throughout Rodriguez's experience, as a student, from his early schooling (including the study he did on his own at home), through his college and graduate studies, to the position he takes, finally, as the writer of "The Achievement of Desire."

2. Stanley Fish, in "How To Recognize a Poem When You See One" (p. 222), argues that the students in his class could see the list of names on the board as a poem because "as members of a literary community they knew what a poem was." Students generally behave as they do because they know how to "do school"; they have become part of a community that thinks and acts in certain predictable ways.

   Membership in this community was never such an easy matter for Rodriguez, although the evidence in "The Achievement of Desire" suggests that it was not difficult for him to enter the community, and once inside he worked hard to stay there. He was a good student. He knew how to do school. In high school, he once read through a list of the "hundred most important books of Western Civilization."

   Imagine that one of Fish's students in the class Fish describes in his essay is a student from a background like Rodriguez's. After attending the class, the student has a conversation with Rodriguez in which he or she tells the students' side of the story and speaks with pleasure of the class's ability to interpret that "poem" so convincingly in such a short period of time. How would Rodriguez respond? What advice would he give to the student about that course and about his or her education generally?

JOHN RUSKIN

JOHN RUSKIN was an important social critic and the leading Victorian art critic. He acquired the passion for beauty that informs all his work from travels to the Continent with his father. This passion was doomed to frustration, however, in the industrial society in which he lived. Ruskin had a particular enthusiasm for Gothic architecture and wanted to revive the kind of culture that had made that style possible, one in which an individual worker—such as a stonemason—could express himself and thereby derive pleasure, as well as wages, from his work. Ruskin thought that industrial society, unless fundamentally changed, would never be capable of producing anything as grand, beautiful, or just as a gothic cathedral.

Ruskin was born in London in 1819 and died there in 1900, just barely putting his foot into our century, and yet his eccentric tastes and his vision of a better world back in a simpler past made its mark on both Victorian society and our own. He took B.A. and M.A. degrees (in 1842 and 1843) at Oxford University, where his skill in looking at buildings was sharpened and tested by the architecture of the many colleges and chapels in a university complex that today remains a gothic cloister in the midst of an industrial city. Ruskin's books include Modern Painters *(5 vols., 1843–60) and* The Stones of Venice *(3 vols., 1851–53).*

During the last thirty years of his life, Ruskin suffered a series of mental breakdowns, which his biographers often attribute to his frustration about the course of English society. He was one of the first to recognize the dangers of "progress" to the environment, and he spoke eloquently throughout his life about the ugliness of modern urban life and its effect on the lives and spirit of those who live in cities. His influence can be seen in the work of William Morris, George Bernard Shaw, and D. H. Lawrence, but also in Tolkein's Lord of the Rings, *in "Dungeons and Dragons," and in the special status we give to folk songs, local crafts, and handmade articles.*

Ruskin was a writer who wanted to teach his readers to pay attention. He once wrote, "You might read all the books in the British Museum (if you could live long enough) and remain an utterly 'illiterate,' uneducated person, but . . . if you read ten pages of a good book, letter by letter—that is to say, with real accuracy—you are forevermore in some measure an educated person." We do not recommend that you read the following selection from The Stones of Venice *letter by letter (whatever that might mean). His prose will take time and attention, however. You will have to give it a chance to teach you how it wants to be read. Ruskin's prose is partly the product of his age, partly the product of the rhythm and cadences of the King James Bible, and partly the product of his own peculiar way of thinking about things. Be patient with it. Don't give in to the temptation to be annoyed by those long sentences or strange, dramatic gestures. Think, rather, about why he might want to talk to you in this way and what, in return, you get if you become his listener.*

The Nature of Gothic

VII. I. SAVAGENESS. I am not sure when the word "Gothic" was first generically applied to the architecture of the North; but I presume that, whatever the date of its original usage, it was intended to imply reproach, and express the barbaric character of the nations among whom that architecture arose. It never implied that they were literally of Gothic lineage, far less that their architecture had been originally invented by the Goths themselves; but it did imply that they and their buildings together exhibited a degree of sternness and rudeness, which, in contradistinction to the character of Southern and Eastern nations, appeared like a perpetual reflection of the contrast between the Goth and the Roman in their first encounter. And when that fallen Roman, in the utmost impotence of his luxury, and insolence of his guilt, became the model for the imitation of civilised Europe, at the close of the so-called Dark ages, the word Gothic became a term of unmitigated contempt, not unmixed with aversion. From that contempt, by the exertion of the antiquaries and architects of this century, Gothic architecture has been sufficiently vindicated; and perhaps some among us, in our admiration of the magnificent science of its structure, and sacredness of its expression, might desire that the term of ancient reproach should be withdrawn, and some other, of more apparent honourableness, adopted in its place. There is no chance, as there is no need, of such a substitution. As far as the epithet was used scornfully, it was used falsely; but there is no reproach in the word, rightly understood; on the contrary, there is a profound truth, which the instinct of mankind almost unconsciously recognises. It is true, greatly and deeply true, that the architecture of the North is rude and wild; but it is not true, that, for this reason, we are to condemn it, or despise. Far otherwise: I believe it is in this very character that it deserves our profoundest reverence.

VIII. The charts of the world which have been drawn up by modern science have thrown into a narrow space the expression of a vast amount of knowledge, but I have never yet seen any one pictorial enough to enable the spectator to imagine the kind of contrast in physical character which exists between Northern and Southern countries. We know the difference in detail, but we have not that broad glance and grasp which would enable us to feel them in their fulness. We know that gentians grow on the Alps, and olives on the Apennines; but we do not enough conceive for ourselves that variegated mosaic of the world's surface which a bird sees in its migration, that difference between the district of the gentian and of the olive which the stork and the swallow see far off, as they lean upon the sirocco wind. Let us, for a moment, try to raise ourselves even above the level of their flight, and imagine the Mediterranean lying beneath us like an irregular lake, and all its ancient promontories sleeping in the sun: here and there an angry spot of thunder, a grey stain of storm, moving upon the burning field; and here and there a fixed wreath of white volcano smoke, surrounded by its circle of ashes; but for the most part a great peacefulness of light, Syria and Greece, Italy and Spain, laid like pieces of a golden pavement into the sea-blue, chased, as we stoop nearer to them, with bossy beaten work of mountain chains, and glowing softly with terraced gardens, and flowers heavy with frankincense, mixed among masses of laurel, and orange, and plumy palm, that abate with their grey-green shadows the burning of the marble rocks, and of the ledges of porphyry sloping under lucent sand. Then let us pass farther towards the north, until we see the orient colours change gradually into a vast belt of rainy green, where the pastures of Switzerland, and poplar valleys of France, and dark forests of the Danube and Carpathians stretch from the mouths of the Loire to those of the Volga, seen through clefts in grey swirls of rain-cloud and flaky veils of the mist of the brooks, spreading low along the pasture lands:

and then, farther north still, to see the earth heave into mighty masses of leaden rock and heathy moor, bordering with a broad waste of gloomy purple that belt of field and wood, and splintering into irregular and grisly islands amidst the northern seas, beaten by storm, and chilled by ice-drift, and tormented by furious pulses of contending tide, until the roots of the last forests fail from among the hill ravines, and the hunger of the north wind bites their peaks into barrenness; and, at last, the wall of ice, durable like iron, sets, deathlike, its white teeth against us out of the polar twilight. And, having once traversed in thought this gradation of the zoned iris of the earth in all its material vastness, let us go down nearer to it, and watch the parallel change in the belt of animal life: the multitudes of swift and brilliant creatures that glance in the air and sea, or tread the sands of the southern zone; striped zebras and spotted leopards, glistening serpents, and birds arrayed in purple and scarlet. Let us contrast their delicacy and brilliancy of colour, and swiftness of motion, with the frost-cramped strength, and shaggy covering, and dusky plumage of the northern tribes; contrast the Arabian horse with the Shetland, the tiger and leopard with the wolf and bear, the antelope with the elk, the bird of paradise with the osprey: and then, submissively acknowledging the great laws by which the earth and all that it bears are ruled throughout their being, let us not condemn, but rejoice in the expression by man of his own rest in the statutes of the lands that gave him birth. Let use watch him with reverence as he sets side by side the burning gems, and smooths with soft sculpture the jasper pillars, that are to reflect a ceaseless sunshine, and rise into a cloudless sky: but not with less reverence let us stand by him, when, with rough strength and hurried stroke, he smites an uncouth animation out of the rocks which he has torn from among the moss of the moorland, and heaves into the darkened air the pile of iron buttress and rugged wall, instinct with work of an imagination as wild and wayward as the northern sea; creations of ungainly shape and rigid limb, but full of wolfish life; fierce as the winds that beat, and changeful as the clouds that shade them.

There is, I repeat, no degradation, no reproach in this, but all dignity and honourableness: and we should err grievously in refusing either to recognise as an essential character of the existing architecture of the North, or to admit as a desirable character in that which it yet may be, this wildness of thought, and roughness of work; this look of mountain brotherhood between the cathedral and the Alp; this magnificence of sturdy power, put forth only the more energetically because the fine finger-touch was chilled away by the frosty wind, and the eye dimmed by the moor-mist, or blinded by the hail; this outspeaking of the strong spirit of men who may not gather redundant fruitage from the earth, nor bask in dreamy benignity of sunshine, but must break the rock for bread, and cleave the forest for fire, and show, even in what they did for their delight, some of the hard habits of the arm and heart that grew on them as they swung the axe or pressed the plough.

IX. If, however, the savageness of Gothic architecture, merely as an expression of its origin among Northern nations, may be considered, in some sort, a noble character, it possesses a higher nobility still, when considered as an index, not of climate, but of religious principle.

In the 13th and 14th paragraphs of Chapter XXI of the first volume of this work, it was noticed that the systems of architectural ornament, properly so called, might be divided into three:—1. Servile ornament, in which the execution or power of the inferior workman is entirely subjected to the intellect of the higher;—2. Constitutional ornament, in which the executive inferior power is, to a certain point, emancipated and independent, having a will of its own, yet confessing its inferiority and rendering obedience to higher powers;—and 3. Revolutionary ornament, in which no executive inferiority is admitted at all. I must here explain the nature of these divisions at somewhat greater length.

Of Servile ornament, the principal schools are the Greek, Ninevite, and Egyptian; but their servility is of different kinds. The Greek master-workman was far advanced in knowledge and power above the Assyrian or Egyptian. Neither he nor those for whom he worked could endure the appearance of imperfection in anything; and, therefore, what ornament he appointed to be done by those beneath him was composed of mere geometrical forms,—balls, ridges, and perfectly symmetrical foliage,—which could be executed with absolute precision by line and rule, and were as perfect in their way, when completed, as his own figure sculpture. The Assyrian and Egyptian, on the contrary, less cognisant of accurate form in anything, were content to allow their figure sculpture to be executed by inferior workmen, but lowered the method of its treatment to a standard which every workman could reach, and then trained him by discipline so rigid, that there was no chance of his falling beneath the standard appointed. The Greek gave to the lower workman no subject which he could not perfectly execute. The Assyrian gave him subjects which he could only execute imperfectly, but fixed a legal standard for his imperfection. The workman was, in both systems, a slave.[1]

X. But in the mediæval, or especially Christian, system of ornament,

---

[1]The third kind of ornament, the Renaissance, is that in which the inferior detail becomes principal, the executor of every minor portion being required to exhibit skill and possess knowledge as great as that which is possessed by the master of the design; and in the endeavour to endow him with this skill and knowledge, his own original power is overwhelmed, and the whole building becomes a wearisome exhibition of well-educated imbecility. We must fully inquire into the nature of this form of error, when we arrive at the examination of the Renaissance schools.

this slavery is done away with altogether; Christianity having recognised, in small things as well as great, the individual value of every soul. But it not only recognises its value; it confesses its imperfection, in only bestowing dignity upon the acknowledgment of unworthiness. That admission of lost power and fallen nature, which the Greek or Ninevite felt to be intensely painful, and, as far as might be, altogether refused, the Christian makes daily and hourly, contemplating the fact of it without fear, as tending, in the end, to God's greater glory. Therefore, to every spirit which Christianity summons to her service, her exhortation is: Do what you can, and confess frankly what you are unable to do; neither let your effort be shortened for fear of failure, nor your confession silenced for fear of shame. And it is, perhaps, the principal admirableness of the Gothic schools of architecture, that they thus receive the results of the labour of inferior minds: and out of fragments full of imperfection, and betraying that imperfection in every touch, indulgently raise up a stately and unaccusable whole.

XI. But the modern English mind has this much in common with that of the Greek, that it intensely desires, in all things, the utmost completion or perfection compatible with their nature. This is a noble character in the abstract, but becomes ignoble when it causes us to forget the relative dignities of that nature itself, and to prefer the perfectness of the lower nature to the imperfection of the higher; not considering that as, judged by such a rule, all the brute animals would be preferable to man, because more perfect in their functions and kind, and yet are always held inferior to him, so also in the works of man, those which are more perfect in their kind are always inferior to those which are, in their nature, liable to more faults and shortcomings. For the finer the nature, the more flaws it will show through the clearness of it; and it is a law of this universe, that the best things shall be seldomest seen in their best form. The wild grass grows well and strongly, one year with another; but the wheat is, according to the greater nobleness of its nature, liable to the bitterer blight. And therefore, while in all things that we see, or do, we are to desire perfection, and strive for it, we are nevertheless not to set the meaner thing, in its narrow accomplishment, above the nobler thing, in its mighty progress; not to esteem smooth minuteness above shattered majesty; not to prefer mean victory to honourable defeat; not to lower the level of our aim, that we may the more surely enjoy the complacency of success. But, above all, in our dealings with the souls of other men, we are to take care how we check, by severe requirement or narrow caution, efforts which might otherwise lead to a noble issue; and, still more, how we withhold our admiration from great excellencies, because they are mingled with rough faults. Now, in the make and nature of every man, however rude or simple, whom we employ in manual labour, there are some powers for better things: some tardy imagination, torpid capacity of emotion, tottering steps of thought, there are, even at the worst; and in most cases it is all our own fault that they *are* tardy or torpid. But they cannot be strengthened, unless we are content to take them in their feebleness, and unless we prize and honour them in their imperfection above the best and most perfect manual skill. And this is what we have to do with all our labourers; to look for the *thoughtful* part of them, and get that out of them, whatever we lose for it, whatever faults and errors we are obliged to take with it. For the best that is in them cannot manifest itself, but in company with much error. Understand this clearly: You can teach a man to draw a straight line, and to cut one; to strike a curved line, and to carve it; and to copy and carve any number of given lines or forms, with admirable speed and perfect precision; and you find his work perfect of its kind: but if you ask him to think about any of those forms, to consider if he cannot find any better in his own head, he stops; his execution becomes hesitating; he thinks, and ten to one he thinks wrong; ten to one he makes a mistake in the first touch he gives to his work as a thinking being. But you have made a man of him for all that. He was only a machine before, an animated tool.

XII. And observe, you are put to stern choice in this matter. You must either make a tool of the creature, or a man of him. You cannot make both. Men were not intended to work with the accuracy of tools, to be precise and perfect in all their actions. If you will have that precision out of them, and make their fingers measure degrees like cog-wheels, and their arms strike curves like compasses, you must unhumanise them. All the energy of their spirits must be given to make cogs and compasses of themselves. All their attention and strength must go to the accomplishment of the mean act. The eye of the soul must be bent upon the finger-point, and the soul's force must fill all the invisible nerves that guide it, ten hours a day, that it may not err from its steely precision, and so soul and sight be worn away, and the whole human being be lost at last—a heap of sawdust, so far as its intellectual work in this world is concerned; saved only by its Heart, which cannot go into the form of cogs and compasses, but expands, after the ten hours are over, into fireside humanity. On the other hand, if you will make a man of the working creature, you cannot make a tool. Let him but begin to imagine, to think, to try to do anything worth doing; and the engine-turned precision is lost at once. Out come all his roughness, all his dulness, all his incapability; shame upon shame, failure upon failure, pause after pause: but out comes the whole majesty of him also; and we know the height of it only, when we see the clouds settling upon him. And, whether the clouds be bright or dark, there will be transfiguration behind and within them.

XIII. And now, reader, look round this English room of yours, about which you have been proud so often, because the work of it was so good and strong, and the ornaments of it so finished. Examine again all those accurate mouldings, and perfect polishings, and unerring adjustments of the seasoned wood and tempered steel. Many a time you have exulted over them, and thought how great England was, because her slightest work was done so thoroughly. Alas! if read rightly, these perfectnesses are signs of a slavery in our England a thousand times more bitter and more degrading than that of the scourged African, or helot Greek. Men may be beaten, chained, tormented, yoked like cattle, slaughtered like summer flies, and yet remain in one sense, and the best sense, free. But to smother their souls within them, to blight and hew into rotting pollards the suckling branches of their human intelligence, to make the flesh and skin which, after the worm's work on it, is to see God, into leathern thongs to yoke machinery with,—this it is to be slave-masters indeed; and there might be more freedom in England, though her feudal lords' lightest words were worth men's lives, and though the blood of the vexed husbandman dropped in the furrows of her fields, than there is while the animation of her multitudes is sent like fuel to feed the factory smoke, and the strength of them is given daily to be wasted into the fineness of a web, or racked into the exactness of a line.

XIV. And, on the other hand, go forth again to gaze upon the old cathedral front, where you have smiled so often at the fantastic ignorance of the old sculptors: examine once more those ugly goblins, and formless monsters, and stern statues, anatomiless and rigid; but do not mock at them, for they are signs of the life and liberty of every workman who struck the stone; a freedom of thought, and rank in scale of being, such as no laws, no charters, no charities can secure; but which it must be the first aim of all Europe at this day to regain for her children.

XV. Let me not be thought to speak wildly or extravagantly. It is verily this degradation of the operative into a machine, which, more than any other evil of the times, is leading the mass of the nations everywhere into vain, incoherent, destructive struggling for a freedom of which they cannot explain the nature to themselves. Their universal outcry against wealth, and against nobility, is not forced from them either by the pressure of famine, or the sting of mortified pride. These do much, and have done much in all ages; but the foundations of society were never yet shaken as they are at this day. It is not that men are ill fed, but that they have no pleasure in the work by which they make their bread, and therefore look to wealth as the only means of pleasure. It is not that men are pained by the scorn of the upper classes, but they cannot endure their own; for they feel that the kind of labour to which they are condemned is verily a degrading one, and makes them less than men. Never had the upper classes so much sympathy with the lower, or charity for them, as they have at this day, and yet never were they so much hated by them: for, of old, the separation between the noble and the poor was merely a wall built by law;

now it is a veritable difference in level of standing, a precipice between upper and lower grounds in the field of humanity, and there is pestilential air at the bottom of it. I know not if a day is ever to come when the nature of right freedom will be understood, and when men will see that to obey another man, to labour for him, yield reverence to him or to his place, is not slavery. It is often the best kind of liberty,—liberty from care. The man who says to one, Go, and he goeth, and to another, Come, and he cometh, has, in most cases, more sense of restraint and difficulty than the man who obeys him. The movements of the one are hindered by the burden on his shoulder; of the other, by the bridle on his lips: there is no way by which the burden may be lightened; but we need not suffer from the bridle if we do not champ at it. To yield reverence to another, to hold ourselves and our lives at his disposal, is not slavery; often, it is the noblest state in which a man can live in this world. There is, indeed, a reverence which is servile, that is to say irrational or selfish: but there is also noble reverence, that is to say, reasonable and loving; and a man is never so noble as when he is reverent in this kind; nay, even if the feeling pass the bounds of mere reason, so that it be loving, man is raised by it. Which had, in reality, most of the serf nature in him—the Irish peasant who was lying in wait yesterday for his landlord, with his musket muzzle thrust through the ragged hedge; or that old mountain servant, who, two hundred years ago, at Inverkeithing, gave up his own life and the lives of his seven sons for his chief?—as each fell, calling forth his brother to the death, "Another for Hector!" And therefore, in all ages and all countries, reverence has been paid and sacrifice made by men to each other, not only without complaint, but rejoicingly; and famine, and peril, and sword, and all evil, and all shame, have been borne willingly in the causes of masters and kings; for all these gifts of the heart ennobled the men who gave, not less than the men who received them, and nature prompted, and God rewarded the sacrifice. But to feel their souls withering within them, unthanked, to find their whole being sunk into an unrecognised abyss, to be counted off into a heap of mechanism, numbered with its wheels, and weighed with its hammer strokes;—this nature bade not,—this God blesses not,—this humanity for no long time is able to endure.

xvi. We have much studied and much perfected, of late, the great civilised invention of the division of labour; only we give it a false name. It is not, truly speaking, the labour that is divided; but the men:—Divided into mere segments of men—broken into small fragments and crumbs of life; so that all the little piece of intelligence that is left in a man is not enough to make a pin, or a nail, but exhausts itself in making the point of a pin, or the head of a nail. Now it is a good and desirable thing, truly, to make many pins in a day; but if we could only see with what crystal sand their points were polished,—sand of human soul, much to be magnified before it can be discerned for what it is,—we should think there might be some loss in it also. And the great cry that rises from all our manufacturing cities, louder than their furnace blast, is all in very deed for this,—that we manufacture everything there except men; we blanch cotton, and strengthen steel, and refine sugar, and shape pottery; but to brighten, to strengthen, to refine, or to form a single living spirit, never enters into our estimate of advantages. And all the evil to which that cry is urging our myriads can be met only in one way: not by teaching nor preaching, for to teach them is but to show them their misery, and to preach to them, if we do nothing more than preach, is to mock at it. It can be met only by a right understanding, on the part of all classes, of what kinds of labour are good for men, raising them, and making them happy; by a determined sacrifice of such convenience, or beauty, or cheapness as is to be got only by the degradation of the workman; and by equally determined demand for the products and results of healthy and ennobling labour.

XVII. And how, it will be asked, are these products to be recognised, and this demand to be regulated? Easily: by the observance of three broad and simple rules:

1. Never encourage the manufacture of any article not absolutely necessary, in the production of which *Invention* has no share.
2. Never demand an exact finish for its own sake, but only for some practical or noble end.
3. Never encourage imitation or copying of any kind, except for the sake of preserving record of great works.

The second of these principles is the only one which directly rises out of the consideration of our immediate subject; but I shall briefly explain the meaning and extent of the first also, reserving the enforcement of the third for another place.

1. Never encourage the manufacture of anything not necessary, in the production of which invention has no share.

For instance. Glass beads are utterly unnecessary, and there is no design or thought employed in their manufacture. They are formed by first drawing out the glass into rods; these rods are chopped up into fragments of the size of beads by the human hand, and the fragments are then rounded in the furnace. The men who chop up the rods sit at their work all day, their hands vibrating with a perpetual and exquisitely timed palsy, and the beads dropping beneath their vibration like hail. Neither they, nor the men who draw out the rods or fuse the fragments, have the smallest occasion for the use of any single human faculty; and every young lady, therefore, who buys glass beads is engaged in the slave-trade, and in a much more cruel one than that which we have so long been endeavouring to put down.

But glass cups and vessels may become the subjects of exquisite invention; and if in buying these we pay for the invention, that is to say for the beautiful form, or colour, or engraving, and not for mere finish of execution, we are doing good to humanity.

XVIII. So, again, the cutting of precious stones, in all ordinary cases, requires little exertion of any mental faculty; some tact and judgment in avoiding flaws, and so on, but nothing to bring out the whole mind. Every person who wears cut jewels merely for the sake of their value is, therefore, a slave-driver.

But the working of the goldsmith, and the various designing of grouped jewellery and enamel-work, may become the subject of the most noble human intelligence. Therefore, money spent in the purchase of well-designed plate, of precious engraved vases, cameos, or enamels, does good to humanity; and, in work of this kind, jewels may be employed to heighten its splendour; and their cutting is then a price paid for the attainment of a noble end, and thus perfectly allowable.

XIX. I shall perhaps press this law farther elsewhere, but our immediate concern is chiefly with the second, namely, never to demand an exact finish, when it does not lead to a noble end. For observe, I have only dwelt upon the rudeness of Gothic, or any other kind of imperfectness, as admirable, where it was impossible to get design or thought without it. If you are to have the thought of a rough and untaught man, you must have it in a rough and untaught way; but from an educated man, who can without effort express his thoughts in an educated way, take the graceful expression, and be thankful. Only *get* the thought, and do not silence the peasant because he cannot speak good grammar, or until you have taught him his grammar. Grammar and refinement are good things, both, only be sure of the better thing first. And thus in art, delicate finish is desirable from the greatest masters, and is always given by them. In some places Michael Angelo, Leonardo, Phidias, Perugino, Turner, all finished with the most exquisite care; and the finish they give always leads to the fuller accomplishment of their noble purposes. But lower men than these cannot finish, for it requires consummate knowledge to finish consummately, and then we must take their thoughts as they are able to give them. So the rule is simple: Always look for invention first, and after that, for such execution as will help the invention, and as the inventor is capable of without painful effort, and *no more.* Above all, demand no refinement of execution where there is no thought, for that is slaves' work, unredeemed. Rather choose rough work than smooth work, so only that the practical purpose be answered, and never imagine there is reason to be proud of anything that may be accomplished by patience and sand-paper.

XX. I shall only give one example, which however will show the reader what I mean, from the manufacture already alluded to, that of glass. Our modern glass is exquisitely clear in its substance, true in its form, accurate in its cutting. We are proud of this. We ought to be ashamed of it. The old Venice glass was muddy, inaccurate in all its forms, and clumsily cut, if at all. And the old Venetian was justly proud of it. For there is this difference between the English and Venetian workman, that the former thinks only of accurately matching his patterns, and getting his curves perfectly true and his edges perfectly sharp, and becomes a mere machine for rounding curves and sharpening edges, while the old Venetian cared not a whit whether his edges were sharp or not, but he invented a new design for every glass that he made, and never moulded a handle or a lip without a new fancy in it. And therefore, though some Venetian glass is ugly and clumsy enough, when made by clumsy and uninventive workmen, other Venetian glass is so lovely in its forms that no price is too great for it; and we never see the same form in it twice. Now you cannot have the finish and the varied form too. If the workman is thinking about his edges, he cannot be thinking of his design; if of his design, he cannot think of his edges. Choose whether you will pay for the lovely form or the perfect finish, and choose at the same moment whether you will make the worker a man or a grindstone.

XXI. Nay, but the reader interrupts me,—"If the workman can design beautifully, I would not have him kept at the furnace. Let him be taken away and made a gentleman, and have a studio, and design his glass there, and I will have it blown and cut for him by common workmen, and so I will have my design and my finish too."

All ideas of this kind are founded upon two mistaken suppositions: the first, that one man's thoughts can be, or ought to be, executed by another man's hands; the second, that manual labour is a degradation, when it is governed by intellect.

On a large scale, and in work determinable by line and rule, it is indeed both possible and necessary that the thoughts of one man should be carried out by the labour of others; in this sense I have already defined the best architecture to be the expression of the mind of manhood by the hands of childhood. But on a smaller scale, and in a design which cannot be mathematically defined, one man's thoughts can never be expressed by another: and the difference between the spirit of touch of the man who is inventing, and of the man who is obeying directions, is often all the difference between a great and a common work of art. How wide the separation is between original and second-hand execution, I shall endeavour to show elsewhere; it is not so much to our purpose here as to mark the other and more fatal error of despising manual labour when governed by intellect; for it is no less fatal an error to despise it when thus regulated by intellect, than to value it for its own sake. We are always in these days endeavouring to separate the two; we want one man to be always thinking, and another to be always working, and we call one a gentleman, and the other an operative; whereas the workman ought often to be thinking, and the thinker often to be working, and both should be gentlemen, in the best sense. As it is, we make both ungentle, the one envying, the other despising, his brother; and the mass of society is made up of morbid thinkers, and miserable workers. Now it is only by labour that thought can be made healthy, and only by thought that labour can be made happy, and the two cannot be separated with impunity. It would be well if all of us were good handicraftsmen in some kind, and the dishonour of manual labour done away with altogether; so that though there should still be a trenchant distinction of race between nobles and commoners, there should not, among the latter, be a trenchant distinction of employment, as between idle and working men, or between men of liberal and illiberal professions. All professions should be liberal, and there should be less pride felt in peculiarity of employment, and more in excellence of achievement. And yet more, in each several profession, no master should be too proud to do its hardest work. The painter should grind his own colours; the architect work in the mason's yard with his men; the master-manufacturer be himself a more skilful operative than any man in his mills; and the distinction between one man and another be only in experience and skill, and the authority and wealth which these must naturally and justly obtain.

XXII. I should be led far from the matter in hand, if I were to pursue this interesting subject. Enough, I trust, has been said to show the reader that the rudeness or imperfection which at first rendered the term "Gothic" one of reproach is indeed, when rightly understood, one of the most noble characters of Christian architecture, and not only a noble but an *essential* one. It seems a fantastic paradox, but it is nevertheless a most important truth, that no architecture can be truly noble which is *not* imperfect. And this is easily demonstrable. For since the architect, whom we will suppose capable of doing all in perfection, cannot execute the whole with his own hands, he must either make slaves of his workmen in the old Greek, and present English fashion, and level his work to a slave's capacities, which is to degrade it; or else he must take his workmen as he finds them, and let them show their weaknesses together with their strength, which will involve the Gothic imperfection, but render the whole work as noble as the intellect of the age can make it.

XXIII. But the principle may be stated more broadly still. I have confined the illustration of it to architecture, but I must not leave it as if true of architecture only. Hitherto I have used the words imperfect and perfect merely to distinguish between work grossly unskilful, and work executed with average precision and science; and I have been pleading that any degree of unskilfulness should be admitted, so only that the labourer's mind had room for expression. But, accurately speaking, no good work whatever can be perfect, and *the demand for perfection is always a sign of a misunderstanding of the ends of art.*

XXIV. This for two reasons, both based on everlasting laws. The first, that no great man ever stops working till he has reached his point of failure; that is to say, his mind is always far in advance of his powers of execution, and the latter will now and then give way in trying to follow it; besides that he will always give to the inferior portions of his work only such inferior attention as they require; and according to his greatness he becomes so accustomed to the feeling of dissatisfaction with the best he can do, that in moments of lassitude or anger with himself he will not care though the beholder be dissatisfied also. I believe there has only been one man who would not acknowledge this necessity, and strove always to reach perfection, Leonardo; the end of his vain effort being merely that he would take ten years to a picture, and leave it unfinished. And therefore, if we are to have great men working at all, or less men doing their best, the work will be imperfect, however beautiful. Of human work none but what is bad can be perfect, in its own bad way.[2]

XXV. The second reason is, that imperfection is in some sort essential to all that we know of life. It is the sign of life in a mortal body, that is to say, of a state of progress and change. Nothing that lives is, or can be, rigidly perfect; part of it is decaying, part nascent. The foxglove blossom,—a third part bud, a third part past, a third part in full bloom,—is a type of the life of this world. And in all things that live there are certain irregularities and deficiencies which are not only signs of life, but sources of beauty. No human face is exactly the same in its lines on each side, no leaf perfect in its lobes, no branch in its symmetry. All admit irregularity as they imply change; and to banish imperfection is to destroy expression, to check exertion, to paralyse vitality. All things are literally better, lovelier, and more beloved for the imperfections which have been divinely appointed, that the law of human life may be Effort, and the law of human judgment, Mercy.

Accept this then for a universal law, that neither architecture nor any other noble work of man can be good unless it be imperfect; and let us be prepared for the otherwise strange fact, which we shall discern clearly as we approach the period of the Renaissance, that the first cause of the fall of the arts of Europe was a relentless requirement of perfection, incapable alike either of being silenced by veneration for greatness, or softened into forgiveness of simplicity.

[2]The Elgin marbles are supposed by many persons to be "perfect." In the most important portions they indeed approach perfection, but only there. The draperies are unfinished, the hair and wool of the animals are unfinished, and the entire bas-reliefs of the frieze are roughly cut.

• • • • • • • • • • • • •

QUESTIONS FOR A SECOND READING

1. On pages 468 and 469 you will find two photographs of the Gothic cathedral at Chartres, in France. The first one, on page 468, shows the view as you approach the cathedral; the other, on page 469, shows detail from the carvings in the main entrance. Before you reread the essay, study these pictures carefully. What do you notice? What would Ruskin have you notice? If there is a difference, how would you explain it? What assumptions guide your vision or determine your point of view? And what about Ruskin—what leads him to notice one part of the facade but to ignore another?

   Ruskin was writing to readers who, he felt, considered Gothic architecture ugly, savage, and crude. Can you imagine such a reader? What would be the expectations or prejudices of those who looked at a cathedral from this point of view? What might they consider beautiful or fine? What does Ruskin assume, in other words, about the tastes and prejudices of his readers?

2. Ruskin says

   > And it is, perhaps, the principal admirableness of the Gothic schools of architecture, that they thus receive the results of the labor of inferior minds; and out of fragments full of imperfection, and betraying that imperfection in every touch, indulgently raise up a stately and unaccusable whole.

   Inferior, imperfect, betrayal, indulgence: these are strange terms to use to describe what is admirable (or, as Ruskin says, "unaccusable") in a work of art. As your reread the chapter, ask yourself what these terms come to represent in the essay. How, that is, does Ruskin use these terms in his argument, and what is required of a reader who is willing to follow it? What metaphors does he develop for the "healthy" life and "good" work, and, finally, what does a reader have to do to keep up with him, to keep believing that good work must be imperfect.

ASSIGNMENTS FOR WRITING

1. On page 461, Ruskin offers three general rules we can use to ensure that we buy only products created through "healthy and ennobling labor." As you think of the things that are yours, particularly those that are important to you, what would you have to give up, or what changes would you have to make in your patterns of consumption, to follow Ruskin's guidelines? In an essay, describe these changes, explain why you would have to make them, and go on, then, to say what you can about the culture and society Ruskin would imagine as ideal in a modern, industrial setting. Would you be willing to live in such a world?

2. At one point in the essay, Ruskin offers two specific challenges to his readers: "And now, reader, look round this English room of yours, about which you have been proud so often, because the work of it was so good and strong, and the ornaments of it so finished"; and "go forth again to gaze upon the old cathedral front, where you have smiled so often at the fantastic ignorance of the old sculptors." Ruskin believed that the perfection of the English room, "if read rightly," was a sign of slavery and degradation, whereas the ugliness and imperfection of the cathedral facade were signs of freedom.

   See if you can extend this challenge to your own immediate surroundings. Look again at something that is part of your local environment—perhaps a building or a room. Look at it for what it says about the life and character of the persons who made it, and for what it says about the culture that values it (or fails to value it). Write an essay in which you explain what you see and how it might be read "rightly." Your job, then, is to extend Ruskin's method of analysis to your world, seen at this point in time. (You should not, however, feel that you have to share Ruskin's conclusions about how things should and should not be made.)

MAKING CONNECTIONS

1. John Berger, in "Ways of Seeing" (p. 48), says "The way we see things is affected by what we know or what we believe." He demonstrates this by showing how critics' perceptions of art are affected by their political beliefs; as a result, he says, they indulge in mystification, "the process of explaining away what might otherwise be evident." As you read Berger's essay, pay particular attention to what he says about history and the effects of "mystification" on our understanding of the past.

   What would Berger say about Ruskin's treatment of Gothic architecture? Would he, for example, say that Ruskin mystifies it or demystifies it? What would he choose as examples to test his contention? And how would he establish whether Ruskin was bringing forward or "explaining away" that which is "evident" in a Gothic cathedral. Write an essay in which you discuss Ruskin's treatment of Gothic architecture in the context of Berger's essay, "Ways of Seeing."

   Note: As you work on this essay, you might ask yourself whether Ruskin's political views determined his way of looking at buildings or whether looking at buildings determined his political views. How would you know?

2. Walker Percy, in his essay "The Loss of the Creature" (p. 394), offers several examples of people having difficulty seeing the things around them: tourists at the Grand Canyon, tourists in Mexico, a Falkland Islander, a student at Sarah Lawrence College. And he talks about the various strategies people use to see what would otherwise remain hidden: "standing on the shoulders of others," getting off the beaten track, apprenticing themselves to a master, "dialectical savorings of the familiar" [continued on p. 470].

Write an essay in which you examine Ruskin through Percy's eyes. What would Percy notice in what Ruskin says and does? What strategy has Ruskin developed to recover what was lost or hidden? Which of Percy's examples does Ruskin most resemble? And, finally, what would Percy see as the limits and possibilities of Ruskin's work?

Note: You might consider writing this essay in Percy's style—telling Ruskin's story, that is, as Percy might tell it.

GLORIA STEINEM

GLORIA STEINEM, one of the leading figures of the contemporary women's movement, is the granddaughter of Pauline Steinem, who was president of a women's suffrage group and representative to the 1908 International Council of Women. Steinem dates her own involvement in feminism from a 1968 Redstockings meeting she attended to gather material on the group for her column in New York *magazine. She has since become one of the most admired, and most controversial, women of our time.*

Steinem was born in 1934 in Toledo, Ohio. After graduating magna cum laude from Smith College in 1956, Steinem served as Chester Bowles Asian Fellow at the University of Delhi and the University of Calcutta, India, from 1956 to 1958. She later became a writer for "That Was the Week That Was" (a weekly television show of political satire), and a member of the National Women's Political Caucus, the Women's Action Alliance, and the Student Non-Violent Coordinating Committee. She was the founding editor of Ms. *magazine and has worked as a writer since 1961, publishing articles in* Esquire, Vogue, Life, Cosmopolitan, Glamour, *and* New York *magazines. She has also written three books, the most recent of which is* Marilyn. *"Ruth's Song" was drawn from her collection of essays,* Outrageous Acts and Everyday Rebellions. *Part of the strength of her criticism of contemporary life is her fair yet passionate assessment of people and issues. In "Ruth's Song," however, Steinem turns from contemporary life to her own life; she writes about her mother and their relationship. The essay's remarkable achievement lies in the balance of passion and clarity Steinem maintains while sorting through difficult memories.*

Ruth's Song (Because She Could Not Sing It)

Happy or unhappy, families are all mysterious. We have only to imagine how differently we would be described—and will be, after our deaths—by each of the family members who believe they know us. The only question is, Why are some mysteries more important than others?

The fate of my Uncle Ed was a mystery of importance in our family. We lavished years of speculation on his transformation from a brilliant young electrical engineer to the town handyman. What could have changed this elegant, Lincolnesque student voted "Best Dressed" by his classmates to the gaunt, unshaven man I remember? Why did he leave a young son and a first wife of the "proper" class and religion, marry a much less educated woman of the "wrong" religion, and raise a second family in a house near an abandoned airstrip; a house whose walls were patched with metal signs to stop the wind? Why did he never talk about his transformation?

For years, I assumed that some secret and dramatic events of a year he spent in Alaska had made the difference. Then I discovered that the trip had come after his change and probably been made because of it. Strangers he worked for as a much-loved handyman talked about him as one more tragedy of the Depression, and it was true that Uncle Ed's father, my paternal grandfather, had lost his money in the stockmarket Crash and died of (depending on who was telling the story) pneumonia or a broken heart. But the Crash of 1929 also had come long after Uncle Ed's transformation. Another theory was that he was afflicted with a mental problem that lasted most of his life, yet he was supremely competent at his work, led an independent life, and asked for help from no one.

Perhaps he had fallen under the spell of a radical professor in the early days of the century, the height of this country's romance with socialism and anarchism. That was the theory of another uncle on my mother's side.

I do remember that no matter how much Uncle Ed needed money, he would charge no more for his work than materials plus 10 percent, and I never saw him in anything other than ancient boots and overalls held up with strategic safety pins. Was he really trying to replace socialism-in-one-country with socialism-in-one-man? If so, why did my grandmother, a woman who herself had run for the school board in coalition with anarchists and socialists, mistrust his judgment so much that she left his share of her estate in trust, even though he was over fifty when she died? And why did Uncle Ed seem uninterested in all other political words and acts? Was it true instead that, as another relative insisted, Uncle Ed had chosen poverty to disprove the myths of Jews and money?

Years after my uncle's death, I asked a son in his second family if he had the key to this family mystery. No, he said. He had never known his father any other way. For that cousin, there had been no question. For the rest of us, there was to be no answer.

For many years I also never imagined my mother any way other than the person she had become before I was born. She was just a fact of life when I was growing up; someone to be worried about and cared for; an invalid who lay in bed with eyes closed and lips moving in occasional response to voices only she could hear; a woman to whom I brought an endless stream of toast and coffee, bologna sandwiches and dime pies, in a child's version of what meals should be. She was a loving, intelligent, terrorized woman who tried hard to clean our littered house whenever she emerged from her private world, but who could rarely be counted on to finish one task. In many ways, our roles were reversed: I was the mother and she was the child. Yet that didn't help her, for she still worried about me with all the intensity of a frightened mother, plus the special fears of her own world full of threats and hostile voices.

Even then I suppose I must have known that, years before she was thirty-five and I was born, she had been a spirited, adventurous young woman who struggled out of a working-class family and into college, who found work she loved and continued to do, even after she was married and my older sister was there to be cared for. Certainly, our immediate family and nearby relatives, of whom I was by far the youngest, must have remembered her life as a whole and functioning person. She was thirty before she gave up her own career to help my father run the Michigan summer resort that was the most practical of his many dreams, and she worked hard there as everything from bookkeeper to bar manager. The family must have watched this energetic, fun-loving, book-loving woman turn into someone who was afraid to be alone, who could not hang on to reality long enough to hold a job, and who could rarely concentrate enough to read a book.

Yet I don't remember any family speculation about the mystery of my mother's transformation. To the kind ones and those who liked her, this new Ruth was simply a sad event, perhaps a mental case, a family problem to be accepted and cared for until some natural process made her better. To the less kind or those who had resented her earlier independence, she was a willful failure, someone who lived in a filthy house, a woman who simply would not pull herself together.

Unlike the case of my Uncle Ed, exterior events were never suggested as reason enough for her problems. Giving up her own career was never cited as her personal parallel of the Depression. (Nor was there discussion of the Depression itself, though my mother, like millions of others, had made potato soup and cut up blankets to make my sister's winter clothes.) Her fears of dependence and poverty were no match for my uncle's possible political beliefs. The real influence of newspaper editors who had praised her reporting was not taken as seriously as the possible influence of one radical professor.

Even the explanation of mental illness seemed to contain more personal fault when applied to my mother. She had suffered her first "nervous breakdown," as she and everyone else called it, before I was born and when my sister was about five. It followed years of trying to take care of a baby, be the wife of a kind but financially irresponsible man with show-business dreams, and still keep her much-loved job as reporter and newspaper editor. After many months in a sanatorium, she was pronounced recovered. That is, she was able to take care of my sister again, to move away from the city and the job she loved, and to work with my father at the isolated rural lake in Michigan he was trying to transform into a resort worthy of the big dance bands of the 1930s.

But she was never again completely without the spells of depression, anxiety, and visions into some other world that eventually were to turn her into the nonperson I remember. And she was never again without a bottle of dark, acrid-smelling liquid she called "Doc Howard's medicine": a solution of chloral hydrate that I later learned was the main ingredient of "Mickey Finns" or "knockout drops," and that probably made my mother and her doctor the pioneers of modern tranquilizers. Though friends and relatives saw this medicine as one more evidence of weakness and indulgence, to me it always seemed an embarrassing but necessary evil. It slurred her speech and slowed her coordination, making our neighbors and my school friends believe she was a drunk. But without it, she would not sleep for days, even a week at a time, and her feverish eyes began to see only that private world in which wars and hostile voices threatened the people she loved.

Because my parents had divorced and my sister was working in a faraway city, my mother and I were alone together then, living off the meager fixed income that my mother got from leasing her share of the remaining land in Michigan. I remember a long Thanksgiving weekend spent hanging on to her with one hand and holding my eighth-grade assignment of *Tale of Two Cities* in the other, because the war outside our house was so real to my mother that she had plunged her hand through a window, badly cutting her arm in an effort to help us escape. Only when she finally agreed to swallow the medicine could she sleep, and only then could I end the terrible calm that comes with crisis and admit to myself how afraid I had been.

No wonder that no relative in my memory challenged the doctor who prescribed this medicine, asked if some of her suffering and hallucinating might be due to overdose or withdrawal, or even consulted another doctor about its use. It was our relief as well as hers.

But why was she never returned even to that first sanatorium? Or to help that might come from other doctors? It's hard to say. Partly, it was her own fear of returning. Partly, it was too little money, and a family's not-unusual assumption that mental illness is an inevitable part of someone's personality. Or perhaps other family members had feared something like my experience when, one hot and desperate summer between the sixth and seventh grade, I finally persuaded her to let me take her to the only doctor from those sanatorium days whom she remembered without fear.

Yes, this brusque old man told me after talking to my abstracted, timid mother for twenty minutes: She definitely belongs in a state hospital. I should put her there right away. But even at that age, *Life* magazine and newspaper exposés had told me what horrors went on inside those hospitals. Assuming there to be no other alternative, I took her home and never tried again.

In retrospect, perhaps the biggest reason my mother was cared for but not helped for twenty years was the simplest: her functioning was not that necessary to the world. Like women alcoholics who drink in their kitchens while costly programs are constructed for executives who drink, or like the homemakers subdued with tranquilizers while male patients get therapy and personal attention instead, my mother was not an important worker. She was not even the caretaker of a very young child, as she had been when she was hospitalized the first time. My father had patiently brought home the groceries and kept our odd household going until I was eight or so and my sister went away to college. Two years later when wartime gas rationing closed his summer resort and he had to travel to buy and sell in summer as well as winter, he said: How can I travel and take care of your mother? How can I make a living? He was right. It was impossible to do both. I did not blame him for leaving once I was old enough to be the bringer of meals and answerer of my mother's questions. ("Has your sister been killed in a car crash?" "Are there German soldiers outside?") I replaced my father, my mother was left with one more way of maintaining a sad status quo, and the world went on undisturbed.

That's why our lives, my mother's from forty-six to fifty-three, and my own from ten to seventeen, were spent alone together. There was one sane winter in a house we rented to be near my sister's college in Massachusetts, then one bad summer spent house-sitting in suburbia while my mother hallucinated and my sister struggled to hold down a summer job in New York. But the rest of those years were lived in Toledo where both my mother and father had been born, and on whose city newspapers an earlier Ruth had worked.

First we moved into a basement apartment in a good neighborhood. In those rooms behind a furnace, I made one last stab at being a child. By pretending to be much sicker with a cold than I really was, I hoped my mother would suddenly turn into a sane and cheerful woman bringing me chicken soup à la Hollywood. Of course, she could not. It only made her feel worse that she could not. I stopped pretending.

But for most of those years, we lived in the upstairs of the house my mother had grown up in and that her parents left her—a deteriorating farm house engulfed by the city, with poor but newer houses stacked against it and a major highway a few feet from its sagging front porch. For a while, we could rent the two downstairs apartments to a newlywed factory worker and a local butcher's family. Then the health department condemned our ancient furnace for the final time, sealing it so tight that even my resourceful Uncle Ed couldn't produce illegal heat.

In that house, I remember:

. . . lying in the bed my mother and I shared for warmth, listening on the early morning radio to the royal wedding of Princess Elizabeth and Prince Philip being broadcast live, while we tried to ignore and thus protect each other from the unmistakable sounds of the factory worker downstairs beating up and locking out his pregnant wife.

. . . hanging paper drapes I had bought in the dime store; stacking books and papers in the shape of two armchairs and covering them with blankets; evolving my own dishwashing system (I waited until all the dishes were dirty, then put them in the bathtub); and listening to my mother's high praise for these housekeeping efforts to bring order from chaos, though in retrospect I think they probably depressed her further.

. . . coming back from one of the Eagles' Club shows where I and other veterans of a local tap-dancing school made ten dollars a night for two shows, and finding my mother waiting with a flashlight and no coat in the dark cold of the bus stop, worried about my safety walking home.

. . . in a good period, when my mother's native adventurousness came through, answering a classified ad together for an amateur acting troupe that performed Biblical dramas in churches, and doing several very corny performances of *Noah's Ark* while my proud mother shook metal sheets backstage to make thunder.

. . . on a hot summer night, being bitten by one of the rats that shared our house and its back alley. It was a terrifying night that turned into a touching one when my mother, summoning courage from some unknown reservoir of love, became a calm, comforting parent who took me to a hospital emergency room despite her terror at leaving home.

. . . coming home from a local library with the three books a week into which I regularly escaped, and discovering that for once there was no need to escape. My mother was calmly planting hollyhocks in the vacant lot next door.

But there were also times when she woke in the early winter dark, too frightened and disoriented to remember that I was at my usual after-school job, and so called the police to find me. Humiliated in front of my friends by sirens and policemen, I would yell at her—and she would bow her head in fear and say "I'm sorry, I'm sorry, I'm sorry," just as she had done so often when my otherwise-kindhearted father had yelled at her in frustration. Perhaps the worst thing about suffering is that it finally hardens the hearts of those around it.

And there were many, many times when I badgered her until her shaking hands had written a small check to cash at the corner grocery and I could leave her alone while I escaped to the comfort of well-heated dime stores that smelled of fresh doughnuts, or to air-conditioned Saturday-afternoon movies that were windows on a very different world.

But my ultimate protection was this: I was just passing through, a guest in the house; perhaps this wasn't my mother at all. Though I knew very well that I was her daughter, I sometimes imagined that I had been adopted and that my real parents would find me, a fantasy I've since discovered is common. (If children wrote more and grownups less, being adopted might be seen not only as a fear but also as a hope.) Certainly, I didn't mourn the wasted life of this woman who was scarcely older than I am now. I worried only about the times when she got worse.

Pity takes distance and a certainty of surviving. It was only after our house was bought for demolition by the church next door, and after my sister had performed the miracle of persuading my father to give me a carefree time before college by taking my mother with him to California for a year, that I could afford to think about the sadness of her life. Suddenly, I was far away in Washington, living with my sister and sharing a house with several of her friends. While I finished high school and discovered to my surprise that my classmates felt sorry for me because my mother *wasn't* there, I also realized that my sister, at least in her early childhood, had known a very different person who lived inside our mother, an earlier Ruth.

She was a woman I met for the first time in a mental hospital near Baltimore, a humane place with gardens and trees where I visited her each weekend of the summer after my first year away in college. Fortunately, my sister hadn't been able to work and be our mother's caretaker, too. After my father's year was up, my sister had carefully researched hospitals and found the courage to break the family chain.

At first, this Ruth was the same abstracted, frightened woman I had lived with all those years, though now all the sadder for being approached through long hospital corridors and many locked doors. But gradually she began to talk about her past life, memories that doctors there must have been awakening. I began to meet a Ruth I had never known.

. . . A tall, spirited, auburn-haired high-school girl who loved basketball and reading; who tried to drive her uncle's Stanley Steamer when it was the first car in the neighborhood; who had a gift for gardening and who sometimes, in defiance of convention, wore her father's overalls; a girl with the courage to go to dances even though her church told her that music itself was sinful, and whose sense of adventure almost made up for feeling gawky and unpretty next to her daintier, dark-haired sister.

. . . A very little girl, just learning to walk, discovering the body places where touching was pleasurable, and being punished by her mother who slapped her hard across the kitchen floor.

. . . A daughter of a handsome railroad-engineer and a schoolteacher who felt she had married "beneath her"; the mother who took her two daughters on Christmas trips to faraway New York on an engineer's free railroad pass and showed them the restaurants and theaters they should aspire to—even though they could only stand outside them in the snow.

. . . A good student at Oberlin College, whose freethinking traditions she loved, where friends nicknamed her "Billy"; a student with a talent for both mathematics and poetry, who was not above putting an invisible film of Karo syrup on all the john seats in her dormitory the night of a big prom; a daughter who had to return to Toledo, live with her family, and go to a local university when her ambitious mother—who had scrimped and saved, ghostwritten a minister's sermons, and made her daughters' clothes in order to get them to college at all—ran out of money. At home, this Ruth became a part-time bookkeeper in a lingerie shop for the very rich, commuting to classes and listening to her mother's harsh lectures on the security of becoming a teacher; but also a young woman who was still rebellious enough to fall in love with my father, the editor of her university newspaper, a funny and charming young man who was a terrible student, had no intention of graduating, put on all the campus dances, and was unacceptably Jewish.

I knew from family lore that my mother had married my father twice: once secretly, after he invited her to become the literary editor of his campus newspaper, and once a year later in a public ceremony, which some members of both families refused to attend as the "mixed marriage" of its day.

And I knew that my mother had gone on to earn a teaching certificate. She had used it to scare away truant officers during the winters when, after my father closed the summer resort for the season, we lived in a house trailer and worked our way to Florida or California and back by buying and selling antiques.

But only during those increasingly adventurous weekend outings from the hospital—going shopping, to lunch, to the movies—did I realize that she had taught college calculus for a year in deference to her mother's insistence that she have teaching "to fall back on." And only then did I realize she had fallen in love with newspapers along with my father. After graduating from the university paper, she wrote a gossip column for a local tabloid, under the name "Duncan MacKenzie," since women weren't supposed to do such things, and soon had earned a job as society reporter on one of Toledo's two big dailies. By the time my sister was four or so, she had worked her way up to the coveted position of Sunday editor.

It was a strange experience to look into those brown eyes I had seen so often and realize suddenly how much they were like my own. For the first time, I realized that she might really be my mother.

I began to think about the many pressures that might have led up to that first nervous breakdown: leaving my sister whom she loved very much with a grandmother whose values my mother didn't share; trying to hold on to a job she loved but was being asked to leave by her husband; wanting very much to go with a woman friend to pursue their own dreams in New York; falling in love with a co-worker at the newspaper who frightened her by being more sexually attractive, more supportive of her work than my father, and perhaps the man she should have married; and finally, nearly bleeding to death with a miscarriage because her own mother had little faith in doctors and refused to get help.

Did those months in the sanatorium brainwash her in some Freudian or very traditional way into making what were, for her, probably the wrong choices? I don't know. It almost doesn't matter. Without extraordinary support to the contrary, she was already convinced that divorce was unthinkable. A husband could not be left for another man, and certainly not for a reason as selfish as a career. A daughter could not be deprived of her father and certainly not be uprooted and taken off to an uncertain future in New York. A bride was supposed to be virginal (not "shop-worn," as my euphemistic mother would have said), and if your husband turned out to be kind, but innocent of the possibility of a woman's pleasure, then just be thankful for kindness.

Of course, other women have torn themselves away from work and love and still survived. But a story my mother told me years later has always symbolized for me the formidable forces arrayed against her.

> It was early spring, nothing was open yet. There was nobody for miles around. We had stayed at the lake that winter, so I was alone a lot while your father took the car and traveled around on business. You were a baby. Your sister was in school, and there was no phone. The last straw was that the radio broke. Suddenly it seemed like forever since I'd been able to talk with anyone—or even hear the sound of another voice.
>
> I bundled you up, took the dog, and walked out to the Brooklyn road. I thought I'd walk the four or five miles to the grocery store, talk to some people, and find somebody to drive me back. I was walking along with Fritzie running up ahead in the empty road—when suddenly a car came out of nowhere and down the hill. It hit Fritzie head on and threw him over to the side of the road. I yelled and screamed at the driver, but he never slowed down. He never looked at us. He never even turned his head.
>
> Poor Fritzie was all broken and bleeding, but he was still alive. I carried him and sat down in the middle of the road, with his head cradled in my arms. I was going to *make* the next car stop and help.
>
> But no car ever came. I sat there for hours, I don't know how long, with you in my lap and holding Fritzie, who was whimpering and looking up at me for help. It was dark by the time he finally died. I pulled him over to the side of the road and walked back home with you and washed the blood out of my clothes.
>
> I don't know what it was about that one day—it was like a breaking point. When your father came home, I said: "From now on, I'm going with you. I won't bother you. I'll just sit in the car. But I can't bear to be alone again."

I think she told me that story to show she had tried to save herself, or perhaps she wanted to exorcise a painful memory by saying it out loud. But hearing it made me understand what could have turned her into the woman I remember: a solitary figure sitting in the car, perspiring through the summer, bundled up in winter, waiting for my father to come out of this or that antique shop, grateful just not to be alone. I was there, too, because I was too young to be left at home, and I loved helping my father wrap and unwrap the newspaper around the china and small objects he had bought at auctions and was selling to dealers. It made me feel necessary and grown-up. But sometimes it was hours before we came back to the car again and to my mother who was always patiently, silently waiting.

At the hospital and later when Ruth told me stories of her past, I used to say, "But why didn't you leave? Why didn't you take the job? Why didn't you marry the other man?" She would always insist it didn't matter, she was lucky to have my sister and me. If I pressed hard enough, she would add, "If I'd left you never would have been born."

I always thought but never had the courage to say: *But you might have been born instead.*

I'd like to tell you that this story has a happy ending. The best I can do is one that is happier than its beginning.

After many months in that Baltimore hospital, my mother lived on her own in a small apartment for two years while I was in college and my sister married and lived nearby. When she felt the old terrors coming back, she returned to the hospital at her own request. She was approaching sixty by the time she emerged from there and from a Quaker farm that served as a halfway house, but she confounded her psychiatrists' predictions that she would be able to live outside for shorter and shorter periods. In fact, she never returned. She lived more than another twenty years, and for six of them, she was well enough to stay in a rooming house that provided both privacy and company. Even after my sister and her husband moved to a larger house and generously made two rooms into an apartment for her, she continued to have some independent life and many friends. She worked part-time as a "salesgirl" in a china shop; went away with me on yearly vacations and took one trip to Europe with relatives; went to women's club meetings; found a multiracial church that she loved; took meditation courses; and enjoyed many books. She still could not bear to see a sad movie, to stay alone with any of her six grandchildren while they were babies, to live without many tranquilizers, or to talk about those bad years in Toledo. The old terrors were still in the back of her mind, and each day was a fight to keep them down.

It was the length of her illness that had made doctors pessimistic. In fact, they could not identify any serious mental problem and diagnosed her only as having "an anxiety neurosis": low self-esteem, a fear of being dependent, a terror of being alone, a constant worry about money. She also had spells of what now would be called agoraphobia, a problem almost entirely confined to dependent women: fear of going outside the house, and incapacitating anxiety attacks in unfamiliar or public places.

Would you say, I asked one of her doctors, that her spirit had been broken? "I guess that's as good a diagnosis as any," he said. "And it's hard to mend anything that's been broken for twenty years."

But once out of the hospital for good, she continued to show flashes of the different woman inside; one with a wry kind of humor, a sense of adventure, and a love of learning. Books on math, physics, and mysticism occupied a lot of her time. ("Religion," she used to say firmly, "begins in the laboratory.") When she visited me in New York during her sixties and seventies, she always told taxi drivers that she was eighty years old ("so they will tell me how young I look"), and convinced theater ticket sellers that she was deaf long before she really was ("so they'll give us seats in the front row"). She made friends easily, with the vulnerability and charm of a person who feels entirely dependent on the approval of others. After one of her visits, every shopkeeper within blocks of my apartment would say, "Oh yes, I know your mother!" At home, she complained that people her own age were too old and stodgy for her. Many of her friends were far younger than she. It was as if she were making up for her own lost years.

She was also overly appreciative of any presents given to her—and that made giving them irresistible. I loved to send her clothes, jewelry, exotic soaps, and additions to her collection of tarot cards. She loved receiving them, though we both knew they would end up stored in boxes and drawers. She carried on a correspondence in German with our European relatives, and exchanges with many other friends, all written in her painfully slow, shaky handwriting. She also loved giving gifts. Even as she worried about money and figured out how to save pennies, she would buy or make carefully chosen presents for grandchildren and friends.

Part of the price she paid for this much health was forgetting. A single reminder of those bad years in Toledo was enough to plunge her into days of depression. There were times when this fact created loneliness for me, too. Only two of us had lived most of my childhood. Now, only one of us remembered. But there were also times in later years when, no matter how much I pled with reporters *not* to interview our friends and neighbors in Toledo, *not* to say that my mother had been hospitalized, they published things that hurt her very much and sent her into a downhill slide.

On the other hand, she was also her mother's daughter, a person with a certain amount of social pride and pretension, and some of her objections had less to do with depression than false pride. She complained bitterly about one report that we had lived in a house trailer. She finally asked angrily: "Couldn't they at least say 'vacation mobile home'?" Divorce was still a shame to her. She might cheerfully tell friends. "I don't know *why* Gloria says her father and I were divorced—we never were." I think she justified this to herself with the idea that they had gone through two marriage ceremonies, one in secret and one in public, but been divorced only once. In fact, they were definitely divorced, and my father had briefly married someone else.

She was very proud of my being a published writer, and we generally shared the same values. After her death, I found a mother-daughter morals quiz I once had written for a women's magazine. In her unmistakably shaky writing, she had recorded her own answers, her entirely accurate imagination of what my answers would be, and a score that concluded our differences were less than those "normal for women separated by twenty-odd years." Nonetheless, she was quite capable of putting a made-up name on her name tag when going to a conservative women's club where she feared our shared identity would bring controversy or even just questions. When I finally got up the nerve to tell her I was signing a 1972 petition of women who publicly said we had had abortions and were demanding the repeal of laws that made them illegal and dangerous, her only reply was sharp and aimed to hurt back. "Every starlet says she's had an abortion," she said. "It's just a way of getting publicity." I knew she agreed that abortion should be a legal choice, but I also knew she would never forgive me for embarrassing her in public.

In fact, her anger and a fairly imaginative ability to wound with words increased in her last years when she was most dependent, most focused on herself, and most likely to need the total attention of others. When my sister made a courageous decision to go to law school at the age of fifty, leaving my mother in a house that not only had many loving teenage grandchildren in it but a kindly older woman as a paid companion besides, my mother reduced her to frequent tears by insisting that this was a family with no love in it, no home-cooked food in the refrigerator; not a real family at all. Since arguments about home cooking wouldn't work on me, my punishment was creative and different. She was going to call up *The New York Times,* she said, and tell them that this was what feminism did: it left old sick women all alone.

Some of this bitterness brought on by failing faculties was eventually solved by a nursing home near my sister's house where my mother not only got the twenty-four-hour help her weakening body demanded, but the attention of affectionate nurses besides. She charmed them, they loved her, and she could still get out for an occasional family wedding. If I ever had any doubts about the debt we owe to nurses, those last months laid them to rest.

When my mother died just before her eighty-second birthday in a hospital room where my sister and I were alternating the hours in which her heart wound slowly down to its last sounds, we were alone together for a few hours while my sister slept. My mother seemed bewildered by her surroundings and the tubes that invaded her body, but her consciousness cleared long enough for her to say: "I want to go home. Please take me home." Lying to her one last time, I said I would. "Okay, honey," she said. "I trust you." Those were her last understandable words.

The nurses let my sister and me stay in the room long after there was no more breath. She had asked us to do that. One of her many fears came from a story she had been told as a child about a man whose coma was mistaken for death. She also had made out a living will requesting that no extraordinary measures be used to keep her alive, and that her ashes be sprinkled in the same stream as my father's.

Her memorial service was in the Episcopalian church that she loved because it fed the poor, let the homeless sleep in its pews, had members of almost every race, and had been sued by the Episcopalian hierarchy for having a woman priest. Most of all, she loved the affection with which its members had welcomed her, visited her at home, and driven her to services. I think she would have liked the Quaker-style informality with which people rose to tell their memories of her. I know she would have loved the presence of many friends. It was to this church that she had donated some of her remaining Michigan property in the hope that it could be used as a multiracial camp, thus getting even with those people in the tiny nearby town who had snubbed my father for being Jewish.

I think she also would have been pleased with her obituary. It emphasized her brief career as one of the early women journalists and asked for donations to Oberlin's scholarship fund so others could go to this college she loved so much but had to leave.

I know I will spend the next years figuring out what her life has left in me.

I realize that I've always been more touched by old people than by children. It's the talent and hopes locked up in a failing body that gets to me; a poignant contrast that reminds me of my mother, even when she was strong.

I've always been drawn to any story of a mother and a daughter on their own in the world. I saw *A Taste of Honey* several times as both a play and a film, and never stopped feeling it. Even *Gypsy* I saw over and over again, sneaking in backstage for the musical and going to the movie as well. I told myself that I was learning the tap-dance routines, but actually my eyes were full of tears.

I once fell in love with a man only because we both belonged to that large and secret club of children who had "crazy mothers." We traded stories of the shameful houses to which we could never invite our friends. Before he was born, his mother had gone to jail for her pacifist convictions. Then she married the politically ambitious young lawyer who had defended her, stayed home and raised many sons. I fell out of love when he confessed that he wished I wouldn't smoke or swear, and he hoped I wouldn't go on working. His mother's plight had taught him self-pity—nothing else.

I'm no longer obsessed, as I was for many years, with the fear that I would end up in a house like that one in Toledo. Now, I'm obsessed instead with the things I could have done for my mother while she was alive, or the things I should have said.

I still don't understand why so many, many years passed before I saw my mother as a person and before I understood that many of the forces in her life are patterns women share. Like a lot of daughters, I suppose I couldn't afford to admit that what had happened to my mother was not all personal or accidental, and therefore could happen to me.

One mystery has finally cleared. I could never understand why my mother hadn't been helped by Pauline, her mother-in-law; a woman she seemed to love more than her own mother. This paternal grandmother had died when I was five, before my mother's real problems began but long after that "nervous breakdown," and I knew Pauline was once a suffragist who addressed Congress, marched for the vote, and was the first woman member of a school board in Ohio. She must have been a courageous and independent woman, yet I could find no evidence in my mother's reminiscences that Pauline had encouraged or helped my mother toward a life of her own.

I finally realized that my grandmother never changed the politics of her own life, either. She was a feminist who kept a neat house for a husband and four antifeminist sons, a vegetarian among five male meat eaters, and a woman who felt so strongly about the dangers of alcohol that she used only paste vanilla; yet she served both meat and wine to the men of the house and made sure their lives and comforts were continued undisturbed. After the vote was won, Pauline seems to have stopped all feminist activity. My mother greatly admired the fact that her mother-in-law kept a spotless house and prepared a week's meals at a time. Whatever her own internal torments, Pauline was to my mother a woman who seemed able to "do it all." "Whither thou goest, I shall go," my mother used to say to her much-loved mother-in-law, quoting the Ruth of the Bible. In the end, her mother-in-law may have added to my mother's burdens of guilt.

Perhaps like many later suffragists, my grandmother was a public feminist and a private isolationist. That may have been heroic in itself, the most she could be expected to do, but the vote and a legal right to work were not the only kind of help my mother needed.

The world still missed a unique person named Ruth. Though she longed to live in New York and in Europe, she became a woman who was afraid to take a bus across town. Though she drove the first Stanley Steamer, she married a man who never let her drive.

I can only guess what she might have become. The clues are in moments of spirit or humor.

After all the years of fear, she still came to Oberlin with me when I was giving a speech there. She remembered everything about its history as the first college to admit blacks and the first to admit women, and responded to students with the dignity of a professor, the accuracy of a journalist, and a charm that was all her own.

When she could still make trips to Washington's wealth of libraries, she became an expert genealogist, delighting especially in finding the rogues and rebels in our family tree.

Just before I was born, when she had cooked one more enormous meal for all the members of some famous dance band at my father's resort and they failed to clean their plates, she had taken a shotgun down from the kitchen wall and held it over their frightened heads until they had finished the last crumb of strawberry shortcake. Only then did she tell them the gun wasn't loaded. It was a story she told with great satisfaction.

Though sex was a subject she couldn't discuss directly, she had a great appreciation of sensuous men. When a friend I brought home tried to talk to her about cooking, she was furious. ("He came out in the kitchen and talked to me about *stew!*") But she forgave him when we went swimming. She whispered, "He has wonderful legs!"

On her seventy-fifth birthday, she played softball with her grandsons on the beach, and took pride in hitting home runs into the ocean.

Even in the last year of her life, when my sister took her to visit a neighbor's new and luxurious house, she looked at the vertical stripes of a very abstract painting in the hallway and said, tartly, "Is that the price code?"

She worried terribly about being socially accepted herself, but she never withheld her own approval for the wrong reasons. Poverty or style or lack of education couldn't stand between her and a new friend. Though she lived in a mostly white society and worried if I went out with a man of the "wrong" race, just as she had once married a man of the "wrong" religion, she always accepted each person as an individual.

"Is he *very* dark?" she once asked worriedly about a friend. But when she met this very dark person, she only said afterward, "What a kind and nice man!"

My father was the Jewish half of the family, yet it was my mother who taught me to have pride in that tradition. It was she who encouraged me to listen to a radio play about a concentration camp when I was little. "You should know that this can happen," she said. Yet she did it just enough to teach, never enough to frighten.

It was she who introduced me to books and a respect for them, to poetry that she knew by heart, and to the idea that you could never criticize someone unless you "walked miles in their shoes."

It was she who sold that Toledo house, the only home she had, with the determination that the money be used to start me in college. She gave both her daughters the encouragement to leave home for four years of independence that she herself had never had.

After her death, my sister and I found a journal she had kept of her one cherished and belated trip to Europe. It was a trip she had described very little when she came home: she always deplored people who talked boringly about their personal travels and showed slides. Nonetheless, she had written a descriptive essay called "Grandma Goes to Europe." She still must have thought of herself as a writer. Yet she showed this long journal to no one.

I miss her, but perhaps no more in death than I did in life. Dying seems less sad than having lived too little. But at least we're now asking questions about all the Ruths and all our family mysteries.

If her song inspires that, I think she would be the first to say: It was worth the singing.

• • • • • • • • • • • •

QUESTIONS FOR A SECOND READING

1. About a third of the way through the essay, Steinem tells a number of stories about her mother. Reread these stories, then ask yourself how each of them represents her mother. What does each story say about her mother's life and Steinem's relationship with her? How did Steinem's image of her mother change from the early set of stories to the later ones?
2. For Steinem, the story about the walk her mother took that ended with the death of her dog represented the "formidable forces" arrayed against her mother. Steinem says that this story shows how her mother tried to save herself. How does it show that? How does Steinem read the incident? What, in other words, does it mean to Steinem?

ASSIGNMENTS FOR WRITING

1. Late in the essay, Steinem writes:

> I still don't understand why so many, many years passed before I saw my mother as a person and before I understood that many of the forces in her life are patterns women share. Like a lot of daugh-

> ters, I suppose I couldn't afford to admit that what had happened to my mother was not all personal or accidental, and therefore could happen to me.

Write an essay describing the forces arrayed against Steinem's mother—the forces Steinem regards as responsible for her mother's transformation—and explain how they affected her mother.

2. How was Steinem affected by her mother's life? Reread the stories she tells about her mother and then write an essay explaining how the circumstances they describe seem to have affected Steinem—both then, as a child, and now, as a writer recalling and reshaping the past. Steinem is careful and precise in telling her mother's story, avoiding the temptation for quick summary and happy endings. Be sure to show equal care and precision in telling Steinem's story.

MAKING CONNECTIONS

1. Dorothy Dinnerstein, in "Higamous-Hogamous" (p. 169), develops a theory about the differences in the freedom of men and of women—the freedom to invest in love and worldly affairs and to make history. She attributes these differences to the fact that children in our culture are raised almost exclusively by their mothers. Write an essay in which you discuss how you think Dinnerstein might explain the transformation of Steinem's mother. (This isn't an opportunity for you to give back Dinnerstein and say that she would attribute the transformation to exclusive mother-raising.) How might she interpret the forces arrayed against Ruth? What would she say about Ruth's relationship with her husband? How might she discuss the way other males in the family treat Ruth, especially during her illness?
2. Like Steinem, Alice Walker, in "In Search of Our Mothers' Gardens" (p. 508), and Richard Rodriguez, in "The Achievement of Desire" (p. 430), write about their families and the past. Consider Steinem and Walker or Rodriguez as cases in point, as writers working to recall and reshape (and thereby understand) the past. How are their essays different? How is the writing different? And to what would you attribute these differences?

STUDS TERKEL

STUDS TERKEL has spent much of his adult life "putting the I back in a Them society," as one critic stated it. Born in New York City in 1912, he graduated from the University of Chicago's law school in 1934. Terkel's first job was as a civil service employee in Washington, D.C., and he has since been a stage actor, movie house manager, radio and television broadcaster, lecturer, columnist, master of ceremonies (at the 1959 and 1960 Newport Folk Festivals), and free-lance writer. His books include Giants of Jazz; Hard Times: An Oral History of the Great Depression; *and* Working, *for which he was nominated for a National Book Award. His most recent book is* The Good War.

Terkel can be said to have made the interview a popular literary form. Unlike Robert Coles ("Entitlement") or Thomas Cottle and Stephen Klineberg ("Ted and Ellie Graziano"), who spent weeks and sometimes years meeting and talking with their subjects, Terkel worked the streets, "on the prowl for a cross-section of urban thought, using no one method or technique." Nevertheless, armed with his tape recorder, he has a remarkable facility for getting people to speak about the things that matter to them. "I realized quite early in this adventure," Terkel said, "that interviews, conventionally conducted, were meaningless. Conditioned clichés were certain to come." What he searched for in buses and bars, in the streets and on the phone, were conversations in which "the sluice gates of dammed up hurts and dreams were opened." Terkel edits and transcribes these conversations, but otherwise the people of his world speak for themselves. Critic Geoffrey Wolff wrote of his work, "People talk miracles to Terkel. They'll confess anything to him for some reason, but the rarest thing he draws from them is their startling decency. And they talk surprising languages: vital, distinct from one another, rich with curious idioms and odd habits of imagination this country has nurtured." This selection presents two of Terkel's interviews from Working.

Roberta Victor and *Eric Nesterenko*

Roberta Victor

She had been a prostitute, starting at the age of fifteen. During the first five or six years, she worked as a high-priced call girl in Manhattan. Later she was a streetwalker . . .

You never used your own name in hustling. I used a different name practically every week. If you got busted, it was more difficult for them to find out who you really were. The role one plays when hustling has nothing to do with who you are. It's only fitting and proper you take another name.

There were certain names that were in great demand. Every second hustler had the name Kim or Tracy or Stacy and a couple others that were in vogue. These were all young women from seventeen to twenty-five, and we picked these very non-ethnic-oriented WASP names, rich names.

A hustler is any woman in American society. I was the kind of hustler who received money for favors granted rather than the type of hustler who signs a lifetime contract for her trick. Or the kind of hustler who carefully reads women's magazines and learns what it is proper to give for each date, depending on how much money her date or trick spends on her.

The favors I granted were not always sexual. When I was a call girl, men were not paying for sex. They were paying for something else. They were either paying to act out a fantasy or they were paying for companionship or they were paying to be seen with a well-dressed young woman. Or they were paying for somebody to listen to them. They were paying for a *lot* of things. Some men were paying for sex that *they* felt was deviant. They were paying so that nobody would accuse them of being perverted or dirty or nasty. A large proportion of these guys asked things that were not at all deviant. Many of them wanted oral sex. They felt they couldn't ask their wives or girl friends because they'd be repulsed. Many of them wanted somebody to talk dirty to them. Every good call girl in New York used to share her book and we all knew the same tricks.

We know a guy who used to lie in a coffin in the middle of his bedroom and he would see the girl only once. He got his kicks when the door would be open, the lights would be out, and there would be candles in the living room, and all you could see was his coffin on wheels. As you walked into the living room, he'd suddenly sit up. Of course, you screamed. He got his kicks when you screamed. Or the guy who set a table like the Last Supper and sat in a robe and sandals and wanted you to play Mary Magdalene. (Laughs.)

I was about fifteen, going on sixteen. I was sitting in a coffee shop in the Village, and a friend of mine came by. She said; "I've got a cab waiting. Hurry up. You can make fifty dollars in twenty minutes." Looking back, I wonder why I was so willing to run out of the coffee shop, get in a cab, and turn a trick. It wasn't traumatic because my training had been in how to be a hustler anyway.

I learned it from the society around me, just as a woman. We're taught how to hustle, how to attract, hold a man, and give sexual favors in return. The language that you hear all the time, "Don't sell yourself cheap." "Hold out for the highest bidder." "Is it proper to kiss a man good night on the first date?" The implication is it may not be proper on the first date, but if he takes you out to dinner on the second date, it's proper. If he brings you a bottle of perfume on the third date, you should let him touch you above the waist. And go on from there. It's a market place transaction.

Somehow I managed to absorb that when I was quite young. So it wasn't even a moment of truth when this woman came into the coffee shop and said; "Come on." I was back in twenty-five minutes and I felt no guilt.

She was a virgin until she was fourteen. A jazz musician, with whom she had fallen in love, avoided her. "So I went out to have sex with somebody to present him with an accomplished fact. I found it nonpleasurable. I did a lot of sleeping around before I ever took money."

A precocious child, she was already attending a high school of demanding academic standards. "I was very lonely. I didn't experience myself as being attractive. I had always felt I was too big, too fat, too awkward, didn't look like a Pepsi-Cola ad, was not anywhere near the American Dream. Guys were mostly scared of me. I was athletic, I was bright, and I didn't know how to keep my mouth shut. I didn't know how to play the games right.

"I understood very clearly they were not attracted to me for what I was, but as a sexual object. I was attractive. The year before I started hustling there were a lot

of guys that wanted to go to bed with me. They didn't want to get involved emotionally, but they did want to ball. For a while I was willing to accept that. It was feeling intimacy, feeling close, feeling warm.

"The time spent in bed wasn't unpleasant. It just wasn't terribly pleasant. It was a way of feeling somebody cared about me, at least for a moment. And it mattered that I was there, that I was important. I discovered that in bed it was possible. It was one skill that I had and I was proud of my reputation as an amateur.

"I viewed all girls as being threats. That's what we were all taught. You can't be friends with another woman, she might take your man. If you tell her anything about how you really feel, she'll use it against you. You smile at other girls and you spend time with them when there's nothing better to do, but you'd leave any girl sitting anywhere if you had an opportunity to go somewhere with a man. Because the most important thing in life is the way men feel about you."

How could you forget your first trick? (Laughs.) We took a cab to midtown Manhattan, we went to a penthouse. The guy up there was quite well known. What he really wanted to do was watch two women make love, and then he wanted to have sex with me. It was barely sex. He was almost finished by the time we started. He barely touched me and we were finished.

Of course, we faked it, the woman and me. The ethic was: You don't participate in a sexual act with another woman if a trick is watching. You always fake it. You're putting something over on him and he's paying for something he didn't really get. That's the only way you can keep any sense of self-respect.

The call girl ethic is very strong. You were the lowest of the low if you allowed yourself to feel anything with a trick. The bed puts you on their level. The way you maintain your integrity is by acting all the way through. It's not too far removed from what most American women do—which is to put on a big smile and act.

It was a tremendous kick. Here I was doing absolutely nothing, *feeling* nothing, and in twenty minutes I was going to walk out with fifty dollars in my pocket. That just made me feel absolutely marvelous. I came downtown. I can't believe this! I'm not changed, I'm the same as I was twenty minutes ago, except that now I have fifty dollars in my pocket. It really was tremendous status. How many people could make fifty dollars for twenty minutes' work? Folks work for eighty dollars take-home pay. I worked twenty minutes for fifty dollars clear, no taxes, nothing! I was still in school, I was smoking grass, I was shooting heroin, I wasn't hooked yet, and I had money. It was terrific.

After that, I made it my business to let my friend know that I was available for more of these situations. (Laughs.) She had good connections.

Very shortly I linked up with a couple of others who had a good call book.

Books of phone numbers are passed around from call girl to call girl. They're numbers of folks who are quite respectable and with whom there is little risk. They're not liable to pull a knife on you, they're not going to cheat you out of money. Businessmen and society figures. There's three or four groups. The wealthy executive, who makes periodic trips into the city and is known to several girls. There's the social figure, whose name appears quite regularly in the society pages and who's a regular once-a-week John. Or there's the quiet, independently wealthy type. Nobody knows how they got their money. I know one of them made his money off munitions in World War II. Then there's the entertainer. There's another crowd that runs around the night spots, the 21 Club . . .

These were the people whose names you saw in the paper almost every day. But I knew what they were really like. Any John who was obnoxious or aggressive was just crossed out of your book. You passed the word around that this person was not somebody other people should call.

We used to share numbers—standard procedure. The book I had I got from a guy who got it from a very good call girl. We kept a copy of that book in a safe deposit box. The standard procedure was that somebody new gave half of what they got the first time for each number. You'd tell them: "Call so-and-so, that's a fifty-dollar trick." They would give you twenty-five dollars. Then the number was theirs. My first book, I paid half of each trick to the person who gave it to me. After that, it was my book.

The book had the name and phone number coded, the price, what the person wants, and the contact name. For four years I didn't turn a trick for less than fifty dollars. They were all fifty to one hundred dollars and up for twenty minutes, an hour. The understanding is: it doesn't get conducted as a business transaction. The myth is that it's a social occasion.

You're expected to be well dressed, well made up, appear glad to see the man. I would get a book from somebody and I would call and say, "I'm a friend of so-and-so's, and she thought it would be nice if we got together." The next move was his. Invariably he'd say, "Why don't we do that? Tonight or tomorrow night. Why don't you come over for a drink?" I would get very carefully dressed and made up . . .

There's a given way of dressing in that league—that's to dress well but not ostentatiously. You have to pass doormen, cabdrivers. You have to look as if you belong in those buildings on Park Avenue or Central Park West. You're expected not to look cheap, not to look hard. Youth is the premium. I was quite young, but I looked older, so I had to work very hard at looking my age. Most men want girls who are eighteen. They really want girls who are younger, but they're afraid of trouble.

Preparations are very elaborate. It has to do with beauty parlors and shopping for clothes and taking long baths and spending money on preserving the kind of front that gives you a respectable address and telephone and being seen at the right clubs and drinking at the right bars. And being able to read the newspapers faithfully, so that not only can you talk about current events, you can talk about the society columns as well.

It's a social ritual. Being able to talk about what is happening and learn from this great master, and be properly respectful and know the names that he mentions. They always drop names of their friends, their contacts, and their clients. You should recognize these. Playing a role . . .

At the beginning I was very excited. But in order to continue I had to turn myself off. I had to disassociate who I was from what I was doing.

It's a process of numbing yourself. I couldn't associate with people who were not in the life—either the drug life or the bustling life. I found I couldn't turn myself back on when I finished working. When I turned myself off, I was numb—emotionally, sexually numb.

At first I felt like I was putting one over on all the other poor slobs that would go to work at eight-thirty in the morning and come home at five. I was coming home at four in the morning and I could sleep all day. I really thought a lot of people would change places with me because of the romantic image: being able to spend two hours out, riding cabs, and coming home with a hundred dollars. I could spend my mornings doing my nails, going to the beauty parlor, taking long baths, going shopping . . .

It was usually two tricks a night. That was easily a hundred, a hundred and a quarter. I always had money in my pocket. I didn't know what the inside of a subway smelled like. Nobody traveled any other way except by cab. I ate in all the best restaurants and I drank in all the best clubs. A lot of people wanted you to go out to dinner with them. All you had to do was be an ornament.

Almost all the call girls I knew were involved in drugs. The fast life, the night hours. At after-hours clubs, if you're not a big drinker, you usually find somebody who has cocaine, 'cause that's the big drug in those places. You wake up at noon, there's not very much to do till nine or ten that night. Everybody else is at work, so you shoot heroin. After a while the work became a means of supplying drugs, rather than drugs being something we took when we were bored.

The work becomes boring because you're not part of the life. You're the part that's always hidden. The doormen smirk when you come in, 'cause they know what's going on. The cabdriver, when you give him a certain address—he knows exactly where you're going when you're riding up Park Avenue at ten o'clock at night, for Christ sake. You leave there and go back—to what? Really, to what? To an emptiness. You've got all this money in your pocket and nobody you care about.

When I was a call girl I looked down on streetwalkers. I couldn't understand why anybody would put themselves in that position. It seemed to me to be hard work and very dangerous. What I was doing was basically riskless. You never had to worry about disease. There were folks who you know took care of themselves and saw the doctor regularly. Their apartments were always immaculate and the liquor was always good. They were always polite. You didn't have to ask them for money first. It was always implicit: when you were ready to leave, there would be an envelope under the lamp or there'd be something in your pocketbook. It never had to be discussed.

I had to work an awful lot harder for the same money when I was a streetwalker. I remember having knives pulled on me, broken bottles held over my head, being raped, having my money stolen back from me, having to jump out of a second-story window, having a gun pointed at me.

As a call girl, I had lunch at the same places society women had lunch. There was no way of telling me apart from anybody else in the upper tax bracket. I made my own hours, no more than three or so hours of work an evening. I didn't have to accept calls. All I had to do was play a role.

As a streetwalker, I didn't have to act, I let myself show the contempt I felt for the tricks. They weren't paying enough to make it worth performing for them. As a call girl, I pretended I enjoyed it sexually. You have to act as if you had an orgasm. As a streetwalker, I didn't. I used to lie there with my hands behind my head and do mathematics equations in my head or memorize the keyboard typewriter.

It was strictly a transaction. No conversation, no acting, no myth around it, no romanticism. It was purely a business transaction. You always asked for your money in front. If you could get away without undressing totally, you did that.

It's not too different than the distinction between an executive secretary and somebody in the typing pool. As an executive secretary you really identify with your boss. When you're part of the typing pool, you're a body, you're hired labor, a set of hands on the typewriter. You have nothing to do with whoever is passing the work down to you. You do it as quickly as you can.

What led you to the streets?

My drug habit. It got a lot larger. I started looking bad. All my money was going for drugs. I didn't have any money to spend on keeping myself up and going to beauty parlors and having a decent address and telephone.

If you can't keep yourself up, you can't call on your old tricks. You drop out of circulation. As a call girl, you have to maintain a whole image.

The trick wants to know he can call you at a certain number and you have to have a stable address. You must look presentable, not like death on a soda cracker.

I looked terrible. When I hit the streets, I tried to stick to at least twenty dollars and folks would laugh. I needed a hundred dollars a night to maintain a drug habit and keep a room somewhere. It meant turning seven or eight tricks a night. I was out on the street from nine o'clock at night till four in the morning. I was taking subways and eating in hamburger stands.

For the first time I ran the risk of being busted. I was never arrested as a call girl. Every once in a while a cop would get hold of somebody's book. They would call one of the girls and say, "I'm a friend of so-and-so's." They would try to trap them. I never took calls from people I didn't know. But on the streets, how do you know who you're gonna pick up?

As a call girl, some of my tricks were upper echelon cops, not patrolmen. Priests, financiers, garment industry folks, bigtimers. On the street, they ranged from *junior* executive types, blue-collar workers, upwardly striving postal workers, college kids, suburban white collars who were in the city for the big night, restaurant workers . . .

You walk a certain area, usually five or six blocks. It has a couple of restaurants, a couple of bars. There's the step in-between: hanging out in a given bar, where people come to you. I did that briefly.

You'd walk very slowly, you'd stop and look in the window. Somebody would come up to you. There was a ritual here too. The law says in order to arrest a woman for prostitution, she has to mention money and she has to tell you what she'll do for the money. We would keep within the letter of the law, even though the cops never did.

Somebody would come up and say, "It's a nice night, isn't it?" "Yes." They'd say, "Are you busy?" I'd say, "Not particularly." "Would you like to come with me and have a drink?" You start walking and they say, "I have fifteen dollars or twelve dollars and I'm very lonely." Something to preserve the myth. Then they want you to spell out exactly what you're willing to do for the money.

I never approached anybody on the street. That was the ultimate risk. Even if he weren't a cop, he could be some kind of supersquare, who would call a cop. I was trapped by cops several times.

The first one didn't even trap me as a trick. It was three in the morning. I was in Chinatown. I ran into a trick I knew. We made contact in a restaurant. He went home and I followed him a few minutes later. I knew the address. I remember passing a banana truck. It didn't dawn on me that it was strange for somebody to be selling bananas at three in the morning. I spent about twenty minutes with my friend. He paid me. I put the money in my shoe. I opened the door and got thrown back against the wall. The banana salesman was a vice squad cop. He'd stood on the garbage can to peer in the window. I got three years for that one.

I was under age. I was four months short of twenty-one. They sent me to what was then called Girls' Term Court. They wouldn't allow me a lawyer because I wasn't an adult, so it wasn't really a criminal charge. The judge said I was rehabilitable. Instead of giving me thirty days, he gave me three years in the reformatory. It was very friendly of him. I was out on parole a couple of times before I'd get caught and sent back.

I once really got trapped. It was about midnight and a guy came down the street. He said he was a postal worker who just got off the shift. He told me how much money he had and what he wanted. I took him to my room. The cop isn't supposed to undress. If you can describe the color of his shorts, it's an invalid arrest. Not only did he show me the color of his shorts, he went to bed with me. Then he pulled a badge and a gun and busted me.

He lied to me. He told me he was a narc and he didn't want to bust me for hustling. If I would tell him who was dealing in the neighborhood, he'd cut me loose. I lied to him, but he won. He got me to walk out of the building past all my friends and when we got to the car, he threw me in (Laughs.) It was great fun. I did time for that—close to four years.

What's the status of the streetwalker in prison?

It's fine. Everybody there has been hustling. It's status in reverse. Anybody who comes in saying things like they could never hustle is looked down on as being somewhat crazy.

She speaks of a profound love she had for a woman who she'd met in prison; of her nursing her lover after the woman had become blind.

"I was out of the country for a couple of years. I worked a house in Mexico. It had heavy velour curtains—a Mexican version of a French whorehouse. There was a reception area, where the men would come and we'd parade in front of them.

"The Mexicans wanted American girls. The Americans wanted Mexican girls. So I didn't get any American tricks. I had to give a certain amount to the house for each trick I turned and anything I negotiated over that amount was mine. It was far less than anything I had taken in the States.

"I was in great demand even though I wasn't a blond. A girl friend of mine worked there two nights. She was Norwegian and very blonde. Every trick who came in wanted her. Her head couldn't handle it all. She quit after two nights. So I was the only American.

"That was really hard work. The Mexicans would play macho. *American tricks will come as quickly as they can. Mexicans will hold back and make me work for my*

money. I swear to God they were doing multiplication tables in their heads to keep from having an orgasm. I would use every trick I knew to get them to finish. It was crazy!

I was teaching school at the same time. I used Alice in Wonderland *as the text in my English class. During the day I tutored English for fifth- and sixth-grade kids. In the evening, I worked in the call house.*

"The junk down there was quite cheap and quite good. My habit was quite large. I loved dope more than anything else around. After a while I couldn't differentiate between working and not working. All men were tricks, all relationships were acting. I was completely turned off."

She quit shooting dope the moment she was slugged, brutally beaten by a dealer who wanted her. This was her revelatory experience. "It was the final indignity. I'd had tricks pulling broken bottles on me, I'd been in razor fights, but nobody had ever hit me." *It was a threat to her status. "I was strong. I could handle myself. A tough broad. This was threatened, so . . ."*

I can't talk for women who were involved with pimp's. That was where I always drew the line. I always thought pimps were lower than pregnant cockroaches. I didn't want anything to do with them. I was involved from time to time with some men. They were either selling dope or stealing, but they were not depending on my income. Nor were they telling me to get my ass out on the street. I never supported a man.

As a call girl I got satisfaction, an unbelievable joy—perhaps perverted—in knowing what these reputable folks were really like. Being able to open a newspaper every morning, read about this pillar of society, and know what a pig he really was. The tremendous kick in knowing that I didn't feel anything, that I was acting and they weren't. It's sick, but no sicker than what every woman is taught, all right?

I was in *control* with every one of those relationships. You're vulnerable if you allow yourself to be involved sexually. I wasn't. They were. I called it. Being able to manipulate somebody sexually, I could determine when I wanted that particular transaction to end. 'Cause I could make the guy come. I could play all kinds of games. See? It was a tremendous sense of power.

What I did was no different from what ninety-nine percent of American women are taught to do. I took the money from under the lamp instead of in Arpege. What would I do with 150 bottles of Arpege a week?

You become your job. I became what I did. I became a hustler. I became cold, I became hard, I became turned off, I became numb. Even when I wasn't hustling, I was a hustler. I don't think it's terribly different from somebody who works on the assembly line forty hours a week and comes home cut off, numb, dehumanized. People aren't built to switch on and off like water faucets.

What was really horrifying about jail is that it really isn't horrifying. You adjust very easily. The same thing with hustling. It became my life. It was too much of an effort to try to make contact with another human being, to force myself to care, to feel.

I didn't care about me. It didn't matter whether I got up or didn't get up. I got high as soon as I awoke. The first thing I'd reach for, with my eyes half-closed, was my dope. I didn't like my work. It was messy. That was the biggest feeling about it. Here's all these guys slobbering over you all night long. I'm lying there, doing math or conjugations or Spanish poetry in my head. (Laughs.) And they're slobbering. God! God! What enabled me to do it was being high—high and numb.

The overt hustling society is the microcosm of the rest of the society. The power relationships are the same and the games are the same. Only this one I was in control of. The greater one I wasn't. In the outside society, if I tried to be me, I wasn't in control of anything. As a bright, assertive woman, I had no power. As a cold, manipulative hustler, I had a lot. I knew I was playing a role. Most women are taught to *become* what they act. All I did was act out the reality of American womanhood.

Eric Nesterenko

He has been a professional hockey player for twenty years, as a member of the Toronto Maple Leafs and the Chicago Black Hawks. He is thirty-eight. He has a wife and three small children.

"I lived in a small mining town in Canada, a God-forsaken place called Flinflan. In the middle of nowhere, four hundred miles north of Winnipeg. It was a good life, beautiful winters. I remember the Northern Lights. Dark would come around three o'clock. Thirty below zero, but dry and clean.

"I lived across the street from the rink. That's how I got started, when I was four or five. We never had any gear. I used to wrap Life *magazines around my legs. We didn't have organized hockey like they have now. All our games were pickup, a never-ending game. Maybe there would be three kids to a team, then there would be fifteen, and the game would go on. Nobody would keep score. It was pure kind of play. The play you see here, outside the stadium, outside at the edge of the ghetto. I see 'em in the schoolyards. It's that same kind of play around the basket. Pure play.*

"My father bought me a pair of skates, but that was it. He never took part. I played the game for my own sake, not for him. He wasn't even really around to watch. I was playing for the joy of it, with my own peers. Very few adults around. We organized everything.

"I see parents at kids' sporting events. It's all highly organized. It's very formal. They have referees and so on. The parents are spectators. The kids are playing for their parents. The old man rewards him for playing well and doesn't reward

him for not doing so well. (Laughs.) The father puts too much pressure on the kid. A boy then is soft material. If you want a kid to do something, it's got to be fun.

"I was a skinny, ratty kid with a terrible case of acne. I could move pretty well, but I never really looked like much. (Laughs.) Nobody ever really noticed me. But I could play the game. In Canada it is part of the culture. If you can play the game, you are recognized. I was good almost from the beginning. The game became a passion with me. I was looking to be somebody and the game was my way. It was my life."

At sixteen, while in high school, he was playing with semi-pro teams, earning two hundred dollars a week. At eighteen, he joined the Toronto Maple Leafs.

There's an irony that one gets paid for playing, that play should bring in money. When you sell play, that makes it hard for pure, recreational play, for play as an art, to exist. It's corrupted, it's made harder, perhaps it's brutalized, but it's still there. Once you learn how to play and are accepted in the group, there is a rapport. All you are as an athlete is honed and made sharper. You learn to survive in a very tough world. It has its own rewards.

The pro game is a kind of a stage. People can see who we are. Our personalities come through in our bodies. It's exciting. I can remember games with twenty thousand people and the place going crazy with sound and action and color. The enormous energy the crowd produces all coming in on the ice, all focusing in on you. It's pretty hard to resist that. (Laughs.)

I was really recognized then. I remember one game: it was in the semi-finals, the year we won the Stanley Cup. I was with Chicago. It was the sixth game against Montreal. They were the big club and we were the Cinderella team. It was three to nothing, for us, with five minutes left to go. As a spontaneous gesture twenty thousand people stood up. I was on the ice. I remember seeing that whole stadium, just solid, row on row, from the balcony to the boxes, standing up. There people were turned on by us. (Sighs.) We came off, three feet off the ice . . . (Softly) Spring of '61.

When Toronto dropped me I said, "I'm a failure." Twenty-two, what the hell does one know? You're the boy of the moment or nothing. What we show is energy and young bodies. We know our time is fleeting. If we don't get a chance to go, it makes us antsy. Our values are instant, it's really hard to bide your time.

Violence is taken to a greater degree. There is always the specter of being hurt. A good player, just come into his prime, cracks a skull, breaks a leg, he's finished. If you get hit, you get hit—with impersonal force. The guy'll hit you as hard as he can. If you get hurt, the other players switch off. Nobody's sympathetic. When you get hurt they don't look at you, even players on your own team. The curtain comes down—'cause it could have been me. One is afraid of being hurt himself. You don't want to think too much about it. I saw my teammate lying there—I knew him pretty well—they put forty stitches in his face. I saw him lying on the table and the doctors working on him. I said, "Better him than me." (Laughs.) We conditioned ourselves to think like that. I think it's a defense mechanism and it's brutalizing.

The professional recognizes this and risks himself less and less, so the percentage is in his favor. This takes a bit of experience. Invariably it's the younger player who gets hurt. Veterans learn to be calculating about their vulnerability. (Laughs.) This takes a little bit away from the play. When I was young, I used to take all sorts of chances just for the hell of it. Today, instead of trying to push through it, I ease up. It takes something off the risk. The older professional often plays a waiting game, waits for the other person to commit himself in the arena.

The younger player, with great natural skill, say Bobby Orr, will actually force the play. He'll push. Sometimes they're good enough to get away with it. Orr got hurt pretty badly the first couple of years he played. He had operations on both knees. Now he's a little smarter, a little more careful, and a little more cynical. (Laughs.)

Cynicism is a tool for survival. I began to grow up quickly. I became disillusioned with the game not being the pure thing it was earlier in my life. I began to see the exploitation of the players by the owners. You realize owners don't really care for you. You're a piece of property. They try to get as much out of you as they can. I remember once I had a torn shoulder. It was well in the process of healing. But I knew it wasn't right yet. They brought their doctor in. He said, "You can play." I played and ripped it completely. I was laid up. So I look at the owner. He shrugs his shoulders, walks away. He doesn't really hate me. He's impersonal.

Among players, while we're playing we're very close. Some of the best clubs I've played with have this intimacy—an intimacy modern man hardly ever achieves. We can see each other naked, emotionally, physically. We're plugged into each other, because we need each other. There have been times when I knew what the other guy was thinking without him ever talking to me. When that happens, we can do anything together.

It can't be just a job. It's not worth playing just for money. It's a way of life. When we were kids there was the release in playing, the sweetness in being able to move and control your body. This is what play is. Beating somebody is secondary. When I was a kid, to really *move* was my delight. I felt released because I could move around anybody. I was free.

That exists on the pro level, but there's the money aspect. You know they're making an awful lot of money off you. You know you're just a piece of property. When an older player's gone, it's not just his body. With modern training methods you can play a long time. But you just get fed up with the whole business. It becomes a job, just a shitty job. (Laughs.)

I'm not wild about living in hotels, coming in late at night, and having to spend time in a room waiting for a game. You've got a day to kill and the game's in back of your mind. It's hard to relax. It's hard to read a good book. I'll read an easy book or go to a movie to kill the time. I didn't mind killing time when I was younger, but I resent killing time now. (Laughs.) I don't want to *kill* time. I want to *do* something with my time.

Traveling in the big jets and going to and from hotels is very tough. We're in New York on a Wednesday, Philadelphia on a Thursday, Buffalo on a Saturday, Pittsburgh on a Sunday, and Detroit on a Tuesday. That's just a terrible way to live. (Laughs.) After the game on Sunday, I am tired—not only with my body, which is not a bad kind of tiredness, I'm tired emotionally, tired mentally. I'm not a very good companion after those games.

It's a lot tougher when things are going badly. It's more gritty and you don't feel very good about yourself. The whole object of a pro game is to win. That is what we sell. We sell it to a lot of people who don't win at all in their regular lives. They involve themselves with *their* team, a winning team. I'm not cynical about this. When we win, there's also a carry-over in us. Life is a little easier. But in the last two or three years fatigue has been there. I'm sucked out. But that's okay. I'd sooner live like that than be bored. If I get a decent sleep, a bit of food that's good and strong, I'm revived. I'm alive again.

The fans touch us, particularly when we've won. You can feel the pat of hands all over. On the back, on the shoulder, they want to shake your hand. When I'm feeling good about myself, I really respond to this. But if I don't feel so good, I play out the role. You have to act it out. It has nothing to do with pure joy. It has nothing to do with the feeling I had when I was a kid.

'Cause hell, nobody recognized me. I didn't have a role to play. Many of us are looking for some kind of role to play. The role of the professional athlete is one that I've learned to play very well. Laughing with strangers. It doesn't take much. It has its built-in moves, responses. There is status for the fans, but there's not a whole lot of status for me. (Laughs.) Not now. I know it doesn't mean very much. I shy away from it more and more. When I'm not feeling good and somebody comes up—"Hello, Eric"—I'm at times a bit cold and abrupt. I can see them withdrawing from me, hurt. They want to be plugged into something and they're not. They may make a slurring remark. I can't do anything about it.

I'm fighting the cynicism. What I'd like to do is find an alter-life and play a little more. I don't have another vocation. I have a feeling unless I find one, my life might be a big anticlimax. I could get a job, but I don't want a job. I never had a job in the sense that I had to earn a living just for the sake of earning a living. I may have to do that, but I sure hope I don't.

I have doubts about what I do. I'm not that sure of myself. It doesn't seem clear to me at times. I'm a man playing a boy's game. Is this a valid reason for making money? Then I turn around and think of a job. I've tried to be a stockbroker. I say to a guy, "I got a good stock, you want to buy it?" He says, "No." I say, "Okay." You don't want to buy, don't buy. (Laughs.) I'm not good at persuading people to buy things they don't want to buy. I'm just not interested in the power of money. I found that out. That's the way one keeps score—the amount of money you earned. I found myself bored with that.

I've worked on construction and I liked that best of all. (Laughs.) I'd been working as a stockbroker and I couldn't stand it any more. I got drunk one Friday night and while I was careening around town I ran into this guy I knew from the past. He said for the hell of it, "Why don't you come and work on the Hancock Building with me?" He was a super on the job. The next Monday I showed up. I stayed for a week. I was interested in seeing how a big building goes up—and working with my hands.

A stockbroker has more status. He surrounds himself with things of status. But the stockbroker comes to see me play, I don't go to see him be a stockbroker. (Laughs.)

The real status is what my peers think of me and what I think of myself. The players have careful self-doubts at times. We talk about our sagging egos. Are we really that famous? Are we really that good? We have terrible doubts. (Laughs.) Actors may have something of this. Did I do well? Am I worth this applause? Is pushing the puck around really that meaningful? (Laughs.) When I'm not pushing that puck well, how come the fans don't like me? (Laughs.) Then there's the reverse reaction—a real brashness. They're always rationalizing to each other. That's probably necessary. It's not a bad way to handle things when you have no control over them. Players who are really put together, who have few doubts, are usually much more in control. If you're recognized by your peers, you're all right.

I still like the physicality, the sensuality of life. I still like to use my body. But the things I like now are more soft. I don't want to beat people. I don't want to prove anything. I have a friend who used to play pro football, but who shares my philosophy. We get into the country that is stark and cold and harsh, but there's a great aesthetic feedback. It's soft and comforting and sweet. We come out of there with such enormous energy and so fit. We often go into town like a couple of fools and get mildly drunk and laugh a lot.

Being a physical man in the modern world is becoming obsolete. The machines have taken the place of that. We work in offices, we fight rules and corporations, but we hardly ever hit anybody. Not that hitting anybody is a solution. But to survive in the world at one time, one had to stand up and fight—fight the weather, fight the land, or fight the rocks. I think there is a real desire for man to do that. Today he has evolved into being more passive, conforming . . .

I think that is why the professional game, with its terrific physicality—men getting together on a cooperative basis—this is appealing to the middle-class man. He's the one who supports professional sports.

I think it's a reflection of the North American way of life. This is one of the ways you are somebody—you beat somebody. (Laughs.) You're better than they are. Somebody has to be less than you in order for you to be somebody. I don't know if that's right any more. I don't have that drive any more. If I function hard, it's against a hard environment. That's preferable to knocking somebody down.

I come up against a hard young stud now, and he wants the puck very badly, I'm inclined to give it to him. (Laughs.) When you start thinking like that you're in trouble, as far as being a pro athlete is involved. But I don't want to be anybody any more in those terms. I've had some money, I've had some big fat times, I've been on the stage.

It's been a good life. Maybe I could have done better, have a better record or something like that. But I've really had very few regrets over the past twenty years. I can enjoy some of the arts that I had shut myself off from as a kid. Perhaps that is my only regret. The passion for the game was so all-consuming when I was a kid that I blocked myself from music. I cut myself off from a certain broadness of experience. Maybe one has to do that to fully explore what they want to do the most passionately.

I know a lot of pro athletes who have a capacity for a wider experience. But they wanted to become champions. They had to focus themselves on their one thing completely. His primary force when he becomes champion is his ego trip, his desire to excel, to be somebody special. To some degree, he must dehumanize himself. I look forward to a lower key way of living. But it must be physical. I'm sure I would die without it, become a drunk or something.

I still like to skate. One day last year on a cold, clear, crisp afternoon, I saw this huge sheet of ice in the street. Goddamn, if I didn't drive out there and put on my skates. I took off my camel-hair coat. I was just in a sort of jacket, on my skates. And I flew. Nobody was there. I was free as a bird. I was really happy. That goes back to when I was a kid. I'll do that until I die, I hope. Oh, I was free!

The wind was blowing from the north. With the wind behind you, you're in motion, you can wheel and dive and turn, you can lay yourself into impossible angles that you never could walking or running. You lay yourself at a forty-five degree angle, your elbows virtually touching the ice as you're in a turn. Incredible! It's beautiful! You're breaking the bounds of gravity. I have a feeling this is the innate desire of man.

(His eyes are glowing.) I haven't kept many photographs of myself, but I found one where I'm in full flight. I'm leaning into a turn. You pick up the centrifugal forces and you lay in it. For a few seconds, like a gyroscope, they support you. I'm in full flight and my head is turned. I'm concentrating on something and I'm grinning. That's the way I like to picture myself. I'm something else there. I'm on another level of existence, just being in pure motion. Going wherever I want to go, whenever I want to go. That's nice, you know. (Laughs softly.)

• • • • • • • • • • • • •

QUESTIONS FOR A SECOND READING

1. Victor and Nesterenko both use one or two dominant metaphors to organize or understand their experiences. Nesterenko, for example, sometimes refers to the hockey rink as "a stage." As you reread, ask yourself what the dominant metaphors are for each of these persons. How might these metaphors be regarded as key factors in both individuals' understanding of their own experience? Bring these metaphors forward, and use them as tools in an investigation of how both Victor and Nesterenko see the world.
2. At one point, Roberta Victor says, "A hustler is any woman in American society," and she makes similar comments several times later in the interview. In fact, much of what she says about women, life in America, and being a hooker has to do with hustling. When you reread her story, locate those instances where she talks about hustling. Is it possible to take her seriously when she says that her experience is like every woman's experience?
3. Find the passage in the Nesterenko interview that strikes you as the key to Nesterenko's character. What does it tell you about him? How can you explain him—what he does, the way he lives—on the basis of this passage and its implications?

ASSIGNMENTS FOR WRITING

1. Roberta Victor said, "After a while I couldn't differentiate between working and not working." These interviews can be read as case studies in an investigation on the boundaries between working and not working. Write an essay in which you define the boundaries between work and nonwork for Victor and Nesterenko. When you are done, look back over what you have

written and consider the degree to which you can or cannot generalize from these two cases.

2. Assume that your role as reader or investigator in these interviews is to reveal something hidden from the subject, to take something that seems unimportant and to make it the most important part of the interview. What do you see or understand in each of the interviews that you think the speaker fails to see or understand about his or her own life? What do you find in each case? Write an essay identifying and explaining your special point of view on either Nesterenko or Victor.

MAKING CONNECTIONS

1. Clifford Geertz, in his essay "Deep Play: Notes on the Balinese Cockfight" (p. 299), discusses cockfighting as the national sport of Bali. He notes that only men play, and that the sport represents more than is first apparent—it reflects the social order and rules of conduct among men in the Balinese culture. For this assignment, consider Eric Nesterenko as a representative of a culture in the same way that Geertz considers men in Bali as representatives of Balinese culture. Write an essay in which you use Geertz's methods to assess professional hockey (through the brief glimpses into professional hockey that the interview provides).
2. Dorothy Dinnerstein, in "Higamous-Hogamous" (p. 169), develops a theory of why women are less free than men, less in control of their lives. Men have more power, she says, and are more inclined toward possessiveness and sexual impulsiveness. She attributes many of the differences between men and women to the fact that children are raised almost exclusively by women, not by men and women together. Write an essay in which you discuss how Roberta Victor would respond to Dinnerstein's conclusions. Note that Victor also talks a great deal about control and freedom; since she says very little about her childhood, however, you must focus on what she says about herself and on how you imagine, from the available evidence, Victor would react to Dinnerstein's impulsivity and sexuality account of the relations between men and women.

ALICE WALKER

ALICE WALKER, the youngest of eight children in a sharecropping family, was born in 1944 in Eatonton, Georgia. She is now one of the most widely read contemporary American novelists. In her work, she frequently returns to scenes of family life—some violent, some peaceful. "I was curious to know," she writes, "why people of families (specifically black families) are often cruel to each other and how much of this cruelty is caused by outside forces. . . . Family relationships are sacred. No amount of outside pressure and injustice should make us lose sight of that fact." In her nonfiction, Walker has helped to define an historical context for the contemporary black artist, a legacy that has had to be recovered from libraries and archives. The essay that follows, "In Search of Our Mothers' Gardens," defines black history as a family matter. It begins by charting the violence done to women who "died with their real gifts stifled within them" and concludes with Walker's recollection of her own mother, a recollection that enables her to imagine generations of black women handing on a "creative spark" to those who follow.

In addition to In Search of Our Mothers' Gardens, *Walker has written novels, including* The Third Life of Grange Copeland *and* The Color Purple *(which won the Pultizer Prize); collections of poems, including* Revolutionary Petunias *and* Good Night Willie Lee, I'll See You in the Morning; *two collections of short stories,* In Love and Trouble *and* You Can't Keep a Good Woman Down, *and a biography of Langston Hughes, She has also served as an editor at* Ms. *magazine. After graduating from Sarah Lawrence College in 1965, she taught at a number of colleges and universities, including Wellesley College and Yale University. She has held a Guggenheim Fellowship and a National Endowment for the Arts fellowship. She lives in San Francisco and teaches at the University of California, Berkeley.*

In Search of Our Mothers' Gardens

> I described her own nature and temperament. Told how they needed a larger life for their expression. . . . I pointed out that in lieu of proper channels, her emotions had overflowed into paths that dissipated them. I talked, beautifully I thought, about an art that would be born, an art that would open the way for women the likes of her. I asked her to hope, and build up an inner life against the coming of that day. . . . I sang, with a strange quiver in my voice, a promise song.
>
> – "Avey," JEAN TOOMER, *Cane*
> *The poet speaking to a prostitute who falls asleep while he's talking*

When the poet Jean Toomer walked through the South in the early twenties, he discovered a curious thing: black women whose spirituality was so intense, so deep, so *unconscious,* they were themselves unaware of the richness they held. They stumbled blindly through their lives: creatures so abused and mutilated in body, so dimmed and confused by pain, that they considered themselves unworthy even of hope. In the selfless abstractions their bodies became to the men who used them, they became more than "sexual objects," more even than mere women: they became "Saints." Instead of being perceived as whole persons, their bodies became shrines: what was thought to be their minds became temples suitable for worship. These crazy Saints stared out at the world, wildly, like lunatics—or quietly, like suicides; and the "God" that was in their gaze was as mute as a great stone.

Who were these Saints? These crazy, loony, pitiful women?

Some of them, without a doubt, were our mothers and grandmothers.

In the still heat of the post-Reconstruction South, this is how they seemed to Jean Toomer: exquisite butterflies trapped in an evil honey, toiling away their lives in an era, a century, that did not acknowledge them, except as "the *mule* of the world." They dreamed dreams that no one knew—not even themselves, in any coherent fashion—and saw visions no one could understand. They wandered or sat about the countryside crooning lullabies to ghosts, and drawing the mother of Christ in charcoal on courthouse walls.

They forced their minds to desert their bodies and their striving spirits sought to rise, like frail whirlwinds from the hard red clay. And when those frail whirlwinds fell, in scattered particles, upon the ground, no one mourned. Instead, men lit candles to celebrate the emptiness that remained, as people do who enter a beautiful but vacant space to resurrect a God.

Our mothers and grandmothers, some of them: moving to music not yet written. And they waited.

They waited for a day when the unknown thing that was in them would be made known; but guessed, somehow in their darkness, that on the day of their revelation they would be long dead. Therefore to Toomer they walked, and even ran, in slow motion. For they were going nowhere immediate, and the future was not yet within their grasp. And men took our mothers and grandmothers, "but got no pleasure from it." So complex was their passion and their calm.

To Toomer, they lay vacant and fallow as autumn fields, with harvest time never in sight: and he saw them enter loveless marriages, without joy; and become prostitutes, without resistance; and become mothers of children, without fulfillment.

For these grandmothers and mothers of ours were not Saints, but Artists; driven to a numb and bleeding madness by the springs of creativity in them for which there was no release. They were Creators, who lived lives of spiritual waste, because they were so rich in spirituality—which is the basis of Art—that the strain of enduring their unused and unwanted talent drove them insane. Throwing away this spirituality was their pathetic attempt to lighten the soul to a weight their work-worn, sexually abused bodies could bear.

What did it mean for a black woman to be an artist in our grandmothers' time? In our great-grandmothers' day? It is a question with an answer cruel enough to stop the blood.

Did you have a genius of a great-great-grandmother who died under some ignorant and depraved white overseer's lash? Or was she required to bake biscuits for a lazy backwater tramp, when she cried out in her soul to paint watercolors of sunsets, or the rain falling on the green and peaceful pasturelands? Or was her body broken and forced to bear children (who were more often than not sold away from her)—eight, ten, fifteen, twenty children—when her one joy was the thought of modeling heroic figures of rebellion, in stone or clay?

How was the creativity of the black woman kept alive, year after year and century after century, when for most of the years black people have been in America, it was a punishable crime for a black person to read or write? And the freedom to paint, to sculpt, to expand the mind with action did not exist. Consider, if you can bear to imagine it, what might have been the result if singing, too, had been forbidden by law. Listen to the voices of Bessie Smith, Billie Holiday, Nina Simone, Roberta Flack, and Aretha Franklin, among others, and imagine those voices muzzled for life. Then you may begin to comprehend the lives of our "crazy," "Sainted" mothers and grandmothers. The agony of the lives of women who might have been Poets, Novelists, Essayists, and Short-Story Writers (over a period of centuries), who died with their real gifts stifled within them.

And, if this were the end of the story, we would have cause to cry out in my paraphrase of Okot p'Bitek's great poem:

> O, my clanswomen
> Let us all cry together!
> Come,
> Let us mourn the death of our mother,
> The death of a Queen
> The ash that was produced
> By a great fire!
> O, this homestead is utterly dead
> Close the gates
> With *lacari* thorns,
> For our mother
> The creator of the Stool is lost!
> And all the young men
> Have perished in the wilderness!

But this is not the end of the story, for all the young women—our mothers and grandmothers, *ourselves*—have not perished in the wilderness. And if we ask ourselves why, and search for and find the answer, we will know beyond all efforts to erase it from our minds, just exactly who, and of what, we black American women are.

One example, perhaps the most pathetic,most misunderstood one, can provide a backdrop for our mothers' work: Phillis Wheatley, a slave in the 1700s.

Virginia Woolf, in her book *A Room of One's Own,* wrote that in order for a woman to write fiction she must have two things, certainly: a room of her own (with key and lock) and enough money to support herself.

What then are we to make of Phillis Wheatley, a slave, who owned not even herself? This sickly, frail black girl who required a servant of her own at times—her health was so precarious—and who, had she been white, would have been easily considered the intellectual superior of all the women and most of the men in the society of her day.

Virginia Woolf wrote further, speaking of course not of our Phillis, that "any woman born with a great gift in the sixteenth century [insert "eighteenth century," insert "black woman," insert "born or made a slave"] would certainly have gone crazed, shot herself, or ended her days in some lonely cottage outside the village, half witch, half wizard [insert "Saint"], feared and mocked at. For it needs little skill and psychology to be sure that a highly gifted girl who had tried to use her gift of poetry would have been so thwarted and hindered by contrary instincts [add "chains, guns, the lash, the ownership of one's body by someone else, submission to an alien religion"], that she must have lost her health and sanity to a certainty."

The key words, as they relate to Phillis, are "contrary instincts." For when we read the poetry of Phillis Wheatley—as when we read the novels of Nella Larsen or the oddly false-sounding autobiography of that freest of all black women writers, Zora Hurston—evidence of "contrary instincts" is everywhere. Her loyalties were completely divided, as was, without question, her mind.

But how could this be otherwise? Captured at seven, a slave of wealthy, doting whites who instilled in her the "savagery" of the Africa they "rescued" her from . . . one wonders if she was even able to remember her homeland as she had known it, or as it really was.

Yet, because she did try to use her gift for poetry in a world that made her a slave, she was "so thwarted and hindered by . . . contrary instincts, that she . . . lost her health. . . ." In the last years of her brief life, burdened not only with the need to express her gift but also with a penniless, friendless "freedom" and several small children for whom she was forced to do strenuous work to feed, she lost her health, certainly. Suffering from malnutrition and neglect and who knows what mental agonies, Phillis Wheatley died.

So torn by "contrary instincts" was black, kidnapped, enslaved Phillis that her description of "the Goddess"—as she poetically called the Liberty she did not have—is ironically, cruelly humorous. And, in fact, has held Phillis up to ridicule for more than a century. It is usually read prior to hanging Phillis's memory as that of a fool. She wrote:

> The Goddess comes, she moves divinely fair,
> Olive and laurel binds her *golden* hair.
> Wherever shines this native of the skies,
> Unnumber'd charms and recent graces rise. [My italics]

It is obvious that Phillis, the slave, combed the "Goddess's" hair every morning; prior, perhaps, to bringing in the milk, or fixing her mistress's lunch. She took her imagery from the one thing she saw elevated above all others.

With the benefit of hindsight we ask, "How could she?"

But at last, Phillis, we understand. No more snickering when your stiff, struggling, ambivalent lines are forced on us. We know now that you were not an idiot or a traitor; only a sickly little black girl, snatched from your home and country and made a slave; a woman who still struggled to sing the song that was your gift, although in a land of barbarians who praised you for your bewildered tongue. It is not so much what you sang, as that you kept alive, in so many of our ancestors, *the notion of song.*

Black women are called, in the folklore that so aptly identified one's status society, "the *mule* of the world," because we have been handed the burdens that everyone else—*everyone* else—refused to carry. We have also been called "Matriarchs," "Superwomen," and "Mean and Evil Bitches." Not to mention "Castraters" and "Sapphire's Mama." When we have pleaded for understanding, our character has been distorted; when we have asked for simple caring, we have been handed empty inspirational appellations, then stuck in the farthest corner. When we have asked for love, we have been given children. In short, even our plainer gifts, our labors of fidelity and love, have been knocked down our throats. To be an artist and a black woman, even today, lowers our status in many respects, rather than raises it: and yet, artists we will be.

Therefore we must fearlessly pull out of ourselves and look at and identify with our lives the living creativity some of our great-grandmothers were not allowed to know. I stress *some* of them because it is well known that the majority of our great-grandmothers knew, even without "knowing" it, the reality of their spirituality, even if they didn't recognize it beyond what happened in the singing at church—and they never had any intention of giving it up.

How they did it—those millions of black women who were not Phillis Wheatley, or Lucy Terry or Frances Harper or Zora Hurston or Nella Larsen or Bessie Smith; or Elizabeth Catlett, or Katherine Dunham, either—brings me to the title of this essay, "In Search of Our Mothers' Gardens," which is a personal account that is yet shared, in its theme and its meaning, by all of us. I found, while thinking about the far-reaching world of the creative black woman, that often the truest answer to a question that really matters can be found very close.

In the late 1920s my mother ran away from home to marry my father. Marriage, if not running away, was expected of seventeen-year-old girls.

By the time she was twenty, she had two children and was pregnant with a third. Five children later, I was born. And this is how I came to know my mother: she seemed a large, soft, loving-eyed woman who was rarely impatient in our home. Her quick, violent temper was on view only a few times a year, when she battled with the white landlord who had the misfortune to suggest to her that her children did not need to go to school.

She made all the clothes we wore, even my brothers' overalls. She made all the towels and sheets we used. She spent the summers canning vegetables and fruits. She spent the winter evenings making quilts enough to cover all our beds.

During the "working" day, she labored beside—not behind—my father in the fields. Her day began before sunup, and did not end until late at night. There was never a moment for her to sit down, undisturbed, to unravel her own private thoughts; never a time free from interruption—by work or the noisy inquiries of her many children. And yet, it is to my mother—and all our mothers who were not famous—that I went in search of the secret of what has fed that muzzled and often mutilated, but vibrant, creative spirit that the black woman has inherited, and that pops out in wild and unlikely places to this day.

But when, you will ask, did my overworked mother have time to know or care about feeding the creative spirit?

The answer is so simple that many of us have spent years discovering it. We have constantly looked high, when we should have looked high—and low.

For example: in the Smithsonian Insitution in Washington, D.C., there hangs a quilt unlike any other in the world. In fanciful, inspired, and yet simple and identifiable figures, it portrays the story of the Crucifixion. It is considered rare, beyond price. Though it follows no known pattern of quilt-making, and though it is made of bits and pieces of worthless rags, it is obviously the work of a person of powerful imagination and deep spiritual feeling. Below this quilt I saw a note that says it was made by "an anonymous Black woman in Alabama, a hundred years ago."

If we could locate this "anonymous" black woman from Alabama, she would turn out to be one of our grandmothers—an artist who left her mark in the only materials she could afford, and in the only medium her position in society allowed her to use.

As Virginia Woolf wrote further, in *A Room of One's Own:*

> Yet genius of a sort must have existed among women as it must have existed among the working class.[Change this to "slaves" and "the wives and daughters of sharecroppers."] Now and again an Emily Brontë or a Robert Burns [change this to "a Zora Hurston or a Richard Wright"] blazes out and proves its presence. But certainly it never got itself on to paper. When, however, one reads of a witch being ducked, of

> a woman possessed by devils [or "Sainthood"], of a wise woman selling herbs [our root workers], or even a very remarkable man who had a mother, then I think we are on the track of a lost novelist, a suppressed poet, or some mute and inglorious Jane Austen. . . . Indeed, I would venture to guess that Anon, who wrote so many poems without signing them, was often a woman. . . .

And so our mothers and grandmothers have, more often than not anonymously, handed on the creative spark, the seed of the flower they themselves never hoped to see: or like a sealed letter they could not plainly read.

And so it is, certainly, with my own mother. Unlike "Ma" Rainey's songs, which retained their creator's name even while blasting forth from Bessie Smith's mouth, no song or poem will bear my mother's name. Yet so many of the stories that I write, that we all write, are my mother's stories. Only recently did I fully realize this: that through years of listening to my mother's stories of her life, I have absorbed not only the stories themselves, but something of the manner in which she spoke, something of the urgency that involves the knowledge that her stories—like her life—must be recorded. It is probably for this reason that so much of what I have written is about characters whose counterparts in real life are so much older than I am.

But the telling of these stories, which came from my mother's lips as naturally as breathing, was not the only way my mother showed herself as an artist. For stories, too, were subject to being distracted, to dying without conclusion. Dinners must be started, and cotton must be gathered before the big rains. The artist that was and is my mother showed itself to me only after many years. This is what I finally noticed:

Like Mem, a character in *The Third Life of Grange Copeland,* my mother adorned with flowers whatever shabby house we were forced to live in. And not just your typical straggly country stand of zinnias, either. She planted ambitious gardens—and still does—with over fifty different varieties of plants that bloom profusely from early March until late November. Before she left home for the fields, she watered her flowers, chopped up the grass, and laid out new beds. When she returned from the fields she might divide clumps of bulbs, dig a cold pit, uproot and replant roses, or prune branches from her taller bushes or trees—until night came and it was too dark to see.

Whatever she planted grew as if by magic, and her fame as a grower of flowers spread over three counties. Because of her creativity with her flowers, even my memories of poverty are seen through a screen of blooms—sunflowers, petunias, roses, dahlias, forsythia, spirea, delphiniums, verbena . . . and on and on.

And I remember people coming to my mother's yard to be given cuttings from her flowers; I hear again the praise showered on her because whatever rocky soil she landed on, she turned into a garden. A garden so brilliant with colors, so original in its design, so magnificent with life and creativity, that to this day people drive by our house in Georgia—perfect strangers and imperfect strangers—and ask to stand or walk among my mother's art.

I notice that it is only when my mother is working in her flowers that she is radiant, almost to the point of being invisible—except as Creator: hand and eye. She is involved in work her soul must have. Ordering the universe in the image of her personal conception of Beauty.

Her face, as she prepares the Art that is her gift, is a legacy of respect she leaves to me, for all that illuminates and cherishes life. She has handed down respect for the possibilities—and the will to grasp them.

For her, so hindered and intruded upon in so many ways, being an artist has still been a daily part of her life. This ability to hold on, even in very simple ways, is work black women have done for a very long time.

This poem is not enough, but it is something, for the woman who literally covered the holes in our walls with sunflowers:

They were women then
My mama's generation
Husky of voice—Stout of
Step
With fists as well as
Hands
How they battered down
Doors
And ironed
Starched white
Shirts
How they led
Armies
Headragged Generals
Across mined
Fields
Booby-trapped
Kitchens
To discover books
Desks
A place for us
How they knew what we
Must know
Without knowing a page
Of it
Themselves

Guided by my heritage of a love of beauty and a respect for strength—in search of my mother's garden, I found my own.

And perhaps in Africa over two hundred years ago, there was just such a mother; perhaps she painted vivid and daring decorations in oranges and yellows and greens on the walls of her hut; perhaps she sang—in a voice like Roberta Flack's—*sweetly* over the compounds of her village; perhaps she wove the most stunning mats or told the most ingenious stories of all the village storytellers. Perhaps she was herself a poet—though only her daughter's name is signed to the poems that we know.

Perhaps Phillis Wheatley's mother was also an artist.

Perhaps in more than Phillis Wheatley's biological life is her mother's signature made clear.

. . . .

QUESTIONS FOR A SECOND READING

1. In the essay, Walker develops the interesting notion of "contrary instincts," particularly when she discusses Phillis Wheatley. The problem for Walker (and others) is that Wheatley would idolize a fair-haired white woman as a goddess of liberty rather than turning to herself as a model, or to the black women who struggled mightily for their identities and liberty. Walker asks, "How could she?" As you reread the essay, pay particular attention to the sections where Walker discusses "contrary instincts." How would you define this term? What kind of answers does this essay make possible to the question "How could she?"
2. As you reread the essay, note particularly the sections where Walker talks about herself. How does she feel about her mother, the history of black women in America, and "contrary instincts"? How would you describe Walker's feelings and attitudes toward herself, the past, and the pressures of living in a predominantly white culture? In considering these questions, don't settle for big words like "honest," "sensitive," or "compassionate." They are accurate, to be sure, but they are imprecise and don't do justice to Walker's seriousness and individuality.

ASSIGNMENTS FOR WRITING

1. What do you consider the most significant passage in this essay? Why do you consider it important? Write an essay where you identify and explain what you see as the most significant passage in this essay. What can you say about it to demonstrate its importance?

2. Walker's essay poses a number of questions about the history of black women in America, including their "creative spirit" in the face of oppressive working and living conditions. At one point, Walker describes her mother's life in the late 1920s after she ran away from home to marry her father. Her mother's difficult life was filled with unrelenting work, yet she managed to keep a "vibrant, creative spirit" alive. Walker asks, "But when, you will ask, did my overworked mother have time to know or care about feeding the creative spirit?" She goes on to say that "the answer is so simple that many of us have spent years discovering it." Write an essay explaining what you think this "simple" answer might be and why it took Alice Walker—or why it would take anyone—so long to find it.

MAKING CONNECTIONS

1. Throughout "Our Time" (p. 519) by John Wideman, Robby talks about his contrary instincts, his ambivalent feelings towards making it in the white world. How can you consider Robby in light of Walker's observations about contrary instincts and the way black women lived in the past? Write an essay in which you explore how John Wideman's understanding of his brother Robby's contrary instincts are different from Alice Walker's understanding of her mother's contrary instincts.
2. Gloria Steinem's mother Ruth (in "Ruth's Song," p. 472) finds self-expression, at least for a while, in her job; but that ends, and she's left alone by a husband whose work involves a great deal of traveling. Even though she does travel with him for a time, her life changes to the point where Steinem calls it a "transformation"—a transformation, Steinem concludes, more the result of forces that affect all women than of personal or accidental forces. On the basis of Walker's and Steinem's mothers' experiences, what can you conclude about the forces that affected their lives? Write an essay in which you discuss these forces. Are they the same for both women? If so, in what ways? If not, how do they differ? Finally, how were the lessons Walker and Steinem learned from their mothers' examples similar? different?

JOHN EDGAR WIDEMAN

JOHN EDGAR WIDEMAN was born in 1941 in Washington, D.C., but spent most of his youth in Homewood, a neighborhood in Pittsburgh. He earned a B.A. from the University of Pennsylvania and is now a professor of English at the University of Wyoming. In addition to the nonfiction work Brothers and Keepers, *from which this selection is drawn, Wideman has published several critically acclaimed novels, including* Sent For You Yesterday, *which won the 1984 PEN/Faulkner Award, and* The Lynchers.

"Stories are letters," Wideman once wrote, "Letters sent to anybody or everybody. But the best kind are meant to be read by a specific somebody. When you read that kind you know you are eavesdropping. You know a real person somewhere will read the same words you are reading and the story is that person's business and you are a ghost listening in." Brothers and Keepers *is a family story, about Wideman and his brother, Robby. John went to Oxford as a Rhodes scholar and Robby went to prison for his role in a robbery and a murder. The section that follows tells part of Robby's story and asks whose business it is to speak of such things and whose business it is to listen. In this account, you will hear the voices of Robby, John, and people from the neighorhood, but also the voice of the writer,*

speaking about the difficulty of writing and the dangers of explaining away the complexity of Robby's life.

In an article called "The Language of Home," Wideman said, "One of the earliest lessons I learned as a child was that if you looked away from something, it might not be there when you looked back. I feared loss, feared turning to speak to someone and finding no one there. . . . Writing forces me to risk ignoring the logic of this lesson. . . . I examine minutely the place I come from, repeat its stories, sing its songs, preserve its language and values, because they make me what I am and because if I don't, who will?"

Our Time

You remember what we were saying about young black men in the street-world life. And trying to understand why the "square world" becomes completely unattractive to them. It has to do with the fact that their world is the GHETTO and in that world all the glamour, all the praise and attention is given to the slick guy, the gangster especially, the ones that get over in the "life." And it's because we can't help but feel some satisfaction seeing a brother, a black man, get over on these people, on their system without playing by their rules. No matter how much we have incorporated these rules as our own, we know that they were forced on us by people who did not have our best interests at heart. So this hip guy, this gangster or player or whatever label you give these brothers that we like to shun because of the poison that they spread, we, black people, still look at them with some sense of pride and admiration, our children openly, us adults somewhere deep inside. We know they represent rebellion—what little is left in us. Well, having lived in the "life," it becomes very hard—almost impossible—to find any contentment in joining the status quo. Too hard to go back to being nobody in a world that hates you. Even if I had struck it rich in the life, I would have managed to throw it down the fast lane. Or have lost it on a revolutionary whim. Hopefully the latter.

I have always burned up in my fervent passions of desire and want. My senses at times tingle and itch with my romantic, idealistic outlook on life, which has always made me keep my distance for reality, reality that was a constant insult to my world, to my dream of happiness and peace, to my people-for-people kind of world, my easy-cars-for-a-nickel-or-a-dime sorta world. And these driving passions, this sensitivity to the love and good in people, also turned on me because I used it to play on people and their feelings. These aspirations of love and desire turned on me when I wasn't able to live up to this sweet-self morality, so I began to self-destruct, burning up in my sensitivity, losing direction, because nowhere could I find this world of truth and love and harmony.

In the real world, the world left for me, it was unacceptable to be "good," it was square to be smart in school, it was jive to show respect to people outside the street world, it was cool to be cold to your woman and the people that loved you. The things we liked we called "bad." "Man, that was a bad girl." The world of the angry black kid growing up in the sixties was a world in which to be in was to be out—out of touch with the square world and all of its rules on what's right and wrong. The thing was to make your own rules, do your own thing, but make sure it's contrary to what society says or is.

I SHALL ALWAYS PRAY

Garth looked bad. Real bad. Ichabod Crane anyway, but now he was a skeleton. Lying there in the bed with his bones poking through his skin, it made you want to cry. Garth's barely able to talk, his smooth, medium-brown skin yellow as pee. Ichabod legs and long hands and long feet, Garth could make you laugh just walking down the street. On the set you'd see him coming a far way off. Three-quarters leg so you knew it had to be Garth the way he was split up higher in the crotch than anybody else. Wilt the Stilt with a lean bird body perched on top his high waist. Size-fifteen shoes. Hands could palm a basketball easy as holding a pool cue. Fingers long enough to wrap round a basketball, but Garth couldn't play a lick. Never could get all that lankiness together on the court. You'd look at him sometimes as he was trucking down Homewood Avenue and think that nigger ain't walking, he's trying to remember how to walk. Awkward as a pigeon on roller skates. Knobby joints out of whack, arms and legs flailing, going their separate ways, his body jerking to keep them from going too far. Moving down the street like that wouldn't work, didn't make sense if you stood back and watched, if you pretended you hadn't seen Garth get where he was going a million times before. Nothing funny now, though. White hospital sheets pulled to his chest. Garth's head always looked small as a tennis ball way up there on his shoulders. Now its a yellow, shrunken skull.

Ever since Robby had entered the ward, he'd wanted to reach over and hide his friend's arm under the covers. For two weeks Gar had been wasting away in the bed. Bad enough knowing Gar was dying. Didn't need that pitiful stick arm reminding him how close to nothing his main man had fallen. So fast. It could happen so fast. If Robby tried to raise that arm it would come off in his hand. As gentle as he could would not be gentle enough. The arm would disintegrate, like a long ash off the end of a cigarette.

Time to leave. No sense in sitting any longer. Garth not talking, no way of telling whether he was listening either. And Robby has nothing more to say. Choked up the way he gets inside hospitals. Hospital smell and quiet, the bare halls and bare floors, the echoes, something about all that he can't name, wouldn't try to name, rises in him and chills him. Like his teeth are chattering the whole time he's inside a hospital. Like his entire body is trembling uncontrollably, only nobody can see it or hear it but him. Shaking because he can't breathe the stuffy air. Hot and cold at the same time. He's been aching to leave since he entered the ward. Aching to get up and bust through the big glass front doors. Aching to pounce on that spidery arm flung back behind Gar's head. The arm too wasted to belong to his friend. He wants to grab it and hurl it away.

Robby pulls on tight white gloves the undertaker had dealt out to him and the rest of the pallbearers. His brown skin shows through the thin material, turns the white dingy. He's remembering the last time in Garth's ward. The hospital stink. Hot, chilly air. A bare arm protruding from the sleeve of the hospital gown, more dried-up toothpick than arm, a withered twig, with Garth's fingers like a bunch of skinny brown bananas drooping from the knobby tip.

Robby had studied the metal guts of the hospital bed,the black scuff marks swirling around the chair's legs. When he'd finally risen to go, his chair scraping against the vinyl floor broke a long silence. The noise must have roused Garth's attention. He'd spoken again.

You're good, man. Don't ever forget, Rob. You're the best.

Garth's first words since the little banter back and forth when Robby had entered the ward and dragged a chair to the side of Gar's bed. A whisper scarcely audible now that Robby was standing. Garth had tried to grin. The best he could manage was a pained adjustment of the bones of his face, no more than a shadow scudding across the yellow skull, but Robby had seen the famous smile. He hesitated, stopped rushing toward the door long enough to smile back. Because that was Gar. That was the way Gar was. He always had a smile and a good word for his cut buddies. Garth's grin was money in the bank. You could count on it like you could count on a good word from him. Something in his face would tell you you were alright, better than alright, that he believed in you, that you were, as he'd just whispered, "the best." you could depend on Garth to say something to make you feel good, even though you knew he was lying. With that grin greasing the lie you had to believe it, even though you knew better. Garth was the gang's dreamer. When he talked, you could see his dreams. That's why Robby had believed it, seen the grin, the bright shadow lighting Garth's face an instant. Out of nothing, out of pain, fear, the certainty of death gripping them both, Garth's voice had manufactured the grin.

Now they had to bury Garth. A few days after the visit to the hospital the phone rang and it was Garth's mother with the news of her son's death. Not really news. Robby had known it was just a matter of time. Of waiting for the moment when somebody else's voice would pronounce the words he'd said to himself a hundred times. *He's gone. Gar's dead.* Long gone before the telephone rang. Gar was gone when they stuck him up in the hospital bed. By the time they'd figured out what ailed him and admitted him to the hospital, it was too late. The disease had turned him to a skeleton. Nothing left of Garth to treat. They hid his messy death under white sheets, perfumed it with disinfectant, pumped him full of drugs so he wouldn't disturb his neighbors.

The others had squeezed into their pallbearers' gloves. Cheap white cotton gloves so you could use them once and throw them away like the rubber ones doctors wear when they stick their fingers up your ass. Michael, Cecil, and Sowell were pallbearers, too. With Robby and two men from Garth's family they would carry the coffin from Gaines Funeral Parlor to the hearse. Garth had been the dreamer for the gang. Robby counted four black fingers in the white glove. Garth was the thumb. The hand would be clumsy, wouldn't work right without him. Garth was different. But everybody else was different, too. Mike, the ice man, supercool. Cecil indifferent, ready to do most anything or nothing and couldn't care less which it was. Sowell wasn't really part of the gang; he didn't hang with them, didn't like to take the risks that were part of the "life." Sowell kept a good job. The "life" for him was just a way to make quick money. He didn't shoot up; he thought of himself as a businessman, an investor not a partner in their schemes. They knew Sowell mostly through Garth. Perhaps things would change now. The four survivors closer after they shared the burden of Gar's coffin, after they hoisted it and slid it on steel rollers into the back of Gaines's Cadillac hearse.

Robby was grateful for the gloves. He'd never been able to touch anything dead. He'd taken a beating once from his father rather than touch the bloody mousetrap his mother had nudged to the back door with her toe and ordered him to empty. The brass handle of the coffin felt damp through the glove. He gripped tighter to stop the flow of blood or sweat, whatever it was leaking from him or seeping from the metal. Garth had melted down to nothing by the end so it couldn't be him nearly yanking off Robby's shoulder when the boys shifted and its weight shot forward. Felt like the coffin full of bricks. Robby stared across at Mike but Mike was a soldier, eyes front, riveted to the yawning rear door of the hearse. Mike's eyes wouldn't admit it, but they'd almost lost the coffin. They were rookie pallbearers and maneuvering down the carpeted front steps of Gaines Funeral Parlor they'd almost let Garth fly out their hands. They needed somebody who knew what he was doing. An old, steady head to show them the way. They needed Garth. But Garth was long gone. Ashes inside the steel box.

They began drinking later that afternoon in Garth's people's house. Women and food in one room, men hitting the whiskey hard in another.

It was a typical project apartment. The kind everybody had stayed in or visited one time or another. Small, shabby, featureless. Not a place to live. No matter what you did to it, how clean you kept it or what kind of furniture you loaded it with, the walls and ceilings were not meant to be home for anybody. A place you passed through. Not yours, because the people who'd been there before you left their indelible marks everywhere and you couldn't help adding your bruises and knots for the next tenants. You could rent a kitchen and bedroom and a bathroom and a living room, the project flats were laid out so you had a room for each of the things people did in houses. Problem was, every corner was cut. Living cramped is one thing and people can get cozy in the closest quarters. It's another thing to live in a place designed to be just a little less than adequate. No slack, no space to personalize, to stamp the flat with what's peculiar to your style. Like a man sitting on a toilet seat that's too small and the toilet too close to the bathtub so his knees shove against the enamel edge. He can move his bowels that way and plenty of people in the world have a lot less but he'll never enjoy sitting there, never feel the deep down comfort of belonging where he must squat.

Anyway, the whiskey started flowing in that little project apartment. Robby listened, for Garth's sake, as long as he could to old people reminiscing about funerals they'd attended, about all the friends and relatives they'd escorted to the edge of Jordan, old folks sipping good whiskey and moaning and groaning till it seemed a sin to be left behind on this side of the river after so many saints had crossed over. He listened to people express their grief, tell sad, familiar stories. As he got high he listened less closely to the words. Faces and gestures revealed more than enough. When he split with Mike and Cecil and their ladies, Sowell tagged along. By then the tacky, low-ceilinged rooms of the flat were packed. Loud talk, laughter, storytellers competing for audiences. Robby half expected the door he pushed shut behind himself to pop open again, waited for bottled-up noise to explode into the funky hallway.

Nobody thinking about cemeteries now. Nobody else needs to be buried today, so it was time to get it on. Some people had been getting close to rowdy. Some people had been getting mad. Mad at one of the guests in the apartment, mad at doctors and hospitals and whites in general who had the whole world in their hands but didn't have the slightest idea what to do with it. A short, dark man, bubble-eyed, immaculately dressed in a three-piece, wool, herringbone suit, had railed about the callousness, the ignorance of white witch doctors who, by misdiagnosing Garth's illness, had sealed his doom. His harangue had drawn a crowd. He wasn't just talking, he was testifying, and a hush had fallen over half the room as he dissected the dirty tricks of white folks. If somebody ran to the hospital and snatched a white-coated doctor and threw him into the circle surrounding the little fish-eyed man, the mourners would tear the pale-faced devil apart. Robby wished he could feed them one. Remembered Garth weak and helpless in the bed and the doctors and nurses flitting around in the halls, jiving the other patients, ignoring Gar like he wasn't there. Garth was dead because he had believed them. Dead because he had nowhere else to turn when the pain in his gut and the headaches grew worse and worse. Not that he trusted the doctors or believed they gave a flying fuck about him. He'd just run out of choices and had to put himself in their hands. They told him jaundice was his problem, and while his liver rotted away and pain cooked him dizzy Garth assured anyone who asked that it was just a matter of giving the medicine time to work. To kill the pain he blew weed as long as he had strength to hold a joint between his lips. Take a whole bunch of smoke to cool me out these days. Puffing like a chimney till he lost it and fell back and Robby scrambling to grab the joint before Garth torched hisself.

When you thought about it, Garth's dying made no sense. And the more you thought the more you dug that nothing else did neither. The world's a stone bitch. Nothing true if that's not true. The man had you coming and going. He owned everything worth owning and all you'd ever get was what he didn't want anymore, what he'd chewed and spit out and left in the gutter for niggers to fight over. Garth had pointed to the street and said, If we ever make it, it got to come from there, from the curb. We got to melt that rock till we get us some money. He grinned then, Ain't no big thing. We'll make it, brother man. We got what it takes. It's our time.

Something had crawled in Garth's belly. The man said it wasn't nothing. Sold him some aspirins and said he'd be alright in no time. The man killed Garth. Couldn't kill him no deader with a .357 magnum slug, but ain't no crime been committed. Just one those things. You know, everybody makes mistakes. And a dead nigger ain't really such a big mistake when you think about it. Matter of fact you mize well forget the whole thing. Nigger wasn't going nowhere, nohow. I mean he wasn't no brain surgeon or astronaut, no movie star or big-time athlete. Probably a dope fiend or gangster. Wind up killing some innocent person or wasting another nigger. Shucks. That doctor ought to get a medal.

Hey, man. Robby caught Mike's eye. Then Cecil and Sowell turned to him. They knew he was speaking to everybody. Late now. Ten, eleven, because it had been dark outside for hours. Quiet now. Too quite in his pad. And too much smoke and drink since the funeral. From a bare bulb in the kitchen ceiling light seeped down the hallway and hovered dimly in the doorway of the room where they sat. Robby wondered if the others felt as bad as he did. If the cemetery clothes itched their skin. If they could smell grave dust on their shoes. He hoped they'd finish this last jug of wine and let the day be over. He needed sleep, downtime to get the terrible weight of Garth's death off his mind. He'd been grateful for the darkness. For the company of his cut buddies after the funeral. For the Sun Ra tape until it ended and plunged them into a deeper silence than any he'd ever known. Garth was gone. In a few days people would stop talking about him. He was in the ground. Stone-cold dead. Robby had held a chunk of crumbly ground in his white-gloved fingers and mashed it and dropped the dust into the hole. Now the ground had closed over Garth and what did it mean? Here one day and gone the next and that was that. They'd bury somebody else out of Gaines tomorrow. People would dress up and cry and get drunk and tell lies and next day it'd be somebody else's turn to die. Which one of the shadows in this black room would go first? What did it matter? Who cared? Who would remember their names; they were ghosts already. Dead as Garth already. Only difference was, Garth didn't have it to worry about no more. Garth didn't have to pretend he was going anywhere cause he was there. He'd made it to the place they all were headed fast as their legs could carry them. Every step was a step closer to the stone-cold ground, the pitch-black hole where they'd dropped Garth's body.

Hey, youall. We got to drink to Garth one last time.

They clinked glasses in the darkness. Robby searched for something to say. The right words wouldn't come. He knew there was something proper and precise that needed to be said. Because the exact words eluded him, because only the right words would do, he swallowed his gulp of heavy, sweet wine in silence.

He knew he'd let Garth down. If it had been one of the others dead, Michael or Cecil or Sowell or him, Garth wouldn't let it slide by like this, wouldn't let it end like so many other nights had ended, the fellows nodding off one by one, stupefied by smoke and drink, each one beginning to shop around in his mind, trying to figure whether or not he should turn in or if there was a lady somewhere who'd welcome him in her bed. No. Garth would have figured a way to make it special. They wouldn't be hiding in the bushes. They'd be knights in shining armor around a big table. They'd raise their giant, silver cups to honor the fallen comrade. Like in the olden days. Clean, brave dudes with gold rings and gold chains. They'd draw their blades. Razor-edged swords that gleam in the light with jewels sparkling in the handles. They'd make a roof over the table when they stood and raised their swords and the points touched in the sky. A silver dagger on a satin pillow in the middle of the table. Everybody roll up their sleeves and prick a vein and go round, each one touching everybody else so the blood runs together and we're brothers forever, brothers as long as blood flows in anybody's arm. We'd ride off and do unbelievable shit. The dead one always with us cause we'd do it all for him. Swear we'd never let him down.

It's our time now. We can't let Garth down. Let's drink this last one for him and promise him we'll do what he said we could. We'll be the best. We'll make it the top for him. We'll do it for Garth.

Glasses rattled together again. Robby empties his and thinks about smashing it against a wall. He's seen it done that way in movies but it was late at night and these crazy niggers might not know when to stop throwing things. A battlefield of broken glass for him to creep through when he gets out of bed in the morning. He doesn't toss the empty glass. Can't see a solid place anyway where it would strike clean and shatter to a million points of light.

My brother has said something about a guy named Garth during one of my visits to the prison. Just a name mentioned in passing. *Garth* or *Gar*. I'd asked Robby to spell it for me. Garth had been a friend of Robby's, about Robby's age, who died one summer of a mysterious disease. Later when Robby chose to begin the story of the robbery and killing by saying, "It all started with Gar dying," I remembered that first casual mention and remembered a conversation with my mother. My mom and I were in the kitchen of the house on Tokay Street. My recollection of details was vague at first but something about the conversation had made a lasting impression because, six years later, hearing Robby say the name *Garth* brought back my mother's words.

My mother worried about Robby all the time. Whenever I visited home, sooner or later I'd find myself alone with Mom and she'd pour out her fears about Robby's *wildness,* the deep trouble he was bound for, the web of entanglements and intrigues and bad company he was weaving around himself with a maddening disregard for the inevitable consequences.

I don't know. I just don't know how to reach him. He won't listen. He's doing wrong and he knows it but nothing I say makes any difference. He's not like the rest of youall. You'd misbehave but I could talk to you or smack you if I had to and you'd straighten up. With Robby it's like talking to a wall.

I'd listen and get angry at my brother because I registered not so much the danger he was bringing on himself, but the effect of his escapades on the woman who'd brought us both into the world. After all, Robby was no baby. If he wanted to mess up, nobody could stop him. Also Robby was my brother, meaning that his wildness was just a stage, a chaotic phase of his life that would only last till he got his head together and decided to start doing right. Doing as the rest of us did. He was my brother. He couldn't fall too far. His brushes with the law (I'd had some, too), the time he'd spent in jail, were serious but temporary setbacks. I viewed his troubles, when I thought about them at all, as a form of protracted juvenile delinquency, and fully expected Robby would learn his lesson sooner or later and return to the fold, the prodigal son, chastened, perhaps a better person for the experience. In the meantime the most serious consequence of his wildness was Mom's devastating unhappiness. She couldn't sustain the detachment, the laissez-faire optimism I had talked myself into. Because I was two thousand miles away, in Wyoming, I didn't have to deal with the day-to-day evidence of Robby's trouble. The syringe Mom found under his bed. The twenty-dollar bill missing from her purse. The times he'd cruise in higher than a kite, his pupils reduced to pinpricks, with his crew and they'd raid the refrigerator and make a loud, sloppy feast, all of them feeling so good they couldn't imagine anybody not up there on cloud nine with them enjoying the time of their lives. Cruising in, then disappearing just as abruptly, leaving their dishes and pans and mess behind. Robby covering Mom with kisses and smiles and drowning her in babytalk hootchey-coo as he staggers through the front door. Her alone in the ravaged, silent kitchen, listening as doors slam and a car squeals off on the cobblestones of Tokay, wondering where they're headed next, wishing, praying Robby will return and eat and eat and eat till he falls asleep at the table so she can carry him upstairs and tuck him in and kiss his forehead and shut the door gently on his sleep.

I wasn't around for all that. Didn't want to know how bad things were for him. Worrying about my mother was tough enough. I could identify with her grief, I could blame my brother. An awful situation, but simple too. My role, my responsibilities and loyalties were clear. The *wildness* was to blame, and it was a passing thing, so I just had to help my mother survive the worst of it, then everything would be alright. I'd steel myself for the moments alone with her when she'd tell me the worst. In the kitchen, usually, over a cup of coffee with the radio playing. When my mother was alone in the house on Tokay, either the TV or a radio or both were always on. Atop the kitchen table a small clock radio turned to WAMO, one of Pittsburgh's soul stations, would background with scratchy gospel music whatever we said in the morning in the kitchen. On a morning like that in 1975, while I drank a cup of coffee and part of me, still half-sleep, hidden, swayed to the soft beat of gospel, my mother had explained how upset Robby was over the death of his friend, Garth.

It was a terrible thing. I've known Garth's mother for years. He was a good boy. No saint for sure, but deep down a good boy. Like your brother. Not a mean bone in his body. Out there in the street doing wrong, but that's where most of them are. What else can they do, John? Sometimes I can't blame them. No jobs, no money in their pockets. How they supposed to feel like men? Garth did better than most. Whatever else he was into, he kept that little job over at Westinghouse and helped out his mother. A big, playful kid. Always smiling. I think that's why him and Robby were so tight. Neither one had good sense. Giggled and acted like fools. Garth no wider than my finger. Straight up and down. A stringbean if I ever saw one. When Robby lived here in the house with me, Garth was always around. I know how bad Robby feels. He hasn't said a word but I know. When Robby's quiet, you know something's wrong. Soon as his eyes pop open in the morning he's looking for the party. First thing in the morning he's chipper and chattering. Looking for the party. That's your brother. He had a match in Garth.

Shame the way they did that boy. He'd been down to the clinic two or three times but they sent him home. Said he had an infection and it would take care of itself. Something like that anyway. You know how they are down there. Have to be spitting blood to get attention. Then all they give you is a Band-Aid. He went back two times, but they kept telling him the same dumb thing. Anybody who knew Garth could see something awful was wrong. Circles under his eyes. Sallow look to his skin. Losing weight. And the poor thing didn't have any weight to lose. Last time I saw him I was shocked. Just about shocked out my shoes. Wasn't Garth standing in front of me. Not the boy I knew.

Well, to make a long story short, they finally took him in the hospital but it was too late. They let him walk the streets till he was dead. It was wrong. Worse than wrong how they did him, but that's how those dogs do us every day God sends here. Garth's gone, so nothing nobody can say will do any good. I feel so sorry for his mother. She lived for that boy. I called her and tried to talk but what can you say? I prayed for her and prayed for Garth and prayed for Robby. A thing like that tears people up. It's worse if you keep it inside. And that's your brother's way. He'll let it eat him up and then go out and do something crazy.

Until she told me Garth's story I guess I hadn't realized how much my mother had begun to change. She had always seemed to me to exemplify the tolerance, the patience, the long view epitomized in her father. John French's favorite saying was, Give 'em the benefit of the doubt. She could get as ruffled, as evil as the rest of us, cry and scream or tear around the house fit to be tied. She had her grudges and quarrels. Mom could let it all hang out, yet most of the time she radiated a deep calm. She reacted strongly to things but at the same time held judgement in abeyance. Events, personalities always deserved a second, slower appraisal, an evaluation outside the sphere of everyday hassles and vexations. You gave people the benefit of the doubt. You attempted to remove your ego, acknowledge the limitations of your individual view of things. You consulted as far as you were equipped by temperament and intelligence a broader, more abiding set of relationships and connections.

You tried on the other person's point of view. You sought the other, better person in yourself who might talk you into relinquishing for a moment your selfish interest in whatever was at issue. You stopped and considered the long view, possibilities other than the one that momentarily was leading you by the nose. You gave yourself and other people the benefit of the doubt.

My mother had that capacity. I'd admired, envied, and benefited infinitely from its presence. As she related the story of Garth's death and my brother's anger and remorse, her tone was uncompromisingly bitter. No slack, no margin of doubt was being granted to the forces that destroyed Garth and still pursued her son. She had exhausted her reserves of understanding and compassion. The long view supplied the same ugly picture as the short. She had an enemy now. It was that revealed truth that had given the conversation its edge, its impact. *They* had killed Garth, and his dying had killed part of her son; so the battle lines were drawn. Irreconcilably. Absolutely. The backside of John French's motto had come into play. Giving someone the benefit of the doubt was also giving him enough rope to hang himself. If a person takes advantage of the benefit of the doubt and keeps on taking and taking, one day the rope plays out. The piper must be paid. If you've been the one giving, it becomes incumbent on you to grip your end tight and take away. You turn the other cheek, but slowly, cautiously, and keep your fist balled up at your side. If your antagonist decides to smack rather than kiss you or leave you alone, you make sure you get in the first blow. And make sure it's hard enough to knock him down.

Before she told Garth's story, my mother had already changed, but it took years for me to realize how profoundly she hated what had been done to Garth and then Robby. The gentleness of my grandfather, like his fair skin and good French hair, had been passed down to my mother. Gentleness styled the way she thought, spoke, and moved in the world. Her easy disposition and sociability masked the intensity of her feelings. Her attitude to authority of any kind, doctors, clerks, police, bill collectors, newscasters, whites in general partook of her constitutional gentleness. She wasn't docile or cowed. The power other people possessed or believed they possessed didn't frighten her; she accommodated herself, offered something they could accept as deference but that was in fact the same resigned, alert attention she paid to roaches or weather or poverty, any of the givens outside herself that she couldn't do much about. She never engaged in public tests of will, never pushed herself or her point of view on people she didn't know. Social awkwardness embarrassed her. Like most Americans she didn't like paying taxes, was suspicious of politicians, resented the disparity between big and little people in our society and the double standard that allowed big shots to get away with murder. She paid particular attention to news stories that reinforced her basic political assumption that power corrupts. On the other hand she knew the world was a vale of tears and one's strength, granted by God to deal with life's inevitable calamities, should not be squandered on small stuff.

In spite of all her temperamental and philosophic resistance to extremes, my mother would be radicalized. What the demonstrations, protest marches, and slogans of the sixties had not effected would be accomplished by Garth's death and my brother's troubles. She would become an aggressive, acid critic of the status quo in all its forms: from the President ("If it wasn't for that rat I'd have a storm door to go with the storm windows but he cut the program") on down to bank tellers ("I go there every Friday and I'm one of the few black faces she sees all day and she knows me as well as she knows that wart on her cheek but she'll still make me show my license before she'll cash my check"). A son she loved would be pursued, captured, tried, and imprisoned by the forces of law and order. Throughout the ordeal her love for him wouldn't change, couldn't change. His crime tested her love and also tested the nature, the intent of the forces arrayed against her son. She had to make a choice. On one side were the stark facts of his crime: robbery, murder, flight; her son an outlaw, a fugitive; then a prisoner. On the other side the guardians of society, the laws, courts, police, judges, and keepers who were responsible for punishing her son's transgression.

She didn't invent the two sides and initially didn't believe there couldn't be a middle ground. She extended the benefit of the doubt. Tried to situate herself somewhere in between, acknowledging the evil of her son's crime while simultaneously holding on to the fact that he existed as a human being before, after, and during the crime he'd committed. He'd done wrong but he was still Robby and she'd always be his mother. Strangely, on the dark side, the side of the crime and its terrible consequences, she would find room to exercise her love. As negative as the elements were, a life taken, the grief of the survivors, suffering, waste, guilt, remorse, the scale was human; she could apply her sense of right and wrong. Her life to that point had equipped her with values, with tools for sorting out and coping with disaster. So she would choose to make her fight there, on treacherous yet familiar ground—familiar since her son was there—and she could place herself, a woman, a mother, a grieving, bereaved human being, there beside him.

Nothing like that was possible on the other side. The legitimacy of the other side was grounded not in her experience of life, but in a set of rules seemingly framed to sidestep, ignore, or replace her sense of reality. Accepting the version of reality encoded in *their* rules would be like stepping into a cage and locking herself in. Definitions of her son, herself, of need and frailty and mercy, of blackness and redemption and justice had all been neatly formulated. No need here for her questions, her uncertainty, her fear, her love. Everything was clean and clear. No room for her sense that things like good and evil, right and wrong bleed into each other and create a dreadful margin of ambiguity no one could name but could only enter, enter at the risk of everything because everything is at stake and no one on earth knows what it means to enter or what will happen if and when the testing of the margin is over.

She could love her son, accept his guilt, accept the necessity of punishment, suffer with him, grow with him past the stage of blaming everyone but himself for his troubles, grieve with him when true penitence began to exact its toll. Though she might wish penance and absolution could be achieved in private, without the intervention of a prison sentence, she understood dues must be paid. He was her son but he was also a man who had committed a robbery in the course of which another woman's son had been killed. What would appall her and what finally turned her against the forces of law and order was the incapacity of the legal system to grant her son's humanity. "Fair" was the word she used—a John French word. She expected them to treat Robby fair. Fairness was what made her willing to give him up to punishment even though her love screamed no and her hands clung to his shoulders. Fairness was what she expected from the other side in their dealings with her and her son.

She could see their side, but they steadfastly refused to see hers. And when she realized fairness was not forthcoming, she began to hate. In the lack of reciprocity, in the failure to grant that Robby was first a man, then a man who had done wrong, the institutions and individuals who took over control of his life denied not only his humanity but the very existence of the world that had nurtured him and nurtured her—the world of touching, laughing, suffering black people that established Robby's claim to something more than a number.

Mom expects the worst now. She's peeped their hole card. She understands they have a master plan that leaves little to accident, that most of the ugliest things happening to black people are not accidental but the predictable results of the working of the plan. What she learned about authority, about law and order didn't make sense at first. It went against her instincts, what she wanted to believe, against the generosity she'd observed in her father's interactions with other Homewood people. He was fair. He'd pick up the egg rolls he loved from the back kitchen door of Mr. Wong's restaurant and not blame Wong, his old talking buddy and card-playing crony, for not serving black people in his restaurant. Wong had a family and depended on white folks to feed them, so Wong didn't have any choice and neither did John French if he wanted those incredible egg rolls. He treated everyone, high and low, the same. He said what he meant and meant what he said. John French expected no more from other people than he expected from himself. And he'd been known to mess up many a time, but that was him, that was John French, no better, no worse than any man who pulls on his britches one leg at a time. He needed a little slack, needed the benefit of that blind eye people who love, or people who want to get along with other people, must learn to cast. John French was grateful for the slack, so was quick to extend it to others. Till they crossed him.

My mother had been raised in Homewood. The old Homewood. Her relations with people in that close-knit, homogeneous community were based on trust, mutual respect, common spiritual and material concerns. Face-to-face contact, shared language and values, a large fund of communal experience rendered individual lives extremely visible in Homewood. Both a person's self-identity ("You know who you are") and accountability ("Other people know who you are") were firmly established.

If one of the Homewood people said, "That's the French girl" or, "There goes John French's daughter," a portrait with subtle shading and complex resonance was painted by the words. If the listener addressed was also a Homewood resident, the speaker's voice located the young woman passing innocently down Tioga Street in a world invisible to outsiders. A French girl was somebody who lived in Cassina Way, somebody you didn't fool with or talk nasty to. Didn't speak to at all except in certain places or on certain occasions. French girls were church girls, Homewood African Methodist Episcopal Zion Sunday-school-picnic and social-event young ladies. You wouldn't find them hanging around anywhere without escorts or chaperones. French girls had that fair, light, bright, almost white redbone complexion and find blow hair and nice big legs but all that was to be appreciated from a distance because they were nice girls and because they had this crazy daddy who wore a big brown country hat and gambled and drank wine and once ran a man out of town, ran him away without ever laying a hand on him or making a bad-mouthed threat, just cut his eyes a certain way when he said the man's name and the word went out and the man who had cheated a drunk John French with loaded dice was gone. Just like that. And there was the time Elias Brown was cleaning his shotgun in his backyard. Brown had his double-barreled shotgun across his knees and a jug of Dago Red on the ground beside him and it was a Saturday and hot and Brown was sweating through his BVD undershirt and paying more attention to the wine than he was to the gun. Next thing you know, *Boom!* Off it goes and buckshot sprayed down Cassina Way, and it's Saturday and summer like I said, so chillens playing everywhere but God watches over fools and babies so nobody hit bad. Nobody hit at all except the little French girl, Geraldine, playing out there in the alley and she got nicked in her knee. Barely drew blood. A sliver of that buckshot musta ricocheted off the cobblestones and cut her knee. Thank Jesus she the only one hit and she ain't hit bad. Poor Elias Brown don't quite know what done happened till some the mens run over in his yard and snatch the gun and shake the wine out his head. What you doing, fool? Don't you know no better all those children running round here? Coulda killed one these babies. Elias stone drunk and don't hear nothing, see nothing till one the men say French girl. Nicked the little French girl, Geraldine. Then Elias woke up real quick. His knees, his dusty butt, everything he got starts to trembling and his eyes get big as dinner plates. Then he's gone like a turkey through the corn. Nobody seen Elias for a week. He's in Ohio at his sister's next time anybody hear anything about Elias. He's cross there in Ohio and still shaking till he git word John French ain't after him. It took three men gon over there telling the same story to get Elias back to Homewood. John French ain't mad. He *was* mad but he ain't mad now. Little girl just nicked is all and French ain't studying you, Brown.

You heard things like that in Homewood names. Rules of etiquette, thumbnail character sketches, a history of the community. A dire warning to get back could be coded into the saying of a person's name, and a further inflection of the speaker's voice could tell you to ignore the facts, forget what he's just reminded you to remember and go on. Try your luck.

Because Homewood was self-contained and possessed such a strong personality, because its people depended less on outsiders than they did on each other for so many of their most basic satisfactions, they didn't notice the net settling over their community until it was already firmly in place. Even though the strands of the net—racial discrimination, economic exploitation, white hate and fear—had existed time out of mind, what people didn't notice or chose not to notice was that the net was being drawn tighter, that ruthless people outside the community had the power to choke the life out of Homewood, and as soon as it served their interests would do just that. During the final stages, as the net closed like a fist around Homewood, my mother couldn't pretend it wasn't there. But instead of setting her free, the truth trapped her in a cage as tangible as the iron bars of Robby's cell.

Some signs were subtle, gradual. The A & P started to die. Nobody mopped filth from the floors. Nobody bothered to restock empty shelves. Fewer and fewer white faces among the shoppers. A plate-glass display window gets broken and stays broken. When they finally close the store, they paste the going-out-of-business notice over the jagged, taped crack. Other signs as blatant, as sudden as fire engines and patrol cars breaking your sleep, screaming through the dark Homewood streets. First Garth's death, then Robby's troubles brought it all home. My mother realized her personal unhappiness and grief were inseparable from what was happening *out there.* Out there had never been further away than the thousand insults and humiliations she had disciplined herself to ignore. What she had deemed petty, not worth bothering about, were strings of the net just as necessary, as effective as the most dramatic intrusions into her life. She decided to stop letting things go by. No more benefit of the doubt. Doubt had been cruelly excised. She decided to train herself to be as wary, as unforgiving as she'd once been ready to live and let live. My mother wouldn't become paranoid, not even overtly prickly or bristling. That would have been too contrary to her style, to what her blood and upbringing had instilled. The change was inside. What she thought of people. How she judged situations. Things she'd say or do startled me, set me back on my heels because I didn't recognize my mother in them. I couldn't account for the stare of pure unadulterated hatred she directed at the prison guard when he turned away from her to answer the phone before handing her the rest-room key she'd requested, the vehemence with which she had cussed Richard Nixon for paying no taxes when she, scraping by on an income of less than four thousand dollars a year, owed the IRS three hundred dollars.

Garth's death and Robby's troubles were at the center of her new vision. Like a prism, they caught the light, transformed it so she could trace the seemingly random inconveniences and impositions coloring her life to their source in a master plan.

I first heard Garth's story in the summer of 1975, the summer my wife carried our daughter Jamila in her belly, the summer before the robbery and killing. The story contained all the clues I'm trying to decipher now. Sitting in the kitchen vaguely distracted by gospel music from the little clock radio atop the table, listening as my mother expressed her sorrow, her indignation at the way Garth was treated, her fears for my brother, I was hearing a new voice. Something about the voice struck me then, but I missed what was novel and crucial. I'd lost my Homewood ear. Missed all the things unsaid that invested her words with special urgency. People in Homewood often ask: You said that to say what? The impacted quality of an utterance either buries a point too obscurely or insists on a point so strongly that the listener wants the meat of the message repeated, wants it restated clearly so it stands alone on its own two feet. If I'd been alert enough to ask that question, to dig down to the root and core of Garth's story after my mother told it, I might have understood sooner how desperate and dangerous Homewood had become. Six years later my brother was in prison, and when he began the story of his troubles with Garth's death, a circle completed itself; Robby was talking to me, but I was still on the outside, looking in.

That day six years later, I talked with Robby three hours, the maximum allotted for weekday visits with a prisoner. It was the first time in life we'd ever talked that long. Probably two and a half hours longer than the longest, unbroken, private conversation we'd ever had. And it had taken guards, locks, and bars to bring us together. The ironies of the situation, the irony of that fact, escaped neither of us.

I listened mostly, interrupting my brother's story a few times to clarify dates or names. Much of what he related was familiar. The people, the places. Even the voice, the words he chose were mine in a way. We're so alike, I kept thinking, anticipating what he would say next, how he would say it, filling in naturally, easily with my words what he left unsaid. Trouble was our minds weren't interchangeable. No more than our bodies. The guards wouldn't have allowed me to stay in my brother's place. He was the criminal. I was the visitor from outside. Different as night and day. As Robby talked I let myself forget that difference. Paid too much attention to myself listening and lost some of what he was saying. What I missed would have helped define the difference. But I missed it. It was easy to half listen. For both of us to pretend to be closer than we were. We needed the closeness. We were brothers. In the prison visiting lounge I acted toward my brother the way I'd been acting toward him all my life, heard what I wanted to hear, rejected the rest.

When Robby talked, the similarity of his Homewood and mine was a trap. I could believe I knew exactly what he was describing. I could relax into his story, walk down Dunfermline or Tioga, see my crippled grandmother sitting on the porch of the house on Finance, all the color her pale face had lost blooming in the rosebush beneath her in the yard, see Robby in the downstairs hall of the house on Marchand, rapping with his girl on the phone, which sat on a three-legged stand just inside the front door. I'd slip unaware out of his story into one of my own. I'd be following him, an obedient shadow, then a cloud would blot the sun and I'd be gone, unchained, a dark form still skulking behind him but no longer in tow.

The hardest habit to break, since it was the habit of a lifetime, would be listening to myself listen to him. That habit would destroy any chance of seeing my brother on his terms; and seeing him in his terms, learning his terms, seemed the whole point of learning his story. However numerous and comforting the similarities, we were different. The world had seized on the difference, allowed me room to thrive, while he'd been forced into a cage. Why did it work out that way? What was the nature of the difference? Why did it haunt me? Temporarily at least, to answer these questions, I had to root my fiction-writing self out of our exchanges. I had to teach myself to listen. Start fresh, clear the pipes, resist too facile an identification, tame the urge to take off with Robby's story and make it my own.

I understood all that, but could I break the habit? And even if I did learn to listen, wouldn't there be a point at which I'd have to take over the telling? Wasn't there something fundamental in my writing, in my capacity to function, that depended on flight, on escape? Wasn't another person's skin a hiding place, a place to work out anxiety, to face threats too intimidating to handle in any other fashion? Wasn't writing about people a way of exploiting them?

A stranger's gait, or eyes, or a piece of clothing can rivet my attention. Then it's like falling down to the center of the earth. Not exactly fear or panic but an uneasy, uncontrollable momentum, a sense of being swallowed, engulfed in blackness that has no dimensions, no fixed points. That boundless, incarcerating black hole is another person. The detail grabbing me functions as a door and it swings open and I'm drawn, sucked, pulled in head over heels till suddenly I'm righted again, on track again and the peculiarity, the ordinariness of the detail that usurped my attention becomes a window, a way of seeing out of another person's eyes, just as for a second it had been my way in. I'm scooting along on short, stubby legs and the legs are not anybody else's and certainly not mine, but I feel for a second what it's like to motor through the world atop these peculiar duck thighs and foreshortened calves and I know how wobbly the earth feels under those run-over-at-the-heel, split-seamed penny loafers. Then just as suddenly I'm back. I'm me again, slightly embarrassed, guilty because I've been trespassing and don't know how long I've been gone or if anybody noticed me violating somebody else's turf.

Do I write to escape, to make a fiction of my life? If I can't be trusted with the story of my own life, how could I ask my brother to trust me with his?

The business of making a book together was new for both of us. Difficult. Awkward. Another book could be constructed about a writer who goes to a prison to interview his brother but comes away with his own story. The conversations with his brother would provide a stage for dramatizing the writer's tortured relationship to other people, himself, his craft. The writer's motives, the issue of exploitation, the inevitable conflict between his role as detached observer and his responsibility as a brother would be at the center of such a book. When I stopped hearing Robby and listened to myself listening, that kind of book shouldered its way into my consciousness. I didn't like the feeling. That book compromised the intimacy I wanted to achieve with my brother. It was as obtrusive as the Wearever pen in my hand, the little yellow sheets of Yard Count paper begged from the pad of the guard in charge of overseeing the visiting lounge. The borrowed pen and paper (I was not permitted into the lounge with my own) were necessary props. I couldn't rely on memory to get my brother's story down and the keepers had refused my request to use a tape recorder, so there I was. Jimmy Olson, cub reporter, poised on the edge of my seat, pen and paper at ready, asking to be treated as a brother.

We were both rookies. Neither of us had learned very much about sharing our feelings with other family members. At home it had been assumed that each family member possessed deep, powerful feelings and that very little or nothing at all needed to be said about these feelings because we all were stuck with them and talk wouldn't change them. Your particular feelings were a private matter and family was a protective fence around everybody's privacy. Inside the perimeter of the fence each family member resided in his or her own quarters. What transpired in each dwelling was mainly the business of its inhabitant as long as nothing generated within an individual unit threatened the peace or safety of the whole. None of us knew how traditional West African families were organized or what values the circular shape of their villages embodied, but the living arrangements we had worked out among ourselves resembled the ancient African patterns. You were granted emotional privacy, independence, and space to commune with your feelings. You were encouraged to deal with as much as you could on your own, yet you never felt alone. The high wall of the family, the collective, communal reality of other souls, other huts like yours eliminated some of the dread, the isolation experienced when you turned inside and tried to make sense out of the chaos of your individual feelings. No matter how grown you thought you were or how far you believed you'd strayed, you knew you could cry *Mama* in the depths of the night and somebody would tend to you. Arms would wrap round you, a soft soothing voice lend its support. If not a flesh-and-blood mother then a mother in the form of song or story or a surrogate, Aunt Geral, Aunt Martha, drawn from the network of family numbers.

Privacy was a bridge between you and the rest of the family. But you had to learn to control the traffic. You had to keep it uncluttered, resist the temptation to cry wolf. Privacy in our family was a birthright, a union card granted with family membership. The card said you're one of us but also certified your separateness, your obligation to keep much of what defined your separateness to yourself.

An almost aesthetic consideration's involved. Okay, let's live together. Let's each build a hut and for security we'll arrange the individual dwellings in a circle and then build an outer ring to enclose the whole village. Now your hut is your own business, but let's in general agree on certain outward forms. Since we all benefit from the larger pattern, let's compromise, conform to some degree on the materials, the shape of each unit. Because symmetry and harmony please the eye. Let's adopt a style, one that won't crimp anybody's individuality, one that will buttress and enhance each member's image of what a living place should be.

So Robby and I faced each other in the prison visiting lounge as familiar strangers, linked by blood and time. But how do you begin talking about blood, about time? He's been inside his privacy and I've been inside mine, and neither of us in thirty-odd years had felt the need to exchange more than social calls. We shared the common history, values, and style developed within the tall stockade of family, and that was enough to make us care about each other, enough to insure a profound depth of mutual regard, but the feelings were undifferentiated. They'd seldom been tested specifically, concretely. His privacy and mine had been exclusive, sanctioned by family traditions. Don't get too close. Don't ask too many questions or give too many answers. Don't pry. Don't let what's inside slop out on the people around you.

The stories I'd sent to Robby were an attempt to reveal what I thought about certain matters crucial to us both. Our shared roots and destinies. I wanted him to know what I'd been thinking and how that thinking was drawing me closer to him. I was banging on the door of his privacy. I believed I'd shed some of my own.

We were ready to talk. It was easy to begin. Impossible. We were neophytes, rookies. I was a double rookie. A beginner at this kind of intimacy, a beginner at trying to record it. My double awkwardness kept getting in the way. I'd hidden the borrowed pen by dropping my hand below the level of the table where we sat. Now when in hell would be the right moment to raise it? To use it? I had to depend on my brother's instincts, his generosity. I had to listen, listen.

Luckily there was catching up to do. He asked me about my kids, about his son, Omar, about the new nieces and nephews he'd never seen. That helped. Reminded us we were brothers. We got on with it. Conditions in the prisons. Robby's state of mind. The atmosphere behind the prison walls had been particularly tense for over a year. A group of new, younger guards had instituted a get-tough policy. More strip searches, cell shakedowns, strict enforcement of penny-ante rules and regulations. Grown men treated like children by other grown men. Inmates yanked out of line and punished because a button is undone or hair uncombed. What politicians demanded in the free world was being acted out inside the prison. A crusade, a war on crime waged by a gang of gung-ho guards against men who were already certified casualties, prisoners of war. The walking wounded being beaten and shot up again because they're easy targets. Robby's closest friends, including Cecil and Mike, are in the hole. Others who were considered potential troublemakers had been transferred to harsher prisons. Robby was warned by a guard. We ain't caught you in the shit yet, but we will. We know what you're thinking and we'll catch you in it. Or put you in it. Got your buddies and we'll get you.

The previous summer, 1980, a prisoner, Leon Patterson, had been asphyxiated in his cell. He was an asthma sufferer, a convicted murderer who depended on medication to survive the most severe attacks of his illness. On a hot August afternoon when the pollution index had reached its highest count of the summer, Patterson was locked in his cell in a cellblock without windows and little air. At four o'clock, two hours after he'd been confined to the range, he began to call for help. Other prisoners raised the traditional distress signal, rattling tin cups against the bars of their cells. Patterson's cries for help became screams, and his fellow inmates beat on the bars and shouted with him. Over an hour passed before any guards arrived. They carted away Patterson's limp body. He never revived and was pronounced dead at 10:45 that evening. His death epitomized the polarization in the prison. Patterson was seen as one more victim of the guards' inhumanity. A series of incidents followed in the ensuing year, hunger strikes, melees between guards and prisoners, culminating in a near massacre when the dog days of August hung once more over the prison.

One of the favorite tactics of the militant guards was grabbing a man from the line as the prisoners moved single-file through an archway dividing the recreation yard from the main cell blocks. No reason was given or needed. It was a simple show of force, a reminder of the guards' absolute power, their right to treat the inmates any way they chose, and do it with impunity. A sit-down strike in the prison auditorium followed one of the more violent attacks on an inmate. The prisoner who had resisted an arbitrary seizure and strip search was smacked in the face. He punched back and the guards jumped him, knocked him to the ground with their fists and sticks. The incident took place in plain view of over a hundred prisoners and it was the last straw. The victim had been provoked, assaulted, and surely would be punished for attempting to protect himself, for doing what any man would and should do in similar circumstances. The prisoner would suffer again. In addition to the physical beating they'd administered, the guards would attack the man's record. He'd be written up. A kangaroo court would take away his *good time,* thereby lengthening the period he'd have to wait before becoming eligible for probation or parole. Finally, on the basis of the guards' testimony he'd probably get a sixty-day sojourn in the hole. The prisoners realized it was time to take a stand. What had happened to one could happen to any of them. They rushed into the auditorium and locked themselves in. The prisoners held out till armed state troopers and prison guards in riot gear surrounded the building. Given the mood of that past year and the unmistakable threat in the new warden's voice as he repeated through a loudspeaker his refusal to meet with the prisoners and discuss their grievances, everybody inside the building knew that the authorities meant business, that the forces of law and order would love nothing better than an excuse to turn the auditorium into a shooting gallery. The strike was broken. The men filed out. A point was driven home again. Prisoners have no rights the keepers are bound to respect.

That was how the summer had gone. Summer was bad enough in the penitentiary in the best of times. Warm weather stirred the prisoners' blood. The siren call of the streets intensified. Circus time. The street blooming again after the long, cold winter. People outdoors. On their stoops. On the corners. In bright summer clothes or hardly any clothes at all. The free-world sounds and sights more real as the weather heats up. Confinement a torture. Each cell a hotbox. The keepers take advantage of every excuse to keep you out of the yard, to deprive you of the simple pleasure of a breeze, the blue sky. Why? So that the pleasant weather can be used as a tool, a boon to be withheld. So punishment has a sharper edge. By a perverse turn of the screw something good becomes something bad. Summer a bitch at best, but this past summer as the young turks among the guards ran roughshod over the prisoners, the prison had come close to blowing, to exploding like a piece of rotten fruit in the sun. And if the lid blew, my brother knew he'd be one of the first to die. During any large-scale uprising, in the first violent, chaotic seconds no board of inquiry would ever be able to reconstruct, scores would be settled. A bullet in the back of the brain would get rid of troublemakers, remove potential leaders, uncontrollable prisoners the guards hated and feared. You were supremely eligible for a bullet if the guards couldn't press your button. If they hadn't learned how to manipulate you, if you couldn't be bought or sold, if you weren't into drug and sex games, if you weren't cowed or depraved, then you were a threat.

Robby understood that he was sentenced to die. That all sentences were death sentences. If he didn't buckle under, the guards would do everything in their power to kill him. If he succumbed to the pressure to surrender dignity, self-respect, control over his own mind and body, then he'd become a beast, and what was good in him would die. The death sentence was unambiguous. The question for him became: How long could he survive in spite of the death sentence? Nothing he did would guarantee his safety. A disturbance in a cell block halfway across the prison could provide an excuse for shooting him and dumping him with the other victims. Anytime he was ordered to go with guards out of sight of other prisoners, his escorts could claim he attacked them, or attempted to escape. Since the flimsiest pretext would make murdering him acceptable, he had no means of protecting himself. Yet to maintain sanity, to minimize their opportunities to destroy him, he had to be constantly vigilant. He had to discipline himself to avoid confrontations, he had to weigh in terms of life and death every decision he made; he had to listen and obey his keepers' orders, but he also had to determine in certain threatening situations whether it was better to say no and keep himself out of a trap or take his chances that this particular summons was not the one inviting him to his doom. Of course to say no perpetuated his reputation as one who couldn't be controlled, a bad guy, a guy you never turn your back on, one of the prisoners out to get the guards. That rap made you more dangerous in the keepers' eyes and therefore increased the likelihood they'd be frightened into striking first. Saying no put you in no less jeopardy than going along with the program. Because the program was contrived to kill you. Directly or indirectly, you knew where you were headed. What you didn't know was the schedule. Tomorrow. Next week. A month. A minute. When would one of them get itchy, get beyond waiting a second longer? Would there be a plan, a contrived incident, a conspiracy they'd talk about and set up as they drank coffee in the guards' room or would it be the hair-trigger impulse of one of them who held a grudge, harbored an antipathy so elemental, so irrational that it could express itself only in a burst of pure, unrestrained violence?

If you're Robby and have the will to survive, these are the possibilities you must constantly entertain. Vigilance is the price of survival. Beneath the vigilance, however, is a gnawing awareness boiling in the pit of your stomach. You can be as vigilant as you're able, you can keep fighting the good fight to survive, and still your fate is out of your hands. If they decide to come for you in the morning, that's it. Your ass is grass and those minutes, and hours, days and years you painfully stitched together to put off the final reckoning won't matter at all. So the choice, difficult beyond words, to say yes or say no is made in light of the knowledge that in the end neither your yes nor your no matters. Your life is not in your hands.

The events, the atmosphere of the summer had brought home to Robby the futility of resistance. Power was absurdly apportioned all on one side. To pretend you could control your own destiny was a joke. You learned to laugh at your puniness, as you laughed at the stink of your farts lighting up your cell. Like you laughed at the seriousness of the masturbation ritual that romanticized, cloaked in darkness and secrecy, the simple, hungry shaking of your penis in your fist. You had no choice, but you always had to decide to go on or stop. It had been a stuttering, stop, start, maybe, fuck it, bitch of a summer, and now, for better or worse, we were starting up something else. Robby backtracks his story from Garth to another beginning, the house on Copeland Street in Shadyside where we lived when he was born.

I know that had something to do with it. Living in Shadyside with only white people around. You remember how it was. Except for us and them couple other families it was a all-white neighborhood. I got a thing about black. See, black was like the forbidden fruit. Even when we went to Freed's in Homewood, Geraldine and them never let me go no farther than the end of the block. All them times I stayed over there I didn't go past Mr. Conrad's house by the vacant lot or the other corner where Billy Shields and them stayed. Started to wondering what was so different about a black neighborhood. I was just a little kid and I was curious. I really wanted to know why they didn't want me finding out what was over there. Be playing with the kids next door to Freed, you know, Sonny and Gumpy and them, but all the time I'm wondering what's round the corner, what's up the street. Didn't care if it was *bad* or good or dangerous or what, I had to find out. If it's something bad I figured they would have told me, tried to scare me off. But nobody said nothing except, No. Don't you go no farther than the corner. Then back home in Shadyside nothing but white people so I couldn't ask nobody what was special about black. Black was a mystery and in my mind I decided I'd find out what it was all about. Didn't care if it killed me, I was going to find out.

One time, it was later, I was close to starting high school, I overheard Mommy and Geraldine and Sissy talking in Freed's kitchen. They was talking about us moving from Shadyside back to Homewood. The biggest thing they was worried about was me. How would it be for me being in Homewood and going to Westinghouse? I could tell they was scared. Specially Mom. You know how she is. She didn't want to move. Homewood scared her. Not so much the place but how I'd act if I got out there in the middle of it. She already knew I was wild, hard to handle. There'd be too much mess for me to get into in Homewood. She could see trouble coming.

And she was right. Me and trouble hooked up. See, it was a question of being somebody. Being my own person. Like youns had sports and good grades sewed up. Wasn't nothing I could do in school or sports that youns hadn't done already. People said, Here comes another Wideman. He's gon be a good student like his brothers and sister. That's the way it was spozed to be. I was another Wideman, the last one, the baby, and everybody knew how I was spozed to act. But something inside me said no. Didn't want to be like the rest of youns. Me, I had to be a rebel. Had to get out from under youns' good grades and do. Way back then I decided I wanted to be a star. I wanted to make it big. My way. I wanted the glamour. I wanted to sit high up.

Figured out school and sports wasn't the way. I got to thinking my brothers and sister was squares. Loved youall but wasn't no room left for me. Had to figure out a new territory. I had to be a rebel.

Along about junior high I discovered Garfield. I started hanging out up on Garfield Hill. You know, partying and stuff in Garfield cause that's where the niggers was. Garfield was black, and I finally found what I'd been looking for. That place they was trying to hide from me. It was heaven. You know. Hanging out with the fellows. Drinking wine and trying anything else we could get our hands on. And the ladies. Always a party on the weekends. Had me plenty sweet little soft-leg Garfield ladies. Niggers run my butt off that hill more than a couple times behind messing with somebody's piece but I'd be back next weekend. Cause I'd found heaven.

Looking back now, wasn't much to Garfield. Just a rinky-dink ghetto up on a hill, but it was the street. I'd found my place.

Having a little bit of a taste behind me I couldn't wait to get to Homewood. In a way I got mad with Mommy and the rest of them. Seemed to me like they was trying to hold me back from a good time. Seemed like they just didn't want me to have no fun. That's when I decided I'd go on about my own business. Do it my way. Cause I wasn't getting no slack at home. They still expected me to be like my sister and brothers. They didn't know I thought youns was squares. Yeah. I knew I was hipper and groovier than youns ever thought of being. Streetwise, into something. Had my own territory and I was bad. I was a rebel. Wasn't following in nobody's footsteps but my own. And I was a hip cookie, you better believe it. Wasn't a hipper thing out there than your brother, Rob. I couldn't wait for them to turn me loose in Homewood.

Me being the youngest and all, the baby in the family, people always said, ain't he cute. That Robby gon be a ladykiller. Been hearing that mess since day one so ain't no surprise I started to believing it. Youns had me pegged as a lady's man so that's what I was. The girls be talking the same trash everybody else did. Ain't he cute. Be petting me and spoiling me like I'm still the baby of the family and I sure ain't gon tell them stop. Thought I was cute as the girls be telling me. Thought sure enough, I'm gon be a star. I loved to get up and show my behind. Must have been good at it too cause the teacher used to call me up in front of the class to perform. The kid's get real quiet. That's probably why the teacher got me up. Keep the class quiet while she nods off. Cause they'd listen to me. Sure nuff pay attention.

Performing always come natural to me. Wasn't nervous or nothing. Just get up and do my thing. They liked for me to do impressions. I could mimic anybody. You remember how I'd do that silly stuff around the house. Anybody I'd see on TV or hear on a record I could mimic to a T. Bob Hope, Nixon, Smokey Robinson, Ed Sullivan. White or black. I could talk just like them or sing a song just like they did. The class yell out a famous name and I'd do the one they wanted to hear. If things had gone another way I've always believed I could have made it big in show business. If you could keep them little frisky kids in Liberty School quiet you could handle any audience. Always could sing and do impressions. You remember Mom asking me to do them for you when you came home from college.

I still be performing. Read poetry in the hole. The other fellows get real quiet and listen. Sing down in there too. Nothing else to do, so we entertain each other. They always asking me to sing or read. "Hey, Wideman. C'mon man and do something." Then it gets quiet while they waiting for me to start. Quiet and it's already dark. You in your own cell and can't see nobody else. Barely enough light to read by. The other fellows can hear you but it's just you and them walls so it feels like being alone much as it feels like you're singing or reading to somebody else.

Yeah. I read my own poems sometimes. Other times I just start in on whatever book I happen to be reading. One the books you sent me, maybe. Fellows like my poems. They say I write about the things they be thinking. Say it's like listening to their own self thinking. That's cause we all down there together. What else you gonna do but think of the people on the outside. Your woman. Your kids or folks, if you got any. Just the same old sad shit we all be thinking all the time. That's what I write and the fellows like to hear it.

Funny how things go around like that. Go round and round and keep coming back to the same place. Teacher used to get me up to pacify the class and I'm doing the same thing in prison. You said your teachers called on you to tell stories, didn't they? Yeah. It's funny how much we're alike. In spite of everything I always believed that. Inside. The feeling side. I always believed we was the most alike out of all the kids. I see stuff in your books. The kinds of things I be thinking or feeling.

Your teachers got you up, too. To tell stories. That's funny, ain't it.

I listen to my brother Robby. He unravels my voice. I sit with him in the darkness of the Behavioral Adjustment Unit. My imagination creates something like a giant seashell, enfolding, enclosing us. Its inner surface is velvet-soft and black. A curving mirror doubling the darkness. Poems are Jean Toomer's petals of dusk, petals of dawn. I want to stop. Savor the sweet, solitary pleasure, the time stolen from time in the hole. But the image I'm creating is a trick of the glass. The mirror that would swallow Robby and then chime to me: You're the fairest of them all. The voice I hear issues from a crack in the glass. I'm two or three steps ahead of my brother, making fiction out of his words. Somebody needs to snatch me by the neck and say, Stop. Stop and listen, listen to him.

The Behavioral Adjustment Unit is, as one guard put it, "a maximum-security prison within a maximum-security prison." The "Restricted Housing Unit" or "hole" or "Home Block" is a squat, two-story cement building containing thirty-five six-by-eight-foot cells. The governor of Pennsylvania closed the area in 1972 because of "inhumane conditions," but within a year the hole was reopened. For at least twenty-three hours a day the prisoners are confined to their cells. An hour of outdoor exercise is permitted only on days the guards choose to supervise it. Two meals are served three hours apart, then nothing except coffee and bread for the next twenty-one. The regulation that limits the time an inmate can serve in the BAU for a single offense is routinely sidestepped by the keepers. "Administrative custody" is a provision allowing officials to cage men in the BAU indefinitely. Hunger strikes are one means the prisoners have employed to protest the harsh conditions of the penal unit. Hearings prompted by the strikes have produced no major changes in the way the hole operates. Law, due process, the rights of the prisoners are irrelevant to the functioning of this prison within a prison. Robby was sentenced to six months in the BAU because a guard suspected he was involved in an attempted escape. The fact that a hearing, held six months later, established Robby's innocence, was small consolation since he'd already served his time in the hole.

Robby tells me about the other side of being the youngest: Okay, you're everybody's pet and that's boss, but on the other hand you sometimes feel you're the least important. Always last. Always bringing up the rear. You learn to do stuff on your own because the older kids are always busy, off doing their things, and you're too young, left behind because you don't fit, or just because they forget you're back here, at the end, bringing up the rear. But when orders are given out, you sure get your share. "John's coming home this weekend. Clean up your room." Robby remembers being forced to get a haircut on the occasion of one of my visits. Honor thy brother. Get your hair cut, your room rid up, and put on clean clothes. He'll be here with his family and I don't want the house looking like a pigpen.

I have to laugh at the image of myself as somebody to get a haircut for. Robby must have been fit to be tied.

Yeah, I was hot. I mean, you was doing well and all that, but shit, you were my brother. And it was my head. What's my head got to do with you? But you know how Mommy is. Ain't no talking to her when her mind gets set. Anything I tried to say was "talking *back*," so I just went ahead to the man and got my ears lowered.

I was trying to be a rebel but back then the most important thing still was what the grown-ups thought about me. How they felt meant everything. Everything. Me and Tish and Dave were the ones at home then. You was gone and Gene was gone so it was the three of us fighting for attention. And we fought. Every crumb, everytime something got cut up or parceled out or it was Christmas or Easter, we so busy checking out what the other one got wasn't hardly no time to enjoy our own. Like a dogfight or cat fight all the time. And being the youngest I'm steady losing ground most the time. Seemed like to me, Tish and Dave the ones everybody talked about. Seemed like my time would never come. That ain't the way it really was, I know. I had my share cause I was the baby and ain't he cute and lots of times I know I got away with outrageous stuff or got my way cause I could play that baby mess to the hilt. Still it seemed like Dave and Tish was the ones really mattered. Mommy and Daddy and Sis and Geral and Big Otie and Ernie always slipping some change in their pockets or taking them to the store or letting them stay over all night in Homewood. I was a jealous little rascal. Sometimes I thought everybody thought I was just a spoiled brat. I'd say damn all youall. I'd think, Go on and love those square turkeys, but one day I'll be the one coming back with a suitcase full of money and a Cadillac. Go on and love them good grades. Robby gon do it his own way.

See, in my mind I was Superfly. I'd drive up slow to the curb. My hog be half a block long and these fine foxes in the back. Everybody looking when I ease out the door clean and mean. Got a check in my pocket to give to Mom. Buy her a new house with everything in it new. Pay her back for the hard times. I could see that happening as real as I can see your face right now. Wasn't no way it wasn't gon happen. Rob was gon make it big. I'd be at the door, smiling with the check in my hand and Mommy'd be so happy she'd be crying.

Well, it's a different story ain't it. Turned out different from how I used to think it would. The worst thing I did, the thing I feel most guilty behind is stealing Mom's life. It's like I stole her youth. Can't nothing change that. I can't give back what's gone. Robbing white people didn't cause me to lose no sleep back then. Couldn't feel but so bad about that. How you gon feel sorry when society's so corrupt, when everybody got their hand out or got their hand in somebody else's pocket and ain't no rules nobody listens to if they can get away with breaking them? How you gon apply the rules? It was dog eat dog out there, so how was I spozed to feel sorry if I was doing what everybody else doing. I just got caught is all. I'm sorry about that, and damned sorry that guy Stavros got killed, but as far as what I did, as far as robbing white people, ain't no way I was gon torture myself over that one.

I tried to write Mom a letter. Not too long ago. Should say I did write the letter and put it in a envelope and sent it cause that's what I did, but I be crying so much trying to write it I don't know what wound up in that letter. I wanted Mom to know I knew what I'd done. In a way I wanted to say I was sorry for spoiling her life. After all she did for me I turned around and made her life miserable. That's the wrongest thing I've done and I wanted to say I was sorry but I kept seeing her face while I was writing the letter. I'd see her face and it would get older while I was looking. She'd get this old woman's face all lined and wrinkled and tired about the eyes. Wasn't nothing I could do but watch. Cause I'd done it and knew I done it and all the letters in the world ain't gon change her face. I sit and think about stuff like that all the time. It's better now. I think about other things too. You know like trying to figure what's really right and wrong, but there be days the guilt don't never go away.

I'm the one made her tired, John. And that's my greatest sorrow. All the love that's in me she created. Then I went and let her down.

When you in prison you got plenty of time to think, that's for damned sure. Too much time. I've gone over and over my life. Every moment. Every little thing again and again. I lay down on my bed and watch it happening over and over. Like a movie. I get it all broke down in pieces then I break up the pieces then I take the pieces of the pieces and run them through my hands so I remember every word a person said to me or what I said to them and I weigh the words till I think I know what each and every one meant. Then I try to put it back together. Try to understand where I been. Why I did what I did. You got time for that in here. Time's all you got in here.

Going over and over things sometimes you can make sense. You know. Like the chinky-chinky Chinaman sittin' on the fence. You put it together and you think, yes. That's why I did thus and so. Yeah. That's why I lost that job or lost that woman or broke that one's heart. You stop thinking in terms of something being good or being evil, you just try to say this happened because that happened because something else came first. You can spend days trying to figure out just one little thing you did. People out there in the world walk around in a daze cause they ain't got time to think. When I was out there, I wasn't no different. Had this Superfly thing and that was the whole bit. Nobody could tell me nothing.

Seems like I should start the story back in Shadyside. In the house on Copeland Street. Nothing but white kids around. Them little white kids had everything, too. That's what I thought, anyway. Nice houses, nice clothes. They could buy pop and comic books and candy when they wanted to. We wasn't that bad off, but compared to what them little white kids had I always felt like I didn't have nothing. It made me kinda quiet and shy around them. Me knowing all the time I wanted what they had. Wanted it bad. There was them white kids with everything and there was the black world Mommy and them was holding back from me. No place to turn, in a way. I guess you could say I was stuck in the middle. Couldn't have what the white kids in Shadyside had, and I wasn't allowed to look around the corner for something else. So I'd start the story with Shadyside, the house on Copeland.

Another place to start could be December 29, 1950—the date of Robby's birth. For some reason—maybe my mother and father were feuding, maybe we just happened to be visiting my grandmother's house when my mother's time came—the trip to the hospital to have Robby began from Finance Street, from the house beside the railroad tracks in Homewood. What I remember is the bustle, people rushing around, yelling up and down the stairwell, doors slammed, drawers being opened and shut. A cold winter day so lots of coats and scarves and galoshes. My mother's face was very pale above the dark cloth coat that made her look even bigger than she was, carrying Robby the ninth month. On the way out the front door she stopped and stared back over her shoulder like she'd forgotten something. People just about shoving her out the house. Lots of bustle and noise getting her through the crowded hallway into the vestibule. Somebody opened the front door and December rattled the glass panes. Wind gusting and whistling, everybody calling out last-minute instructions, arrangements, goodbyes, blessings, prayers. My mother's white face calm, hovering a moment above it all as she turned back toward the hall, the stairs where I was planted, halfway to the top. She didn't find me, wasn't looking for me. A thought had crossed her mind and carried her far away. She didn't know why so many hands were rushing her out the door. She didn't hear the swirl of words, the icy blast of wind. Wrapped in a navy-blue coat, either Aunt Aida's or an old one of my grandmother's, which didn't have all its black buttons but stretched double over her big belly, my mother was wondering whether or not she'd turned off the water in the bathroom sink and deciding whether or not she should return up the stairs to check. Something like that crossing her mind, freeing her an instant before she got down to the business of pushing my brother into the world.

Both my grandfathers died on December 28. My grandmother died just after dawn on December 29. My sister lost a baby early in January. The end of the year has become associated with mournings, funerals; New Year's Day arrives burdened by a sense of loss, bereavement. Robby's birthday became tainted. To be born close to Christmas is bad enough in and of itself. Your birthday celebration gets upstaged by the orgy of gift giving on Christmas Day. No matter how many presents you receive on December 29, they seem a trickle after the Christmas flood. Plus there's too much excitement in too brief a period. Parents and relatives are exhausted, broke, still hung over from the Christmas rush, so there just isn't very much left to work with if your birthday comes four short days after Jesus'. Almost like not having a birthday. Or even worse, like sharing it with your brothers and sister instead of having the private oasis of your very own special day. So Robby cried a lot on his birthdays. And it certainly wasn't a happy time for my mother. Her father, John French, died the year after Robby was born, one day before Robby's birthday. Fifteen years and a day later Mom would lose her mother. The death of the baby my sister was carrying was a final, cruel blow, scaring my mother, jinxing the end of the year eternally. She dreaded the holiday season, expected it to bring dire tidings. She had attempted at one point to consecrate the sad days, employ them as a period of reflection, quietly, privately memorialize the passing of the two people who'd loved her most in the world. But the death of my father's father, then the miscarriage within this jinxed span of days burst the fragile truce my mother had effected with the year's end. She withdraws into herself, anticipates the worst as soon as Christmas decorations begin appearing. In 1975, the year of the robbery and murder, Robby was on the run when his birthday fell. My mother was sure he wouldn't survive the deadly close of the year.

Robby's birthday is smack dab in the middle of the hard time. Planted like a flag to let you know the bad time's arrived. His adult life, the manhood of my mother's last child, begins as she is orphaned, as she starts to become nobody's child.

I named Robby. Before the women hustled my mother out the door into a taxi, I jumped down the stairs, tugged on her coattail and reminded her she'd promised it'd be Robby. No doubt in my mind she'd bring me home a baby brother. Don't ask me why I was certain. I just was. I hadn't even considered names for a girl. Robby it would be. Robert Douglas. Where the Douglas came from is another story, but the Robert came from me because I liked the sound. Robert was formal, dignified, important. Robert. And that was nearly as nice as the chance I'd have to call my little brother Rob and Robby.

He weighed seven pounds, fourteen ounces. He was born in Allegheny Hospital at 6:30 in the evening, December 29, 1950. His fingers and toes were intact and quite long. He was a plump baby. My grandfather, high on Dago Red, tramped into the maternity ward just minutes after Robby was delivered. John French was delighted with the new baby. Called him Red. A big fat little red nigger.

December always been a bad month for me. One the worst days of my life was in December. It's still one the worst days in my life even after all this other mess. Jail. Running. The whole bit. Been waiting to tell you this a long time. Ain't no reason to hold it back no longer. We into this telling-the-truth thing so mize well tell it all. I'm still shamed, but here it is. You know that TV of youall's got stolen from Mommy's. Well, I did it. Was me and Henry took youall's TV that time and set the house up to look like a robbery. We did it. Took my own brother's TV. Couldn't hardly look you in the face for a long time after we done it. Was pretty sure youall never knowed it was me, but I felt real bad round youns anyway. No way I was gon confess though. Too shamed. A junkie stealing from his own family. See. Used to bullshit myself. Say I ain't like them other guys. They stone junkies, they hooked. Do anything for a hit. But me, I'm Robby. I'm cool. I be believing that shit, too. Fooling myself. You got to bullshit yourself when you falling. Got to do it to live wit yourself. See but where it's at is you be doing any goddamn thing for dope. You hooked and that's all's to it. You a stone junkie just like the rest.

Always wondered if you knew I took it.

Mom was suspicious. She knew more than we did then. About the dope. The seriousness of it. Money disappearing from her purse when nobody in the house but the two of you. Finding a syringe on the third floor. Stuff like that she hadn't talked about to us yet. So your stealing the TV was a possibility that came up. But to me it was just one of many. One of the things that could have happened along with a whole lot of other possibilities we sat around talking about. An unlikely possibility as far as I was concerned. Nobody wanted to believe it was you. Mom tried to tell us how it *could* be but in my mind you weren't the one. Haven't thought about it much since then. Except as one of those things that make me worry about Mom living in the house alone. One of those things making Homewood dangerous, tearing it down.

I'm glad I'm finally getting to tell you. I never could get it out. Didn't want you to think I'd steal from my own brother. Specially since all youall done to help me out. You and Judy and the kids. Stealing youall's TV. Don't make no sense, does it? But if we gon get the story down mize well get it all down.

It was a while ago. Do you remember the year?

Nineteen seventy-one was Greens. When we robbed Greens and got in big trouble so it had to be the year before that, 1970. That's when it had to be. Youns was home for Christmas. Mommy and them was having a big party. A reunion kinda cause all the family was together. Everybody home for the first time in a long time. Tish in from Detroit. David back from Philly. Youns in town. My birthday, too. Party spozed to celebrate my birthday too, since it came right along in there after Christmas. Maybe that's why I was feeling so bad. Knowing I had a birthday coming and knowing at the same time how fucked up I was.

Sat in a chair all day. I was hooked for the first time. Good and hooked. Didn't know how low you could feel till that day. Cold and snowing outside. And I got the stone miseries inside. Couldn't move. Weak and sick. Henry too. He was wit me in the house feeling bad as I was. We was two desperate dudes. Didn't have no money and that Jones down on us.

Mommy kept asking, What's wrong with you two? She was on my case all day. What ails you, Robby? Got to be about three o'clock. She come in the room again: You better get up and get some decent clothes on. We're leaving for Geral's soon. See cause it was the day of the big Christmas party. Geral had baked a cake for me. Everybody was together and they'd be singing Happy Birthday Robby and do. The whole bit and I'm spozed to be guest of honor and can't even move out the chair. Here I go again disappointing everybody. Everybody be at Geral's looking for me and Geral had a cake and everything. Where's Robby? He's home dying cause he can't get no dope.

Feeling real sorry for myself but I'm hating me too. Wrapped up in a blanket like some damned Indin. Shivering and wondering how the hell Ima go out in this cold and hustle up some money. Wind be howling.

Snow pitching a bitch. There we is. Stuck in the house. Two pitiful junkies. Scheming how we gon get over. Some sorry-assed dudes. But it's comical in a way too, when you look back. To get well we need to get money. And no way we gon get money less we go outside and get sicker than we already is. Mom peeking in the room, getting on my case. Get up out that chair, boy. What are you waiting for? We're leaving in two minutes.

So I says, Go on. I ain't ready. Youns go on. I'll catch up with youns at Geral's.

Mommy standing in the doorway. She can't say too much, cause youns is home and you ain't hip to what's happening. C'mon now. We can't wait any longer for you. Please get up. Geral baked a cake for you. Everybody's looking forward to seeing you.

Seem like she stands there a hour begging me to come. She ain't mad no more. She's begging. Just about ready to cry. Youall in the other room. You can hear what she's saying but you can't see her eyes and they tearing me up. Her eyes begging me to get out the chair and it's tearing me up to see her hurting so bad, but ain't nothing I can do. Jones sitting on my chest and ain't no getup in me.

Youns go head, Mommy. I'll be over in a little while. Be there to blow them candles out and cut the cake.

She knew better. Knew if I didn't come right then, chances was I wasn't coming at all. She knew but wasn't nothing she could do. Guess I knew I was lying too. Nothing in my mind cept copping that dope. Yeah, Mom. Be there to light them candles. I'm grinning but she ain't smiling back. She knows I'm in trouble, deep trouble. I can see her today standing in the doorway begging me to come with youns.

But it ain't meant to be. Me and Henry thought we come up with a idea. Henry's old man had some pistols. We was gon steal em and hock em. Take the money and score. Then we be better. Wouldn't be no big thing to hustle some money, get the guns outa hock. Sneak the pistols back in Henry's house, everything be alright. Wouldn't even exactly be stealing from his old man. Like we just borrowing the pistols till we score and take care business. Henry's old man wouldn't even know his pistols missing. Slick. Sick as we was, thinking we slick.

A hundred times. Mom musta poked her head in the room a hundred times.

What's wrong with you?

Like a drum beating in my head. What's wrong with you? But the other thing is stronger. The dope talking to me louder. It says get you some. It says you ain't never gon get better less you cop.

We waited long as we could but it didn't turn no better outside. Still snowing. Wind shaking the whole house. How we gon walk to Henry's and steal them pistols? Henry live way up on the hill. All the way up Tokay then you still got a long way to go over into the projects. Can't make it. No way we gon climb Tokay. So then what? Everybody's left for Geral's. Then I remembers the TV youns brought. A little portable Sony black-and-white, right? You and Judy sleeping in Mom's room and she has her TV already in there, so the Sony ain't unpacked. Saw it sitting with youall's suitcases over by the dresser. On top the dresser in a box. Remembered it and soon's I did I knew we had to have it. Sick as I was that TV had to go. Wouldn't really be stealing. Borrow it instead of borrowing the pistols. Pawn it. Get straight. Steal some money and buy it back. Just borrowing youall's TV.

Won't take me and Henry no time to rob something and buy back the TV. We stone thieves. Just had to get well first so we could operate. So we took youns TV and set the house up to look like a robbery.

I'm remembering the day. Wondering why it had slipped completely from my mind. I feel like a stranger. Yet as Robby talks, my memory confirms details of his recollection. I admit, yes. I was there. That's the way it was. But *where* was I? Who was I? How did I miss so much?

His confessions make me uncomfortable. Instead of concentrating on what he's revealing, I'm pushed into considering all the things I could be confessing, should be confessing but haven't and probably won't ever. I feel hypocritical. Why should I allow my brother to repose a confidence in me when it's beyond my power to reciprocate? Shouldn't I confess that first? My embarrassment, my uneasiness, the clinical, analytic coldness settling over me when I catch on to what's about to happen.

I have a lot to hide. Places inside myself where truth hurts, where incriminating secrets are hidden, places I avoid, or deny most of the time. Pulling one piece of that debris to the surface, airing it in the light of day doesn't accomplish much, doesn't clarify the rest of what's buried down there. What I feel when I delve deeply into myself is chaos. Chaos and contradiction. So how up front can I get? I'm moved by Robby's secrets. The heart I have is breaking. But what that heart is and where it is I can't say. I can't depend on it, so he shouldn't. Part of me goes out to him. Heartbreak is the sound of ice cracking. Deep. Layers and layers muffling the sound.

I listen but I can't trust myself. I have no desire to tell everything about myself so I resist his attempt to be up front with me. The chaos at my core must be in his. His confession pushes me to think of all the stuff I should lay on him. And that scares the shit out of me. I don't like to feel dirty, but that's how I feel when people try to come clean with me.

Very complicated and very simple too. The fact is I don't believe in clean. What I know best is myself and, knowing what I know about myself, clean seems impossible. A dream. One of those better selves occasionally in the driver's seat but nothing more. Nothing to be depended upon. A self no more or less in control than the countless other selves who each, for a time, seem to be running things.

Chaos is what he's addressing. What his candor, his frankness, his confession echo against. Chaos and time and circumstance and the old news, the bad news that we still walk in circles, each of us trapped in his own little world. Behind bars. Locked in our cells.

But my heart can break, does break listening to my brother's pain. I just remember differently. Different parts of the incidents he's describing come back. Strange thing is my recollections return through the door he opened. My memories needed his. Maybe the fact that we recall different things is crucial. Maybe they are foreground and background, propping each other up. He holds on to this or that scrap of the past and I listen to what he's saved and it's not mine, not what I saw or heard or felt. The pressure's on me then. If his version of the past is real, then what's mine? Where does it fit? As he stitches his memories together they bridge a vast emptiness. The time lost enveloping us all. Everything. And hearing him talk, listening to him try to make something of the nothing, challenges me. My sense of the emptiness playing around his words, any words, is intensified. Words are nothing and everything. If I don't speak I have no past. Except the nothing, the emptiness. My brother's memories are not mine, so I have to break into the silence with my own version of the past. My words. My whistling in the dark. His story freeing me, because it forces me to tell my own.

I'm sorry you took so long to forgive yourself. I forgave you a long time ago, in advance for a sin I didn't even know you'd committed. You lied to me. You stole from me. I'm in prison now listening because we committed those sins against each other countless times. I want your forgiveness. Talking about debts you owe me makes me awkward, uneasy. We remember different things. They set us apart. They bring us together searching for what is lost, for the meaning of difference, of distance.

For instance, the Sony TV. It was a present from Mort, Judy's dad. When we told him about the break-in and robbery at Mom's house, he bought us another Sony. Later we discovered the stolen TV was covered by our homeowner's policy even though we'd lost it in Pittsburgh. A claim was filed and eventually we collected around a hundred bucks. Not enough to buy a new Sony but a good portion of the purchase price. Seemed a lark when the check arrived. Pennies from heaven. One hundred dollars free and clear since we already had the new TV Mort had surprised us with. About a year later one of us, Judy or I, was telling the story of the robbery and how well we came out of it. Not until that very moment when

I caught a glimpse of Mort's face out of the corner of my eye did I realize what we'd done. Judy remembers urging me to send Mort that insurance check and she probably did, but I have no recollection of an argument. In my mind there had never been an issue. Why shouldn't we keep the money? But when I saw the look of surprise and hurt flash across Mort's face, I knew the insurance check should have gone directly to him. He's a generous man and probably would have refused to accept it, but we'd taken advantage of his generosity by not offering the check as soon as we received it. Clearly the money belonged to him. Unasked, he'd replaced the lost TV. I had treated him like an institution, one of those faceless corporate entities like the gas company or IRS. By then, by the time I saw the surprise in Mort's face and understood how selfishly, thoughtlessly, even corruptly I'd behaved, it was too late. Offering Mort a hundred dollars at that point would have been insulting. Anything I could think of saying sounded hopelessly lame, inept. I'd fucked up. I'd injured someone who'd been nothing but kind and generous to me. Not intentionally, consciously, but that only made the whole business worse in a way because I'd failed him instinctively. The failure was a measure of who I was. What I'd unthinkingly done revealed something about my relationship to Mort I'm sure he'd rather not have discovered. No way I could take my action back, make it up. It reflected a truth about who I was.

That memory pops right up. Compromising, ugly. Ironically, it's also about stealing from a relative. Not to buy dope, but to feed a habit just as self-destructive. The habit of taking good fortune for granted, the habit of blind self-absorption that allows us to believe the world owes us everything and we are not responsible for giving anything in return. Spoiled children. The good coming our way taken as our due. No strings attached.

Lots of other recollections were triggered as Robby spoke of that winter and the lost TV. The shock of walking into a burgled house. How it makes you feel unclean. How quickly you lose the sense of privacy and security a house, any place you call home, is supposed to provide. It's a form of rape. Forced entry, violation, brutal hands defiling what's personal, and precious. The aftershock of seeing your possessions strewn about, broken. Fear gnawing at you because what you thought was safe isn't safe at all. The worst has happened and can happen again. Your sanctuary has been destroyed. Any time you walk in your door you may be greeted by the same scene. Or worse. You may stumble upon the thieves themselves. The symbolic rape of your dwelling place enacted on your actual body. Real screams. Real blood. A knife at your throat. A stranger's weight bearing down.

Mom put it in different words but she was as shaken as I was when we walked into her house after Geral's party. Given what I know now, she must have been even more profoundly disturbed than I imagined. A double bind. Bad enough to be ripped off by anonymous thieves. How much worse if the thief is your son? For Mom the robbery was proof Robby was gone. Somebody else walking round in his skin. Mom was wounded in ways I hadn't begun to guess at. At the root of her pain were your troubles, the troubles stealing you away from her, from all of us. The troubles thick in the air as that snow you are remembering, the troubles falling on your head and mine, troubles I refused to see . . .

Snowing and the hawk kicking my ass but I got to have it. TV's in a box under my arm and me and Henry walking down Bennett to Homewood Avenue. Need thirty dollars. Thirty dollars buy us two spoons. Looking for One-Arm Ralph, the fence. Looking for him or that big white Cadillac he drives.

Wind blowing snow all up in my face. Thought I's bout to die out there. Nobody on the avenue. Even the junkies and dealers inside today. Wouldn't put no dog out in weather like that. So cold my teeth is chattering, talking to me. No feeling in my hands but I got to hold on to that TV. Henry took it for a little while so's I could put both my hands in my pockets. Henry lookin bad as I'm feeling. Thought I was gon puke. But it's too goddamn cold to puke.

Nobody in sight. Shit and double shit's what I'm thinking. They got to be somewhere. Twenty-four hours a day, seven days a week somebody doing business. Finally we seen One-Arm Ralph come out the Hi Hat.

This TV, man. Lemme hold thirty dollars on it.

Ralph ain't goin for it. Twenty-five the best he say he can do. Twenty-five don't do us no good. It's fifteen each for a spoon. One spoon ain't enough. We begging the dude now. We got to have it, man. Got to get well. We good for the money. Need thirty dollars for two hits. You get your money back.

Too cold to be standing round arguing. The dude go in his pocket and give us the thirty. He been knowing us. He know we good for it. I'm telling him don't sell the TV right away. Hold it till tomorrow we have his money. He say, You don't come back tonight you blow it. Ralph a hard motherfucker and don't want him changing his mind again about the thirty so I say, We'll have the money tonight. Hold the TV till tonight, you get your money.

Now all we got to do is find Goose. Goose always be hanging on the set. Ain't nobody else dealing, Goose be out there for his people. Goose an alright dude, but even Goose ain't out in the street on no day like this. I know the cat stays over the barbershop on Homewood Avenue. Across from Murphy's five-and-ten. I goes round to the side entrance, the alleyway tween Homewood and Kelly. That's how you get to his place. Goose lets me in and I cop. For some reason I turn up the alley and go toward

Kelly instead of back to Homewood the way I came in. Don't know why I did it. Being slick. Being scared. Henry's waiting on the avenue for me so I go round the long way just in case somebody pinned him. I can check out the scene before I come back up the avenue. That's probably what I'm thinking. But soon's I turn the corner of Kelly, Bam. Up pops the devil.

Up against the wall, Squirrel.

It's Simon and Garfunkel, two jive undercover cops. We call them that, you dig. Lemme tell you what kind of undercover cops these niggers was. Both of em wearing Big Apple hats and jackets like people be wearing then but they both got on police shoes. Police brogans you could spot a mile away. But they think they slick. They disguised, see. Apple hats and hippy-dip jackets. Everybody knew them chumps was cops. Ride around in a big Continental. Going for bad. Everybody hated them cause everybody knew they in the dope business. They bust a junkie, take his shit and sell it. One them had a cousin. Biggest dealer on the Hill. You know where he getting half his dope. Be selling again what Simon and Garfunkel stole from junkies. Some rotten dudes. Liked to beat on people too. Wasn't bad enough they robbing people. They whipped heads too.

Soon's I turn the corner they got me. Brams me up against the wall. They so lame they think they got Squirrel. Think I'm Squirrel and they gon make a big bust. We got you, Squirrel. They happy, see, cause Squirrel dealing heavy then. Thought they caught them a whole shopping bag of dope.

Wearing my double-breasted pea coat. Used to be sharp but it's raggedy now. Ain't worth shit in cold weather like that. Pockets got holes and the dope dropped down in the lining so they don't find nothing the first time they search me. Can tell they mad. Thought they into something big and don't find shit. Looking at each other like, What the fuck's going on here? We big-time undercover supercops. This ain't spozed to be happening to us. They roughing me up too. Pulling my clothes off and shit. Hands all down in my pockets again. It's freezing and I'm shivering but these fools don't give a fuck. Rip my goddamn pea coat off me. Shaking it. Tearing it up. Find the two packs of dope inside the lining this time. Ain't what they wanted but they pissed off now. Take what they can get now.

What's this, Squirrel? Got your ass now.

Slinging me down the alley. I'm stone sick now. Begging these cats for mercy. Youall got me. You got your bust. Lemme snort some the dope, man. Little bit out each bag. You still got your bust. I'm dying. Little taste fore you lock me up.

Rotten motherfuckers ain't going for it. They see I'm sick as a dog. They know what's happening. Cold as it is, the sweat pouring out me. It's sweat but it's like ice. Like knives cutting me. They ain't give back my coat.

Snowing on me and I'm shaking and sweating and sick. They can see all this. They know what's happening but ain't no mercy in these dudes. Henry's cross the street watching them bust me. Tears in his eyes. Ain't nothing he can do. The street's empty. Henry's bout froze too. Watching them sling my ass in their Continental. Never forget how Henry looked that day. All alone on the avenue. Tears froze in his eyes. Seeing him like that was a sad thing. Last thing I saw was him standing there across Homewood Avenue before they slammed me up in the car. Like I was in two places. That's me standing there in the snow. That's me so sick and cold I'm crying in the empty street and ain't a damn thing I can do about it.

By the time they get me down to the Police Station, down to No. 5 in East Liberty, I ain't no more good, sure nuff. Puking. Begging them punks not to bust me. Just bout out my mind. Must have been a pitiful sight. Then's when Henry went to Geral's house and scratched on the window and called David out on the porch. That's when youall found out I was in trouble and had to come down and get me. Right in the middle of the party and everything. Henry's sick too and he been walking round Homewood in the cold didn't know what to do. But he's my man. He got to Geral's so youall could come down and help me. Shamed to go in so he scratched on the window to get Dave on the porch.

Party's over and youns go to Mommy's and on top everything else find the house broke in and the TV gone. All the stuff's going through my mind. I'm on the bottom now. Low as you can go. Had me in a cell and I was lying cross the cot staring at the ceiling. Bars all round. Up cross the ceiling too. Like in a cage in the zoo. Miserable as I could be. All the shit staring me in the face. You're a dope fiend. You stole your brother's TV. You're hurting Mommy again. Hurting everybody. You're sick. You're nothing. Looking up at the bars on the ceiling and wondering if I could tie my belt up there. Stick my neck in it. I wanted to be dead.

Tied my belt to the ceiling. Then this guard checking on me he starts to hollering.

What you doing? Hey, Joe. This guy's trying to commit suicide.

They take my clothes. Leave me nothing but my shorts. I'm lying there shivering in my underwear and that's the end. In a cage naked like some goddamn animal. Shaking like a leaf. Thinking maybe I can beat my head against the bars or maybe jump down off the bed head first on the concrete and bust my brains open. Dead already. Nothing already. Low as I can go.

Must have passed out or gone to sleep or something, cause it gets blurry round in here. Don't remember much but they gave back my clothes and took me Downtown and there was a arraignment next morning.

Mommy told me later, one the cops advised her not to pay my bond.

Said the best thing for him be to stay in jail awhile. Let him see how it is inside. Scare im. But I be steady beggin. Please, please get me out here. Youns got soft-hearted. Got the money together and paid the bond.

What would have happened if you left me to rot in there till my hearing? Damned if I know. I probably woulda went crazy, for one thing. I do know that. Know I was sick and scared and cried like a baby for Mommy and them to get me out. Don't think it really do no good letting them keep me in there. I mean the jail's a terrible place. You can get everything in jail you get in the street. No different. Cept in jail it's more dangerous cause you got a whole bunch of crazies locked up in one little space. Worse than the street. Less you got buddies in there they tear you up. Got to learn to survive quick. Cause jail be the stone jungle. Call prison the House of Knowledge cause you learns how to be a sure nuff criminal. Come in lame you leave knowing all kinds of evil shit. You learn quick or they eats you up. That's where it's at. So you leave a person in there, chances are they gets worse. Or gets wasted.

But Mom has that soft heart anyway and she ain't leaving her baby boy in no miserable jail. Right or wrong, she ain't leaving me in no place like that. Daddy been talking to Simon and Garfunkel. Daddy's hip, see. He been out there in the street all his life and he knows what's to it. Knows those guys and knows how rotten they is. Ain't no big thing they catch one pitiful little junkie holding two spoons. They wants dealers. They wants to look good Downtown. They wants to bust dealers and cop beaucoup dope so's they can steal it and get rich. Daddy makes a deal with them rats. Says if they drop the charges he'll make me set up Goose. Finger Goose and then stay off Homewood Avenue. Daddy says I'll do that so they let me go.

No way Ima squeal on Goose but I said okay, it's a deal. Soon's I was loose I warned Goose. Pretend like I'm trying to set him up so the cops get off my ass but Goose see me coming know the cops is watching. Helped him, really. Like a lookout. Then dumb motherfuckers got tired playing me. Simon got greedy. Somebody set him up. He got busted for drugs. Still see Garfunkel riding round in his Continental but they took him off the avenue. Too dangerous. Everybody hated them guys.

My lowest day. Didn't know till then I was strung out. That's the first time I was hooked. Started shooting up with Squirrel and Bugs Johnson when Squirrel be coming over to Mom's sometimes. Get up in the morning, go up to the third floor, and shoot up. They was like my teachers. Bugs goes way back. He started with Uncle Carl. Been shooting ever since. Dude's old now. Call him King of the Junkies, he been round so long. Bugs seen it all. You know junkies don't hardly be getting old. Have their day then they gone. Don't see em no more. They in jail or dead. Junkie just don't have no long life. Fast life but your average dopehead ain't round long. Bugs different. He was a pal of Uncle Carl's back in the fifties. Shot up together way back then. Now here he is wit Squirrel and me, still doing his thing. Everybody knows Bugs. He the King.

Let me shoot up wit em but they wouldn't let me go out in the street and hustle wit em. Said I was too young. Too green.

Learning from the King, see. That's how I started the heavy stuff. Me and Squirrel and Bugs first thing in the morning when I got out of bed. Mom was gone to work. They getting themselves ready to hit the street. Make that money. Just like a job. Wasn't no time before I was out there, too. On my own learning to get money for dope. Me and my little mob. We was ready. Didn't take us no time fore we was gangsters. Gon be the next Bugs Johnson. Gon make it to the top.

Don't take long. One day you the King. Next day dope got you and it's the King. You ain't nothing. You lying there naked bout to die and it don't take but a minute. You fall and you gone in a minute. That's the life. That's how it is. And I was out there. I know. Now they got me jammed up in the slammer. That's the way it is. But nobody could tell me nothing then. Hard head. You know. Got to find out for myself. Nobody could tell me nothing. Just out of high school and my life's over and I didn't even know it. Too dumb. Too hardheaded. I was gon do it my way. Youns was square. Youns didn't know nothing. Me, I was gon make mine from the curb. Hammer that rock till I was a supergangster. Be the one dealing the shit. Be the one running the junkies. That's all I knew. Street smarts. Stop being a chump. Forget that nickel-dime hoodlum bag. Be a star. Rise to the top.

You know where that got me. You heard that story. Here I sit today behind that story. Nobody to blame but my ownself. I know that now. But things was fucked up in the streets. You could fall in them streets, Brother. Low. Them streets could snatch you bald-headed and turn you around and wring you inside out. Streets was a bitch. Wake up some mornings and you think you in hell. Think you died and went straight to hell. I know cause I been there. Be days I wished I was dead. Be days worser than that.

. . . .

QUESTIONS FOR A SECOND READING

1. Wideman said that his mother had a remarkable capacity for "trying on the other person's point of view." Wideman tries on another point of view himself, speaking to us in the voice of his brother, Robby. As you reread this selection, note the passages spoken in Robby's voice and try to infer Rob-

by's point of view from them. If you look at the differences between John and Robby as evidenced by the ways they use language to understand and represent the world, what do you notice?

2. Wideman talks about three ways he could start Robby's story: with Garth's death, with the house in Shadyside, and with the day of Robby's birth. What difference would it make in each case if he chose one and not the others? What's the point of presenting all three?

3. Robby's mother, brother, and friends point to Garth's death as a turning point in Robby's life. Why do you think they see it as a turning point? When you go back to the excerpt, look closely at the relationship between Garth and Robby. Why was Garth so important to Robby? You might simply say that he was Robby's friend, but friends become friends for reasons. What did Garth mean to Robby? Why did Garth's death affect Robby as it did?

ASSIGNMENTS FOR WRITING

1. Wideman tells Robby's story in this excerpt, but he also tells the story of his neighborhood, Homewood; of his mother; and of his grandfather, John French. Write an essay telling their stories and explaining what they have to do with Robby's.

2. At several points in the essay, Wideman discusses himself as a writer and describes the problems he faces in writing this piece. Why do you think he talks about them here—why not keep quiet and hope that no one notices? Write an essay defining the problems Wideman faces and explain why you think he raises them as he does.

• • • • • • • • • • • • • •

MAKING CONNECTIONS

1. Robby in "Our Time" and Marya in Joyce Carol Oates's "Theft" (p. 353) both feel out of place. They speak about themselves as outsiders, and they do things, such as stealing, that are unacceptable to the larger society. The tensions of their lives are defined by their precarious relations to rules. If you look at them as cases in point, what can you say about the feelings and experiences that made them who they are, people who are not altogether what they would like to be? Write an essay in which you talk about Robby and Marya as examples of a general problem in growing up and entering the world.

2. In his essay, "Entitlement" (p. 89), Robert Coles says, "more than once I have insisted that each individual has his or her own unique way of pulling together the various elements of mental life. I have wanted, however, to

suggest a common manner of response toward life among children of a certain class and background." The tension in Coles's work is between his need to see general processes and his desire to preserve the identity and integrity of the individual. We know little of Robby's early childhood, but the techniques Coles uses to discuss wealthy children can nevertheless be applied to Robby's story. Write an essay in which you examine both Robby's "unique way of pulling together the various elements of mental life" and Robby as an example of a "common manner of response toward life among children of a certain class and background." How does John Wideman help you make this distinction between unique and common responses?

Assignment Sequences

THE ASSIGNMENT SEQUENCES that follow are different from the single writing assignments at the end of each essay. The single writing assignments are designed to give you a way back into the works you have read. They define the way you, the reader, can work on an essay by writing about it—testing its assumptions, probing its examples, applying its way of thinking to a new setting or to new material. A single assignment might ask you to read what Freire has to say about education and then, as a writer, to use Freire's terms and methods to analyze a moment from your own schooling. The single assignments are designed to demonstrate how a student might work on an essay, particularly an essay that is long or complex, and they are designed to show how pieces that might seem daunting are open, manageable, and managed best by writing.

The assignment sequences have a similar function, but with one important difference. Instead of writing one paper, or working on one or two selections from the book, you will be writing several essays and reading several selections. Your work will be sequential as well as cumulative. The work you do on Freire, for example, will give you a way of beginning with

Emerson, or with Adrienne Rich. It will give you an angle of vision. You won't be a newcomer to such discussions. Your previous reading will make the new essay rich with association. Passages or examples will jump, as if magnetized, and demand your attention. And by reading these essays in context, you will see each writer as a single voice in a larger discussion. Neither Freire, nor Emerson, nor Rich, after all, has had the last word on the subject of education. It is not as though, by working on one of the essays, the subject is wrapped up, ready to be put on the shelf.

The sequences are designed, then, so that you will not only be working on essays, but on a subject, like education (or taboos, or entitlement, or the composing process), a subject that can be examined, probed, and understood through the various frames provided by your reading. Each essay becomes a way of seeing a problem or a subject; it becomes a tool for thinking, an example of how a mind might work, a way of using language to make a subject rich and alive. In the assignment sequences, your reading is not random. Each sequence provides a set of readings that can be unified into a project.

The sequences allow you to participate in an extended academic project, one with several texts and several weeks' worth of writing. You are not just adding one essay to another (Freire + Emerson = ?) but trying out an approach to a subject by revising it, looking at new examples, hearing what someone else has to say, and beginning again to take a position of your own. Projects like these take time. It is not at all uncommon for professional writers to devote weeks or even months to a single essay, and the essay they write does not mark the end of their thinking on the subject, but only one stage. Similarly, when readers are working on a project, the pieces they read accumulate on their desks and in their minds and become part of an extended conversation with several speakers, each voice offering a point of view on a subject, a new set of examples, or a new way of talking that resonates with echoes from earlier reading.

A student may read many books, take several courses, write many papers; ideally each experience becomes part of something larger, an education. The work of understanding, in other words, requires time and repeated effort. The power that comes from understanding cannot be acquired quickly—by reading one essay or working for a few hours. A student, finally, is a person who choreographs such experiences, not someone who passes one test only to move on to another. And the assignment sequences are designed to reproduce, although in a condensed period of time, the rhythm and texture of academic life. They invite you to try on its characteristic ways of seeing, thinking, and writing. The work you do in one week will not be lost when it has bearing on the work you do in the next. If an essay by Walker Percy has value for you, it is not because you proved to a teacher that you read it, but because you have put it to work and made it a part of your vocabulary as a student.

Here, then, is what you can expect as you work with a sequence. You will need to read each essay twice, the second time with the "Questions for a Second Reading" and the assignment sequence in mind. Before the second reading you should, in other words, read through the sequence to get a sense of where you will be headed. The essays you write for each assignment in a sequence might be thought of as work-in-progress. Your instructor will tell you the degree to which each essay should be finished—that is, the degree to which it should be revised and edited and worked into a finished performance. From the perspective of the project, however, each piece you write is part of a larger body of work. You might think of each sequence as a revising exercise, where the revision looks forward to what comes next as well as backward to what you have done. This form of revision asks you to do more than complete a single paper; it invites you to resee a subject or reimagine what you might say about it from a new point of view. You should feel free, then, to draw on your earlier work when you work on one of the later assignments. There is every reason for you to reuse ideas, phrases, sentences, even paragraphs as your work builds from one week to the next. The advantage of work-in-progress is that you are not starting over completely every time you sit down to write. You've been over this territory before. You've developed some expertise in your subject. There is a body of work behind you.

The sequences bring together several essays from the text and ask you to imagine them as an extended conversation, one with several speakers. The assignments are designed to give you a place in the conversation as well, to allow you to speak in turn and, to take your place in the company of other writers. This is the final purpose of the assignment sequence: after several weeks' work on the essays and on the subject that draws them together, you will begin to establish your own point of view. You will develop a position from which you can speak with authority, drawing strength from the work you have done as well as from your familiarity with the people who surround you.

This book brings together some of the most powerful voices of our culture. They speak in a manner that asks for response. The assignments at the end of each chapter and, with a wider range of reference, the assignment sequences here at the end of the book demonstrate that there is no reason for a student, in such company, to remain silent.

SEQUENCE ONE

The Aims of Education

Paulo Freire — *The "Banking" Concept of Education*
Adrienne Rich — *When We Dead Awaken: Writing as Re-Vision*
Ralph Waldo Emerson — *The American Scholar*
Stanley Fish — *How to Recognize a Poem When You See One*

YOU HAVE BEEN in school for several years, long enough for your experiences in the classroom to seem natural, inevitable. The purpose of this sequence is to invite you to step outside a world you may have begun to take for granted, to look at the ways you have been taught and at the unspoken assumptions behind your education. The six assignments that follow bring together four essays that discuss how people (and particularly students) become trapped inside habits of thought. These habits of thought (they are sometimes referred to as "structures" of thought) become invisible (or seem natural) because of the ways our schools work or because of the ways we have traditionally learned to use language when we speak, read, or write.

Three of the essays you will read (by Freire, Rich, and Emerson) argue that there are revolutionary ways of using language that can enable a person to break free from limited or limiting ways of thinking. The four assignments that accompany them provide an opportunity for you to test the arguments in individual essays by weighing them against your own experience as a student or to test them by looking at the experience of others.

The last two assignments are exercises in revision. An essay by Stanley Fish provides a point of view that could be said to oppose those of the other writers in this sequence. You are given a chance to revise one of your earlier essays by bringing in this alternate point of view. The last assignment provides an occasion for you to draw material from all the essays you have written into a final and more comprehensive general statement on the proper uses of reading and writing in a college education.

ASSIGNMENT 1

Applying Freire To Your Own Experience as a Student [Freire]

> The teacher talks about reality as if it were motionless, static, compartmentalized, and predictable. Or else he expounds on a topic completely alien to the existential experience of the students. His task is to "fill" the students with the contents of his narration—contents which are detached from reality, disconnected from the totality that engendered them and could give them significance. Words are emptied of their concreteness and become a hollow, alienated, and alienating verbosity.
>
> – PAULO FREIRE
> *The "Banking" Concept of Education*

Surely all of us, anyone who has made it through twelve years of formal education, can think of a class or an occasion to serve as a quick example of what Freire calls the "banking" concept of education, where students are turned into "containers" to be "filled" by their teachers. If Freire is to be useful to you, however, he must do more than call up quick examples. He should allow you to say more than that a teacher once treated you like a container or that a teacher once gave you your freedom.

Write an essay that centers on a rich and illustrative incident from your experience (perhaps, but not necessarily, from your experience in school), and read it (that is, interpret it) as Freire would. You will need to tell a story from your own experience, and also to comment on it—to see it and understand it as though you were continuing or extending Freire's project. You will need to be able to provide important details: things that were said and done; a careful description of setting; perhaps the exact wording of an assignment, a textbook, or a teacher's comments.

Freire would not want you, however, to work "passively" or "mechanically," as though you were following orders. He would want you to make your own mark on the work he has begun. You should use your example, in other words, as a way of testing and examining things that Freire says, particularly those things he says that you find difficult or that you don't understand as well as you would like.

ASSIGNMENT 2

Studying Adrienne Rich as a Case in Point [Freire, Rich]

> The truth is, however, that the oppressed are not "marginals," are not men living "outside" society. They have always been "inside"—inside the structure which made them "beings for others." The solution is not to "integrate" them into the structure of oppression, but to transform that structure so that they can become "beings for themselves." Such transformation, of course, would determine the oppressors' purposes; . . .
>
> – PAULO FREIRE
> *The "Banking" Concept of Education*

> For a poem to coalesce, for a character or an action to take shape, there has to be an imaginative transformation of reality which is no way passive. . . . Moreover, if the imagination is to transcend and transform experience it has to question, to challenge, to conceive of alternatives, perhaps to the very life you are living at that moment. You have to be free to play around with the notion that day might be night, love might be hate; nothing can be too sacred for the imagination to turn into its opposite or to call experimentally by another name. For writing is re-naming.
>
> – ADRIENNE RICH
> *When We Dead Awaken: Writing as Re-Vision*

Both Rich and Freire talk repeatedly about transformations—about transforming structures, transforming the world, transforming the way language is used, transforming the relations between people. In fact, the changes in Rich's poetry might be seen as evidence of her transforming the structures from within which she worked. And, when Freire takes a situation we think of as "natural" (teachers talking and students sitting silent) and names it "banking education," he makes it possible for students and their teachers to question, challenge, conceive of alternatives, and transform experience. Each, in other words, can be framed as an example in the language of the other—Freire in Rich's terms, Rich in Freire's. For both, this act of transformation is something that takes place within and through the use of language.

Adrienne Rich's essay, "When We Dead Awaken: Writing as Re-Vision," could be read as a statement about the aims of education, particularly if the changes in Rich's work are taken as evidence of something the poet learned to do. Rich talks about teachers, about people who helped her to reimagine her situation as a woman and a poet, and about the work she had to do on her own. It is interesting to ask whether Rich might be an example of what Freire is talking about when he talks about "an authentic form of thought and action" or about "the *emergence* of consciousness" and "*critical intervention* in reality."

For this assignment, take one of the early poems Rich presents as an example ("Aunt Jennifer's Tigers" or "The Loser") and use it as a way of testing and extending Freire's argument. What, for example, might you point to in the poem as evidence of a "structure" of oppression? In what ways, if you look both at the later poems and at what Rich says about her work, could these structures be said to have been transformed? What problems did she pose for herself? What acts of cognition were involved? In what ways might Rich be said to have been having a "dialogue" with her own work? Who was the teacher here (or who were the teachers) and what did the poet learn to do?

You should try to use Rich's example to work out some of the more difficult or mysterious things that Freire says about the way people can bring about change.

ASSIGNMENT 3

Performing an Emersonian Reading of "The American Scholar" [Emerson]

> One must be an inventor to read well. As the proverb says, "He that would bring home the wealth of the Indies, must carry out the wealth of the Indies." There is then creative reading, as well as creative writing. When the mind is braced by labor and invention, the page of whatever book we read becomes luminous with manifold allusion. Every sentence is doubly significant, and the sense of our author is as broad as the world."
>
> – RALPH WALDO EMERSON
> *The American Scholar*

"Every sentence is doubly significant, and the sense of our author is as broad as the world." This is one of those sentences (and it is part of one of those passages) that is grand and inspiring but also potentially empty and useless. After all, what does it mean to say that the sense of an author can be "as broad as the world"? It is possible, however, for you to put Emerson to the test by performing an Emersonian reading of Emerson's "The American Scholar"—by seeing if you can do what he says you should be able to do when you read.

As an exercise, choose one sentence from "The American Scholar" and explain how it could be said to be "doubly significant." When you are done, go on to show how the section surrounding it could be said, then, to become "luminous" with manifold allusion, and how, finally, the sense of your author could be said to be "as broad as the world."

Then, as a separate short essay, write an explanation of what it does and does not mean, so far as you can tell from your experience, to be an Emersonian reader. You might find it useful at this point to go back and reread "The American Scholar" in order to find other statements from Emerson you can use in making your case.

ASSIGNMENT 4

The American Scholar 150 Years Later [Emerson]

In the three numbered sections of "The American Scholar," Emerson speaks of "the education of the scholar by nature, by books and by action." Choose the argument he makes that seems to you to be the most powerful or most interesting, and apply it to the curriculum at your own school. If you use your own school as an example, what does the education of an American scholar look like 150 years or so after Emerson's address to students and teachers at Harvard?

You might need to search out your college catalog or whatever documents your school has prepared to explain its curriculum. As you begin thinking about your essay, you could imagine that you are writing a piece for an alumni magazine, or perhaps a position paper to be presented to a faculty committee charged with reviewing undergraduate education.

ASSIGNMENT 5

Confronting an Alternate Point of View [Freire, Rich, Emerson, Fish]

> The conclusion, therefore, is that all objects are made and not found, and that they are made by the interpretive strategies we set in motion. . . . No one of us wakes up in the morning and (in French fashion) reinvents poetry or thinks up a new educational system or decides to reject seriality in favor of some other, wholly original, form of organization. We do not do these things because we could not do them, because the mental operations we can perform are limited by the institutions in which we are *already* embedded.
>
> – STANLEY FISH
> *How to Recognize a Poem When You See One*

Fish seems to be arguing that we cannot make fundamental changes in what we do or what we know "because the mental operations we can perform are limited by the institutions in which we are *already* embedded." This seems to stand in striking opposition to arguments made by Freire, Rich, and Emerson. What can you make of what Fish says in light of the work you have already done in this assignment sequence? Does Fish know something these others don't know? Is he more of a realist? Does he have a better sense of what students can and cannot do? Or could he be said to somehow be wrong? And, if so, how?

Perhaps the best way for you to bring Fish into the work you have already done is to literally work him into something that you have already written. For example, you have written from within the point of view of Freire, Emerson, and Rich. What would happen to any of those essays if you brought in relevant examples, terms, or arguments from "How to Recognize a Poem When You See One"?

For this assignment, go back to rework one of the essays you have written in this sequence by bringing in Stanley Fish. (You might begin by rereading Fish's essay and noting those sections you most want to work with.) You might think of Fish as someone who *also* has something to say about the aims of education, a person who has said something that simply can't be ignored.

You will be revising your earlier essay, but the revision here will require some major changes. Rather than taking what you had written, getting back inside its argument, and making it tighter, you will be bringing in material that has the potential to upset or perhaps transform what you have said. You will have to consider another point of view and establish its position in a discussion you have already begun.

ASSIGNMENT 6

Putting Things Together [Freire, Rich, Emerson, Fish]

This is the final assignment of this sequence, and it is the occasion for you to step back and take stock of all that you have done. Perhaps the best way for you to do this is by making a statement of your own about the role of reading and writing in an undergraduate education. You might, for example, write a document for students who will be entering your school for the first time, telling them what they should expect or what they should know about reading and writing if they want to make the most of their education. Or, as in assignment four, this might be an essay written for an alumni magazine or a paper for a faculty committee charged with reviewing undergraduate education.

You should feel free to draw as much as you can from the papers you have already written, making your points through examples you have already examined, perhaps using your own work with these assignments as an example of what students might be expected to do.

SEQUENCE TWO

Entitlements

Robert Coles — *Entitlement*
John Wideman — *Our Time*
Studs Terkel — *Roberta Victor*
Alice Walker — *In Search of Our Mothers' Gardens*

THE FOUR ASSIGNMENTS that follow ask you to think about what people inherit from their parents and the environments in which they grow up. First, you're asked to read an essay by the psychologist Robert Coles about the entitlements of children from wealthy families. The second assignment invites you to see entitlements differently (yet similarly) by coming to grips with the life of Robby Wideman, a young black man in prison. For the third assignment, you read an interview by Studs Terkel with a prostitute, Roberta Victor, who feels she inherited a set of values and beliefs from American society. Then, for the final assignment, you read Alice Walker's essay, "In Search of Our Mothers' Gardens," and write about her sense of what black women inherit, *and* you're asked to place her with the other "cases" you've studied, so as to allow yourself to make comparisons and draw conclusions about a broad range of entitlements. You can imagine this sequence, then, as your reworking of the project Coles begins. He offers terms and explanations from his work with children from wealthy families, and you have the opportunity to extend and revise his project by considering people (or cases) that he didn't.

ASSIGNMENT 1

Awareness of Entitlements [Coles]

> Each child . . . is also influenced by certain social, racial, cultural, or religious traditions, or thoroughly idiosyncratic ones—a given family's tastes, sentiments, ideals, say. The issue is "class"; but the issue is not only class.
>
> I would use the word "entitlement" to describe what, perhaps, all quite well-off American families transmit to their children—an important psychological common denominator, I believe: an emotional expression, really, of those familiar, class-bound prerogatives, money and power. The word was given to me, amid much soul-searching, by the rather rich parents of a child I began to talk with almost two decades ago, in 1959. I have watched those parents become grandparents, seen what they described as "the responsibilities of entitlement" get handed down to a new generation.
>
> – ROBERT COLES
> *Entitlement*

In his discussion of entitlement, Coles tells a number of stories about families—the lawyer-stockbroker's family, the mine owner's family, the patrician Yankee family from Westchester County, the family from the Garden District of New Orleans, and the powerful Florida grower's family. These families differ in significant ways, even though they share certain traits common to monied, powerful people.

For this assignment, select one of these family stories and write an essay in which you show how an awareness of these entitlements is conveyed to the children. Specifically, what are these entitlements? What is their source? How do these entitlements influence the children who receive them? Which of the entitlements are class related and which are "thoroughly idiosyncratic"?

You can imagine your job here is to perform a "close reading," a careful analysis of one family handing down values, traditions, tastes, and sentiments to their children. You'll want to do a more thorough job than Coles has done, though.

ASSIGNMENT 2

Robby Wideman's Entitlement [Coles, Wideman]

> I have always burned up in my fervent passions of desire and want. My senses at times tingle and itch with my romantic, idealistic outlook on life, which has always made me keep my distance from reality, reality that was a constant insult to my world, to my dream of happiness and peace, to my people-for-people kind of world, my easy-cars-for-a-nickel-or-a-dime sorta world. And these driving passions, this sensitivity to the love and good in people, also turned on me because I used it to play on people and their feelings. These aspirations of love and desire turned on me when I wasn't able to live up to this sweet-self morality, so I began to self-destruct, burning up in my sensitivity, losing direction, because nowhere could I find this world of truth and love and harmony.
>
> – JOHN EDGAR WIDEMAN
> *Our Time*

Like the youngsters in Coles's study, Robby Wideman had dreams and expectations about himself and his future. Like those children, he inherited values, beliefs, and ideals from his family and from others. What, do you imagine, did John French, his mother, his brothers, and his friends—especially Garth—pass along to him? How does what they give him influence what eventually happens to him?

Write an essay tracing Robby's inheritances from other people and describe his family as Coles does for the youngsters in his study. Remember, that, as Coles says, it won't do to reduce people to "clear-cut, consistent psychological or cultural characteristics," or to make simplistic statements such as "Robby inherited dreams because his family didn't have any money or power." Your job, likes Coles's, is to show Robby as an individual, influenced by a unique family and set of friends.

To do this assignment, you'll want to read Robby's story at least twice, once to develop a sense of him and his family and a second time to begin mapping out specifically what he received from different individuals. You might find it helpful to mark especially important passages in the selection and then, on a separate sheet of paper, list what those passages tell you about Robby's social and psychological inheritances, including how they affected him and how he reacted to them.

ASSIGNMENT 3

Roberta Victor [Coles, Terkel]

> A hustler is any woman in American society. I was the kind of hustler who received money for favors granted rather than the type of hustler who signs a lifetime contract for her trick. Or the kind of hustler who carefully reads women's magazines and learns what it is proper to give for each date, depending on how much money her date or trick spends on her. . . . The overt hustling society is the microcosm of the rest of the society. The power relationships are the same and the games are the same. Only this one I was in control of. The greater one I wasn't. In the outside society, if I tried to be me, I wasn't in control of anything. As a bright, assertive woman, I had no power. As a cold, manipulative hustler, I had a lot. I knew I was playing a role. Most women are taught to become what they act. All I did was act out the reality of American womanhood.
>
> – STUDS TERKEL
> *Roberta Victor* and *Eric Nesterenko*

Roberta Victor has strong ideas about herself and about women in American society. You have read a great deal about peoples' inheritances and the powerful influences of families and friends, but Victor makes few references to her friends and none at all to her family. Nevertheless, she continually refers to what she learned from society and its definitions of women and their roles.

Coles said, "More than once I have insisted that each individual has his or her own unique way of pulling together the various elements of mental life. I have wanted, however, to suggest a common manner of response toward life among children of a certain class and background." Roberta Victor seems equally concerned (although probably for different reasons) to suggest that her life is a "common manner of response" among women who grow up in American culture. What, however, might you say about her unique way of defining her relation to others: women, men, people generally? Victor says, "All I did was act out the reality of American womanhood." What is the nature of this reality, as Victor sees it? The question for this assignment is not whether Victor's response is true or not. Whether it is true or not, she offers it as her way of seeing the world. The question this assignment raises is how you might see her as one instance of a common response women make to their situation and as an individual. Your job, then, is to write an essay in which you paint another Coles-like portrait, this time to throw what light you can on Roberta Victor and the life to which she feels entitled. Like Coles, you want to resist the desire to generalize until you are satisfied that the generalizations haven't kept you from seeing the person before you.

ASSIGNMENT 4

Not Saints, But Artists: Developing Your Own Theory [Coles, Wideman, Terkel, Walker]

> For these grandmothers and mothers of ours were not Saints, but Artists; driven to a numb and bleeding madness by the springs of creativity in them for which there was no release. They were Creators, who lived lives of spiritual waste, because they were so rich in spirituality—which is the basis of Art—that the strain of enduring their unused and unwanted talent drove them insane. Throwing away this spirituality was their pathetic attempt to lighten the soul to a weight their work-worn, sexually abused bodies could bear.
>
> – ALICE WALKER
> *In Search of Our Mothers' Gardens*

In the last three assignments you have begun to develop a sense of the power of entitlements—for both the wealthy and the poor. In this essay, Alice Walker offers her thoughts on the inheritance of black women. In particular, she's interested in what happens to the creativity of black women and how that creativity is or isn't passed along. For this assignment describe this inheritance in an essay of your own, and compare it to the inheritances you encountered in the other essays you read and wrote about.

Since you will want to back up your explanations and conclusions with specific examples, you might ask yourself whether Wideman's and Walker's views of the inheritance of blacks have elements in common, and whether Victor's views of women's roles in American society have elements in common with Walker's views of black women. You'll also want to consider Coles's advice about seeing both "social, racial, cultural, or religious traditions" and "thoroughly idiosyncratic" traditions as you draw your conclusions. That is, you'll want to write about Walker and her mother as individuals and as another case in a series of cases from which you draw comparisons and conclusions to make your final statement about entitlements.

SEQUENCE THREE

Experts and Expertise

John Ruskin — The Nature of Gothic

Thomas Kuhn — *The Historical Structure of Scientific Discovery*

Annie Dillard — *The Fixed*

Clifford Geertz — *Deep Play: Notes on the Balinese Cockfight*

Walker Percy — *The Loss of the Creature*

THE FIRST FOUR ASSIGNMENTS in this sequence invite you to look at the world through the eyes of experts: John Ruskin, Thomas Kuhn, and Clifford Geertz. This can be heady and exciting work. You are given the chance to think about familiar settings or experiences through the imaginations of thinkers who have had a profound affect on contemporary culture. In his essay, "The Nature of Gothic," for example, John Ruskin looks at the buildings and objects that surround him and thinks about the way they were made and the quality of life of the people who worked to make them. You will be asked to conduct a similar inventory and to see what connections you can make between architecture or consumer goods and the values they represent. Thomas Kuhn provides a way of charting the "structure" of a discovery. You will be asked to use his method to analyze the discoveries Annie Dillard records in her essay, "The Fixed." Clifford Geertz, in "Deep Play," argues that the Balinese cockfight is a story the Balinese tell themselves about themselves. With Geertz as a model, you will be given the opportunity to interpret a characteristic scene from the culture around you.

In each case, you are given the opportunity to work alongside these thinkers as an apprentice, carrying out work they have begun. The final assignment in the sequence will ask you to look back on what you have done, to take stock, and to draw some conclusions about the potential and consequences of this kind of intellectual apprenticeship.

ASSIGNMENT 1

Going Forth Again to Gaze on a Familiar Setting [Ruskin]

> Go forth again to gaze upon the old cathedral front, where you have smiled so often at the fantastic ignorance of the old sculptors: examine once more those ugly goblins, and formless monsters, and stern statues, anatomiless and rigid; but do not mock at them, for they are signs of the life and liberty of every workman who struck the stone; a freedom of thought, and rank in scale of being, such as no laws, no charters, no charities can secure; but which it must be the first aim of all Europe at this day to regain for her children.
>
> – JOHN RUSKIN
> *The Nature of Gothic*

Ruskin addresses you fairly aggressively as *his* reader: "Go forth and look again at the old cathedral front," he says to you. Or, in another section, "And now, reader, look round this English room of yours."

You are not in an English room. You are not his nineteenth-century contemporary. And you are not, most likely, in a position to have a first-hand look at the front of a Gothic cathedral (although you will find some photographs of a gothic cathedral on pages 468 and 469, after Ruskin's essay). Ruskin directs your attention, and he is quite certain about what you will see, about what the "signs" in these landscapes mean. The perfection of the English room, "if read rightly," is a sign of slavery and degradation, while the ugliness and imperfection of the cathedral facade are signs of life and liberty.

For this assignment, see if you can extend Ruskin's challenge to your own immediate surroundings. Look again at something that is part of your local environment—perhaps a building or a room—and look at it for what it says about the life and character of the persons who made, and for what it says about the culture that values it (or fails to value it). Write an essay in which you explain what you see and how it might be "read rightly." Your job, then, is to extend Ruskin's method of analysis to your world, seen at this point in time.

Note: You should not feel that in carrying on Ruskin's project, you are bound to share Ruskin's politics—to say what he does about industrialization or the working class. There are those who would argue that you cannot adopt a method (a way of seeing) without adopting a political stance.

When you have finished your essay, you might ask yourself whether it is possible to imitate Ruskin's way of seeing architectural or domestic detail without coming to similar conclusions about production and consumption.

ASSIGNMENT 2

The Historical Structure of a Discovery, Scientific or Otherwise [Kuhn]

> Though the sorts of discoveries we have here been examining are undoubtedly additions to scientific knowledge, they are also something more. In a sense that I can now develop only in part, they also react back upon what has previously been known, providing a new view of some previously familiar objects and simultaneously changing the way in which even some traditional parts of science are practiced. Those in whose area of special competence the new phenomenon falls often see both the world and their work differently as they emerge from the extended struggle with anomaly which constitutes the discovery of that phenomenon.
>
> – THOMAS KUHN
> *The Historical Structure of Scientific Discovery*

Kuhn's essay, "The Historical Structure of Scientific Discovery," presents an interesting challenge to the general reader. It is not a particularly difficult essay to understand—the examples are not overly technical or arcane, and the terms, with few exceptions, are drawn from the general language of academic discussion. And yet it is hard to know what to *do* with this essay. The examples Kuhn draws on and the examples one might hold up as similar cases in order to test or extend his argument belong to the scientific community. To put it simply, few of us have ready access to examples of advanced scientific experimentation and discovery. This was not a problem with Ruskin's essay. We could easily move from Ruskin's English room to rooms of our own.

If you cannot work with Kuhn's examples, you can work with his terms, terms that can be put to use to examine discoveries outside of science, including discoveries that *do* belong to your immediate repertoire of examples. From this angle, the challenge of Kuhn's essay is to figure out what it might mean to say that a discovery has a "historical structure"—a prehistory, an internal history, and a posthistory. These are unusual terms.

As Kuhn said, however, he had to fashion "a new vocabulary and new concepts" for analyzing a discovery as an event with a context. This assignment is a chance for you to put his terms to work.

Write an essay that describes and analyzes a discovery whose "history" you know well. Most likely it will be a discovery of your own—a time when you changed your mind, when you saw something that you knew well or had taken for granted in a new way. This event may be one that occurred in school (even in a science lab), but it may also have occured at home or on the streets or in sports. You should not feel, in other words, that you have to describe a Discovery (with a capital D), something on a par with the discovery of oxygen. At the same time, the event you describe should be significant enough that (in Kuhn's terms) there was some struggle involved, and you emerged from the experience seeing both the world and yourself differently. You should describe what happened (and in enough detail that others might share your sense of its significance), and discuss it in Kuhn's terms, analyzing its "historical structure."

ASSIGNMENT 3

Performing a Kuhnian Analysis of Dillard's "The Fixed" [Kuhn, Dillard]

> Fish gotta swim and birds gotta fly; insects, it seems, gotta do one horrible thing after another. I never ask why of a vulture or shark, but I ask why of almost every insect I see.
>
> – ANNIE DILLARD
> *The Fixed*

Dillard is not a scientist, at least not strictly speaking, but she does set out to study nature, and she does come to something like a discovery. One interesting question to ask of "The Fixed" is how Dillard does what she does. What, in other words, is her method? Kuhn can be helpful in a project like this.

Write an essay in which you apply Kuhn's terms and method of analysis to the story of discovery you find in Dillard's essay, treating her work as a systematic process and examining its "prehistory" and internal structure.

ASSIGNMENT 4

Seeing Your World through Anthropological Eyes [Geertz]

> The culture of a people is an ensemble of texts, themselves ensembles, which the anthropologist strains to read over the shoulders of those to whom they properly belong.
>
> — CLIFFORD GEERTZ
> *Deep Play: Notes on the Balinese Cockfight*

Geertz talks about "reading" a culture while peering over the shoulders of those to whom it properly belongs. In "Deep Play," he "reads" the cockfight over the shoulders of the Balinese. But the cockfight is not a single event to be described in isolation. It is itself a "text," one that must be understood in context. Or, as Geertz says, the cockfight is a "Balinese reading of Balinese experience, a story they tell themselves about themselves."

The job of the anthropologist, Geertz says, is "formulating sociological principles, not . . . promoting or appreciating cockfights." And the question for the anthropologist is this: "What does one learn about such principles from examining culture as an assemblage of texts?" Societies, he says, "like lives, contain their own interpretations. One has only to learn how to gain access to them."

Anthropologists are expert at gaining access to cultures and at performing this kind of complex reading. One of the interesting things about being a student is that you have the opportunity to (or you have to) act like an expert even when, properly speaking, you are not. For this assignment, write an essay in which you prepare a Geertzian reading of some part of our culture you know well (sorority rush, window shopping in a shopping mall, studying in the library, decorating a dorm room, tailgate parties at the football game, whatever). Ideally, you should go out and observe the behavior you are studying, looking at the players and taking notes with your project in mind. You should imagine that you are working in Geertz's spirit, imitating his method and style and carrying out work that he has begun.

ASSIGNMENT 5

On Experts and Expertise [Ruskin, Kuhn, Geertz, Percy]

> The whole horizon of being is staked out by "them," the experts. The highest satisfaction of the sightseer (not merely the tourist but any layman seer of sights) is that his sight should be certified as genuine. The worst of his impoverishment is that there is no sense of impoverishment.
>
> I refer to the general situation in which sovereignty is surrendered to a class of privileged knowers, whether these be theorists or artists. A reader may surrender sovereignty over that which has been written about, just as a consumer may surrender sovereignty over a thing which has been theorized about. The consumer is content to receive an experience just as it has been presented to him by theorists and planners. The reader may also be content to judge life by whether it has or has not been formulated by those who know and write about life.
>
> – WALKER PERCY
> *The Loss of the Creature*

In the last four assignments you were asked to try on "Ruskinian," "Kuhnian" and "Geertzian" ways of seeing the world through the lens of their work. You looked at what you had read or done, and at scenes from your own life, casting your experience in the terms of others.

Percy, in "The Loss of the Creature," offers what might be taken as a critique of such activity. His method for analyzing the experience of tourists and students can be applied to your own with these assignments. "A reader," he says, "may surrender sovereignty over that which has been written about, just as a consumer may surrender sovereignty over a thing which has been theorized about." Geertz, Kuhn, and Ruskin have all been presented to you as, in a sense, "privileged knowers." You have been asked to model your own work on their example.

It seems safe to say that, at least so far as Percy is concerned, surrendering sovereignty is not a good thing to do. According to Percy there are, however, ways for a student to "rescue the specimen," ways for a person to "recover the creature."

If Percy were to read over your work in these assignments, how do you think he would describe what you have done? If he were to take your work as an example in his essay, where might he place it? And how does his reading of your work fit with your sense of what you have done? Would Percy's assessment be accurate, or is there something he is missing, something he failed to see?

Write an essay in which you describe and comment on your work in this sequence, looking at it both from Percy's point of view and from your own, but viewing that work as an example of an educational practice, a way of reading (and writing) that may or may not have benefits for the reader.

Note: You will need to carefully review those earlier papers and mark sections that you feel might serve as interesting examples in your discussion. You want to base your conclusions on the best evidence you can. When you begin writing, it would be best if you refer to the writer of those earlier papers as a "he" or a "she" who played certain roles and performed his or her work in certain characteristic ways. You can save the first person, the "I," for the person who is writing and looking back on those texts.

SEQUENCE FOUR

Observing Taboos

Sigmund Freud — *Taboo and the Ambivalence of Emotions*
Saul Bellow — *A Silver Dish*
Joyce Carol Oates — *Theft*

THE FIVE ASSIGNMENTS in this sequence ask you to think about what it means to observe taboos. They ask you to interpret, reconstruct, and apply complex ideas about a phenomena that Sigmund Freud claims is at work in both cultures and individuals. The first three assignments are designed to help you understand Freud's long and complicated essay, "Taboo and the Ambivalence of Emotions." The first asks you for your personal interpretation of Freud's taboo stories, the second for your reconstruction of his ideas, and the third for your "reading" of a present-day taboo. Assignment four asks you to interpret the behavior of the main characters in Saul Bellow's "A Silver Dish" in light of Freud's essay. Assignment five invites you to apply Freud's discussion of taboos about touching to Joyce Carol Oates's story, "Theft."

ASSIGNMENT 1

The Taboo Stories [Freud]

> A dance is given and a song is sung in which the slain enemy is mourned and his forgiveness is implored: "Be not angry," they say, "because your head is here with us; had we been less lucky, our heads might have been exposed in your village. We have offered the sacrifice to appease you. Your spirit may now rest and leave us at peace. Why were you our enemy? Would it not have been better that we should remain friends? Then your blood would not have been spilt and your head would not have been cut off."
>
> – SIGMUND FREUD
> *Taboo and the Ambivalence of Emotions*

This quote is from one of the stories Freud tells as he develops his analysis of taboo practices among various races. Freud tells three kinds of stories in his description and explanation of taboo: "The Treatment of Enemies" (from which the quote is taken), "The Taboo of Rulers," and "The Taboo of the Dead."

For this assignment, read these three groups of stories (pp. 263–284) without reading the rest of the essay—save that for the next assignment. Although Freud uses these stories to explain the presence of taboos in cultures,—contending that they are very much like neuroses in individuals—if you study the stories and draw your own conclusions about taboos before you read Freud's, you'll be in a better position to understand his. When you read them, pay attention to the stories rather than to his remarks about them. You might think of the stories as case studies or tales of people living together. What do they tell you? Some certainly involve strange behaviors and rituals. What are they? Who is involved?

Write an essay in which you discuss what you think it means to be a person who holds or observes a taboo. How are the rituals created and acted out? Why do you suppose they exist? What effects do they have on the people involved?

Although you are not devoting your attention to Freud's comments about taboo in this assignment, you won't be able to avoid them; but remember, however, that this essay is your explanation of taboo, not his. If something he says reflects your own thinking, then use it; but do not simply repeat his interpretation.

ASSIGNMENT 2

Freud's Interpretation [Freud]

> Taboo is a very primitive prohibition imposed from without (by an authority) and directed against the strongest desires of man. The desire to violate it continues in the unconscious; persons who obey the taboo have an ambivalent feeling toward what is affected by the taboo. The magic power attributed to taboo goes back to its ability to lead man into temptation; it behaves like a contagion, because the example is contagious, and because the prohibited desire becomes displaced in the unconscious upon something else. The expiation for the violation of a taboo through a renunciation proves that a renunciation is at the basis of the observance of the taboo.
>
> – SIGMUND FREUD
> *Taboo and the Ambivalence of Emotions*

Freud's thinking about people's problems has had an enormous effect on us and on the language we use to explain ourselves. In the next three assignments, you will be working with his ideas about cultural and individual taboos.

In the first assignment, you wrote your interpretation of the taboo stories. Now for this assignment, concentrate on what Freud is saying about taboos. Write an essay that defines, according to Freud, taboo and the ambivalence of emotions, the double meanings or feelings, associated with a taboo. What, in other words, does Freud say it means to hold a taboo, to be a person who observes a taboo and, consequently, expresses an ambivalence of emotions over the taboo?

You might consider reading this essay at least three times. It is a difficult selection, partly because of the translation and partly because it poses tough conceptual problems. Your first reading can be used to get the feel for it, realizing that you're reading it more for a feel for the language and for how Freud's mind works. During your second reading, you might mark the margins to identify sections where Freud offers significant insights on the characteristics of taboos and the mixed emotions associated with them. Your third reading can be used to review the essay and to note important points that you may have missed earlier.

ASSIGNMENT 3

Present-Day Taboos [Freud]

> We may ask what we have gained from the comparison of taboo with compulsion neurosis and what value can be claimed for the interpretation we have given on the basis of this comparison? Our interpretation is evidently of no value unless it affords a better understanding of taboo than was otherwise possible. . . . We must decide, however, what we want to look for. The assertion concerning the genesis of taboo, namely, that it was derived from a primitive prohibition which was once imposed from without, cannot, of course be proved. We shall therefore seek to confirm those psychological conditions for taboo with which we have become acquainted in the case of compulsion neurosis. How did we gain our knowledge of these psychological factors in the case of neurosis? Through the analytical study of symptoms, especially the compulsive actions, the defense reactions, and the obsessive commands.
>
> – SIGMUND FREUD
> *Taboo and the Ambivalence of Emotions*

Now that you have written about Freud's notions of taboo and the mixed feelings associated with the objects of taboo, we want you to consider his ideas in relation to culture and individuals today.

Freud claims that when it comes to prohibitions—especially those pertaining to compulsive and obsessive actions—cultures and individuals mirror each other. He makes his point through the use of stories about the treatment of enemies, rulers, and the dead.

For this assignment, choose an interesting taboo from present-day American culture and write an essay hypothesizing about its origins.

Although this is a theoretical problem, you should make it concrete by using examples to illustrate the taboo as Freud does with his three kinds of stories. You will need to write about situations and people you know. Ask yourself how the taboo is acted out. What is the prohibition? Who does it affect? What problems does the prohibition solve or create and in what ways? What are the mixed emotions associated with the taboo? How are they expressed? What personal, individual prohibitions, compulsions, obsessions, or defensive reactions might have been responsible for the taboo?

ASSIGNMENT 4

A Freudian View of Bellow's "A Silver Dish" [Freud, Bellow]

> Pop had no more religion than you could find in the Yiddish paper, but he made Woody promise to bury him among Jews, and that was where he lay now, in the Hawaiian shirt Woody had bought for him at the tilers' convention in Honolulu. Woody would allow no undertaker's assistant to dress him, but came to the parlor and buttoned the stiff into the shirt himself, and the old man went down looking like Ben-Gurion in a simple wooden coffin, sure to rot fast. That was how Woody wanted it. At the graveside, he had taken off and folded his jacket, rolled up his sleeves on thick freckled biceps, waved back the little tractor standing by, and shoveled the dirt himself. His big face, broad at the bottom, narrowed upward like a Dutch house. And, his small good lower teeth taking hold of the upper lip in his exertion, he performed the final duty of a son.
>
> – SAUL BELLOW
> *A Silver Dish*

In this story, we meet an interesting character named Morris, Woody Selbst's father or, as Woody calls him, Pop. Morris came to America as a boy after being deserted by his parents in Liverpool, England. When his son Woody was fourteen years old, Pop left his "difficult Christian wife and his converted son and his small daughter" for a woman named Halina, whom he lived with for the next forty years. Throughout the story, we learn that Morris had no use for his Christian wife, the Reverend Doctor Kovner, and Mrs. Skoglund. He seems to have liked Woody, although he sometimes took advantage of him. The story begins with a question about Pop's death: "What do you do about death—in this case, the death of an old father? If you're a modern person, sixty years of age, and a man who's been around, like Woody Selbst, what do you do?"

Pop's death might be seen as a struggle for Woody; after all, taboos and all that is associated with them can cause problems for people. The situation that Woody is in, then, can be seen as another "Taboo of the Dead" story. For this assignment, write an essay interpreting the story from the standpoint of Freud's ideas about taboos of the dead.

To do the assignment, you'll want to read the Bellow story at least twice, once to grasp the story and a second time to focus on how Woody talks and behaves in response to his father's death. You'll also want to reread the section of the Freud essay titled "The Taboo of the Dead." Ask yourself what Woody does and does not allow himself to think and do in the face of his father's death. What are his ambivalent feelings? How can Woody be said to have taboos about death?

ASSIGNMENT 5

Stealing and Touching Taboos [Freud, Oates]

> . . . in the case of taboo, the nucleus of the neurotic prohibition is the act of touching, whence we derive the name "touching phobia" or *delire de toucher*. The prohibition extends not only to direct contact with the body but also to the figurative use of the phrase as "to come into contact" or "be in touch with some one or something." Anything that leads the thoughts to what is prohibited and thus calls forth mental contact is just as much prohibited as immediate bodily contact; this same extension is also found in taboo.
>
> – SIGMUND FREUD
> *Taboo and the Ambivalence of Emotions*

This assignment resembles the previous one, in which you were asked to give a Freudian interpretation of Woody and Pop Selbst. Here we ask you to take a Freudian perspective on Marya, one of the main characters in the Joyce Carol Oates story, "Theft."

Marya can't stand to be touched herself, yet she is preoccupied with touching other people by stealing from them. On a double date with her friend Imogene, she bolts from Matthew when he tries to hold her, and later, when Imogene and Marya fight, she shouts, "Don't you touch me! What do you mean, touching *me!*" She withdraws when Imogene clasps her hands after a play, and she admits that her reputation as an intellectual protects her from others, keeps them at a distance. There are also other instances of her withdrawing from contact with others.

Your assignment is to write an essay showing how Freud might explain Marya's problem. Although we've given you some examples from "Theft" that outline the problem, you'll have to reread the story and examine Marya's behavior carefully if you hope to understand it. To consider her problem through Freud's eyes, you will also want to reread his essay, noting what he says about touching and trying to apply it to Marya.

SEQUENCE FIVE

A Way of Composing

Paulo Freire — The "Banking" Concept of Education

John Berger — *Ways of Seeing*

Adrienne Rich — *When We Dead Awaken: Writing as Re-Vision*

THIS SEQUENCE is designed to offer a lesson in writing. The assignments will stage your work (or the process you will follow in composing a single essay) in a pattern common to most writers: drafting, revising, and editing. You will begin by identifying a topic and writing a first draft; this draft will be revised several times and prepared as final copy.

This is not the usual writing lesson, however, since you will be asked to imagine that your teachers are Paulo Freire, John Berger, and Adrienne Rich and that their essays were addressed immediately to you as a writer, as though these writers were sitting by your desk and commenting on your writing. In place of the conventional vocabulary of the writing class, you will be working from passages drawn from their essays. You may find that the terms these teachers use in a conversation about writing are unusual—they are not what you would find in most composition textbooks, for example—but the language is powerful and surprising. This assignment sequence demonstrates how these writers could be imagined to be talking to you while you are writing, and it argues that you can make use of a theoretical discussion of language—you can do this, that is, if you learn to look through the eyes of a writer eager to understand his or her work.

Your work in these assignments, then, will be framed by the words of Freire, Berger, and Rich. Their essays are not offered as models, however. You will not be asked to write like Freire, Berger, or Rich. Their essays are offered as places where a writer can find a vocabulary to describe the experience of writing. Writers need models, to be sure. And writers need tips or techniques. But above all writers need a way of thinking about writing, a way of reading their own work from a critical perspective, a way of seeing and understanding the problems and potential in the use of written language. The primary goal of this assignment sequence is to show how this is possible.

ASSIGNMENT 1

Posing a Problem for Writing [Freire]

> Students, as they are increasingly posed with problems relating to themselves in the world and with the world, will feel increasingly challenged and obliged to respond to that challenge. Because they apprehend the challenge as interrelated to other problems within a total context, not as a theoretical question, the resulting comprehension tends to be increasingly critical and thus constantly less alienated. Their response to the challenge evokes new challenges, followed by new understandings; and gradually the students come to regard themselves as committed.
>
> – PAULO FREIRE
> *The "Banking" Concept of Education*

One of the arguments of Freire's essay, "The 'Banking' Concept of Education" is that students must be given work that they can think of as theirs; they should not be "docile" listeners but "critical co-investigators" of their own situations "in the world and with the world." The work they do must matter, not only because it draws on their experience but also because that work makes it possible for students to better understand (and therefore change) their lives.

This is heady talk, but it has practical implications. The work of a writer, for example, to be real work must begin with real situations that need to be "problematized." "Authentic reflection considers neither abstract man nor the world without men, but men in their relations with the world." The work of a writer, then, begins with stories or anecdotes, with examples drawn from the world you live in or from reading that could somehow be said to be yours. It does not begin with abstractions, with theses to be proven or ideas to be organized on a page. It begins with memories or observations that become, through writing, verbal representations of your situation in the world; and, as a writer, you can return to these representations to study them, to consider them first this way and then that, to see what form of understanding they represent and how that way of seeing things might be transformed. As Freire says, "In problem-posing education, men develop their power to perceive critically *the way they exist* in the world *with which* and *in which* they find themselves; they come to see the world not as a static reality, but as a reality in process, in transformation."

For this assignment, locate a moment from your own recent experience (an event or a chain of events) that seems rich or puzzling, that you feel you do not quite understand but that you would like to understand better (or that you would like to understand differently). Write the first draft of an essay in which you both describe what happened and provide a way of seeing or understanding what happened. You will need to tell a story with much careful detail, since those details will provide the material for you to work on when you begin interpreting or commenting on your story. It is possible to write a paper like this without stopping to think about what you are doing. You could write a routine essay, but that is not the point of this assignment. The purpose of this draft is to pose a problem for yourself, to represent your experience in such a way that there is work for you to do on it as a writer.

You should think of your essay as a preliminary draft, not a finished paper. You will have the opportunity to go back and work on it again later. You don't need to feel that you need to say everything that can be said, nor do you need to feel that you have to prepare a "finished" essay. You need to write a draft that will give you a place to begin.

When you have finished, go back and reread Freire's essay as a piece directed to you as a writer. Mark those sections that seem to offer something for you to act on when you go back later to revise your essay.

ASSIGNMENT 2

Giving Advice to a Fellow Student [Berger]

> Yet when an image is presented as a work of art, the way people look at it is affected by a whole series of learnt assumptions about art. Assumptions concerning:
>
> Beauty
> Truth
> Genius
> Civilization
> Form
> Status
> Taste, etc.
>
> – JOHN BERGER
> *Ways of Seeing*

Berger suggests that problems of seeing can also be imagined as problems of writing. He calls this problem "mystification." "Mystification is the process of explaining away what might otherwise be evident." Here is one of his examples of the kind of writing he calls mystification:

> Hals's unwavering commitment to his personal vision, which enriches our consciousness of our fellow men and heightens our awe for the ever-increasing power of the mighty impulses that enabled him to give us a close view of life's vital forces.

This way of talking might sound familiar to you. You may hear some of your teachers in it, or echoes of books you have read. Teachers also, however, will hear some of their students in that passage like that. Listen, for example, to a passage from a student paper:

> Walker Percy writes of man's age-old problem. How does one know the truth? How does one find beauty and wisdom combined? Percy's message is simple. We must avoid the distractions of the modern world and learn to see the beauty and wisdom around us. We must turn our eyes again to the glory of the mountains and the wisdom of Shakespeare. It is easy to be satisfied with packaged tours and *Cliff's Notes*. It is more comfortable to take the American Express guided tour than to rent a Land Rover and explore the untrodden trails of the jungle. We have all felt the desire to turn on the TV and watch "Dallas" rather than curl up with a good book. I've done it myself. But to do so is to turn our backs on the infinite richness life has to offer.

What is going on here? What is the problem? What is the problem with the writing—or with the stance or the thinking that is represented by this writing? (The student is writing in response to Walker Percy's essay, "The Loss of the Creature," one of the essays in this book. You can understand the passage, and what is going on in the passage, even if you have not read Percy's essay. Similarly, you could understand the passage about Franz Hals without ever having seen the paintings to which it refers. In fact, what it says could probably be applied to any of a hundred paintings in your local museum. Perhaps this is one of the problems with mystification.)

For this assignment, write a letter to the student who wrote that paragraph. You might include a copy of the passage, with your marginal comments, in that letter. The point of your letter is to give advice—to help that student understand what the problem is and to imagine what to do next. You can assume that he or she (you chose whether it is a man or a woman) has read both "The 'Banking' Concept of Education" and "Ways of Seeing." To prepare yourself for this letter, reread "Ways of Seeing" and mark those passages that seem to you to be interesting or relevant in light of whatever problems you see in the passage above.

ASSIGNMENT 3

Writing a Second Draft [Freire, Berger]

> Problem-posing education, as a humanist and liberating praxis, posits as fundamental that men subjected to domination must fight for their emancipation. To that end, it enables teachers and students to become Subjects of the educational process by overcoming authoritarianism and an alienating intellectualism; it also enables men to overcome their false perception of reality. The world—no longer something to be described by deceptive words—becomes the object of that transforming action by men which results in their humanization.
>
> – PAULO FREIRE
> *The "Banking" Concept of Education*

There is a difference between writing and revising, and the difference is more than a difference of time and place. The work is different. In the first case you are working on a subject—finding something to say and getting words down on paper (often finding something to say *by* getting words down on paper). In the second, you are working on a text, on something that has been written, on your subject as it is represented by the words on the page.

Revision allows you the opportunity to work more deliberately than you possibly can when you are struggling to put something on the page for the first time. It gives you the time and the occasion to reflect, question, and reconsider what you have written. The time to do this is not always available when you are caught up in the confusing rush of composing an initial draft. In fact, it is not always appropriate to challenge or question what you write while you are writing, since this can block thoughts that are eager for expression and divert attention from the task at hand.

The job for the writer in revising a paper, then, is to imagine how the text might be altered—and altered, presumably, for the better. This is seldom a simple, routine, or mechanical process. You are not just copying-over-more-neatly or searching for spelling mistakes.

If you take Freire or Berger as guides, revision can be thought of as a struggle against domination. One of the difficulties of writing is that what you want to say is sometimes consumed or displaced by a language that mystifies the subject or alienates the writer. The problem with authoritarianism or alienating intellectualism or deceptive words is that it is not a simple matter to break free from them. It takes work. The ways of speaking and thinking that are immediately available to a writer (what Berger calls "learnt assumptions") can be seen as obstacles as well as aids. If a first draft is driven by habit and assisted by conventional ways of thinking and writing, a second can enable a writer to push against habit and convention.

For this assignment, read back through the draft you wrote for assignment one, underlining words or phrases that seem to be evidence of the power of language to dominate, mystify, deceive, or alienate. And then, when you are done, prepare a second draft that struggles against such acts, that transforms the first into an essay that honors your subject or that seems more humane in the way it speaks to its readers.

ASSIGNMENT 4

Writing as Re-Vision [Rich]

> For a poem to coalesce, for a character or an action to take shape, there has to be an imaginative transformation of reality which is no way passive. And a certain freedom of mind is needed—freedom to press on, to enter the currents of your thought like a glider pilot, knowing that your motion can be sustained, that the buoyancy of your attention will not be suddenly snatched away. Moreover, if the imagination is to transcend and transform experience, it has no question, to challenge, to conceive of alternatives, perhaps to the very life you are living at that moment. You have to be free to play around with the notion that day might be night, love might be hate; nothing can be too sacred for the imagination to turn into its opposite or to call experimentally by another name. For writing is re-naming.
>
> – ADRIENNE RICH
> *When We Dead Awaken: Writing as Re-Vision*

This is powerful language, and it is interesting to imagine how a writer might put such terms to work. For this assignment, go back to the draft you wrote for assignment three and look for a section where the writing is strong and authoritative, where you seemed, as a writer, to be most in control of what you were doing. If, in that section, you gave shape and definition (perhaps even a name) to your experience, see what you can do to "transcend and transform" what you have written. Play around with the notion that day might be night, love might be hate; nothing should be too sacred for your imagination to turn into its opposite or call experimentally by another name.

Rewrite that section of your essay, but without throwing away or discarding what you had previously written. The section you work on, in other words, should grow in size as it incorporates this "playful" experimentation with another point of view. Grant yourself the "freedom to press on" even if the currents of your thought run in alternate directions—or turn back on themselves.

ASSIGNMENT 5

Preparing a Final Draft [Freire, Berger, Rich]

> Their response to the challenge evokes new challenges, followed by new understandings; and gradually the students come to regard themselves as committed.
>
> – PAULO FREIRE
> *The "Banking" Concept of Education*

A piece of writing is never really finished, but there comes a point in time when a writer has to send it to an editor (or give it to a teacher) and turn to work on something else. This is the last opportunity you will have to work on the essay you began in assignment one. To this point, you have been working under the guidance of expert writers: Freire, Berger, and Rich. For the final revision, you are on your own. You have their advice and (particularly in Rich's case) their example before you. You have your drafts, with the comments you've received from your instructor (or perhaps your colleagues in class). You should complete the work, now, as best you can, honoring your commitment to the project you have begun and following it to its fullest conclusion.

Note: When you have finished working on your essay and you are ready to hand it in, you should set aside time to proofread it. This is the work of correcting mistakes, usually mistakes in spelling, punctuation, or grammar. This is the last thing a writer does, and it is not the same thing as revision. You will need to read through carefully and, while you are reading, make corrections on the manuscript you will turn in.

The hard work is locating the errors, not correcting them. Proofreading requires a slowed-down form of reading, where you pay attention to the marks on the page rather than to the sound of a voice or the train of ideas, and this form of reading is strange and unnatural. Many writers have learned, in fact, to artificially disrupt the normal rhythms of reading by reading their manuscripts backwards, beginning with the last page and moving to the first; by reading with a ruler to block out the following lines; or by making a photocopy, grabbing a friend, and taking turns reading out loud.

SEQUENCE SIX

Ways of Seeing

Walker Percy — *The Loss of the Creature*
John Berger — *Ways of Seeing*
Richard Rodriguez — *The Achievement of Desire*
Clifford Geertz — *Deep Play: Notes on the Balinese Cockfight*

THIS SEQUENCE is designed to give you a way of reading the opening essay, "The Loss of the Creature." This is not a simple essay, and it deserves more than a single reading. There are nine assignments in this sequence, all of which offer a way of rereading (or revising your reading) Percy's essay; and, in doing so, they provide one example of what it means to be an expert or a critical reader.

"The Loss of the Creature" argues that people have trouble seeing and understanding the things around them. Percy makes his point by looking at two exemplary groups: students and tourists. The opening three assignments provide a way for you to work on "The Loss of the Creature" as a single essay, as something that stands alone. You will restate its argument, test its implications, and tell a "Percian" story of your own. A similar procedure is used for John Berger's "Ways of Seeing," an essay that provides a second point of view (and a second set of examples) for a person studying "ways of seeing." Then, Rodriguez and Geertz provide alternate ways of talking about the problems of "seeing." And, in addition, they provide examples you can use to extend Percy's argument further; both of them can be thought of as representative Percian examples: Rodriguez as a student, and Geertz as a tourist. The final assignment is the occasion for you to step forward as an expert, a person who has something to add to the conversation Percy began.

ASSIGNMENT 1

Who's Lost What in "The Loss of the Creature"? [Percy]

> Our complex friend stands behind his fellow tourists at the Bright Angel Lodge and sees the canyon through them and their predicament, their picture taking and busy disregard. In a sense, he exploits his fellow tourists; he stands on their shoulders to see the canyon.
>
> Such a man is far more advanced in the dialectic than the sightseer who is trying to get off the beaten track—getting up at dawn and approaching the canyon through the mesquite. This strategem is, in fact, for our complex man the weariest, most beaten track of all.
>
> – WALKER PERCY
> *The Loss of the Creature*

Percy's essay is not difficult to read, and yet there is a way in which it is a difficult essay. He tells several stories—some of them quite good stories—but it's hard to know what he's getting at, just what point it is that he is trying to make. If he is making an argument, it is not the sort of argument that is easy to summarize. And if the stories (or anecdotes, perhaps) are meant to serve as examples, they are not the sort of examples that quickly add up to a single, general conclusion or that serve to clarify a point or support a thesis. In fact, at the very moment at which you expect Percy to come forward and talk like an expert (to pull things together, sum things up, or say what he means), he often gives you yet another story—as though another example, rather than a general statement, would get you closer to what he is saying.

There are, at the same time, terms and phrases in this essay to suggest that this is an essay with a point to make. Percy talks, for example, about "the loss of sovereignty," "symbolic packages," "sovereign individuals," "consumers of experience," "a universe disposed by theory," "dialectic," and it seems safe to say that these phrases are meant to name or comment on key scenes, situations, and characters in the examples. You could go to the dictionary to see what these words might mean, but the problem for a reader of this essay is to see what the words might mean for Percy as he is writing the essay, telling those stories, and looking for terms he can use to make those stories say more than what they appear to say (about a trip to the Grand Canyon, or a trip to Mexico, or a Falkland Islander, or a student at Sarah Lawrence College). This is an essay, in other words, that seems to break some of the rules of essay writing and to make unusual (and interesting) demands on a reader. There's more for a reader to do here than follow a discussion from its introduction to its conclusion.

As you begin working on Percy's essay (that is, as you begin rereading), you might begin with the stories. They fall roughly into two groups (stories about students and those about tourists), raising the question of how students and tourists might be said to face similar problems or confront similar situations.

Choose two stories that seem to you to be particularly interesting or puzzling. Go back to the text and review them, looking particularly for the small details that seem to be worth thinking about. (If you work with the section on the tourists at the Grand Canyon, be sure to acknowledge that this section tells the story of several different tourists—not everyone comes on a bus from Terre Haute; not everyone follows the same route.) Then, in an essay, use the stories as examples for your own discussion of Percy's essay and what it might be said to be about.

Note: You should look closely at the differences between the two examples you choose. The differences may be more telling than the similarities. If you look only at the similarities, then you are tacitly assuming that they are both examples of the same thing. If one example would suffice, then presumably Percy would have stopped at one. It is useful to assume that he added more examples because one wouldn't do, because he wanted to add another angle of vision, to qualify, refine, extend, or challenge the apparent meaning of the previous examples.

ASSIGNMENT 2

Telling a "Percian" Story of Your Own [Percy]

> The situation of the tourist at the Grand Canyon and the biology student are special cases of a predicament in which everyone finds himself in a modern technical society—a so-

> ciety, that is, in which there is a division between expert and layman, planner and consumer, in which experts and planners take special measures to teach and edify the consumer.
>
> – WALKER PERCY
> *The Loss of the Creature*

For this assignment, you should tell a story of your own, a story that is suggested by the stories Percy tells—perhaps a story about a time you went looking for something or at something, or a time when you did or did not find a dogfish in your Shakespeare class. You should imagine that you are carrying out a project that Walker Percy has begun, a project that has you looking back at your own experience through the lens of "The Loss of the Creature." You might also experiment with some of his key terms or phrases (like "dialectic" or "consumer of experience," but you should choose the ones that seem the most interesting or puzzling—the ones you would want to work with, that is.) These will help to establish a perspective from which you can look at and comment on the story you have to tell.

ASSIGNMENT 3

Complex and Common Readings of "The Loss of the Creature" [Percy]

> I do not refer only to the special relation of layman to theorist. I refer to the general situation in which sovereignty is surrendered to a class of privileged knowers, whether these be theorists or artists. A reader may surrender sovereignty over that which has been written about, just as a consumer may surrender sovereignty over a thing that has been theorized about. The consumer is content to receive an experience just as it has been presented to him by theorists and planners. The reader may also be content to judge life by whether it has or has not been formulated by those who know and write about life.
>
> The dialectic of sightseeing cannot be taken into account by planners, for the object of the dialectic is nothing other than the subversion of the efforts of the planners.
>
> – WALKER PERCY
> *The Loss of the Creature*

Percy charts several routes to the Grand Canyon: you can take the packaged tour; you can get off the beaten track; you can wait for a disaster; you can follow the "dialectical movement which brings you back to the beaten track but at a level above it." This last path (or "strategem"), he says, is for the complex traveller: "Our complex friend stands behind his fellow tourists at the Bright Angel Lodge and sees the canyon through them and their predicament, their picture taking and busy disregard. In a sense, he exploits his fellow tourists; he stands on their shoulders to see the canyon."

When Percy talks about students studying Shakespeare or biology, he says that "there is nothing the educator can do" to provide for the student's need to recover the specimen from its educational package. "Everything the educator does only succeeds in becoming, for the student, part of the educational package."

Percy, in his essay, is working on a problem, a problem that is hard to name and hard to define, but it is a problem that can be located in the experience of the student and the experience of the tourist and overcome, perhaps, only by means of certain strategies. This problem can also be imagined as a problem facing a reader: "A reader may surrender sovereignty over that which has been written about, just as a consumer may surrender sovereignty over a thing that has been theorized about."

The "complex" traveller sees the Grand Canyon through the example of the common tourists with their "predicament, their picture taking and busy disregard." He or she "stands on their shoulders" to see the canyon. What happens if you apply these terms—*complex* and *common*—to reading? What strategies might a complex reader use to recover his or her sovereignty over that which has been written (or that which has been written about)?

For this assignment, write an essay that demonstrates a common and a complex reading of "The Loss of the Creature." Your essay should have three sections (and you could number them, if you choose).

The first two sections should each represent a way of reading the essay. One should be an example of the work of a common reader, a reader who treats the text the way the common tourists treat the Grand Canyon. The other should be an example of the work of a complex reader, a reader with a different set of strategies or a reader who has found a different route to the essay. You should feel free to draw on either or both of your previous essays for this assignment, revising them as you see fit to make them represent either of these ways of reading. Or, if need be, you may choose to start all over again.

The third section of your paper should look back and comment on the previous two sections. In particular, you might address these questions: What does the complex reader see or do? And why might a person prefer one reading over another? What is to be gained or lost?

ASSIGNMENT 4

Berger's Example of a Way of Seeing [Berger]

> We are not saying that there is nothing left to experience before original works of art except a sense of awe because they have survived. The way original works of art are usually approached—through museum catalogues, guides, hired cassettes, etc.—is not the only way they might be approached. When the art of the past ceases to be viewed nostagically, the works will cease to be holy relics—although they will never re-become what they were before the age of reproduction. We are not saying original works of art are now useless.
>
> – JOHN BERGER
> *Ways of Seeing*

There is a way in which Berger offers another story about tourists—tourists going to a museum to see paintings; to buy postcards, gallery guides, reprints and T-shirts featuring the image of the Mona Lisa. Like Percy, he argues that there are problems in the way we see or don't see things before us, problems that can be located in and overcome by strategies or approaches.

For Berger, what we lose if we fail to see properly is history: "If we 'saw' the art of the past, we would situate ourselves in history. When we are prevented from seeing it, we are being deprived of the history which belongs to us." It is not hard to figure out who, according to Berger, prevents us from seeing the art of the past. He says it is the ruling class. It is difficult, however, to figure out what he says gets in our way and what all this has to do with "history."

For this assignment, write an essay explaining what, as you read Berger, it is that gets in the way when we look at pictures, paintings, or images, and what this has to do with history.

Note: Since "The Loss of the Creature" is now the one sure piece of common ground for the readers and writers among your classmates, you might find it useful, while discussing the more difficult or elusive ideas in Berger, to make reference to Percy's argument and his key terms and examples.

ASSIGNMENT 5

Applying Berger's Methods to Vermeer's Woman Pouring Milk [Berger]

> A people or a class which is cut off from its own past is far less free to choose and to act as a people or class than one that has been able to situate itself in history. That is why—and this is the only reason why—the entire art of the past has not become a political issue.
>
> – JOHN BERGER
> *Ways of Seeing*

Berger says that the real question facing those who care about art is this: "To whom does the meaning of the art of the past properly belong? To those who can apply it to their own lives, or to a cultural hierarchy of relic specialists?" As Berger's reader, you are invited to act as though the meaning of the art of the past belonged to you. Look again at the painting by Vermeer, "Woman Pouring Milk," that is included in the essay on page 70. Berger includes the painting, but without much discussion, as though he were, in fact, leaving it for you to work on by yourself.

Write an essay that shows others how they might best look at and see that painting (or the reproduction printed in this book). You should offer this lesson in the spirit of John Berger. You should imagine that you are carrying out a project he has begun, perhaps as his apprentice.

ASSIGNMENT 6

A Way of Seeing Your Way of Seeing [Berger]

> What we make of that painted moment when it is before our eyes depends upon what we expect of art, and that in turn depends upon how we have already experienced the meaning of paintings through reproductions.
>
> – JOHN BERGER
> *Ways of Seeing*

Return now to the essay you wrote on Vermeer's "Woman Pouring Milk," and look at your essay as an example of a way of seeing, one of several ways a thoughtful person might approach and talk about that painting. You have not, to be sure, said everything there is to say about the painting. What you wrote should give you evidence of a person making choices, a person with a point of view, with expectations and strategies that have been learned through prior experience.

For this assignment, study what you have written and write an essay that comments on its way of seeing (or "reading") "Woman Pouring Milk." Here are some questions to guide you in preparing your commentary:

What expectations about art are represented by the example of the person you see at work in your essay?

What is the most interesting or puzzling or significant thing that viewer was able to see in this painting? How would you characterize a viewer who would notice *this* and take it as central to an understanding of the painting?

What do you suppose that viewer must necessarily have missed or failed to see? What other approaches might have been taken? What are the disadvantages in the approach you see in the essay?

Is there anything you might point to as an example of "mystification" in that essay? ("Mystification" was the term Berger used to characterize writing that sounds like this: "Hals's unwavering commitment to his personal vision, which enriches our consciousness of our fellow men and heightens our awe for the ever-increasing power of the mighty impulses that enabled him to give us a close view of life's vital forces.") Is there anything you might point to as an example of mystification's opposite?

Berger said, "If we 'saw' the art of the past, we would situate ourselves in history." As you look back over your essay, what does any of what you wrote or saw (or failed to write or see) have to do with your position in "history"?

Berger says that what you write depends on how you have already experienced the meaning of paintings. What are the characteristic features in the work of a person who has learned from Berger how to "experience the meaning of paintings"? If you were to get more training in this—in the act of looking at paintings and writing about them—what would you hope to learn?

ASSIGNMENT 7

Richard Rodriguez as One of Percy's Examples [Percy, Rodriguez]

> Those who would take seriously the boy's success—and his failure—would be forced to realize how great is the change any academic undergoes, how far one must move from one's past. It is easiest to ignore such considerations. So little is said about the scholarship boy in pages and pages of educational literature. Nothing is said of the silence that comes to separate the boy from his parents. Instead, one hears proposals for increasing the self-esteem of students and encouraging early intellectual independence. Paragraphs glitter with constellations of terms like "creativity" and "originality." (Ignored altogether is the function of imitation in a student's life.)
>
> – RICHARD RODRIGUEZ
> *The Achievement of Desire*

"The Achievement of Desire" is the second chapter in Richard Rodriguez's autobiography, *Hunger of Memory: The Education of Richard Rodriguez.* The story Rodriguez tells is, in part, a story of loss and separation, of the necessary sacrifices required of all those who take their own education seriously. To use the language of Percy's essay, Rodriguez loses any authentic or sovereign contact he once had with the world around him. He has become a kind of "weary traveller," deprived of the immediate, easy access he once had to his parents, his past, or even to his own thoughts and emotions. And whatever he has lost, it can only be regained now—if it can be regained at all—by a complex strategy.

If Percy were to take Rodriguez's story—or a section of it—as an example, where would he place it and what would he have to say about it? If Percy were to add Rodriguez (perhaps the Rodriguez who read Hoggart's *The Uses of Literacy* or the Rodriguez who read through the list of the "hundred most important books of Western Civilization") to the example of the biology student or the Falkland Islander, where would he put Rodriguez and what would he say to place Rodriguez in the context of his argument?

For this assignment, write two short essays. In the first essay you will read Rodriguez's story through the frame of Percy's essay. If you look from this point of view, what would Percy notice and what would he say about what he notices?

Rodriguez, however, also has an argument to make about education and loss. For the second essay, consider the following questions: What does Rodriguez offer as the significant moments in his experience? What does he have to say about them? And what might he have to say to Walker Percy? Is Percy one who, in Rodriguez's terms, can take seriously the scholarship boy's success and failure?

Your job, then, is to set Percy and Rodriguez against each other, to write about Rodriguez from Percy's point of view, but then in a separate short essay to consider as well what Rodriguez might have to say about Percy's reading of "The Achievement of Desire."

ASSIGNMENT 8

The Anthropologist as a Person with a Way of Seeing [Geertz]

> For the anthropologist, whose concern is with formulating sociological principles, not with promoting or appreciating cockfights, the question is, what does one learn about such principles from examining culture as an assemblage of texts?
>
> — CLIFFORD GEERTZ
> *Deep Play: Notes on the Balinese Cockfight*

You've gone from tourists to students and now, at the end of this set of readings, you have another travel story before you. The final essay, "Deep Play: Notes on the Balinese Cockfight," was written by an anthropologist. Anthropologists, properly speaking, are not really tourists. There is a scholarly purpose to their travel and, presumably, they have learned or developed the complex strategies necessary to get beyond the preformed "symbolic complex" that would keep them from seeing the place or the people they have travelled to study. They are experts, in other words, not just any "layman seer of sights." One question to ask of "Deep Play" is whether Geertz has solved the problem of seeing that Percy outlines.

Anthropologists are people who observe (or in Geertz's terms "read") the behavior of other people. But their work is governed by methods, by ways of seeing that are complex and sophisticated. They can do something that the ordinary tourist to Bali (or Mexico or the Grand Canyon) cannot. They have different ways of situating themselves as observers and they have a different way of thinking (or writing) about what they have seen.

What is it, then, that anthropologists do and how do they do what they do?

If "Deep Play" were your only evidence, how might you describe the work of an anthropologist? Write an essay in which you look at "Deep Play" section by section, describing on the basis of each the methods of an anthropologist. In each case, you have the chance to watch Geertz at work. (Your essay, then, might be divided into seven sections.) When you have worked through "Deep Play" section by section, bring all the pieces together in a final discussion that examines how these various skills fit together to define an anthropologist's special way of seeing.

ASSIGNMENT 9

Taking Your Turn in the Conversation [Percy, Berger, Rodriguez, Geertz]

> I refer to the general situation in which sovereignty is surrendered to a class of privileged knowers, whether these be theorists or artists. A reader may surrender sovereignty over that which has been written about, just as a consumer may surrender sovereignty over a thing which has been theorized about. The consumer is content to receive an experience just as it has been presented to him by theorists and planners. The reader may also be content to judge life by whether it has or has not been formulated by those who know and write about life.
>
> – WALKER PERCY
> *The Loss of the Creature*

It could be argued that all of the work you have done in these assignments has been preparing you to test the assumptions of the opening essay of this sequence, "The Loss of the Creature." You've read several accounts of the problems facing tourists and students, people who look at and try to understand that which is before them. You have observed acts of seeing, reading, and writing that can extend the range of examples provided by Percy. And you have, of course, your own work before you as an example of a student working under the guidance of a variety of experts. You are in a position, in other words, to speak in response to Percy with considerable authority. This last assignment is the occasion for you to do so.

For this assignment, you might imagine that you are writing an article for the journal that first printed "The Loss of the Creature." You can assume, that is, that your readers are expert readers. They have read Percy's essay. They know what the common reading would be and they know that they want something else. This is not an occasion for summary, but for an essay that can enable those readers to take a next step in their thinking. You may challenge Percy's essay, defend and extend what it has to say, or provide an angle you feel others will not have seen. You should feel free to draw as much as you can on the writing you have already done, working sections of those papers into your final essay. Percy has said what he has to say. It is time for you to speak, now, in turn.

SEQUENCE SEVEN

What Are We Talking about When We Talk about Love?

Raymond Carver — What We Talk about When We Talk about Love

Thomas Cottle and Stephen Klineberg — *Ted and Ellie Graziano*

Saul Bellow — *A Silver Dish*

THE FIRST THREE ASSIGNMENTS in this sequence invite you to comment on what different people talk about when they talk about love. In two stories and an interview, several very different people confront the difficult subject of love. The characters in the Carver story talk directly about love, yet they seem to be stuck and their conversation is elusive. Ted and Ellie Graziano hardly ever talk directly about love, but they act out an argument that might be said to say very much about it. The third story, by Saul Bellow, brings forward another enactment of love, this time through the eyes of a son who has just buried his father. The fourth and final assignment asks you to conclude your project about what people talk about when they talk about love by taking a critical stance towards the people you studied and what they said.

ASSIGNMENT 1

What Are They Talking About? [Carver]

> "What do any of us really know about love?" Mel said. "It seems to me we're just beginners at love. We say we love each other and we do, I don't doubt it. I love Terri and Terri loves me, and you guys love each other too. You know the kind of love I'm talking about now. Physical love, that impulse that drives you to someone special, as well as love of the other person's being, his or her essence, as it were. Carnal love and, well, call it sentimental love, the day-to-day caring about the other person. But sometimes I have a hard time accounting for the fact that I must have loved my first wife too. But I did, I know I did. So I suppose I am like Terri in that regard. Terri and Ed." He thought about it and then he went on. "There was a time when I thought I loved my first wife more than life itself. But now I hate her guts. I do. How do you explain that? What happened to that love? What happened to it, is what I'd like to know. I wish someone could tell me . . ."
>
> – RAYMOND CARVER
> *What We Talk about When We Talk about Love*

It's possible to read this story a number of times and still keep asking, "What are these people talking about? How *do* they explain love?" Terri, Mel, Laura, and Nick all make a number of observations, but they never seem to reach any conclusion or agreement, and the precise nature of their disagreements is elusive. At the same time, it's possible to feel that much has been said here. The question, then, is what *do* they talk about when they talk about love?

Write an essay in which you address these questions. What is love to each of these people? What are they trying to say to each other about it?

ASSIGNMENT 2

What's Love to the Grazianos? [Cottle and Klineberg]

> Ted's mouth closed; he nodded sarcastically. "Escapee from a mental . . . This is what I have to take. Every day of my life. I am totally alone, making it possible for four human beings to lead their lives with a little dignity." His voice had quieted somewhat. "Four ungrateful human beings. I don't have a soul to talk to in this house. I see the way people are living. I see the way people are dying, and we're not getting any of it. Either one. I can't even afford to get us ground in the cemetery. Has that, Mrs. Big Mouth, ever crossed that brilliant brain of yours? Where, exactly, would you like them to put my corpse when I die if I don't arrange for a plot? Here? Would you like it in the kitchen maybe? Just where do the poor die? You ever think of that? That, too, is part of the future. Maybe that's what they mean by destiny. Huh? You ever think of that? I've got to arrange that too, pal."
>
> — THOMAS COTTLE AND STEPHEN KLINEBERG
> *Ted and Ellie Graziano*

Ted and Ellie Graziano touch on one sensitive subject after another in their interview, but they never talk directly about love, even though they say they love each other. Sometimes they sound like Mel and Terri from the Carver story, and at other times, they seem more involved with each other in their arguments than any of Carver's characters.

What are the Grazianos arguing about? What are their disagreements? What do their disagreements have to do with love?

For this assignment, select three or four passages from the interview that you think best represent what Ted and Ellie talk about when they talk about love. Write an essay in which you discuss what these passages tell you about the Grazianos and and how they understand love.

ASSIGNMENT 3

Woody Selbst's Struggles in the Name of Love [Bellow]

> . . . for the rest of the week Woody was busy, had jobs to run, office responsibilities, family responsibilities. He lived alone; as did his wife; as did his mistress; everybody in a separate establishment. Since his wife, after fifteen years of separation, had not learned to take care of herself, Woody did her shopping on Fridays, filled her freezer. He had to take her this week to buy shoes. Also, Friday night he always spent with Helen—Helen was his wife de facto. Saturday he did his big weekly shopping. Saturday night he devoted to Mom and his sisters. So he was too busy to attend to his own feelings except, intermittently, to note to himself, "First Thursday in the grave." "First Friday, and fine weather." "First Saturday; he's got to be getting used to it." Under his breath he occasionally said, "Oh, Pop."
>
> – SAUL BELLOW
> *A Silver Dish*

In the Saul Bellow story, "A Silver Dish," Woody Selbst struggles with his love for his father, his wife, his mistress, and his family.

Write an essay in which you characterize Woody's love for the different people in his life, especially for his father, Morris. Ask yourself how his love for these people compares to his love for his father. In what ways could it be said to be similar? different? What passages or moments in the story can you use to explain and illustrate these similarities or differences?

ASSIGNMENT 4

Taking a Position [Carver, Cottle and Klineberg, Bellow]

In the past three assignments, you have considered a number of different perspectives on love. For this assignment, write an essay in which you take a position in relation to these characters. Who makes sense? Who is crazy? In what respects do you think they are wrong or right?

In a sense, you will be giving your own views on love in this essay, but you will be doing it indirectly, by commenting on the examples of the people you've read about. It's a difficult subject; discussions of love tend to disintegrate into generalizations and abstractions, so you'll want to refer frequently to the experiences of the characters you're commenting on. Back up your conclusions with examples of their actions and comments. You will also want to base your responses on your experiences. When you comment on Ted and Ellie, for example, you'll want to base your remarks on what you know about them *and* what you know about husbands and wives from your own experience with people you have known. The same will be true when you write about Woody and Morris Selbst—use what you know about real fathers and sons as a basis for your comments about them. This is an opportunity for you to draw conclusions about love based on what you know and what you have learned from studying these characters. You have the last word on the subject; but be careful, you don't want your essay to sound like a greeting card or a cute list of what love is or is not.

SEQUENCE EIGHT

Women's Lives

Gloria Steinem — *Ruth's Song (Because She Could Not Sing It)*

Thomas Cottle and Stephen Klineberg — *Ted and Ellie Graziano*

Dorothy Dinnerstein — *Higamous-Hogamous*

THE *FIVE ASSIGNMENTS* in this sequence ask you to think about the relations between men and women. In assignment one, you are asked to read and comment on Gloria Steinem's candid and moving essay about her mother. In assignment two, you are introduced to Ted and Ellie Graziano who, in a compelling interview, reveal the tensions in their relationship. Assignment three invites you to construct a theory to explain the issues faced by these three women—Gloria Steinem, Steinem's mother, and Ellie Graziano. And in the fourth assignment, you are asked to read and comment on a theoretical essay by Dorothy Dinnerstein that proposes an explanation for the problems men and women have in their relationships with each other. The last assignment asks you to revise the theory you developed in assignment three in light of Dinnerstein's observations and the use you can or cannot make of her work.

ASSIGNMENT 1

Ruth Steinem's Transformation [Steinem]

> The family must have watched this energetic, fun-loving, book-loving woman turn into someone who was afraid to be alone, who could not hang on to reality long enough to hold a job, and who could rarely concentrate enough to read a book.
>
> Yet I don't remember any family speculation about the mystery of mother's transformation. To the kind ones and those who liked her, this new Ruth was simply a sad event, perhaps a mental case, a family problem to be accepted and cared for until some natural process made her better. To the less kind or those who resented her earlier independence, she was a willful failure, someone who lived in a filthy house, a woman who simply would not pull herself together.
>
> – GLORIA STEINEM
> *Ruth's Song (Because She Could Not Sing It)*

Steinem tells her mother's story through a series of recollections, which show her changing from a strong, independent woman to someone who, as Steinem says, "was afraid to be alone, who could not hang on to reality long enough to hold a job." The ostensible cause of these changes was a breakdown, but Steinem isn't satisfied with that explanation. She writes:

> I still don't understand why so many, many years passed before I saw my mother as a person and before I understood that many of the forces in her life are patterns women share. Like a lot of daughters, I suppose I couldn't afford to admit that what had happened to my mother was not all personal or accidental, and therefore could happen to me.

If what happened to Steinem's mother was not completely the result of personal or accidental factors, what caused it? What are the personal and accidental causes of her breakdown and what else is there? What does Steinem mean, for example, when she refers to "forces" in her mother's life and "patterns women share"? And what do these "forces" and "patterns women share" have to do with her mother's breakdown?

Write an essay explaining the forces at work in the life of Steinem's mother, those that were unique to Steinem's mother, those that bear on Gloria Steinem's life, and those that represent these "patterns women share."

ASSIGNMENT 2

Ted and Ellie Graziano
[Cottle and Klineberg]

> Ellie Graziano asks Tom Cottle ". . . Are you still asking the same questions?"
>
> "Same questions, I suppose."
>
> "About working and living and everything, eh?"
>
> "Yeah, that about covers it."
>
> – THOMAS COTTLE AND STEPHEN KLINEBERG
> *Ted and Ellie Graziano*

Now that you have written about Steinem's mother's difficulties, we want you to examine a thicker slice of life than you have had to deal with so far.

Your task for this assignment is to try to understand Ted and Ellie Graziano. It's a big job; although Ted and Ellie are products of our society, their problems are uniquely theirs; so don't be surprised if you see them differently than someone else would who approached them from a different angle. That's the way it is with thick slices of life.

We know the Grazianos' difficulties involve big issues—"working and living and everything," as Ellie says—and that their problems cause them great trouble and pain. We know, too, that they haven't been able to solve them. They do talk a lot, however; they give clues about their hopes, and their differences are evident in the metaphors they choose to represent life. At one point, for instance, Ted portrays life as a football game, and he chides Ellie for not seeing it his way. At another point, we learn that Ted and Ellie see time differently. They do reveal themselves, that is, in both their actions and their language. Consequently, you will want to pay attention not only to what they do but what they say and how they say it. What, for example, do their metaphors tell you?

Write an essay explaining what you think is going on between Ted and Ellie Graziano. In what respect are their problems uniquely theirs, and how might their lives and how they understand them be influenced by broader forces? What kind of people are they? What do they do? not do? What do you learn about them from their relationships with others? What do they believe? value? love? despise? fear? Be sure to account for why you think they are the way they are by going back to the interview and finding the evidence you marked or took notes on to support your ideas. In other words, use those sections that give you insight into Ted and Ellie to explain and substantiate what you think is going on between them.

ASSIGNMENT 3

Developing a Theory [Cottle and Klineberg]

Now that you have read and written about the lives of three women (Steinem, Steinem's mother, and Ellie Graziano), it is time to develop a theory about the personal, accidental, and other forces that shape the experience of women.

Write an essay in which you discuss these forces as they are represented in the lives of the women you've read and written about. Do not try to develop a theory derived from the experience of women in general; the authors of the essays present their stories as they do to emphasize important issues specific to these women. Draw conclusions about the forces affecting *those women* and explain why you think these forces evolved.

To write this essay, you'll need to move back and forth between the stories and your theory. Use examples from the stories and pay attention to the explanations offered by the writers. Feel free to draw on your work in the last two essays as well. You might locate those moments in your essays where you commented on the problems and forces at work in Steinem's, Steinem's mother's, and Ellie Graziano's life. What did you have to say about them? Did you notice similarities? differences? common patterns? What draws the lives of these women together? A good part of what you do will involve seeing patterns and making connections between events that at first may seem unconnected.

This is a first draft that you will revise for assignment five, so don't insist on perfection. Your job now is to start developing a theory that can be refined later.

ASSIGNMENT 4

"Mother-raising" [Dinnerstein]

> . . . man's monopoly of history-making follows from the sexual standard. As the unpossessed possessor of woman he is freer than she is to come and go—geographically and psychologically—from the place where they are intimate: It is he, not she, who can leave what belongs to him—to go to a war or a laboratory, to spend all night writing or painting—with-

> out violating the terms of ownership. . . . Since it is he whose sexual impulsivity is legitimate, while she is expected to be receptive and undemanding, it is he, not she, at whose initiative erotic energy can with propriety be withdrawn from love and invested in worldly affairs: She, not he, is the one who must wait when the other turns away and be sexually available when he comes back. Finally, since personal sentiment is less closely tied to sex for him than for her, it is easier for him to uproot himself from their private realm when the public realm pulls at him: He is the one who has more passion to spare in history.
>
> — DOROTHY DINNERSTEIN
> *Higamous-Hogamous*

According to Dinnerstein, men are freer than women—freer to do as they please, to invest in love or worldly affairs, to make history. Dinnerstein argues that this occurs because we live in a culture where children are raised primarily by women.

Your job in this assignment is to write an essay explaining Dinnerstein's perspective and whether or not you consider it an adequate explanation of why men are freer than women.

After you've read the essay twice, once to get your bearings and again to devote attention to the effects of "mother-raising," ask yourself how "mother-raising" affects male and female children. How do gender-related patterns of possessiveness, jealousy, erotic impulsivity, sexual excitement, and personal sentiment result from this practice? What else might be influential? What is your feeling about Dinnerstein's argument? Does she develop an adequate (or compelling or crazy) explanation of why men are freer than women? And, finally, is her's an argument that you think needs or ought to be made—an argument, in other words, that addresses an important or significant problem?

ASSIGNMENT 5

Revising Your Theory
[Steinem, Cottle and Klineberg, Dinnerstein]

In assignment three you began to develop a theory about the forces that shape women's lives. Now that you have read Dinnerstein's essay, revise your theory to make your final statement about the forces that shape women's lives. Dinnerstein stands ready to enter into what you're doing, but how you'll use her, how she'll influence what you have to say about the lives of these women, is up to you. She's a theorist and she has strong ideas, but this is your theory, and like all people who develop theories, the decisions on how you use or address other theorists remains with you.

There are a number of ways to approach this assignment, and you might want to pull your thoughts together by discussing patterns or themes or influences or beliefs that can account for behaviors in the lives of the women you have been studying. Support your claims for such things as similarities, differences, and common patterns by drawing on material in the essays and in your earlier papers. You should feel free to revise anything you may have said in other papers, and you should also feel free to use work from your other papers and from class discussions to help make your case. Remember, this is your theory, and it's yours to literally make up, to create.

ACKNOWLEDGMENTS

(*Continued from page ii*)